The Globalization of Legal Education

The Globalization of Legal Education

A Critical Perspective

Edited by

BRYANT GARTH & GREGORY SHAFFER

OXFORD
UNIVERSITY PRESS

Oxford University Press is a department of the University of Oxford. It furthers the University's objective of excellence in research, scholarship, and education by publishing worldwide. Oxford is a registered trade mark of Oxford University Press in the UK and certain other countries.

Published in the United States of America by Oxford University Press
198 Madison Avenue, New York, NY 10016, United States of America.

Library of Congress Cataloging-in-Publication Data
Names: Garth, Bryant, editor. | Shaffer, Gregory, editor.
Title: The globalization of legal education : a critical perspective /
Bryant Garth & Gregory Shaffer.
Description: New York, NY : Oxford University Press, [2022] |
Includes bibliographical references and index.
Identifiers: LCCN 2021056152 (print) | LCCN 2021056153 (ebook) |
ISBN 9780197632314 (hardback) | ISBN 9780197632338 (epub) |
ISBN 9780197632321 (updf) | ISBN 9780197632345 (online)
Subjects: LCSH: Law—Study and teaching. | Law and globalization.
Classification: LCC K100 .G56 2022 (print) | LCC K100 (ebook) |
DDC 340.071/1—dc23/eng/20220118
LC record available at https://lccn.loc.gov/2021056152
LC ebook record available at https://lccn.loc.gov/2021056153

DOI: 10.1093/oso/9780197632314.001.0001

1 3 5 7 9 8 6 4 2

Printed by Integrated Books International, United States of America

Note to Readers
This publication is designed to provide accurate and authoritative information in regard to the subject matter covered. It is based upon sources believed to be accurate and reliable and is intended to be current as of the time it was written. It is sold with the understanding that the publisher is not engaged in rendering legal, accounting, or other professional services. If legal advice or other expert assistance is required, the services of a competent professional person should be sought. Also, to confirm that the information has not been affected or changed by recent developments, traditional legal research techniques should be used, including checking primary sources where appropriate.

(Based on the Declaration of Principles jointly adopted by a Committee of the American Bar Association and a Committee of Publishers and Associations.)

You may order this or any other Oxford University Press publication by visiting the Oxford University Press website at www.oup.com.

Contents

List of Authors   xi

PART I. INTRODUCTION

1. The Globalization of Legal Education: A Critical Perspective   3
   Bryant Garth and Gregory Shaffer
   I.   Historical Perspectives   10
   II. Theoretical Approaches   16
        A. Transnational Legal Ordering   17
        B. Comparative Sociology of Legal Professions   19
   III. General Themes: The Transnational Meets the Local in
        Legal Education Reform   23
   IV. An Introduction to and Thematic Reading of the Book's Chapters 28
        A. Transnational Processes in the Reform of Legal Education   29
        B. Global Law Schools   44
        C. Transnational Flows of Students, Faculty, and Judges in the
           Constitution of Legal Fields   61
   V.   Final Remarks   69

PART II. TRANSNATIONAL PROCESSES IN THE REFORM OF LEGAL EDUCATION

2. Strategic Philanthropy and International Strategies: The Ford
   Foundation and Investments in Law Schools and Legal Education   79
   Ron Levi, Ronit Dinovitzer, and Wendy H. Wong
   I.   Introduction   79
   II. The Ford Foundation, Law, and International Justice   80
   III. The Ford Foundation and Legal Education   82
        A. Legal Education as Training for International Democracy and
           Citizenship   82
        B. Legal Education as Expertise for Social Change   93
        C. Human Rights and Civil Rights   101
        D. Legal Education and Legal Institutions for Development Abroad 107
        E. Turning to International Organizations   114
   IV. Conclusion   115

3. The Transnationalization of Legal Education on the
Periphery: Continuities and Changes in Colonial Logics for a
"Globalizing" Africa   123
Michelle Burgis-Kasthala
   I. Introduction   124
   II. The Role of Law and Legal Education in Colonial Africa   127
   III. Decolonization during the Cold War: The Promise and the
      Failure of Law and Legal Education in the African "Developmental
      University," 1950s–1970s   129
   IV. From Privatization to Commercialization: Impoverishment of
      African Higher Education as Recolonization, 1970s–1990s   137
   V. African Legal Education in the Twenty-first Century:
      Regionalization and Internationalization vs. Globalization
      and Neocolonialism   141
   VI. Conclusion   148

4. Legal Education in South Africa: Racialized Globalizations,
Crises, and Contestations   157
Ralph Madlalate
   I. Introduction   157
   II. The Origins of Legal Education in South Africa: Colonial
      Apartheid as Context   158
     A. The Ideology of Apartheid Legal Education   165
   III. Regearing Legal Education Post-apartheid: Facing
      and Contesting Transformation   168
   IV. Transformation and Its Discontents: Crises in the Age
      of Globalization   173
   V. Conclusion   179

5. Battles Around Legal Education Reform in India: From
Entrenched Local Legal Oligarchies to Oligopolistic Universals   185
Yves Dezalay and Bryant Garth
   I. India: Colonial Path Dependencies Revisited: An Embattled
      Senior Bar, the Marginalization of Knowledge, and
      Internationalized Challengers   189
   II. The Bar   199
   III. Challenges to the Elite Bench and Bar   203
   IV. Conclusion   209

6. Asian Legal Education's Engagement with Policy   213
Veronica L. Taylor
   I. Introduction   213
   II. Prologue: Talking about Rule of Law in Yangon   215
   III. Legal Education's Knowledge Mandate   218

IV. Shaping Law School Engagement with Policy in Asia   220
   A. The PRC: The Case of the Disappearing Legal Clinic   221
   B. The Philippines: Declining to Engage   224
   C. Indonesia: The Scholarship Vacuum   226
   D. Japan: Capture and Capitulation   229
V. Conclusion   232

7. Transnational Legal Networks and the Reshaping of Legal
Education in Latin America: The Case of SELA   238
Javier Couso
   I. Introduction   238
   II. The "Latin American Seminar on Constitutional and Political
Theory" (SELA)   240
   III. SELA's Annual Meeting   242
   IV. SELA's Ethos and Purpose   244
   V. Conclusion   248

PART III. GLOBAL LAW SCHOOLS

8. The Unstoppable Force, the Immovable Object: Challenges for
Structuring a Cosmopolitan Legal Education in Brazil   253
Oscar Vilhena Vieira and José Garcez Ghirardi
   I. Globalization, Return to Democratic Rule, and the Need for
Innovative Legal Professionals in Brazil   253
   II. Traditional Legal Education and Political Perspectives in Brazil   255
   III. Three Main Challenges Attached to Offering Global-Oriented
Legal Education in Brazil   261
   IV. Three Traps: Legal Colonialism, Academic Solipsism,
and Elitism   265
      A. Legal Colonialism   267
      B. Academic Solipsism   269
      C. Elitism   271
   V. Conclusion   272

9. Isolation and Globalization: The Dawn of Legal Education in
Bhutan   276
David S. Law
   I. Introduction   276
   II. Three Impressions: Isolation, Tradition, Anxiety   278
   III. The History of Bhutan's First Law School   281
   IV. Curriculum   285
   V. Faculty   292
      A. Faculty Training   293
      B. Faculty Recruitment   294

VI. Admissions 296
VII. International Influences 298
    A. India 300
    B. The United States 301
    C. Austria 302
    D. Other Countries 303
VIII. Conclusion 304

10. China and the Globalization of Legal Education:
A Look into the Future 308
Philip J. McConnaughay and Colleen B. Toomey
    I. STL in the Beginning 312
    II. STL's Pivot to China 316
    III. The Influence of Shenzhen and the Rest of the Non-West 319
    IV. Some Advantages and Challenges of Being Part
of a Chinese University 325
    V. Conclusion 329

11. Who Wants the Global Law School? 333
Kevin E. Davis and Xinyi Zhang
    I. Introduction 333
    II. Derived Demand 335
        A. Globalization and the Demand for Transnational Legal Services 335
        B. Demand for Multijural Lawyers 336
        C. Derived Demand for Multijural Legal Education 338
        D. Evidence of Derived Demand for Multijural Legal Education 340
    III. A Theory of Constructed Demand 340
        A. Limitations of Derived Demand 340
        B. An Alternative to Derived Demand 344
    IV. NYU Law Abroad 346
        A. Background 348
        B. Evidence of Derived Demand 353
        C. Evidence of Constructed Demand 356
    V. Conclusion 360

12. "Have Law Books, Computer, Simulations—Will Travel":
The Transnationalization of (Some of) the Law Professoriate 366
Carrie Menkel-Meadow
    I. Introduction: The Peripatetic Law Professor and Her
Data Sources 366
    II. Some Illustrations from CTLS and Points Beyond 372
    III. Comparisons to Other Forms of Global Legal Education 378
    IV. Assessing Impacts? 385
        A. Curriculum and Pedagogy 386
        B. Research and Scholarship 389

C. Cultural Competency or "Capability"   390
D. Institutional Sensitivity, Competence, and Innovation   391

PART IV. TRANSNATIONAL FLOWS OF
STUDENTS, FACULTY, AND JUDGES IN THE
CONSTITUTION OF LEGAL FIELDS

13. Who Rules the World? The Educational Capital of the
     International Judiciary   403
     Mikael Rask Madsen
       I. Studying the International Judiciary   406
      II. How International Are International Judges? Studying at
           Home or Abroad?   409
     III. Elite Universities and the International Judiciary   416
      IV. Discussion and Conclusion   423

14. Cross-Border Student Flows and the Construction of
     International Law as a Transnational Legal Field   428
     Anthea Roberts
       I. Transnational Student Flows   430
           A. Cross-Border Flows of Students in General   431
           B. The Globalization of Legal Education   438
           C. Implications for the Divisible College   443
      II. Educational Backgrounds of Professors   448
           A. Tracking Educational Diversity   449
           B. Explaining Educational Diversity   450
               1. Lack of Educational Diversity: Russia and France   451
               2. Intermediate Educational Diversity: China and the United States   455
               3. *Significant Educational Diversity: The United Kingdom
                   and Australia*   458
           C. Implications for the Divisible College   461
     III. Conclusion   469

15. International Law Student Mobility in Context:
     Understanding Variations in Sticky Floors, Springboards,
     Stairways, and Slow Escalators   476
     Carole Silver and Swethaa S. Ballakrishnen
       I. Trends in International Legal Education   482
      II. Mobile Pathways: Sticky Floors, Springboards, Stairways,
           and Slow Escalators   492
     III. Glocal Trends: Local Contexts, Global Repercussions   501
      IV. Discussion   504
       V. Conclusion   513

Index   521

List of Authors

Swethaa S. Ballakrishnen is Assistant Professor of Law at the University of California Irvine School of Law.

Michelle Burgis-Kasthala is a Lecturer in Public International Law at the University of Edinburgh, Edinburgh Law School.

Javier Couso is Professor of Law at Universidad Diego Portales (Chile), and at Utrecht University (The Netherlands).

Kevin E. Davis is Beller Family Professor of Business Law at New York University School of Law.

Yves Dezalay is Director Emeritus of the Centre National de la Recherche Scientifique.

Ronit Dinovitzer is a Professor of Sociology, University of Toronto and Faculty Fellow, American Bar Foundation.

Bryant Garth is Distinguished Professor of Law Emeritus at the University California, Irvine School of Law.

José Garcez Ghirardi is Professor of Law at Fundação Getulio Vargas, Direito, São Paulo, Brazil.

David S. Law is the Sir Y.K. Pao Chair in Public Law at the University of Hong Kong.

Ron Levi is Professor of Sociology and Global Affairs at the University of Toronto.

Ralph Madlalate is Research Fellow, Harvard Law School, Center on the Legal Profession.

Mikael Rask Madsen is Professor of Law and Director of iCourts, Centre of Excellence for International Courts, University of Copenhagen.

Philip J. McConnaughay is Dean and Professor of Law at Peking University School of Transnational Law, and a former Vice Chancellor of Peking University Shenzhen Graduate School.

Carrie Menkel-Meadow is Distinguished Professor of Law (and Political Science) at the University of California, Irvine, and A.B. Chettle Professor of Law, Dispute Resolution and Civil Procedure Emerita at Georgetown University.

Anthea Roberts is Professor of Global Governance at the School of Regulation and Global Governance (RegNet), Australian National University, Australia.

Gregory Shaffer is Chancellor's Professor of Law and Political Science at the University of California, Irvine School of Law.

Carole Silver is a Professor of Global Law and Practice at Northwestern University Pritzker School of Law in Chicago, IL.

Veronica L. Taylor is Professor of Law and Regulation at the School of Regulation and Global Governance (RegNet), Australian National University, Australia.

Colleen B. Toomey is Senior Associate Dean, Columbia University School of International and Public Affairs, and former Vice Dean of Peking University School of Transnational Law.

Oscar Vilhena Vieira is Dean of Fundação Getulio Vargas, Direito, São Paulo, Brazil.

Wendy H. Wong is Professor, Department of Political Science, University of Toronto.

Xinyi Zhang is a PhD student in the Department of Sociology at New York University.

PART I
INTRODUCTION

1

The Globalization of Legal Education

A Critical Perspective

Bryant Garth and Gregory Shaffer

Legal academics and practitioners in recent decades increasingly emphasize the so-called "globalization" of legal education. The diffusion of the Juris
Doctor (JD) degree to Australia, Hong Kong, Japan, and South Korea, as
well as the advent of a very similar Juris Master (JM) degree in China and a
shift in the late 1980s and beyond to a new, US-influenced format in India,
exemplify shifts toward US legal education practices (Flood 2014). The
global and Americanizing trend is evident on the websites of law schools
around the globe, with many law schools competing to be the most "global"
in terms of their faculty, curricula, teaching methods, and students. Less
pronounced but related to the literature on legal globalization is that on
"transnationalization" and transnational processes, which is a strong component of the move toward globalization in legal education. As this book shows,
if we look to see what is celebrated as part of globalized law schools and faculties, we see increased cross-border flows of professors and students, teaching
of transnational legal subjects, development of particular forms of teaching
practice such as legal clinics, explicit focus on transnational rankings, and
transnationalized scholarly communities sharing teaching and research
methods and approaches across domains of law.

These trends do not mean that globalization in law simplistically equals
Americanization, that influences are unidirectional, that local factors are
less important than global, or that there are not counter and competing
trends. At this moment, the processes that we show in this book make US
influences paramount in this self-conscious legal globalization—but not because US practices are inherently superior. Our approach in this book is critical, seeking to understand the processes behind the globalization of legal
education. These processes involve global hierarchies and competition for
influence, marketization, the global spread of corporate law firms, major

Bryant Garth and Gregory Shaffer, *The Globalization of Legal Education* In: *The Globalization of Legal Education.*
Edited by: Bryant Garth & Gregory Shaffer, Oxford University Press. © Oxford University Press 2022.
DOI: 10.1093/oso/9780197632314.003.0001

inequalities in access to the credentials to get ahead in the global economy, and links between globalization and generational warfare against entrenched local legal hierarchies.

This chapter introduces the book's themes and presents how the individual chapters illuminate them. We begin by drawing on law school websites to illustrate the widespread emphasis on features of legal education most identified with the United States. We then situate today's globalizing trends in relation to interconnected histories, especially the histories of empire and colonization; globalization is not new. We next introduce two theoretical approaches, which stem from the orientation of each of the co-editors' scholarship. One is the study of transnational legal orders and the other is the comparative sociology of the legal profession. We believe that together they provide useful vantage points to understand the phenomena explored in this book. After discussing the book's themes, we present the chapters in light of them through the two theoretical perspectives we bring.

We begin with a brief look at websites to document how law schools in different countries market themselves in "global" terms. Consider some Asian examples. Chinese University of Hong Kong (CUHK LAW), befitting that global city, states: "The outstanding quality of our taught programmes is acknowledged worldwide and evidenced by collaborations with many leading law schools in the world. The cutting-edge research conducted by our professors from 20 different jurisdictions and by our research students with equally diverse backgrounds generates significant impact. CUHK LAW offers a truly agile and global learning and research environment." The emphasis here is on connections with "leading law schools," "worldwide" recognition now seen in global rankings, "cutting-edge" research no doubt defined by "global standards," and a wide assortment of globally diverse professors and students. KoGuan Law School in Shanghai, named after a key Chinese-American philanthropic supporter who made his fortune in the information technology industry after obtaining a law degree from New York Law School, states on its website: "In the age of globalization, legal education has transcended national boundaries. The legal challenges faced, and the practice of law have become increasingly, more global in character. An international perspective is a fundamental component of the competencies needed by every lawyer and legal academic." KoGuan emphasizes foreign exchange programs as a key to learning these competencies.

The two Singapore competitors echo similar sentiments. The Law Dean at National University of Singapore states that "NUS Law is Asia's Global Law

School. Widely regarded as the region's leading law school, we also see our-selves as part of a global conversation about the study and practice of law. This global perspective infuses our academic programme—from the diverse courses that we offer, taught by faculty from most major jurisdictions, to the exchange arrangements we have with other top law schools around the world." More than CUHK, it also emphasizes the globalization of the academic program. The Law Dean at the Singapore Management School, in parallel, emphasizes its faculty's transnational, elite, educational backgrounds: "Our distinguished faculty are educated at such reputable universities as Oxford, Cambridge and Harvard, just to name a few. Our research agenda and publi-cation are equally top classed."

The emphasis on faculty who are graduates from globally elite law schools in the legal centers of the world is not unusual on these websites. They em-phasize global jobs as well. Melbourne Law School states, for example, "Melbourne Law School JD students can participate in exchange programs, undertake a dual degree at one of our partnered universities overseas and apply for an international internship during their degrees. A Melbourne Law School degree also prepares graduates for global careers. More than one-third of our graduates have worked or are working in international locations."

In Germany, Bucerius Law School, funded by one of the largest German foundations, created by Gerd Bucerius, a German judge, lawyer, politi-cian, and founding publisher of the weekly newspaper *Die Zeit*, advertises that its "international approach to legal education remains a unique feature among German high education institutions. Our internationality presents itself in four main areas: (1) International Research, (2) Global Partner Network, (3) International Study Programs, and (4) Internationalized cur-riculum for our LL.B. students." Exchange is a key part of Bucerius's inter-nationalization, but also emphasized are international research, including interdisciplinary research, and the presence of foreign faculty as part of the program. Emphasizing multinational jobs for graduates, the Sciences Po Law School in Paris lists on its website a group of "partners" that suggests where the graduates may go: "Clifford Chance, Gide Loyrette Nouel, August & Debouzy, Berthelot, Bredin Prat, De Gaulle, Fleurance et Associés, Dechert LLP, Hogan Lovells, Latournerie Wolfrom Avocats, Quinn Emanuel Erquhart & Sullivan, LLP, Vivant Chiss, and White & Case LLP." The rise of corporate law firms—and the profession of the "avocat d'affaires" (business lawyer)—is one component of this globalization of legal education.

New law schools in emerging economies likewise position themselves as global law schools. In India, Jindal Global Law School succinctly explains its vision of the global: "JGLS imparts a rigorous and multi-disciplinary legal education with a view of producing world-class legal professionals, scholars, leaders and public servants. . . . The School's expert faculty comes from across the globe and engages in critical scholarship that contributes to public debates both in India and abroad." The emphasis on interdisciplinarity and scholarly participation in global dialogues is again stressed as key elements of a global law school. Similarly, in Brazil, Fundação Getulio Vargas Law School in São Paulo (FGV DIREITO SP) states, "To meet the demands of today's market, DIREITO SP students are prepared to work in public and private organizations and to dialogue with other fields of knowledge, so that they can positively and profoundly influence the legal scenario in Brazil and in other nations." DIREITO SP highlights the importance of engaged teaching, reflected in many of these law schools' websites. Going against traditional teaching involving boring lectures often delivered by assistants to professors, and research that takes the form of commentaries on codes, the website stresses the "calling" "to be a school with PhD Professors and students fully dedicated to teaching and research and committed to constant innovation, both in using participatory methods of teaching and conducting research— preferably empirical, collective, and of public interest—with high level of quality."

Across these schools' websites, we see themes of interdisciplinarity and participation in global scholarly debates; engaged teaching; internationalized faculty through exchange and hiring; internationalized student exchange; global positions for graduates, including in corporate law firms; and at least nods—and often much more—to a curriculum that covers transnational legal domains. While not a random sample, it is notable that the websites most emphasizing globalization are often new schools, including new private ones such as Bucerius, FGV São Paulo, Jindal, and new public ones such as Sciences Po and KoGuan. Private philanthropy is often central to the schools' reform efforts. They often were conceived as alternatives and even challengers to traditional law schools, as in the case of Bucerius, FGV, Jindal, and Sciences Po. Other times they are seeking to compete with the more traditional schools and approaches, as with KoGuan and Melbourne (the first in Australia to convert from undergraduate legal education to a JD). Or their position in entrepôts, such as Singapore and Hong Kong, internationalizes the schools by definition. There is notably less emphasis on the global in the law school websites traditionally at the top in many locales, such as Harvard, Oxford, the University of Sydney, or Yale. That does not mean that the curriculum or faculty hiring has not shifted, but it is interesting that it is less part of their marketing.

In the former colonial power of Great Britain, one of the leading examples of a commitment to the global is the Dickson Poon School of Law (King's College London), named after an entrepreneur from Hong Kong in the field of luxury goods: "Our faculty are at the cutting-edge of international legal scholarship and are committed to exploring the role of law in solving today's global problems through a transnational lens that transcends national borders. . . . Our teaching is led by internationally respected, leading academics, visiting lecturers and practitioners from global law firms. . . . The courses we offer are informed by our research expertise and you are encouraged to engage with issues at the cutting-edge of your studies, giving you the skills and confidence to engage with complex legal issues and global challenges." Following a huge gift from its namesake, which was the largest ever to a UK law school, and its aggressive hiring of international professors, the school rose significantly in the UK rankings.

Within the United States, there is less emphasis on the themes of schools located outside of the United States in large part because much of what is promoted as "global"—engaged teaching, interdisciplinary research, participatory education, preparation for global jobs—is modeled on the US law school. There is, for example, less emphasis in US law schools on international faculty coming from outside the United States, although, as Anthea Roberts shows, the numbers are also increasing (Chapter 14). The US law schools have already built tight connections with corporate law firms to hire graduates, which is a feature that the globalized law schools outside of the United States stress to distinguish themselves. The volumes from the GLEE project (Globalization, Lawyers and Emerging Economies) led by David Wilkins out of Harvard show that "global" educational reforms are closely related to the remarkable spread of US-style corporate law firms around the globe that service global business. Although the volumes on Brazil (Gross Cunha, Gabbay, Ghirardi, Trubek, and Wilkins eds. 2018) and India (Wilkins, Khanna, and Trubek eds. 2017) focus on the rise of corporate law firms, they include chapters on legal education that illuminate the connections between legal education reform and corporate law.

Nevertheless, within the United States, some schools have aimed to position themselves through their "global" brands or programs. New York

University School of Law, the pioneer "global law school" (Chapter 11) in the United States, remains strongly committed to that brand, which it adopted in 1995, the year that the World Trade Organization was created. NYU's website proclaims:

> The Law School's global and international law program integrates world-leading research with the preparation of students to make major impacts in a world that is fast-changing, increasingly interconnected, and often contentious and challenged. Our faculty and curriculum are unsurpassed, with about 50 courses, seminars, clinics and other experiential classes each year covering the spectrum of core "public" and "private" international law fields; . . . NYU Law's global law work is strongly interdisciplinary, integrating faculty expertise in economics, sociology, anthropology, history, and philosophy.

Stanford is a recent addition to those emphasizing the global, creating a new W.A. Franke Global Law Program in 2019, "spearheaded" by Professor Rob Daines, a former "investment banker at Goldman Sachs where he helped clients structure transnational deals." The website asserts: "Our innovative model for training tomorrow's law and business leaders is comprised of four elements: (1) a global quarter: an intensive, 10-week immersion in international law and finance (2) a foundational course on global legal practice (3) courses that combine rigorous classroom training with intensive overseas study trips (4) greater integration of comparative law and international issues into existing core courses."

This book advances empirical study regarding the processes through which law schools have changed their approaches in terms of hiring, international exchange, scholarship, and curriculum. Some of the change is largely symbolic. Most legal education remains local, as, for example, a critical study of "global" law schools in Latin America showed (Montoya 2010). But that does not mean that globalization has failed to spur significant change, whether in self-designated global law schools or more broadly within law schools. For example, we know that transnational legal fields such as human rights, international economic law, international commercial arbitration, rule of law promotion, and others have earned places in many law schools' hiring and curricula. This volume cannot chronicle the extent of the globalization of law schools nor detail all the manifestations of that globalization. But, as the quoted websites suggest, there is a remarkable amount of attention to this phenomenon that, for the most part, is taken for granted as an indicator of progress.

Most of the literature on this phenomenon is promotional. The small but growing scholarship on the globalization of law schools tends to consist of inventories of relative successes or critiques of the law schools that have, or have not, embraced modern practices. Examples include books edited by Klabbers and Sellers (2008), Jamin and van Caenegem (2016), and Gane and Hui Huang (2016). There are, in parallel, books on the globalization of clinical education, one of the major components of reform in many places (Wilson 2017), and a useful volume on Asia (Steele and Taylor 2010). Some of the literature contends that innovation is now coming from the east and south (Chesterman 2017), which is no doubt true but not inconsistent with an orientation toward the northern consensus on what "modern" looks like. The editors or authors of these volumes rarely seek to explain why these reforms are on the agenda, why they are contested, or what their implications might be.

The chapters in this volume provide empirical evidence of the transnational diffusion of approaches to legal education, together with insights from a critical approach to these processes. What diffuses and how it diffuses to different places at different times depends on the local situation in the importing country. The reforms, or various parts of reforms, such as promotion of interdisciplinary scholarship or even hiring of full-time professors, may run into barriers that cannot be overcome, depending on the local context. For example, scholars view the move to the JD in Japan as a dramatic failure in contrast to the same process in South Korea (Taylor, Chapter 6). Similarly, the new and meritocratic national law schools in India have not displaced traditional local law schools nor the importance of personal relationships in recruitment into the prestigious world of Indian advocates (Dezalay and Garth, Chapter 5). The remarkably innovative FGV DIREITO in São Paulo is challenged every day because its position is "out of place" in the Brazilian world of legal education (Vilhena Vieira and Garcez Ghirardi, Chapter 8). Yet, the processes are still in play, and the website rhetoric, competition for rankings, and practical observation (Menkel-Meadow, Chapter 12) show that changes have taken place in many areas, including in clinical legal education and in teaching new areas such as dispute processing, including international commercial arbitration.

This book does not take a position on what constitutes "best practices" in legal education.[1] Rather, this book seeks to understand the processes of legal

---

[1] We support, in our own context of US legal education, most of what is discussed in terms of reform in the book's chapters, such as multidisciplinary work on law, legal clinics, attention to the

education reform and resistance and point to what these processes mean for law, lawyers, and governance. The book seeks to understand the forces driving these processes and to evaluate their implications. Its substantive chapters provide critical insights into how these transnational processes operate in different jurisdictions around the world in light of globalization and local competition. Taken together, the chapters show how norms regarding legal education move across jurisdictions and shape legal education practices transnationally, as well as the challenges and limits these processes face.

This introductory chapter lays the groundwork for this study. It places this inquiry into the context of broader scholarly debates about the impact of globalization on legal education. We note that, although there is much material in this book and elsewhere on forces and trends in the globalization of law schools, there remains little available quantitative data on changes in teaching styles, research approaches, hiring criteria, and internationalized curricula. The absence of such research is understandable, since the shape of "globalization" in any given context depends largely on how influences are received locally—where reforms may be hotly contested. This book helps map avenues for future research.

I. Historical Perspectives

Global law schools are not a new phenomenon. From a historical perspective, the globalization of legal education can be traced to medieval Italy. Children of feudal lords, aristocrats, nobility, and church officials began to study at what became the University of Bologna. The recently rediscovered Corpus Juris of Roman Law and the emergence of scholars explicating that work led ambitious and well-connected individuals to seek to acquire expertise in Roman civil law and the emerging canon law (the latter in part based on Roman civil law) (Brundage 2008). The power of that expertise, combined with its embeddedness in elite social capital, helped broker solutions to the many jurisdictional and other conflicts of a rapidly changing era—including the rise of the Italian City States (Martines 1968). These successes spurred

politics of law in broader policy context, awareness of law in transnational context given the complexity of problem-solving in an economically globalized world, and the need to address the broader challenge of unequal access to legal education and its reproduction of hierarchy. Part of the mandate for a critical examination of how these reforms are spreading globally is to explore the complexity of local contexts rather than take sides.

imitators elsewhere, such as in Paris and Oxford. The structure of legal education based on the model developed in Bologna evolved in different but related ways in England and on the continent (Dezalay and Garth 2021). These European models then were exported as part of the age of imperialism.

The age of empire from the late eighteenth to the twentieth century was a propitious period for the development of professions such as law. As in the present, a technological revolution was central to the expanded role of what Kris Manjapra (2019) calls "the semiperipheral hand" to highlight the position of intermediaries between the imperial centers and activities in the colonies. As noted by Manjapra, "the world system was marked by an unprecedented acceleration of communication, exchange, and circulation in the nineteenth century, . . . [and] the semiperipheral hand played the functional role making goods, labor, ideas, and services move faster—faster accumulation of land and labor products, faster ships and distribution technologies, faster transfers of credit, faster transfers of information." He refers to "a planetary military-fiscal-scientific-agricultural-industrial complex" that "relied on gentlemanly capital, which was anchored in imperial metropolitan centers, and on managerial and information capital that maintained webs of connection and communication between metropolitan centers and the imperial peripheries." Attorneys were at the top of his list of these knowledge intermediaries: "those functions were historically provided by attorneys, mercenaries, army officers, surveyors, engineers, travel writers, Man Fridays, secretaries, translators, and scientific advisors who helped produce and manage colonial frontiers of difference and helped create pathways of circulation and appropriation across those frontiers" (Manjapra 2019).

The current phenomenon of the creation of global law schools is therefore a new but path-dependent version of what existed in the age of empire. In the British empire, for example, local elites in colonial settings, either through their own resources or through British efforts to co-opt them with scholarships, came to England to study at Oxford or Cambridge and even join the Inns of Court. Prominent leaders of independence movements, including Jawaharlal Nehru in India and Lee Kwan Yew in Singapore, used both the credibility that they gained from their credentials abroad and the tools that they learned to make the case for independence and their own leading roles in independence movements (Dezalay and Garth 2010). From the perspective of the British empire, individuals from the colonies not only gained a superior education in England, but, in turn, brought enlightenment back to the colonies. The English-educated lawyers prospered enormously as well within the British Raj. Not surprisingly, foreign-educated leaders continued to follow the colonial practices that they knew well, including in legal education, after independence. They saw those practices as the most modern of the time. Arguments couched in "modernity" continue in contemporary debates about global legal education.

This history helps clarify the core and periphery phenomenon that we also see today, which varies over time and by region. The terms "core" and "periphery" are relative and relational ones, where there are many examples, including regional examples such as African students going to South Africa to study today. Yet they also reflect longer histories. The core of the law in the British Empire, for example, was identified with London's courts and the Queen's or King's Counsel who practiced in them (Benton and Ford 2016). The QCs who practiced in the courts that forged the leading precedents and their applications were ipso facto the most prominent legal advocates in the empire. Accordingly, when there was crucial litigation within the colonies, the top advocates from London typically were sought for their expertise and authority. The same held true for the writing of the constitutions of the formal colonies when they became independent states (Shaffer, Ginsburg, and Halliday 2019; Kumarasingham 2019). These colonial patterns tended to survive the demise of the great European empires. There remains a strong influence, for example, of English and French law and legal education, respectively, in the former English and French colonies (discussed in Chapters 3 and 14). There is also a strong German influence in countries such as China, Japan, and South Korea, which imported German legal approaches under pressure from Western powers to demonstrate that they were "civilized" and "modern" according to western standards (Zhang 2018; Hattori 1963; for the strong German influence in India in the nineteenth century, see Manjapra 2014).

The flow of people and ideas continues to reflect this core and periphery phenomenon, as in the past. Ambitious and well-connected people tend to come to what they see as the core to study, and then bring back ideas and enhance their status and credibility in the peripheries. The flow of students, as Anthea Roberts shows (Chapter 14), tends to follow patterns set in the colonial era. Students from francophone Africa with the opportunity to study abroad tend to favor France and especially Paris for legal study. The credentials they obtain will be recognized at home—in part because predecessor elites obtained the same credentials during and after the colonial period. Moreover, the material that they learn is naturally relevant to legal systems set up by the French and modeled on the French civil codes. The same holds true for former British, Portuguese, and Spanish colonies, where there has been a long tradition of local elites going to colonial capitals to build their credibility and a claim to the "superior" education at the core of the legal system that still reigns to a great degree in their countries. Even where there are no longer linguistic fits, such as with Indonesia and its former colonial relationship with the Netherlands, students from Indonesia may be more likely to go to the Netherlands than other countries to study abroad, even if the language of instruction is in English (*id.*).

The competition between and among empires is a strong part of the history of globalized law schools. Facilitated by technological advances in communication and travel, such competition helped drive greater imperial investment in law in the late nineteenth and early twentieth century (Mazower 2012). It then helped spur enhanced US efforts to reform legal education abroad after World War II (Levi, Dinovitzer, and Wong, Chapter 2). Countries in the core hoped to bolster the legitimacy of their empires through increasing efforts to provide education for colonial subjects beginning late in the nineteenth century, especially for those with elite status, such as Brahmins in India and the Javanese elite in Indonesia. In this way, they hoped to respond to criticisms at home and abroad. For example, the British increased their investment in law in response to challenges at home to the economic exploitation of the colonies (Dezalay and Garth 2010). The Dutch similarly responded by seeking to invest more in the "civilizing mission" within their colonies. By increasing training in law and administration, and by giving local elites more of a role in governance, they aimed to enhance the legitimacy of their empires at home, within the colonies, and internationally. Locals were co-opted, but, in turn, they also co-opted the colonists while pursuing their own interests (Benton and Ford 2016). As today, they could at the same time be critical of empires and hegemons while supporting the use of the expertise they learned in the imperial capitals.

The latest wave of globalization of legal education follows the rise of the United States in the competition for global leadership and hegemony. The United States became a colonial power in the late nineteenth century, most notably in the Philippines and Puerto Rico (Burbank and Cooper 2010), while also participating in the creation of colonial enclaves imposed on China, where the United States located a district court from 1906 to 1943 within the jurisdiction of the Ninth Circuit to handle disputes involving Americans (Ruskola 2013). The United States, however, also sought to position itself as an "anti-imperial" empire, urging the granting of independence to countries under colonial domination, the development of the rule of law, and policies of free trade consistent with an "open door" (Dezalay and Garth 2010; Coates 2016). Legal and economic missionaries, mainly from the private sectors, began to promote these policies in the nineteenth century in places such as Japan and China and accelerated and extended such efforts throughout the twentieth century (Kroncke 2016).

Beginning in the 1950s, the support of legal education reform (as well as education in economics) became both a private and US governmental priority. As assessed in Chapter 2, however, US legal educational reform efforts at that time, including in Brazil, Chile, India, Japan, and South Korea, were not very successful. US ambitions, together with those of many local actors, to encourage—depending on the setting—full-time professors, more engaged teaching, scholarly inquiry beyond the interpretation of codes, more practical instruction, and less formalism in instruction and practice, failed (Gardner 1980; Krishnan 2004). Critics charge that the programs illustrated legal imperialism, but that is somewhat too simplified (Gardner 1980). In fact, there was already a cadre of local reformers seeking to import educational reforms inspired by US examples, in part, because of the growing importance of the United States in the world.

Today, there is even greater local demand for legal education reform modeled on the United States. From a historical perspective, this local demand parallels the growth of US power and influence, especially as it peaked in the 1990s and early 2000s. The influence of US law spread, facilitating and regulating market transactions, as exemplified by contract law and contract practices used for commercial transactions, corporate governance standards, approaches to environmental law, trade law, and human rights law. Relatedly, post–Cold War globalization and market liberalization spurred the proliferation of US-style corporate law firms along with the investment banks that keep them busy. Competition and marketization spread to the global law school world as well. Finally, as in the age of empire, dramatic advances in technology, above all the digital revolution, were central to overcoming obstacles to the globalization of law and legal education. The availability of email communication, e-libraries, and e-journals, for example, along with less expensive global travel, brought access back and forth from centers and peripheries. Students and professors from around the globe in law and other fields could draw easily on the most respected scholars in the most prestigious sites. The technology also facilitated rankings in scholarship and among academic institutions.

Rankings, in turn, shape processes of globalization and transnationalization. In particular, as Hamann and Schmidt-Wellenburg (2020: 173) argue in a recent study of rankings generally, "rankings themselves contribute to the transnationalization of the academic field by lending specific milieus, paradigms, agents, and strategies symbolic authority from transnational sources, i.e., private corporations, media corporations, and data providers." That role is "far from impartial and equitable." It advances

> a global circulation of expertise and knowledge that conforms to English-language, journal-based publication cultures; has value in its practical application; or corresponds to political and market interests. The resulting geographies of higher education display striking disparities between the economically prospering regions in North America, Europe, East Asia, and Australia, and large parts of South America, Africa, and Asia . . . Academic rankings do not only accompany these processes by interconnecting fields, circumventing the authority of nation-states, and tapping transnational sources of authority. They also lend processes of transnationalization moral integrity by allowing for a clear conscience of meritocracy and transparency.

The authors note also, citing Espeland and Sauder (2007), that "[t]he irony of a meritocratic belief in rankings that do not depict but recreate social orders seems to escape the subjectivized actors the more they are engaged in the game."

Those at the top of local legal professions have long capped their local legal education with study abroad. But what followed the global trend toward US-style corporate law, and to a lesser extent international human rights law, shifted the direction of the flows—now encouraged also by global rankings. Where once Latin American lawyers would have scoffed at the relevance of US law to practice or teaching in Latin America, now US degrees became the most prestigious global credentials (Chapters 14 and 15), although of course there are still many other sites and programs that attract ambitious lawyers. The ascendency of corporate law firms also fueled the demand for local legal education reform. Those attuned to the practices of corporate firms often lead attacks on formalism in legal education in favor of a more practice-oriented curriculum and an emphasis on problem-solving—which is identified with

US educational practice. For example, the founding dean of FGV Direito in São Paulo (discussed in Chapter 8), Ary Oswaldo Mattos Filho, had earlier established one of the most important corporate law firms in Brazil.

History teaches, finally, that global hierarchies and domestic politics change. The rise of emergent powers, such as China, could affect the role, structure, and substance of international law in trade, investment, and other domains, particularly in relation to sovereignty (Ginsburg 2020; Shaffer and Gao 2020). This shift could reflect a return to earlier patterns of dominance. Spanning from 1368 to 1841, China, Korea, Vietnam, and Japan "maintained peaceful and long-lasting relations with one another" (Kang 2010: 3), with China being "the dominant military, cultural, and economic power in the system" (*id.*)—a "hegemon . . . operating under a presumption of inequality, which resulted in a clear hierarchy and lasting peace." Historians call it a "tribute" system, which involved travel, educational exchange, and gifts. In the process, other countries "consciously copied Chinese institutional and discursive practices in part to craft stable relations with China." As a result, "there was no intellectual challenge to the rules of the game until the late nineteenth century and the arrival of the Western powers." China could gain the same kind of role in the future, perhaps this time with more focus on law and lawyers. During the period of the Cold War, as another example, leftists who received educational credentials from Russia or, for Latin America, Cuba, were privileged in local leftist movements (Castañeda 1993). Today, even in countries where legal institutions are most clearly established (including in the United States), religious groups, populist political parties, and authoritarian movements could reduce law's importance in national and transnational governance. Although the future unfolds as we write, common patterns still characterize these long-standing transnational processes that shape national and global rules and governance practices.

II. Theoretical Approaches

There are different ways of framing the study of the globalization and transnationalization of legal education. One is simply to compare law schools and faculties of law according to various criteria. For example, one could assess how global is the composition of the students and the professors, how transnational is the curriculum, how well is the curriculum designed for practice in transnational and international organizations, corporate law firms, multinational corporations, and transnational nongovernmental organizations (NGOs), or what career paths do graduates actually pursue. This kind of systematic cataloguing is unavailable today, but it would certainly be interesting to have it. Such data could facilitate assessment of transnational diffusion and ordering of legal education practices, a critique of imperial influences, and a search for "best practices."

In this book, we combine theoretical perspectives to examine these phenomena. One theoretical framework—that of transnational legal ordering—addresses how legal norms are constructed, flow, settle and unsettle, affecting legal practice across jurisdictions. Another—the comparative sociology of the legal profession—examines imperial competition, hierarchies of power, how legal fields connect to power, and the way that transnational processes of legal education reform both challenge and reinforce local and transnational hierarchies. Our goal is to show how these approaches combine to illustrate and explain the interaction of transnational processes and domestic settings in the field of legal education.

A. Transnational Legal Ordering

The theoretical framework of transnational legal orders is a processual theory developed to challenge methodological nationalism in the study of law. From this sociolegal perspective, "transnational legal ordering" consists of the transnational construction and flow of legal norms across borders (Shaffer 2013), which can give rise to transnational legal orders when the norms settle in practice and transcend borders (Halliday and Shaffer 2015). The transnationalization of legal education can serve as a mechanism for transnational legal ordering that affects law and practice in different substantive domains. By training elites on particular subjects in similar ways, including through the cross-border exchange of students, professors, pedagogies, and ideas, transnational processes shaping legal education can potentially facilitate a common conceptualization of "problems" in social life and legal responses to them. In this way, legal educational reforms potentially can facilitate the transnational flow of legal norms in different subject areas, from corporate and business law to human rights and constitutional law.

Transnational legal ordering tends to begin with the framing and construction of a "problem" (Halliday and Shaffer 2015), such as the problem of how to reform legal education to adapt to contemporary challenges.

Problems are not natural. They are social constructions reflecting social norms and movements, actors pursuing particular interests, and competitive processes of marketization. Contests regarding the framing of problems and their resolution are thus frequent. Through economic and cultural globalization, the framing of these problems more likely becomes transnationalized.

These transnational processes potentially can give rise to a "transnational legal order," which Halliday and Shaffer (2015) define as a collection of formalized legal norms and associated organizations and actors that authoritatively order the understanding and practice of law across national jurisdictions. Scholars seek to understand how such orders are created, maintained, legitimated, resisted, and challenged, facilitating the settlement and unsettlement of legal norms across levels of social organization. On the one hand, transnational legal ordering can have deep effects within states, shaping not only laws but also state institutions, the role of markets, the development of legal professions, and broader normative framings. On the other hand, legal developments within states recursively can affect developments in international law and institutions.

Legal education can be both a symptom and a mechanism for these transnational changes. It can be a symptom, for example, when new corporate elites and other actors seek particular types of training of law students, and new law schools work to meet these incipient demands. Similarly, it can be a symptom of economic and cultural globalization and normative diffusion more broadly. In turn, it can be a mechanism for the conveyance of different conceptualizations of problems and the appropriate legal response through exchanges of students, professors, teaching methodologies, and ideas. States and entrepreneurs may invest in new law schools, in particular, with an eye to participate in the shaping of transnational legal ordering processes, as well as to address domestic challenges in light of transnationally exchanged ideas and experiences.

Participants in the reform of legal education include entrepreneurs who wish to improve legal education, whether to better contribute to problem solving in various domains of social life, or simply to anticipate and meet market demand. These processes potentially can be "progressive" to address particular national challenges, such as access to justice, advancement of civil, political, economic, social, and cultural rights, or of particular development perspectives of the Global South in international settings. They also can reflect power differentials when they respond to and help institutionalize practices that are characterized as "universals," but that do not serve all states and individuals equally. Entrepreneurs conceive of "problems" to be addressed in particular ways, reflecting particular ideological predispositions, as well as cultural and socioeconomic backgrounds. Issues of core and periphery are reflected in the weight given to solutions that gain traction in the centers of the legal and political world, both internationally and nationally.

Key to this transnational perspective is its attention to both norm carriers and local practices. Norms regarding legal education practices do not travel by themselves. They are conveyed by actors, as exemplified by the study of the Ford Foundation's efforts in South American in Chapter 2, of colonial processes in Africa and India in Chapters 3, 4, and 5, and of transnational networks of professors in Chapters 7 and 14. At times, these actors may simply aim to advance their individual careers, as in the case of student flows addressed in Chapters 14 and 15. At others, they may work to shape international and transnational law and institutions, as reflected in Chapters 8 and 10.

How transnational processes play out at the local level, however, is anything but determined. Transnational processes always confront local settings, with their traditions and configurations of interest and power, which may resist them. The study of transnational processes of the reform of legal education thus must include a comparative sociology of the legal professions that is grounded in both transnational and domestic contexts.

B. Comparative Sociology of Legal Professions

The comparative sociology of legal professions of Dezalay and Garth starts with a sociological and political observation that lawyers—more precisely the "legal field"—serve state power and that such service is often critical for lawyer prosperity (Dezalay and Garth 2010). Law and lawyers provide legitimacy to power and, in exchange, the holders of power—domestically or transnationally—agree to be governed by law (although they do not always submit to law in practice). Governance in the language of law reinforces power, while also potentially constraining it. From this vantage, processes of transnational legal ordering can serve existing power configurations and help to sustain them, while also being used to challenge them.

The goal of this sociology is to uncover the power structures and processes that shape and transform the role of law and lawyers nationally and transnationally. Legal change involves both reproduction and revolution. The comparative study of legal professions illuminates how reform processes play out in different settings, including why local investment in legal education reform occurs in particular places, the extent to which it aligns with US models and the spread of corporate law firms, and with what impact. This approach focuses on interconnected histories and the national legal fields produced out of these histories. The structure of national legal hierarchies is a crucial factor that shapes how legal education reforms are received (Dezalay and Garth 2021).

Legal hierarchies within the profession develop in relation to, and are embedded in, state power. The histories of legal professions in different countries are interconnected, but there are also particular national histories that lead to different hierarchical structures—sustained also by different educational structures and approaches (Dezalay and Garth 2021). To date, as suggested in Chapters 13 and 14, transnational legal ordering, often backed by international courts and law schools with transnational curricula, has not changed the fact that both national and transnational legal careers develop out of positions in national legal professions.

A comparative, sociological perspective foregrounds how national legal hierarchies differ from country to country. In the United States, partners in corporate law firms are typically at the top of the hierarchy (Dinovitzer and Garth 2020). Their power comes in part from their service as brokers connecting economic and corporate power with state power, as reflected in the "revolving door" between top administrative and political officials and leaders in Wall Street and K Street business lobbies. Legal education is both embedded in and constitutive of this hierarchical structure. The leading law schools have very close, almost symbiotic relationships with elite corporate firms, and the top law graduates almost as a rule start their careers in corporate law (Dinovitzer and Garth 2020). The leading partners, as part of the link between economic and state power, move from time to time into government positions where they help use the law to regulate but not disrupt their powerful clients.

We see different hierarchies in the legal profession across countries. In Brazil, notable jurists are at the top of the legal profession, typically serving as a professor, politician, public intellectual, member of a prominent family, and broker to economic and political capital that also may be familial (Dezalay and Garth 2002). Legal education is symbiotic with the maintenance of this hierarchy. In India, at the top are the grand advocates, the lawyers in India's high courts who typically descend from generations of judges and advocates trained in the British Empire, and who reproduce this hierarchy through personal relations and apprenticeships that require family capital (Dezalay and Garth, Chapter 5). The weak role of legal education in India helps sustain the power of the grand advocates and judges.

These groups at the top, connected closely with structures of political, economic, and social power, may become complacent, conservative, and resistant to change, which works fine for them when state and economic power are stable. But in times of change, outsider groups within and outside of the legal profession can challenge them. A major challenge for the reform of legal education is that the legal establishment tends to use its position to tip the balance away from merit and scholarly capital in favor of familial and social capital. The globalization of legal education that we present in this book is in part a challenge to the relative complacency of these groups in Brazil, India, and other places through a more US-oriented meritocratic approach.

These challenges to power often arise through changes in imperial relationships and the forces of competition between and among former imperial powers and new hegemonic ones. The rise of intensified transnational legal ordering in the late twentieth and early twenty-first century closely relates to US hegemony in the post–Cold War period. Legal entrepreneurs at the end of the Cold War produced and built on existing theories supportive of the new global balance of power—US hegemony through establishing a market-oriented "legalist empire" (Coates 2016)—which political actors, such as Warren Christopher in the Clinton administration, embraced. Elite law found its place as part of this hegemony, supporting human rights, free trade, privatization, arbitration, and the spread of corporate law firms around the globe that further diffused US legal models. Transnational legal orders such as for international trade with the World Trade Organization at its pinnacle, fitted and reinforced this new balance of power, which actors like the Ford Foundation recognized (Chapter 2).

Yet the success of a legalist empire cannot be assured for the future. Major changes nationally and internationally threaten this privileging of law and open doors for trade. Authoritarian regimes, for example, may favor a rule *by* law that supports authoritarianism, or they may decide that law entails too much restraint and they do not need lawyers to legitimate their rule. It is easy to find leaders today whose evolving relationship to law is tenuous. Global changes in balance of power—such as the rise of China—may bring hegemonic approaches to global governance that do not privilege law, lawyers, and transnational legal ordering. Nonetheless, US approaches, which helped promote legal, economic, and political changes in many places, still resonate. China has responded to them by often mimicking and repurposing US legal models for its own ends (Shaffer and Gao 2020).

US strength has helped to foster the global diffusion of financialization and neoliberalism[2] in the past four decades, and this global development has shaped the attractiveness of particular local legal education reforms. In practice, interactions between reformers and those traditionally at the top of existing national legal hierarchies often entail a two-part process. Traditional legal oligarchies first resisted corporate law firms, which were an innovation very foreign to local ideals of professionalism. The corporate law firms were first cabined to serve almost exclusively foreign clients. But these corporate firms found a place, in part, by co-opting local legal elites (involving a process of mutual benefit). This foothold made it possible for entrepreneurs, including the descendants of the largely unsuccessful law and development movement of the 1970s (Trubek and Galanter 1974), to seek to challenge the existing legal hierarchy and spur a legal revolution through reform of legal education in ways that are consistent with US tenets. Legal revolutions, as Berman (1983) shows, do not occur just through changes within the legal field, but also through links with outsiders (Dezalay and Garth 2021). In the case of legal education, reformers are more meritocratic and scholarly than those they target. In challenging the complacent legal establishment, they can gain influence and power by aligning with emerging political (or other potentially powerful) movements that can benefit from the legal legitimacy provided. The huge contributions of wealthy entrepreneurs to law schools seeking to redefine educational models are prominent examples, as seen in the funding of KoGuan Law School in Shanghai, Dickson Poon in London, Jindal in India, and Bucerius in Germany.

Major "successes," when they occur, depend on how the local context interacts with the transnational "model" exported. This interaction shapes what pieces of a model take hold, and in what manner, whether emanating from the United States or elsewhere. The relative successes and failures of legal education reform are ultimately a function of domestic struggles, or "palace wars," that become transnationalized in light of the resources and legitimacy that transnational norms offer (Dezalay and Garth 2002). In some

---

[2] By neoliberalism, we refer to a shift toward market liberalization and a greater role for market mechanisms across areas of social life. Neoliberalism, however, is a multifaceted concept, which variously refers to "finance capitalism," "market fundamentalism," and the "commodification" of culture (Rodgers 2018).

settings, for example, scholars import "Law and Economics," while in others they import "Critical Legal Studies," as scholarly approaches. In each case, they aim to shape approaches to substantive law and policy, from competition and business law to social rights and antidiscrimination law. There will always be contenders for new "revolutions" in legal education, as global and domestic contexts and contests change. There could even be radical movements, such as in China during the Anti-Rightist Movement and the Cultural Revolution, that close down or marginalize law schools and minimize the role of law and lawyers.

In sum, although evolving global hierarchies shape what is seen as "modern" in legal education and thus affect the extent and shape of transnational ordering, national political, economic, and social power are vital, affecting where and to what extent reforms take root. It is noteworthy, for example, that leaders of the democracy movement in South Korea seized on the US JD model not because they valued the model as such, but because this kind of reform was a means to undermine the legal oligarchy that propped up authoritarian governments and the chaebols in South Korea. It is not that the entrepreneurs for legal education reform were pro–United States. In fact, they saw the United States as shoring up the authoritarians. But the prestige of the US model and its attractiveness to the rising corporate law firms in Seoul made the JD reform a promising way to attack, and ultimately close, the Judicial Research and Training Institute thought to be central to the conservatism and complicity of prosecutors and judges with the status quo (Dezalay and Garth 2021). The relative success of reform in legal education, in turn, affects what defines a good law professor, what legal scholarship should be and how it should be assessed, what is good legal teaching, and even what defines a good legal argument. The websites we discussed at the beginning of this chapter clearly reflect the rise of this modernity in legal education that mimics US standards of excellence.

III. General Themes: The Transnational Meets the Local in Legal Education Reform

The collection of studies in this volume provides critical insights regarding the context and implications of the globalization of law schools across countries. Six interconnected themes emerge. We highlight these themes here, before discussing how the individual chapters illustrate them.

First, we focus particularly on efforts to shape legal education outside the United States in the image of the United States, which is part of *a longer history of transnational ordering*. It is, for example, an extension of the anti-imperial imperialism that began in the late nineteenth century as the United States was becoming a major player in international affairs and attempted to build a "legalist empire" (Coates 2016). One aspect of that legalism was investment in international courts and other institutions. After World War II, the cosmopolitan and internationalist elite in the United States sought to engage US and foreign law schools to promote lawyers to become progressive leaders of moderate change. The Ford Foundation was a major player in this relatively idealistic law and development movement (Chapter 2), whose model for the kind of lawyer needed was the US corporate lawyer-statesperson at the top of the US legal hierarchy. In the short term, it was not successful in changing the formalistic, conservative, and narrow approach of the faculties of law in places like Brazil, Chile, and India. However, the end of the Cold War, coupled with new technologies and global rankings, enhanced the impact of US legal education models.

That impact does not mean that US schools are always at the top. The relationship is more complex, as suggested by Hamann and Schmidt-Wellenburg (2020: 169). They argue that business schools, which were invented in the United States and globalized, with the help of philanthropy, in the 1950s and 1960s, changed through the criteria used by the *Financial Times*. The *FT ranking* "managed to redefine what these schools are about, putting more emphasis on the traits of European business schools, thereby opening and altering the US-American field." The change was in the interests in the long term of "the top US business schools . . . [as] they are now able to draw on resources on a global scale and have managed to proliferate their model, albeit slightly altered, worldwide." The same process could happen for law schools. The *QS* international rankings of law schools, for example, in contrast to rankings from within the United States, has metrics that include the ratio of international faculty to total faculty and the ratio of international students to total students. US schools may lose ground on these factors, but they benefit overall through the transnationalizing of key aspects of the US model. The re-export of aspects of the US model now comes from Britain, Germany, France, Australia, and other places.

Second, curiously, the recent and more successful efforts to move legal education abroad into a new direction that challenged the traditional, local, legal elites, *comes predominantly from the demand side*, especially as these countries deepen their connections to the global economy. The law and development movement of a generation earlier influenced some of the actors, but the rise and legitimation of corporate law firms globally increased demand, which was consistent with the legalist empire that the US sought to build in the post–Cold War period. This involved even greater investment in courts, legalization, and institutionalization, which facilitated the rise of transnational legal orders (Halliday and Shaffer 2015). Cosmopolitan actors, outside of conservative and traditional legal elites in many countries, saw the changed situation as an opportunity to push harder against the conservatism of legal education and legal practice. This change, which advantaged US law schools at the center of the global hierarchy, shifted somewhat the flow of law students from peripheries to cores. Unlike the idealism of the law and development movement, which sought to create lawyer statespersons as moderate reformers, much of this recent transformation is about *building elite careers in corporate law and in the institutions that sustain them, including law schools.*

The demand is not just for corporate law, as there are parallel drives for an enhanced role for constitutional, civil, political, and social rights, including through enforcement by courts and an enhanced role for NGOs. This parallel drive is captured in the chapters on the creation of FGV Direito (Chapter 2), the constitutional law ambitions of those who participate in the SELA network in Latin America (Chapter 7), the goals of those working to make law more responsive to policy in Africa (Chapter 4) and Asia (Chapter 6), and the aims of the collaborative Center for Transnational Law in London (Chapter 12). As the websites quoted at the beginning of this introduction show, a central aim also has been the desire of new and reformed law schools to produce scholarship that contributes to global debates as well as local reform. Their students and professors may then join and contribute to the reform of international and national institutions, thereby shaping transnational legal ordering processes (Shaffer 2021).

Third, changes in legal education oriented toward globalization depend on the way in which the contested "legal revolution" emanating from the United States (and other allies around the globe) *interacts with local legal hierarchies and political dynamics* (Dezalay and Garth 2021). The contrast between South Korea's JD experience versus that of Japan exemplifies how local context matters. The reformers in Japan had no real political allies. South Korean legal education reformers, however, were closely linked to the democracy movement, which gained power and used legal education reform to undermine (at least somewhat) the power of prosecutors and judges who had sustained the authoritarian government and its legacy. More subtle is the watering down of the ambitious innovations of the National Law Schools in India through the governance of the very conservative elite Indian bench and bar.

Fourth, *core-periphery relationships "tilt" the production of legal imports and exports, including in legal education.* Changes in global legal hierarchies may occur and vary by regional context, and changes in domestic legal politics may undermine the strength and prestige of the models at the core. Yet transnational processes help define what is a successful argument in legal debates, what constitutes the most influential legal scholarship, and what the top qualifications are for hiring legal scholars. These processes have tilted international law and transnational legal orders toward US models and more generally those of the Global North and West. The book's authors from the Global South, as reflected in the chapters on South Africa, SELA, and FGV Direito, confirm that they are subject to national and transnational hegemonic relationships that they cannot overturn, but they work within and harness them for their own purposes.

Fifth, the structural tilt is *not inconsistent with a realistic "transnational optimism."* The goal of many programs is to gain access to and harness global and transnational debates about legal education, transnational law, and legal reform. In order to play, as the chapter on FGV Direito underlines, it does not help to ignore the hierarchies and pretend that there is no such thing as transnational economic law, for example. Scholars and students conversant in such subjects increase their clout by mastering the language of the debates, even if the debates are structured through global hierarchies. Latin American scholars from SELA, schooled in US theories and approaches, for example, are leading global commentators on trends in constitutional law. Participation in such transnational debates may serve to legitimize particular frames of transnational legal ordering, but it is still participation in processes that would continue with or without these scholars' input. Legal education reformers, drawing on transnational debates, may in fact make a "better" law school. But they cannot credibly win recognition globally if they advocate, as they could, for cheaper and more efficient law schools with traditional, part-time professors delivering formal lectures to large numbers of students.

Scholars of transnational legal ordering may be optimistic or pessimistic in relation to structures of power. Yet there is still agency exercised in constituting, debating, and reforming such structures. Indeed, sensitivity to power imbalances may lead to an openness to reforms rather than taking the status quo for granted. Menkel-Meadow makes this point by arguing that international exchange and study leads to more "humility" about what seems natural and normal, especially for those who look down from the "upstairs" position within existing structures. Structural sociology teaches that the world is not flat, unlike what Thomas Friedman famously argued in 2005, and that legal hierarchies reproduce themselves and serve to moderate reforms for their own purposes and those they serve. But acting as if the world is flat may also be consequential.

Finally, the ticket for admission into scholarly debates, corporate law firms, and other organizations consistent with transnationalization *is not evenly distributed, including within any one country.* The diffusion of US approaches to education and markets has helped produce a dichotomy between a mass of law schools—1,000 or more in some countries—and students at an elite few law schools open only to a select group. Those who benefit must have a background that allows them to learn English and excel on standardized tests. They frequently must pay the costs that have risen dramatically in many law schools, including the Indian elite schools, FGV Direito, and African law schools under the encouragement of the World Bank. If they then decide to go abroad to pursue the most valued credentials, they must pay very high travel and tuition costs, particularly to the United States, where scholarships are few and tuitions high. Menkel-Meadow notes, for example, that students at the Center for Transnational Law have in common that they are all from relatively privileged backgrounds. The SELA network too is open only by invitation, and those invited are from the elites educated abroad at Yale and comparable places. In this respect, the globalization of legal education reflects an economic and skills divide that has become salient in the United States, to which transnational legal ordering both contributes and is called to address. This highly skewed meritocracy lends even greater weight to those few who can attend the global brand names, such as Oxford, Cambridge, Harvard, and Yale (as reflected in Chapter 13 on "who rules the world" of the international judiciary).

IV. An Introduction to and Thematic Reading of the Book's Chapters

The purpose of this Section IV is not just to introduce the chapters, but to provide a thematic reading of them in light of our respective theoretical approaches of transnational legal ordering and the sociology of the legal profession. One should of course fully read the rich chapters for their full exposes of the book's themes. In this section, we "converse" with them in light of our approaches.

We have organized the book's chapters into three parts, respectively regarding transnational processes, global law schools, and academic flows. The first part, comprising Chapters 2–7, uncovers the transnational processes that lie behind the globalization of legal education. There are of course other processes than those we can capture in this book, including, for example, the Erasmus exchanges, the marketization of legal education within Europe, and the continuing influence of German legal science on countries with civil codes. We focus, in particular, on how and why the US model has gained particular influence, a phenomenon that has not been adequately studied. We begin with the work of the Ford Foundation, which has been a key player in setting the stage for what we see today. The next chapter provides a broad look at Africa, where legal education approaches went from weak colonial investment to a kind of seesaw of reform and lack of reform depending on trends among donor groups like the Ford Foundation and donor states competing at times for ascendency. Next, we look at legal education in South Africa, both a regional legal center and a place of huge inequality traced to apartheid and colonialism. We then explore India, which advanced reforms in the late 1980s, with some help from Ford, but which took off only after Ford had given up on reform prospects there. Then we move to other countries in Asia, where again much of the story of legal education reform begins elsewhere, within donor states and foundations, but where the highly variable local impacts depend on local political economy dynamics. The last chapter in this section describes the highly successful and organically developed "Seminario en Latinoamérica de Teoría Constitucional y Política" (Latin American Seminar on Constitutional and Political Theory), also known as SELA. This North-South dynamic reveals how the globalization of legal education unfolds.

The second part, comprising Chapters 8–12, presents variations on the theme of the global law school, with each chapter covering a single law school: FGV Direito in São Paulo; the new (and first) law school in Bhutan, Jigme Singye Wangchuck School of Law; the Peking School of Transnational Law in Shenzhen; New York University's Global Law School; and the Georgetown Center for Transnational Legal Studies in London. Finally, the third part, consisting of Chapters 13–15, examines the flow of people around the globe into and out of the leading, globally recognized, law schools and faculties of law. We first look at the judges of international courts to assess the educational backgrounds of this part of the "invisible college" of international law. We next examine the global movement of students and faculty that shape the study and understanding of "international law." We then conclude with a study of non-US students coming to US law schools—the most-sought after destinations for students seeking law degrees from abroad, who become, in turn, potential conveyors of transnational legal norms.

A. Transnational Processes in the Reform of Legal Education

1. The Ford Foundation as Catalyst. Chapters 2–5 are devoted to the processes of diffusion of a US model of legal education into the Global South. We begin with the chapter by Ron Levi, Ronit Dinovitzer, and Wendy H. Wong on the evolution of Ford Foundation programs on law and legal education since the 1950s. Ford is central to the long history of US agendas in legal education reform. Ford Foundation leaders understood academic trends and political subtleties and positioned the Foundation to bring a progressive synthesis to policy experiments and initiatives at home and abroad. Other foundations such as Rockefeller played similar roles, but the Ford Foundation took the lead.

Locally, the Ford Foundation in the 1950s sought to strengthen the role of elite lawyers in relatively progressive governance. At home, this meant investment in updating comparative and international capacity in elite law schools to ensure that professors and graduates would engage with issues of foreign policy consistent with the enlarged role of the United States after World War II. An "international sensibility" was essential for lawyers to help lead and insure global engagement that would protect US interests abroad. In addition, Ford sought to educate "able foreign leaders" to encourage lawyers abroad to gain strong positions with an eye toward facilitating moderate progressive social change to stave off Communism. One prime example in the

1950s was a foray into India to try to move elite lawyers to a more progressive and respected position in governance. The Foundation found, however, that the Indian bar was highly resistant to change. The same effort was made in the "law and development" programs of the late 1960s and 1970s, again with disappointing results.

The chapter emphasizes the work on legal education in Chile. The goal of the grants to Chile was to work with small groups of local reformers to build law schools with full-time professors, which was not at all the norm at the time; hire scholars and teachers who would not hew dogmatically to formalism and who would embrace interdisciplinary approaches and problem-solving (as in the United States after Legal Realism); and form clinics for more practical education (following the Foundation's major efforts to expand legal clinics in US law schools). The program to upgrade legal education, as the authors point out, sought to "disrupt established hierarchies" in order to create a new kind of lawyer who would play a progressive role in development through harnessing a new set of tools beyond stale legal formalism. In the authors' words: "By converting law from its place as traditional and formalistic analysis, this register of law and development sought to build up legal training as *problem-solving*." The reformers wanted to translate the ideal of the American bar as adept at managing social change. As in India, they were not successful in this attempt at conversion. The Foundation, following famous self-criticisms by US participants in the programs, backed off of legal educational reform.

The Foundation largely stayed out of legal education reform abroad until the late 1970s. Responding to opportunities in the changing global environment, the Foundation quickly moved to invest in law, clinical legal education, legal exchange, and legal scholarship in and about China after its reopening of legal education in the late 1970s. A number of leading law professors in China, educated before the Communist victory but still active in building legal institutions after that victory, resurfaced after persecution in the Anti-Rightist Campaign and the Cultural Revolution.

They had international ties before the purges, and they quickly embraced exchange with the United States for themselves and their students after they regained positions in the newly reopened legal academy. US-trained lawyers, it was hoped, might move China in a pro-West and pro-Democracy direction. Columbia Law School was a key recipient of Foundation funds for these exchanges. Investment in building clinical legal education throughout China formed another large part of that investment. Clinical lawyers, it was hoped, might help to train and create lawyers who would promote rights strategies within China. Changes within China, however, thwarted that hope, as Chapter 6 on legal education reform in Asia shows. Nonetheless, the law schools in China have become thoroughly globalized in terms of their scholarship, their intellectual debates, and their connections to corporate law firms. Moreover, their students are the leading source of graduate law students in the United States (Chapter 15). The Foundation helped build, in short, a strong role for internationalized lawyers and law in China, but not legal liberalism. In contrast, the investment in legal clinics in South Africa was a key element in the move against apartheid and the establishment of democracy (Chapter 4).

Finally, we highlight the Foundation's shift in emphasis at the end of the Cold War in the 1990s, when US global hegemony was largely uncontested. By this time, the Foundation had aligned with a new US, anti-statist, economic orthodoxy shared by Democrats and Republicans. The growth of the state was increasingly seen by foundations such as Ford with suspicion, so that there was less appetite to provide advice to government and more appetite to privilege independent expertise and groups beyond the state, including to foster legal strategies for change. The enthusiasm for law expanded along with particular US models for law's globalization, as reflected in the spread of corporate law firms, US models of regulation, human rights, international criminal law, international trade through the World Trade Organization, and expanded international commercial and investment arbitration.

From the perspective of the Ford Foundation, it was critical to support global legalization processes. The reports stressed the objectives of advanced training of scholars and practitioners in the fields of international organizations and international law, education to enhance public understanding of the role of international organizations and law in furthering world peace, and research and policy analysis on important multilateral institutions. The Foundation's long commitment to legal education reform abroad facilitated the building of global exchanges and markets in legal education.

In short, the chapter shows that the Ford Foundation sought to build up a world where progressive and internationalized lawyers played leadership roles in the United States and could connect with counterparts abroad who would embrace the same kind of role—becoming moderate reformers who would help build trade and investment, democracy, and resistance to Communism. The Foundation felt that success in that venture required a new kind of lawyer, which required a new kind of legal education.

These efforts to export US modes of legal education had limited success at the time. The study shows how exporting models is only part of the story, and needs to be complemented by attention to importers. On the one hand, China after the Cultural Revolution aggressively imported some ideas from the United States and sought to build exchange relationships, create corporate law firms top down, and encourage scholarship embedded in Western scholarly communities. On the other hand, in India and Brazil (addressed in Chapters 5 and 8), there was a delayed impact. Locals who had participated in law and development were among the leaders of new calls for change a generation after law and development when the establishment and legitimation of corporate law firms increased the local demand for a more "modern" kind of law teaching.

2. Core and Periphery: Legal Education in Africa. Chapter 3, by Michelle Burgis-Kasthala, focuses on Africa. Africa can only be understood in relation to core and periphery relations that are evident but not emphasized in the preceding chapter. As she makes clear, "We need to flip our thinking . . . on Africa to regard it intellectually as the most pronounced and concentrated site of transnationalised education *because of its peripheral status.*" She refers to "epistemic dependency" as well as issues of financial dependency. Accordingly, "the continent also possesses extreme degrees of internationalisation, whether through its student mobility or dependence on foreign funding and epistemic resources."

Colonial legal investment was very weak in the English colonies that are her main focus in this chapter. As Burgis-Kasthala notes, "the British were suspicious of the disruptive power of legal education, especially as 'the Indian nationalist movement had been led by lawyers." After African contributions to the war effort in World War II, the British encouraged legal education in Africa through scholarships at the Inns of Court, rather than development of law schools in Africa. African students at the Inns of Court by the early 1960s greatly outnumbered the law students "of all English-language universities of Middle Africa."

After independence, African law schools built on African lawyers' Inns of Court experience, which unified much of the legal profession in these countries. In doing so, they adopted a curriculum and general approach to law that followed the relatively narrow approach of the British, reflected in formal teaching and weak and formalistic scholarship. The number of law schools in Africa increased substantially, with some forty-three African universities having a law faculty by 1972.

In addition to the British, "new players in the region: the US, China, the Soviet Union and US private charitable entities provided a range of direct and indirect aid contributions to higher education." At the time, UNESCO was the leading international organization promoting legal education, and it sought to support legal education in furtherance of development. But what kind of education supported law and development was "understood quite differently between various donors. Given Cold War rivalries too, higher education served as a site of competing hegemonic projects and pressures so that African perspectives were often overlooked."

From the US side, as in Latin America and India, "technical competence was not enough for fostering social transformation; a broad-based social education for lawyers was required so that they could play a central role in all sectors of society." As in Latin America, the Ford Foundation created an ambitious program, known as SAILER (Staffing of African Institutions of Legal Education and Research), which promoted an alternative to the British approach to legal education. US scholars "embrace[d] more clinical methods, which aimed at students' active resolution of 'real' social problems" (Harrington and Manji 2003). This "law and development" pedagogical approach "embodied an instrumentalist reading of both law and legal education, which could play a seminal role in the transformation of society." The British effort ended in the early 1960s, followed by the US SAILER program, in each case through the same critiques of Law and Development that also terminated programs in Latin America (Krishnan 2012).

The British story is further interesting because it provides an example of how international experiences help produce innovations that take root in the core. Legal Realist–influenced professors from Britain, notably William Twining and Robert Stevens (a Brit educated in the United States and a professor at Yale), were part of the program. Twining notes in his autobiography that the experience in Dar es Salaam helped spur the "law in context" approach: "The absence of textbooks, the fact that we were dealing with several countries and jurisdictions, the heady political atmosphere and the rapidity of change combined to make it virtually impossible to teach or learn law as a static system of abstract rules. We were forced by circumstance to be contextual, critical, comparative and to be concerned with how to think about dynamic problems and values" (Twining 2019). Twining met Stevens at Dar es Salaam and then again at Yale. Stevens "was already an iconoclastic critic of the English Bar and English legal education ... He and I persuaded Weidenfeld and Nicolson to try to break the near-monopoly of Butterworths and Sweet and Maxwell over academic law publishing in UK by launching a series of 'counter-textbooks'. Our aim was 'to subvert and revolutionise' the prevailing orthodoxy in English legal education." The influential "Law in Context" series produced by this collaboration continues to flourish and challenge traditional British legal scholarship.

With the debt crisis, the rise of neoliberalism, the attitude of key donors toward legal education in Africa changed. The World Bank became the major player, and UNESCO, which had played a major role, became marginalized. UNESCO's embrace of "dependency theory" led to the US withdrawal from it in 1984, followed by the United Kingdom and other countries. The World Bank stepped in. Its orthodoxy at the time was that human capital investment should not include investment in tertiary education, which only rewarded individual actors: "Although the Bank re-embraced higher education in its 1994 Report and has since worked strategically with UNESCO to reverse negative trends from the latter part of the 20th century, the long-term effects of these foreign policies continue to mar the African landscape." Burgis-Kasthala sees "this period as one of re-colonisation most directly through the IFIs [International Financial Institutions] and foreign NGOs, but far more profoundly, for the nature of African thought itself." The movement was from "privatization to commercialization."

Law schools gained a greater role in the 1990s, but the role of "re-colonized" legal education placed African legal education squarely in the periphery. Law faculties have been assigned very poor positions in global rankings, and they have been assimilated into the "broader trend of the growing role of transnational regulation within a globalising knowledge economy." Those who can find places in that world thrive: "Lawyers equipped with the skills and networks provided by training in elite law schools can move deftly through a range of jurisdictional zones. Resources are required though to begin such a journey and for most law students in Africa, the chances of entry are extremely limited. The best routes are through scholarships to prestigious Northern law schools or to the continent's regional legal training hubs, such as South Africa."

Legal education in Africa, buffeted by changing hegemons and legal and economic changes in the West, finally has a recognized role. But it is largely dependent on and oriented toward serving a privileged minority able to gain access to the "globalized legal education" that will embed them in global businesses, organizations, and to some extent NGOs, all of which have Northern cores and African peripheries. We will get hints of the continuing story in Chapter 15, when we trace the paths of African and other non-US students trying to build their competitiveness in the global marketplace through US JD degrees.

This chapter extends hope for reform along the lines of progressive law akin to that promoted in the United States. On the one hand, "the biggest challenge remains at the epistemic level in (re)thinking 'Africa' and law's role in its social transformation." On the other hand, "Law can serve as a tool of social transformation for a decolonial future, but it can also facilitate entrenched, colonial and neo-colonial forms of dependency." Despite the peripheral relationship of African legal education, if it produces enough members of a global legal elite with that orientation (which challenges the approach of existing local legal elites), they could at least open the knowledge economy to different voices, even though largely speaking the same legal language as a ticket to enter the discussion. This conclusion raises the complexity of how to define success—including the question of what it means to be "counter-hegemonic"—in legal education reform in a world where what is "modern" and even "innovative" is also "imperial." Many chapters take up that issue, but it is directly the focus of Chapter 8 regarding the challenges of establishing a new law school in Brazil.

3. Legal Education in South Africa: Racialized Globalizations, Crises, and Contestations. Chapter 4, by Ralph Madlalate focuses on South Africa, which looks at first glance to be one of the relative winners in legal globalization, especially within Africa. Students from all over Africa and beyond come to study there, its law schools are the highest ranked in Africa, and there is a thriving corporate bar. The legacies of colonialism and apartheid are still very present, however, leading to a stratification by race and class very present in legal education today, giving rise to movements attacking the "global" in the South African context.

As was typical of the British Empire, the first lawyers in South Africa were British educated. Local law schools did not arrive until the late nineteenth and early twentieth centuries, and divided into British and Dutch language schools, focusing on the "cores" of the British common law on the one hand, and Roman Dutch Law on the other. Rhodes Scholarships later built up the connections between London and legal education in South Africa. A few Black South Africans managed to gain admission through study in Britain, but not through Rhodes Scholarships. Apartheid in 1948 entrenched and legalized the racial divide. With apartheid, "the government strategically expanded opportunities for black students in an effort to train staff for the

administrations of quasi-independent 'Bantustans,'" which led to the creation of law faculties at the Universities of Fort Hare, the North, Zululand,
Bophuthatswana and Transkei. The legacy of apartheid was very strong.
Despite these new law schools, "in 1994 African, Indian and Colored lawyers
made up a mere 14 percent of the profession, with the remainder consisting
of white lawyers." There were prosperous private law firms, but very few non-
whites had positions in them. Nevertheless, African South African lawyers
such as Nelson Mandela challenged legalized apartheid and were leaders of
independence. Another legacy was a narrow positivism: "legal education of
this era was premised on narrow, technical and positivist approaches to law
which elided engagement with the racialized social context in which the law
operated." The new constitution after independence and the experience of
public interest law in the 1970s brought hope that law would be more oriented toward social justice.

Criticisms, such as that by the Council of Higher Education, reflect local
and global concerns—first of all, there are "too few African South African
instructors." Teaching was criticized also: "too often, students were assessed,
either wholly or substantially, on their rote learning ability." Positivism was
still an obstacle: "law faculties 'have not yet fully internalised the notion of
"transformative constitutionalism"—either in their curricula or among the
entire corpus of staff and students.'" Research rankings have brought globalized change. Medlalate quotes a scholar noting: "Academics, especially from
those universities that have bought into the rating system, now concentrate
far more on their international profiles and faculties are less inward-looking
than before and encourage contact with sister institutions around the world.
This has begun to break the isolation and insular thinking that characterized
the apartheid years and it may well encourage more theoretical, discipline-
orientated research over more practice-orientated approaches."

The historically English faculties of law, led in global rankings by the
University of Cape Town, attract students from the region as well as from
South Africa: "the major destinations for international students are the
country's historically white institutions, . . . [which] boast internationally
recognized research outputs, faculties that include 'former Rhodes Scholars
and Alexander von Humboldt fellows', 'exceptionally strong and varied international ties' and 'students from all over South Africa, Africa—and at LLM
level from many other parts of world.'"

In contrast, there are enormous challenges for the historically black universities and law faculties and for the historically disadvantaged Africans

more generally. The research requirements do not fit the apartheid-created universities, these schools lack resources, and they face other problems. Yet they play a crucial role "in educating black lawyers." As we see in India in the next chapter, the deeper problem is *who* has access to the so-called top law schools which provide gateways to the top positions. As Madlatate notes, fundamental is "students' ability to succeed in higher education given the educational challenges they face before university, not least the important role of language."

This two-tier and racialized "meritocratic" division, unlike in the United States or India, is not without challenge. The year 2015 saw the "(re-)emergence of university students as a powerful force in the country's higher education system. Organized around slogans including #RhodesMustFall and #FeesMustFall, these movements introduced a radical anti-colonial critique of higher education in South Africa." These criticisms, whatever their success, suggests that it is naïve to expect that the mantra of meritocracy will thwart criticism of globalization when the mantra creates structures through which only a few, mostly from advantaged backgrounds, gain admission to a few privileged law faculties and schools, and then gain the rewards of the few elite positions available in a globalized political economy.

4. Transformations and Contests over Legal Education in India. Chapter 5, by Yves Dezalay and Bryant Garth, looks at the Indian example of legal education reform and seeks to place it in the context of a "legal revolution" associated with financialization of the economy, neoliberalism, the rise of corporate law firms, and the reform of legal education aligned with these other features. The establishment of the National Law School in Bangalore in 1986 resulted from a mix of Indian entrepreneurs promoting the US model to upgrade and modernize legal education at a particular time of challenge for the legal profession in India. A faction of the elite recognized the need to provide more openness and legitimacy to the very conservative legal hierarchy led by senior advocates and judges of high courts and the Supreme Court. That establishment was embarrassed by the weak role the Supreme Court played during the emergency declared in the mid-1970s by Indira Gandhi. The long process culminated in the creation of one underfinanced law school, the National Law School at Bangalore, which sought to produce public interest lawyers who would take advantage of Public Interest Litigation unleashed by the Supreme Court after the debacle of the Emergency. After financial challenges threatened to end the experiment, the Ford Foundation provided funds to allow its survival.

Fortuitously, the first class graduated just at the time of the liberalization of the economy in 1991, and the first and subsequent classes pursued the resultant legal opportunities in new corporate law firms modeled explicitly on US law firms (Ballakrishnen 2019; Krishnan 2004, 2005). The success of the first National Law School led to the proliferation of twenty or more built on the same model in subsequent decades. These schools are open to those who do well on standardized tests, charge a tuition that is high by Indian standards, seek to have more engaged teaching, and try to provide an Americanized approach.

They are deemed to represent a major upgrade in Indian legal education, joined now by private alternatives led by the Jindal Global Law School, funded by an Indian billionaire industrialist, Naveen Jindal, the Chancellor of Jindal Global Law School. JGLS is even more embedded in US legal education than the National Law Schools with close ties to Harvard and Indiana in particular.

The weakness of the National Law Schools, rarely noted by scholars of legal education reform, is that in order to gain the acquiescence of the Indian bar to operate, they gave complete control of the schools to the Senior Advocates and Judiciary, which have no incentive to promote substantial change. From the perspective of reformers, the National Law Schools are underfunded, the professors underpaid and disrespected by the bench and bar, and there is little opportunity for professors at all but a few of the schools to undertake scholarly research.

Meanwhile, the Senior Advocates and Judiciary thrive despite criticism that they stubbornly resist what a "modern" legal education offers: sophisticated legal arguments fortified with interdisciplinary insights versus forensic artifice and lack of preparation; focused hearings versus endless rambling; and more meritocratic entry from more diverse groups versus personal connections and long family dynasties. Hierarchy within the bar continues to reproduce itself through family capital leading to apprenticeships out of schools that barely teach, such as the Government Law College in Mumbai. The Senior Advocates thrive because they are essential in big cases in order to gain the attention of the top judiciary that come from the same social world.

Yet the legal revolution is challenging this legal oligarchy. The corporate law firms, which continue to hire National Law School graduates, are increasingly looking for ways to bypass the Senior Advocates. Their hiring and promotion practices are notably meritocratic (Ballakrishnen 2019). Meritocratic graduates who receive Rhodes Scholarships and other scholarships to study abroad are increasingly returning and promoting scholarship about the courts and advocacy from independent bases in think tanks and some of the law schools, including Jindal. These think tanks and Jindal, in turn, are funded by major corporations and entrepreneurs, not lawyers, who also encourage an upgrading of legal scholarship and practice and are impressed with the elite credentials of the young founders of these groups. This combination of meritocratic, scholarly, international, economic, and even political capital, is working to upgrade the careers of legal academics, challenge the bar where it is vulnerable, and put pressure on the bar's method of reproduction in favor of more meritocratic selection. To date, however, the bar is closed to this effort. One indicator is that no National Law School graduate has become a judge or Senior Advocate.

More than a generation after law and development, there is a pretty strong movement to upgrade and modernize legal education, building on the National Law Schools. The demand has become much stronger. It is only a matter of time until the bar will have to recognize the force of these challenges and retool for what the latest legal revolution defines as modern. What is modern, once more, is deeply embedded in the global community of corporate law firms, global NGOs, and the transnational legal ordering of business and other areas of law.

5. The Efforts and Limits to Engage Lawyers with Policy in Asia. Chapter 6, by Veronica Taylor, follows a number of these themes into other parts of Asia. The chapter takes up a normative challenge that is part and parcel of global efforts to modernize legal education. There are again donor countries and foundations in the story, but the United States is not always a major player. The theme, however, is one that comes initially from US legal education, but it is reinterpreted and adapted in the different Asian contexts. It is the need for law schools and their professors to become scholarly actors in issues of intellectual debate and reform. Historically, that has not been the case either in the British model of legal education nor in the continental model. Very formal analysis of cases in Britain and codes on the Continent were the norm. Taylor asks whether "a 'revival' of law in some Asian states . . . is reflected in a 'knowledge to policy' process by law schools?" She asks, "in what ways do Asian law schools influence the state or broker norms that are part of the globalization of law, and with what kinds of drivers, partners, politics and constraints?" The goal is for law schools to adopt a model that touches on politics and political controversy at home and abroad.

After describing donor projects addressing the rule of law and transitional justice in Myanmar, Taylor looks at the role of legal academics. First, it is striking that, while, "Well-paid jobs and preferment were open to young, English-speaking, 'reform-minded' legal intermediaries, . . . there have been fewer opportunities for legal academics and other government employees." They cannot compete with the cosmopolitan reformers integrated already into a global donor community of legal reformers. Further, even the tentative efforts to instill the idea of law school "knowledge to policy" engagement hit resistance. Partly, the university leaders may have had a different politics than the new regime, but there is also some nationalistic resentment "of pressure to accept international legal norms or sanctions." Taylor points to "universal themes within this skirmishing." Instead of embracing a new internationally inspired role, there is a "struggle to insulate the law school at a national university from global engagement that may have ramifications for domestic politics."

Transformations in legal education and in the legal profession, once more, are contested. They are generally effective only if they are part of a broader political and social movement. The previous chapter on India, for example, suggests that the new pressure to transform and modernize the Indian legal elite—the grand advocates and high court judges—is gaining momentum because of the support of certain parts of the government, corporate philanthropy, the new corporate law firms, and the opinions of transnational corporate law firms.

Taylor provides a mix of case studies to illustrate similar themes. The rise of the clinical education movement in China, much of which was funded by the Ford Foundation, is the first example. The focus on access to justice and legal empowerment, she says, did not survive the turn to "rule by law" in the past decade in China. Thus, "the clear implication here is that Chinese law schools do not have an unfettered ability to advance into an engagement or nascent policy space like clinical legal education, even if they are producing a public good, if that conflicts with the Party's fear of 'empowerment' translating into social instability." Although there was some real success in building a strong position for an internationalized legal elite, that did not translate to investment in "liberal legalism" (Zhang and Ginsburg 2019).

The discussion of Indonesia is instructive. Taylor notes the transnational debate about how Indonesian law schools should relate to the modernist push we have seen generally: "A scholarly debate has simmered across decades about the mission of the Indonesian law school—whether it should teach 'pure law' [as a legacy from the Dutch], whether it should serve the national interest and teach 'progressive law', or whether it should have a more socio-legal, empirically-informed cast." Part of the debate, as elsewhere, is whether "the formalist character of legal education in Indonesia [is] an impediment," which would be "consistent with [Simon] Chesterman's thesis about the constraining power of colonial models." The Chesterman thesis does not say, but could have said, "constraining" in comparison to the US model. There does not seem to be much local resonance for reform of legal education in Indonesia so far. Only the private Indonesia Jentera Law School offers a different model.

Another repeated issue is the impact of international funders within the local legal market. In Indonesia, for example, there are experienced lawyers capable of getting the positions offered by funders, but these projects have "the effect of taking the most productive staff out of the law school, paying them a premium to work for an outside organization, and framing the law schools as 'recipients' of aid, rather than as agents and genuine partners in the design and implementation of the projects." Despite this embedded hegemonic relationship, Taylor nevertheless is hopeful that the new and more creative partnering with Australia might be more effective in building local commitments to evidence-based policies "that advance social equity."

Finally, Taylor concludes with the failure of the adoption of the US graduate law school model in Japan, in contrast to South Korea. The inability to make the bar exam less of an obstacle, through the resistance of the legal establishment, effectively killed any liberal impetus in Japanese reforms. The bar passers now generally are those who study law at both the undergraduate and graduate levels, instead of bringing other perspectives to law through wide-ranging undergraduate experiences. The crushing dominance of the bar exam and the need to teach to it also undermines social engagement. Some of the new law schools did seek to "deliver a distinctive style of socially-engaged and practical legal education that would have been a departure from the abstract rote-learning of the past," with foreign law professors teaching some courses, such as international commercial law courses in English, and with "skills training through clinical education and mooting." However, "fifteen years into the experiment, arguably none of reform goals has been achieved, and instead the law schools' knowledge mandate has shrunk." Taylor highlights the issue of "design" in Japan compared to South Korea, which did not keep the undergraduate law programs open. That design issue closely relates to the fact that the South Korean reform, unlike that in Japan, overcame the resistance from the legal oligarchy because it joined with a "democracy movement" challenging authoritarian government, the chaebols, and the complicity of the legal system in protecting that reactionary alliance (Dezalay and Garth 2021).

6. A Yale-Forged, Transnational Scholarly Network in Latin America. The last chapter in this section, Chapter 7, by Javier Couso, takes us to Latin America and an extraordinarily successful North-South venture, the "Seminario en Latinoamérica de Teoría Constitucional y Política" (Latin American Seminar on Constitutional and Political Theory), also known as SELA. Couso himself has been active in this group since 2001. The network constituted by this group, as Couso points out, "brings together legal scholars from Latin America's most important law schools, and one of the U.S.'s most prestigious centers of legal education, Yale Law School." SELA represents one of the most consequential networks contributing to global legal education in Latin America in the last two decades." Couso states upfront that there is a core-periphery or hegemonic relationship, noting the "the role that it plays in furthering U.S. conceptions of law and legal education throughout Latin America," but this is not inconsistent with embracing the contribution of SELA in improving scholarship and legal education in Latin America.

This annual seminar began in 1995 through the entrepreneurship of Owen Fiss of Yale Law School, who, with some of his Latin American students, sought to build a seminar to keep together networks that had developed around the Argentine liberal legal philosopher Carlos Nino, who had died very suddenly. SELA's membership has always been by invitation only. It began with Yale and a few law schools in Argentina and Chile, and then expanded to include a good portion of the leading law schools in Latin America. Rigorously intellectual, the seminar works with plenary sessions and critiques of individual papers. As Couso notes, "while in the first years of SELA the papers were commissioned by the Yale faculty, since the mid 2000s they started to be selected in a competitive way by the Organizing Committee, from abstracts submitted by the members of the network." Yale provides most, but not all, of the financial and administrative support.

Intellectually, "[t]he paradigm that frames most of the debates taking place at a typical SELA meeting is a liberal-egalitarian one. Thus, the kind of authors most likely to be cited in the papers are Ronald Dworkin, H.L.A. Hart, John Rawls, Owen Fiss, Robert Alexy, Catherine Mackinnon, Reva Siegel, Carlos Nino, Jürgen Habermas, Tom Scanlon and Thomas Nagel, as well as scores of Anglo-American and European scholars who work within that tradition." The network has broadened to include critical legal studies, law and society, feminist jurisprudence, and other disciplinary approaches, but the seminar has maintained "its liberal democratic and egalitarian outlook."

The Latin American scholars, at the beginning mostly with graduate law degrees from Yale, were ambitious. They sought "a cultural shift in Latin America's legal academy" that drew on their Yale educations. They sought "the gradual construction of a community of scholars sharing a 'common language', 'a certain vision of law', and an 'intellectual style' characterized by sharp, analytical, and horizontal debates." This was not the prevailing "language" or "style" in Latin America. SELA provided a meeting place and supporting network for "scholars from different countries of the region sharing the above-stated conceptions." There was a very clear target. The network was expected to help their members "confront the hierarchical, parochial and formalistic traditional legal discourse then prevailing in Latin America." They hoped to become influential players and reformers in their own legal systems.

SELA's launching was at a propitious time. Democratic transition brought a new focus on public law. The conservatism of the legal establishment and the judiciary during the dictatorship periods spurred the young legal challengers. There was "strong criticism of the way the judiciaries—and more broadly, the legal systems—had behaved during the wave of brutal military dictatorships in the preceding decades," such that "a new generation of legal scholars was starting to challenge the old one."

As we have seen repeatedly, "[t]he most common criticism issued by the new generation against the judiciary and the legal academy was its 'formalism.' By this, they meant the mechanical application of statutory law, even in cases where it led to utter violation of important constitutional values (with the material injustice that came with it)." Accordingly, "most original SELA members shared the notion that courts can be important actors on behalf of social justice, through an active enforcement of the constitutional principle of substantive equality," including through engaging with international courts, and, in particular, the Inter-American Court of Human Rights. A final and related theme that contributed to SELA's original cohesion was the strong indictment shared by its members of the way legal education and research was being conducted in Latin America at the time. SELA's launching "coincided with the constitution of the first fully professional academic communities in Argentina, Chile, Peru and Colombia." This reform agenda replaced "teaching by prestigious litigants and lawyers on an hourly basis, using legal treatises written by themselves in their spare time," with "a legal academy made of scholars devoted to full-time teaching and research, as happens in the legal academy of most of the Global North." These scholars were part of "an important 'struggle' to replace what was seen as an obsolete—and deeply flawed—legal academy with a more professional and modern one."

Couso raises the question of whether SELA presents an example of legal imperialism, noting that, "SELA has been a way to transmit U.S. legal ideas to Latin America. It also involves a link between top Latin American law schools and prestigious academic institutions in the United States." More generally, the mission involved "the 'modernization' of the legal field in Latin America." Yet, he maintains, the process was "almost communitarian," rather than imperial, and it was successful in a number of respects.

Regarding SELA's influence, Couso concludes by noting "the disproportionate number of presidents of universities and deans of law schools, justices of supreme and constitutional courts, and highly influential legal scholars that have been members of SELA." Their careers show the growing legitimacy in Latin America of the scholarly approaches and legal politics that originally were identified especially with the United States. The old guard may still exist, but its power is much diminished.

Many of these law schools have reformed toward engaging full-time professors, valuing interdisciplinary scholarship that meets "global" standards, and instituting clinics and transnationalized curricula. We see one example from Brazil in the next chapter—FGV Direito in São Paulo—where Oscar Vilhena Vieira, the current dean and co-author of the chapter, is also an active participant in the SELA seminars and network. That chapter also shows how these reforms from the public law side complement the institutionalization of large corporate law firms and processes of transnational legal ordering. It adds to the complexity of the question raised in several chapters. What does it mean to talk about hegemonic and counterhegemonic approaches to legal education?

B. Global Law Schools

1. FGV Direito, São Paulo: A Global Law School in Brazil. Chapter 7, by Oscar Vilhena Vieira and José Garcez Ghirardi, critically examines their own

law school, Fundação Getulio Vargas (FGV) Direito, São Paulo, which has now been in operation for eighteen years. The title of this inspiring chapter, "The Unstoppable Force, the Immovable Object: Challenges for Structuring a Cosmopolitan Legal Education in Brazil," perfectly captures the contest between the advocates of a new global revolution in legal education and a local (in this case Brazilian) legal oligarchy embedded in economic, social, and political power. The authors stress that the story of FGV Direito "illustrates the difficulties to implement a new paradigm for legal education in an emerging South. It also suggests that any successful attempt at reform in this area depends on the institution's ability to strike a politically workable, educationally sensible balance between global demands and local realities, between new and traditional paradigms."

Prior to the split with Portugal in 1822, there were no law faculties in Brazil. The first was established in 1827 to train the legal bureaucracy. There was from the start "an enduring propensity to be encyclopedic, with courses usually closely following the structure of the major codes" enacted almost a century later in Brazil and based on European models. But more important than study were networks: "Beyond the impact that the goal of forming State bureaucrats had on curricula and teaching priorities, the vicinity to power which characterized law schools also importantly affected their institutional dynamics. Not unlike the English Inns of Court, Brazilian Law schools were primarily *loci* for networking and jockeying for advantageous positions." As a result, "technical legal expertise was less important than political acumen, as the ability to ingratiate oneself to the right colleagues was key to success in a country where legal and political elites were virtually identical. Students who prioritized lessons and books over socializing were often ridiculed as *rábulas*, a derogatory term used to designate petty-minded lawyers."

Professors were part-time teachers with private legal practices and links to politics and business. They were "praised according to their standing on the public stage. More often than not, it was their success outside the academy that validated their position as scholars. Higher Court Justices, state ministers and secretaries, alongside with the most successful and prestigious private lawyers of the day, were considered natural professors to an institution that aimed at preparing for government office." Accordingly, "the selection of new professors, in tandem with this practice, seemed to depend more on personal allegiances than on academic achievement." Academic research involved mainly the production of outlines and commentaries on codes. The analysis and teaching were highly formalistic. This was the model that the SELA reformers also attacked.

There were some criticisms from Brazilian legal scholars of the "formalism, teacher-centered pedagogy, lecturing and parochialism," but this system, organized around the eminent "jurist" professor, politician, and notable, was deeply embedded in structures of power. The law and development efforts to challenge this hierarchy in the 1960s and 1970s failed. The main "reform" in legal education in the neoliberal-oriented 1990s was to marketize it by deregulation. The number of law schools rose from 165 in 1995 to over 1,300 in 2015—largely through increases in private law schools, with the hope that market competition would foster improvements in legal education. This deregulation and dramatic increase in the number of law schools occurred in many other countries, including China and India.

FGV Direito challenged the traditional law schools in numerous ways. First, the faculty was selected to gather scholars with international experience, advanced degrees, and the ability to participate in "cosmopolitan academic dialogues" and interdisciplinary debates. Second, the curriculum was transnationalized in order to "respond to a more complex, globalized and entrepreneurial context, both in the private and public spheres." New required undergraduate courses included: "Crime and Society; Regulation and Development; Corporate Procedural Law; Law and Economics; Global Law; Law and Development; Law and Arts." There was also a new Global Law program bringing visiting professors and encouraging domestic students to study abroad. Recognizing the school's challenge to prevailing national approaches, FGV Direito became active in the Law School Global League, a group of more than twenty like-minded law schools around the world. The school moved away from "the letter-of-the law, statute-commentary syllabuses which characterize traditional legal teaching." Instead, "FGV Direito SP implemented a student-centered methodology designed to foster problem-solving abilities and to lead students to think critically about Law." These innovations in engaged and full-time teaching and globally sophisticated research meant that FGV Direito made no place in its structure for the Brazilian jurist/professors who are at the top of the Brazilian professional hierarchy. This was a bold innovation.

The authors recognize that, like SELA, it is easy to criticize this institution as "as an attempt to merely transplant US/European models to a regional context. At worst, it may be perceived as a spearhead to the agenda of North cultural dominance." Some critics on the left, indeed, say that FGV represents a US-oriented "neoliberal" program designed to train corporate lawyers. The founding dean of FGV Direito São Paulo was Ary Oswaldo Mattos Filho, a supporter of the earlier law and development program of the 1970s, who later created a very successful corporate law firm in São Paulo at a time when there were very few such law firms. The current dean, Oscar Vilhena Vieira, comes from the human rights world, but, as noted earlier, has links to US approaches to scholarship and education through SELA and its networks.

The legal imperialism criticism, however, misses the point of the school. As stated by the authors, "The best path to take seems that of being clear about the choices one is making and explicit about the reasons for making them." They do not dispute that they are facilitating a kind of modernization consistent with the legal revolution of corporate law firms, financialization, and transnational approaches to issues of governance, including human rights. They note, however, that "the workings of international financial markets, organizations and agencies, the problems of refugees, environmental hazards and terrorism, affect the country and pressure its legal and political institutions to respond to them. These problems will not go away simply by being ignored, nor will Brazil's capacity to handle them be improved if no action is taken." The traditional law schools had ignored these issues and global transformations that deeply affect Brazil.

The authors recognize that, at the same time, "in the international arena, these problems have been shaped and dealt with, from a legal viewpoint, by instruments and dynamics mirroring, unsurprisingly, those of the global North powers leading the globalization process. This hegemony is hardly surprising and has been described and discussed at length." Nevertheless, they contend, legal actors "have to be taught the rules currently shaping the game so that they can operate, question and eventually contribute to shape these rules. A refusal to learn or teach the grammar in which global transactions are made denies the country the much-needed skills of being able to question it." The school, in other words, aims, in part, to help Brazilians build legal capacity to participate in shaping the rules of the game, even though the rules structurally reflect hegemonic power (Shaffer 2021).

FGV Direito's powerful challenge to the traditional legal hierarchy and the legal education system that supports it is not naive. It will not topple the Brazilian hierarchy. Yet it does aim to foster deliberation toward change. As the authors write, "even though there are numerous examples of resistance, and criticism against a more problem-oriented, interdisciplinary and globalized approach to law, a new dialogue has begun." FGV Direito, in fact, plays a significant role in refurbishing and upgrading schools such as the University of São Paulo (USP), the most prestigious law school in Brazil. The students at all the elite law schools, including USP, are well aware of the advantages of study abroad, including especially the United States. Some of these graduates find their way to the FGV faculty, where they maintain their networks with USP's professors and students.

Although it is not the focus of the chapter, the ongoing dialogues point to the truism that legal revolutions not only can be resisted, but also co-opted. Brazil's economic reforms over several decades have been led by economists and mostly resisted by the jurists of the most prestigious law faculties. FGV is helping make law and Brazilian lawyers more relevant to issues around Brazil's participation in the global economy. The result of FGV Direito's leadership affects the teaching and research in USP through interchange and common experiences. Yet it could go the other way as well. FGV Direito could, in theory, seek to increase its local position by moving closer to the traditional law schools, such as by hiring or allowing internal development of prestigious jurist/professors, with perhaps a reduced emphasis on teaching. The dynamics of these struggles will play out over time.

It is interesting in this respect that the first corporate law firms in Brazil were initially outside of and challenging the mainstream of the profession, and they served mainly international clients as well. The pioneering firm of Pinheiro Neto, in particular, in the 1990s rejected allowing professors to join the firm and allowing partners to get involved in politics. The law firms have now made their peace with the jurists, who are now involved in corporate law firms, and who indeed often recruit their own students according to the traditional model. Successful challenges to the traditional elite, whether in Brazil or India, are more likely to update and rebuild the elite than to topple it from positions deeply embedded in political, economic, and social power.

2. Modeling a Nation's First Law School: Bhutan. Chapter 9, by David S. Law, examines the Jigme Singye Wangchuck School of Law (JSW) in Bhutan, which opened in 2017 and became the first law school in that country. The school started with a "clean slate," but it also sought global credibility and the adoption of global best practices. Graduates from the first class, with only twenty-five students, were supposed to become "elite lawyers, judges, and bureaucrats." The law school is also in part a nation-building exercise, as Law notes. It aims to build legal autonomy from India while also contributing to building the global identity of Bhutan as the pioneer of the concept of Gross National Happiness. There is a compulsory course in "Law

and Gross National Happiness," as well as requirements in Buddhist philosophy, environmental law, "Appropriate Dispute Resolution," and "Penal Code & Restorative Justice" (in place of Criminal Law).

JSW offers a five-year undergraduate LLB program. The school is free of any economic fees for the students. The curriculum includes all kinds of global as well as locally oriented classes: "To the extent that there is an international or global version of some subject on the curricular wish list, JSW has been happy to embrace that version. And to the extent that there is not, JSW has been happy to develop unique offerings of its own." The school offers clinics as well. As a result, "pedagogy at JSW is, like Bhutanese law itself, an eclectic mix: it reflects the heterogeneity of the faculty and ranges from lecturing (in philosophy), to almost fully Socratic instruction (in torts), to simulation and experiential learning."

The chapter recognizes that JSW could not really operate on a blank slate: "In the absence of raw materials for constructing a system of law or legal education that could plausibly be described as autochthonous, resistance to foreign models is not an option, and necessity is the mother of imitation. The case of legal education in Bhutan illustrates the extent to which globalization is often not a matter of choice but of necessity." Accordingly, "outsiders have been essential to the creation and design of JSW at every step of the way, from the hiring and training of faculty to the design of the curriculum, to the construction of the campus." Law stresses the challenges of bridging the local and the global: "On the other hand, Bhutanese policy is focused intently on maintaining local control of the development process and bolstering national identity and autonomy. . . . In legal education as in other domains, the challenge for Bhutan is to find ways of obtaining outside help while not only preserving but enhancing local ownership and identity."

While seeking to build autonomy from India, where Bhutanese lawyers had been educated in the past, JSW also decided to embrace the five-year program of India's National Law Schools, which also were subject to transnational curricular influences. This move was almost natural since the National Law Schools were modeled on the US law school. Bhutanese leaders also shared criticisms of traditional Indian law schools that had, in part, inspired the creation of India's National Law Schools:

[T]he term used to describe traditional Indian pedagogy is "chalk and talk": an instructor stands at a chalkboard and speaks from "dusty yellow notes" that have barely changed in decades. India's elite National Law

Schools sought to address these ills in the late 1990s with a significantly revamped and interdisciplinary curriculum that expanded the course of study from three to five years, but they are still afflicted by what one graduate described as "low-paid, bad instructors."

As we stressed earlier, this ongoing challenge reflects the dominance of the very conservative senior advocates and judges over India's National Law Schools. In a sense, Bhutan picked up the baton of the modernist challengers to the Indian legal establishment.

The strong US influence, which is consistent with that challenge, came from personal networks, funding, and the serendipity of a relationship with White and Case, a US-based, transnational law firm with which the founders consulted from the start. Relationships to a few US law schools also proved fruitful, such as with Stanford and George Washington. The international hierarchy that the flow of professors and students from the periphery to the core exemplifies (Chapters 14 and 15) was bound to play a role in this and any other efforts to build world-class law schools, just as for Jindal Global Law School and FGV Direito São Paulo. That relationship is reflected in the background of the president of the law school, Her Royal Highness Princess Sonam Dechan Wangchuck, who has an undergraduate degree from Stanford and a Harvard LLM.

This hierarchy also appears in the foreign faculty hired, including a vice dean, Michael Peil, who had been at Washington University School of Law. The goal of encouraging all the Bhutanese faculty at JSW "to obtain LL.M. degrees from various countries in the English-speaking world, mainly the United States and Australia" also illustrates these hierarchies. Nonetheless, as stressed in Chapter 8 regarding FGV, the embrace of a US-inspired legal revolution reflects not just hegemonic relationships but also an opportunity both to better participate in international policy debates and to address domestic challenges. Law concludes that "American influence will remain considerable, albeit unsystematic and uncoordinated."

3. A Transnational Law School in China. Chapter 10, by Philip J. McConnaughay and Colleen B. Toomey, takes up the story of another notable global experiment, this time in Shenzhen, a city in the heart of the Pearl Delta and at the forefront of China's embrace of economic globalization, serving "as a principal gateway for China's 'Belt and Road Initiative.'" The Peking University School of Transnational Law (STL) admitted its first class in 2008. STL was a local initiative that seems to have no relationship

to foreign donors or sponsors. Hai Wen, an economics professor with a US PhD, became Chancellor of Peking University's Shenzhen Graduate Campus, and came up with the idea after observing that a growing number of Chinese students were going abroad to seek JD degrees from US law schools (as Chapter 15 shows). The goal was to establish a law school on Peking University's Shenzhen campus that "would offer an American JD, in English; be competitive academically with the very best U.S. law schools; and charge tuition and fees that would be dramatically lower than those a growing number of Chinese graduate students were paying for U.S.-based legal education." In the words of the founding dean, the aim was for STL graduates to enjoy identical professional opportunities so that they can "walk out and work for Paul Hastings, Akin Gump and other similar firms."

The founders intended not just to have a US-modeled law school. It was to grant JD degrees with full accreditation from the American Bar Association (ABA). They had support for accreditation from many corporate law firm leaders in China and elsewhere, eager to hire lawyers trained for those firms. After securing approval in China, they hired Founding Dean Jeffrey Lehman, formerly dean of the University of Michigan Law School.

The US legal recession helped to kill this prospect, however. As a reminder that globalization is contested at home and abroad, the lawyers within the ABA, especially in a recession dominated by the rhetoric of "too many lawyers," felt that there should be no competition from lawyers produced in China or anywhere else outside the United States. Prior to the bad news in 2012, the STL JD curriculum had gone ahead with a small resident faculty and "visiting scholars recruited from the very best U.S. law schools . . . together with U.S. practitioners who were among the profession's most esteemed, including two former ABA presidents." The former ABA presidents modeled the US "lawyer-statesperson" role identified with corporate lawyers at the top of the US legal profession. The school thus presented the ideal of elite law in the United States, which we also saw in the Ford Foundation's programs (Chapter 2).

The founders aimed to build this model in China. The school's identification with China's leading research university—Bei-da, Peking University—plus the attraction of the JD, attracted students to it. Early enthusiasm was reflected in a commitment by the government of Shenzhen "to fund a new signature building for the law school designed by the leading architectural firm Kohn Pederson Fox of New York."

After the prospect of ABA accreditation evaporated, the leaders of STL refocused on STL's China law Juris Master (JM) curriculum, which had existed only to comply with China's educational regulations. The school did not offer the LLB, which remains the most prestigious law degree in China. The JM degree they were authorized to offer was created in 1998, partly in response to the shift toward JDs in South Korea and Japan. There was optimism at the time that it would be the main vehicle for training practicing lawyers in China (Erie 2009: 67), but the challenge to the LLB degree's status was not successful (*id.*). The school nonetheless has done well, and it has excelled in placing its students in elite law firms, despite its inability to offer the highest prestige degree.

STL decided to retool to offer both the JM and the JD in a four-year program. Their revisions in the curriculum "recognize that China law and civil codes, although based largely on the civil law codes of Germany, in fact reflect a host of customary, communist, Soviet, American and other influences." The niche they sought was combining the civil and common law "in a way that is directly analogous to the juxtaposed legal traditions of Shenzhen and Hong Kong." STL focused research and teaching on the hybrid transnational legal approaches that China might employ for the Belt and Road Initiative (Erie 2021; Shaffer and Gao 2020). It particularly sought scholars who focused on "new and emerging mechanisms of transnational governance, such as the multinational networks of public, private, national and international actors that are producing transnational norms and regulatory structures independently of national government action with respect to such matters of transnational concern as climate change, technology transfer, food safety, energy and natural resource protection." It also seeks scholars who are able to address "the legal systems of major Belt and Road countries" for "transactions and commercial dispute resolution involving non-Western parties." In reflection of the school's name, first-year students take a year-long course in "Transnational Legal Practice," which focuses on legal literacy in English and essentials of Common Law analysis and advocacy.

The ambitions of STL are significant, reflected in its location in what aspires to be "China's Silicon Valley." STL aims to train Chinese students to be participants in the shaping of transnational legal ordering. In this way, it hopes to build from US models while also "challenging as never before prevailing assumptions of a global convergence of law around the Western legal tradition." In this way, it can train lawyers that are responsive to preferences among Asian parties to address "relational" concerns contractually, such as through a duty of "good faith" and principles of "equity," coupled with "dispute resolution clauses [that] might require more flexible procedures or more elastic notions of impartiality so that mediation and arbitration may be blended more easily with the same decision-maker. And so forth." In this way, STL can train elite lawyers for China's Belt and Road Initiative that "portend significant non-Western influence on the development of commercial and legal practices and principles, both within the region and globally." It thereby will provide legal support for "China's global economic ascension."

STL, as other *avant garde* global schools, promotes an agenda of domestic legal education reform. As the authors note, "legal education in China still is largely theoretical and provided via one-way lecturing to large numbers of students, often hundreds at a time. The study of law is not based on the case method, classes are not interactive, the acquisition of professional skills is not a priority, and the overall academic rigor of most law programs is not high. In a very real way, the reform of STL's China law curriculum is creating a new model of J.M. legal education for China."

STL pursues its ambitions through building from US legal education models that involve "rigorous analytic thinking, the ability to see all sides of an issue, the ability to solve complex problems creatively, and the ability to persuade, both orally and in writing." It does so through use of the "case method" and "interactive classes." STL has responded to the growing role of advanced technologies and financial services in Asia's rise and economic globalization more generally, with an internationalized curriculum that supports related legal services, such as in intellectual property, law and biotechnology, bilingual contracts, cross-cultural dispute resolution, international banking, and other cutting-edge areas. The school also sponsors an entrepreneurship clinic that advises on the legal needs of start-up companies in Shenzhen's "incubator." STL includes a strong comparative element in its preparation of students for such transnational practice.

STL faces some bureaucratic challenges, including the limitation on the number of students and, to a lesser extent, the inability to offer the LLB; but it has found an identity and connection to the Pearl Delta and the Belt and Road Initiative. Professional placement of STL graduates appears to have been highly successful, with close to 100 percent of graduates securing positions by graduation with domestic and international law firms and companies, state-owned enterprises, or government. The destination of students has shifted in interesting ways over the last ten years, reflective of changes in the market for legal services in China. During STL's early years, well over 50 percent of graduates went to Beijing, and 25 percent or more joined international law firms, often abroad. In recent years, almost as many graduates have joined Shenzhen law firms and companies as have gone to Beijing (about 30 percent of graduates to each location), with graduates overwhelmingly, regardless of destination, joining Chinese law firms and companies over international firms. The shift reflects the fact that Chinese law firms continue to capture an increasing share of both inbound and outbound international legal work involving China and Chinese companies.

The impact of STL on legal education in China is hard to predict. The JM did not gain prestige because of the long history of prizing graduates of the top undergraduate faculties of law, who then go on to get LLMs (Erie 2009). STL is also relatively small, regulated by quota allocated by the Ministry of Education to Chinese universities, with only 79 graduates in 2019, although it may now admit 155 students in each entering class, for a total student population of 620. Nonetheless, the scholarly and teaching focus of STL could, as with FGV Direito, help the country participate more effectively in shaping transnational governance through law. China is much better positioned economically to exercise such influence.

STL, in sum, has elements in common with other globalized law schools, such as the three Hong Kong law faculties, JSW in Bhutan, the Jindal Global Law School, FGV Direito, and a number of Australian law faculties. They compete, for example, for expatriate professors to internationalize their schools. As shown by Roberts in Chapter 14, a core and periphery phenomenon continues to affect their positioning. Nonetheless, with China's rise and its transnational ambitions, STL reflects an attempt at modernization of legal education along a US model while adapting it to a world in which China is rapidly developing and, more recently, becoming more assertive in global governance (Shaffer 2021).

4. The Original "Global Law School": NYU. Chapter 11, by Kevin E. Davis and Xinyi Zhang, moves to the United States and the original US "global law school," New York University School of Law. Their chapter assesses why students from NYU decide to take advantage of NYU semester-long programs, notably in Shanghai, Paris, and Buenos Aires. The authors critique "the derived demand theory," which in this case means that, "if globalization generates demand for multijural lawyers, then prospective students will demand multijural legal training from law schools," such as that available from these study-abroad programs.

It is interesting to compare this global law school with those already discussed. First, it is squarely in the core, habituated to the scholarly and teaching approaches that are now promoted by law schools such as Jindal, FGV Direito, STL, and JSW to challenge traditional approaches and hierarchies outside the United States. Domestically, however, NYU occupies a similar position to many of the law schools that have globalized. As noted for China by Wang, Liu, and Li (2017), the national schools mostly likely to invest in "globalization" are those who see the investment as a way to compete with the most elite schools, which are naturally more complacent. Certainly, we find more complacency in the most elite Brazilian schools, notably University of São Paulo and the schools that traditionally produce the elite of grand advocates in India, such as the Government Law College in Mumbai. It is not a surprise that new schools or schools outside of—but close enough to compete with—the elite schools embedded in political and economic power seek to distinguish themselves with a global brand. NYU fits this profile perfectly, and the global initiative helped push NYU into the top five of US law schools.

Twenty years ago, under the leadership of an entrepreneurial dean, John Sexton, NYU established the Global Law School Program, later renamed the Hauser Global Law School after major donors to the program. The Global Law School Program had a "global faculty" "invited to teach repeatedly at the NYU campus in New York," but not actually on the NYU faculty. Other components included a global scholars' program for recruiting foreign graduate students, and support for curricular innovations and research from a transnational perspective.

Currently, as the authors note, NYU Law is not the only globalized law school in the US, as others followed its lead: "Other top-ranked US law schools . . . expanded their numbers of visiting faculty and many US law schools expanded LLM programs aimed at students from overseas. In addition, there was a broad consensus in the US legal academy around the need to adopt a transnational perspective on curriculum design and academic research." Still, NYU remains the elite law school that is most branded as "global."

Sexton went on to be president of NYU, and he continued to push the theme of globalization as key to the identity of the university: "He almost immediately expanded NYU's network of overseas facilities for hosting New York-based students studying abroad. He also launched an ambitious plan to build two new campuses overseas, one in Abu Dhabi and the other in

Shanghai." Accordingly, if the Global Law School was designed "to bring the world to NYU," new programs in law and elsewhere try to bring NYU to the world. The law school version of this is NYU Law Abroad.

NYU Law Abroad allows NYU Law students—3Ls, 2Ls, and LLMs—to study for a semester in NYU facilities in one of three locations: Buenos Aires, Paris, and Shanghai. A committee of the law school's board of trustees, citing the "increasingly global nature of law practice, in areas ranging from climate change to commerce and war crimes to taxes," and the increasing importance as well of "knowledge of local languages," proposed that NYU Law School "develop . . . a more ambitious, integrated program that combines language training, cultural education, and foreign practice opportunity (through internships and clinics) with formal course study in other countries." The first group of students to go overseas went in the second semester of 2014. Enrollment in the Buenos Aires and Paris programs, but less so the Shanghai program, became consistently at or near their full capacities.

From the domestic viewpoint, NYU is solidifying its leadership in the global law school space. It attracts students and inspires alumni to give and build the brand. Domestically, the stakes of success or failure in accomplishing the program's goals are not that important. Part of the reason is that, as the authors point out, there is no real competitive advantage for students who spend the semester at NYU Law Abroad. The ranking of NYU and student grades are the leading criteria determining who gets the competitive law firm positions. Moreover, the vast majority of the students have jobs before they enter the program. Indeed, NYU Law strongly discourages third-year students without a permanent job offer—needed to build NYU's placement statistics—from leaving New York, recognizing that the experience abroad will not make a difference.

The provocative question raised by the authors is why students go and what they get out of the program. Students reported seeking to work on language skills, and many noted that they picked up some skills and experiences that helped them in their work after graduation. Program alumni also note "personal benefits they gained from the program, such as cultural immersion and making close friends," having fun, and the appeal of the specific sites. Some chose "to study abroad in attempts to diversify their law school experience," to "take more risks" because they already had a job, and "as the 'last chance' they have to be able to live in and travel around a different part of the world *for fun*."

The authors raise the question of how these choices fit into the Bourdieusian concept of "habitus" as applied to the law students. The term refers to internalized orientations or strategies that shape their approach to competing within a particular field, such as law. Anticipating Chapter 15, we can suggest that in many countries, especially China, the internalized habitus orients ambitious and well-connected students toward study abroad, especially in the United States. Whether they study abroad for the prestige and connections, the experience, or the substance of what they learn, one cannot say, but the substance of most one-year LLM programs in the United States is thin. The goal for most students coming to the United States is explicitly instrumental, however (Chapter 15). The habitus that leads US students abroad, however, is more of a mystery.

NYU students are united by the habitus of immersion in a very competitive race almost from birth to get into the top schools, to excel, and to have a choice of the top jobs (which most students agree on) (Markovits 2019). But a group of students seeks this experience abroad for fun and other non-instrumental reasons. The gloss of a foreign experience, in the United States and elsewhere, can be one way the privileged legitimate and maintain their status and deepen their contacts, even if they are doing it for fun. But pretty clearly, for most US law graduates, already with the credentials to be taken seriously in the core, the worth of study abroad is nowhere near as valuable as it is for graduates from the periphery.

5. A Transnational Consortium Led by Georgetown from the US Capital. Chapter 12, by Carrie Menkel-Meadow, has two themes that we highlight. One is to assess the experience of the Center for Transnational Legal Studies (CTSL), which has now been open for twelve years. She helped found the center and has participated greatly in its design and teaching. The second major theme is to draw on her experience teaching, speaking, and evaluating law schools at home and abroad to assess the phenomena of transnationalization and globalization. We shall treat the two themes separately, beginning with CTLS, which was conceived at Georgetown University but involves many law schools from around the globe. It is "a program of legal education for students from over 20 different countries, who study together, where no one is 'home,' in London, and are taught by professors from different institutions, educated in many different legal systems—civil, common, religious (e.g. Shari'a) and hybrid systems of law, on many different subjects."

The founding schools were Georgetown Law School and King's College (United Kingdom), Melbourne (Australia), Frei Universitat (Germany),

ESADE (Spain), Hebrew University (Israel), Fribourg (Switzerland), Universidad di São Paulo (Brazil), University of Torino (Italy), University of Toronto (Canada), and National University of Singapore. Currently, there are twenty schools: the founders minus Universidad di São Paulo, plus four more schools from Europe, three from Latin America, two from Asia, including China and South Korea, and one from New Zealand. The 150 to 175 students spend a semester or full year taught by faculty from participating schools. The students receive a "Certificate in Transnational Legal Studies" and credit for their work in their home institutions.

The curriculum is remarkably transnational and comparative. From the beginning, first year of the program, there has been a required "Global Practice Exercise" to begin the first week and start the students working together. The 2019–2020 curriculum also includes mandatory courses and colloquia on transnational law, and a mix of electives from public and private transnational law. The professors were from the United States, Europe, and National University of Singapore.

The classrooms appear to be very engaged with the innovative programming and pedagogy: "For many students in this course, engagement with issues of the 'law in action' or socio-legal approaches to law, as well as theoretical and philosophy of law questions, were a departure from their more conventional doctrinal courses at home." Menkel-Meadow concludes the analysis as follows:

> The founding of CTLS . . . was an effort to create a totally new institution—a place for transnational, comparative and international legal study, without a "home" institution. Although many institutions came together to found and fund this program, the idea was that teaching, and, eventually administration, would be shared by all the institutions participating to create something different from, and "free-standing" from, more conventional law schools. . . . My anecdotal experience is that those who have studied at CTLS are much more likely to seek legal work in international institutions and transnational practices around the world, but this could clearly be the effect of self-selection into the program in the first place.

The program exemplifies transnationalism, both in its practice and in its aims.

The program is reminiscent of SELA with its facilitation of exchange and debate among scholars and students from many different places. It has the

North-South dimension of SELA as well, but probably for financial reasons, the South is not as active in the CTLS as in the SELA network that is largely funded and administered by Yale. Georgetown also is notable for not making this a strictly Georgetown program, branded like the NYU Global Law School, but instead has fostered a transnational collaboration among law schools. Finally, and we will return to this subject below, this program's embrace of the transnational is remarkable.

One sees Menkel-Meadow in the program. She characterizes herself in this chapter as an "optimistic transnationalist," drawing on Thomas Friedman's observation in *From Beirut to Jerusalem* (1989) that he learned at Oxford that people from different parts of the world could learn from and change opinions through constructive engagement among people with very different backgrounds and ideologies. She embraces legal pluralism and transnational law in a legal world that is "more varied, horizontal and complex with both overlapping and also potentially conflicting rulings. There is no Supreme Court of the World to smooth out conflicting interpretations." Those who gain the tools of a transnational legal education are ready for the key positions in the global economy. Indeed, "graduates of cosmopolitan transnational legal programs may have more commonalities with each other in their elite statuses than they may have with their own countrymen," but at the same time there may be ways to open access to this kind of elite education.

A key point for Menkel-Menkel is that "law and legal rules are chosen not given (except in some colonial and religious based legal systems)," which makes the "study of different choices made in different legal systems" important. "At both theoretical and practical levels, truly transnational legal education raises questions about legal hegemony, diffusion, and transplantation of legal ideas, practices and power." But there also is an "increasing influence of non-American sources and interpretations of law. True transnational legal education should induce a form of humility about any one way of 'solving' legal problems and an openness to other legal configurations and interpretations."

Therefore, she emphasizes that, in the program, "[w]e no longer totally accept the 'rightness' of 'laid down' civil codes or legal institutions of the past, or the 'superiority' of particular groups over others (at least in theory, if not in world-wide practice!)." We "aspire" to "learn from everyone—social pluralism produces legal pluralism." She understands that this aspiration faces structural challenges: "As we know from past encounters with 'law and . . . . (development, colonialism and intellectual imperialism)', ambitious and perhaps hegemonic projects (e.g. democracy building and good governance, not to mention economic development and promotion of particular legal or economic systems) will be subject to economic and political factors beyond our control as educators and scholars." Recognizing such political and economic factors, however, does not preclude optimism:

> [W]hat I am still certain of, in the current era, troubling though it is for the flourishing of transnational cooperation, is that innovation and influence in law, in education, in culture and yes, even in politics, travels in multiple directions now. The diversity and growth in transnational legal programs now on offer are promoting a "globalization of legal education" that in my view . . . is, in fact, a qualitative good.

This chapter is not necessarily inconsistent with chapters on FGV Direito, Africa, SELA, and Bhutan, which are the most self-conscious about how power differentials, hierarchies, hegemonic relationships, and empires play a major role in what defines a globalized law school and its teaching of transnational law. These chapters reveal tilts to the North even where all are open and where many approaches appear to be on the table. The efforts of the Ford Foundation to build modern law schools, now evolved into global law schools, and to strengthen transnational law and legal institutions, is a recognition, on the other side, that cosmopolitan and progressive interests in the United States—as well as US economic interests—thrive in a world where law, courts, legal NGOs, and corporate law firms also thrive.

Transnational optimists, such as Menkel-Meadow, are cognizant of this political economy, but that is not inconsistent with working to make transnational rules better and more open to non-US or generally non-Northern participation. As she writes, "True transnational and comparative legal education allows professors to challenge the received wisdom of their own legal educations, often formed within single legal systems, establishing a sort of intellectual hegemony in their minds and legal education practices, and when well-practiced allows both students and professors from different legal environments to learn from each other." The last section of the book now turns to the political economy of core and periphery, North-South, and the role it plays in legal education in today's world.

C. Transnational Flows of Students, Faculty, and Judges in the Constitution of Legal Fields

1. The Educational Backgrounds of Judges on International Courts. Chapter 13, by Mikael Rask Madsen, asks "Who Rules the World? The Educational Capital of the International Judiciary." Madsen takes up the question of where the more than three hundred judges in international courts (ICs), which have proliferated in recent decades with the rise of international law and processes of transnational legal ordering (Shaffer and Coye 2020), received their legal education. The study, he notes, cannot examine in depth how international courts are embedded in "transnational power elites," and vice versa, which would show more precisely how these courts relate to global hierarchies, core and periphery relationships, and national powers. As Madsen states, "it is not the institutions as such, in this case ICs, that are seen as governing the world but the transnational power elites constituting and instituting them."

Nevertheless, it is helpful to understand this power elite in international and transnational courts through their educational credentials. What kinds of credentials are valued stems in part from a path dependency built by the North and stemming from the Permanent Court of International Justice in the post–World War I period. The kinds of capital valued at that time left a mark that set a pattern—a strong valuation of academic capital, for example.

A key question for Madsen "is the relative internationalization of the international judiciary in terms of education." He asks: "are international judges national legal champs promoted to international tasks? Or, alternatively, are they internationally trained and thereby part of a more cosmopolitan segment of the legal profession?" After conducting "a comparative analysis of the judges at nine international courts based in Africa, Europe, Latin America, and the Caribbean," he finds that these judges are not "denationalized" cosmopolitans as often depicted by critics. Citing an in-depth study of the European Court of Human Rights, he notes that the judges were "very often powerful domestic actors who had been promoted to international posts due to important national careers and who maintained deep connections to their home states. In other words, although they were international when sitting at the ECtHR, they were in practice first and foremost prestigious senior lawyers in their domestic fields." The combination of national and international experience and links is one way that more powerful countries can influence the construction of transnational legal norms. The judges themselves serve as intermediaries between the international and the national in the construction and the conveyance of transnational norms. From the perspective of transnational legal ordering, as Madsen notes, judicial appointment strategies appear to tacitly aim to ensure "that knowledge and know-how of national legal systems are both available and likely to influence the outlook of the system at large."

Madsen notes that there are increases over time in study abroad among the international court judges, with the greatest numbers in non-European international courts such as in Africa and the Caribbean, suggesting that those in more peripheral countries have a greater need to gain internationally prestigious degrees to advance nationally to the courts. He also asks which universities claim the most international judges. The hierarchy is instructive: Cambridge (38), University of London (33), Harvard (25), the University of Paris (24), Oxford (19), Columbia (14), Yale (11), Madrid (10), Bonn (10), and NYU (10) are the leaders. Examining more closely, Madsen also notes the importance of the National Autonomous University of Mexico (UNAM) and Moscow State University. UNAM occupies a recognized place in the training of a number of Latin American judges, while Moscow has trained "East European judges particularly from neighboring countries of the former Soviet Union." He shows that another circle worth noting is in Kampala, Uganda, "where a number of African judges have received training." We also see the role of such regional and global markets—different manifestations of cores and peripheries—in the next chapter by Anthea Roberts. But Madsen's main point is that those markets operate mainly to build, and to build from, national careers.

Madsen summarizes by noting that, in fact, international courts are not occupied by a transnational elite with particular cosmopolitan legal credentials. Rather, the "international sphere of law to a large extent is a continuation of domestic forms of reproducing elites. The different patterns observed in this study between, for example, Europe and Africa are in fact not differing from the regional models of producing elites. While European elites typically pursue elite education in their top national universities, African elites are more likely to go abroad."

2. Academic Flows and the Creation of Transnational Legal Fields. Anthea Roberts, in Chapter 14, takes a different topic but applies a complementary analysis in "Cross-border Student Flows and the Construction of International Law as a Transnational Legal Field." Her initial question is parallel to Madsen's: What kinds of national and transnational educational

trajectories make national careers in international law, and how do the national trajectories translate into positions of influence within the field of international law? She thus looks at another (and no doubt overlapping) branch of the "invisible college" associated with international and transnational law. One question is, how unified is this group? Roberts responds, "it might be better to understand the transnational field of international law as comprising a 'divisible college' of international lawyers marked by patterns of difference and dominance."

Her approach is not to focus only on international law, however. She examines the flow of people—professors and students—to suggest the role of educational flows in the construction and evolution of transnational and international fields generally. There is a strong core and periphery in the flow of both students and professors. She notes that "these transnational flows reflect and reinforce certain nationalizing, denationalizing, and westernizing influences that characterize the field of international law." These flows facilitate processes of transnational legal ordering that have a particular structural tilt.

> When students only study law in their own state, they are more likely to develop a nationalized approach to international law, though this depends in part on the state in which they study. When they cross borders to study international law, this has a denationalizing effect as they are exposed to another national approach to international law and a different community of international law professors and students. However, because students typically move toward core, Western states, transnational legal education often introduces or reconfirms a western orientation. As many of these students return home to practice or teach after their studies, these movements create pathways for ideas, approaches and materials to move from core states to periphery and semi-periphery ones.

The take-away is pretty straightforward:

> These educational patterns reflect and reinforce some of the hierarchies and inequalities that characterize the international legal field more generally, including the disproportionate power of legal elites in core states to define the "international" in their own image and to transpose their national ideas, materials, and approaches onto the international plane. These patterns of difference and dominance are central to understanding the

construction of international law as a transnational legal field and are at odds with the self-image of universality that the field likes to project.

Law students flow to the core, represented especially by the United States, the United Kingdom, and France. There are also regional flows, as Madsen noted as well, in this case best exemplified by Australia and South Africa. The flow is also affected by the history of colonialism and imperial competition that continues. China, to date, sends many law students to the United States, the United Kingdom, and Japan. Relatively few students from those countries go to China. However, "Chinese law schools are beginning to offer LLM programs in English designed to attract students from around the world. The Chinese government is offering tens of thousands of scholarships to Chinese universities to foreign students, scholars, and diplomats, including a significant number to individuals coming from Africa." There is a competition to gain influence. China seeks "to build up its soft power by sensitizing foreign students to Chinese views, customs, and preferences, and to cultivate professional and personal networks that will carry on into the future." It remains to be seen whether China's rise will provide Chinese views a greater foothold in other countries (Ginsburg 2020), especially those along the Belt and Road Initiative (Shaffer and Gao 2020).

The flow of students reflects "multiple core/periphery relationships in legal education based on language and legal families." Roberts suggests that the first two waves of globalization of legal thought "occurred first through colonization and then through legal educational routes following ex-colonial pathways." The flows from ex-colonies to France and the United Kingdom illustrate the continuing importance of language and prior colonial relationships. The third wave, however, is a "broad movement toward core, English-speaking states, most notably the United States and the United Kingdom, in view of the general importance of these states as educational destinations, the emergence of English as the educational and business global lingua franca, and the dominance of US and UK firms in the market of 'global' law firms." The current globalization of law schools also reflects this third wave. The hierarchy that pulls students to the centers of the corporate law world, such as the United States and the United Kingdom, also catalyzes educational reforms in national law schools that emulate the practices of law schools at those centers.

The recent role of the United States reflects a change in what is perceived as the core of legal education. Roberts notes that, "in the nineteenth and early twentieth centuries, universities in civil law states played a far more prominent role in Western legal education and thought." US international lawyers gained credibility and legitimacy within the United States, for example, by study in Europe. This core has shifted in response to changing hierarchies in the law and legal education, reflecting global hierarchies that shift but remain contested. These hierarchies ultimately impact what constitutes international and transnational law, and thus the makeup and stability of transnational legal orders.

As Roberts shows, students and legal ideas flow in opposite directions as part of transnational processes, helping to shape transnational legal ordering. As regards scholars and their ideas, "the asymmetric nature of these student flows means that legal academics at elite schools in core states are prone to be highly influential in constituting the transnational field of international law; . . . international law academics and practitioners often complete part of their legal education at a handful of elite law schools in a small number of core states." More generally,

> legal ideas and materials typically move in the opposite direction to transnational student flows. . . . Students moved primarily within legal families and from peripheral and semiperipheral states (former colonies) to core states (former colonial masters). By contrast, legal sources moved in the opposite direction. The textbooks of core states contained few references to legal materials from other legal systems. The textbooks of peripheral and semiperipheral countries contained numerous references to foreign case law, which came predominantly from core countries and especially from those within the same legal family tree. . . . In this way, the national approaches of some states are able to assert disproportionate influence in defining the "international."

The United States, as the most prestigious destination for legal education, has fewer numbers of international law academics but an outsize influence.

With respect to professors, there is variation in the degree of internationalization of countries' law faculties. As regards the United States, it is noteworthy that over two-thirds of international law academics have no diversity in their educational background, and those that do generally received their first degree abroad, "often before completing a second or third law degree in the United States or elsewhere." In other words, "almost all of the diversity of education in the US law academy comes from inbound rather than outbound diversity, which reflects the United States' status as a core state."

A minority of faculty with international backgrounds brings some different perspectives to the elite US law schools, but the larger point is that they are hired according to the criteria of excellence within the elite US academy. Similarly, for transnational networks such as SELA, the diversity comes with a confirmation of the "legal language" of what constitutes outstanding scholarship. Roberts notes provocatively that "[i]t may well be that the more 'international' a field becomes, the more it dollarizes on particular currency, reflecting and reinforcing certain hierarchical relationships that inhibit hetereogenity."

There are clear implications for the study of transnational legal orders generally. Roberts writes, "these patterns of diversity and difference, and hierarchy and heterogeneity, also create a template for understanding the construction of transnational legal orders." New perspectives are absorbed, as the optimistic legal transnationalists note, but the field has a tilt that remains constitutive. This tilt is not the result of a conspiracy. It just means that international hierarchies are built into global governance, including through formal international law and deeper processes of transnational legal ordering.

3. The Magnet of US Law Schools. Chapter 15, by Carole Silver and Swethaa S. Ballakrishnen, entitled "International Law Student Mobility in Context: Understanding Variations in Sticky Floors, Springboards, Stairways, and Slow Escalators," looks closely at the students who come to the United States for law degrees. The number has increased dramatically in recent decades for several reasons. One is the core and periphery phenomenon noted by Roberts in the previous chapter. But another is the strictly domestic desire among core country law schools to gain revenues from international students to compete in law school rankings. As a result, "today nearly 80% of all law schools [in the United States] offer at least one post-JD degree program for international law graduates, reflecting an approximate doubling of the law schools offering such a program over the last ten years." The number of students in such programs more than doubled from 2004 to 2016, reaching almost 10,000 students. In addition, an increasing number of international students enroll in JD programs. Indeed, "the percentage of international students in mainstream JD programs not only has increased substantially in the last decade but also has surpassed other domestic minority

groups in certain instances, and this is particularly the case in law schools ranked at the top of the U.S. News rankings."

The authors point to some key factors on the demand side. In many ways, as Roberts also notes, one might have expected colonial patterns to continue, with a rough divide defined by "civil law" and "common law." Certainly, until the 1980s, Brazilian or Argentine lawyers, as two examples, would have deemed an LLM from the United States largely worthless in the context of their domestic legal practices. What changed? As the authors write, "the rise of the United States as an important site for educating international lawyers occurred roughly in tandem with the ascendance of U.S. law firms in the global market for legal services and during a period when U.S. higher education also increasingly was valorized." Further, "[a]s legal practice became more remunerative and prestigious around the world, international lawyers and law graduates could throw off the pretense of scholarship and justify pursuit of a graduate degree on other grounds."

The authors examine the motives for coming to the United States from the late 1990s to the early 2000s on the basis of surveys. In contrast to the students at NYU going abroad largely for reasons such as the attractiveness of the destination and the opportunity to have fun, most of the non-US LLM students were very instrumental. Now, "students talk about the LLM as advancing their career opportunities, helping them strengthen their English language skills, and in gaining the cultural exposure that comes with living outside of their home countries—all motivations for pursuing an LLM that were expressed by the LLMs who graduated between 1996 and 2000." But "LLMs today also increasingly describe the degree as a means to another end—whether the bar, a U.S.-based practice experience or both—that *itself* is necessary in order for the LLM credential to serve as a mark of distinction in the student's home country." We can understand this change as reflecting an increase in competition that requires even better and more prestigious US credentials.

The increased number of non-US nationals in JD programs reflects this increased competition. The authors find, "overall, as a percentage of all JDs in all ABA-approved law schools, non-resident aliens increased from 1.78% of the JD student body in 2011 to 3.32% in 2017." Significantly, "there were more non-resident aliens than Black students at half of the Top-20 law schools in 2017, up from only 10% in 2011." These trends implicate access to corporate law jobs in the United States, since these foreign students may qualify for and take advantage of law firm diversity programs. They typically come from relatively more privileged backgrounds than many diverse students from the United States.

The authors focus their chapter on the Asian component of the LLM and JD programs: "The biggest Asian sending countries for legal studies, according to these data, were China, South Korea and Japan, which together account for over one-third of the total number of visa approvals for international students to study law in both degree levels, combined." From the perspective of the Asian students that the authors interviewed, reasons for the JD included "the dilution of the LLM as a credential" and the need to take the bar examination in the United States. Some start with the LLM and decide to convert it to a JD, as many schools permit, and others enroll in JD programs after obtaining a first degree in the United States.

There are many reasons to seek LLMs and JDs in the United States. The pull of the core lures many students to make the trip. But the authors note that the advanced degree does not reward all equally. They posit that there are "four kinds of metaphorical pathways: *sticky floors, springboards, stairways,* and *slow escalators.*" These categories suggest that the value of LLMs and JDs depends on many factors. Students are not always rewarded, and the rewards vary enormously depending on individual and social context. In general, however, "getting an LLM is a passport of sorts. But with the globalized demands of legal services markets, . . . returning LLMs gain advantages in their home countries both because of the practical advantages the LLM offers (training in international law, exposure to new networks, etc.) as well as its signaling 'halo' advantages, which come from being associated with an international law school from a high status country." In addition, returnees may gain other advantages, "such as using the LLM to create contacts and networks with a global legal community and even locally, and drawing language and cultural capital from this association." The increasing number of students getting a JD, they note, may disrupt the market for LLMs who return home, since the JD is treated very differently.

This globalization of the JD means that non-US JDs also could disrupt domestic JD markets. One phenomenon that is reportedly prevalent in Australia, for example, is that Chinese or Australian-born Chinese law graduates are favored by Australian law firms focused on the China trade, which is Australia's most important trading partner. The rise of China has an impact on the value of Chinese linguistic and cultural capital in corporate law firms (and many other businesses), reflecting China's rise and its potential indirect impact on transnational legal ordering processes. In the process, these students can "become conduits for the flow of transnational legal norms and legal practices, such as drafting particular kinds of documents," as for China's Belt and Road Initiative.

V. Final Remarks

The study of the globalization of legal education is typically understood in terms of how law schools improve and adapt traditional, locally focused curricula to the "demands" of globalization. The critical perspective of these chapters shows that a closer look at transnational processes reveals a much more complex, evolving picture. Global and local hierarchies, global and local contests for power and influence, the rise of corporate law firms, inequalities of access to rewarding and prestigious careers associated with globalization, and a range of evolving core-periphery relationships complicate the task of understanding this dimension of legal globalization and how it leads—or not—to a kind of transnational order in legal education.

Returning to the themes we introduced previously in Section III, all the chapters reflect the relevance of long colonial and imperial histories, as well as the rise of US hegemony that reached its zenith in the 1990s and early 2000s. That hegemonic power supported a greater role for law in governance through processes of transnational legal ordering, affecting the rules of the game internationally and domestically. US actors, such as the Ford Foundation, recognized the consistency of such transnational legal ordering with US interests, which could be advanced through relatively open trade, investment, and democratic legal orders that respected international human rights. US hegemonic power was both recognized and reflected in the self-conscious programs of legal reformers around the world, such as those active in SELA, FGV São Paulo, and Jindal Global Law School.

Second, what fuels many of the reforms is the rise of the corporate law firms engaged in transnational transactions. These law firms reflect a broader financial and neoliberal revolution in business, and they work alongside investment banks, private equity, hedge funds, accounting firms, and graduates of MBA programs that have proliferated, in parallel, outside the United States and globalized. Aspiring elite students seek admission to the leading law schools, which, in practice, offer the best access to transnational corporate law firms. These law school degrees, blazed on curriculum vitae, serve as professional entry points locally and transnationally. The cutting-edge programmatic features that circulate among ambitious law schools play into corporate law firm demands for pragmatic "problem-solving" and "interdisciplinary" skills.

Third, local contexts continue to entangle with, and thus remain central to, these globalization processes, just as in the past. Varying degrees of resistance and adaptation affecting the shape of reforms are detailed in the book's chapters, such as on India (where we see ongoing conservatism in the elite bench and bar), China (where the JM program did not dislodge the LLB and liberal activism fell flat when the regime clamped down on dissent), and elsewhere in Asia (where the ideal of enlightened policy promotion through law schools encountered frequent political pushback). Similarly, the chapters on SELA and FGV São Paulo show the need to take account of local hierarchies and traditionally embedded approaches to law in assessing educational reform endeavors.

Fourth, there remains a structural tilt favoring (relative) cores over (relative) peripheries, which technological changes facilitate. Information and communication technologies have sped up the flows of ideas and scholarly approaches, including through the ability to rank legal education practices in ways consistent with dominant approaches in the core. Some law schools outside of the core may obtain relatively high rankings, but the rankings overall serve to legitimate and spread the basic traits of the top schools in the core. Indeed, in today's world, one could not credibly advance a global rankings system that did not deploy criteria that placed Harvard and Oxford at or near the top.

Fifth, one can remain a "transnational optimist" despite these structural tilts. That optimism reflects a pragmatic approach to transnational legal ordering. On the one hand, transnational processes can be useful for local actors who are contesting local hierarchies and prevailing conservative practices, as captured in many of this book's chapters. On the other hand, local actors aim to enhance their voices in global debates. The authors of the chapter on FGV are most explicit in stressing this latter point, as they seek to find a way to play within rules that come from the North and especially the United States. Legal actors, they contend, "have to be taught the rules currently shaping the game so that they can operate, question and eventually contribute to shape these rules. A refusal to learn or teach the grammar in which global transactions are made denies the country the much-needed skills of being able to question it." The websites of many schools talk about faculty contributions to global debates, while not contesting the global structures. Some contend that China could do so, given its increasing economic clout (Ginsburg 2020). So far, however, China has mostly worked within the current rules and structures to advance Chinese interests for its own ends, as have Brazil and India (Shaffer 2021). Optimism for most countries outside of the core, nonetheless, generally means obtaining a voice and seeking some modifications and applications that take their interests into account. In the process, they can make the rules appear more legitimate and inclusive, while reflecting the same or a similar structural tilt.

Finally, we discussed the way that globalization processes have increased meritocracy while at the same time exacerbating inequality. The trend away from "public" law schools toward private funding of legal education by very wealthy individuals tied to business interests contributes to these developments. Competition over "rankings" drives the need for private funding, which can blur distinctions between "public" and "private" legal education, as tuitions and fees escalate. The rise in prominence of global rankings, in turn, depreciates the value of degrees from most of the South, while appreciating those from Northern centers of power. The costs of travel to such schools, the acquisition of linguistic skills and cultural competence, and inflation in the kinds of degrees needed (such as from the LLM to the JD), create enormous barriers, even though there are some scholarships available. Travel by relatively privileged elites from outside the global centers, in parallel, can change career opportunities in the centers when foreign students obtain key positions in the North in law firms and faculties of law that promote "diversity."

This book melds two theoretical perspectives addressing these processes of transnational ordering. The framework of transnational legal ordering examines how legal education can serve both as a producer of transnational legal norms and as a symptom of broader transnational processes. Transnational legal ordering processes became more prominent with the rise of US hegemony, US emphases on law and rights, US-modeled, transnational corporate practice, norm-driven NGOs, and private philanthropy. Legal education reform, from this vantage, is both vehicle and outcome. The approach of the comparative sociology of the legal profession, complementarily, focuses on enduring national competitions in which transnational processes become entangled with local hierarchies. It stresses, in particular, the historical contexts that produced transnational structures consistent with US-inspired legal educational approaches, as well as their relation to local structures. Both approaches assess how the direct and indirect diffusion of

US approaches affects the role of law and lawyers distinctively in different national contexts. In bringing together these theoretical perspectives, this book assesses both what drives transnational normative "consensus" over what constitutes "good," "modern" legal education, and enduring national competitions within the legal profession that disrupt any such "consensus." These entanglements of transnational and local processes, which occur within transnational and local structures, define the field of legal education globally and locally.

References

Ballakrishnen, Swethaa (2019). "Just Like Global Firms: Unintended Gender Parity and Speculative Isomorphism in India's Elite Professions, *Law and Society Review* 53(1): 108–140.

Benton, Laura and Lisa Ford (2016). *Rage for Order: The British Empire and the Origins of International Law, 1800–1850.* Harvard University Press.

Berman, Harold J. (1983). *Law and Revolution: The Formation of the Western Legal Tradition.* Harvard University Press.

Brundage, James (2008). *The Medieval Origins of the Legal Profession.* University of Chicago Press.

Burbank, Jane and Frederick Cooper (2010). *Empires in World History. Power and the Politics of Difference.* Princeton.

Castañeda, Jorge (1993). *Utopia Unarmed: The Latin American Left after the Cold War.* Knopf.

Chesterman, Simon (2017). "The Fall and Rise of Legal Education in Singapore," *Singapore Journal of Legal Studies* 2017(2): 201–214.

Coates, Benjamin (2016). *Legalist Empire: The United States, Civilization, and International Law in the Early Twentieth Century.* Oxford University Press.

Cunha, Luciano Gross, Jose Garcez Ghirardi, David M. Trubek, and David B. Wilkins (2018). "Globalization, Lawyers, and Emerging Economies: The Case of Brazil," in Luciana Gross Cunha, Daniela Monteiro Gabbay, Jose Garcez Ghirardi, David M. Trubek, and David B. Wilkins, eds., *The Brazilian Legal Profession in the Age of Globalization: The Rise of the corporate Legal Sector and its Impact on Lawyers and Society.* Pp. 1–32. Cambridge University Press.

Dezalay, Yves and Bryant Garth (2002). *The Internationalization of Palace Wars: Lawyers, Economists, and the Contest to Transform Latin American States.* University of Chicago Press.

Dezalay, Yves and Bryant Garth (2010). *Asian Legal Revivals: Lawyers in the Shadow of Empire.* University of Chicago Press.

Dezalay, Yves and Bryant Garth (2021). *Law as Reproduction and Revolution: An Interconnected History.* University of California Press.

Dinovitzer, Ronit and Bryant Garth (2020). "The New Place of Corporate Law Firms in the Structuring of Elite Legal Careers," *Law and Social Inquiry* 45(2): 339–371.

Erie, Mathew (2009). "Legal Education Reform in China Through U.S.-Inspired Transplants," *Journal of Legal Education* 59(1): 60–96.

Erie, Mathew (2021). "Chinese Law and Development," *Harvard International Law Journal* 62(1): 51–115.

Espeland, Wendy and Michael Sauder (2007). "Rankings and Reactivity: How Public Measures Recreate Social Worlds," *American Journal of Sociology* 113(1): 1–40.

Flood, John (2014). "The Global Contest for Legal Education," in Fiona Westwood and Karen Barton, eds., *The Calling of Law*. Pp. 13–34. Ashgate.

Gane, Christopher and Robin Hui Huang, eds. (2016). *Legal Education in the Global Context: Opportunities and Challenges*. Ashgate.

Gardner, James (1980). *Legal Imperialism*. University of Wisconsin Press.

Ginsburg, Tom (2020). "Authoritarian International Law," *American Journal of International Law* 114(2): 221–260.

Halliday, Terence and Gregory Shaffer (2015). *Transnational Legal Orders*. Cambridge University Press.

Hamann, Julian and Christian Schmidt-Wellenburg (2020). "The Double Function of Rankings. Consecration and Dispositif in Transnational Academic Fields," in Christian Schmidt-Wellenburg and Stefan Bernhard, eds., *Charting Transnational Fields: Methodology for a Political Sociology of Knowledge*. Pp. 160–178. Routledge.

Harrington, J.A. and A. Manji (2003). "'Mind with Mind and Spirit with Spirit': Lord Denning and African Legal Education," *Journal of Law and Society* 30(3): 376–399.

Hattori, Tataaki (1963). "The Legal Profession in Japan: Its Historical Development and Present State," in Robert Taylor von Mehren, ed., *Law in Japan: The Legal Order in a Changing Society*. Pp. 109–187. Harvard.

Jamin, Christoph and William van Caenegem, eds. (2016). *The Internationalisation of Legal Education*. Springer.

Kang, David C. (2010). *East Asia Before the West: Five Centuries of Trade and Tribute*. Columbia University Press.

Klabbers, Jan and Mortimer Sellers (2008). *The Internationalization of Law and Legal Education*. Springer.

Kluttz, Daniel N. and Neil Fligstein (2016). "Varieties of Sociological Field Theory," in Seth Abrutyn, ed., *Handbook of Contemporary Sociological Theory*. Pp. 185–204. Springer.

Krishnan, Jayath (2004). "Professor Kingsfield Goes to Delhi: American Academics, the Ford Foundation, and the Development of Legal Education in India," *American Journal of Legal History* 46(4): 447–499.

Krishnan, Jayath (2005). "From the ALI to the ILI: The Efforts to Export an American Legal Institution," *Vanderbilt Journal of Transnational Law* 38(5): 1255–1294.

Krishnan, Jayanth (2012). "Academic SAILERS: The Ford Foundation and the Efforts to Shape Legal Education in Africa, 1957–1977," *American Journal of Legal History* 52(3): 261–324.

Kronche, Jedidiah (2016). *The Futility of Law and Development: China and the Dangers of Exporting American Law*. Oxford.

Kumarasingham, Harshan (2019). "A Transnational Actor on a Dramatic Stage—Sir Ivor Jennings and the Manipulation of Westminster Style Democracy in Pakistan," in Gregory Shaffer, Tom Ginsburg, and Terence Halliday, eds., *Constitution-making and Transnational Legal Order*. Pp. 55–84. Cambridge University Press.

Manjapra, Kris (2014). *Age of Entanglement: German and Indian Intellectuals Across Empire*. Harvard University Press.

Manjapra, Kris (2019). "The Semiperipheral Hand: Middle Class Service Professionals of Imperial Capitalism," in Christof Dejung, David Motadel, and Jürgen Osterhammel, eds., *The Global Bourgeoisie: The Rise of the Middle Classes in the Age of Empire*. Pp. 184–204. Princeton University Press.

Markovits, Daniel (2019). *The Meritocracy Trap: How America's Foundational Myth Feeds Inequality, Dismantles the Middle Class, and Devours the Elite*. Penguin.

Martines, Lauro (1968). *Lawyers and Statecraft in Renaissance Florence*. Princeton University Press.

Mazower, Mark (2012). *Governing the World: The History of an Idea, 1815 to the Present*. Penguin Books.

Montoya, Juny (2010). "The Current State of Legal Education Reform in Latin America: A Critical Appraisal," *Journal of Legal Education* 59(4): 545–566.

Rodgers, Daniel (2018). "The Uses and Abuses of Neoliberalism," *Dissent* 65(1): 78–87.

Ruskola, Teemu (2013). *Legal Orientalism: China, the United States, and Modern Law*. Harvard University Press.

Shaffer, Gregory (2013). *Transnational Legal Orders and State Change*. Cambridge University Press.

Shaffer, Gregory (2021). *Emerging Powers and the World Trading System: The Past and Future of International Economic Law*. Cambridge University Press.

Shaffer, Gregory and Carlos Coye (2020). "From International Law to Jessup's Transnational Law, from Transnational Law to Transnational Legal Orders," in Peer Zumbansen, ed., *The Many Lives of Transnational Law: Critical Engagements with Jessup's Bold Proposal*. Pp. 126–152. Cambridge University Press.

Shaffer, Gregory and Henry Gao (2020). "A New Chinese Economic Order?," *Journal of International Economic Law* 23(3): 607–635.

Shaffer, Gregory, Tom Ginsburg, and Terence Halliday (2019). *Constitution-making and Transnational Legal Order*. Cambridge University Press.

Steele, Stacey and Kathryn Taylor, eds. (2010). *Legal Education in Asia: Globalization, Change and Context*. Routledge.

Thornton, Margaret (2012). *Privatising the Public University: The Case of Law*. Routledge.

Trubek, David M. and Marc Galanter (1974). "Scholars in Self Estrangement: Reflections on the. Crisis in Law and Development Studies," *Wisconsin Law Review* 1974 (4): 1062–1102.

Twining, William (2019). *Jurist in Context*. Cambridge University Press.

Wang, Zhizhou, Sida Liu, and Xueyao Li (2017). "Internationalizing Chinese Legal Education in the Early Twenty-First Century," *Journal of Legal Education* 66(2): 238–266.

Wilkins, David, Vikramaditya Khanna, and David Trubek, eds. (2017). *The Indian Legal Profession in the Age of Globalization: The Rise of the Corporate Legal Sector and Its Impact on Lawyers and Society*. Cambridge University Press.

Wilkins, David B., David M. Trubek, and Bryon Fong (2019). *Globalization, Lawyers, and Emerging Economies: The Rise, Transformation, and Significance of the New Corporate Legal Ecosystem in India, Brazil, and China*. HLS Center on the Legal Profession Research Paper No. 2019-1.

Wilson, Richard (2017). *The Global Evolution of Clinical Legal Education*. Cambridge University Press.

Zhang, Taisu (2018). "The Development of Comparative Law in China," in Matthias Reimann and Reinhardt Zimmerman, eds., *Oxford Handbook of Comparative Law*. Pp. 228–257. Oxford. 2d ed.

Zhang, Taisu and Tom Ginsburg (2019). "Legality in Contemporary Chinese Politics," *Virginia Journal of International Law* 58(2): 306–389.

PART II

TRANSNATIONAL PROCESSES IN THE REFORM OF LEGAL EDUCATION

2

Strategic Philanthropy and International Strategies

The Ford Foundation and Investments in Law Schools and Legal Education

Ron Levi, Ronit Dinovitzer, and Wendy H. Wong

I. Introduction

The Ford Foundation has had a storied role in funding educational efforts across areas of study. Domestically and abroad, the Foundation has relied on grants to universities to incite change by funding new scholarly perspectives and educational practices (Cohen 2017; Khurana, Kimura, and Fourcade 2011; Gemelli 1998; Krige 1999). It has constructed new forms of expertise, legitimated new scholarly orthodoxies, and provided support to new competitors for power and prestige (Dezalay and Garth 2002). By investing in education it could also support heterodox ideas to challenge dominant perspectives and hierarchies (Khurana, Kimura, and Fourcade 2011: 8).

One example is the Ford Foundation's dramatic reshaping of the field of management education. Between 1951 and 1964, Ford's grantmaking reshaped graduate management schools in the United States, from vocational schools to academically grounded institutions. This happened by funding centers of excellence such as Harvard, and by reallocating support from other disciplines in the behavioral sciences toward management education. In so doing, Ford legitimated a new expertise in economics that would redefine the relationship between business and government. The success of these investments at home and abroad were further secured through homologies between the leadership of the Foundation and new academic leaders of these business schools (Khurana, Kimura, and Fourcade 2011).

Another example is the Ford Foundation's support for European studies. The content and scope of its support for this field shifted depending on

Ron Levi, Ronit Dinovitzer, and Wendy H. Wong, *Strategic Philanthropy and International Strategies* In: *The Globalization of Legal Education*. Edited by: Bryant Garth & Gregory Shaffer, Oxford University Press. © Oxford University Press 2022.
DOI: 10.1093/oso/9780197632314.003.0002

political conjunctures in the United States and Europe. As with business schools, it depended on the presence of individuals within countries who could pursue Ford's vision of this intellectual field, and help to secure the academic institutions in which it would flourish (Cohen 2017).

In this chapter, we focus on the role of the Ford Foundation in legal education. Ideals of human rights, social justice, and international development have long been identified as core to the Foundation's grantmaking (Wong, Levi, and Deutsch 2017). Legal education, both within the United States and abroad, were central "learned strategies" for advancing these ideals (Dezalay and Garth 2002: 8). Yet we argue that funding for legal education went beyond this: funding legal education and law schools was also a way to more broadly legitimate lawyers and legal expertise in state reform, within the United States and internationally (Krishnan 2004).

We rely on a data set of all grantmaking by the Ford Foundation to law schools and the field of legal education, from the 1950s to the early 2000s. Echoing the analyses of management education and European studies, investments in legal education varied geographically and substantively over this era, reflecting changing domestic and international politics. In some decades, the Foundation's focus on legal education was resolutely domestic, including civil rights within the United States. At other times, the investments were internationally directed in ways that encouraged law schools to create links between US-based law professors and elites abroad. Over time, these investments allowed the Foundation to fund legal education projects that would focus on changing US foreign policy needs.

We conclude that the Ford Foundation's investments in legal education promoted the reliance on legal expertise as a tool for addressing problems of governance, domestically and abroad. This would create new international interlocutors for US-based law professors, and underwrite the idea that lawyers would be seen as leaders on statecraft internationally.

II. The Ford Foundation, Law, and International Justice

The Ford Foundation was central to developing fields of international justice. The broad contours of Ford's influence are known through accounts of prominent recipients and program officers (McClymont and Golub 2000). Recent work further finds that during a key period of 1970–1989 there was significant convergence in Ford grantmaking in the United States and abroad, across civil and political rights and economic, social, and cultural rights (Wong, Levi, and Deutsch 2017).

Ford's rights promotion included educational investments. As is well known, Ford funded academic projects in Chile that would lay the ground-work for the democratic resistance against repression in Chile and beyond, while tracking US foreign policy interests (Korey 2007: 25–28). This chapter investigates the size and scope of these investments in law schools and legal education. We obtained data from the Rockefeller Archive Center on every grant provided by the Ford Foundation to 2003. The database of 42,671 grants spans from January 1936 to September 2003. Because of significant missing data in the early years, we focus on 1950–2003 for this analysis.

To code for this project we began by identifying the set of grants broadly related to law and social justice. These were grants in which the program name and program field indicated that the grant was related to civil society, international affairs with a focus on rights or law, social justice, or human rights. This identified 5,091 grants. To identify those within legal educa-tion, we narrowed this set further by relying on the name of the grantee and the purpose of the grant specified in these data.[1] This resulted in 721 legal education-related grants. We supplement these data with textual and budget material from Ford Foundation Annual Reports, archival research we pur-sued through the Rockefeller Archive Center, and the secondary literature on the Ford Foundation.

Following this strategy, we analyzed budget data from the Ford Foundation from 1950 through 2003. Figure 2.1 shows that over $1.3 billion was invested in the broad justice field over time, with increases over the decades. Figure 2.1 also shows that Ford's investment in this field has been met with sustained attention to legal education. The height of legal education's share occurred in the 1950s, with early investments in law schools coming to represent nearly half of law-related grantmaking in that decade, and since the 1970s at nearly 10 percent of such funding.

In the following we draw out how these investments in legal education were tailored to political and strategic needs of different eras—and that

---

[1] Within these grants, we define them as related to legal education if the "purpose of the grant" contained the following keywords: school of law, law school, legal education, legal studies, legal training, lawyer training, law teachers, law professor, or law faculty. In addition, within these law and social justice grants, grants were defined as legal education if the grantee was a law school, or was a university and the "purpose of the grant" indicated law or legal education.

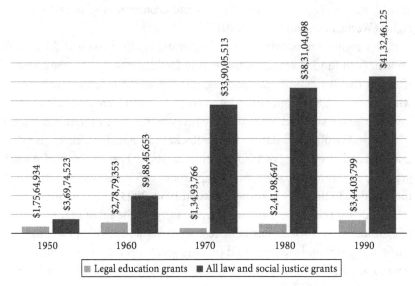

Figure 2.1. Totals of All Law and Social Justice Grants and Legal Education Grants, by Decade

investments in legal education were part of a broader strategy of influencing state reform, both within the United States and abroad.

III. The Ford Foundation and Legal Education

A. Legal Education as Training for International Democracy and Citizenship

The early years of the 1950s to 1960s were particularly important for Ford's investments in law and justice, and reflected the concerns of the US state in the years following World War II. Concern over the Soviet Union loomed large in the early years of the Ford Foundation, alongside a broader production of Sovietology in the United States (Solomon 2000; Engerman 2009). Following Henry Ford II, the first director of the Ford Foundation was Paul Hoffman, who had just completed his tenure as the administrator for the Marshall Plan after having served as the president of Studebaker. The Marshall Plan itself was, of course, a mechanism to fortify Europe against communism through economic and political cooperation. As Hoffman reflected in an interview,

"We had been persuaded by Jean Monnet and others that there was no hope for progress of a compartmentalized Europe and that in the post-war world, Europe's future would be dim unless there was close cooperation among the Marshall Plan countries" (Brooks 2003).

The emphasis on internationalization, anti-Communism, and US security—conjoined with an emphasis on the role of law schools and the academy—was continued by Rowan Gaither, a California lawyer and legal academic (having taught briefly at the University of California Law School after the war) who had long been a bridge between the academy and the military. Gaither had been an original trustee of the Rand Corporation and an assistant director of the defense-centered Radiation Laboratory at MIT, where Ford provided funding for the 1948 reconfiguration of the Rand Corporation from its original connection with the Douglas Aircraft Company (Hounshell 1997: 242; Snead 1999).

On meeting Gaither through the MIT funding proposal, Henry Ford II asked him to join the Foundation, and to write a report on its objectives (Snead 1999: 51). He was asked to focus on "what men need to live more fruitful lives" (Korey 2007: 8). Gaither's report came to highlight five program areas that mirrored his own expertise and networks: (1) the establishment of peace and a world order of law and justice; (2) the bolstering of democracy and freedom; (3) the strengthening of the economy; (4) general and civic education; (5) expansion of knowledge of human conduct (Gaither 1949: 49–99; Fleishman 2007: 225; Korey 2007: 9).

The Gaither report highlighted law, justice, and education. The report argued for the importance of long-term rather than defensive thinking, and for the importance of Foundation funding for projects of society building unencumbered by politics (Snead 1999: 51). It would be transformative for Ford, and led to the creation of an International Division within the Foundation. While the Rockefeller Foundation saw an earlier turn to internationalism in relief work after World War I (Solomon and Krementsov 2001), Ford's International Division became central to the funding of international legal education.

As president of the Foundation, Paul Hoffman was enthusiastic about the Gaither report. To take on controversial approaches to problems internationally, Hoffman drew on Gaither's vision to expand Ford's operations to developing nations in Africa, Asia, Latin America, and the Middle East (McCarthy 1997: 131). Hoffman himself would focus much of his interests

on foreign affairs and civil liberties and in expanding US influence beyond
Europe (Raucher 1985: 81–88).[2]

Though Hoffman himself did not pursue his initial hopes to attend law
school, law professors would quickly gain prominence in the Foundation
and its reorientation toward international strategies. This would include
concerns over the Soviet Union, a battle that would bring parallel attention
to Latin America, Asia, and Africa. A central player was Robert Maynard
Hutchins, a past dean of Yale Law School (and president of the University
of Chicago), where he was a promoter of Legal Realism in response to traditional, formalist, doctrinal study. Hutchins's eminence derived from being
at the intersection of the legal academy and the state. As William Korey
explains, Hutchins was seen as "the 'wunderkind' of the higher educational
world" whom Hoffman appreciated, and Hutchins saw the Foundation's direction "as providing a panorama and opportunity for an especially gifted
person, like himself, 'to save the world,'" including through educational and
international projects (Korey 2007: 12).

The theory of building knowledge to enhance freedom resonated with elite
approaches to law during this time, with legal realism at institutions such
as Yale and Columbia emphasizing integration with the social sciences and
building strong institutions rather than an exclusive emphasis on doctrines
and concepts (Kalman 1986). Though decades after Hutchins had been dean,
Yale Law School was emphasizing a policy-oriented approach to international law. This New Haven "World Public Order" approach, with thinkers
such as Harold Lasswell and Myres McDougal at its helm, emphasized international law as based on attaining basic values, several of which are similar
to those offered by Gaither in his report to the Ford Foundation. An early
address outlining this approach was, tellingly, titled "The Law School of the
Future: From Legal Realism to Policy Science in the World Community"
(McDougal 1947).[3] The interdisciplinary goal was to place international law
in the service of problem-solving to reach politically set goals of achieving a
world community (Åkermark 1997: 62–66; Chen 2007).

---

[2] On retiring from the Foundation, Hoffman spoke with President Eisenhower and indicated that
this would allow him to accept "spot assignments" for the president (New York Times 1953). In 1966,
Hoffman would go on to become the first administrator of the UN Development Program.

[3] This included a course on the World Community and Law, noting that "[t]he institutions,
practices and doctrines traditionally known as international law will require a reassessment and a
determination of the extent to which they promote or retard the world community, with suggestion of appropriate improvement and alternatives"—taught by Lasswell and McDougal (McDougal
1947: 1352; Carlston 1948).

The Ford Foundation's interest in funding legal education projects was thus set as early as 1950, with a focus on international connections, the promotion of peace, democracy, justice, and the economy, and enhancing US security. In 1953, Gaither himself began as Foundation president, with investment in public policymaking that attended to links between nonprofit organizations, industry, government, and social science research (Dowie 2001: 5). As an early history of the Foundation notes, "[i]f Hoffman was the glittering ringmaster of a philanthropic circus, Gaither is the hardworking transmission belt between the Ford millions and the outside world" (Macdonald 1989: 155). Gaither's clear focus was the Foundation's international strategy and the security of the United States. It is telling that upon leaving the Foundation presidency in 1956, Gaither chaired the US presidential panel and report on "Deterrence & Survival in the Nuclear Age."

Legal education funding in the early years of the 1950s—during the years of Rowan Gaither, Paul Hoffman, and Robert Maynard Hutchins—was particularly notable. This included establishing programs in international legal education at Stanford, Columbia, Michigan, Harvard, and Yale. As we demonstrated above, the 1950s saw a high-water mark of nearly half of all justice funding going to legal education programs. When drilling down into the annual data, we see in Figure 2.2 that in the middle years of the 1950s, legal education funding came to over 90 percent of the Foundation's grantmaking budget across all justice work.

In 1952, the Foundation provided a grant to Harvard Law School to fund training and research on taxation policies in underdeveloped countries;

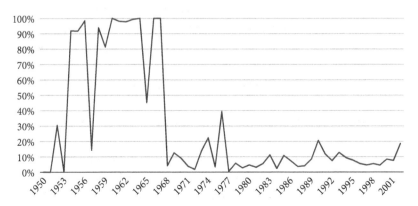

Figure 2.2. Legal Education Grants as a Percent of All Law and Social Justice Grants

Harvard also attracted funding from the US government, the United Nations, and foreign governments. The argument was that taxation policies had as much to do with development as did population pressure or land reform. Among the funded activities was the training of US, UN, and foreign officials at Harvard, "studies of the relation of United States taxation to American private investment abroad," and research on how tax policy relates to economic development (Ford Foundation Annual Report 1952).

In 1954, the Foundation reported on a grant of $350,000 to promote the exchange of law students and teachers between American and Japanese universities. This began with Japanese professors coming to the United States, reflecting the legal academic elite of both countries: Harvard, Stanford, and the University of Michigan, along with the Universities of Kyoto, Tohoku, Tokyo, Chuo, Keio, and Waseda (Ford Foundation Annual Report 1954):

> The need for cooperative research and study arises out of postwar changes in Japanese laws. Originally drawn largely from German sources, the legal system of modern Japan was extensively revised during the Occupation and now has a considerable deposit of elements of Anglo-American legal traditions, in addition to those of German and Japanese origin. The new Japanese Constitution embodies many of the democratic ideals and institutions found in the United States Constitution; there has also been enacted in recent years important legislation similar to that of the United States in such fields as criminal law and procedure, corporation law, labor law, antimonopoly law and tax law.

This reflected the view that legal education was how to reimagine Japan after the war. This was echoed by David Cavers, a Harvard Law School Professor and chairman of the Committee on International Legal Studies. Cavers had, earlier in the 1950s, been tasked at Harvard Law School with the project of creating a "World School of Law" (Harvard Crimson 1951). Cavers explained that a need for this Ford-funded program arose because US law schools had originally been left out of the internationalization effort, due to

> our belated realization of the predicament which the bold experiment of the United States in transplanting American laws and legal institutions into the Japanese system had created for the legal profession and the legal scholars of Japan. American law faculties had not been participants in that experiment, nor were they, of course, committed to strive for its success. However, the

risk that such an experiment would fail because the transplanted laws had not been properly understood and hence could not be properly employed and evaluated was one to which American law schools, as institutions responsible for the exposition and transmission of the American legal tradition, could not remain insensitive (Cavers 1963: xvii).

By 1955, there was massive investment by the Foundation in international legal education. The Foundation focused on the role that lawyers play in American public life, and, by implication, the role they can take up in public life abroad:

Lawyers traditionally have played a prominent role in American public life. From their ranks come many of our governmental, business and community leaders. Out of the Foundation's general interest in the development of effective leadership in public affairs has grown support for programs intended by the law schools to give Americans trained in law better understanding of law in its relation to governmental affairs, both domestic and international, to business and economic activities across national boundaries, and to the society in which law operates (Ford Foundation Annual Report 1955: 57).

The Ford Foundation thus created a program of Support for International Legal Studies, with a nearly $8 million investment to ensure US legal leadership in internationalization. Described as "Education for Democracy," elite law schools—Harvard, Yale, Columbia, and Chicago in the main, as well as Stanford, Michigan, and Berkeley—would receive these funds over a ten-year period. While mainly for international legal studies, this extended beyond comparative or international law, with the Foundation instead highlighting "the legal aspects of a broad range of public and private activities in foreign countries and across national borders" (Ford Foundation Annual Report 1955: 59).

Embedded in this vision was an understanding of lawyers as problem-solvers for new democracies and as a corps that could broker relations on behalf of the United States at a time of rapid change worldwide:

The sum of $7,825,000 was granted to seven law schools *for the training of lawyers, both as professional men and as citizens to work with increased understanding across national boundaries.* The growing complexity of international relationships, both public and private, brought about by the rapid development of many international organizations, the multitudinous and varying transactions between governments, the intricacies of international trade and investment, all insistently call for swift and expanding development of academic courses *to keep pace with hurrying events* [emphasis ours] (Ford Foundation Annual Report 1955: 8).

This urgency was matched with a broad set of skills that the new funding of international legal studies sought to produce. These were to position US lawyers with the ability to harness, quickly, the worldwide opportunities of the 1950s and to build American links for elite foreign lawyers. The program would have the following general objectives (Ford Foundation Annual Report 1955: 59):

1. to make training in foreign and international legal problems available in the normal course of legal education for American law students;
2. to make training in United States law and legal thought available to able foreign lawyers, many of whom occupy or will occupy positions of importance in their own countries;
3. to provide intensive training to specialists whose careers in business, government, or otherwise, will involve foreign and international activities; and
4. to engage in research that will benefit the general student, the specialist, the teacher, the practitioner and the interested public.

The ambition to internationalize legal studies extended beyond this program. The American Law Institute, for instance, received a $300,000 grant to work on how domestic US law would affect the conduct of American foreign relations (Ford Foundation Annual Report 1955: 60). Duke University and the American Society of International Law received funds to host meetings and regional workshops across the country on international law; and Yale Law School would receive support to broaden its training of law professors, with the Foundation noting Yale's prominence in producing law professors for the country (Ford Foundation Annual Report 1955: 60–61).

As early as 1951, Carl Spaeth, then dean at Stanford Law School (who had earlier worked in Latin America and the US State Department), proposed to the Ford Foundation the creation of a Center for Asian Studies. Spaeth then spent the 1952–1954 period as director of the Foundation's Overseas Activities before returning to Stanford (Sutton 1987). Over the first four years of the International Legal Studies program, over $11 million was provided by the Foundation, 80 percent of which was allocated to just fourteen US law schools (Ford Foundation Annual Report 1958: 78). Building on its earlier work on Japan, Ford made grants to foreign institutions—including the University of Delhi, the Egyptian Society of International Law, and the Indian Law Institute. While the Foundation originally contemplated strengthening Indian law faculties and perhaps funding an Indian law institute, Spaeth, who was tapped by the Foundation to travel to India to explore potential opportunities for legal education reform, warned against moving quickly in this uncertain environment (Krishnan 2004). The result was faculty exchanges between the United States and India, including legal elites such as Clark Byse and Carl Spaeth (Krishnan 2004: n.43). It also included a five-week conference at Stanford focused on public law subjects and law for social change, and a four-month stay in India for Spaeth himself, who became concerned with the small percentage of Indian law students entering legal practice, while continuing to caution the Foundation on the complexities of reforming legal education abroad without attending to local contexts (Krishnan 2004).

These investments can also help to explain some of the intellectual shifts occurring in the US legal academy. The intellectual "Rise Era" in comparative constitutional law during the post–World War II period (Fontana 2011: 48) is captured by the Ford Foundation's ambitions for elite law. Ford invested in law professors as part of opening up the US legal profession, so that elite US legal scholarship would become more global and comparative. The aim was to create legal specialists who would build new academic expertise attuned to legal questions from abroad. It was about changing how the US legal profession would see itself, by inserting comparative and international law into the fabric of legal study.

Figure 2.3 provides a summary of the application by Harvard University, which foregrounds that its primary purpose is "to help improve leadership in American public life by giving Americans trained in law, from whose ranks come many of our governmental, business, and community leaders." This is precisely the phrase used by the Ford Foundation, describing "Education for Democracy"—"a better understanding of and competence in international affairs," through training in "international and foreign problems." As an ancillary purpose, we also see the "training to able men from foreign countries."

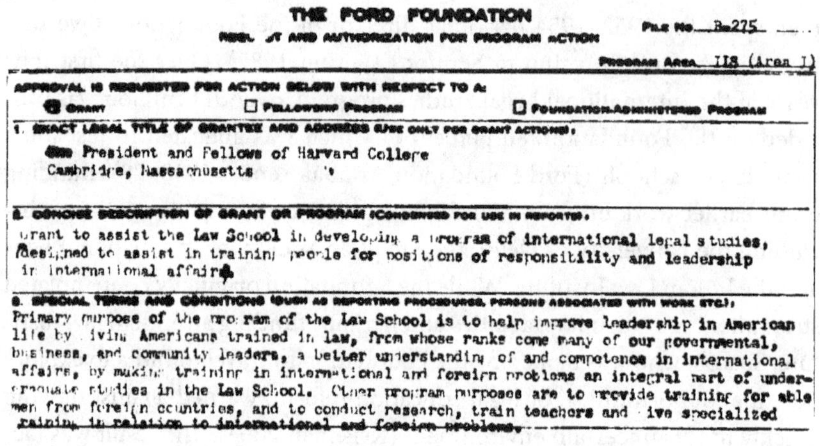

Figure 2.3. Summary of the Application by Harvard University

Education for democracy would turn on elite law schools' training of law students for both private enterprise and leadership in the state.

We argue that this combination—the facilitative role of commercial lawyers, as well as the general social leadership that lawyers could provide—made funding legal education particularly attractive to the Foundation during this time. This would, we argue, allow the Foundation to invest in broadening the legal field and the rules of the game of the US legal profession. This is evident in the Foundation's articulation, one year later, of legal education as forming both the *legal specialist* as well as the *lawyer-citizen*. The legal specialist had to do with the growth in governmental and private transactions between states, with an emphasis on commercial lawyering: "[i]ndividual lawyers, *more likely now to be called on to represent clients with international interests*, are required to know international law and to understand at least the general outlines of foreign legal systems" (emphasis added). The second role reflected social standing, rather than solely lawyers' professional positions: "Sound American relations with other countries depend fully as much on the lawyer-citizen, however, as they do on the legal specialist. In the United States, as in many other countries, the lawyer is an articulate and influential member of his community and frequently a public official." The Foundation seemed particularly interested in funding programs to create an international sensibility among US law students and faculty members (Ford Foundation Annual Report 1956).

This can also be seen through the photos selected for the Ford Foundation's Annual Reports. As we see in the following figures, the first photo chosen to represent the international legal studies is of an Indian law professor speaking at Stanford (Figure 2.4); this is followed the next year by a photo of foreign law students being trained in the United States (Figure 2.5); and two years later by a photo of a US lawyer who took a leave from his law firm to attend the University of Chicago for training in foreign law (Figure 2.6).

The photo of Tom Nicholson illustrates this internationally minded US lawyer who could move across national borders, working both with private clients and government. Nicholson, a naval lieutenant during the war and graduate of Andover, Princeton, and the Sorbonne, worked for the information office of the State Department after his military service. After graduating from the University of Chicago Law School, he practiced law in the city, taking time to study international law in Chicago, Hamburg, and Brussels. He went on to chair a UNESCO conference on the New Europe, and in the mid-1960s joined Mayer Brown & Platt, where he practiced until retirement (Princeton Alumni Weekly 2002).

This coupling of legal education with internationalism would soon shift. In 1956, Henry Heald, an engineer and academic leader who was the chancellor

Indian legal scholar addresses seminar at Stanford under Foundation-supported program of international legal studies

Figure 2.4. Indian Law Professor Speaking at Stanford, 1955 Annual Report

*American law schools are training a growing number of foreign
students like those from Chile, Colombia and Egypt in front
row of jury box at university moot court. Schools also are
establishing programs to teach foreign law and culture in U.S.*

Figure 2.5. Photo of Foreign Law Students Being Trained in the United States,
1956 Annual Report

International Legal Studies

Deep in the stacks of the University of Chicago's law library,
a young lawyer, Thomas Nicholson, prepares a seminar report on a problem in international civil law. Nicholson took
a leave of absence from his job in order to do graduate
work under Chicago's program in international legal studies,
one of several supported by the Foundation to train experts
in foreign law.

Figure 2.6. US Lawyer Who Took a Leave from His Law Firm to Attend the
University of Chicago for Training in Foreign Law, 1958 Annual Report

of New York University, became president of the Ford Foundation. Heald had been closely involved with education reforms of school systems in both Chicago and New York City, and was appointed by Rockefeller to chair a Committee on Higher Education for New York State (Farber 1975). Under Heald's tenure, internationally focused education gained greater prominence, with the Foundation's International Affairs program becoming "something like plenipotentiary powers across the Atlantic" (Sutton 2001: 88). Yet it is science education that became important to internationalism, rather than the behavioral sciences promoted by Gaither (Magat 1979: 29; Macdonald 1989: xiv). There continued to be significant giving to US educational institutions (Macdonald 1989: xiii), including law schools: yet this opened a new opportunity for legal education funding to focus on civil society and social change, domestically and abroad.

B. Legal Education as Expertise for Social Change

Central to this shift was William Pincus, a program officer with Ford, who in 1958 worked with the National Legal Aid and Defender Association to develop a grant proposal that would emphasize legal aid clinics within law schools (Ogilvy 2009). This was part of a generational shift. Pincus had worked in the federal Bureau of the Budget and the first and second Hoover Commissions prior to joining the Ford Foundation. He saw himself as "a child of the Roosevelt era, a child of the Depression," who was interested in government's capacity to improve the conditions of everyday life" (Pincus 2000: 20). Pincus was legally trained, though while in law school at George Washington University also worked in Roosevelt's administration (Pincus 2000).

At Ford, Pincus was tapped by a vice president, Dyke Brown, to review the "zillions of applications from the law world" coming to the Foundation. Pincus, who had spent limited time in government legal practice, had himself been concerned during law school about the disconnect between law teaching and the world of practice (particularly given the presence of war veterans in class with him). He was unenthusiastic about these proposals, since he did not see how they would improve the administration of justice. He thus approached the director of the National Legal Aid Association, which had been turned down by Ford for general support, to instead develop a model for clinical legal education to be staffed by law students (Pincus 2000).

Pincus's argument for this model of clinical legal education was based on a parallel with medical school training (Ogilvy 2009; Pincus 2000). This was precisely the same analogy to medicine that Jerome Frank at Yale Law School—who, among many left-leaning law professors of the time, also served in the Roosevelt administration—articulated, arguing for "clinical-lawyer" law schools (Frank 1933; Moran 2018; Ogilvy 2009). This was thus once again an extension of Yale's legal realism, following attempts by New Deal law professors to teach more courses on administrative law upon their return from the federal government. Clinics would build students' conceptual understanding of law, by giving them real-world experience that fit with legal realist goals (Moran 2018: 147).

As an academic idea clinics had not gained much traction nor federal funding (Moran 2018; Ogilvy 2009). The idea, though, found support through the Ford Foundation and its reimagined investments in law schools. Frustrated with the law-based funding applications he was charged to review, Pincus worked with the National Legal Aid Association, and developed an $800,000 Ford Foundation grant for law-school-based clinics. The early years of this model, known as the Council of Legal Clinics, met with limited success—including resistance, in some law schools, to the language of "clinical" education, which for example was inapposite with the interdisciplinary focus of the University of Chicago. Yet with changing political and professional trends, the program grew and came to be known as COEPR (Council on Education in Professional Responsibility), and CLEPR (Council of Legal Education for Professional Responsibility) by the late 1960s.

This heralded and anticipated the beginning of a new age in American lawyering, with a focus on civil rights at home, a topic that had been avoided by the American Bar Association prior to that point (Moran 2018). Clinical legal education would also accommodate rising student demand in civil rights. While intellectual battles within legal realism led to some early law school resistance to the language of clinical education, legally trained New Dealers would draw on these intellectual underpinnings as a next stage of legal realism. This would lay the seeds, in the 1950s, for how US legal education would be reformatted in the 1960s and 1970s.

Ford Foundation projects from the 1960s onward would draw on these developments in legal education. From the mid-1960s through the late 1970s, the Ford Foundation turned to an emphasis on international economic development, with a focus on India, China, and Latin America. This was led by McGeorge Bundy, who began as Ford Foundation president in 1966, a post he would hold until 1979. Bundy came to Ford with impeccable academic and social capital credentials. He had worked with the Council on Foreign Relations, served as the youngest dean of Arts and Sciences at Harvard University, and was National Security Advisor for both John F. Kennedy and Lyndon Johnson. Bundy's family members were personal friends of the Rockefellers, who had close ties to the Ford Foundation through the 1950s and 1960s (DeSocio 2017). Since the 1950s, it had been a reputational strategy of the Foundation to recruit academic stars to leverage their reputation (Pincus 2000: 10), and Bundy fit the profile to a tee.

McGeorge Bundy came from a personal and professional tradition steeped in foreign policy interests (Korey 2007: 61). Though Bundy was himself not a lawyer, he enjoyed close connections to elite law. His father was Harvey Hollister Bundy, a third-generation lawyer and Harvard Law School graduate who worked closely with Henry Stimson when he served as secretary of war during World War II. His mother was of Boston's most prominent and powerful families, and the daughter of Lawrence Lowell, a Harvard Law professor who became president of Harvard University for over two decades. And the Bundys were also family friends of US Supreme Court Justice Felix Frankfurter, who over time came to be a mentor to McGeorge Bundy, and offered him (along with his brother) a judicial clerkship despite his lack of legal education (Dalin 2017: 172).

In McGeorge Bundy's view, law "must be an active, not a passive force" for change (Hershkoff and Hollander 2000: 91). As we see in Figure 2.1 (above), funding for justice broadly, as well as for legal education specifically, increased in the 1960s, along with a high percentage of legal education funding. Echoing the shift toward clinical legal education, within the United States, Ford spent considerable funds to promote law clinics and access to justice, along with legal defense funds for Native Americans and Puerto Ricans. Grantmaking allotted to questions of minority rights litigation within the United States expanded dramatically under McGeorge Bundy's tenure, coming to over one-third of all of the Ford Foundation's annual giving in 1968 (Hershkoff and Hollander 2000: 91; MacDonald 2006; McCutcheon 2000a). This included grants for policy-oriented research. This also matched a broader turn to law as part of the war on poverty and a remaking of lawyers as agents for social change (Garth and Sterling 1998).

Internationally, the 1960s were focused on economic development, with an emphasis on Asia, India, and Latin America, as well as concerns over Communism. Tied to this were lawyers, with a concern throughout the decade on connecting the needs of developing countries and new nations with a strategy around the rule of law. Formally, the International Legal Studies program ended in 1958—yet it persisted through the early 1960s by offering fellowship support in "international legal studies" to US-based law professors. Approximately four professors received fellowships annually. What is particularly notable is that a good number of these recipients had not been doing international work as such but were instead specialists on domestic legal topics, who were funded to internationalize the reach of domestic US law thinking. These were prominent recipients, including Kenneth Culp Davis from the University of Minnesota Law School, Daniel Mandelker from Indiana University School of Law, E. Allan Farnsworth and Maurice Rosenberg from Columbia University School of Law, Victor Stone from the University of Illinois, Herbert Morris, from UCLA, and John Whelan from Georgetown University (Ford Foundation Annual Report 1959, 1960, 1962, 1963).

As the Foundation pursued work in development issues internationally, lawyers were funded along with economists, as a bid to upgrade the expertise and knowledge base used by governments abroad and with law as the language of governance (Dezalay and Garth, Chapter 5). Internationally oriented funding for law schools and legal education were thus retooled and reimagined around communism and decolonization (see also Engerman 2009). Grants were made to ensure that US lawyers could galvanize lawyers worldwide—including an early grant, in 1960, to the Committee on World Peace through Law, established by the American Bar Association (with funding to the American Bar Foundation). McGill University received a grant to its Institute for Air and Space Law (including problems of jet transportation, supersonic civil aircraft, manned and unmanned missiles, and space exploration) (Ford Foundation Annual Report 1963). Columbia University received funding for a project on the law of communist countries. Conferences were funded over how independence and decolonization would affect international agreements, partly through Columbia University in collaboration with others, for both American and European lawyers and law students (Ford Foundation Annual Report 1963, 1964).

A major grant of the 1960s was to a new entity, created by the Carnegie Endowment for International Peace, called the International Legal Center (ILC). Ford, Rockefeller and others had by the late 1950s joined the Carnegie Endowment in funding the Hague Academy of International Law, to modernize the Academy during a time of decolonization (Scott-Smith 2007). The ILC received a start-up grant of $3 million from the Ford Foundation in 1966 and was designed to position lawyers as experts in development issues, both at home and abroad:

> Working with U.S., foreign, and international agencies, foundations, universities, and practicing lawyers and jurists, the center will stimulate and support systematic study of the role of law in international relations and the development of modern nations. The center will also be concerned with recruitment and training to expand the ranks of lawyers, social scientists, and others qualified to work on problems of law and development; and with projects to help developing countries establish legal institutions essential to the functioning of modern, free societies (Ford Foundation Annual Report 1966).

The ILC provided an opportunity for many in the Ford Foundation network to advance themselves or their proteges through fellowship opportunities and offering Ford staff members international opportunities at the end of their terms. This notably included John Howard, a graduate of the University of Chicago Law School with a PhD in chemistry from Harvard, who became its director after sixteen years at the Foundation (Dezalay and Garth 1996: 72; Merryman 2000: 482; Krishnan 2012: 313).

Compared with the focus of the 1950s, grantmaking to international legal education of the 1960s emphasized law and development. Figure 2.7 draws on the Ford budget data, and shows that legal education projects outside the United States would amount to nearly one-third of legal education funding that decade.

This turn to law and development included the reform of legal education and law schools abroad. This shift in the Foundation is articulated in recollections of James Gardner, a Ford Foundation program officer:

> It is safe to say that in the 60's the Foundation, the ILC and many international organizations—and lawyers—waffled from some general objective to advance human welfare to the idea that law somehow contributes importantly to development, and hence to the advance of human welfare. Thus, drawn to the legal sector, it seemed but a small and relatively secure step to a rationale focusing on the idea that lawyers were central figures in the functioning of law in a developmental context, and hence to an

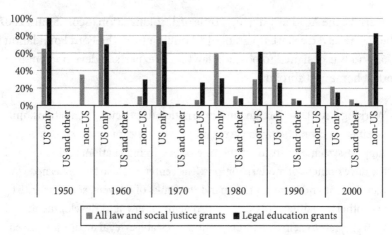

Figure 2.7. Distribution of Legal Education vs. All Law and Social Justice Grants by Location

institutional extrapolation of that rationale, and the idea that that the way to get at lawyers was through legal education (López Valdez 1975: 7).

One quarter of the funding for the ILC was directed to two Chilean law schools: the Universities of Chile and Concepcion and the Catholic University of Valparaiso. The funding was for "modernization" of their curriculum and staffing, and collaboration with North American law professors and students. This language of modernization reflected the dominant thinking on development, here expanded to capture law and legal expertise. Such modernization would fund full-time faculty and research, create networks among faculty, and mirror US-style legal education by disrupting the teaching of doctrinal legal education (López Valdez 1975).

The Ford funding of law and development sought to disrupt established hierarchies abroad by conceiving of law as central to improving national development. By converting law from its place as traditional and formalistic analysis, this register of law and development sought to build up legal training as *problem-solving*. This management of social change was imagined to have been the success of US lawyers at home, and it permeated the law and development moment (López Valdez 1975: 25 n.22). For instance, as part of this modernization Ford would fund, within legal training, "a basic course in the social sciences" (Ford Foundation Annual Report 1967: 54). The theory of law and development was that lawyers could discern and ask questions about "underlying social maladies," which would in turn be "more responsive to popular desires" (Trubek 1972: 38).[4]

This extended to Africa. Among the ILC activities that captured Ford's attention was its work on introducing "modern techniques" of teaching law abroad, including temporarily staffing African law schools with US law professors, and placing "young American lawyers abroad for training and service with governmental agencies of developing countries" (Ford Foundation Annual Report 1968). These efforts, devised by John Bainbridge at Columbia Law School (from which he was also a graduate), came to be known as "SAILER," an acronym for the Staffing of African Institutions of Legal Education and Research, and turned on exchange and fellowship opportunities for US professors and law students, and African students who came to the United States to pursue graduate law degrees (Krishnan 2012). In so doing, SAILER also provided a safe haven for African lawyers during times of conflict, such as in Ethiopia and Nigeria (Krishnan 2012). As a SAILER alumnus and retired partner from Cravath, Swaine & Moore would later indicate, the program "has had a lasting impact in many ways as the students and teachers involved matured into leaders in their countries" (Saxon 2006).

Efforts to reform legal education in India persisted in the 1960s, with close connections to the Indian Law Institute and Delhi University. Having learned from prior efforts of the 1950s, these programs increasingly included Indian legal elites. Yet they now faced local discomfort regarding the presence of Americans in Indian universities (Krishnan 2004: 466–467), and it was difficult for the Foundation to change existing hierarchies around legal education and its relative social standing (Dezalay and Garth, Chapter 5).

Within the United States, a signal investment of the Ford Foundation would be the extension of clinical legal education. With Pincus at its helm, approximately $10 million in grant funding was distributed to US law schools from 1968 to 1980 through CLEPR (Pincus 2000; Stuckey 1996; Ogilvy 2009). This funding was part of retooling legal education to meet the needs of the civil rights era. This was despite some contestation from within law schools over whether this was sufficiently "academic" in nature (e.g., Wilson 2017; Moran 2018; Holland 1999). It also reimagined legal education

---

[4] These efforts in Chile, as with Colombia, were interrupted by political change in the mid-1970s, including an ascendancy in power of conservative law professors (Frühling 2000: 57).

away from the studied distance that the organized bar had been keeping from civil rights. These clinics would instead meet student interest in civil rights (Sandefur and Selbin 2009), a concern that was articulated by the chair of the Curriculum Committee for the American Association of Law Schools in 1968:

> Fundamental changes must be made soon. It is not only that law students over the country are reaching the point of open revolt, but also that law faculties themselves, particularly the younger members, share with the student the view that legal education is too rigid, too uniform, too narrow, too repetitious and too long (Stuckey 1996: 252–253).

This model of clinical legal education would also be part of what became exported abroad, including through CLEPR funds (Ogilvy 2009: 19). The Ford Foundation budget data reflects this turn to civil rights and law school clinics. From being largely ignored in the 1950s, funding targeting access and equity accounts for almost half of legal education funding throughout the 1960s, with development accounting for an additional 20 percent of this funding.[5]

Under the tenures of Henry Heald and McGeorge Bundy, Ford reflected US academic trends toward thinking of law as a policy-oriented social science, an extension of earlier roots in legal realism (Garth and Sterling 1998). Both non-lawyers, during their tenures law would be identified with problem-solving—and legal education would provide the Foundation with a platform, in the United States and abroad, to disrupt conservative elements in the profession and the state generally. This suggests some continuity with the earlier role for law in the Foundation: in both the 1950s and the 1960s, lawyers were seen as central to state leadership, and links across nations would occur through legal networks. This could include new cadres of lawyers to be invested in, or in some situations where lawyers were seen as conservative roadblocks to development, the Foundation would position US-style legal education as a model for breaking up professional divisions of labour and social conservatism (Dezalay and Garth 2002).

---

[5] Analyses on file with authors.

C. Human Rights and Civil Rights

These reforms of legal education abroad, though, produced resistance within the Foundation. A 1971 report expressed concerns within the legal academy over exporting a US model abroad (Frühling 2000: 56). In 1974, Ford staff suggested that the way the Foundation had pursued its international agenda—through government cooperation and building university programs abroad—ought not be the only paths, given the challenging political contexts in many of their countries of interest.

Two years later, Bundy endorsed a move to begin supporting activity and research by academics and NGOs outside of their countries of focus (Carmichael 2001: 251). Latin America was an obvious case. As local interlocutors faced government repression, it was clear that not only did they require support to find refuge elsewhere but that external actors, including US law professors, needed to get involved in many cases Ford was interested in (Frühling 2000). Ford's internationalization strategy would thus go beyond the funding and promotion of legal education abroad, to funding law professors engaged on these issues within the United States.

This turn to domestic law schools soon converged with the Foundation's growing concerns over fairness within the US justice system, with an emphasis on issues of justice, civil rights, and equality, and with attention to poverty, health, and education internationally (Wong, Levi, and Deutsch 2017). For example, the ILC received funds for a domestic project on convicted persons in the criminal justice system, on the basis that it "would apply throughout the criminal justice system and across national borders" (Ford Foundation Annual Report 1971). The ILC also received a grant to explore creating an International Development Law Advisory Service that "would advise and represent developing nations in international transactions," and pursue education and training to create technical expertise (Ford Foundation Annual Report 1974). This shift is again reflected in the choice of photos in annual reports, such as those reproduced in Figure 2.8 (Ford Foundation Annual Report 1970).

These concerns over rights and equity would lead to continued investment in justice issues—but not necessarily legal education. Despite being among the most generous years for grantmaking at the Foundation, legal education projects in the 1970s fell to half of the funding provided in the 1960s (Figure 2.1, above), and approximately 10 percent of all justice-oriented grants, with much of it to US institutions.

Figure 2.8. US Justice Systems and Agricultural Projects in Indonesia, 1970 Annual Report

The Foundation was instead taking an explicit turn toward human rights grantmaking. This did not come easily, since many in the Foundation—despite its support for civil rights work—regarded human rights as outside its remit. Yet a key prompt for this turn lay in Ford's response to the Chilean coup, when Ford staff in Chile, who had been working on legal education and development reforms in the 1960s, broke with the US intelligence services and found ways to support the Allende government through the legal logic of human rights (Dezalay and Garth 2006). Ford Foundation funding for the Catholic Vicariate of Solidarity thus began in 1978, then the Argentine Centro de Estudios Legales y Sociales beginning in 1981, and later extending to Peru (Frühling 2000: 63).

The human rights turn also led to different grantmaking projects for Ford. A key example is South Africa, where grantmaking for legal education and law school projects began in 1973. The first investment was a conference held at the University of Natal-Durban to bring US experts on clinical legal education to South Africa, credited as bringing the idea of public interest law to the country (Golub 2000a: 23). The legal clinic model—born from the legal realism movement and extended by Bill Pincus as a way to have domestic legal education meet changing social demands—became part of the Foundation's strategy for responding to apartheid over the 1970s (McCutcheon 2000a: 269).

This turn to human rights abroad and to civil rights in the United States became a major shift in the Foundation in 1979, under the leadership of Franklin Thomas, the first African American president of the Foundation. A lawyer, Thomas grew up in Brooklyn and was the son of West Indian immigrants. Having attended Columbia University on an academic scholarship, and then serving four years in the US Air Force Reserve Officer Training Corps, he went on to graduate from Columbia Law School. He worked as an Assistant US Attorney in New York, and was named Deputy Police Commissioner in Charge of Legal Matters for the NYPD. He then moved into community development, and was appointed by Senator Robert Kennedy to lead the Bedford Stuyvesant Restoration Corporation.

The Foundation's focus on law and social justice that had been built in the path from Gaither to Bundy was now reinforced by Franklin Thomas. Yet the 1970s recession led to financial constraints on the Foundation, and mirroring Thomas's own trajectory and connections, Ford would now focus on using law as a strategy to alleviate poverty and vulnerability within the United States (Hershkoff and Hollander 2000). Thomas identified legal initiatives as the key to addressing society's "sensitive and unyielding problems," such as civil rights and poverty (Hershkoff and Hollander 2000: 92). With the election of Ronald Reagan in 1980, resistance to civil rights successes was also pursued through the courts, leading to ever greater focus on law as a tool for social reform (Dezalay and Garth 2006; Hershkoff and Hollander 2000: 93). Rather than being separated in the Foundation's international portfolio, human rights and social justice became a uniform funding category within the Foundation (Rosenfield and Wimpee 2015: 26). Domestic legal projects gained further attention, defined through the domestic civil rights and antiwar movements (Korey 2007: 61). The focus on human rights led to Foundation investments in the Fund for Free Expression, Helsinki Watch, and in turn Americas Watch, which became attractive to Ford because of their ability to engage domestic elites on human rights issues abroad (Dezalay and Garth 2006; Wong, Levi, and Deutsch 2017). The later emergence of Human Rights Watch then came to reflect an ever more legalistic approach to the human rights field (Dezalay and Garth 2006), with ever greater prominence on law as state critique (Garth and Sterling 1998; Jenson and Levi 2013).

While some have criticized the domestic focus of foundation giving during this time (Heydemann and Kinsey 2010: 234), Ford did continue to invest in targeted countries. This notably included China. Funding in China extended an earlier investment in teaching Chinese studies within the United States to an effort to rebuild law schools in 1979 and to the Foundation's establishment of an office in Beijing in 1988. As one program officer indicated, once law was seen as a way to engage with China, legal education was privileged since this "would have a major multiplier effect on other future law programs" (McCutcheon 2000a: 166). A 1982 conference led to the prominent US-China Committee for Legal Education Exchange (CLEEC), funding hundreds of students and scholars until the end of Thomas's tenure, with grantees in later years actively pursuing Chinese legal reform projects. This included creation of the Wuhan Center in 1992, which became an exemplar in China for university- and student-based legal clinics (McCutcheon 2000a: 159–171, 183; Edwards 2009).

Similarly the Ford Foundation was, from 1973 onward, making grants in Latin America, South Africa, and South Asia, including legal clinics, university-based centers, and legal consciousness raising activities (Frühling 2000; Golub 2000a, 2000b, 2000c). In South Africa the Ford Foundation took a central role in the fight against apartheid, with an emphasis on legal approaches including funding for the Centre for Applied Legal Studies (CALS) at Wits University, and the public interest Legal Resources Centre (LRC) (Wits University n.d.). During this time, Franklin Thomas chaired the Study Commission on US Policy Toward Southern Africa, established by the Rockefeller Foundation in 1977 (Thomas 1981). The Commission's recommendations included supporting public interest organizations and noted the achievements of the LRC (Thomas 1981: 440). This emphasis on the role of law for promoting change in South Africa found key intellectual counterparts in the United States and the United Kingdom (Abel 1995; Iya 1995). As Franklin Thomas recollected, "[w]e were helping to reinforce black South Africans' notion that they had rights, that they could go to court, and that they could get a favorable court ruling enforced" (Golub 2000a: 19).

The fight against apartheid also provided an opportunity to export the US model of clinical legal education. As early as 1973, Bill Pincus as president of CLEPR made a presentation at a legal aid conference held at the University of Natal to discuss US-based approaches to clinical legal education (McQuoid-Mason 2004: 31 n.16; Pincus 1974). Funded by Ford, the conference "provided a jump-start for clinics in South Africa," with ten established clinics by the end of the 1970s (De Klerk 2005: 930). Yet while these seeds for South African legal clinics were sown, it was in the late 1970s—during Franklin Thomas's leadership—that these grew in size and prominence (Golub 2000a: 23). Data from Foundation annual reports show that by the 1980s, projects in South Africa received a substantial share of legal education funds.

Funding clinical legal education projects also allowed the Foundation to forge strategic alliances with South African elites. In attendance at the 1973 meeting and supportive of these clinics was the storied South African jurist and commercial lawyer Sydney Kentridge. Kentridge was born in Johannesburg and raised in a liberal Jewish family, and by the late 1970s had already defended Nelson Mandela and represented Stephen Biko's family (Golub 2000a; Gapper 2013). Kentridge went on to help launch the new South African LRC, cofounded by his spouse Felicia, who came from a family of lawyers (her mother being the first woman barrister in South Africa) (Legal Resources Centre 2015), and who had set up a legal clinic for the poor at Witwatersrand University in the early 1970s. Felicia Kentridge had also developed a public interest law center in Johannesburg, which garnered the support of Lloyd Cutler in the United States, and, with it, financial support from Ford, Carnegie, and Rockefeller (Battersby 2015).

Similarly, another cofounder of the LRC, Geoff Budlender, had been a student activist in the 1970s who graduated from the law faculty at the University of Cape Town and served as the director general of the Department of Land Affairs during Mandela's presidency (Budlender 1999; Budlender 2012). Budlender had visited the United States in 1978 through a State Department visitors' program and met with visiting public interest lawyers, the NAACP, and the ACLU. Budlender (2012: 3) recalled that "I was very interested in what they were doing, it seemed to me it really provided interesting models for what we might be able to do, so I became very keen to be part of something like that . . . which led to the establishment of the LRC." The LRC would soon be directed by none other than Arthur Chaskalson, a leading commercial lawyer who would, among others, be part of Nelson Mandela's defense team. Parallel engagements would lead to the creation of the Centre for Applied Legal Studies at Witwatersrand University, led by John Dugard who was the immediate past dean of Witwatersrand's faculty and a prominent human rights professor (Golub 2000a: 23–24; Duke University n.d.).

It seems that the turn to clinical legal education models would allow the Foundation to invest in legal education abroad, without the same backlash it experienced when exporting US models of legal education. The South African context demonstrates that these clinics could be taken up by local elites, who would mobilize these clinics as part of social reform struggles. In other words, clinical legal education provided the Foundation with a transnational bridge for linking social issues in the United States and abroad, including by connecting efforts for racial justice at home with the struggle against apartheid in South Africa. Law schools and legal education would thereby be identified as institutions for social change. This specific form of investment in legal education has led to the continued prominence of law clinics in South African law schools, with continued Ford Foundation funding through the 1990s (De Klerk 2005: 931; Wilson 2017: 231).

Of course, whether different locales adopted legal clinics turned on shifting conditions and the structural positions of agents who were available to adopt and build political space and professional constituencies for these exports (Dezalay and Garth 2002; Halliday and Shaffer 2015). For instance, Figure 2.9 demonstrates that there were parallel investments in legal education elsewhere during this time. In Latin America, this would include legal clinics such as the Inter-American Legal Services Association, yet it took later investment by Ford in the 1990s for these clinic to overcome more conventional forms of legal education (Carrillo and Yaksic 2011: 89; Castro-Buitrago et al. 2011; Frühling 2000). In the terms of field sociology, some of these are "half-failed transplants," with unanticipated detours yet which still produce local consequences for importers (Dezalay and Garth 2002: 246).

We conclude that legal education funding was important to Ford's strategies during the 1970s. The turn to human rights and civil rights led to an expansion of projects focused on on-the-ground advocacy and legal services,

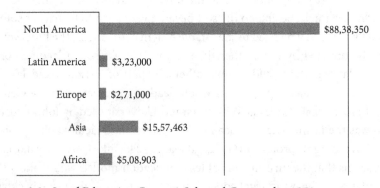

Figure 2.9. Legal Education Grants y Selected Geography, 1970s

thereby repositioning law schools as instrumental for social change and for connecting with domestic, foreign, and international nongovernmental organizations. This came with less appetite to provide advice to government (Heydemann and Kinsey 2010; Hershkoff and Hollander 2000). Yet it coincided well with the approach to legal education taking place within the United States, which emphasized clinical work and litigation for social change, and which became seen as a successful model for others to import.

D. Legal Education and Legal Institutions for Development Abroad

The Foundation continued to provide significant support to law schools and legal education in the 1980s and 1990s. Partly as a result of accretion, the grants given were now diverse, including local and domestic institutions, ranging from a focus on employment and education for minorities through a grant to UC Berkeley, support for research on violence in São Paulo, investments in public interest law across Eastern Europe, and support for legal aid clinics in South Africa (see, e.g., Golub 2000a; McCutcheon 2000b).

Yet a central element of the 1980s lay in the Ford Foundation's engagement with China. The Foundation had been viewed with distrust in China for decades (Hu and Rerup 2015: 24). And when diplomatic relations were restored with China in 1979, this provided an opportunity for Ford to engage—which it did through investments in legal education. As elsewhere in previous decades, investments in China began by attending to the research and networks of elite law professors, along with formal attention to legal clinics later in the 1990s (Pottenger 2004: 68).

Investing in legal education was particularly attractive to the Ford Foundation (and to engaged US law schools) because of the Chinese plan, as of 1978, to establish a law school in each of China's provinces and autonomous regions. Over the 1980s, the number of law schools in China grew by 500 percent (from 10 to 48), with the number of law students increasing twenty-fold over (Carmichael 1988a: 3–4; Lubman 1999). With no private bar and limited foreign opportunities, the vast majority of these new graduates found work in the state (Minzner 2013). Ford recognized that this emphasis on law schools was core to post-Mao China's modernization strategy, and its state reforms in industry, agriculture, science and technology, and national defense (Ford Foundation 1986: 3). Ford saw the Chinese investment in law schools as an attempt to reform arbitrary abuse and as needing rules to govern economic relations to attract foreign capital and technology (1986: 4).

An important plank of this Ford Foundation investment was the Chinese Academy of Social Sciences (CASS), with collaborations on economics, law, and international relations. The Academy was itself interested in focusing on law, and as of 1979 the Foundation was involved in encouraging contacts among US and Chinese law professors (Hu and Rerup 2015). In 1980, a Ford Foundation delegation visited China to explore possible connections on law and legal institutions. It was led by Frank Sutton, the vice president of Ford's international division who held a PhD in Sociology from Harvard University, where decades earlier he had written a dissertation on radical Marxism in an effort to understand communist rationales (Sutton 1950; Leibner and Green 2008: 4; Carmichael 1988a: 4). This then led to lectures being financed, both in China and the United States, by law professors, including Frank Sutton in 1980, Louis Henkin, Alan Dershowitz, Whitmore Grey, Oscar Schachter, and others. It was anticipated that new teaching would include interdisciplinary courses connecting law with sociology, psychology, and current trends in Western legal theory (Carmichael 1988a: 4, 7; Carmichael 1985: 5).

By 1982, a committee of US legal scholars and CASS cosponsored a conference in China, which represented "the first such meeting between legal experts from the two countries" since 1949 (Ford Foundation Annual Report 1988: xiv). Connections with CASS were soon extended to "include leading universities and ministry-related research centers" (Ford Foundation Annual Report 1988: xiv). This became a highly significant program for the Ford Foundation. Over a seven-year period in the 1980s, 140 Chinese law teachers and law students were brought to the United States with Ford support, and a China Centre for American Law Study was established in China to host US law professors teaching in the summer months to Chinese lawyers. For the Ford Foundation, the benefits to influencing state transformation were clear:

> These activities have contributed to the training of a new generation of law teachers who are increasingly involved in offering in-service training to Chinese legal officials, judges and lawyers, drafting new laws and regulations, providing legal services to Chinese individuals and institutions, and conducting related public education campaigns. And the graduates taught by the law teachers trained under the program are now at work as judges in the emerging Chinese court system, as prosecuters [*sic*] and lawyers in the revitalized prosecution office and law firms, and as legal

experts in government agencies. In addition, several younger American scholars have been trained in Chinese law in China (Carmichael 1988b: 5).

Over the 1980s and 1990s, what came to be known as CLEEC (Committee on Legal Education Exchange with China), would bring over two hundred scholars and students from China to the United States, and train hundreds of others in summer programs, in addition to training law librarians (Pottenger 2004: 68; McCutcheon 2000c: 167). Several individuals took on elite positions as law school deans and senior administrators in China, as vice presidents of the Supreme People's Court, in important law firms, and in Chinese government agencies (Pottenger 2004: 68; McCutcheon 2000c: 168). At Wuhan University, it was reported that CLEEC participants "are now the backbone of the University law faculty" (McCutcheon 2000c: 169). By 1998, several of the key advisors to the new Chinese premier, Zhu Rongi, were prior Ford grantees (Hu and Rerup 2015: 30). Furthermore, not all CLEEC's participants in the United States returned to China. About one-third stayed in the United States, and the American co-chair of CLEEC assessed that these Chinese lawyers with graduate degrees were in high demand domestically. This may also have reflected an abeyance strategy, with a greater number of CLEEC participants apparently returning to China following 1992 reforms in the wake of the Tiananmen Square protests (McCutcheon 2000c: 168).

The success of CLEEC's alumni in China is part of this story. With Chinese law schools growing dramatically, a focus of the 1980s was broadly on scholarly workshops, knowledge building, and elite academic networks between China and the United States, including support for Harvard Law School's East Asian Legal Studies program (McCutcheon 2000c: 165). This included building knowledge about China to understand the changes and consequences of Chinese development (McCutcheon 2000c: 165).

This is exemplified by a series of grant proposals between 1983 and 1988 from Columbia University Law School to fund legal education exchanges under the rubric of human rights and social justice. Led by law professors Randle Edwards and Walter Gellhorn, Columbia had played a central role since the early 1980s in promoting legal education exchanges with China. The 1983 funding proposal, for instance, would provide LLM scholarships for young Chinese faculty members, visiting scholarships for established Chinese faculty members, graduate study and research in China for US-based faculty, along with study tours, the exchange of library materials, and scholarly workshops. The first such workshop was scheduled to be held in

China in 1984, on "Legal Problems of International Trade and Investment" (the workshop appears to have been held at Wuhan University in 1985). Investments in legal education would include the creation and strengthening of law faculties and legal research, but also the training of legislative drafters in China.

Peter Geithner, who initiated Ford's China-focused grantmaking, would explain to a program officer that in growing the budget on China, the decision to focus on legal education was to "take the long view," with a later program officer Mark Sidel referring to the "major multiplier effect" of investing in legal education (McCutcheon 2000c: 166). This is echoed in an internal 1988 memo at Ford, recommending two more years of funding to Columbia University for strengthening Chinese legal education (Carmichael 1988b). The vision was one of state reform through law, with the hope that legal reform would "prevent abuses of individual rights" following the Cultural Revolution, the administration of "increasingly complex economic relationships between consumers and producers, between workers and management, and between the state and individual urban entrepreneurs and farmers," and identifying the need for legal regulation so China can "attract foreign investment and expand trade with the world community" (Carmichael 1988a: 3).

Creation of a group of US-trained Chinese legal scholars was core to the Ford strategy: in this same memo, Foundation staff are to provide continued support because new responsibilities are being "shouldered by the participating Chinese law faculties," with foreign trained junior faculty now providing training to Chinese legal practitioners and conducting public education campaigns (1988a: 6–7). Indeed by the time of the terminal grant to Columbia in 1988, nearly all the funds requested were for graduate study and research in the United States, with a small amount requested for graduate study and research in China. In other words, Ford's investments in law and legal education twinned an international and domestic strategy for Chinese state reform.

Investments in Chinese legal education in the 1980s had at their core an emphasis on academic networks and comparative law. This was understood as central to state reform in China. This relationship of legal institutions to change and reform is implicit in the conclusion of a Ford Foundation Annual Report (1988: xvii) toward the end of the decade, noting that "as China completes its first decade of reform, maintaining the balance between order and change has been an enormously difficult task," and that "[o]ld political and legal institutions must be adapted and new ones established to mediate and regulate the competition of interests that is bound to intensify."

By the end of the 1980s, Foundation staff indicated that they would be recommending other approaches to Chinese legal development. This included training for judges and legislative drafters, and developing new fields of law in Chinese law schools and research institutions. In 1988 the Foundation opened its office in Beijing, which would support training for judges and legislative research and drafting (including the main Chinese organizations involved in legislative drafting) and then the procuracy, with an emphasis on rights and governance in the early 1990s (Ford Foundation Annual Report 1988: xvi). The political sensitivities of the latter work were managed through Ford's local connections and partners, including the prominent Administrative Law Research Group that was a Ford grantee (McCutcheon 2000c: 160–171).

The 1980s and 1990s also saw Ford Foundation investments in judicial education. This followed the same logic of building connections between elites—but now beyond connections in the United States, to internationalize the Chinese judiciary more broadly. In 1999 the Foundation provided $200,000 to the Senior Judges Training Center to invite foreign specialists to China and to provide study and training opportunities for Chinese judges in Canada, Japan, the Soviet Union, Western Europe, and the United States (Ford Foundation Annual Report 2000: 61). Parallel funding for legislative drafting was instrumental in supporting the Administrative Law Research Group, which drew on the alumni and experience of CASS and CLEEC in drafting new legislation that opened the scope for individuals in China to sue the state, for a new criminal procedure law, and for a law on women's rights (McCutcheon 2000c: 171–173).

From 1986 to 1988, the Ford Foundation invested over $8 million in China-related activities—including law, as well as economics and international relations (Ford Foundation Annual Report 1988: xiv, xvii). By the end of the 1980s, the Ford annual budget for access to social justice, legal services, and education relating to China was just over $1.1 million, of which $800,000 went to Columbia and just over $170,000 to China-based institutions, including the Chinese Academy of Social Sciences (Ford Foundation Annual Report 1988). Other funders would join Ford in building and strengthening Chinese law faculties, including the Henry R. Luce and Chinn Ho foundations, and the United States Information Agency (Ford Foundation Annual Report 1988: xv).

Perhaps the most striking investments in China in the 1990s was a turn to clinical legal education and the "law in action" over formal doctrinal law (McCutcheon 2000c). This had been contemplated in the 1980s as part of exposing China to US approaches to legal education (Carmichael 1988b: 7), and gained vigor through the late 1990s (Phan 2005; Pottenger 2004; Taylor, Chapter 5). Clinical approaches began in seven Chinese law schools and spread throughout China with the creation of the Committee of Chinese Clinical Legal Educators (Phan 2005: 128-129, 136)—with Ford further sponsoring exchanges and partnerships for Chinese students with clinical programs in US law schools (Phan 2005: 129 n.66). It is important to signal that there was a deep connection here with Ford's earlier investments in Chinese legal education: Wan E'Xiang, who was at the time a faculty member at Wuhan University (and has since become a member of the Supreme People's Court), had been a beneficiary of Ford fellowships to study at Michigan and Yale law schools and led the charge to develop clinical education at Wuhan (Yanmin and Pottenger 2011: 91-92).

Early investments, in other words, set the stage for the Foundation's later impact on clinical legal education in China throughout the 1990s. Yet whereas earlier projects were focused on the writing of legal rules and the establishment of legal elites, these clinical opportunities have spurred social justice approaches within China that emphasize rights protection (McCutcheon 2000c: 166). Over time the emphasis has been on connecting Chinese and US law school clinics, in particular at Yale, and with the Committee of Chinese Clinical Legal Educators seeking to develop models of legal clinics (Yanmin and Pottenger 2011). These networks have been particularly useful given government pressure on these clinics, realities that the clinics are run by law teachers who do not specialize in clinical approaches, that law school curricula are very heavy, and that American models of clinical legal education are often inapposite in civilian systems (Phan 2005; Yanmin and Pottenger 2011).

Overall, the Ford Foundation's investments in legal education—through CLEEC, the Committee of Chinese Clinical Legal Educators, or more direct training of prosecutors and judges—have had a significant imprint on the Chinese legal profession. Ford is seen as the most significant foreign NGO in China on matters relating to rights, justice, and democratic governance (Hu and Rerup 2015: 12). Ford's investments in Chinese legal education have built out law schools to respond to changing social needs, often by promoting local elites and networking them with US law schools. As the Foundation would report, "By mid-1989, 124 Chinese law teachers from nine participating Chinese institutions will have spent from three months to two years in the United States" (Ford Foundation Annual Report 1988: xv). The move from development and modernization to social justice and individual claims against the state show how Chinese legal education has been a battleground for refiguring law both as a tool of statecraft and social justice.[6]

Finally, we note that China was not the only focus of Ford's legal education investments at this time. We return to South Africa briefly to note that during the 1980s, the institutes created with earlier Ford funds grew in prominence, with research reports, "justice and society" conferences through which judges met progressive lawyers, and university center support for the South African labor movement. This tied together the interests of labor and civil rights, including funding for legal aid to black and multiracial unions, training for black trade unionists in legal matters, and reports on industrial health and safety (Ford Foundation Annual Report, 1982: 26). In 1985 the trustees approved a $1.9 million special appropriation dedicated to the "expansion of educational opportunities to prepare black South Africans for positions of present and future leadership, development of public interest law and legal services, and strengthening of black community-based self-help organizations." Spurring these initiatives was the desire "to find opportunities to help meet the human needs of oppressed blacks in ways that also contribute to preparing them for the day when they will assume their rightful role-first as full partners in negotiation of their country's future, then as potential leaders of a democratic South African government" (Ford Foundation Annual Report, 1986: xiii–xiv). And as political tides shifted in 1990, and building on the success of the CALS (Ford Foundation Annual Report 1986), Ford provided funds to university-based grantees, such as the University of the Western Cape, to support exiles returning to South Africa—who were working with ANC teams on legal elements of the country's transition—and to connect grantees to civil rights lawyers in the United States (Golub 2000a).

---

[6] This had limits. As a Ford discussion paper notes, "the downturn" in the US-China relationship in the mid-1990s led to "increased suspicion" about the Foundation (Hu and Rerup 2015: 30).

E. Turning to International Organizations

The mid-1980s had already brought increasing attention to public international law, including a 1984 project on "International Organizations and Law." This trend reflected how to navigate the end of the Cold War, along with concern over globalization and cooperation with industrialized countries: "[b]oth in the North and in the South," the Foundation reported, "there are mixed feelings about the many implications of interdependence" (Ford Foundation Annual Report 1990).

The end of the Cold War, the Rwandan war, the early years of the Bosnian war, and wars in Afghanistan and Nepal were some of the conflicts worrying the United States. Economic growth globally and the Beijing Conference on women's rights were two opportunities that also captured US attention. It was apparent that "the mood of the Foundation seemed to have shifted from optimism to considerable uncertainty about the changing global order" (Rosenfield and Wimpee 2015: 32).

In 1996, Susan Berresford took up the helm at Ford, remaining in the role until 2007. Berresford was the first woman as Ford president, and was neither a lawyer nor an academic. Prior to becoming president, Berresford served the Foundation as vice president, in charge of worldwide programming and investments. By the time of her appointment the Foundation was witnessing a turn to international needs, including enhancing international cooperation and reducing poverty and injustice. While asserting that any changes would not be drastic (Arenson 1996), Berresford compared her own trajectory to the Foundation history, arguing that interconnections between the domestic and the international had been Franklin Thomas's goal throughout (Brier 2009).

With Foundation assets growing, after her first year in office Berresford reorganized grantmaking to focus on the three pillars of poverty, peace, and social justice, and a broad category for education, media, arts, and culture (Rosenfield and Wimpee 2015: 32). Attuned to international questions, Berresford opened Foundation offices in Russia and China (Rosenfield and Wimpee 2015). This allowed connections with past grantees and for Ford to be part of a broader set of US engagements in law and business. As an early employee in the Moscow office recalls, "in Moscow, at the words 'Ford Foundation' the doors of Baker and Mackenzie, Price Waterhouse and Citibank seemed to fly open" (McAuley 2018). Legal clinics were created in China during the 1990s, with continued human rights work in Latin America and impact litigation in Eastern Europe (Frühling 2000; McCutcheon 2000a: 269, 2000c: 180, 2000b: 234). Toward the end of the twentieth century, massive granting was directed to international fellowships for disadvantaged professionals abroad—including a partnership for higher education in Africa, and a scholar rescue fund in the wake of 9/11. Foundation historians note that during Berresford's tenure "Foundation staff thus explicitly took into account the new global context, increasing opportunities for inclusion" (Rosenfield and Wimpee 2015: 35).

Implicitly harkening back to its earlier view of the 1950s, the Foundation positioned law and legal education as core to the problem-solving needed to reach consensus around complex challenges. It was now tied to strengthening international law: "World events of 1991 heightened awareness of international organizations and international law as the best hope for global peace and security" (Ford Foundation Annual Report 1991: 112). To do so, the Foundation recounted, required "advanced training of scholars and practitioners in the fields of international organizations and international law, education to enhance public understanding of the role of international organizations and law in furthering world peace, and research and policy analysis on important multilateral institutions" (p.112).

From an $840,000 investment in 1985, the International Affairs program in 1990 increased its expenditures to $6.7 million, with US law schools receiving the lion's share of these funds. Approximately $4 million was given to twenty-three US law schools for fellowships, internships, and activities to attract students and scholars to the study of public international law and to improve teaching in the field and links with the United Nations. For instance, in 1990, the Foundation's Scholar in Residence, Sir Brian Urquhart, and Erskine Childers, both former senior UN officials, completed a study on "A World in Need of Leadership: Tomorrow's United Nations," co-sponsored by the Ford Foundation and the Swedish Dag Hammarskjöld Foundation (Urquhart and Childers 1996).

IV. Conclusion

The funding of legal education by Ford can be conceived as a private transnational legal ordering that coupled law, governance, and the state (Shaffer 2016). Over time and across countries, the Foundation invested in legal education as a professional node to address development, diplomacy, and political change. This would converge with US-based concerns around social justice, commerce, inequality, and the legal system.

Political eras shaped the Ford Foundation's funding of legal education worldwide. The focus on international law and legal studies that predominated in the 1950s and 1960s was recreated differently in later decades—though the project has consistently been to produce and legitimate lawyers through education and cosmopolitan networks. In this way, Ford investments have built up lawyers as a professional group with an expertise for reforming states and powerful organizations. We see this in Japan, China, South Africa, across Latin America, and in international organizations—and with deep connections to US law and legal networks.

Political eras also produced headwinds. Take, for example, the counterfactual example of legal education in India. Jayanth Krishnan (2004) stunningly demonstrates that, by the 1980s, the Ford Foundation had shifted away from investing in legal education out of a sense that grassroots initiatives were better bets for reform efforts—a conclusion that the Foundation reached in the wake of Indira Gandhi's suspension of the constitution, but also as a result of a report from Bob Cole from UC Berkeley Law School, who, while advocating for continued funding of legal education efforts, expressed concern over the capacity of Indian law schools to achieve meaningful change given the structure of legal work, the lack of diversity in the bar, and the comparative lack of prestige of Indian lawyers.

Yet even in the face of such headwinds, the field of legal education that Ford funded worldwide would lead to new position-takings and recursive effects. Krishnan (2004: 474–475) demonstrates that N.R. Madhava Menon met US law professors engaged with Ford while at Delhi University. He then spent a sabbatical at Columbia University Law School, also going to Northwestern University for a workshop on law and social science in India, taught by law and society notables Marc Galanter and Red Schwartz, and funded by the ILC, a Ford grantee. Menon later convinced the Foundation to invest nearly $1 million in supporting the National Law School, despite Ford's reservations—and despite Galanter too being skeptical of this plan (Krishnan 2004: 485 n.279). The point here is that the networks and exposure of law professors abroad to US models would produce and legitimate cosmopolitan lawyers—so their own influence would later keep Ford in the field of legal education, in the face of retrenchment and reservation.

In other words, legal education funding is not only about styles and models of law teaching. The Ford Foundation identified law early as a tool for problem-solving. Foundation funding would link importers of legal education projects abroad with exporters in the United States. Its investments in legal education promoted the development of legal expertise to address global problems. The malleability of legal frameworks—and the cosmopolitan legitimacy they produce—allows them to fit a wide array of problems and situations across countries. These legal education projects would then provide reformers with the status and authority necessary to overturn entrenched hierarchies abroad.

These same investments would also benefit US-based lawyering by exposing domestic law schools to the world. Exporting would connect elite law schools to potential reformers and powerful agents abroad. Challenges of development, diplomacy, and political change could converge with US-based concerns around trade, social justice, inequality, and the legal system. In short, Ford's investments in legal education fostered a US-defined model that closely connected lawyers with governance worldwide, providing law schools with the tools, resources, and symbolic legitimacy needed in each era.

Globally, the Ford Foundation has often helped to build greater autonomy for legal education from the state, while more tightly coupling legitimated elites abroad to the thinking about law and the state generated in US law schools. For example, US lawyers had been perceived since the 1950s as moderates who could modernize the state. Where legal elites abroad were perceived as antagonistic to state reform, Ford's material and symbolic capital could be invested in new legal approaches that could help undermine entrenched conservative oligarchies and disrupt entrenched hierarchies. Across political conjunctures, new models of legal expertise would enjoy reach, relevance, and recognition—through which the Ford Foundation would invest in foundational debates in statemaking.

References

Abel, R. (2015). *Politics by Other Means: Law in the Struggle against Apartheid, 1980–1994*. Routledge.

Åkermark, A.S. (1997). *Justifications of Minority Protection in International Law* (Vol. 50). Martinus Nijhoff.

Arenson, K.W. (1996). "At Ford Foundation, a New Chief and a New Style," *New York Times*.

Battersby, J. (2015). "Felicia Kentridge Obituary," *The Guardian*. July 5.

Brier, J. (2009). *Infectious Ideas: US Political Responses to the AIDS Crisis*. University of North Carolina Press.

Brooks, P. (2003). "Paul G. Hoffman," in Steve Neal, ed., *HST: Memories of the Truman Years*. Pp. 155–162. Southern Illinois University Press.

Budlender, G. (1999). Oral History: Geoffrey Budlender. http://www.columbia.edu/cu/lweb/digital/collections/oral_hist/carnegie/pdfs/geoffrey-budlender.pdf.

Budlender, G. (2012). Constitutional Court Oral History Project: Geoffrey Budlender. http://www.historicalpapers.wits.ac.za/inventories/inv_pdfo/AG3368/AG3368-B11-001-jpeg.pdf.

Carlston, K. (1948). "Teaching of International Law in Law Schools," *Columbia Law Review* 48: 516.

Carmichael, W.D. (2001). "The Role of the Ford Foundation" in C.E. Welch, ed., NGOs and Human Rights: Promise and Performance. Philadelphia: University of Pennsylvania Press.

Carmichael, W.D. (1985). "Support to Strengthen Legal Education and Research in China, Supplement No. 1." Memorandum: Recommendation for Grant/FAP Action, To: Franklin A. Thomas; Grantee: Columbia University. 83-666A. Rockefeller Archive Center. Ford Foundation Fund Files (FA715). May 30.

Carmichael, W.D. (1988a). "Support to Strengthen Legal Education and Research in China, Supplement No. 3." Memorandum: Recommendation for Grant/FAP Action, To: Franklin A. Thomas; Grantee: Columbia University. 830-666C. Rockefeller Archive Center. Ford Foundation Fund Files (FA715). April 28.

Carmichael, W.D. (1988b). "Support to Strengthen Legal Education and Research in China, Supplement No. 4." Memorandum: Recommendation for Grant/FAP Action, To: Franklin A. Thomas; Grantee: Columbia University. 83-666D. Rockefeller Archive Center. Ford Foundation Fund Files (FA715). December 8.

Carrillo, A.J. and N.E. Yaksic (2011). "Re-imaging the Human Rights Law Clinic," *Maryland Journal of International Law* 26: 80.

Castro-Buitrago, E., N. Espejo-Yaksic, M. Puga, and M. Villarreal (2011). *Clinical Legal Education in Latin America: Toward Public Interest*. Oxford University Press.

Cavers, D. (1963). "The Japanese American Program for Cooperation in Legal Studies," in A.T. von Mehren, ed., *Law in Japan: The Legal Order in a Changing Society XV*. Pp. XV–XXXVIII. Publisher: Cambridge, Harvard University Press.

Chen, L. (1993). "Perspectives from the New Haven School," *American Society of International Law Proceedings*. 87: 398.

Cohen, A. (2017). "The Atlantic Structuration of European Studies," *Revue française de science politique* 67(1): 69–96.

Dalin, D.G. (2017). *Jewish Justices of the Supreme Court: From Brandeis to Kagan*. Brandeis University Press.

De Klerk, W. (2005). "University Law Clinics in South Africa," *South African Law Journal* 122: 929.

DeSocio, R.J. (2017). *Clash of Dynasties: Why Gov. Nelson Rockefeller Killed JFK, RFK, and Ordered the Watergate Break-In to End the Presidential Hopes of Ted Kennedy*. AuthorHouse.

Dezalay, Y. and B. Garth (2002). *The Internalization of Palace Wars: Lawyers, Economists, and the Contest to Transform Latin American States*. University of Chicago Press.

Dezalay, Y. and B. Garth (2006). "From the Cold War to Kosovo: The Rise and Renewal of the Field of International Human Rights," *Annual Review of Law and Social Science* 2: 231–255.

Dezalay, Y. and B. Garth (1996). *Dealing in Virtue: International Commercial Arbitration and the Construction of a Transnational Legal Order*. University of Chicago Press.

Dezalay, Y. and B. Garth (2002) (eds.). "Legitimating the New Legal Orthodoxy," in *Global Prescriptions: The Production, Exportation, and Importation of a New Legal Orthodoxy*. Pp. 306–334.

Dezalay, Y. and B. Garth (2018). "Battles around Legal Education Reform: From Entrenched Local Legal Oligarchies to Oligopolistic Universals: India as a Case Study," *UC Irvine J. International Transnational & Comparative Law* 3: 143.

Dowie, M. (2001). *American Foundations: An Investigative History*. MIT Press.

Duke University (n.d.). John Dugard, Visiting Distinguished Professor. https://web.arch ive.org/web/20110305163838/http://www.law.duke.edu/fac/dugard/.

Edwards, R.R. (2009). "Thirty Years of Legal Exchange with China: The Columbia Law School Role," *Columbia Journal of Asian Law* 23: 3.

Engerman, D.C. (2009). *Know Your Enemy: The Rise and Fall of America's Soviet Experts*. Oxford University Press.

Farber, M.A. (1975). "Dr. Henry Heald of Ford Fund Dead," *New York Times*. Nov. 25.

Fleishman, J.L. (2007). *The Foundation: A Great American Secret*. Public Affairs.

Fontana, D. (2011). The Rise and Fall of Comparative Constitutional Law in the Postwar Era. *Yale Journal of International Law*, 36(1):1–53.

Ford Foundation (1952–2000). Annual Report. New York: Ford Foundation.

Frank, J. (1933). "Why Not a Clinical Lawyer-School?," *University of Pennsylvania Law Review and American Law Register* 81(8): 907–923.

Frühling, H. (2000). "From Dictatorship to Democracy: Law and Social Change in the Andean Region and the Southern Cone of South America," in M. McClymont and S. Golub, *Many Roads to Justice: The Law Related Work of Ford Foundation Grantees around the World*. Pp. 55–87. Ford Foundation.

Gaither, H. Rowan Jr. (1949). "The Report of the Study for the Ford Foundation on Policy and Program" (Rep. Detroit: Ford Foundation). http://www.transatlanticperspectives. org/document.php?rec=18 (last accessed April 7, 2020).

Gapper, J. (2013). "Lunch with the FT: Sydney Kentridge," *Financial Times*. January 18, 2013.

Garth, B. and J. Sterling (1998). "From Legal Realism to Law and Society: Reshaping Law for the Last Stages of the Social Activist State," *Law and Society Review* 32(2): 409–472.

Gemelli, G. (1998). *The Ford Foundation and Europe (1950's–1970's): Cross-Fertilization of Learning in Social Science and Management*. European Interuniversity Press.

Golub, S. (2000a). "Battling Apartheid, Building a New South Africa," in *Many Roads to Justice: The Law-Related Work of Ford Foundation Grantees Around the World*. Pp. 19–54. Ford Foundation.

Golub, S. (2000b). "From the Village to the University: Legal Activism in Bangladesh," in *Many Roads to Justice: The Law Related World of Ford Foundation Grantees Around the World*. Pp. 127, 136–141. Ford Foundation.

Golub, S. (2000c). "Participatory Justice in the Philippines," in Mary McClymont and Stephen Golub, eds. *Many Roads to Justice–The Law Related Work of Ford Foundation Grantees Around the World*. Pp. 197–231. Ford Foundation.

Halliday, T.C. and G. Shaffer (2015). "Researching Transnational Legal Orders." Pp. 475–528. Transnational Legal Orders.

Harvard Crimson (1951). "Cavers Named Dean to Head Law Research," March 21. Accessed April 7, 2020. https://www.thecrimson.com/article/1951/3/21/cavers-named-dean-to-head-law/.

Hershkoff, H. and D. Hollander (2000). "Rights into Action: Public Interest Litigation in the United States," in *Many Roads to Justice: The Law Related World of Ford Foundation Grantees Around the World*. Pp. 89, 91–95. Ford Foundation.

Heydemann, S. with R. Kinsey (2010). "The State and International Philanthropy: The Contribution of American Foundations, 1919–1991," in H.K. Anheier and D.C. Hammack, eds., *American Foundations: Roles and Contributions*. Pp. 205–236. Brookings Institution.

Holland, L.G. (1999). "Invading the Ivory Tower: The History of Clinical Education at Yale Law School," *Journal of Legal Education* 49: 504.

Hounshell, D. (1997). "The Cold War, RAND, and the Generation of Knowledge, 1946–1962," *Historical Studies in the Physical and Biological Studies* 27(2): 237–267.

Hu, Y. and C. Rerup, (2015). Structuring an Authoritarian Country with Western Concepts of Human Rights: Institutional Entrepreneurship as "Symbiotic Transformation" between Actor and Context. Accessed April 7, 2020. https://www.egosnet.org/jart/prj3/egos/data/uploads/Awards/BSPA-2015_st-08_Hu+Rerup.pdf.

Jenson, J. and R. Levi (2013). "Narratives and Regimes of Social and Human Rights: The Jackpines of the Neoliberal Era," in P. Hall and M. Lamont, eds., *Social Resilience in the Neoliberal Era*. Pp. 69–98. Cambridge University Press.

Iya, P.F. (1995). "Addressing the Challenges of Research into Clinical Legal Education Within the Context of the New South Africa," *South African Law Journal* 112: 265.

Kalman, L. (1986). *Legal Realism at Yale, 1927–1960*. UNC Press.

Khurana, R., K. Kimura, and M. Fourcade (2011). *How Foundations Think: The Ford Foundation as a Dominating Institution in the Field of American Business Schools*. Working Paper 11–070 (Boston, MA: Harvard Business School).

Korey, W. (2007). *Taking on the World's Repressive Regimes: The Ford Foundation's International Human Rights Policies and Practices*. Palgrave Macmillan.

Krige, J. (1999). "The Ford Foundation, European Physics and the Cold War," *Historical Studies in the Physical and Biological Sciences* 29(2): 333–361.

Krishnan, J.K. (2004). "Professor Kingsfield Goes to Delhi: American Academics, the Ford Foundation, and the Development of Legal Education in India," *American Journal of Legal History* 46(4): 447–499.

Krishnan, J.K. (2012). "Academic SAILERS: The Ford Foundation and the Efforts to Shape Legal Education in Africa, 1957–1977," *American Journal of Legal History* 52(3): 261–324.

Legal Resources Center (2015). Statement from the LRC on Learning of the Death of Lady Felicia Kentridge. Accessed April 7, 2020. https://web.archive.org/web/20150721132411/http://lrc.org.za/press-releases/3507-statement-from-the-lrc-on-learning-of-the-death-of-lady-felicia-kentridge.

Leibner, G. and J.N. Green (2008). "New Views on the History of Latin American Communism," *Latin American Perspectives* 35(2): 3–8.

Lubman, S.B. (1999). *Bird in a Cage: Legal Reform in China after Mao*. Stanford University Press.

Mac Donald, H. (2006). "*This* Is the Legal Mainstream? Law School Clinics Are Stuck in the Sixties," *City Journal* (Winter).

MacDonald, D. (1989). *The Ford Foundation: The Men and the Millions*. New Brunswick: Transaction Publishers.

Magat, R. (1979) ed. "Processes of Philanthropic Management," in *The Ford Foundation at Work*. Pp. 27–45. Springer.

McAuley, M. (2018). "The Early Years of the Moscow Office," *The LAFF Society*, 2. http://www.laffsociety.org/OldNews.asp?PostID=992.

McCarthy, K. D. (1997). "From Government to Grassroots Reform: The Ford Foundation's Population Programs in South Asia, 1959–1981," in Hewa, S. (ed.) Philanthropy and Cultural Context: Western Philanthropy in South, East, and Southeast Asia in the 20th Century. Lanham, MD: University of America.

McClymont, M.E. and S. Golub (2000). *Many Roads to Justice: The Law-Related Work of Ford Foundation Grantees Around the World*. Ford Foundation.

McCutcheon, A. (2000a). "University Legal Aid Clinics: A Growing International Presence with Manifold Benefits," in McClymont, M.E., and S. Golub, eds. *Many Roads to Justice: The Law-related Work of the Foundation Grantees Around the World*. Pp. 267–282. Ford Foundation.

McCutcheon, A. (2000b). "Eastern Europe: Funding Strategies for Public Interest Law in Transitional Societies," in McClymont, M.E., and S. Golub, eds. *Many Roads to Justice: The Law-related Work of the Foundation Grantees Around the World*. Pp. 233–234. Ford Foundation.

McCutcheon, A. (2000c). "Contributing to Legal Reform in China," in McClymont, M.E., and S. Golub, eds. *Many Roads to Justice: The Law-related Work of the Foundation Grantees Around the World*. Pp. 159–196. Ford Foundation.

McDougal, M.S. (1947). "The Law School of the Future: From Legal Realism to Policy Science in the World Community," *Yale Law Journal* 56(8): 1345–1355.

McQuoid-Mason, D.J. (2004). "Access to Justice and the Role of Law Schools in Developing Countries: Some Lessons from South Africa: Pre-1970 until 1990: Part I," *Journal for Juridical Science* 29(3): 28–51.

Merryman, J. (2000). "Law and Development Memoirs I: The Chile Law Program," *American Journal of Comparative Law* 48(3): 481–499.

Minzner, C.F. (2013). "The Rise and Fall of Chinese Legal Education," *Fordham International Law Journal* 36: 334.

Moran, R.F. (2018). "The Three Ages of Modern American Lawyering and the Current Crisis in the Legal Profession and Legal Education," *Santa Clara Law Review* 58: 453.

New York Times (1953) "Paul Hoffman's New Role." February 7, 14.

Ogilvy, J.P. (2009). "Celebrating CLEPR's 40th Anniversary: The Early Development of Clinical Legal Education and Legal Ethics Instruction in US Law Schools," *Clinical Law Review* 16: 1.

Phan, P.N. (2005). "Clinical Legal Education in China: In Pursuit of a Culture of Law and a Mission of Social Justice," *Yale Human Rights and Development Law Journal* 8: 117.

Pincus, W. (1974). *Legal Clinics in the Law Schools*. P. 123. Faculty of Law, University of Natal.

Pincus, W. (2000). Transcription of the Oral History Interview with Bill Pincus. Accessed April 7, 2020. https://www.law.edu/_media/imported-media/NACLE/pincus.pdf.

Pottenger, J. (2004). "Role of Clinical Legal Education in Legal Reform in the People's Republic of China: Chicken, Egg-or Fox," *International Journal of Clinical Legal Education* 4: 65.

Princeton Alumni Weekly (2002). Memorial: Thomas Laurence Nicholson '45. Accessed April 7, 2020. https://paw.princeton.edu/memorial/thomas-laurence-nichol son-%E2%80%9945.

Raucher, A.R. (1985). *Paul G. Hoffman: Architect of Foreign Aid*. University of Kentucky Press.

Rosenfield, P. and R. Wimpee (2015). *The Ford Foundation: Themes, 1936–2001*. Rockefeller Archive Center.

Sandefur, R. and J. Selbin (2009). "The Clinic Effect," *Clinical Law Review* 16: 57.

Saxon, W. (2006). "John S. Bainbridge, 90, Legal Educator for African Leaders, Dies," *New York Times*, February 6 Section A, 21.

Scott-Smith, G. (2007). "Attempting to Secure an 'Orderly Evolution': American Foundations, The Hague Academy of International Law and the Third World," *Journal of American Studies* 41: 509–532.

Shaffer, G. (2016). "Theorizing Transnational Legal Ordering," *Annual Review of Law and Social Science* 12: 231–253.

Snead, D.L. (1999). *The Gaither Committee, Eisenhower, and the Cold War*. Ohio State University Press.

Solomon, S.G. (2000). "'Through a Glass Darkly': The Rockefeller Foundation's International Health Board and Soviet Public Health," *Studies in History and Philosophy of Science Part C: Studies in History and Philosophy of Biological and Biomedical Sciences* 31(3): 409–418.

Solomon, S.G. and N. Krementsov (2001). "Giving and Taking across Borders: The Rockefeller Foundation and Russia, 1919–1928," *Minerva* 39(3): 265–298.

Stuckey, R.T. (1996). "Education for the Practice of Law: The Times They Are-A-Changin'," *Nebraska Law Review* 75: 648.

Sutton, F. (1987). "The Ford Foundation: The Early Years," *Daedalus* 116(1): 41–91.

Sutton, F. (2001). "The Ford Foundation's Transatlantic Role and Purposes, 1951–81," *Review (Fernand Braudel Center)* 24(1):77–104.

Sutton, F.X. (1950). "The Radical Marxist." Doctoral dissertation, Harvard University.

Taylor, V. (Forthcoming). *Contesting Legal Education's Engagement with Policy* (in this volume).

Thomas, F.A. (Chair) (1981). *Study Commission on US Policy toward Southern Africa (US). South Africa/time Running Out*. Constitutional Rights Foundation.

Trubek, D.M. (1972). "Toward a Social Theory of Law: An Essay on the Study of Law and Development," *Yale Law Journal* 82(1): 1–50.

Urquhart, B. and E. Childers (1996). *A World in Need of Leadership: Tomorrow's United Nations. A Fresh Appraisal*. Dag Hammarskjold and Ford Foundation.

Valdez, A. (1975). "Developing the Role of Law in Social Change: Past Endeavors and Future Opportunities in Latin America and the Caribbean," *Lawyer of the Americas* 7(1): 1–28.

Wilson, R. (2017). *The Global Evolution of Clinical Legal Education: More than a Method*. Cambridge University Press.

Wong, W.H., R. Levi, and J. Deutsch (2017). "The Ford Foundation. P82-100," in L. Seabrooke and L.F. Henriksen, eds., *Professional Networks in Transnational Governance*. Pp. 82–100. Cambridge University Press.

Yanmin, C. and J.L. Pottenger (2011). "The 'Chinese Characteristics' of Clinical Legal Education," in Frank S. Bloch, ed. *The Global Clinical Movement: Educating Lawyers for Social Justice*. Pp. 87–104. Oxford University Press.

3

The Transnationalization of Legal Education on the Periphery

Continuities and Changes in Colonial Logics for a "Globalizing" Africa

Michelle Burgis-Kasthala[*]

The postcolonial African university provided a particular vantage point from which to produce academic knowledge about a world shaped and divided by contradictory, and structurally antagonistic, social forces. In these accounts, the world comprised of competing (and often irreconcilable) economic, social, political, and cultural entities that could not be conceptualized as simply various instantiations of the same "global" reality.

—Isaac Kamola 2013, at 51

Recognizing the diversification, differentiation and expansion of higher education systems in Africa and the need to adapt the existing legal instruments and practices in order to promote the mobility of students, teachers and researchers at the national, continental and international levels.

Preamble, Revised Convention on the
Recognition of Studies, Certificates, Diplomas, Degrees and
Other Academic Qualifications in Higher Education in —African
States, December 2014 (the Addis Ababa Convention)

[*] Senior Lecturer in Public International Law, University of Edinburgh. Many thanks to the wonderful feedback of Sara Dezalay and the research assistance of Maddy Godwin.

Michelle Burgis-Kasthala, *The Transnationalization of Legal Education on the Periphery* In: *The Globalization of Legal Education.* Edited by: Bryant Garth & Gregory Shaffer, Oxford University Press. © Oxford University Press 2022.
DOI: 10.1093/oso/9780197632314.003.0003

I. Introduction

As centers of learning situated within particular matrices of power and economy, universities have always straddled a variety of local and nonlocal institutional and epistemic rationalities. Yet the breadth and depth of recent transnational trends in higher education suggest not only a quantitative, but potentially qualitative, change in the role of universities for servicing elites within a modern and globalizing knowledge economy. Accordingly, a vast literature on the so-called globalization of higher education has emerged that tends to characterize the sector's evolution as either a story of opportunity or crisis (Chou, Kamola, and Pietsch 2016). Perhaps paradoxically, while Africa lags at the bottom of certain higher education globalization indicators, such as university league tables and per capita student spending, the continent also possesses extreme degrees of internationalization, whether through its student mobility or dependence on foreign funding and epistemic resources.

It is the contention of this chapter that it is only in studying higher education *on the periphery*—in Africa—that we come to appreciate the pronounced contradictions and tensions inherent at the core of higher education today. We need to flip our thinking then on Africa to regard it intellectually as the most pronounced and concentrated site of transnationalized education *because of its peripheral status*. As this volume on the transnationalization of higher education is concerned with the specific focus of *legal* education, where possible, this chapter grounds its general narrative in examples of law and legal education across the continent, while noting the highly uneven availability of materials. Whether in (post)colonial Africa or capitals in the metropole, the success of the legal academy depends on its ability to ensure a semi-autonomous relationship with the state and the market. Legal education then is a barometer of prevailing configurations of power/knowledge in a given society. In the case of (post)colonial Africa, legal education continues to manifest significant epistemic and institutional dependence on and dominance from Northern law schools and markets. Law and legal education are therefore a lens through which to assess the possibility of a truly equitable form of transnational higher education today.

Perhaps more significantly for this volume and this chapter is to develop *critical* approaches for appraising the phenomenon of transnational legal education. This chapter argues that thinking through the idea of "Africa" can provide such a critical lens in forcing us to rethink the role of legal education in the twenty-first century in a context of widening material and epistemic inequality. Continental countermovements such as regionalization cannot compete with the sheer predominance of Northern knowledge institutions, but their recent renaissance at least allows us the chance to evaluate the extent to which we are witnessing a shift from "the university in Africa" to the "African university" (Kamola 2014: 604). Greater Chinese support for higher education especially since 2000 also points to other possible pathways. Are counterhegemonic practices possible in Africa, and what role in particular does law play?

Even more simply in accounting for legal education in Africa, we first need to re-evaluate the idea of "Africa" itself in understanding its variegated experiences of globalization. Typically, Africa as an idea is either radically overdetermined or underdetermined. "Africa" regularly figures in modern parlance as an image of a large territorial land mass with underdetermined cultural variation. This lack of detail ensures that the idea serves as a trope for all things different, faltering or other. Such generalizations through use of the continental category of "Africa" produce a large part of the globe and its people as beset by existential lack. Counterhegemonic reactions to this reduction of Africa can play out then through pan-African initiatives, whether at the educational level or a range of legal, political, and cultural connections. Yet countering such gestures is the simultaneous overdetermination or fragmentation of Africa, particularly in the international non/governmental grey literature which disaggregates the continent into North Africa (which is then often aligned racially/linguistically with Arab West Asia) and sub-Saharan Africa. Such accounts ensure a bifurcated mental map and the scholarly challenge of forming a continent-wide account of various policies.

Given the vastly disparate level of available material about different African countries and regions, this chapter cannot hope for any degree at systematicity. Instead, it seeks to interrogate the idea of "Africa" itself alongside "globalization" through shifts in education policy during colonialism until the present. Ferguson here is useful, first on Africa in general as a

category through which a "world" is structured—a category that (like all categories) is historically and socially constructed . . . but also a category that is "real", that is imposed with force, that has a mandatory quality; a category within which and according to which, people must live (Fergueson 2006: 5).

And second for his critique of the tendency to characterize globalization through the notion of "transnational flows" as for him, "[c]apital is *globe-hopping*, not *globe-covering*" (Fergueson 2006: 38). This requires then a focus on

> the social relations that selectively constitute global society; the statuses and ranks that it comprises; and the relations, rights, and obligations that characterize it. To take seriously African experiences of the global requires that any discussion of "globalization" and "new world orders" must first of all be a discussion of social relations of membership, responsibility, and inequality on a truly planetary scale (Fergueson 2006: 23).

"Africa" then is an idea and a place that is constantly remade, and here in this chapter, I consider the role of higher education and especially legal education in shaping its future.

The chapter comprises five sections. First, in Section II, I explore how colonial legal relations continued to shape legal education and institutions in Africa after independence. In Sections III and IV, I sketch out the nature of legal education within the context of postindependence policies spanning the periods of optimism and then radical degeneration in the higher education sector until the mid-1990s. Section V begins by considering the role of international donors with their renewed support for higher education from the 1990s. I situate this policy shift within broader neoliberal mindsets, which have radically reshaped the role of the university in African society. This century has accordingly witnessed a steady increase in student enrolments internationally, regionally, subregionally, and nationally, but often in profoundly inequitable ways (Chesterman 2009). New law schools in Africa abound whether as public or private universities but they are prohibitively expensive for many Africans, where tertiary enrollment rates of 7 percent lag far behind other regions (Boly 2018: 18). Accordingly, the chapter ends by considering the possibilities and limitations of higher education generally and legal education specifically in Africa, particularly through regionalization and harmonization efforts. It is noteworthy that significant gaps in available data prevent any comprehensive analysis of legal education in Africa, and linguistic barriers have oriented me to concentrate on Anglophone Africa.

II. The Role of Law and Legal Education
in Colonial Africa

Literature on the role of legal education in the modern nation-state highlights how the training of local elites in the semi-autonomous field of law plays a crucial role in the development and legitimation of state policy and rule (Dezalay and Garth 2011). Yet in precolonial Africa, this interrelationship between the state and the legal profession was largely absent in a context of a variety of parastate and imperial state-formations. Particularly in the north of the continent, Islamic *madāris* (schools) contributed significantly to the training of scholars able to resolve disputes whether in the presence or absence of a state. Indeed, the world's oldest university, Al-Azhar in Cairo, which began classes in 975, has maintained a strong tradition in Islamic law education under a range of foreign rulers as well as in the era of decolonization. Yet once European powers began to rule the continent, bifurcated legal systems emerged that tended to separate "state" or "public" colonial law from indigenous, customary practices. Such divisions persist, for example, across much of northern Africa with its rich Islamic law tradition where "private law" retains strong *sharīʿa* influences, whereas French civil law predominates for the remaining legal areas.[1] Such divisions are also evident in the continuing division between customary and state law in many African jurisdictions.

Although Africa possessed an ancient academic tradition, the advent of colonialism meant that most institutions were either overshadowed or simply destroyed (Teferra 2007: 557). Today, Africans are aware of these centers of learning, but for Mamdani, "this historical fact is of marginal significance for contemporary African higher education . . . [because the] organization of knowledge production in the contemporary African university is everywhere based on a disciplinary mode developed in Western universities over the 19th and 20th centuries" (Mamdani 2011). Colonial powers had no intention of replacing such indigenous centers of learning across the "dark continent." Whether at the primary, secondary, or tertiary levels, education for Africans was not a priority for colonial overlords. In Francophone Africa, education was feared in general for its ability to instill resistance in the minds

---

[1] This is not simply a product of European colonial rule, but it also arises from the nature of Ottoman law itself, which increasingly favored rule through the *kanun* (secular law) as opposed to *sharīʿa* to address normative gaps, and the power of the *ulema*, which supported a radically dispersed practice of legal interpretation.

of local subjects (Devarajan, Monga, and Zongo 2011: 135). Similarly, the British were suspicious of the disruptive power of legal education (Ndulo 2002: 489), especially as "the Indian nationalist movement had been led by lawyers" (Ghai 1987: 751).

Given that the bifurcated customary and colonial legal system funneled almost all African legal issues into the customary system, it was also easy to neglect the training of local lawyers competent in both systems. British expatriates and Asians tended to populate the echelons of colonial bureaucracies and courts. Local Africans could provide forms of legal assistance as there was no formalized accreditation system, but demand for such services was not significant (Ghai 1987: 489–490). Yet colonial powers had to provide better opportunities for professional education as a result of the undeniable contribution made by African troops and societies during the Second World War. Accordingly, privileged Africans took up scholarships to study at universities in the metropole in the hope of embodying colonial, modernizing mentalities on their return (Devarajan, Monga, and Zongo 2011: 135–136). In the case of British African subjects seeking legal training, however, it was not universities but Inns of Court that provided their entry into legal practice.[2] For example in Nigeria, this approach was formalized in 1945 when only those admitted to practice as barristers in Scotland, Ireland, or England were able to work in the jurisdiction (Manteaw 2007: 913). Later in 1959, out of 1,251 students enrolled at the Inns, 842 were from overseas, including 438 from common law Africa (the largest number being from Nigeria) (Thomas 1971: 6). Armed with this new knowledge, Dezalay points out that

> lawyers in the colonial *margins* were positioned as allies of the Empire through the interlocking of law and literacy, as much as they were embedded in local nodes of power. They were at once, thus, collaborators and rebels, the necessary kingpins of the Empire while, as the "fighting brigade of the people", central cogs in its demise (Dezalay 2017: 25).[3]

---

[2] This was a particularly problematic aspect of colonial education during the early years of decolonization as pointed out in the Tananarive Conference Report: "In some countries, by tradition, certain professional training, e.g. in law and engineering, is wholly or in part in the hands of the professions themselves rather than the responsibility of the universities. This cannot be so in Africa, and the universities must be prepared to accept a wider range of professional training courses in response to local needs, whether or not such courses form part of the European university pattern" (UNESCO 1962).

[3] We can also conceive of indigenous lawyers as "a Frankenstein of colonial creation, doing much to dislodge the colonial establishment that gave them their profession[al] life" (Oguamanam and Pue 2007: 783).

Thus, during the colonial period, and despite its many constraints, indigenous lawyers could enter the legal arena in a form of dialogue and negotiation about the nature of foreign rule (Karkwaivanene 2016: 333–349).[4] This fundamentally political reading of law would come to inform approaches to law and legal education in the early years of decolonization.

On the eve of independence in Africa, then, legal education for local Africans had improved, but with highly problematic and elitist results. Because training for the British bar focused on litigation, developing the skills to act as a solicitor was overlooked. Accordingly, both during and after independence in British Africa, there was no distinction drawn between barristers and solicitors, with a heavy bias toward seeing the law as that which played out in the courtroom. Prevailing legal cultures favored private and commercial practice too and so lawyers had little interest or skill in public interest litigation (Manteaw 2007: 916). This tiny cadre of lawyers was also wholly inadequate for emerging African states. For example, in 1961 in Tanganyika (later Tanzania), only one out of 100 lawyers was African; less than 10 of around 300 Kenyan lawyers; and around 20 out of 150 in Uganda. Some states contained no lawyers whatsoever at the dawn of independence (Manteaw 2007: 915–916). More significantly in terms of indigenous legal education, in 1961, there were "five times as many African students in the Inns of Court in London as there are in all the law departments (659) of all English-language universities of Middle Africa" (UNESCO 1962: 109 and 149).

III. Decolonization during the Cold War: The Promise and the Failure of Law and Legal Education in the African "Developmental University," 1950s–1970s

It was in spite of and yet because of these shortcomings that higher education became a central tenet of postindependence developmental planning for the newly liberated African continent. Lofty aspirations for an African-centered approach to higher education had to accommodate the reality of a radically underresourced tertiary sector. For example, in 1950 out of thirty-four countries, only eleven had a university, yet by 1962, twenty-eight did. Over the same period, university numbers tripled from sixteen to forty-one

---

[4] Also see Karekwaivanene 2016 and Karekwaivanene 2017.

along with a 600 percent increase in student enrollments (Carrol and Samoff 2004b: 77).[5] Thus, for Mamdani, "the African university was mainly a postcolonial development" (Mamdani 2012: 87).

From its inception in 1945 until today, UNESCO has played a unique role in the higher education of Africa, particularly in serving as a forum for agenda setting and as an information hub. During its first two decades in particular, UNESCO "aimed to shape higher education institutions according to the development needs of newly formed nations" (Lebeau and Sall 2011: 130). Thus emerged the idea of the "developmental university" in the Third World, which "promoted a curriculum organized around learning that could be productively applied immediately" (Lebeau and Sall 2011: 131).

Africa's "powerful faith" (Lebeau and Sall 2011: 68) in the promise of development through higher education is best captured in the official documentation from the 1962 Tananarive Conference on the Development of Higher Education in Africa. This UNESCO-sponsored event brought together thirty-one African member and associate members of UNESCO. Not only did it set out a comprehensive vision about the role of higher education for the coming decades across the continent, but it also served as a forum for international dialogue between African officials, UN personnel, and (foreign) tertiary sector experts who formulated background reports to inform the discussion and recommendations. Its unanimously approved introductory statement is worth quoting at length as it captures the hope felt across the continent at the time:

> The establishment and development of university institutions in Africa raise fundamental issues of their precise role in African life. Should they merely perform the traditional functions which the universities of Europe have performed for centuries for their societies? Should they take on additional roles which, while radically distinguishing them from the older European institutions, fit them nevertheless for greater service to the African society? Can they effectively cope with the immediate and urgent demands made of them for the improvement of African society and at the same time remain loyal to the world standards of higher education institutions? African universities like their counterparts elsewhere have the responsibility to advance the frontiers of knowledge through teaching and research . . . The

---

[5] An extreme example is that of Cairo University, which had 2,027 students during its first year. By 1983, although its buildings were designed to accommodate a maximum of 35,000 students, enrollments reached 150,000 students (Farag 2007: 700).

African university cannot deviate radically from this basic pattern without losing its international identity . . . Consequently, in addition to the traditional role of giving a broad liberal education, African universities must reflect the needs of the African world by providing African society with men and women equipped with skills that will enable them to participate fully and usefully in the economic and social development of their continent . . .

. . . Until recent times, education in Africa was entirely or mainly centred on the study of foreign civilizations. The mission of a university is to define and confirm the aspirations of the society which it is established to serve. The mission of African universities cannot be different. While wishing to make its full contribution to the universal stock of knowledge, African higher education must aspire to give African peoples their rightful place and to cement African unity for ever . . .

. . . African institutions of higher education are at once the main instrument of national progress, the chief guardian of the people's heritage and the voice of the people in the international councils of technology and scholarship. This triple role, progressive, conservative and collaborative, is an excitingly challenging one. The Tananarive Conference is confident that African higher education can and will rise successfully to this challenge (UNESCO 1962: 1–3).

This vision of higher education as socially transformative emphasized "practical" subjects such as agriculture and engineering, along with the social sciences.[6] Scholars of law and economics in particular would serve as continental trailblazers in public administration and developmental policy creation.[7] According to such a "modernizing" mentality then, law and legal education was largely a technical tool for overall social improvement and "Relevance!" became the watchword (Carrol and Samoff 2004b: 79). Yet technical competence was not enough for fostering social transformation; a broad-based social education for lawyers was required so that they could

---

[6] For example, in relation to Nigeria, see Oloruntoba 2014: 344; and Paul 1987: 18–28 and 21–22.

[7] UNESCO 1962, 54–55. "It must be admitted that, in certain respects, the economist, the statistician, the lawyer and the sociologist must be more highly qualified in Africa than in other countries, for they will have less data and information (particularly of a statistical kind) at their disposal, they will be more isolated intellectually and forced to rely principally on their own knowledge and to trust to their imagination and personal judgment in situations in which their counterparts in the developed countries would consult specialists in other branches of study. However, this is felt to apply only to a comparatively small number of high-level specialists, such as economists responsible for the programming of development, managerial staff, economic advisers for government departments, research workers and, of course, university teachers themselves."

play a central role in all sectors of society (Kapinga 1992, 879). Writing from Tanzania in 1975, Harvey suggested that the

> good lawyer is the one who knows also something of the society in which the law operates and the processes by which the law may change and be changed by that society. Thus we teach the law as it exists in East Africa today, but we do not stop there; we use this law as a firm base upon which future developments may be considered. In this way we hope to be able to produce lawyers who will have thoroughly mastered the techniques of the law . . . But over and above all these, they will have studied the law against the social and economic background of the East African jurisdictions, and will be in a good position to offer useful contributions to discussions on the problem of the law that ought to be in East Africa (Kapinga 1992: 880).

Whether through legal or nonlegal training, then, the developmentalist university and the developmental state were closely linked in this period of rapid institution building (Lebeau and Sall 2011: 131).

Yet while serving the interests of the new nationalist political elite, universities were also increasingly viewed with suspicion. "Officialdom came to equate critical thought with a critique of nationalism and the nationalism elite. Indeed, the university occupied a contradictory location, for the university was an incubator of not only critical through but also a political counter-elite" (Mamdani 2012: 87). A fine balance was required that could accommodate the university as a site of training for new policy formation as well as an autonomous sphere for critical thought.[8] This required "putting sheer numbers of scholars in place and creating a significant density of institutional life" whose realization across the continent was rare.[9]

Such political antagonisms over the university's role were heightened by the far more pressing challenge of funding constraints. Accordingly, foreign intervention was crucial in underwriting these efforts not only in sheer financial terms but also intellectually. Most pressing of course was that despite a significant state commitment to tertiary education funding, such sums failed to meet student enrollment projections, as contained in the Tananarive Conference. In 1962, there were 459 law students enrolled in middle Africa (Manteaw 2007: 917). Participants at the Conference sought to increase this

---

[8] On these tensions, also see Oloruntoba 2014: 344.
[9] Nigeria and South Africa were two such examples: Mamdani 2012: 88.

number to 3,075 by 1980. Such a projected increase required law schools. By 1972, 43 African universities housed a law faculty. Former colonial states as well as new players in the region—the United States, China, the Soviet Union, and US private charitable entities—provided a range of direct and indirect aid contributions to higher education. The main contributors in Africa from the 1950s to the 1970s were two national agencies—the United States Agency for International Development (USAID) and the British Inter-University Council for Higher Education Overseas (backed by the British Overseas Development Administration)—together with France and four major private philanthropic organizations—the Ford Foundation, the Rockefeller Foundation, the W.K. Kellogg Foundation, and the Carnegie Corporation of New York (Coleman and Court 1993: 14). Support from the Soviet Union, while not as large in monetary terms as the contributions from Britain or France, was also important. Between 1981 and 1983, external support to African education from Britain, France, the United States, and Eastern Europe and Cuba was $206.2 million, $39.9 million, $36.3 million, and $40 million, respectively (Carrol and Samoff 2004b: 86). Donors funded the creation of new universities,[10] university infrastructure, materials, scholarships,[11] faculty exchanges, training initiatives, and "student airlifts" (Ogachi 2009: 334). All contributions were committed to improving higher education as part of development, but this relationship was understood quite differently between various donors. Given Cold War rivalries too, higher education served as a site of competing hegemonic projects and pressures so that African perspectives were often overlooked.

For legal education, such foreign financial contributions came hand in hand with sustained intellectual oversight and steering of both the curriculum and pedagogical approaches. In contrast to the colonial practice of legal training in the metropole, the "developmental university" of postindependence Africa required the creation of a legal curriculum from scratch. Given the pressing need for lawyers and with only "slight local variations,

---

[10] Such as the USAID supported University of Nigeria, Nsukka, which is based on the American university model.

[11] For example, the African Scholarship Program of U.S. Universities funded more than 1,000 scholarships for African students between 1961 and 1965 (Carrol and Samoff 2004b: 78). Conversely, the Soviet Union established the Lumumba Friendship University in Moscow, which in Khrushchev's words in 1960 would "give aid to colonial and neo-colonial Third-World countries in the training of their national cadres of engineers, agricultural specialists, doctors, teachers, economists, and specialists." The Institute of Law opened in 1995 and has an extensive international law teaching profile as well as interest in international and comparative legal education. See the website: *Institute of Law*, http://www.rudn.ru/en_new/?pagec=1278.

the British legal education curriculum was introduced wholesale in African countries" (Manteaw 2007: 919). Such a pragmatic move ensured that those serving lawyers trained in Britain could continue, yet in reality, the effects were more sustained as the model has continued often unchanged until today (Kahn-Fogel 2012: 754–755).

In 1960, London commissioned Lord Denning to produce a report on the African law curriculum and system of accreditation for legal practice (Committee on Legal Education for Students from Africa 1961). "Denning saw a need for a cadre of professional lawyers, trained in the English style; unlike the latter, his ideal of lawyering in Africa was conservative and non-instrumental" (Harrington and Manji 2003: 377–378). The Report recommended the familiar two-tiered common law system of a university degree followed by a one-year "apprenticeship" "through complete submission to an experienced master" (Harrington and Manji 2003: 393). Part of the rationale for this was to ensure that foreign-trained lawyers—particularly in Britain—could gain practical African-based skills. Yet the effect of such a seeming division between law as theory and law as practice—in spite of the developmental aims of legal education—was to underprepare students for broadly conceived public interest legal work (Harrington and Manji 2003: 393). Such legal training favored the colonial focus on private and commercial litigation along with the new dimension of assisting in the administration of courts and governments (Manteaw 2007: 919). Broader social transformation through legal education though fell outside Denning's vision as well as the traditional British pedagogical model.

Even decades after the Denning Report, the United Kingdom's significant intellectual influence continued to pervade the common law world of Africa, demonstrated through the reliance on UK legal rules, textbooks (Ghai 1987: 755–760), and teachers (at least in the early period), as well as its key jurisprudential regional hub in South Africa. Thus, writing in 2002, Ndulo argued that in former British colonies

[m]ost of the rules come directly from English textbooks; it is easier to learn British rules than local rules in the African context because, despite over forty years of independence, the difficulties of working with local materials are formidable. Until recently, law reports containing cases decided by the African courts were often not available. There are very few books and other local published materials; when they do exist, they are often out of print or very difficult to obtain (Ndulo 2002: 492).

Britain's prominent position within the international legal education market ensures that retaining hallmarks of the British curriculum is a double-edged sword for African universities seeking to decolonize their teaching and their societies.

While Britain capitalized on its colonial preeminence in shaping the early independence agenda for Anglophone legal education, the US-led "law and development" movement soon became the most significant foreign influence across Anglophone Africa in the 1960s "Development Decade."[12] Although "official American aid agencies had little interest in law and legal education" (Paul 1987: 23), the Ford Foundation in particular stepped into the breach with its ambitious SAILER scheme (Staffing of African Institutions of Legal Education and Research) for a number of newly independent states between 1962 and1977. Implementation of the scheme comprised three parts: (1) funding senior American legal scholars to spend time in African law schools; (2) funding recent American law graduates to serve as teaching fellows in Africa; and (3) providing Western academic leadership for certain law schools (Krishnan 2012: 280–281). In contrast to the British method, these US scholars "embrace[d] more clinical methods which aimed at students' active resolution of 'real' social problems" (Harrington and Manji 2003: 396–397). This "law and development" pedagogy (of "liberal law and public policy curriculum, and academic entrepreneurialism") (Krishnan 2012: 283) embodied an instrumentalist reading of both law and legal education,[13] which could play a seminal role in the transformation of society.[14] Narrow and technical skill would not be enough; instead, a number of US and indigenous educators stressed the importance of a broad-based intellectual journey for the African law student in this era (Krishnan 2012: 302–303).[15]

---

[12] Particularly following the Conference on Legal Education in Accra and Legon, Ghana in 1962 (Bainbridge 1972: 71).

[13] For a thoughtful consideration of law as instrumentalism, see Ghai 199: 8–20.

[14] Captured forcefully in the words of Friedman, who "taught a number of seminars on public corporations and foreign investment in various African countries" in the 1960s: "The contemporary lawyer . . . in the developing nations must become an active and responsible participant in development plans" (quoted in Paul 1987: 22).

[15] For Geraghty, the "'Law and Development' movement of the 1960's and early 1970's was an attempt by American law professors and foundations to teach and import Western legal codes, educational, and legal systems to Africa to support economic development" (Geraghty and Quansah 2008: 56).

As was the case for the scholarly trend (Trubek and Galanter 1974), such partnerships came into question by the 1970s in the midst of a variety of political shifts, including the Vietnam War, a growing African desire for local teachers, and a re-evaluation of law's role in the developmental state (Paul 1987: 23). In the latter years of SAILER, more Africans were sponsored to study in the United States or Britain instead of Americans serving as teachers and university leaders on the continent (Krishnan 2012: 267). Looking back to his own participation in this endeavor, one academic captures this shift from optimism to realism—whether on the part of Africans or their foreign counterparts:

> I have suggested that we were all moved by the spirit of the times, a Zeitgeist, when we set forth to build legal education and research in Africa. The times change, and with it their prevailing spirit. The years since ... have been full of doubts and criticisms of what we tried to do. We have read and heard charges of legal imperialism and chauvinistic devotion to American law and legal education directed at efforts not only in Africa but all over the world. There was certainly naiveté and ignorance that was quickly recognized and led to the efforts to make law and development into a serious field of research. But I believe that the rise of criticism had less to do with errors and follies we may have committed than with a broad change in the Zeitgeist. The whole conception of development that guided us in the early years came to be seriously questioned or rejected by the turn of 1970's. Governments were less benevolently regarded, planning was "in crisis", and faith withered in the powers of foreign assistance to build national institutions. We came into a time of emphasis on equity and direct efforts to meet the basic needs of the poorest. University development was criticized as favoring national elites and foundation interests in law shifted toward legal aid to the poor and human rights (Sutton 1986: 23–24).

Despite the demise of such direct US professional influence, we shall see how differing agendas framed within the metropole would continue to have a profoundly detrimental effect on higher education as a whole in the decades to come.

IV. From Privatization
to Commercialization: Impoverishment of African Higher
Education as Recolonization, 1970s–1990s

If the key trends in higher education immediately following independence were nation building through the university, these ideals came under sustained internal and external criticism by the 1970s within the shadow of the debt crisis. Both foreign and state-based funding for the sector had failed to ensure the degree of transformation envisaged. Foreign disillusionment with increasingly corrupt state elites, many of whom had been schooled in faltering domestic institutions, came to put pressure on the African university. Where once universities were regarded by state bureaucrats as allies, they were increasingly regarded as problematic and hostile spaces of political unrest. Various forms of state control as well as financial neglect would ensure that universities strayed further from their founding goals all the while encouraging political opposition. During this period then, the "nature of colleges and universities changed gradually from 'the production of knowledge and skills to create wealth and modernize African societies' as stated at the 1972 Accra African Union Workshop, to training civil servants, mainly to provide employment and contribute to sociopolitical stability" (Devajaran and Zongo 2011: 137).

Faced already with a looming economic crisis, universities were further hit by a general shift in (Northern) donor mindsets, which had given up on the idea of development through higher education by the mid-1970s. For example, the 1975 UK government's white paper, "The Changing Emphasis in British Aid Policy: more help for the poorest," sums up the renewed emphasis on "basic education" *as opposed to* higher education (Lebeau and Sall 2011: 133).[16] UNESCO continued to try and bridge the increasing division in policy outlooks pitting liberal developmentalism on the part of the Global North with dependency theory readings about underdevelopment from the Global South. Yet in 1984, the United States revoked its UNESCO membership, and this was followed by the United Kingdom and Singapore a year later. This truncated the Council's budget by a quarter, and it "ensured that UNESCO's leadership role in education reform, and thus the expansion of

---

[16] This idea was institutionalized in the 1990 World Conference on Education for All (Haddad 1990).

education systems the funding UNESCO advocated, was interrupted" (Kim and Boyle 2013: 124).

While the fortunes of the Council waned, the World Bank became ever more powerful as a donor of education so that by the 1980s, its contributions almost doubled those of the United Nations (Lebeau and Sall 2011: 134). Like the 1975 UK white paper, the World Bank was highly suspicious of investing in higher education. World Bank policy was informed by human capital theory and the resulting utilitarian emphasis on investing in "manpower needs" (Carrol and Samoff 2004a: 9), which tended to suggest a far greater rate of return for public investments in education at the primary level (Lebeau and Sall 2011: 135).[17] Within this theory, higher education could be regarded more as an investment with far higher returns to the private individual rather than the economy as a whole. Such market-based interpretations of higher education failed to appreciate the social dimensions of educational transformation. Concerns about brain drain and a corresponding narrow transposition between education costs and its threatened loss to African societies meant that the Bank actively discouraged tertiary sector funding whether directly for donor states or even for nondonor states with its extensive agenda-setting influence. For example, public recurrent expenditure per tertiary student in sub-Saharan Africa fell from $6,461 in 1975 to $2,365 in 1983 (Carrol and Samoff 2004a: 4).[18] Although the Bank re-embraced higher education in its 1994 Report and has since worked strategically with UNESCO to reverse negative trends from the latter part of the twentieth century, the long-term effects of these foreign policies continue to mar the African landscape.[19]

Faced with shrinking budgets, governments and universities were forced to reassess the financing of higher education in response to structural adjustment programs. Traditionally, the state had favored the financing of higher

---

[17] Also see Bloom, Canning, and Chan 2006: 2.

[18] See also Nesiah 2013: 378.

[19] In the words of Hon. Mrs. Ann Therese Ndong-Jatta, Secretary of State for Education of the Republic of The Gambia in 2002, "A condition for qualifying for World Bank assistance in the education sector was for African countries to divert resources from higher education and channel them instead towards primary and basic education . . . African Governments protested that in the matter of providing education to their people, it was not a question of either primary or secondary, or indeed higher education . . . Needless to say, with the tremendous pressures that come along with World Bank and IMF conditionalities, they lost the battle, and higher education in Africa virtually went under. To this day, many countries have not been able to recover from that onslaught on African higher education. Some of our finest institutions have thus almost been destroyed, thanks to the imposition of bad policies from partners who, in the first place, came out professing to help us. What we received from them was the kiss of death" (quoted in Carrol and Samoff 2004a: 1).

education, often providing free tuition and living expenses in a national context where family contributions to primary and secondary education were the norm. Such state support for higher education embodied the belief in education and especially higher education as central to Africa's decolonizing trajectory. This model came under increasing pressure at the national level as well as the international level by the international financial institutions (IFIs) and their introduction of structural adjustment policies (SAPs) to Africa in the late 1970s. As well as actively discouraging tertiary education in this period, the World Bank was the main actor during the 1980s and 1990s seeking a realignment of university funding and governance structures. Along with calls for greater university sector autonomy and accountability to stakeholders, the Bank pushed for cost-sharing that would require private contributions from students. The wholesale reconfiguration of state-society relations was now possible for the Bank through such policies. Thus, for Federici, SAPs, as tantamount to recolonization, "signalled the end of the 'social contract' that had shaped [students'] relation to the state ... which had made education the key to social advancement and participatory citizenship" (Federici 2012).

Often in a desperate bid to secure funds, universities had to open themselves up to ever-larger student numbers as well as a range of quasi-commercial activities such as consultancy report-writing (Oloruntuba 2014: 345). This is captured brilliantly in Mamdani's account of the crisis that shook his own university of Makerere, which

> joined an infatuation with privately sponsored students to an extreme decentralisation that in turn fed it. Different constituencies pushed decentralisation for their own reasons. The World Bank believed that the most effective way to promote market forces in the university was to give maximum freedom to revenue-earning units. Within the university, decentralisation was advocated in the language of justice: its often radical promoters in different Faculties argued that the university belongs to those who work in it, particularly the academic staff, and that student fees are the rightful returns of the labour of the academic staff. Even if this version of privatisation was weighted in favour of the academic staff, there was still no room for a larger public interest in this reformed conception (Mamdani 2007).

Mamdani documents how it was the faculty of law that was the most ideologically committed to decentralization (Mamdani 2007: 197). Part of the reason for this was because it was relatively well placed in generating revenue and wanted greater control of funds. Opening the faculty up to private paying students would generate even more income, and so during the 1990s there was a significant increase in fee-paying law students (from 61 in 1993–1994 to 150 in 1996–1997) (Mamdani 2007: 197). Student numbers rose dramatically in little more than a decade from 86 to 392 (Mamdani 2007: 55), while government funding contracted and general academic standards fell (Mamdani 2007: 165).

Mamdani's discussion about the pressures faced by African universities highlights the way in which this was never simply about the problems of limited financial resources. Instead, Mamdani in relation to Makerere and in his work more generally points to the epistemic dependency that has arisen from Africa's place in the (neoliberal) world. Once the optimism of decolonization and the promise of the national university rang hollow with the onset of the debt crisis, it is helpful to think about this period as one of recolonization most directly through the IFIs and foreign NGOs, but far more profoundly, for the nature of African thought itself. Mamdani marks this shift through the experience of Makere from privatization to commercialization.

> Privatisation was an external relationship between the market and the university, whereby the university opened up its gates to fee-paying students but did not change its curriculum to suit the demands of the market. Commercialisation, however, led to a deep-seated transformation, involving not only the external relation between the university and the market but also the internal process of knowledge production in the university and internal relations between different academic units (Mamdani 2007: 118).

Such logics of commercialization have only intensified in the twenty-first century.

We can also account for the law faculty's policies by situating them within the international context of legal education funding specifically. We saw how there was significant commitment from public and private donors to legal education across Africa between the 1950s and 1970s. Later, however, "external donors (non-African governments and foundations) . . . all but abandoned their support of African legal education" (Geraghty and Quansah 2008: 54).[20] The failure of law and development eventually led donors to

---

[20] For example, "The Partnership for Higher Education in Africa, launched in 2000 by the Carnegie Corporation, the Ford Foundation, the John D. and Catherine T. MacArthur Foundation, and the

favor the "development law" model (Geraghty and Quansah 2008: 545–556), which emphasized local capacity building and "good governance," with a focus on judicial training rather than legal education as a whole. Rather than embracing legal education and its link to development in general, instead it would come to inform specific policy alleviation programs reflecting international blueprints like the Millennium Development Goals with their "tertiary-level human resource development" training in a range of legal subjects, including commercial, mining, contract, land, trade, and human rights law.[21] Such a technocratic emphasis on legal education reflects broader donor preferences that have increasingly shifted from funding a range of university subjects in favor of only those deemed directly supportive of neoliberal developmental logics, such as science, economics, and especially information and communication technology (ICT).[22] Kapinga documents, for example, how IFI privatization policies in Tanzania in the 1980s encouraged students to favor studying tax, company, and commercial law subjects that were sometimes taught by visiting Northern academics. As in the case of Makerere in Uganda, "[a] conservative and bourgeois approach to the teaching of law has, by and large, now descended upon the [Dar es Salaam] Faculty [of Law]" (Kapinga 1992: 883).

V. African Legal Education in the Twenty-first Century: Regionalization and Internationalization vs. Globalization and Neocolonialism

"A new era of higher education in Africa began in the late 1990s, as leading think tank institutions and major donors elevated the status of higher education . . . to a major policy and resource agenda item" (Teferra 2007: 567). While still burdened by chronic resource shortages and increasing student

Rockefeller Foundation (which now includes the Kresge Foundation, the William and Flora Hewlett Foundation, and the Andrew Mellon Foundation) has not provided support for legal education in Africa and appears to have no plans to do so."

[21] In its 2009 Report, the World Bank surveys particular policies for their higher education effects in the Poverty Reduction Strategy Papers (PRSPs) of fourteen sub-Saharan African states (The World Bank 2009). For background on the place of higher education in PRSPs, see Bloom, Canning, and Chan 2006: 6–7.

[22] For example, Oloruntoba notes that in a World Bank funded project, US$230 million was provided to Nigeria to support science and technology in Nigeria. No funds were provided for the social sciences (Oloruntoba 2014: 348).

enrolments,[23] African universities at least entered the twenty-first century on a wave of international policy convergence supportive once again of higher education. Despite some undoubted gains for African higher education and legal education in particular, the further intensification of the globalization of higher education, I argue, serves to exacerbate inequalities within, across, and beyond African states and societies.[24] Resulting internationalization, regionalization, and subregionalization efforts can only partially counter the predominant neoliberal optics of seeing education as a (tradable) service commodity within a highly unequal, globalizing knowledge economy (Lebeau and Sall 2011: 143).

As was the case at the end of the twentieth century, the World Bank and UNESCO continue to serve as the principle higher education policymakers at the international level. They have forged a sometimes uncomfortable partnership in the sector. As mentioned previously, the World Bank became an increasingly important actor in the field during the age of structural adjustment programs when higher education was abandoned in favor of "education for all." This shortsighted approach, however, was first questioned by the Bank itself in its 1994 report, "Higher Education, The Lessons of Experience," which nevertheless continued to uphold its push for privatization (Lebeau and Sall 2011: 136–137).[25] The nature of this knowledge has changed too with UNESCO conceding by 2009 that "[i]t appears that the modern university has shifted its orientation from social knowledge to market knowledge" (Meek, Teichler, and Kearney 2009: 53).[26] In its 1999, the World Bank showed that there was a positive link between investment in higher education and economic development. It then convened a joint taskforce with UNESCO, which led to the 2000 report, "Higher Education in Developing Countries: Peril and Promise." Here, it was conceded that "[n] arrow—and, in our view, misleading—economic analysis has contributed to the view that public investment in universities and colleges brings meagre

[23] For some useful student enrolment statistics, see Varghese 2016.

[24] Africa is only the most extreme example of higher education inequalities resulting in the wake of intensified globalization. See generally Altbach 2007: 124.

[25] Robertson summarizes the four reform strategies of the report as: "(i) greater differentiation of institutions, including the development of private ones; (ii) incentives for public institutions to diversify sources of funding, including cost sharing with students, (iii) redefining the role of government in higher education, and (iv) introducing policies designed to give priority to quality and equity objectives" (Robertson 2009: 120).

[26] In particular, see the 1998 World Development Report, "Knowledge for Development," which according to Robertson "laid the foundations for much of the Bank's [knowledge economy] work over the next decade" (Robertson 2009: 121).

returns compared to investment in primary and secondary schools, and that higher education magnifies income inequality" (The World Bank 2000: 10). The report corrected any lingering doubts on this and urged significant support for the sector through an emphasis on the knowledge economy and globalization.

The convergence of international agency discourses (the World Bank, OECD, World Trade Organization, and European Union) and key bilateral donors on the role of higher education in so-called knowledge-led economic development "provided the analytical concepts for such agencies to appear as legitimate with a greater capacity to interfere more directly and more openly in national higher education matters" (Lebeau and Sall 2011: 138). The World Bank–created knowledge economy index is one such policy tool, which ranks economies based on "the favorability for knowledge development within the economic and institutional regime; education; innovation; and information and communications technology" (Bloom, Canning, and Chan 2006: 9). African states perform very badly within such rankings, which fail to capture particular challenges faced across the continent.[27]

The push for global standards in measuring higher education is symptomatic of the key, interrelated trends of globalization and internationalization that accelerated around the turn of the century. Much of the high-level donor reporting in the 1990s and 2000s centers on ways to enhance the provision of higher education within a globalizing world that has come to rely more and more on trade in services and hence the knowledge economy. Scholarship on the globalization of higher education either tends to present the topic as one of *opportunity* in relation to increased student, academic, and knowledge movement or one of *crisis* due to the overemphasis on universities as sites of job training and commodification within "Americanised" strictures (Chou, Kamola, and Pietsch 2016).

Typically, in the higher education literature, internationalization is presented as a potentially positive counterweight to the inexorable forces of globalization (Altbach 2007: 123). Knight is cited regularly in the literature, and she has defended her "neutral" definition of "internationalization" for its focus on educational functions and objectives. Accordingly, the definition she advances for internationalization is "the process of integrating an international, intercultural or global dimension into the purpose, functions (primarily teaching/learning, research, service) or delivery of higher education"

---

[27] Robertson discusses some other World Bank "knowledge" indicators (Robertson 2009).

(Knight 2013: 85). Typically, internationalization entails "sending students to study abroad, setting up a branch campus overseas, or engaging in some type of inter-institutional partnership" (Haddad 2009: iv). To this we can also add "multinationalization," which "refers to academic programs or institutions located in one country offering degrees, courses, certificates, or other qualifications in other countries" (Altbach 2007: 123). Such practices often occur in regional contexts, such as Africa's higher education setting examined later.

Such characterizations of internationalization are helpful, but they capture only some of the dynamics at play, especially once we turn our gaze back to the African higher education sector.[28] The Bank has continued to push for "good governance," "autonomous" public universities and increasingly privatized forms of research and teaching within a funding environment that for African states has been fragmented and still highly skewed toward disproportionate sums for scholarships to the metropole and donor-driven research projects,[29] rather than investing in African national and regional initiatives.[30] UNESCO research in particular is an invaluable resource for revealing the profoundly problematic aspects of internationalized education:

> Inequality among national higher education systems as well as within countries has increased in the past several decades. The academic world has always been characterized by centers and peripheries. The strongest universities, usually because of their research prowess and reputation

[28] For example, Jowi 2009 notes the many negative and positive implications of internationalization. Also see Singh 2010.

[29] In the words of Rockefeller Foundation Country Representative in Nairobi, David Court, "one has resources, the other would like them. In order to gain access, the applicant can hardly avoid adjusting the manner of his approach to accord with the known or perceived preferences of the donor in a process of self restriction and hence, reduction of freedom and that changes in donor interests are bound to provoke a corresponding response by scholars leading to take on topics, which are lower personal or institutional priority than those of the external agendas" (quoted by Zeleza 2002 in Oloruntoba 2014: 347).

[30] One-quarter of international aid provided to the education sector in sub-Saharan Africa (approximately US$600 million annually average 2002 to 2006) is allocated to higher education. The bulk of this aid is bilateral and is also highly fragmented owing to the lack of donor coordination. Unfortunately, the impact of this aid on national capacity building is limited because only 26 percent of this aid is direct and invested locally. The lion's share of bilateral aid consists of scholarships benefiting the universities in the host countries of the African students abroad. Multilateral aid is geared toward sector investment at the local level, but is still inadequate. Indeed, priority is still accorded to basic education for all, although there are encouraging signs of diversification from the African Development Bank and the World Bank, as aid is increasingly being provided in the form of overall budgetary support and governments are submitting requests to international organizations pertaining to other priorities (financial crisis, food crisis, and the energy crisis) (Haddad 2009: 9). Also see The World Bank 2010.

for excellence, are seen as centers. African universities for example, have found it extremely challenging and complex to find their footing on the global higher education stage—they barely register on world institutional rankings and league tables and produce a tiny percentage of the world's research output (Haddad 2009: 18).

Despite the possibilities of "differentiated academic systems," UNESCO points out that instead there is a "tendency towards isomorphism" where all universities aspire to follow one model (Haddad 2009: 18) or, in the words of Nyamnjoh, for Africa, "mimicry" of Northern knowledge (Nyamnjoh 2012: 336). Chou et al. also question this UNESCO narrative by noting the "*apparent isomorphism* of transnational higher education" (Chou, Kamola, and Pietsch 2016). Global metrics enable leading tertiary institutions in the Global North to capitalize on their prestige and gain preponderance in the "new imperial" marketplace of internationalized education.[31] In such a profoundly inequitable system where some US university endowments are larger than the GDP of African countries, higher education in Africa must not only be assessed along "global," "neutral" metrics. Instead, if such universities are to be "African universities" rather than simply "universities in Africa" (Kamola 2014: 604), then their approach to research and teaching must speak not only to global elites but to local, national, subregional, and regional *political* concerns. Most profoundly, this requires a commitment to critical intellectual inquiry even in the face of a variety of contrary pressures.[32]

Various regional initiatives have been pursued as a way to consolidate African tertiary resources and expertise and potentially counter the "brain drain" that often occurs in the wake of overseas study.[33] There is now a vast

---

[31] See Naidoo 2011.

[32] This is captured by Kamola's account of the University of Cape Town's (UCT) treatment of Mamdani during his time at the Centre for African Studies 1996–1999 and his course, "Problemtizing Africa," which was rejected by the university, prompting Mamdani's departure. For Kamola, "'pursuit of excellence' within 'any university' is not only the ability to claim a racially diversified faculty and student body (although this is important), or for that matter to point out UCT's 'global' ranking, but rather to foster an environment in which one's world can be swayed by the 'winds of political change.' In the case of UCT, Mamdani thinks excellence should be measured in terms of how well the school helps students embrace the radical political and intellectual potential of post-apartheid South Africa" (Kamola 2011: 160–161). In 2018 Mamdani was appointed as an Honorary Professor at UCT's Centre of African Studies almost twenty years after his initial, challenging time there. See https://www.news.uct.ac.za/article/-2018-05-30-mamdani-rejoins-uct. Also noteworthy is the way in which the UCT as a "historically white," privileged institution has been at the forefront of the recent Rhodes Must Fall movement seeking to decolonize the university and its curriculum (Luckett 2016). Also see Mamdani 2008.

[33] On the "brain drain." see Jowi 2012.

literature exploring the similarities and differences between the globalization, internationalization, and regionalization of higher education, whether in Africa or beyond. Typically, globalization is contrasted with the complementary practices of regionalization and internationalization. As was the case in relation to internationalization, Knight's definition of regionalization is regularly cited: regionalization is the "process of building closer collaboration and alignment among higher education actors and systems within a defined area or framework called a region" (Knight 2013: 349). Although she concedes that in Africa this can speak to a variety of linguistic, geographic, and cultural subregions, she argues that typically the region is synonymous with the continent as a whole.[34] Of note here are a variety of regional and subregional associations (such as the Association of African Universities, the Southern African Regional Universities Association, and the Inter University Council for East Africa),[35] journals, and conferences centered on fostering greater collaboration in teaching and research.[36] Harmonization of teaching courses through the Addis Adaba Convention, December 2014, is perhaps the most significant development in enabling alignment in course delivery across the continent. Although Africa was ahead of the harmonization curve in first producing the Arusha Agreement in 1981,[37] ratifications were small and more recent harmonization efforts need to be understood within the context of global harmonization trends dominated by Europe's Bologna process[38] (often transmitted by UNESCO),[39] countered by the African aspiration to preserve and enhance indigenous training and expertise.

It is beyond the scope of this chapter to explore these regional initiatives in detail, but at the very least we need to situate such efforts within a broader pattern of the neoliberalization of higher education, whether in Africa or beyond. Taylor cautions against a view of regionalization as a simple

> counter-reaction in the direction of regional autarkies. Instead, it delineates a consolidation of politico-economic spaces contesting with one another within the capitalist global economy. It is clear that there are no "natural" regions, and that regions have to be constructed. That existing regionalist

---

[34] For a recent appraisal, see Knight and Woldegiorgis 2017.
[35] On the latter, see Jowi 2009: 263–281.
[36] For example, see Teferra 2007: 567. Also see Sehoole and de Wit 2014.
[37] On harmonization, see Knight 2013.
[38] For some critical appraisals of the impact of the Bologna framework in Africa, see Croché and Charlier 2012; Shawa 2008.
[39] See Hartmann 2008.

projects reflect the impulses of a neo-liberal world order is of consequence of the environment within which regional elites find themselves (Taylor 2003 314).

Applying this to higher education in Africa, it is clear that although African elites can try to construct alternative institutional and even epistemic logics, their chances of success will be limited in a landscape constituted by the sheer scale of material inequalities.

The transnationalization of legal education, then, is a response to the growing role of transnational regulation within a globalizing knowledge economy. Lawyers equipped with the skills and networks provided by training in elite law schools can move deftly through a range of jurisdictional zones. Resources are required though to begin such a journey, and for most law students in Africa, the chances of entry are extremely limited. The best routes are through scholarships to prestigious Northern law schools or to the continent's regional legal training hubs, such as South Africa, with new opportunities now also being offered by China.[40]

With its own well-established university tradition, links to British law and the English language, post-apartheid South Africa is the most important site for training African lawyers seeking to enter transnational legal practice. South Africa has also fostered a range of social justice grassroots initiatives with an emphasis on the legal clinic model inside and outside the country.[41] While South African universities can try to forge a uniquely 'African' curriculum,[42] particularly for those students seeking to ride the wave of profitable international corporate and commercial practice, then, time and again, "global" models trump their indigenous counterparts (Klaaren 2015). This is partly the result of the limited material resources available to South Africa due to its relatively weak global position.[43]

---

[40] While not supportive of legal education as a priority, China has massively increased its contribution to African higher education especially since the founding of the Forum for Africa-China Cooperation (FOCAC) in 2000. Most noteworthy is the 20+20 Cooperation Plan for Chinese and African Institutions of Higher Education launched in 2009, which supports China's most recent plans to offer 50,000 scholarships to African students to study in China as contained in the FOCAC Action Plan 2019–2021: https://focacsummit.mfa.gov.cn/eng/hyqk_1/t1594297.htm (see Section 4.3). For an overview of Chinese contributions to African higher education, see Gu 2017.

[41] For a discussion about the influence of South African clinical legal education in Nigeria, see Krishnan and Ajagbe 2018: 235–238.

[42] For a fascinating account of Mamdani's attempt to create an African curriculum, see his overview in Mamdani, 1998: 63–75 and Kamola 2011.

[43] On the limited possibilities of South Africa's mediating position between other African states and the global market, see Alden and Schoemen 2015; and Ogunnubi and Akinola 2017.

VI. Conclusion

Whether for legal education in particular, or higher education in general, the case of Africa demonstrates how its peripheral status in a globalizing knowledge economy makes it especially vulnerable to a range of interrelated material and epistemic forms of domination. We can see this even in relation to the majority of African scholars this chapter has engaged with. While their critical reflections offer valuable insights into countering Northern hegemonies, we also need to acknowledge how such scholars themselves are often linked into privileged Northern networks of higher education. Ferguson reminds us that "the 'global' does not 'flow', thereby connecting and watering contiguous spaces: it hops instead, efficiently connecting the enclaved points in the network while excluding (with equal efficiency) the spaces that lie between the points."[44] Today, most of the privileged enclaves of legal education and practice exist in the Global North. If Africa wants to benefit from such possibilities and profits, it is hard to envisage how it could do so with a sufficient degree of epistemic and material autonomy. This does not mean that regional efforts in the development of shared curriculum and training should not be pursued, but in seeking to conceive of a worthwhile legal education model for modern Africa, the biggest challenge remains at the epistemic level in (re) thinking "Africa" and law's role in its social transformation. Law can serve as a tool of social transformation for a decolonial future, but it can also facilitate entrenched colonial and neocolonial forms of dependency. Prey to the vagaries of a transnational market in higher education, African law schools must balance a range of competing interests, too many of which serve to further exacerbate Africa's disparities in its (epistemic and legal) wealth.

References

Aiyedun, A. and A. Ordor (2012). "Accessing Justice within Plural Normative Systems in Africa: Case Study of South Africa," *African Journal of Clinical Legal Education and Access to Justice* 1: 49–72.

Alden, C. and M. Schoemen (2015). "South Africa's Symbolic Hegemony in Africa," *International Politics* 52(2): 239–254

Altbach, P.G. (2007). "Globalization and the University: Realities in an Unequal World," in J.J. Forest and P.G. Altbach, eds., *International Handbook of Higher Education.* Pp. 121–139. Springer.

---

[44] Ferguson 2006: 47.

Altbach, P.G., L. Reisberg, and L.E. Rumbley (2009). *Trends in Global Higher Education: Tracking an Academic Revolution: A Report Prepared for the UNESCO 2009 World Conference on Higher Education.* United Nations Educational, Scientific and Cultural Organization.

Arjona, C., J. Anderson, F. Meier, and S. Robart (2015). "What Law for Transnational Legal Education? A Cooperative View of an Introductory Course to Transnational Law and Governance," *Transnational Legal Theory* 6(2): 253–286.

Arowosegbe, J.O. (2016). "African Scholars, African Studies and Knowledge Production on Africa," *Africa* 86(2): 324–338.

Arthurs, H.W. (2009). "Law and Learning in an Era of Globalization," *German Law Journal* 10(1): 629–640.

Bainbridge, J.S. (1972). *The Study and Teaching of Law in Africa: Survey of Institutions of Legal Education in Africa.* Fred B Rothman & Co.

Basedow, J. (2014). "Breeding Lawyers for the Global Village: The Internationalisation of Law and Legal Education, "in W. Van Caenegem and M. Hiscock, eds., *The Internationalisation of Legal Education: The Future Practice of Law.* Pp. 1–18. Edward Elgar Publishing Limited.

Blommaert, J. (2000). "Language in Education in Post-colonial Africa: Trends and Problems," *Conference on Language Policy—Trends and Perspectives.* Conference on Language Policy—Trends and Perspectives, City University of Hong Kong. https://www.researchgate.net/publication/290446865_Language_in_education_in_post-colonial_Africa_Trends_and_problems

Bloom, D.E., D. Canning, and K. Chan (2006). Higher Education and Economic Development in Africa. Accessed June 8, 2018. http://ent.arp.harvard.edu/AfricaHigherEducation/Reports/BloomAndCanning.pdf. https://www.researchgate.net/publication/281028088_Higher_Education_and_Economic_Growth_in_Africa

Boly, H., H. Boukary, A. Byll-Cataria, T. Chehidi, K. Kinyanjui, and D. Teferra, eds. Continental Education Strategy for Africa: 2016–2025. Accessed June 8, 2018. https://au.int/sites/default/files/documents/29958-doc-cesa_-_english-v9.pdf.

Botha, M.M. (2010). "Compatibility Between Internationalizing and Africanizing Higher Education in South Africa," *Journal of Studies in International Education* 14: 200–213.

Boulle, L. (2014). "Isolationism, Democratisation and Globalisation: Legal Education in a Developing Country," in W. Van Caenegem and M. Hiscock, eds., *The Internationalisation of Legal Education: The Future Practice of Law.* Pp. 48–69. Edward Elgar Publishing Limited.

Britz, J.J. and S. Ponelis (2012). "Social Justice and the International Flow of Knowledge with Specific Reference to African Scholars," *Aslib Proceedings: New Information Perspectives* 64(5): 462–477.

Caplow, S. and M. Fullerton (2005). "Co-teaching International Criminal Law: New Strategies to Meet the Challenges of a New Course," *Brooklyn Journal of International Law* 31(1): 103–127.

Carl, B.M. (1986). "Peanuts, Law Professors, and Third World Lawyers," *Third World Legal Studies* 5: 1–13.

Carrol, B. and J. Samoff (2004a). *Conditions, Coalitions, and Influence: The World Bank and Higher Education in Africa.* Annual Conference of the Comparative and International Education Society, Salt Lake City.

Carrol, B. and J. Samoff (2004b). "The Promise of Partnership and Continuities of Dependence: External Support to Higher Education in Africa," *African Studies Review* 47(1): 67–199.

Chesterman, S. (2008). "The Globalisation of Legal Education," *Singapore Journal of Legal Studies* 2008: 58–67.

Chesterman, S. (2009). "The Evolution of Legal Education: Internationalization, Transnationalization, Globalization," *German Law Journal* 10(6–7): 877–888.

Chesterman, S. (2014). "Doctrine, Perspectives and Skills for Global Practice," in W. Van Caenegem and M. Hiscock, eds., *The Interationalisation of Legal Education: The Future Practice of Law*. Pp. 183–192. Edward Elgar Publishing Limited.

Chorev, N. and A. Schrank (2017). "Professionals and the Professions in the Global South," *Sociology of Development* 3: 197–210.

Chou, M-H., I. Kamola, and T. Pietsch (2016). "Introduction: the Transnational Politics of Higher Education," in M-H. Chou, I. Kamola, and T. Pietsch, eds., *The Transnational Politics of Higher Education: Contesting the Global/Transforming the Local*. Pp. 1–21. Routledge.

Clegg, S. (2016). "The Necessity and Possibility of Powerful 'Regional' Knowledge: Curriculum Change and Renewal," *Teaching in Higher Education* 21(4): 457–470.

Coleman, J.S., D. Court, and the Rockefeller Foundation Nairobi, Kenya (1993). *University Development in the Third World: The Rockefeller Foundation Experience*. Pergamon Press.

Combining Learning and Legal Aid: Clinics in Africa. Report on the First All-African Colloquium on Clinical Legal Education, 23–28 June 2003 (2003). Accessed June 8, 2018. https://www.opensocietyfoundations.org/sites/default/files/southafrica_20030 628.pdf.

Committee on Legal Education for Students from Africa (1961), Report of the Committee on Legal Education for Students from Africa. H.M.S.O. Cmnd. No. 1255.

Coper, M. (2014). "Internationalisation and Different National Philosophies of Legal Education: Convergence, Divergence and Contestability," in W. Van Caenegem and M. Hiscock, eds., *The Internationalisation of Legal Education: The Future Practice of Law*. Pp. 21–47. Edward Elgar Publishing Limited.

Croché, S. and J.-É. Charlier (2012). "Normative Influence of the Bologna Process on French-speaking African Universities," *Globalisation, Societies and Education* 10(4): 457–472.

Davis, G. (2008). *Report to Council of Australian Law Deans (Summary)*. International Conference on the Future of Legal Education, 200 Georgia State University, College of Law, Atlanta.

Day, L.E., M. Vandiver, and R. Janikowski (2003). "Teaching the Ultime Crime: Genocide and International Law in the Criminal Justice Curriculum," *Journal of Criminal Justice Education* 14: 119–131.

Devarajan, S., C. Monga, and T. Zongo (2011). "Making Higher Education Finance Work for Africa," *Journal of African Economies* 20(3): 133–154.

Dezalay, S. (2015). "Les Juristes en Afrique: Entre Trajectoires D'Etat, Sillons d'Empire et Mondialisation," *Politique africaine* 138(2): 5–23.

Dezalay, S. (2017). "Lawyers' Empire in the (African) Colonial Margins," *International Journal of the Legal Profession* 24(1): 25–32.

Dezalay, Y. and B. Garth (2011). "State Politics and Legal Markets," *Comparative Sociology* 10(1): 38–66.

Donovan, N., ed. (2009). The Enforcement of International Criminal Law. Accessed June 8, 2018. https://reliefweb.int/sites/reliefweb.int/files/resources/603D8E48589F6DD1C 12577E70039FB54-Aegis_Jan2009.pdf.

Draft Declaration and Action Plan of the 1st African Higher Education Summit on Revitalizing Higher Education for Africa's Future: March 10–12, 2015, Dakar, Senegal (2015). Accessed June 8, 2018. http://www.africa-platform.org/sites/default/files/resources/summit-declaration-and-action-plan.pdf.

Farag, I.E., J.J. Forest, and P.G. Altbach (2007). *International Handbook of Higher Education*. Springer.

Faundez, J. (2000). "Legal Reform in Developing and Transition Countries—Making Haste Slowly," *Law, Social Justice and Global Development Journal* 2000(1). http://www2.warwick.ac.uk/fac/soc/law/elj/lgd/2000_1/faundez/.

Federici, S. (2012). African Roots of US University Struggles: From the Occupy Movement to the Anti-Student-Debt Campaign. Accessed June 8, 2018. http://eipcp.net/transver sal/0112/federici/en.

Ferguson, J. (2006). *Global Shadows: Africa in the Neoliberal World Order*. Duke University Press.

Garth, B. (2013). "Crises, Crisis Rhetoric, and the Competition in Legal Education: A Sociological Perspective on the (Latest) Crisis of the Legal Profession and Legal Education," *Stanford Law and Policy Review* XXIV: 503–532.

Geraghty, T.F. and E.K. Quansah (2007). "African Legal Education: A Missed Opportunity and Suggestions for Change: A Call for Renewed Attention to a Neglected Means of Securing Human Rights and Legal Predictability," *Loyola University Chicago International Law Review* 5: 87–105.

Geraghty, T.F. and E.K. Quansah (2008). "Reform of Legal Education in Ethiopia: The Ethiopian Experience in the Context of History, the Present and the Future," *Reprinted in Journal of Ethiopian Law* 22: 49–74.

Gevers, C., A. Wallis, and C. James (2013). *Positive Reinforcement: Advocating for International Criminal Justice in Africa*. Southern Africa Litigation Centre.

Ghai, Y. (1987). "Law, Development and African Scholarship," *The Modern Law Review* 50(6): 750–776.

Ghai, Y. (1991). "The Role of Law in the Transition of Societies: The African Experience," *Journal of African Law* 35(1–2): 8–20.

Gibson, F. (2012). "Community Engagement in Action: Creating Successful University Clinical Legal Internship," *African Journal of Clinical Legal Education and Access to Justice* 1: 1–30.

Greenbaum, L. (2015–2016). "Legal Education in South Africa: Harmonizing the Aspirations of Transformative Constitutionalism with Our Education Legacy," *New York Law School Law Review* 60: 463–491.

Gu, M. (2017). "The Sino-African Higher Educational Exchange: How Big Is It and Will It Continue?," *World Education + Reviews*. https://wenr.wes.org/2017/03/the-sino-african-higher-educational-exchange-how-big-is-it-and-will-it-continue

Haddad, G. (2009). In UNESCO, ed., *Thematic Studies Synthesis: Realized in the context of the Task Force for Higher Education in Africa*. United Nations Educational, Scientific and Cultural Organization.

Haddad, W., N. Colletta, N. Fisher, M. Lakin, and R. Rinaldi (1990). *Final Report: World Conference on Education for All: Meeting Basic Learning Needs*. WCEFA Inter-Agency Commission.

Harrington, J.A. and A. Manji (2003). "'Mind with Mind and Spirit with Spirit': Lord Denning and African Legal Education," *Journal of Law and Society* 30(3): 376–399.

Hartmann, E. (2008). "Bologna Goes Global: A New Imperialism in the Making?," *Globalisation, Societies and Education* 6(3): 207–220.

Iya, P.F. (2003). "From Lecture Room to Practice: Addressing the Challenges of Reconstructing and Regulating Legal Education and Legal Practice in the New South Africa," *Third World Legal Studies* 16: 141–160.

Iya, P.F. (2005). "Enhancing the Teaching of Human Rights in African Universities: What Role for Law School Clinics?," *Journal of Clinical Legal Education* 7 (August): 20–28.

Jessup, G. (2006). "Development Law: Squaring the Circle, Advancing Human Rights in Africa," *Human Rights Review* 7 (April–June): 96–111.

Jowi, J.O. (2009). "Internationalization of Higher Education in Africa: Developments, Emerging Trends, Issues and Policy Implications," *Higher Education Policy* 22(3): 263–281.

Jowi, J.O. (2012). "African Universities in the Global Knowledge Economy: The Good and Ugly of Internationalization," *Journal of Marketing for Higher Education* 22(1): 153–165.

Kahn-Fogel, N.A. (2012). "The Troubling Shortage of African Lawyers: Examination of a Continental Crisis Using Zambia as a Case Study," *University of Pennsylvania Journal of International Law* 33(3): 719–789.

Kalhan, A. (2012–2013). "Thinking Critically about International and Transnational Legal Education," *Drexel Law Review* 5: 285–296.

Kamola, I.A. (2011). "Pursuing Excellence in a 'World-Class African University: The Mamdani Affair and the Politics of Global' Higher Education," *Journal of Higher Education in Africa* 9(1–2): 147–168.

Kamola, I. (2013). "Why Global? Diagnosing the Globalization Literature Within a Political Economy of Higher Education," *International Political Sociology* 7: 41–58.

Kamola, I. (2014). "The African University as 'Global' University," *PS: Political Science and Politics* 47: 604–607.

Kanywanyi, J.L. (1989). "The Struggle to Decolonise and Demystify University Education: Dar's 25 Years Experience on the Faculty of Law (October 1961–October 1985)," *Eastern African Law Review* 16(1): 1–70.

Kapinga, W.B.L. (1992). "The Legal Profession and Social Action in the Third World: Reflections on Tanzania and Kenya," *African Journal of International and Comparative Law* 4: 874–891.

Karekwaivanene, G.H. (2011). "'It Shall Be the Duty of Every African to Obey and Comply Promptly': Negotiating State Authority in the Legal Arena, Rhodesia 1965–1980," *Journal of Southern African Studies* 37(2): 333–349.

Karekwaivanene, G.H. (2016). "'Through the Narrow Door': Narratives of the First Generation of African Lawyers in Zimbabwe," *Africa* 86(1): 59–77.

Karekwaivanene, G.H. (2017). *The Struggle over State Power in Zimbabwe: Law and Politics since 1950*. Cambridge University Press.

Kayombo, J.J. (2015). "Strategic Harmoinzation of Higher Education Systems: The Dominance of Cross-State Organizations, Government Treaties and International Conferences in Higher Education Accreditation and Quality Assurance," *Journal of Literature, Language and Linguistics* 5: 26–30.

Kim, M. and E.H. Boyle (2013). "Neoliberalism, Transnational Education Norms, and Education Spending in the Developing World, 1983–2004," in G. Shaffer, ed., *Transnational Legal Ordering and State Change.* Pp. 121–147. Cambridge University Press.

Klaaren, J. (2015). "African Corporate Lawyers and Globalization," *International Journal of the Legal Profession* 22: 226–242.

Klabbers, J. and J. Sellers (2008). *The Internationalization of Law and Legal Education.* Springer.

Knight, J. (2013). "The Changing Landscape of Higher Education Internationalisation— For Better or Worse?," *Perspectives: Policy and Practice in Higher Education* 17: 84–90.

Knight, J. (2013). "Towards African Higher Education Regionalization and Harmonization: Functional, Organizational and Political Approaches," in A.W. Wiseman and C.C. Wolhuter, eds., *Development of Higher Education in Africa: Prospects and Challenges.* Pp. 347–373. Emerald.

Knight, J. and J. Mcnamara, *Transnational Education: A Classification Framework and Date Collection Guidelines for International Programme and Provider Mobility.* Accessed June 8, 2018. https://www.britishcouncil.org/sites/default/files/tne_classific ation_framework-final.pdf.

Knight, J. and E.T. Woldegiorgis, eds. (2017). *Regionalization of African Higher Education: Progress and Prospects.* Sense Publishers.

Krishnan, J.K. (2012). "Academic SAILERS: The Ford Foundation and the Efforts to Shape Legal Education in Africa, 1957–1977," *American Journal of Legal History* 52(3): 261–324.

Krishnan, J.K. and K. Ajagbe (2018). "Legal Activism in the Face of Political Challenges: The Nigerian Case," *Journal of the Legal Profession* 42: 197–241.

Lebeau, Y. and E. Sall (2011). "Global Institutions, Higher Education Development," in R. King, S. Marginson, and R. Naidoo, eds., *Handbook on Globalization and Higher Education.* Pp. 129–148. Edward Elgar Publishing.

Luckett, K. (2016). "Curriculum Contestation in a Post-colonial context: A View from the South," *Teaching in Higher Education* 21(4): 415–428.

Mamdani, M. (1998). "Is African Studies to Be Turned into a New Home for Bantu Education at UCT?," *Social Dynamics* 24: 63–75.

Mamdani, M. (2007). *Scholars in the Marketplace: The Dilemmas of Neo-Liberal Reform at Makerere University, 1989–2005.* Council for the Development of Social Science Research in Africa.

Mamdani, M. (2008). "Higher Education, the State, and the Marketplace," *Journal of Higher Education in Africa* 6(1): 1–10.

Mamdani, M. (2011). "The Importance of Research in a University," *Pambazuka News.* April 21. https://www.pambazuka.org/resources/importance-research-university.

Mamdani, M. (2012). *Define and Rule: Native as Political Identity.* Harvard University Press.

Manning, C. (2007). *Brain Drain and Brain Gain: A Survey of Issues, Outcomes and Policies in the Least Developed Countries (LDCs).* UNCTAD: The Least Developed Countries Report 2007 Background Paper. Australian National University.

Manteaw, S.O. (2007). "Legal Education in Africa: What Type of Lawyer Does Africa Need?," *McGeorge Law Review* 39(4): 903–976.

Meek, V.L., U. Teichler, and M-L. Kearney, eds. (2009). *Higher Education, Research and Innovation: Changing Dynamics, Report on the UNESCO Forum on Higher Education,*

Research and Knowledge, 2001-2009. Accessed June 8, 2018. http://unesdoc.unesco.org/images/0018/001830/183071E.pdf.

Mukhopadhyay, S. (2015). "West Is Best? A Post-colonial Perspective on the Implementation of Inclusive Education in Botswana," *KED Journal of Educational Policy* 12: 19–39.

Naidoo, R. (2011). "Rethinking Development: Higher Education and the New Imperialism," in R. King, S. Marginson, and R. Naidoo, eds., *A Handbook of Globalization and Higher Education.* Pp. 40–58. Edward Elgar.

Ndulo, M. (2002). "Legal Education in Africa in the Era of Globalization and Structural Adjustment," *Penn State International Law Review* 20(3): 487–503.

Ndulo, M. (2014). "Legal Education in an Era of Globalisation and the Challenge of Development," *Journal of Comparative Law in Africa* 1: 1–24.

Nesiah, V. (2013). "A Flat Earth for Lawyers without Borders? Rethinking Current Approaches to the Globalization of Legal Education," *Drexel Law Review* 5: 371–390.

Nyamnjoh, F.B. (2012). "'Potted Plants in Greenhouses': A Critical Reflection on the Resilience of Colonial Education in Africa," *Journal of Asian and African Studies* 47(2): 129–154.

Ogachi, O. (2009). "Internationalization *vs* Regionalization of Higher Education in East Africa and the Challenges of Quality Assurance and Knowledge Production," *Higher Education Policy* 22(3): 331–347.

Oguamanam, C. and W.W. Pue (2007). "Lawyers' Professionalism, Colonialism, State Formation, and National Life in Nigeria, 1900–1960: 'The Fighting Brigade of the People,'" *Social Identities* 13(6): 769–785.

Ogunnubi, O. and A. Akinola (2017). "South Africa and the Question of Regional Hegemony in Africa," *Journal of Developing Societies* 33(4): 428–447.

Okafor, O.C. and D.C.J. Dakas (2009). "Teaching 'Human Rights in Africa' Transnationally: Reflections on the Jos-Osgoode Virtual Classroom Experience," *German Law Journal* (6–7)10: 959–968.

Okebukola, P. ed. (2015). *Towards Innovative Models for Funding Higher Education in Africa.* Association of African Universities.

Oketch, M. (2016). "Financing Higher Education in Sub-Saharan Africa: Some Reflections and Implications for Sustainable Development," *Higher Education Studies* 72(4): 525–539.

Oloruntoba, S.O. (2014). "Social Sciences as Dependency: State Apathy and the Crisis of Knowledge in Nigerian Universities," *Social Dynamics* 40(2): 338–352.

Oyewole, O. (2013). "African Harmonisation: An Academic Process for a Political End?," *Chronicle of African Higher Education* January (2013): 1–4.

Paul, J.C.N. (1987). "American Law Teachers and Africa: Some Historical Observations," *Journal of African Law* 31(1–2): 18–28.

Robertson, S.L. (2009). "Market Multilateralism, the World Bank Group and the Asymmetries of Globalising Higher Education: Toward a Critical Political Economy Analysis," in R. M. Bassett and A. Maldanado-Maldanado, eds, *International Organizations and Higher Education Policy: Thinking Globally, Acting Locally?,* Pp. 113–131. Taylor and Francis.

Saint, W., C. Lao, and P. Materu (2009). *Legal Frameworks for Tertiary Education in Sub-Saharan Africa: The Quest for Institutional Responsiveness.* World Bank.

Sarker, S.P. (2013). "Empowering the Underprivileged: The Social Justice Mission for Clinical Legal Education in India," *International Journal of Clinical Legal Education* 19: 321–339.

Scoville, R.M. (2017). "International Law in National Schools," *Indiana Law Journal* 92(4): 1449–1507.

Sehoole, C. and H. de Wit (2014). "The Regionalisation, Internationalisation and Globalisation of African Higher Education," *International Journal of African Higher Education* 1: 217–241.

Shawa, L.B. (2008). "The Bologna Process and the European Gain: Africa's Development Demise?," *European Education* 40(1): 97–106.

Singh, M. (2010). "Re-orientating Internationalisation in African Higher Education Globalisation," *Societies and Education* 8: 269–282.

Sornarajah, M. (2016). "On Fighting for Global Justice: The Role of a Third World International Lawyer," *Third World Quarterly* 37(11): 1972–1989.

Tamanaha, B.Z. (1995). "Review: The Lessons of Law-and-Development Studies," *The American Journal of International Law* 89(2): 470–486.

Tamanaha, B.Z. (2011). "The Primacy of Society and the Failures of Law and Development," *Cornell International Law Journal* 44(2): 209–247.

The Task Force on Higher Education and Society (2000). *Higher Education in Developing Countries: Peril and Promise.* The World Bank.

Taylor, I. (2003). "Globalization and Regionalization in Africa: Reactions to Attempts at Neo-liberal Regionalism," *Review of International Political Economy* 10: 310–330.

Teal, F. (2010). Higher Education and Economic Development in Africa: a Review of Channels and Interactions Centre for the Study of African Economies: University of Oxford. Accessed June 8, 2018. https://pdfs.semanticscholar.org/dafb/8fa2b3ebc1c23 16d9967e2e1e7186dbd4c80.pdf.

Teferra, D. (2007). "Higher Education in Sub-Saharan Africa," in J.J.F. Forrest and P.G. Altbach, eds., *International Handbook of Higher Education.* Pp. 557–69. Springer.

Teferra, D. (2013). "Introduction," in D. Teferra, ed., *Funding Higher Education in Sub-Saharan Africa.* Pp. 1–12. Palgrave Macmillan.

Terretta, M. (2017). "Anti-Colonial Lawyering, Postwar Human Rights, and Decolonization across Imperial Boundaries in Africa," *Canadian Journal of History* 52(3): 448–478.

Thomas, K. (2012). *Internationalisation: Establishing a Collective Understanding of the Issues.* Presentation at the Higher Education Academy.

Thomas, P.A. (1971). "Legal Education in Africa: With Special Reference to Zambia," *Northern Ireland Legal Quarterly* 22: 3–37.

Thornton, M. (2009). "The Law School, the Market and the New Knowledge Economy," *German Law Journal* 10(6–7): 641–668.

Trebilcock, M. (2012). "The Rule of Law and Development: In Search of the Holy Grail," *The World Bank Legal Review* 3: 207–240.

Triggs, G. (2014). "The Internationalisation of Legal Education: An Opportunity for Human Rights?," in W. Van Caenegem and M. Hiscock, eds., *The Internationalisation of Legal Education: The Future Practice of Law.* Pp. 209–222. Edward Elgar Publishing Limited.

Trubek, D.M. and M. Galanter (1974). "Scholars in Self-Estrangement: Some Reflections on the Crisis in Law and Development Studies in the United States," *Wisconsin Law Review.* (1974(4)): 1062–1102.

UNCTAD (2012). "Chapter 4: From Mobilizing the Diaspora: From Brain Drain to Brain Gain," in UNCTAD, ed., *The Least Developed Countries Report 2012: Harnessing Remittances and Diaspora Knowledge to Build Productive Capacities.* Geneva. United Nations Conference on Trade and Development: https://unctad.org/system/files/offic ial-document/ldc2012_en.pdf.

UNESCO (1962). *The Development of Higher Education in Africa: Report of the Conference on the Development of Higher Education in Africa,* Tananarive.

UNESCO (2004). *Higher Education in a Globalized Society: UNESCO Education Position Paper.* United Nations Educational, Scientific and Cultural Organization.

UNESCO (2009). *Thematic Studies Synthesis: Realized in the context of the Task Force for Higher Education in Africa.* United Nations Educational, Scientific and Cultural Organization.

Van Caenegem, W. (2014). "Ignoring the Civil Law/Common Law Divide in an Integrated Legal World," in W. Van Caenegem and M. Hiscock, eds., *The Internationalisation of Legal Education: The Future Practice of Law.* Pp. 145–172. Edward Elgar Publishing Limited.

Van Der Merwe, Hj. and G. Kemp (2016). *International Criminal Justice in Africa: Issues, Challenges and Prospects.* Srathmore University Press.

Varghese, N.V. (2016). "Reforms and Changes in Governance of Higher Education in Africa: An Overview," in N.V. Varghese, ed., *Reforms and Changes in Governance of Higher Education in Africa.* Pp. 21–39. International Institute for Education Planning: UNESCO.

Wandela, E.L. (2014). *Tanzania Post-Colonial Educational System and Perspectives on Secondary Science, Education, Pedagogy, and Curriculum: A Qualitative Study.* DePaul University.

Woldegiorgis, E.T. (2013). "Conceptualizing Harmonization of Higher Education Systems: The Application of Regional Integration Theories on Higher Education Studies," *Higher Education Studies* 3: 12–23.

Woldegiorgis, E.T., P. Jonck, and A. Goujon (2015). "Regional Higher Education Reform Initiatives in Africa: A Comparative Analysis with the Bologna Process," *International Journal of Higher Education* 4(1): 241–253.

Woldetensae, D.Y. (2012). *Vision of the African Union on the Role of Higher Education in Africa's Development.* Africa-U.S. Higher Education Initiative Partners' Meeting, 2012, Addis Ababa.

The World Bank (2000). *Higher Education in Developing Countries: Peril and Promise.* The International Bank for Reconstruction and Development.

The World Bank (2009). *Accelerating Catch-up: Tertiary Education for Growth in Sub-Saharan Africa.* The International Bank for Reconstruction and Development.

The World Bank (2010). *Financing Higher Education in Africa.* The International Bank for Reconstruction and Development.

4

Legal Education in South Africa

Racialized Globalizations, Crises, and Contestations

Ralph Madlalate

I. Introduction

Legal education in South Africa has a peculiar provenance. Like many products of the colonial era, the country's legal education system has been shaped by a process "of unabashed and of conscious empire building and lawgiving, in which transfers of legal knowledge and legal institutions took place" (Chanock 2001: 30). Central to this process was a commitment to racial subordination, exclusion, and its ambiguities. As such, the pathway into the legal profession has been, and remains, a site of contest imbued with colonial and apartheid ideology. This chapter traces the development of South African legal education situating it in the context of globalizations past and present. Section II provides a vignette of the larger narrative of racial oppression in South Africa from the vantage point of legal education. This picture does little to capture the indignity of life for the "colonized" many, nor indeed does it account for the African law which operated prior to the colonial encounter (Chanock 1985). What it illustrates, however, is the embeddedness of racial oppression rooted in the colonial project within the South African legal system. This colonial-apartheid context is, I submit, crucial to understanding the development of the country's legal education system and its contestations in apartheid's wake. This section illustrates that precursors to contemporary globalization have been significant and in some instances have foreshadowed current trends in transnational interconnectivity. This is exemplified by the flow of practitioners and students between the colony and the metropole, which laid enduring circuits between the country and the global north as Roberts illustrates in this volume. As a result, some quarters of legal education such as historically white universities have a long history of global integration. Yet other segments, notably historically black universities, reflect

Ralph Madlalate, *Legal Education in South Africa* In: *The Globalization of Legal Education.* Edited by:
Bryant Garth and Gregory Shaffer, Oxford University Press. © Oxford University Press 2022.
DOI: 10.1093/oso/9780197632314.003.0004

the marginalization and underdevelopment which plagues African higher education more broadly (Popescu 2015; Ndulo 2002). These distinctions reflect the fact that legal education is a product of a racially constructed settler colonial state, which for much of the country's development prioritized the development of its euro-descendant population at the expense of the indigenous African population. This section also shows that, quite apart from passive bystanders, law schools have been central to producing the legal agents of the colonial and apartheid era, including those who promoted it and those who resisted it.

Sections III and IV examine the responses to the country's history of segregation in legal education and the changes it has undergone in the post-apartheid era. This period is characterized by the fall of apartheid in 1994 and the drive to remediate its legacy of racial inequities through a process of transformative constitutionalism (Klare 1998). This period has also coincided with the rapid expansion of globalization which influenced post-apartheid South Africa through the adoption of global human rights discourse, economic reforms, and increased regional and global economic interconnectivity. These sections illustrate that, despite modifications, the inequities of the colonial-apartheid era, meted out along racial lines, haunt the present. This is evident across many law faculties which have struggled to meet the country's aspiration of transformation in both demographic representation and epistemic reimagining amid students' calls for decolonized education. Moreover the vast gap between historically white and black institutions manifests in divergent institutional priorities. While the country's elite universities vie for global rankings, international partnerships, and highly skilled faculty, its historically black universities are plagued by resource shortages, large class sizes, and underequipped facilities. In this way, the country's legal education institutions' attempts to engage with the contemporary facets of globalization remain shaped by the pernicious aspects of globalizations past.

II. The Origins of Legal Education in South Africa: Colonial Apartheid as Context

The advent of law in South Africa is inextricably tied to conquest, colonial lawgiving, and competition between British and Dutch settlers (Worden 2012). This process created what Lester (2001: 6) terms "geographies of connection" between Western Europe and South Africa entrenched through exchange in commodities, labor, and capital. These commercial ties laid the foundations for imperial webs in which sovereignty came to be asserted, connecting spatially and temporally disparate peoples in networks of empire (Ward 2009). Pursuant to the transnational economic interweaving of the age, early lawyers arrived from the Netherlands in the late seventeenth century; settling in what became the Cape Colony, they brought with them a system of Roman-Dutch law. This legal system, itself a hybrid of Roman legal principles rationalized by Dutch renaissance jurists, was instituted at the expense of the indigenous African legal system, which was confined to a secondary position relevant only among the area's African inhabitants (Wildenboer 2010; Iya 2001). The marginal position of African law was a reflection of the peripheral status of African people themselves. African hopes of equal participation in the nascent colony were progressively denied, entrenching racial inequality (Terreblanche 2002; Thompson 2001). Like indigenous people in other parts of Africa, they saw the creation of a colonial outpost from which they were denied equal membership, becoming colonial subjects rather than citizens (Mamdani 1996).

The British assumed control of the Cape Colony at the turn of the nineteenth century, marking the beginning of increased British influence in the legal system. English law became the dominant legal system in without jettisoning Roman-Dutch law, which formed the bulk of the country's common law (Botha 1924). The influence of the British law in the Cape Colony was cemented by the Charter of Justice of 1827, which sought to organize the practice of law. In the absence of a local system of legal education, the charter allowed the Supreme Court of the Cape Colony to regulate entry into the profession. It provided for the Court to admit to practice "such persons as shall have been admitted as Barristers in England or Ireland or Advocates in the Court of Sessions of Scotland, or to the Degree of Doctor of Laws at our Universities of Oxford, Cambridge, or Dublin to act as Barristers or Advocates" (Erasmus 2015: 223; Kaburise 2001). This gave the legal system a transnational quality as legal practitioners moved between the metropole and the colony both privately and within the colonial service.

The development of a local system of legal education began in 1857 with the creation of a "Certificate of Higher Class in Law and Jurisprudence" at what is now the University of Cape Town (UCT). Its inaugural professor, Johannes Brand, was a member of the colonial elite, having taken his LLD at Leiden before being admitted to the English bar and returning to the Cape to found a successful practice in law (Cowen and Visser 2004). This program produced the country's first domestically trained lawyers. It was superseded in 1874 as the UCT launched its Bachelor of Laws (LLB) program. The program taught a combination of Roman, Roman-Dutch, and English law. Although its jurisprudential orientation was dominated by English positivism it retained a commitment to keeping Roman-Dutch law alive at the Cape (Chanock 2001; Cowen and Visser 2004; Greenbaum 2009). Thus aspirant law students could acquire legal education locally as well as abroad by the mid-nineteenth century.

The turn of the twentieth century marked a key point in the country's development. South Africa was unified in 1910, consolidating British Colonies in the Cape and Natal with Afrikaner colonies in the Orange Free State and Transvaal into a single national entity under British rule. Excluded from this union were the indigenous African population and colored and Indian people. Patently, this development was measured to increase white despotism, as Mamdani writes, "the union was forged around one key principle, rule by decree over natives; in the person of the governor, the union was like an armed fist over native heads" (1996: 63). In this increasingly racialized milieu, the expansion of local legal education gathered momentum. In 1918, the UCT law program was institutionalized into a department, becoming the country's first law faculty. In 1921, law departments were established at the University of Stellenbosch and the University of the Witwatersrand (Wits) in Johannesburg. Stellenbosch relied on Afrikaans as the language of instruction and emphasized Roman-Dutch law, while Wits operated in English and launched its legal certificate program to cater for growing mining and related industries in Johannesburg (Hunt 1963; Kahn 1997; Cowen and Visser 2004). Legal education of this period was divided not only along cultural and linguistic lines but also into different programs of study. English-speaking universities such as Wits and UCT adopted a liberal arts approach situating legal education among other disciplines. The University of South Africa and Afrikaans universities' approaches to legal education centered around law with few nonlegal courses included in the curriculum (Midgley 2010). Following these models, universities' law faculties were founded in other parts of the country.

During this period, African students were not officially barred from higher education, indeed the first African medical students at UCT and Wits were admitted in the early 1900s.[1] African law students, however, were not admitted into the country's law faculties until the middle decades of the

---

[1] In the main these were health science students motivated by the state's desire to ensure the availability of some black health workers to serve the black population. See Murray 1982.

twentieth century. In an early iteration of transnational student flows, they along with their white counterparts studied abroad if they had the means. This process was not immune to the racial divisions of the day. For instance, white students' educational ties to the metropole were strengthened by personal capital and initiatives such as the Rhodes scholarship, which functioned as tools to further the globalization of knowledge (Schaeper and Schaeper 2010). These students returned to take up prized positions in the legal profession and legal academy. UCT's early full-time law professors George Willie and John Wylie in the twentieth century exemplify this trend (Cowen and Visser 2004).[2] The same could not be said for African students. Notable examples of African lawyers who trained abroad include Alfred Mangena, who trained at Lincoln's Inn in 1903 before being called to the bar in 1908, becoming the first black South African to qualify as a barrister in the United Kingdom. Mangena returned to South Africa in 1910 and sought admission as an attorney.[3] His admission was granted by the Court but not before the Law Society had opposed his admission on the basis of his being a member of "one of the native races" (Mangena v Law Society 1910 TPD 649). Richard Msimang was the first black South African to qualify as a solicitor of England and Wales in 1912. Msimang, like Mangena before him, attained his legal education in the metropole, reading law at Queens College, in Somerset. Msimang returned to South Africa and was admitted as an attorney in June 1913. Pixely ka Isaka Seme, one of the founders of the African National Congress, took a cosmopolitan path to the legal profession. He attended Columbia University in New York, where he completed his Bachelor of Arts, picked up an American accent, and gave his prize winning speech, "The Regeneration of Africa," rejecting racism and colonization (Killingray 2012; Ngqulunga 2017). He then went on to Oxford University to read law. While he did not complete his legal studies at Oxford, he did complete his legal training, being called to the bar at Middle Temple in London. Seme returned to South Africa in 1910 where he was admitted as an attorney

---

[2] George Willie was born in Graaf Reinet South Africa and attended school in England before going on to obtain his BA LLB at Cambridge before being called to the bar at Middle Temple in 1903. John Wylie studied law at the University of Edinburgh, and London receiving his MA LLB there before being admitted as an advocate of the Scottish Bar.

[3] The Law Society argued that allowing Africans to practice would encourage litigation among Africans and undermine the state's policy of directing all African issues through the Natives administration. The courts declined to accept the Law Society's argument and found no reason in law that barred Africans from practice. After its unsuccessful legal challenge, the Law Society refused to admit African lawyers, thus hampering their ability to find chambers or to build a successful practice through administrative means.

(Ngcukaitobi 2018). These British-trained lawyers returned to South Africa to find racial tensions on the rise, which limited their prospects of successfully practicing as lawyers. They did, however, through their presence and organizing activities, challenge the racial orthodoxy, while also contributing to a broader narrative of lawyer-resistance to colonialism (Gibbs 2020; Oguamanam and Pue 2007; Krishnan and Ajagbe 2018).

In this period, law faculties were oriented toward training legal practitioners. Master's and Doctoral degrees in law were not available locally. Those seeking to earn postgraduate degrees in law studied abroad. To regulate entry into the legal profession for graduates, who were now by and large locally trained, Parliament enacted the Attorneys, Notaries and Conveyancers Admission Act in 1934. This act laid the basis of the country's two-part system of legal education. The first part being academic, and the second premised on vocational training as an apprentice to an established lawyer (Greenbaum 2009). Both phases were influenced by entrenched racial biases. University admission decisions and racial policy were at the discretion of the universities themselves. Wits and UCT pursued an "open" model where admissions were based primarily on academic criteria; Afrikaans universities instituted a color bar remaining closed to black students (Murray 1982; Cowen and Visser 2004). It was only in the 1940s that Africans were admitted to study law at the country's English-speaking universities. This situation reflected the prevailing racial sentiments but was also motivated by a desire to prevent Africans from competing with white legal professionals (Murray 1982). To be sure, English universities were only partially "open." For instance, Wits had a policy of "academic non-segregation and social segregation" (B. Murray 1990: 650). This curious policy required that black students be treated impartially in all academic matters but ensured that they remained segregated from the rest of the student body in residence, sports, and social gatherings.

In this hostile environment, African students experienced marginalization and discrimination from some of their peers and instructors. The history of the Wits School of Law's most famous nongraduate student illustrates the peculiar difficulties faced by African students in accessing legal education in the 1940s. Nelson Mandela enrolled at Wits School of Law as the first African student to enroll since it became "open" to all races in 1943. Like many of his instructors, Mandela could only commit part of his time to his legal studies. Indeed, the law faculty was inchoate and meager by contemporary standards, with only a handful of full-time faculty, the majority of the faculty being engaged in legal practice (Kahn 1989; Murray 2016). Mandela wrote his final examinations for his LLB three times. He was unsuccessful each time. Finally, he wrote to the then dean of the Wits Faculty of Law, Professor H.R. Hahlo, requesting that he receive credit for the courses he had passed and asking that he be allowed to write supplementary examinations in the remaining courses. The request was met unsympathetically and denied by the law faculty. Mandela subsequently abandoned his LLB and sought instead to be admitted as an attorney by completing the attorney's examination. He was admitted as an attorney in 1951 (Murray 2016).

Despite the financial and academic hurdles facing black students, a greater problem may have been subtle and overt discrimination they experienced in "open" universities. In his autobiography, Mandela recalls then Dean Hahlo's racism and misogyny, saying, "his view was that law was a social science and that women and Africans were not disciplined enough to master its intricacies. He once told me I should not be at Wits but studying for my degree through UNISA" (Mandela 1995: 90). Mandela was not alone in experiencing racial discrimination within the "open" Wits institution. Duma Nokwe, a law student in this era, recalls the gratuitous advice given to him by then Dean Hahlo, who said "that he [Nokwe] should give up law as he was wasting his time, since Africans were incapable of passing the law examinations" (Joseph 1963: 168). Spurred on by this affront, Nokwe became the first African to graduate from Wits School of Law in 1955, passing his law examinations and enrolling as an advocate. Nokwe joined Mandela and others in resisting apartheid within the African National Congress. The experiences of Mandela and Nokwe highlight not only the tradition of lawyer resistance to colonial-apartheid but also the prejudice that permeated certain quarters of the "open" white universities. However, duplicitous as it was, this space of multiracial legal education was fleeting and contracted with the emergence of apartheid.

The rise of apartheid in 1948 had profound effects on South African legal culture and influenced the development of legal education. In this context, racial and ethnic discrimination, already a hallmark of the colonial period, took on increasingly juridical forms. In the apartheid era, university admissions became increasingly politicized in line with the government's racial policies. The government's laissez-faire policy on higher education changed with the coming to power of the National Party. In 1950, the government instituted a blanket ban on the admission of foreign African students. Constraints on admissions policies increased with the passing of the Extension of University Education Act in 1959. Contrary to its title, this law restricted black students' access to "white" universities, requiring special ministerial approval before they could be admitted. Institutions, such as Wits and UCT, which had previously admitted modest numbers of black law students, now had to revise their admissions policies (Murray 1990).

Apartheid in higher education also ushered in an era of separate and unequal tuition. This saw the establishment of distinct institutions for students based on their racial designation. "African," "Indian," and "colored" persons were sorted into institutions which corresponded with their racial classification. The government strategically expanded opportunities for black students in an effort to train staff for the administrations of quasi-independent "Bantustans." This saw the creation of law faculties at the Universities of Fort Hare, the North, Zululand, Bophuthatswana, and Transkei. The expansion of black universities was calculated to entrench segregation and meant that numbers of black students at white institutions dwindled. While there were some pockets of excellence, on the whole these were lower tier institutions, located far away from commercial centers in rural areas and lacking the facilities and resources to compete with "white" universities (Iya 2001; Gibbs 2020).

The differences among universities ensured graduates from "black" law schools were looked down upon as they sought employment at leading firms (Greenbaum 2009; Murray 1982). Despite the segregated legal education system, some African law students managed to tap into channels of transnational education, which were the preserve of white South Africans. For instance, Sandile Ngcobo and Sisi Khamepe, both graduates of the University of Zululand, went on to receive the LLM degrees at Harvard Law School receiving Fulbright and Harvard South Africa fellowships, respectively, before going on to sit on the country's highest court. To be sure, those who managed to graduate from black institutions constituted an elite few, for most prospective lawyers were screened out before higher education. Although there was no strict prohibition on Africans entering the legal profession, the effects of decades of structural racial discrimination ensured that few Africans would attain the educational requirements required to pursue a career in legal practice. This grim reality was ensured by the system of Bantu education enacted in 1953, which prepared Africans for employment in only the most menial occupations. Under Bantu education policy, the missionary schools which had educated early African lawyers were forced to lower the quality of their curriculums or close. Thus narrowing one of the pathways that had produced the country's first black lawyers (Pruitt 2002; Broun 2000).

Under apartheid, the country's stratified social structure was mirrored in legal education, which offered a hierarchical range of pathways into the profession. Students had the option of pursuing one of three qualifications depending on their racial classification. The first, and most prized, was the LLB degree, which usually comprised a two- or three-year postgraduate degree, preceded by an undergraduate degree in the arts, commerce, or science. The second pathway was a Baccalaureus Procurationis (B Proc), which replaced the law certificate program in 1979 and qualified graduates to practice as attorneys. A third path was the Baccalaureus Juris (B Juris). This program was three years long and qualified graduates, often those of black universities, to work in the public administration of justice either as prosecutors or magistrates. The second and third routes were favored by black universities which adopted a more pragmatic law centered curriculum (Greenbaum 2009).

The structure of legal education under apartheid, with its color bars and tiers of academic qualifications, was designed to reproduce social inequalities. Judged by this wicked standard, it was a success. In 1994, African, Indian, and colored lawyers made up a mere 14 percent of the profession, with the remainder consisting of white lawyers (Pruitt 2002). The culmination of racial discrimination in legal education and the market ensured that the legal profession was a white domain; one dominated overwhelmingly by men. In the corporate legal sector, white firms enjoyed the bulk of commercial work, reaping the benefits of the country's integration with European and North American corporations. The few African firms were on the whole relegated to less lucrative and prestigious areas of practice (Iya 1997). The judiciary was overwhelmingly white, with very few women represented. Legal academia was no different with virtually no black scholars. The situation was only marginally improved by the numbers of black instructors at black universities (Greenbaum 2009; Pruitt 2002).

A. The Ideology of Apartheid Legal Education

The country's checkered social context shaped the content of legal education. The racially discriminatory order was bolstered by the prevalent ideology of legal education. The legal education of this era was premised on narrow, technical, and positivist approaches to law, which elided engagement with the racialized social context in which the law operated. This approach was buttressed by a doctrine of parliamentary sovereignty, which gave primacy to legislation and left few avenues to challenge state policy. Teaching decontextualized law allowed universities to function within the settler-colonial polity, producing local elites for the corporate services market and the bench while rarely posing a threat to the apartheid order. Legal education under apartheid found itself mired in the paradoxes of colonial modes of thought, as Dlamini points out:

> To admit that the great bulk of South African law was unjust and discriminatory would have created another moral conflict for many law teachers. Besides the fact that apartheid was meant to protect white people in this country, the attitude of white people in general has been that black people are different from them. Their institutions, including their law, has largely been regarded as primitive, undeveloped and uncivilized. South African law, on the other hand, has been regarded as the epitome of civilization, development and modernity. Its imposition on blacks was therefore regarded by its custodians as a boon to them (1992: 600).

The preoccupation with maintaining white supremacy ensured that South African legal education remained premised on its hybrid civil law–common law system, which emphasized traditional methods of legal reasoning which tended toward maintaining the repressive social order. This bred parochialism, closing the country off to major geopolitical developments such as the Atlantic Charter and the rise of international human rights norms, encapsulated by the UN Declaration on Universal Human Rights of 1948. This insularity also precluded engagement with significant regional developments such as the creation of African legal education in the 1960s. This position was in stark contrast to the legal education movements taking place in decolonizing African countries, as Burgis-Kasthala (Chapter 3) illustrates in this volume. However, the legal education of this era resists categorization as purely parochial. Instead, it was marked by inconsistencies and internal contradictions, as Boulle observes:

> There was a quasi-global dimension in four respects. The first was a historical reach in references to the great civil lawyers of the eighteenth century, in particular those from Holland, but also from French and Swiss civil lawyers. This was supplemented by references to modern civil law scholars, in particular those from Germany. Secondly, there were references to Roman law

sources such as Justinian's Corpus Iuris Civilis from the sixth century AD, an even greater historical reach, sometimes reinforced by the use of original Latin texts in student assessment requirements. Thirdly, there were necessary references to English common law, particularly in commercial areas such as corporations or insolvency, and extensively in adjectival disciplines such as the laws of evidence and procedure. Finally, there were occasional references to other systems based on Roman law, such as Scots or Sri Lankan law (2014: 53).

The lack of basic acknowledgment of principles of justice shrouded legal education in apartheid's callousness and stilted South African legal thought. However, the dominant position was not monolithic. The 1970s saw the emergence of law clinics which adopted a more contextualized approach to law, placing the realities of the many facing apartheid's harsh legal edifice at the center of their work. These clinics, supported by the Ford Foundation, provided legal services for indigent clients while training students in legal skills (Klerk 2005; Maisel 2006; McClymont and Golub 2000). Their socially oriented work buttressed the work of other organizations such as the Centre for Applied Legal Studies at Wits, which provided popular human rights education and the Legal Resources Centre, which conducted strategic litigation, challenging aspects of the apartheid order through legal means (Abel 1995).

The pernicious impact of apartheid on legal education was reflected in the proceedings of the Truth and Reconciliation Commission where professional bodies, including the General Council of the Bar (GCB), the Association of Law Societies (ALS), and the Society of Law Teachers conceded that under apartheid: "Legal education and training had been largely uncritical of unjust legal dogma and practice. Those few academics who had dared to speak out had received insufficient support from their colleagues and institutions" (Truth and Reconciliation Commission of South Africa 1999: 96–97). As the Commission observed, the country's institutions of legal education were complicit in maintaining apartheid rule by law. The Commission noted in particular the abetting role of legal academia, condemning "[l]aw teachers who chose to concentrate on 'safe' areas of the law or to teach in such a way that no critical ability was imparted to the students. [And] Students who chose to be blinded by the glamour and material returns of the conventional mainstream of the profession, neglecting [their] potential role as fighters for justice for all in South Africa" (Truth and Reconciliation Commission of South Africa 1999: 102–103).

III. Regearing Legal Education Post-apartheid: Facing and Contesting Transformation

The fall of apartheid in the early 1990s marked the beginning of a new chapter in South Africa's history. Nelson Mandela captured the spirit of the age, proclaiming: "[T]he time has come for South Africa to take up its rightful and responsible place in the community of nations" (Mandela 1993: 97). As Mandela asserted, the "new" South Africa would seek to be a global actor, guided by human rights norms and involved in regional as well as international affairs. The promise of transformation was particularly pertinent for the legal profession. For elite firms, this period ushered in an age of globalization which saw the country's largely white law firms at the center of new economic opportunities, partnering with international firms and expanding their operations across the continent (Klaaren 2015). For legal education, however, the country's transition from authoritarianism to democracy was fraught with uncertainty and contestations. The tension was manifest in the disjuncture between the country's human rights–centered transformational aspiration and its reality of conservative positivist legal education. In this context, Klare observed that "South Africa's legal culture and legal education are in need of a transformation or leavening that will bring them into closer harmony with the values and aspirations enacted in the Constitution" (1998: 151). Transformation discourse in legal education is premised on demographic diversification of staff and student profiles (Centre for Applied Legal Studies 2014), coupled with epistemic transformation and the creation of a legal culture which conforms with the principles enshrined in the Constitution (Davis 2015). The state, universities, and the private sector have been influential in shaping both.

In 1994, legal education was firmly controlled by white academics (Iya 1997). Importantly, however, the transition to democracy created greater opportunities for individual black lawyers and black lawyers' organizations to influence legal education. As Midgley points out, the influence of black lawyers increased as "a number of black lawyers either returned to, or came to, South Africa with qualifications from other countries, some of which had systems quite foreign to that in South Africa. Some, mainly returning South Africans, found themselves in government; others, often from East and West Africa, were academic appointments" (Midgley 2010: 102–103). These lawyers and organizations such as the Black Lawyers Association (BLA) and National Association of Democratic Lawyers (NADEL) had, under apartheid, supported the entry of black lawyers into the profession through continuing legal education and capacity building for black lawyers once they entered the profession. The transitional period saw them wield greater influence in the debates about transformation in the legal profession. Some of these lawyers, now in influential government positions, urged transformation in the legal profession from within the state and private sector.

The state played a leading role in reforming legal education, establishing a National Consultative Forum in 1994 to promote dialogue among key stakeholders in legal education. Following this conference, a unit was established within the Department of Justice to articulate a policy for transformation in the legal profession (Greenbaum 2015; Whitear-Nel and Freedman 2015). In 1995, the Department of Justice published its "Justice Vision 2000," a policy document which made it clear that the future of the legal profession would differ markedly from that of the apartheid era. A key concern the document considered was how to ensure that the legal profession was demographically representative of broader society. While stopping short of providing recommendations, it outlines key challenges facing legal education. These include the question of how to best transform the system of legal education, values that legal education should adopt, and the extent to which legal education should be geared toward private practice. Another concern was how to allocate resources so as to ensure the transformation of the legal profession and representation for disadvantaged groups (Ministry of Justice 1995).

With transformation firmly on the agenda, attention turned to the disparate pathways into the legal profession. In 1995, the Department of Justice requested the deans of South African law schools, representatives of the legal profession, and government officials to make submissions for a new framework for legal education. In formulating its report, this task group drew heavily on the First Report on Legal Education and Training by the Lord Chancellor's Advisory Committee on Legal Education and Conduct in England. This task group has been criticized for its limited consultative process and relying too heavily on the English model while failing to engage its local context (Whitear-Nel and Freedman 2015; Woolman, Watson, and Smith 1997). Following the English position, the task group argued that faculties should determine the content of their curricula. Ironically, this latitude, premised on academic freedom, allowed many faculties to stall, circumvent, and undermine transformation efforts, adopting a business as usual approach to legal education despite the country's vast legal changes (Greenbaum 2015).

With curriculum reform left largely to individual institutions, the debate turned to how to reform the entry qualification framework in order to facilitate entry into the profession for underrepresented groups. Here the concern appears to have been creating a national qualification that addressed local inequities, rather than a desire to reproduce a global standard. To fast-track entry into the legal profession for historically disadvantaged groups, the task group proposed an undergraduate LLB degree taught over four years as the single entry qualification for legal practice. On this issue there was clear dissensus among stakeholders. As Midgley observes: "the response from the professions and from the universities was defensive and focused primarily on maintaining the status quo—under the guise of maintaining academic and professional standards, and thereby the status of the legal professions, and protecting the public from lawyers that were either incapable or inadequately prepared and who should not be offering legal services to the public" (2010: 105). The universities, led by historically English institutions, were largely opposed to the introduction of a single LLB criteria, arguing that the program would diminish their academic integrity by making them responsible for practical training, which they argued was the responsibility of the profession. On the other hand, black universities were more amenable to the change given that the proposed change was not too dissimilar from their traditional B Proc and B Juris offerings. A compromise was reached, making the four-year LLB the entry qualification common among all universities. The task group agreed that while the content of the curriculum would not be fixed, it would be grounded in the local context and move away from the eurocentric model. It would also feature some vocational skills and emphasize legal ethics to satisfy the concerns of the profession (Whitear-Nel and Freedman 2015). The Qualification of Legal Practitioners Amendment Act was passed in 1997 to give effect to this change, and the new qualification was offered in 1998.

The new LLB attempted to balance academic rigor and skills development. It also had the aim of increasing participation in legal education for disadvantaged black students for whom the financial costs of the previous pathways were prohibitively high. It is not the only qualification option, however. The influence of the market saw more universities supplement their traditional BA LLB offerings by introducing a five-year BCom LLB (see Figure 4.1),

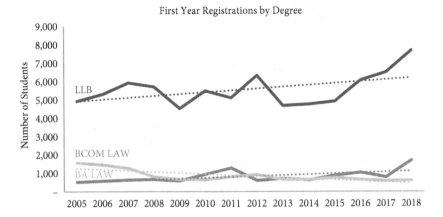

Figure 4.1
Source: Law Society of South Africa 2018.

which attracted students interested in working in the corporate legal sector (Midgley 2010; Greenbaum 2015).

Of the three qualification options available, registrations data suggest that the LLB is the preferred route into the legal profession among students. Between 2005 and 2018, the vast majority of registrants opted for the LLB. Indeed, there is an inverse relationship between LLB and BCom Law degrees among first-year, first registrations. This sees first-year LLB registrations growing annually, on average, 3.5 percent while first-year BCom Law registrations declined at –7 percent in the same period.

The transition from apartheid also saw a restructuring of higher education "from a fragmented and structurally racialised system of 36 public and more than 300 private institutions in 1994 to a relatively (at least formally) more integrated system of 26 public universities" (Department of Higher Education and Training 2015). For law schools, this meant merging some institutions and rebranding as smaller schools and technikons were incorporated into larger universities (Midgley 2010). The result was consolidation into seventeen public law schools. The public legal education system is overseen by the Department of Education, which subsidizes institutions according to a national policy. The department's policy prioritizes improving academic activity, transformation and ensuring that previously disadvantaged groups enjoy greater access to education. Midgley describes this policy as "a steering mechanism"—"a goal-directed, distributive mechanism which relates government funds to academic activity and output"—and funds will be allocated, amongst others, according to government's policy priorities and academic activity which leads to "improvements in the social and economic conditions of the country" (Midgley 2010: 112).

While some private institutions have emerged in the post-apartheid era, they have not significantly captured the legal education market. One such institution, Monash University of Australia, became the country's first foreign university when it established its Johannesburg campus in 2001 under its internationalization plan (Setswe 2013). The venture, however, was short-lived, with the university selling its undertaking to the Independent Institute of Education, South Africa's largest private higher education provider, in 2018 (Monash University 2018).[4] The university now operates under the IIE MSA moniker and offers a post-graduate LLB program, which promises graduates "the ability to participate in an increasingly complex and dynamic local and global economy" (IIE MSA 2021). The number of privately educated law graduates may be set to increase. Recently, the Independent Institute of Education won a major legal battle when the Constitutional Court ruled in favor of allowing LLB graduates of accredited private institutions to enroll as candidate attorneys with law societies under the Legal Practice Act of 2014 (Independent Institute of Education v Kwazulu-Natal Law Society 2020 (2) SA 325 CC).

Another key area of public involvement has been the provision of local ratings for researchers through the National Research Foundation (NRF). The NRF supports research and innovation by encouraging researchers to partner with international institutions and collaborators. The introduction of ratings in law has had important consequences for legal education. As Midgley points out, "[a]cademics, especially from those universities that have bought into the rating system, now concentrate far more on their international profiles and faculties are less inward-looking than before and encourage contact with sister institutions around the world. This has begun to break the isolation and insular thinking that characterized the apartheid years and it may well encourage more theoretical, discipline-orientated

---

[4] Monash University reported, "MSA has operated as a joint venture between US-based majority owner Laureate Education (75 per cent) and Monash University (25 per cent) since 2013. In 2017, both Monash University and Laureate agreed to explore the possibility of concluding the joint venture, having determined that the next phase of development of the campus would be best managed under custodianship of a local operator better suited to operate in the South African education market.

"The IIE operates across 21 sites in South Africa offering registered and accredited higher education programmes from Higher Certificate to Masters level at its Varsity College, Vega, and Rosebank College campuses and 35,000 students at Higher Education level."

research over more practice-orientated approaches" (Midgley 2010: 117). Thus this mechanism has provided an incentive to researchers to not only raise the quality of the research but also to locate it within a broader global context.

The profession, represented by the Law Society, has also been influential in shaping post-apartheid legal education. While the Law Society is primarily concerned with vocational training for attorneys, it also exerts influence on academic legal education. Perhaps unsurprisingly given its affiliation with the profession, the Law Society has lobbied for greater practical skills and training, focusing on practice management. The Law Society has also expressed its concern about the numeracy and literacy skills of law graduates. To remedy these shortcomings, it has partnered with some universities to shape curricula. The Law Society has leveraged financial support as a means of advancing its policy. Partnering with the Attorneys Fidelity Fund, it has incentivized universities to adopt projects that serve the interests of the profession by offering financial assistance to programs that incorporate its objectives (Midgley 2010).

IV. Transformation and Its Discontents: Crises in the Age of Globalization

As the dust settled on the post-apartheid reforms to legal education, a less than optimal picture emerged. On one hand, the number of graduates had increased, as did the numbers of black and female graduates. Indeed, the growth of female LLB graduates outpaced that of males between 2009 and 2017, growing on average 8 percent compared to 3 percent among males. Following contemporary legal trends in other parts of the world (Michelson 2013), in 2017, females constituted 57 percent of the total LLB graduating class (Law Society of South Africa 2018). Between 2009 and 2017, the number of Africans in the LLB graduate population grew an average of 14 percent each year (3,062 African LLB graduates in 2017), far surpassing the average annual growth of Indian (6 percent) and colored (6 percent). The white population, in contrast, stagnated at an average annual growth of 1 percent between 2009 and 2017 (see Figure 4.2). Despite the marked diversification of legal education, the legal profession remained dominated by white lawyers, a trend which was particularly pronounced in the corporate hemisphere (Klaaren 2020). These developments take place as the country's

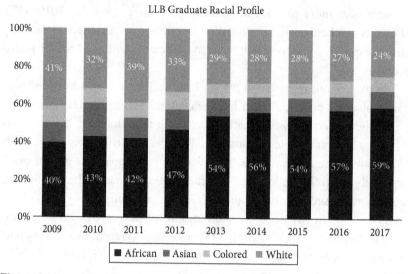

Figure 4.2
Source: Law Society of South Africa 2010–2018.

elite firms have sought to expand their regional influence, establishing tie-ups and establishing offices on the continent.

Yet as the number of graduates increased, so too did complaints from the profession regarding the quality and preparedness of law graduates for legal practice. In particular, a chorus of stakeholders in the attorney's profession, the public sector, and the judiciary expressed their concern at new LLB graduates' perceived lack of writing and numeracy skills. Many put these deficiencies down to the legal education system, and the four-year LLB in particular. Some argued for the reintroduction of a longer route toward legal qualification as had been the case under apartheid (Dibetle 2007). The opposing view was advanced by the chair of the South African Law Deans Association (SALDA), Midgley who, noting the necessities of raising standards to improve skills, favored maintaining the four-year curriculum in order to allow graduates to enter the market sooner and thus contribute to the economy (Dibetle 2007).

The growing discord surrounding legal education culminated in a conference in May 2013, convened jointly by the SALDA and the profession represented by the LSSA and the GCB. This conference was pointedly titled "LLB Summit: Legal Education in Crisis?" Its aim was to address problems surrounding the LLB curriculum, its deficiencies, and graduates' preparedness for the legal services market (Van Niekerk 2013). Among the outcomes of this summit was the creation of a working group comprised of legal academics and members of the Council on Higher Education (CHE), the body responsible for accrediting law faculties, to engage in a process of national standard setting for the LLB, led by legal academics. The process considered substantive legal knowledge, skills, and competencies, including literacy and numeracy as well as professional ethics and social justice concerns (Dicker 2013; Whitear-Nel and Freedman 2015). Following consultations, in 2015, the task group articulated a national LLB standard. This standard sets out the purpose and orientation of legal education. Its preamble outlines the significance of law to the country's nation-building project, affirming:

> Legal education as a public good should be responsive to the needs of the economy, the legal profession and broader society. It must produce skilled graduates who are critical thinkers and enlightened citizens with a profound understanding of the impact of the Constitution on the development of the law, and advancing the course of social justice in South Africa. Moreover, the law graduate must be equipped to discharge his or her social and professional duties ethically and efficaciously. Therefore, higher education must also be responsive to globalisation and the ever evolving information-technology (Council on Higher Education 2015: 7).

Another outcome of the Legal Education in Crisis summit was an undertaking to conduct a national review of the LLB program to assess all legal education institutions for reaccreditation. This review represents the most comprehensive analysis of post-apartheid legal education. Perhaps unsurprisingly given the country's deep historical inequities, the LLB review finds extensive disparities between institutions. Indeed, the review observes that "the gap between well-resourced and poorly-resourced faculties is wide" (Council on Higher Education 2018: 61). Many of these differences track the inequities of legal education under apartheid, and others reflect divergent approaches adopted by law schools in the post-apartheid era. The council expressed reservations on whether reforms to legal education were efficacious, finding that "it is doubtful whether the four-year first degree LLB programme is fit-for-purpose—to substantively meet the requirements set for legal education in the Standard" (Council on Higher Education 2018: 50). To remedy this deficiency, the CHE recommended that students be required to complete a degree in the arts or in commerce prior to undertaking a law degree or that the LLB be extended to five years to allow for the inclusion in the curriculum of nonlaw courses. The CHE also observed the persistence of rudimentary modes of tuition noting that "too often, students were assessed, either wholly or substantially, on their rote learning ability" (Council on Higher Education 2018: 57).

The review is critical of universities in a number of important areas. Not least among these was the goal of transformation. Here the CHE found that with few exceptions law faculties "have not yet fully internalised the notion of 'transformative constitutionalism"—either in their curricula or among the entire corpus of staff and students (Council on Higher Education 2018: 52). As such, the demographic composition of faculties remains problematic, with too few African South African instructors. The review found that no faculty, save the University of the Western Cape, "is representative of the national demographics" and that white staff are overrepresented on most faculties (Council on Higher Education 2018: 58).

Globalization is another matter on which legal education is sharply divided. While the country has positioned itself as a regional hub for international students in Southern Africa and Africa more broadly, perhaps unsurprisingly, the major destinations for international students are the country's historically white institutions; the universities of Cape Town, Stellenbosch, Witwatersrand, Pretoria, and Kwazulu Natal host the majority of these students (Kwaramba 2012). In its review, the CHE found inconsistent approaches to globalization of curricula across universities although it was generally satisfied. It asserted:

> The requirement of globalisation in the LLB Standard seems to have been adequately met by most faculties, with their various LLB programmes offering suites of modules, both core and elective, which address globalisation. However, in some faculties, although students are exposed to modules like Public International Law, Private International Law and Business Law, these modules are focused on preparing students for practicing law in South Africa—and not as a response to globalization . . . By contrast, some faculties have sought to reinforce the "globalisation" of their LLB programme, by revising the curriculum to more deeply infuse regional, continental and global developments in the law (Council on Higher Education 2018: 19–20).

While much of the discontent surrounding legal education has stemmed from stakeholders such as the state, the market, and universities, 2015 saw the (re-)emergence of university students as a powerful force in the country's higher education system (Andrews 2018). Organized around slogans such as #RhodesMustFall and #FeesMustFall, these movements introduced a radical anticolonial critique of higher education in South Africa. These student movements argue that the curricula, methods, and iconography of higher education retain remnants of the colonial era. As such, these "fallist" student movements reject the modest reforms of past generations, drawing on the ideas of Biko and Fanon to put black consciousness and decolonization squarely on the agenda (Ahmed 2017). The movement also draws attention to the cost of higher education which, for many, remains prohibitively high. While not specifically aimed at legal education, the fallist movements have had profound impact on law faculties, fueling greater urgency to Africanize amidst growing criticism of the constitutional settlement and the notion of transformative constitutionalism itself (Modiri 2018; Sibanda 2020). The growing calls for decolonization have not escaped the CHE, which in its LLB review found that, much like the goal of transformative constitutionalism, the goal of decolonization in curricula remains largely unmet. As the council observed:

> Decolonisation speaks to the need to transform the LLB curriculum and the teaching and learning content of applicable modules in a manner that, while mindful of constitutional norms and principles, steers a clear path between the need to "Africanise" the curriculum and the need to educate students on the globalized environment within which law is practised. African-based themes and an African context must permeate law teaching far more than is currently the case—but in a way that does not neglect the importance of maintaining a global perspective on national and international law (Council on Higher Education 2018: 54).

Building on calls for decolonized legal education, law students from fifteen of the country's seventeen law faculties hosted a "Law Students' Conference on the Decolonisation and Africanisation of Legal Education in 2019" (Lansink and Jegede 2020). This conference, held at the university of Venda, a historically black university, advanced new themes which seek to disrupt the orthodoxy of South African legal education (Letsoalo and Pero 2020). The emergence of de-colonial discourse and a push toward Africanization understandably lags behind other African states in which these ideas were articulated early in the postindependence era (Ghai and McAuslan 1970). It does, however, promise to reinvigorate and challenge South African legal education, bringing it closer to the concerns of the majority of the population, who have been marginalized for much of its development. These debates, raised in the context of seemingly recurring student protests, underscore the enduring crises in legal education as evidenced by persistent racialized structural inequities between institutions.

The crisis is borne out by the struggles of former Bantustan universities such as Walter Sisulu University (WSU), formerly the University of Transkei. This historically black institution was established to produce Bantustan technocrats and has struggled to transition to a comprehensive developmental institution in the post-apartheid era. After years of malaise, it lost its LLB accreditation in 2018 owing to its mismanagement and lack of qualified teachers and adequate facilities, including functional classrooms (Council on Higher Education 2018). The university has since regained its accreditation after addressing a number of issues, including the instructors and educational facilities. Some of the blame for the institution's woes may lie elsewhere, however. As Ngcukaitobi, chair of the WSU council, argues, the Department of Education's research centered funding formula "is largely biased against black universities, because most of these institutions are not research intensive" (Macupe 2021). The challenges facing black universities are not limited to WSU. Former Bantustan University of Zululand has seen student protests over the adequacies of accommodation facilities which students describe as "inhumane" (Macupe 2019). Similarly, the University of Fort Hare, once a training ground for the African elite, was in jeopardy as it was placed under administration following a protracted governance crisis (Linden 2019). The challenges at historically black universities are particularly problematic given their role in educating black lawyers. In 2017, 22 percent (1,118) of the total LLB graduating class received their education from former Bantustan institutions.

At the other end of the spectrum, the country's elite institutions boast internationally recognized research outputs, faculties that include "former Rhodes Scholars and Alexander von Humboldt fellows," "exceptionally strong and varied international ties," and "students from all over South Africa, Africa—and at LLM level from many other parts of world" (Cowen and Visser 2004: 145). Contemporary tensions in higher education are fueled by the persistent cleavage between the country's well-resourced institutions and its underserved population. While much of the attention in debates over legal education centers on university education (Quinot and Van Tonder 2015), the problems may stem from elsewhere. As Godfrey points out, his interviews with legal practitioners suggest that the cause of graduates' underpreparedness was down to the education they received prior to university. The inadequacies, he argues, are inherent in the country's unequal education system, which is not only divided along racial and class lines but also exhibits a prominent rural urban divide. As a result, universities are not adequately prepared to address these deficiencies (Godfrey 2009). Indeed, the focus on the duration of the LLB tends to elide deeper questions about students' ability to succeed in higher education given the educational challenges they face before university, not least the important role of language. South Africa is a multilingual country with eleven official languages, yet university education is conducted largely in English or Afrikaans. As result, many students find themselves learning in a second or third language, which compounds literacy and numeracy problems (Balfour 2007; Dladla 2020). This fact is not lost on the Department of Education, which asserts that "the lack of epistemological transformation is further reflected in the role of language in higher education . . . the language issue is undoubtedly one of the main obstacles to academic success for the majority of black students" (Department of Education 2008).

V. Conclusion

The narrative of globalization in South Africa's legal education is, like much of its history, a segregated one. The deep racialized inequalities between law faculties have produced a fragmented legal education system in which the benefits of globalization are unequally distributed. The stubborn persistence of racialized inequalities in the South African legal education and its legal profession are legacies of colonial and apartheid history. This legacy has proved Janus-faced, at once allowing the country's legal education system to develop as a regional hub for higher education, bearing connections to higher education institutions in the metropole, attracting international students, and favorable rankings. Yet on the on the other the hand, it has excluded the majority of the society. Its colonial origins now put the country's systems of higher education in a quandary amid calls for universities to function as institutions as engines for social justice, which blare alongside competing calls for universities to position themselves as global institutions, prioritize the metrics of global success, and market themselves to a wider international audience (Swartz et al. 2019). This fractured social context has defined the character of South African legal education since its inception and ensured that contemporary processes of globalization are prefigured by the inequities that characterized earlier globalization under colonial rule. As such, the challenge that legal education faces amidst increasing global interconnectivity is a long-standing one: how to ensure equity in its legal education.

References

Abel, Richard (1995). *Politics by Other Means: Law in the Struggle against Apartheid, 1980–1994.* Routledge.

Ahmed, Kayum (2017). "#RhodesMustFall: Decolonization, Praxis and Disruption," *Journal of Comparative & International Higher Education* 9: 8–13.

Andrews, Penelope (2018). "Race, Inclusiveness and Transformation of Legal Education in South Africa," in Rosalind Dixon and Theunis Roux, eds., *Constitutional Triumphs, Constitutional Disappointments: A Critical Assessment of the 1996 South African Constitution's Local and International Influence.* Pp. 223–251. Cambridge University Press.

Balfour, Robert (2007). "University Language Policies, Internationalism, Multilingualism, and Language Development in South Africa and the UK," *Cambridge Journal of Education* 37(1): 35–49.

Botha, Graham (1924). "Early Legal Practitioners of the Cape Colony," *South African Law Journal* 41(3): 255–261.

Boulle, Laurence (2014). "Isolationism, Democratisation and Globalisation: Legal Education in a Developing Country," in William van Caenegem and Mary Hiscock eds., *The Internationalisation of Legal Education.* Pp. 48–69. Edward Elgar Publishing.

Broun, Kenneth (2000). *Black Lawyers, White Courts: The Soul of South African Law.* Ohio University Press.

Centre for Applied Legal Studies (2014). Transformation of the Legal Profession. https://www.wits.ac.za/media/wits-university/faculties-and-schools/commerce-law-and-management/research-entities/cals/documents/programmes/gender/Transformation%20of%20the%20Legal%20Profession.pdf.

Chanock, Martin (1985). *Law, Custom, and Social Order: The Colonial Experience in Malawi and Zambia.* African Studies Series 45. Cambridge University Press.

Chanock, Martin (2001). *The Making of South African Legal Culture 1902–1936: Fear, Favour and Prejudice.* Cambridge University Press. 1st ed.

Council on Higher Education (2015). Qualifications Standard for Bachelor of Laws (LLB). https://www.univen.ac.za/docs/Standards_for_Bachelor_of_Laws_ %20LLB%20final%20version_20150921.pdf.

Council on Higher Education (2018). The State of the Provision of the Bachelor of Laws (LLB) Qualification in South Africa. http://www.derebus.org.za/wp-content/uploads/2019/06/CHE_LLB-National-Report_2018.pdf.

Cowen, Daniel and Denis Visser (2004). *The University of Cape Town Law Faculty: A History 1859–2004.* Siber Ink.

Davis, Dennis (2015). "Legal Transformation and Legal Education: Congruence or Conflict?," *Acta Juridica* 18: 172–188.

Department of Education (2008). Report of the Ministerial Committee on Transformation and Social Cohesion and the Elimination of Discrimination in Public Higher Education Institutions.https://ukzn.ac.za/wp-content/miscFiles/publications/Repo rtonHEandTransformation.pdf.

Department of Higher Education and Training (2015). Reflections on Higher Education Transformation. https://www.justice.gov.za/commissions/FeesHET/docs/2015-HESummit-Annexure05.pdf.

Dibetle, Monako (2007). "Quality of Law Degrees Questioned," *The Mail & Guardian.* November 14. https://mg.co.za/article/2007-11-14-quality-of-law-degrees-que stioned/.

Dicker, Leon (2013). "The 2013 LLB Summit," *Advocate.* August.

Dladla, Thokozani (2020). "Breaking The Language Barrier In Legal Education: A Method for Africanising Legal Education," *Pretoria Student Law Review* 14(1): 12.

Dlamini, Charles (1992). "The Law Teacher, the Law Student and Legal Education in South Africa," *South African Law Journal* 109(4): 17.

Erasmus, Hennie (2015). "The Beginnings of a Mixed System or, Advocates at the Cape during the Early Nineteenth Century, 1828–1850," *Fundamina* 21(2): 219–233.

Ghai, Yash and Patrick McAuslan (1970). *Public Law and Political Change in Kenya a Study of the Legal Framework of Government from Colonial Times to the Present.* Oxford University Press.

Gibbs, Timothy (2020). "Apartheid South Africa's Segregated Legal Field: Black Lawyers and the Bantustans," *Africa* 90(2): 293–317.

Godfrey, Shane (2009). "The Legal Profession: Transformation And Skills," *South African Law Journal* 126(1): 91–123.

Greenbaum, Lesley (2009). "A History of the Racial Disparities in Legal Education in South Africa," *John Marshall Law Journal* 3(1): 1–18.

Greenbaum, Lesley (2015). "Legal Education in South Africa: Harmonizing the Aspirations of Transformative Constitutionalism with Our Educational Legacy I. Twenty Years of South African Constitutionalism," *New York Law School Law Review* 60(2): 463–492.

Hunt, Peter (1963). "South Africa—The Faculty of Law, University of the Witwatersrand, Johannesburg Legal Education Supplement," *Journal of African Law* 7(2): 120–125.

IIE MSA (2021) "IIE Bachelor of Laws (LLB) Fact Sheet" https://www.iiemsa.co.za/fact-sheet/bachelor-of-laws-llb/

Iya, Philip (1997). "Reform of Legal Education in South Africa: Analysis of the New Challenge of Change," *The Law Teacher* 31(3): 310–325.

Iya, Philip (2001). "The Legal System and Legal Education in Southern Africa: Past Influences and Current Challenges," *Journal of Legal Education* 51(3): 355–362.

Joseph, Helen (1963). *If This Be Treason.* Andre Deutsch

Kaburise, John (2001). "The Structure of Legal Education in South Africa," *Journal of Legal Education* 51(3): 363–71.

Kahn, Ellison (1989). "The Wits Faculty of Law, 1922–1989: A Story with a Personal Touch," *Consultus* 2(2): 103–112.

Kahn, Ellison (1997). "The Wits Faculty of Law Turns 75: Ruminations on Its Yesterday, Today and Tomorrow by an Old-Stager," *South African Law Journal* 114(3): 511–541.

Killingray, David (2012). "Significant Black South Africans in Britain before 1912: Pan-African Organisations and the Emergence of South Africa's First Black Lawyers," *South African Historical Journal* 64(3): 393–417.

Klaaren, Jonathan (2015). "African Corporate Lawyering and Globalization," *International Journal of the Legal Profession* 22(2): 226–42.

Klaaren, Jonathan (2020). "South Africa: A Profession in Transformation," in Richard Abel, Ole Hammerslev, Hilary Sommerlad, and Ulrike Schultz, eds., *Lawyers in 21st-Century Societies.* Pp. 535–46 Hart Publishing.

Klare, Karl (1998). "Legal Culture and Transformative Constitutionalism," *South African Journal on Human Rights* 14(1): 146–188.

Klerk, Willem De (2005). "University Law Clinics In South Africa," *South African Law Journal* 122(4): 929–950.

Krishnan, Jayanth and Kunle Ajagbe (2018). "Legal Activism in the Face of Political Challenges: The Nigerian Case," *Journal of the Legal Profession* 42(2): 197–241.

Kwaramba, Marko (2012). "Internationalisation of Higher Education in Southern Africa with South Africa as a Major Exporter," *Journal of International Education and Leadership* 1: 22.

Lansink, Annette and Ademola Oluborode Jegede (2020). "Introduction to the Pretoria Student Law Review: Special Edition on the Decolonisation and Africanisation of Legal Education," *Pretoria Student Law Review* 14: ix–xv.

Law Society of South Africa (2018). Statistics For Legal Profession 2017/2018. https://www.lssa.org.za/wp-content/uploads/2019/11/LSSA-STATS-DOC-2017-18.pdf.

Letsoalo, Mankhuwe Caroline and Zenia Pero (2020). "Historically White Universities and the White Gaze: Critical Reflections on the Decolonisation of the LLB Curriculum," *Pretoria Student Law Review* 1(1): 1–11.

Linden, Aretha (2019). "Maladministration' Blamed as University of Fort Hare Placed under Administration," *TimesLIVE.* April 29. https://www.timeslive.co.za/news/south-africa/2019-04-29-maladministration-blamed-as-university-of-fort-hare-placed-under-administration/.

Macupe, Bongekile (2019). "UniZulu Students' Accommodation Conditions Are 'Inhumane'—The Mail & Guardian." https://mg.co.za/article/2019-04-26-00-unizulu-students-accommodationconditions-are-inhumane/.

Macupe, Bongekile (2021). "Ngcukaitobi, the New Sheriff at Walter Sisulu University," *The Mail & Guardian.* February 21.https://mg.co.za/education/2021-02-21-ngcukaitobi-at-walter-sisulu-university/.

Maisel, Peggy (2006). "Expanding and Sustaining Clinical Legal Education in Developing Countries: What We Can Learn from South Africa," *Fordham International Law Journal* 30(2): 374–420.

Mamdani, Mahmood (1996). *Citizen and Subject: Contemporary Africa and the Legacy of Late Colonialism.* Princeton University Press. 1st ed.

Mandela, Nelson (1993). "South Africa's Future Foreign Policy," *Foreign Affairs* 72(5): 86–97.

Mandela, Nelson (1995). *Long Walk to Freedom: The Autobiography of Nelson Mandela.* Back Bay Books.

McClymont, Mary and Stephen Golub, eds. (2000). *Many Roads to Justice: The Law-Related Work of Ford Foundation Grantees around the World.* Ford Foundation.

Michelson, Ethan (2013). "Women in the Legal Profession, 1970–2010: A Study of the Global Supply of Lawyers," *Indiana Journal of Global Legal Studies* 20(2): 1071–1137.

Midgley, Rob (2010). "South Africa: Legal Education in a Transitional Society," in *Stakeholders in the Law School*. 31. Pp. 97–126. Bloomsbury Publishing Plc.

Ministry of Justice (1995). Justice Vision 2000—A Strategic Plan for the Transformation and Rationalisation of the Administration of Justice. https://www.gov.za/sites/default/files/gcis_document/201409/justicevision2000s0.pdf.

Modiri, Joel M. (2018). "Conquest and Constitutionalism: First Thoughts on an Alternative Jurisprudence," *South African Journal on Human Rights* 34(3): 300–325.

Monash University. (2018). "Change of Ownership for Monash South Africa" https://www.monash.edu/news/articles/change-of-ownership-for-monash-south-africa

Murray, Bruce (1990). "Wits as an 'Open' University 1939–1959: Black Admissions to the University of the Witwatersrand," *Journal of Southern African Studies* 16(4): 649–676.

Murray, Bruce (2016). "Nelson Mandela and Wits University," *The Journal of African History* 57(2): 271–292.

Murray, Bruce (1982). *Wits, the Early Years: A History of the University of the Witwatersrand, Johannesburg, and Its Precursors, 1896–1939*. Witwatersrand University Press.

Ndulo, Muna (2002). "Legal Education in Africa in the Era of Globalization and Structural Adjustment," *Penn State International Law Review* 20(3): 487–503.

Ngcukaitobi, Tembeka (2018). *The Land Is Ours: South Africa's First Black Lawyers and the Birth of Constitutionalism*. Penguin Books, an imprint of Penguin Random House.

Ngqulunga, Bongani (2017). *The Man Who Founded the ANC: A Biography of Pixley Ka Isaka Seme*. Penguin Books.

Oguamanam, Chidi and Wes Pue (2007). "Lawyers' Professionalism, Colonialism, State Formation, and National Life in Nigeria, 1900–1960: 'The Fighting Brigade of the People,'" *Social Identities* 13(6): 769–785.

Popescu, Florentin (2015). "South African Globalization Strategies and Higher Education," *Procedia—Social and Behavioral Sciences* 209(December): 411–418.

Pruitt, Lisa (2002). "No Black Names on the Letterhead? Efficient Discrimination and the South African Legal Profession," *Michigan Journal of International Law* 23(3): 545–676.

Quinot, Geo and SP Van Tonder (2015). "The Potential of Capstone Learning Experiences in Addressing Perceived Shortcomings in LLB Training in South Africa," *Potchefstroom Electronic Law Journal/Potchefstroomse Elektroniese Regsblad* 17(4): 1350.

Schaeper, Thomas and Kathleen Schaeper (2010). *Rhodes Scholars, Oxford and the Creation of an American Elite*. Berghahn Books. Rev. ed.

Setswe, Geoffrey. (2013). "Private higher education in Africa: The Case of Monash South Africa," *Africa Education Review*, 10(1): 97–110.

Sibanda, Sanele (2020). "When Do You Call Time on a Compromise? South Africa's Discourse on Transformation and the Future of Transformative Constitutionalism," *Law, Democracy & Development* 24(1): 384–412.

Swartz, Rebecca, Mariya Ivancheva, Laura Czerniewicz, and Neil Morris (2019). "Between a Rock and a Hard Place: Dilemmas Regarding the Purpose of Public Universities in South Africa," *Higher Education* 77(4): 567–583.

Terreblanche, Sampie (2002). *A History of Inequality in South Africa 1652-2002*. University of KwaZulu-Natal Press.

Thompson, Leonard (2001). *A History of South Africa, Third Edition*. Yale University Press. 3d ed.

Truth and Reconciliation Commission of South Africa (1999). "Truth and Reconciliation Commission of South Africa Report," *Choice Reviews Online* 37(3): 37-1803–37-1803.

Van Niekerk, Carmel (2013). "The Four-Year Undergraduate LLB: Where to from Here?," *Obiter* 34(3): 533–544.

Ward, Kerry (2009). *Networks of Empire: Forced Migration in the Dutch East India Company.* Cambridge University Press.

Whitear-Nel, Nicola and Warren Freedman (2015). "A Historical Review of the Development of the Post-Apartheid South African LLB Degree—With Particular Reference to Legal Ethics," *Fundamina* 21(2): 234–250.

Wildenboer, Liezl (2010). "The Origins of the Division of the Legal Profession in South Africa: A Brief Overview," *Fundamina* 16(2): 199–225.

Woolman, Stuart, Pam Watson, and Nicholas Smith (1997). "Toto, I've a Feeling We're Not in Kansas Any More: A Reply to Professor Motala and Others on the Transformation of Legal Education in South Africa," *South African Law Journal* 114(1): 30–64.

Worden, Nigel (2012). *The Making of Modern South Africa: Conquest, Apartheid, Democracy.* Wiley-Blackwell. 5th ed.

5

Battles Around Legal Education Reform in India

From Entrenched Local Legal Oligarchies to Oligopolistic Universals

Yves Dezalay and Bryant Garth

This chapter focuses on battles around legal education reform, which have long played a strategic role in competing law and development efforts around the world. Numerous books and articles discuss what global law schools should be, what kind of teaching and clinical programs make for best practices, the quality of academic research, and the possibilities of access into the legal profession (Gane and Huang 2016; Jamin and van Caenegem 2016). The specific institutional focus of the studies—on categories such as the bar, the solicitors branch, faculties of law and law schools, judges, or even the "legal complex"—tends to neglect processes of capital conversion that characterize the law and lawyers in different settings. The categories must be deconstructed to see what goes into the law and the legal profession. One way to see processes of transformation and capital conversion is to draw on interconnected histories that reveal similarities and differences.

Our work on legal education focuses on three dimensions of a "legal revolution" in the sense employed by Harold Berman in his famous books on law and revolution (1983, 2003). Berman began with explanations of the Gregorian revolution in the tenth century and then applied the same analysis to the Protestant Reformation. In each case, he highlighted how learned capital of relatively marginal scholarly groups linked with emerging political movements and ultimately provided legitimacy and continuity for the new regime. The new law retained a connection to the established powers but also took on the new forms of capital made valuable through the state and social transformation/revolution. Legal education and learned law are thus important battlegrounds in legal revolutions.

Yves Dezalay and Bryant Garth, *Battles Around Legal Education Reform in India* In: *The Globalization of Legal Education.* Edited by: Bryant Garth & Gregory Shaffer, Oxford University Press. © Oxford University Press 2022. DOI: 10.1093/oso/9780197632314.003.0005

The first dimension of the recent revolution which we focus on is a new imperial or hegemonic relationship that is gaining power in relation to the older colonial relationships. It involves the ascendency of the United States globally after World War II and especially the end of the Cold War. With that ascendency came a revolution in the governance of the state and economy that diffused broadly throughout the world (Dezalay and Garth 2021). The global rise of large corporate law firms is one key legal component of this revolution, which also includes deregulation and privatization (Gross Cunha et al. 2018; Wilkins et al. 2017).

The second dimension is therefore the rise of what is often called the "financialization" of the economy, the neoliberal revolution, or the Big Bang of deregulation. One aspect of this transformation is a stagnation and relative impoverishment of the stock of public capital (which comprised state-owned companies, banks, and much less debt in the three decades after World War II) versus a huge accumulation of private capital associated with the so-called "one percent" (or more accurately one-tenth of one percent) and a corresponding accumulation of government debt (Piketty 2017). The public and private fortunes are reversed.

The third dimension is a transformation seen in legal education and the legal profession. In one sense, there is a huge proliferation of law schools in many countries of the world, including the United States, to some extent, with about 200 law schools; Mexico (Pérez Hurtado 2010), Brazil (Vilhena Vieira and José Garcez Ghirardi, this volume, Chapter 7), and India (Gingerich and Robinson, 2017), each of which has more than 1,000 faculties of law; and China, with some 600 law schools (Wang et al. 2017). The legal professions of places such as Japan (Rosen 2017), Korea (Lee 2019), and Hong Kong (Jones 2009) have also grown substantially, even if relatively small compared to the others. From one perspective, the proliferation suggests a growing openness to the legal profession and an increase in the importance of law in state governance. Yet the story also parallels the story of financialization. There is a vast difference between the very few institutions at the top and the numerous institutions at the bottom.

Many of the elite public schools are relatively open on the basis of meritocratic criteria, but it is extremely difficult to get into them unless one comes from a family able to put resources into costly primary and secondary schools. And the tuitions and fees are going up for many of the public schools, which compete with a new cohort of private schools that have entered the market with the aim largely of producing corporate lawyers. In any event, the differences between the elite and rank-and-file are dramatic.

In the United States, for example, law professors at elite schools make triple the salaries of those at low-ranked schools, and law graduates able to obtain corporate law jobs start their careers at more than double the salaries of those who start in the government or in small firms, with the gap increasing over time (Dinovitzer et al. 2004). The percentage of law graduates starting at corporate law firms of more than 250 lawyers, according to the After the JD (AJD) longitudinal study of law graduates who commenced their careers in 2000, was about 18 percent at a time of a good market in the United States, and the percentage remaining in such firms at year thirteen was about 8 percent (and there are also substantial differences between the firms that have more than 250 lawyers) (Dinovitzer 2014). The elite equity partners at the US firms come disproportionately from elite schools. There are therefore "magic circles" in law firms and in law schools that disproportionately reap the profits of business law (and also public interest law). The key lawyers arguing in the U.S. Supreme Court and taking major positions in government come from the same elite circles (Biskupic et al. 2014).

We do not have specific comparable data on other countries, but the differences are certainly as great given the gaps between the leading law schools and a mass of marginal schools. Further, the numbers of those who work in the so-called corporate hemisphere are relatively smaller, and the opportunity to gain access to the large corporate law firms from non-English-speaking countries depends also on knowledge of English, which relates also to one's social position and ability to travel. There are strong social, financial, and cultural barriers to entry into these internationally oriented corporate law firms and even to the faculties of law that train their recruits.

The legal revolution that goes with the revolution in governance, involving law schools, faculties of law, and corporate law firms, can be seen more specifically as part of a contested process—with legal education as a key battleground. There are both entrenched and even embattled elites resisting the forces promoting change, as well as elites using multiple positions and connections to absorb and solidify the changes. In many situations, the process of change is exacerbated by what can be seen as a relative decline in the value of scholarly capital in comparison to family and social capital. The decline makes it easier for new groups to ally with emerging but marginal scholarly communities bringing new investment in scholarship. The new system supported by the reformers is more embedded in finance and markets, and more academically selective about who obtains the key positions. It represents a key tool in reconfiguring academia and in the relation between academia and practice in different countries. The local battles about law and legal education, then, depend on a mix of professional and social hierarchies and relationships to hegemonic powers.

South and East Asia provide a nice setting for exploring these processes. Indeed, we focus on Asia in our book (Dezalay and Garth 2021) because it is at the core of the revolution that we wish to analyze. It combines colonial legacies embedded in powerfully entrenched and homogeneous legal hierarchies and institutions—notably the grand advocates in India, the Judicial Research and Training Institute in Korea, and the Legal Research and Training Institute in Japan. More generally, in four of the five countries we focus on in the larger work, which includes Hong Kong and China as well, there is a traditional alliance between an elite bar and high judges, with academics in a largely subordinate position. There is a rise of newcomers (outsiders) both in international law firms and in local clones of US corporate law firms, building on a powerful mix of outside resources (including global finance, Ivy League campuses, and legacies of Cold War hegemony).

These new sites for the reproduction of producers and diffusion/importation of new forms of financial/legal excellence complement each other in the relative success of this offensive. The two camps and their resources are relatively well defined, but the outcome of these battles differs depending on their respective strengths in each setting. And apart from Japan (Rosen 2017: 271–272), it seems that the old guard is mainly fighting a rearguard battle which aims at delaying and restricting the entry to the inner core hierarchy of judicial institutions while also slowing the rise of the newcomers. In each case, in addition, defensive strategies risk backfiring and promoting a diaspora of ambitious and well-connected law graduates. The case study of India provides a particularly vivid illustration of such battles.

This chapter's general theoretical framework sees law as a cultural bank holding symbolic capital. This phenomenon is easy to see in India. The power and history of the Parsi and the Brahmins are embedded within Indian law as family capital (Dezalay and Garth 2010; Sharafi 2014). The connections to the state here as elsewhere are also part of the value of legal capital, as are connections to the leading family businesses and landowning families. Family capital can be converted into other forms of capital that become more important at particular times and in particular places, such as moving from law into economics and land into finance. Law and the institutions in the legal field provide places of exchange for capital conversion. The hierarchies within the field also determine receptivity to new forms of capital including both learned capital and family capital. The elite of the bench and bar in India are at the top of the profession and guard the temple of Indian law (Galanter and Robinson 2017). In the United States, in contrast, corporate lawyers hold the dominant role. Other countries have different hierarchies.

From the beginning of law and development in the 1950s, the US approach has been to challenge the existing guardians of the temple outside the United States in order to promote universals consistent with US hegemony. US foundations and others have sought to "modernize" legal elites to become moderate leaders in development and governance instead of conservative backers of a propertied class seen as enemies of reform and development. The stories of legal education reform are therefore combinations of export efforts and import efforts that may disagree in many respects—but unite in seeking to disrupt the existing hierarchies and upgrade the quality of legal argument and legal scholarship (Krishnan 2005, 2004; Gardner 1980).

I. India: Colonial Path Dependencies Revisited: An Embattled Senior Bar, the Marginalization of Knowledge, and Internationalized Challengers

Recent accounts of the Indian legal profession note the powerful position of the grand advocates, an elite of high court and supreme court barristers who operate in tandem with the elite judiciary. Galanter and Robinson note that India's grand advocates are an "elite handful of lawyers" that have "flourished in the age of globalization" (2017: 455). Wilkins and Khanna note the perception among in-house counsel that "a small number of Grand Advocates . . . dominate the Indian advocacy market"—essential especially "when the stakes were high" (Wilkins and Khanna 2017). Ballakrishnen's recent report on India notes that the story of the bar is one of continuity, with familial capital remaining important and limiting entry to the flourishing elite barrister practices (2020). The corporate law firms, Ballakrishnen also finds, have changed. They broke somewhat with their historical path and became relatively meritocratic without the overt gender bias dominant in the bar (Ballakrishnen 2019).

The bar appears therefore to be an example of highrestricted entry—providing control over the market—among a relatively small group for which family capital is critical to get access to a pupillage. The top advocates reap substantial monopoly profits. The corporate bar, except for the leaders and dominant partners of the top firms (Int. 1 2017), does not do quite as well, but it too is relatively prosperous compared to those who make up the rank-and-file of the profession. And in contrast to the advocates in the bar, the corporate firms hire on relatively meritocratic grounds. In particular, they provide lucrative jobs for those who graduate from the relatively new and meritocratic national law schools (Gingerich and Robinson 2017).

The scholarly accounts described above each emphasize one aspect of the current situation, highlighting the contrast between the two sectors—the bar and the corporate law firms. Our account relates the two accounts and emphasizes also that the Indian legal aristocracy was built through colonialism and has always existed in a peripheral, dominated relationship. The Indian legal aristocracy has tended to be quite conservative except in relation to support for the independence movement. The great wealth of the "Nabobs of the law" prior to independence and during the golden age of the bar after independence depended on connections to the British legal core and on service on behalf of large landholders (Dezalay and Garth 2010: 151–157). The conservatism of the legal elite led Nehru to accuse the bench and bar of engineering a "purloined state" characterized by attacks in the courts on Nehru's progressive policies in the 1950s and 1960s. The elite of the bar, with a few exceptions, resisted policies that would reduce the power of their traditional clients (Williams 2020).

The bunker mentality adopted by the traditional legal elite, protecting itself and its market, helped to depreciate the prestige of law and legal careers. As was well documented in the 1960s and 1970s, law was not the choice of talented individuals without strong family contacts in the legal profession, despite efforts of the Ford Foundation and others to find a point of entry to improve teaching and scholarly research as a way to modernize the profession (Krishnan 2005, 2004). The best students chose engineering or medicine rather than law, with the Indian Institutes of Technology providing a well-documented point of entry for those able to excel on the entrance examinations.

Criticisms of the conservatism of the legal profession opened up possibilities for new ideas and contacts seeking to adapt to and ally with new local and global governing hierarchies. In particular, as discussed more later, entrepreneurs in law took advantage of a hegemonic restructuring that increased the relative value of US-made-and-exported legal expertise. The period after the emergency declared by Indira Gandhi in the mid-1970s was a key period for this entrepreneurship.

The support of the Indian Supreme Court for the emergency gave rise to a larger reformist element among the legal elite, and that opposition provided an opportunity to regain the bar's stature. Led by entrepreneurial activists in the bench and bar, the Supreme Court itself and the senior bar improved their image with the development of public interest litigation, with some assistance from the Ford Foundation (Dezalay and Garth 2010: 186–188). The timing also made more salient the existing momentum for reform of legal education centered at the University of Delhi. In particular, the idea of a new national law school outside of the existing law faculties gained support from Upendra Baxi's critique and suggestions for reform, published later (Baxi 1976). It also drew on the successes of the Indian institutes of technology and the Indian institutes of management, themselves in part inspired by US higher education.

Baxi, the best known Indian legal academic, obtained an SJD from the University of California, Berkeley, taught in Australia, and then came back to the University of Delhi. He taught from the 1970s to mid-1990s there, served as dean and in many other capacities, and moved to the University of Warwick in the mid-1990s. His career is closely connected to the rise of public interest litigation and the development of the national law schools. The following quote taken from a recently published examination of the founding of the national law schools notes the impact of Baxi and elite members of the bar and judiciary:

Justice M. Hidayatullah spearheaded the concept of a Law School on the lines of Harvard Law School, which would be led by a diverse and dedicated group of faculty and law scholars, would be autonomous in nature, completely self-financed, not take any financial aid from Government or regulatory bodies and in turn not permit their interference. The vision of Justice Hidayatullah was discussed in a number of LEC meetings. Prof. Upendra Baxi, eminent jurist who was [sic] co-opted member of LEC undertook the spadework and the entire legal education scenario of the country was set to undergo a metamorphosis (Mathur 2017).

The aspiration was to create an Indian version of Harvard.

After a set of events well documented by Krishnan (204: 484–488), N.R. Madhava Menon, a protégé of Justice Krishna Iyer, one of the leaders of public interest litigation on the Indian Supreme Court, established the National Law School of India University (NLSIU), the first national law school (NLS), located in Bangalore. Since that time he has been one of the key promoters of legal education reform. Menon has written an autobiography of his experience as a founder (2009).

The five-year curriculum, Menon noted, was inspired largely by US law schools and was much more rigorous than the three-year BA of the existing law faculties. The school also had very limited resources when it opened in 1987, but the Ford Foundation, which had long hoped to upgrade legal education and scholarship in India, stepped in with an $800,000 grant "at a crucial time when the law school was finding it difficult to continue operations (i.e.1989–1994)" (id.). The fortuitous timing of the NLSIU helped ensure its success but turned it away from the initial mandate to create a new generation of advocates aligned with public interest litigation. The first graduates emerged just after economic liberalization, and they instead eagerly embraced the new opportunities in the corporate law firms.

An international team, including Marc Galanter, William Twining, and Savitri Gunasekhere from Colombo, reviewed the achievements of NLSIU and concluded that it had "fully met the objectives of being a centre of excellence that serves as a pace setter for Indian legal education" (Menon 2009: 54). The success of NLSIU then inspired the national law school in Hyderabad (officially the National Academy of Legal Studies and Research (NALSAR)), which opened in 1998, and then the model really took off. There are now some twenty-three national law schools spread throughout India—with varying claims to affinity with the original model. The national law schools have also influenced legal education outside of the NLS sector. The number of three-year LLB programs is diminishing, with relatively few prominent holdouts such as Delhi University and the Government Law College in Mumbai. Recently, for example, the Pravin Gandhi School of Law affiliated with the University of Mumbai switched its emphasis to a five-year LLB program away from a three-year evening program.

Entrepreneurial opportunities toward increasingly influential US expertise were further enhanced by the restructuring of the Indian economy, especially under Prime Minister Manmohan Singh, bringing the end of the Indian "Licensing Raj" and opening up the economy to much more foreign trade and investment. This set of economic reforms opened space for new and expanded Indian solicitor firms and for global corporate law firms serving India from outside the country. Law firms retooled quite dramatically in relation to the transformation of the economy (Nanda et al. 2017: 69). Many graduates of the national law schools moved into these firms, and students there reportedly compete now for slots within the national and global corporate law firms (Gingerich and Robinson 2017). As Jay Krishnan noted in 2013, the law firm growth is relatively recent, reflecting the impact of the dramatic economic changes (2013: 24 n.76). Of the forty top firms named in a survey, eight started between 1991 and 1999, and fifteen began after 2000 (*id.* at 20). To a certain extent, in fact, the bar complains now about the relative lack of interest among the national law school graduates in careers in the bar (Int. 20 2017).

The first point is that the national law schools occupy a relatively tiny niche within Indian legal education. We are not, therefore, examining the vast majority of law faculties and law graduates. There are some 1.3 million lawyers in India, more than 1,200 law schools and faculties of law, and perhaps 45,000 law students. There are roughly 30,000 applications for the 1,500 to 2,000 positions in the national law schools (Gingerich and Robinson 2017). The Common Law Admission Test, established in 2008, allows students to take one examination while applying to national law schools throughout the country. The process is similar in this respect to the Indian institutes of technology.

The standardized tests used by the national law schools require English proficiency, and the fees of about $2,500 per year deter a great number of applications as well. A recent study of students at NLSIU confirms that they come disproportionately from high incomes and high castes (Jain et al. 2016: 28, 32). Brahmins made up 26.5 percent of students and other upper castes 32.5 percent, with the numbers likely higher if they included those who did not report (*id.* at 28). Some 30 percent of NLSIU students come from Tier 1 (major) cities, but that is a decline from 50 percent, suggesting a more provincial trend although not away from urban settings. Most students have parents that are fluent in English (*id.* at 35). There are also a small number of students in the "reserved" group for "scheduled castes" and similar groups. The report suggests that those with more advantage do better in school, participate heavily in the moot court competitions, and get prestigious jobs upon graduation. (*id.* at 14–15). As others have suggested, it is very difficult to come from outside the elites and excel in law school in India (Basheer et al. 2017: 578). Shamnad Basheer's creative and tenacious efforts to expand the chances for outsiders to gain success in the national law schools illustrates the tremendous obstacles they face (*id.*).

Parallel to the Indian institutes of technology (IIT), the caste elites are not distinguished especially by wealth or property, but by an ability to embody the accepted meritocratic values. As a scholar of the IITs suggests, "they are able to inhabit a universal worldview precisely because of a history of accumulated privilege, a history that allows them a unique claim to certain forms of self-fashioning" (Subramanian 2015: 296). "Whereas at an earlier moment, status might have been more explicitly tied to caste, the social bases of merit continue to be constituted in ways that allow the same social groups to inhabit merit as an embodied ideal" (*id.*). They are selected because of their achievement—which tends to coincide with caste.

The legal press in India reports on the high-prestige positions that graduates obtain from the national law schools. Recently the NALSAR in Hyderabad reported as follows. Out of seventy-four graduating students, the fifty-eight who participated in the campus recruiting program all got positions. Those positions included ten Shardul Amarchand Mangaldas, six Cyril Amarchand Mangaldas, five Luthra & Luthra, four Trilegal, three AZB & Partners, two Khaitan & Co, two P&C Legal, and two S&R Associates, with a few other firms hiring one. On the in-house side, the RPG Group hired five, while ICICI Bank hired four students. Others reportedly planned to "pursue careers in academia, policy making, judicial and civil services, et cetera." They reported offers to attend "the University of California at Berkeley . . . , the participating universities for the European Masters in Law and Economics program, the Faculty of Law, Oxford University, and Faculty of Law, Cambridge University, University of California at Los Angeles, Cornell University, and the London School of Economics" (Reddy 2017). Some planned on taking civil service exams, and one was taking a judicial exam. Two reportedly were planning on becoming advocates or clerking for a court. Similar results came from the other law schools reporting in the media, including Bangalore and Gujarat NLU (*id.*; Gingerich and Robinson 2017). A dean of a more traditional law school noted that the (Int. 2 2017) law firms preferred to hire from the national law schools than from the traditional schools.

These data are somewhat misleading, however. First, many leave the law firms after a relatively short time. One observer stated that half of the graduates of national law schools leave the practice of law within ten years for other careers such as business, design, and journalism (Int. 3 2017). An examination of the LinkedIn members identified with the national law schools in Hyderabad and Bangalore, which seems to capture a good portion of the alumni, suggests that many are still in law firms, but quite a number are in business, in-house counsel, legal education, or alternative careers. NLSIU has 5,441 alumni listed, which no doubt includes those who have participated in a range of programs, but it is interesting that the breakdown includes many or even most in careers other than legal careers (linked in 2018). Clearly, a large group is not in legal careers. Of the legal component, the largest employers listed are the leading corporate law firms and the bar. The list shows a number at the top law firms and in the bar, but the numbers in relation to the number of graduates is not high. Krishnan's research on the frequency generally of individuals leaving corporate law firms—"peeling off"—also suggests that graduates are not in general making their careers in the large corporate law firms (Krishnan 2013: 31–32).

As Krishnan notes, lawyers leave in part because the leading corporate law firms generally are of two types: family-dominated or dominated by a few individuals. Interviews confirmed this situation today, suggesting that there are very few "true partnerships" (*id.*; Int. 4 2017). One young lawyer in a law firm with his father in Mumbai notes that family-operated businesses often feel comfortable giving their legal work to the children of a long-standing lawyer (Int. 5 2017). The new firms started by many of those who leave tend then to replicate the structures they left behind (Krishnan 2013: 54–56). Starting salaries are also relatively low. A small firm might pay 40,000 Indian rupees per month, a large one 50,000, and a few firms such as the two Amarchand firms pay some 150,000 rupees a month, producing annual salaries of $7,500 to less than $30,000 (often augmented to some extent with bonuses).

Many who leave the law firms also seek to gain a foothold at the bar by teaming up with an established advocate. Krishnan shows how difficult it is to make it that way and break into the hierarchical advocacy world (*id.* at 38, 56–57). One of the frequent observations about the graduates of the national law schools is that, after almost thirty years of producing lawyers, no graduate has become a grand advocate or a judge (Int. 6 2017). The meritocratic criteria of the national law schools do not so far overcome the strong familial capital required for a career at the bar, which then can lead to judicial appointments. Indeed, advocates promoting their sophisticated expertise can be seen as "too modern for the court" or "incapable of playing by rules" because lacking inside knowledge of the rules (Int. 7 2017).

The world of the bench and bar also has a very strong impact on both the law firms and the national law schools, which are embedded deeply in the world of elite advocacy and the judiciary. The law firms can be divided into three general categories. The first is what *Legally India* terms the "Big Seven" (Legally India 2016). The big seven law firms gained prominence or were established after economic liberalization. They include Cyril Amarchand Mangaldas, with 601 lawyers; Khaitan and Co., with 485; Shardul Amarchand Mangaldas & Co., with 430; AZB & Partners, with 375; Luthra & Luthra, with 336; J. Sagar Associates, with 302; and Trilegal, with 221. They are the most important corporate law firms. Another group is the older firms established by expatriates in the colonial era, such as Crawford Bayley, established in 1830. Other firms in this category include Little & Co. and Mulla & Mulla (Nanda et al. 2017). These were the most prominent firms prior to liberalization, but they did not move to adapt to the new situation, and a very few partners dominated the firm and the profits. They were eclipsed by the newer and more entrepreneurial firms, which also attracted more new associates because of the promise—ultimately not realized—that firms would be more egalitarian in sharing the profits and partnership places. The remainder of the corporate legal sector is comprised of many small firms serving some aspect of the corporate business. Still, the current "big seven" has a "quasi monopoly" on major transactions (Wilkins and Khanna 2017: 144).

For all the law firms, it is necessary to have access to the leading advocates in order to be successful for clients in litigation. One of the larger firms reported the importance of access to the "face value" of the fifteen or so advocates that they utilized (Int. 8 2017). Nanda, Wilkins, and Fong note that the older firms survive in part because they are so connected with the elite bar. Their niche generally is the places where "old-line connections and prestige remain salient . . . for big Indian companies"—in particular, for real estate and regulatory issues (Nanda et al. 2017: 74). Furthermore, "[t]hese firms also have long-standing relationships with many of India's top grand advocates and high court judges"—"when the matter is really sensitive and the CEO needs someone he can really trust to navigate the bureaucracy or the courts . . . " (*id.* at 75).

There are other ways that the law firms connect to the networks around the bench and bar. Two of the most prominent of the big seven law firms, each of which has very prominent women in key positions, illustrate familial embeddedness. Pallavi Shroff, a key partner in the Delhi firm of Shardul Amarchand Mangaldas & Co., is the wife of Shardul Shroff, the chair of the firm and inheritor with his brother of his father's prominent firm. She is also the daughter of well-known retired Supreme Court Justice P.N. Bhagwati, one of the justices also most identified with public interest litigation. The Shroffs also link closely to the Gujarati community and Reliance, one of the major corporate groups (*id.* at 78). Khaitan and Co. similarly is closely connected to the Marwari community from Kolkata and Aditya Birla Group (*id.*). Further, Zia Mody, the founder of AZB and partners, is the daughter of Soli Sorabjee, another famous Indian jurist and former attorney general of India. Mody started the firm after ten years as an advocate. Reportedly she became tired of the male-dominated bar and took advantage of her University of Cambridge law degree, Harvard LLM, and family capital to start what has become one of the most successful law firms in India.

The law firm sector has grown substantially since economic liberalization, but it does not appear to be growing very much today. After an initial expansion of the corporate legal services market under liberalization, the market appears to have stagnated—perhaps in part because of the limited local opportunities and products offered in litigation (*id.*; Int. 9 2017). The corporate law firms in varying degrees are linked up with the familial world of the elite bench and bar, even though a number of those in the corporate bar are also pressing for some change.

The connections between the elite bench and bar to the national law schools is extremely close. The governing boards of the national law schools are dominated by members of the elite of the bar and the judiciary. More generally, legal education is regulated by the Bar Council—the organ of the advocates. The Bar Council, for example, prescribes twenty-six mandatory courses, limits teaching by practitioners, and limits class size to sixty (Gingerich and Robinson 2017). It also imposed an all-India bar examination in 2010. Leaders of the relatively marginal All India Law Teachers' Organization argue that the Bar Council should have "no role" in the teaching program of the law schools, but there is no likelihood of change (Int. 10 2017). The Bar Council is still in charge.

The hierarchical connection between the judiciary and the national law schools is even stronger. Key judges generally decide whom to hire as the dean or vice chancellor of a national law school. One vice chancellor spoke of meeting a key judge for dinner and then getting offered the position (Int. 11 2017). According to one knowledgeable observer, potential deans "cow-tow to the local judiciary," forming a "small cabal" (Int. 12 2015). The chancellor of each school is a judge, with the chief justice of the Indian Supreme Court the chancellor of the NLSIU by virtue of the chief justice position. One critic of the NLS vice chancellors, in fact, stated that once they are appointed, they spend all their time and energy trying to gain stature within the world of the elite bench and bar (Int. 12 2015). The dependence of each NLS on the vice chancellor's clout magnifies the importance of those ties. Faculties have very weak voices so that the schools are "personality driven" by the vice chancellor Ballakrishnen 2014; Int. 14 2017). Interviewees noted that when a capable vice chancellor left the NLS Kolkata, for example, the school went back to the "dark ages" (Int. 15 2017).

The influence of the judiciary is quite pronounced. The ability to get local government funding, according to interviews, depends on the work of members of the judiciary who lobby their local government—which must pay some attention since they appear frequently before those judges. It is also quite clear that the funding levels for most of the national law schools are not very high, which puts pressure on them to increase tuition fees. Finally, the more recently established NLS tend to have substantial local restrictions placed on them (e.g., number of students that must be local). Recently, legislation that would reserve 50 percent of the NLSIU spots for locals has alarmed alumni (Aji 2017).

Very high teaching loads are the norm in the NLS with the major exception currently being the NLS Delhi, which is very well funded and focused, under the current vice chancellor, on significantly increasing the research output. More generally, the spread of the national law schools has not substantially raised the prestige and profile of legal academics in India. Many interviewees noted that there is still no real career in legal academia. One law graduate in a different PhD program noted that there is no real job as "law professor." It is a "dead end" (Int. 12 2017). The NLS phenomenon, others noted, did not change the faculty model of professors as just "teachers." The "main focus is teaching" at the national law schools, even though the teaching itself is not that high quality (Int. 13 2017). There is "not much time for research," and there are no "structures to build up" to promote a better position for faculty members (Int. 14 2017). There is little focus on the "quality of faculty" or "research agendas" (Int. 16 2017). The faculty of the national law schools from our observations tends to be relatively young, and many faculty members do not stay in teaching. The group includes many who did not succeed in litigation and a number who are not on the "tenure track" (Ballakrishnen 2009).

The long-standing effort to upgrade law teaching and legal scholarly research, supported by a number of Ford Foundation initiatives beginning in the 1950s, has so far had limited success (Dasgupta 2010). The best and brightest law graduates do not seek careers as law professors. There is a recognition among many we interviewed that more legal academics are producing research, and the number of academic scholars today is much greater than in the past. But interviewees also report that the journals are "dead" and that the advances are quite limited (Int. 17 2017). While many people in India can name judges or senior advocates, legal scholars, with the exception of Upendra Baxi, are unknown even in the legal profession (Int. 18 2017). The national law schools, moreover, are the relatively elite tip of the iceberg. There are more than a thousand other public and private schools with lower pay—including a large number of private schools that pay half of what the public schools pay (Int. 10 2017). Only the private Jindal Global Law School near Delhi (Jindal), discussed below, and the well-funded national law school in Delhi appear to have a commitment to encourage scholarly productivity.

The pressure to change comes mainly from those who go abroad. Many who go become part of a brain drain, but a group of relatively young lawyers with elite credentials suggests that more are returning. As noted by one interviewee, "increasingly people are coming back," the legal academy is more "exciting" than in the past, and many see "teaching as a vehicle" for research (Int. 19 2017). They hope for a "recapturing and reinvesting of the brain drain." What they learned abroad and is valued abroad, however, is still unevenly recognized or even devalued in India (Ballakrishnen 2012). We examine these groups after the discussion of the bar.

II. The Bar

The tightly connected elite of the bench and bar remains at the top of the legal hierarchy. It is dominated especially by well-connected elites, including Brahmins and upper castes and the Parsi elite in Mumbai (Sharafi 2014; Int. 5 2017 (noting the connections between Parsi businesses and Parsi law firms)). The grand advocates are at the top of the hierarchy. Galanter and Robinson point out that seniority is part of this relationship (2017). Since judges face compulsory retirement at sixty-one (and at sixty-five in the Supreme Court), they are often younger than the senior advocates and may have looked up to or even learned their practices from them. As just noted, this elite of the bar and bench has a very strong impact on legal education, on the governance of the national law schools, on the hiring of the vice chancellors who govern the schools, on the funding of the schools, and also in providing social capital that helps make up the elite of the corporate law firms.

The bar has participated in initiatives such as the national law schools and public interest litigation that have enhanced the legitimacy of the profession and opened up to more meritocratic and high-quality entrants. But it is still a legal elite that is essentially inbred and very restrictive in entry. As noted previously, the graduates of the national law schools have not had much success in this sector of the legal profession.

The conservative nature of the bar is quite evident. Its attitude toward the law professors is apparently much like it was traditionally in the United Kingdom: the professors are not highly respected. One interviewee noted that professors at one NLS sought to eliminate Saturday classes in part to encourage research, and the governing board rejected the request because, in their opinion, "law professors don't work anyway" (Int. 15 2017). One interviewee noted that there is a "large disconnect between academics and practice," and the feeling of superiority is mutual (Int. 19 2017). The narrowness of the prevailing view of law practice is captured by a lawyer in a social science PhD program who had trouble renewing the license to belong to the bar. The authority thought that interdisciplinary academic study about law was inconsistent with the position of a member of the bar (Int. 12 2017).

The issue of the quality of the advocacy came up in a number of interviews (also see Galanter and Robinson 2017; Wilkins and Khanna 2017: 146). From the side of the law firms, the interviewees reported the need for the "face value" of the fifteen or so advocates that they use, but the interviewees also said that the abilities of the elite bar are "lower and lower" (Int. 3 2017). The problem, in part, is that the elite advocates have too many cases. They also do not use technology in their arguments. They rely on "court craft" and "no depth" (Int. 3 2017). A former law firm lawyer suggested a "blinkered vision of law," that there are very few quality lawyers in the bar, that the bar is "mediocre," and that "80 percent were unprepared" (Int. 18 2017). Interestingly, a number also of the in-house counsel studied by Wilkins and Khanna reported "great frustration with the quality of these top advocates" (2017: 146).

Well-trained lawyers armed with the experience of Oxford, Cambridge, or US law schools, coupled with experience in an international law firm, find that they are "overtrained" for litigation in India (Int. 8 2017; Ballakrishnen 2012). The senior advocates do not have time for complex points, and it is by no means clear that, if they did, the judges would embrace them. There is no "market for top-level legal argument," in the words of a senior partner in a law firm (Int. 3 2017). Arbitration to avoid the courts is no answer, according to the same partner, because judgments must be enforced in the courts (Int. 3 2017). One young lawyer reported that he left the practice of law because of this disconnect between what he was trained for and what he could use in litigation in India.

Interviewees stated that there were some prominent exceptions among the bench and the bar. Most frequently named were two justices of the Supreme Court from prominent legal families. One is Justice Dhananjaya Yashwant Chandrachud, whose father Shri Y.V. Chandrachud was the longest serving chief justice of India. Chandrachud graduated in economics and mathematics from St. Stephen's College in New Delhi in 1979, obtained his LLB degree from Delhi University in 1982, and obtained an LLM degree from Harvard University in 1983. The other is Justice Rohinnton Fali Nariman. Nariman is the son of Fali Sam Nariman, a leading senior advocate. The younger Nariman received his early education in Mumbai, with a B.Com. degree from Shri Ram College of Commerce. He completed his LLB from the Faculty of Law, University of Delhi, and then obtained an LLM from Harvard Law School. He practiced law in New York for a year as well. His career in India went fast, mixing family capital and meritocratic credentials. The bar had to amend the rules to allow him to become a senior advocate at the age of thirty-seven. He reportedly is the first Harvard alumnus to serve as a justice at the Supreme Court of India.

Family capital remains vital for careers in the bar and on the bench. The system for promotion into the judiciary is secret and subject to some criticism. Selection to the high courts and to the Supreme Court takes place through a closed colloquium and, as one observer noted, it results in enduring legal names that tend to be upper caste: from Mumbai, as the example of Nariman suggests, among the Parsi elite (Int. 12 2017). The impact of selection to a high court or supreme court, in addition, endures beyond retirement, since retired judges gain many influential positions related to politics and the law after their service on the judiciary (Robinson 2015: 353).

Interestingly, in a recent speech to the bar association in Mumbai, Justice Chandrachud raised some judicious criticisms about the closed nature of the bar. (Chandrachud 2016). After praising the bar as an "assembly line of brilliance," he talked of "our outmoded way of working" and the "perception that the bar is closed." He lamented the talented individuals who "never went to the supreme court," and argued that it is "an issue of grave concern" that there is "talent" with "no access to centers of power." He stated that it was important to "open up our bar to a true meritocracy."

The national law schools, as noted, have not provided an effective meritocratic pipeline into the elite bar. One leading lawyer with a family firm in Mumbai noted that for the leading lawyers in Mumbai, whether practicing in firms or as advocates, the likely choice of law schools would be the Government Law College (GLC) (Int. 20 2017), and the same would be true for New Delhi with the University of Delhi law faculty (Int. 12 2017). The reasons are twofold: the exam threshold is difficult to pass for admission to an NLS, and the networks around the GLC are essential to success in Mumbai.

Admission to the GLC is not easy. Many are turned down. Yet several locals within the elite legal world noted that children of judges and elite advocates get in despite lacking the top credentials. One graduate noted that if one has "no connections," it will be very difficult to find the mentors at the bar necessary for success (Int. 12 2017); on the other hand, a faculty member says that the GLC students without connections have the time and capacity to find them (Int. 21 2017). No one disputes the value of family capital in careers starting at the GLC. Similarly, neither graduates nor faculty argue that there is any real teaching at the GLC. Classes meet from 7:30 a.m. to 10:30 a.m., and busy practitioners may not show up to teach if something else comes up. There is in any event "no need to attend classes" (Int. 21 2017). The students essentially spend all their time apprenticing with the advocates who congregate at the Bombay High Court one block from the GLC. There are conscientious professors nevertheless who help, for example, to organize a law review, but scholarly capital pales in importance to family capital. Interestingly, however, one faculty member reported that there were currently three GLC students at Harvard (Int. 21 2017). One administrator noted that leading US schools recruit at the GLC, and that as many as 25 percent study abroad—despite the lack of academic rigor at the GLC (Int. 22 2017). The social capital suffices.

The portrait of the bar reveals a legal elite that is very inbred and restricted in entry. There is no way to mix the legal milieu. The graduates of the national law schools, who treat their law degrees similar to the engineering graduates of the Indian institutes of technology, have to find another path of meritocracy versus a small subset of a national elites around the courts and advocacy. Further, with the growth of trade, corporations, and investment, there are opportunities for a professional class to serve the state, and big corporations, with new and more "modern" expertise. The corporate law firms, as noted, which rebuilt their approach after the era of conveyancing and some banking relationships, are one place where some of this upgrading has taken place, but they are limited by the world of a very conservative elite bench and bar. These challengers likely circumscribe the possibilities for the grand advocates, keep them out of some new markets, and therefore limit the opportunities for new advocates to gain entry to the rarified levels now dominated by very senior advocates. Those senior advocates are still necessary for access to the higher courts, but much energy is now spent looking for ways around this path.

III. Challenges to the Elite Bench and Bar

The challenges and pressures for change tend to come from the outside. As noted, at least one of the top Supreme Court justices, with multiple degrees from abroad, has sought to modernize from within. But the highly internationalized elite are the more general source of change. It includes many who have studied abroad, including individuals with Rhodes Scholarships, and a number who have returned from the United States or from positions in the English "magic circle" law firms or variants in Australia. A good proportion have advanced degrees from the United Kingdom, but the United States has become more attractive for study abroad in recent years (Ballakrishnen 2012). The voices of these relatively young elites are evident in the litany of criticisms captured in the preceding section. A number of graduates of the NLS have teaching and research positions abroad. They, too, participate in these debates. It is indicative that a recent review article of law and social science research about India emphasizes the work of those who are from India, but work abroad (Sharafi 2015). Within India, in addition, there are now clear alliances of this internationalized group with business and philanthropy promoting a modernized "good governance" within India.

The leading internationalized law firms within India are part of the offensive. One top litigation partner with experience abroad noted the impact of the bar's narrowness. The partner argued that in transactional work the leading law firms could grow and take advantage of foreign clients and their own local and transnational expertise (Int. 3 2017). But in litigation they were still blocked; they could not deploy their expertise or their abilities to draw on technological innovations. This mismatch also limits the growth of the Indian legal market. Some firms are trying to build their own in-house litigation expertise to work with, or go around, the advocates, but the possibilities of bypassing are still pretty limited.

The earlier offensive to upgrade legal knowledge, combined with social activism, was not very successful despite the efforts of the Ford Foundation (Krishnan 2004; 2005). In contrast, the new offensive goes with, and gained momentum with, the economic liberalization that began in 1991. The professional milieu around finance and business associated with liberalization can take advantage of the mix of social capital and corporate connections, but any move into law has been blocked by the insular legal profession. This problem is evident from the relatively limited career opportunities even for the graduates of the national law schools, who tend to come from the social group with resources, but not family legal capital. The "global meritocratic" quality of the top graduates is indicated by the high number of NLS graduates who obtain Rhodes Scholarships.

There is a new, legally educated elite, therefore, and it has its own hierarchies and trappings linked to the national law schools. But to jump anywhere past the limited extensions that this new elite status can offer (i.e., firms, global organizations, think tanks, some in-house counsel positions), or to jump into the mainstream legal elite, requires different forms of capital. The law graduates from the national law schools have profiles similar in this respect to the graduates of the Indian institutes of technology (Subramanian 2015), but they do not have the opportunity in India to mix engineering, social science, technology, and law in the way that it is done in the Silicon Valley, for example.

One potential remedy for the economic liberals is to open up the legal services markets, but the bar has strongly opposed competition from abroad within India (Coe 2016). There is more momentum now than in the past for a limited opening, but there are still "snags." The opening would undoubtedly have an impact, perhaps in two ways. On the one hand, it may weaken the power of the Indian corporate law firms, since the global law firms have advantages facilitating large-scale transactions. As suggested by Wilkins and Khanna, "foreign firms were more likely to handle important matters involving M&A, civil liability, and arbitration" (2017: 157). The global firms may also attract more Indian nationals back to India because of the relative openness of those firms for advancement (Nanda et al. 2017: 106). At the same time, as Nanda, Wilkins, and Fong point out, the traditional firms founded in the colonial era by British lawyers "might actually be seen as more valuable" if the market is opened up because of their unique ties with regulatory authorities, the grand advocates, and the courts (2017: 106).

Many of those who go abroad become interested in research and teaching, and they increase some of the pressure within India. Many stay abroad. There are at least six individuals teaching in the United States, the United Kingdom, and Singapore (Int. 23 2017). A number of them nevertheless want to "recapture and reinvest the brain drain" (Int. 19 2017). They overinvest in technical scholarly sophistication in part because of the challenge they face in India to break into the world dominated by the bar. Not surprisingly, they often aim their research precisely at the quality of the courts and the judiciary, seeking transparency as another way to challenge the conservatism. But they have not succeeded in breaking down the walls. Despite requiring PhDs, as do the British, scholarly research at the national law schools is very limited, including at the top ones, and the position of law professor is still not widely respected, and does not offer an attractive career path.

Nevertheless, there are some very prominent examples of research successes, such as the research at the NLS Delhi on the death penalty, which also provide some transparency while drawing on empirical legal research approaches imported from the United States. Anup Surendranath, the law professor in charge of the project, is a graduate of NALSAR in Hyderabad with an Oxford PhD gained through scholarship assistance. His death penalty research led the chief justice of the Indian Supreme Court in 2014 to name him the deputy registrar (research) in the Supreme Court of India. According to his website, "The only other instance of an academic being invited to the supreme court for a similar assignment was almost thirty years ago, in the late 1980s, under Chief Justice P.N. Bhagwati" (National Law School of India, Delhi 2015).

Other examples are think tanks created by individuals returning from abroad and well aware of the limited opportunities to deploy their knowledge and expertise. Vidhi represents a particularly notable example (Vidhi 2020). According to its website,

The Vidhi Centre for Legal Policy is an independent think tank doing legal research and assisting government in making better laws. Vidhi is committed to producing legal research of the highest standard with the aim of informing public debate and contributing to improved governance. Vidhi works with Ministries of the Government of India and State Governments, as well as other public institutions, providing research and drafting support at various stages of law-making (id.).

Vidhi also conducts independent research, including, it reports, on "Judicial Reform: Research in this area takes a data-driven approach to suggesting reforms that address the problem of judicial delays" (*id.*).

More than thirty professionals working with Vidhi are listed on the website. The research director and founder is Arghya Sengupta, a graduate of the NLSIU and Oxford, where he was a Rhodes Scholar. His PhD at Oxford was on the independence and accountability of the Indian higher judiciary. The credentials of the group are stellar, with degrees from the national law schools, US, British, and other graduate programs, and experience that includes work with the corporate law firms.

The genesis of the group was among graduate students in Oxford, who noted the "inadequate legal research" that formed the basis of the government's work on an Indian-US nuclear deal (Int. 19 2017). The group included two from Oxford, one from Harvard, and one from Delhi, and they believed that the there was a "gap in the system" (Int. 19 2017). The government had high-quality input on economics and policy, but not good law. This group acted to remedy the problem for the nuclear agreement, and they were successful in gaining credibility and attention despite their very young ages. They decided to build on this work and create a think tank to occupy the space of high-quality legal research. They observed that there was no perceived problem in government litigation, in any event under the control of the bar, but the quality of legal expertise generally needed upgrading. They used their capital from their studies abroad and the Rhodes Scholarship, even though only in their early twenties, to find independent funding. They were successful, and Vidhi began in 2013 as the "first legal think tank." They were also very careful to avoid "advocacy" or other activities that could taint the "expertise" (Int. 19 2017).

Suggesting some appetite for an upgrade in legal expertise as part of good governance, they succeeded in raising money not from the legal profession but from philanthropy, including substantial support from Rohini Nilekani, part of the Infosys community. Vidhi does not pay high salaries, but it tries to pay roughly half of what the associates in law firms make. They work with other disciplines and other think tanks, with some circulation among such think tanks as the Center for Policy Research in New Delhi. There are also links to the national law schools and to the Jindal Global Law School. They belong to the group challenging the traditional, and conservative, world of the bench and bar.

The Jindal Global Law School is the first high-profile private law school in India and also the first to focus specifically on academic scholarship (Kumar 2017). It is the brainchild of Raj Kumar, a representative of the diaspora reinvesting in India. He has degrees from, among other places, Delhi, Oxford (where he went as a Rhodes Scholar), Harvard, and the University of Hong Kong. In 2009, he became the founding vice chancellor of the Jindal Global Law School. Kumar was teaching at the University of Hong Kong, and he became convinced that the national law schools had not succeeded in bringing Indian legal education as far as necessary. In particular, he believed that research was not sufficiently emphasized. Drawing on US capital and US institutions for initial support, and drawing on the success of the private Indian School of Business, he went searching for philanthropy to build a $100 million private law school. He succeeded, ultimately, with the Jindal grant, drawing on wealth generated from the Jindal steel empire. Still, tuition had to be set quite high according to Indian standards. It is now equal to about $10,000 per year. The school offers a five-year LLB/BA, a three-year LLB, and a one-year LLM.

After beginning with a law school, Jindal Global University now has a business school, a liberal arts and humanities school, a communications and journalism school, and a school of international affairs. Jindal this way seeks to build interdisciplinary connections around law that are missing from the traditional faculties of law and the national law schools. Jindal has numerous relationships with schools abroad, and the faculty includes a number of expatriates. Notably, some one-third of the faculty members are graduates of one of the national law schools. Faculty salaries are relatively high for India, and there are centers focused on research. The teaching loads are not light, and the scholarly output is a little uneven, but the professors are well integrated into the global and, especially, US scholarly worlds (id.).

A third area challenging traditional legal knowledge in India comes not from within the various law schools, but rather in the social science departments, especially at the prestigious Jawaharlal Nehru University in New Delhi (JNU). The Law and Social Sciences Research Network (LASSnet), organized by the Centre for the Study of Law and Governance at JNU, has held a number of conferences. It draws on and challenges legal scholarly capital in several ways. The key individual organizing this network is Pratiksha Baxi, a sociologist at the Centre and the daughter of Upendra Baxi. This interdisciplinary work offers an option that law graduates may pursue to avoid the narrowness of legal scholarship and the precariousness of the law professor position.

This terrain of expertise challenging the conservatism of the elites of the bench and bar is mainly a detour around Indian hierarchies. It builds on foreign capital—especially from the United Kingdom and the United States—to push beyond the conservatism. This terrain provides some outlet for the hundreds, or even thousands, of individuals who receive good educations yet are locked out of the very conservative, and embattled, bar elite. These efforts have not touched the elite of the bar in a substantial way to date, but the aging elite of the bar faces a threat that may render their enduring conservatism and bunker mentality obsolete.

The challenge to the traditional bar, it should be noted, should not be portrayed as a meritocracy versus inherited legal positions. The challengers themselves have substantial resources from within current Indian society and from abroad. Jindal is funded by a large business, and it often takes business-generated wealth to attend. It takes resources to do well on the tests for admission to the national law schools and to benefit from study abroad on NLS degrees. The think tanks, in particular Vidhi, also connect to major businesses seeking to upgrade the quality of governance in India, including law. It took connections to that wealth and cosmopolitan capital—Oxford and Harvard degrees—to gain entry to those groups and build Vidhi. These approaches allow law graduates to branch out and to challenge and perhaps surround the traditional elite, but they represent a palace war mainly among elites.

Compared to the QCs in England who are embedded in oligarchy, politics, and the business class, as well as entry into the knowledge world of Oxford and Cambridge, the senior advocates in India appear narrow and embattled. They do not enrich and renew their knowledge, which appears to be decades behind the United States and the United Kingdom. Contrary to the relatively optimistic conclusion of Galanter and Robinson about the status of the grand advocates today (2017), that status is hardly the same as when, for example, the Parsi in Mumbai and the Brahmins in Madras were central to economic and social life on the path to independence. The bar made a comeback through the reaction to the emergency and the creation of public interest law, but the same individuals who gained credibility at that moment dominate the elite of the bar today.

The elite grand advocates, high court, and Supreme Court judges face challenges from those more attuned to the globally ascendant expertise and set of technologies (*id.*). But the embattled elite remain able to assert their influence over many of the ostensible challengers within legal education and within the solicitors' firms. The challengers are more meritocratic and less dependent on family capital, and they therefore provide a countermovement to the traditionally closed legal profession of India. But the challengers do not represent the graduates of the more than 1,000 law schools that now exist in India. They represent a counter elite, with professional and business parents, high-caste backgrounds, and resources that allow them to excel on the exams necessary to attend the national law schools or Jindal, pay the tuition, and gain the international capital necessary to mount challenges to the embedded local hierarchies.

IV. Conclusion

Legal education reform in India is closely associated with the legal revolution linked to US-style globalization, financialization, and the growth of private markets. The rise of national law schools and the Jindal Global Law School are part of that revolution, which involves more meritocratic entrance into the profession, upgraded legal instruction and faculty credentials, upgraded advocacy, and internationalized and interdisciplinary scholarship. The rise operates in tandem with the rise of corporate law firms linked to the new law schools. As elsewhere, this more meritocratic course, coupled with a great expansion in access to the legal profession, exacerbates inequality on the basis of access to such education, upbringing, and linguistic skills essential to gain entry into one of the top law schools and to elite careers, especially in the corporate law firms. The various magic circles of the legal elite are open to only a very few with privileged backgrounds.

The revolution also meets some strong resistance, largely connected to the embattled elite in India built on family capital and entrenched in the elite judiciary and bar. The resistance of these elites helps prevent the development of academic careers, sustained legal and interdisciplinary scholarship, quality teaching, and the higher quality of legal argument and advocacy that a relatively young and internationalized legal elite seeks to effectuate. With many paths blocked for the young elite, we see them using their international capital, and connections to business and philanthropy, to build think tanks, a few pockets of interdisciplinary research, and higher quality faculty in the national law schools, the internationally oriented Jindal Global Law School, and in networks in the social sciences. They represent a strong Indian challenge to the elite bench and bar, but not so strong at this point that the elite bar's monopolistic returns are threatened.

References

Aji, Sowmya (2017). "Karnataka to Reserve 50 Percent Seats in NLSIU for Local Students, Economic," *Times.* June 20. http://economictimes.indiatimes.com/industry/services/education/karnataka-to-reserve-50-percent-seats-in-nlsiu-for-local-students/articleshow/59239084.cms

Ballakrishnen, Swethaa (2009). "Where Did We Come From? Where Do We Go? An Enquiry into the Students and Systems of Legal Education in India," *Journal of Commonwealth Law and Legal Education* 7(2): 133–54.

Ballakrishnen, Swethaa (2012). "Homeward Bound: What Does a Global Legal Education Offer the Indian Returnees?," *Fordham Law Review* 80(6): 2441–2480.

Ballakrishnen, Swethaa (2014). "'Why I Am Not a Lawyer'—An Institutional Analysis of the Indian National Law School Model and Its Implications for Global Legal Education," in Lokendra Malik, ed., *The State of Legal Education in India: Essays in Honour of Professor Ranbir Singh.* Pp. 131–152. Lexis Nexis.

Ballakrishnen, Swethaa (2019). "Just Like Global Firms: Unintended Parity and Speculative Isomorphism in India's Elite Professions," *Law and Society Review* 53(1): 108–140.

Ballakrishnen, Swethaa (2020). "Present and Future: A Revised Sociological Portrait of the Indian Legal Profession," in Richard Abel, Ole Hammerslev, Hilary Sommerlad, and Ulrike Schultz, eds., *Lawyers in 21st Century Society.* Pp. 713–33. Hart Publishing.

Basheer, Shamnad, K.V. Krishnaprasad, Sree Mitra, and Prajna Mohapatra (2017). "The Making of Legal Elites and the IDIA of Justice," in David Wilkins, Vikramaditya Khanna, and David Trubek, eds., *The Indian Legal Profession in the Age of Globalization: The Rise of the Corporate Legal Sector and Its Impact on Lawyers and Society.* Pp. 578–605. Cambridge University Press.

Baxi, Upendra (1976). "Notes Towards a Socially Relevant Legal Education," *Journal of the Bar Council of India* 5: 23.

Berman, Harold J. (1983). *Law and Revolution: The Formation of the Western Legal Tradition.* Harvard University Press.

Berman, Harold J. (2003). *Law and Revolution II: The Impact of the Protestant Reformations on the Western Legal Tradition.* Belknap Press of Harvard University Press.

Biskupic, Joan, Janet Roberts, and John Shiffman (2014). "Special Report: At U.S. Court of Last Resort, Handful of Lawyers Dominate Docket," *Reuters,* December 8. https://www.reuters.com/investigates/special-report/scotus/.

Chandrachud, Honorable Justice D. Y. (2016). "Address by Hon'ble Justice D Y Chandrachud at the Sesquicentenary event of the BombayBar Association on 19th November 2016." https://www.youtube.com/watch?v=mIy02Wrbt0E.

Coe, Aebra (2016). "Plans to Open Up Legal Sector in India Hit a Snag," *Law 360.* October 4. https://www.law360.com/articles/848269/plans-to-open-up-legal-sec tor-in-india-hit-a-snag.

Dasgupta, Lovely (2010). "Reforming Indian Legal Education: Linking Research and Teaching," *Journal of Legal Education* 59(3): 432.

Dezalay, Yves and Bryant Garth (2010). *Asian Legal Revivals: Lawyers in the Shadow of Empire*. University of Chicago Press.

Dezalay, Yves and Bryant Garth (2021). *Law as Reproduction and Revolution: An Interconnected History*. University of California Press.

Dinovitzer, Ronit (2014). "Practice Setting," in G. Plickert, ed., *After the JD: Third Results from a National Study of Lawyer Careers*. Pp. 25–30. NALP Foundation.

Dinovitzer, Ronit, Bryant Garth, Richard Sander, Joyce Sterling, and Gita Wilder (2004). *After the JD: First Results of a National Study of Legal Careers*. NALP Foundation.

Galanter, Marc and Nick Robinson (2017). "Grand Advocates: The Traditional Elite Lawyers," in David Wilkins, Vikramaditya Khanna, and David Trubek, eds., *The Indian Legal Profession in the Age of Globalization: The Rise of the Corporate Legal Sector and Its Impact on Lawyers and Society*. Pp. 455–485. Cambridge University Press.

Gane, Christopher and Robin Hui Huang, eds. (2016). *Legal Education in the Global Context: Opportunities and Challenges*. Ashgate.

Gardner, James (1980). *Legal Imperialism*. University of Wisconsin Press.

Gingerich, Jonathan and Nick Robinson (2017). "Responding to the Market: The Impact of the Rise of Corporate Law Firms on Elite Legal Education in India," in David Wilkins, Vikramaditya Khanna, and David Trubek, eds., *The Indian Legal Profession in the Age of Globalization: The Rise of the Corporate Legal Sector and Its Impact on Lawyers and Society*. Pp. 519–547. Cambridge University Press.

Gross Cunha, Luciana, Daniela Monteiro Gabbay, Jose Garcez Ghirardi, David M. Trubek, and David B. Wilkins, eds. (2018). *The Brazilian Legal Profession in the Age of Globalization: The Rise of the Corporate Legal Sector and Its Impact on Lawyers and Society*. Cambridge University Press.

Jain, Chirayu, Spadika Jayaraj, Sanjana Muraleedharan, and Harjas Singh (2016). *The Elusive Island of Excellence A Study on Student Demographics, Accessibility and Inclusivity at National Law School 2015-16*. National Law School Bangalore.

Jamin, Christoph and William van Caenegem, eds. (2016). *The Internationalisation of Legal Education*. Springer.

Jones, Carol (2009). "Producing the Producers: Legal Education in Hong Kong," in Stacey Steele and Kathryn Taylor, eds., *Legal Education in Asia*. Pp. 107–136. Routledge.

Krishnan, Jayath (2004). "Professor Kingsfield Goes to Delhi: American Academics, the Ford Foundation, and the Development of Legal Education in India," *American Journal of Legal History* 46(4): 447–499.

Krishnan, Jayath (2005). "From the ALI to the ILI: The Efforts to Export an American Legal Institution," *Vanderbilt Journal of Transnational Law* 38(5): 1255–1294.

Krishnan, Jayath (2013). "Peel-Off Lawyers: Legal Professionals in India's Corporate Law Firm Sector," *Socio-legal Review* 9(1): 1–59.

Kumar, C. Raj (2017). "Experiments in Legal Education in India: Jindal Global Law School and Private Nonprofit Legal Education," in David Wilkins, Vikramaditya Khanna, and David Trubek, eds., *The Indian Legal Profession in the Age of Globalization: The Rise of the Corporate Legal Sector and Its Impact on Lawyers and Society*. Pp. 606–630. Cambridge University Press.

Lee, Jae-Hyup (2009). "Legal Education in Korea: Some Thoughts on Linking the Past and the Future," *Kyung Hee Law Review* 44: 605–623.

Legally India (2016). A Ranking of India's 25 Largest Law Firms. December 15. http://www.legallyindia.com/law-firms/india-25-largest-law-firms-by-headcount-00011 130-816.

Mathur, Justice N.N. (2017). National Law Universities, Original Intent & Real Founders. July 24. http://www.livelaw.in/national-law-universities-original-intent-real-founders/.

Menon, N.R. Madhava (2009). *Turning Point: The Story of a Law Teacher*. Universal Law Publishing.

Nanda, Ashish, David B. Wilkins, and Bryon Fong (2017). "Mapping India's Corporate Law Firm Sector," in David Wilkins, Vikramaditya Khanna, and David Trubek, eds., *The Indian Legal Profession in the Age of Globalization: The Rise of the Corporate Legal Sector and Its Impact on Lawyers and Society*. Pp. 69–114. Cambridge University Press.

National Law School of India (2020). Linked-in Alumni. Accessed February 4, 2020. https://www.linkedin.com/school/national-law-school-of-india-university/people/.

National Law School of India, Delhi (2015). Faculty: Anup Surendranath. http://nludelhi.ac.in/pep-fac-new-pro.aspx?Id=42/.

Pérez Hurtado, Luis Fernando (2010). "Content, Structure, and Growth of Mexican Legal Education," *Journal of Legal Education* 59(4): 567–597.

Piketty, Thomas (2017). "Public Capital, Private Capital," *Le blog de Thomas Piketty*. March 14. http://piketty.blog.lemonde.fr/2017/03/14/public-capital-private-capital/.

Reddy, B. Varun (2017). "NALSAR Class of 2017: Conclusion of Recruitment Process," *SCC Online Blog*. May 2. http://blog.scconline.com/post/2017/05/02/nalsar-class-of-2017-conclusion-of-recruitment-process/.

Robinson, Nick (2015). "Closing the Implementation Gap: Grievance Redress and India's Social Welfare Programs," *Columbia Journal of Transnational Law* 53(2): 321–362.

Rosen, Dan (2017). "Japan's Law School System: The Sorrow and the Pity," *Journal of Legal Education* 66(2): 267–288.

Sharafi, Mitra (2014). *Law and Identity in Colonial South Asia: Parsi Legal Culture, 1772–1947*. Cambridge University Press.

Sharafi, Mitra (2015). "South Asian Legal History," *Annual Review of Law and Social Science* 11(1): 309–336.

Subramanian, Ajantha (2015). "Making Merit: The Indian Institutes of Technology and the Social Life of Caste," *Comparative Studies in Society and History* 57(2): 291–322.

Vidhi Centre for Legal Policy (2020). https://vidhilegalpolicy.in/about (10 February).

Wang, Zhizhou, Sida Liu, and Xueyao Li (2017). "Internationalizing Chinese Legal Education in the Early Twenty-First Century," *Journal of Legal Education* 66(2): 238–266.

Wilkins, David, Vikramaditya Khanna, and David Trubek, eds. (2017). *The Indian Legal Profession in the Age of Globalization: The Rise of the Corporate Legal Sector and Its Impact on Lawyers and Society*. Cambridge University Press.

Wilkins, David B. and Vikramaditya S. Khanna (2017). "Globalization and the Rise of the In-house Counsel Movement in India," in David Wilkins, Vikramaditya Khanna, and David Trubek, eds., *The Indian Legal Profession in the Age of Globalization: The Rise of the Corporate Legal Sector and Its Impact on Lawyers and Society*. Pp.114–169. Cambridge University Press.

Williams, Alexander (2020). "Imagining the Post-colonial Lawyer: Legal Elites and the Indian Nation-State," *Asian Journal of Comparative Law* 15(1): 156–186.

6

Asian Legal Education's Engagement with Policy

Veronica L. Taylor

I. Introduction

Law is a normative profession. Legal education involves producing and transmitting legal knowledge in ways that articulate, inculcate, and defend those norms. Thus, for example, the Faculty of Law at Universitas Indonesia has, as its mission:

> Preparing FHUI as a "prominent law faculty" at a superior level within Southeast Asia and [realizing its] competitive power *by building on the technology, culture, character and morals of Indonesia* [emphasis added] (FHUI 2020).

When legal education takes place in universities, we see this normative work occurring through legal research and publishing; through classroom teaching; and through service to the university or the legal profession. Increasingly, "engagement" is being added as a dimension of law school. "Engagement" means the work that extends beyond the university, through partnership with external actors in government, industry, or civil society. It includes activities such as collaborative research with an industry or government or nongovernment partner; executive education; policy advice given to government or civil society organizations; or paid consultancies.

In some places, the shorthand expression for engagement between the university and the public sector is "knowledge to policy." In this form of engagement, academics actively participate in public policy debates, and they provide theoretical and applied research and data that can inform decision-making by policymakers, including the judiciary. That knowledge may be generated through activities such as clinical legal education or advocacy,

Veronica L. Taylor, *Asian Legal Education's Engagement with Policy* In: *The Globalization of Legal Education.*
Edited by: Bryant Garth & Gregory Shaffer, Oxford University Press. © Oxford University Press 2022.
DOI: 10.1093/oso/9780197632314.003.0006

pro bono work for nonprofit groups, contributions to legislative reform or government policy reviews, or from interaction with regional or global governance institutions. The "knowledge" being tendered to policymakers may reach them directly and publicly through publication or consultation, or it may be offered in closed discussions, or it may be brokered through intermediaries such as advocates, lobbyists, and civil society organizations.

Legal academics in systems such as the United States, the United Kingdom, and Australia are rewarded for participating in these forms of "engagement" or "knowledge to policy" activities because they seem to combine some of the altruistic values of legal practice[1] with the potential to influence government, business, or civil society for the public good. At the same time, this kind of university engagement has a political edge: governments expect universities to deliver public goods that go beyond pure research or conventional teaching. The demand that universities serve the needs of government encapsulates the perennial tension between scholars and teachers who want to defend the inherent value of quiet, considered production of knowledge that is protected by academic freedom, and a state that seeks to align the production of knowledge with current government policy. The state's demand that universities "engage" is framed as a legitimate expectation and a form of return on public and private "investment" in higher education.[2] Complicating the conversation is the entry of other, non-state actors, from the private sector, from civil society groups, and from international domains.

Although expressed in slightly different terms in different places and enforced in different ways, balancing the different expectations of these multiple stakeholders about how law schools should produce and share knowledge—and of what kind—is a challenge common to the corporatized university in postindustrial societies, and to universities in developing and middle-income countries. How this kind of normative contestation is managed and reflected in the design of legal education institutions[3] in Asia is the issue that I seek to highlight in this chapter.

---

[1] By altruistic values I mean values that resonate with the legal profession's claim to act for the benefit of society, rather than for personal gain or profit. Those need not have a particular political cast, but they are often characterized as progressive values such as human rights, the rule of law, and distributive social justice (e.g. Halliday and Karpik, 1998)

[2] Cuts to university funding in Australia are routinely described by government as 'efficiency dividends', for example: https://www.go8.edu.au/article/media-minister-simon-birmingham-faces-university-revolt-funding

[3] University-based legal education in the contemporary world comes in many institutional forms, each with their own histories, path dependencies and political economy. For the purposes of this chapter, I collapse these differences between 'law schools', 'law faculties' and public policy schools located in public and private universities and call all of these legal education providers 'law schools'.

Chesterman (2015) has argued that part of the colonial history of Asia was deliberate underinvestment in universities, which debilitated legal education; a situation that persisted until a recent wave of reforms to legal education. Dezalay and Garth (2010) also trace cycles of colonial investment and disinvestment in law (and legal education) in Asia, and the ways in which this determines the ability of a legal profession to accrue and mobilize legal, social, and family capital, which in turn affects the degree to which they may function independently and challenge state authority. The question that this chapter poses, then, is whether what Dezalay and Garth have termed a "revival" of law in some Asian states (2010) is reflected in a "knowledge to policy" process by law schools. In what ways do Asian law schools influence the state or broker norms that are part of the globalization of law, and with what kinds of drivers, partners, politics, and constraints? To answer these questions conclusively would require a thorough empirical study. Instead, this chapter sketches a series of policy engagement examples from China, Japan, Indonesia, Myanmar, and the Philippines. The examples chosen are ones in which the altruistic or liberal legal values are at issue, where transnational or global influences are visible, and where multiple stakeholders are using the law school as a site for developing or thwarting avenues for normative development and policy influence. The aim of the chapter is to draw attention to policy engagement as an understudied element of legal education institutions in Asia.

II. Prologue: Talking about Rule of Law in Yangon

To illustrate policy engagement by law schools as contested terrain, we start with an example from Myanmar, prior to the civilian government being ousted by a military coup in February 2021. My institution, the Australian National University (ANU) has a formal partnership with Yangon University (YU), as do many other international actors, including Oxford University, the National University of Singapore, the University of Washington, and Nagoya University, among others. One element of that has been a multiyear project funded by the Australian Department of Foreign Affairs and Trade (DFAT) to strengthen legal education in Myanmar, through support for curriculum redesign and help to boost the research capability of YU's law faculty. At the request of colleagues at YU, we then designed a workshop on rule of law, Security Sector Reform (SSR), and Sustainable Development Goal

(SDG) 16 (peace, justice, and strong institutions)—to help build awareness of national reporting obligations for Myanmar under the SDG framework.[4] YU colleagues self-reported limited ability to contribute to policy discourse in Myanmar. What they did not say explicitly was that, despite YU's proud intellectual history dating from 1920, decades of subordination by the military had rendered their political status peripheral. One dimension of this was that law had been taught for decades without the benefit of political science, which has only recently been reinstated as a discipline within Myanmar's universities.

The "theory of change" for this activity, then, was to provide a working understanding of these concepts, so that academics in that law faculty and in the political science faculty could better engage in policy discussions domestically. Ancillary goals included positioning them to work more effectively with each other, and with the many international organizations and donor projects promoting those concepts in Myanmar. The latter were a source of disquiet among academics, because the transition to a civilian government led by the National League for Democracy (NLD) in 2017 created a "parallel economy" for legal reform led by international actors. Well-paid jobs and preferment were open to young, English-speaking, "reform-minded" legal intermediaries, but there have been fewer opportunities for legal academics and other government employees (Simion 2021).

As in many repressive regimes, the legal profession in Myanmar during military rule had been kept small and proto-professional, without the expertise or prestige that would allow it to directly influence the universities. More significantly, law itself had been used almost exclusively as a tool of social control (Cheesman 2015). When one of the country's most celebrated lawyers, U Ko Ni, was assassinated (Crouch 2016), this was widely believed to be the work of one or more senior military figures. His killing was both a reminder of the impunity of the former regime and of their ability to control Aung San Suu Kyi, for whom U Ko Ni had been both senior advisor and architect of her constitutional role as "State Counsellor."

Against this background we understood the sensitivity of publicizing a workshop using terms such as "rule of law" and "SSR," and so we offered to describe it in different language. However, we were assured it was fine: everyone was excited. The workshop date was then suddenly canceled because the necessary Ministry of Education approval had not arrived. Through its

---

[4] See https://sustainabledevelopment.un.org/sdg16.

university rectors, the Ministry checked and approved every event that was held on university campuses or in which its academic staff participated. What we had not fully understood was that most of the rectors are also members of the USDP, the party ousted by the NLD in 2017. The USDP remains closely aligned with the military, and it is widely believed that the military has advised rectors to do what they can to "gum up the works" for foreign initiatives at Myanmar's universities. In this case, however, the permission did come through, and we were able to reschedule and proceed.

Colleagues from another Australian university were less fortunate. They began a workshop on transitional justice in a regional location, only to receive a call hours later from the capital, Naypyidaw, demanding that it be canceled. "Rule of law" is a concept that has been endorsed and adopted by Aung San Suu Kyi, as de facto head of state, but "transitional justice" is not something that she, her party, or the military wished to discuss. The political settlement that made possible the short-lived transition to civilian government in Myanmar did not include a reckoning for past (and current) abuses by the military (who continue to control Myanmar's internal ministries) as part of the deal (Callahan 2017). This was acutely obvious in the period following the 2018 political standoff between UN investigators and the Myanmar State in relation to independent reporting on the systemic killing and expulsion of Rohingya Muslim communities in Rakhine State. Having refused the United Nations' representatives access to Rakhine State, the government refused to accept their findings, which included genocide and crimes against humanity by the military and responsibility by multiple actors for the displacement of 700,000 as refugees (OHCHR, 2018).

Against this highly charged political background, it is hardly surprising that political elites had considerable ambivalence toward legal education reforms in which international partners were offered capacity development that had a normative edge. The (then) NLD government readily acknowledged that their universities needed to be redeveloped if Myanmar was to have any hope of developing economically or engaging meaningfully as a member of the Association of South East Asian Nations (ASEAN). Yet there was a palpable lack of domestic momentum to overhaul either law school staff or what they teach. The reason may have been that the government lacked traction with the university leaders who were agents for the previous military regime, or because of the well-publicized policy bottlenecks that occur in a political party with a single autocratic leader (Callahan 2017), or because no one was confident that there would not be a return to military rule after the general elections in November 2020. Those who feared a military coup were proven correct in February 2021 when the military seized control of the country following the re-election of the NLD government. Those who feared the vulnerability of universities were also proven correct: the civil disobedience movement resistance to the military junta resulted in tens of thousands of lecturers being dismissed, and hundreds of lecturers and students being arrested, tortured and killed (Reuters 2021).

As Simion (2021) shows very effectively, political elites of all colors in Myanmar were wary about the normative ideas that external donors were bringing in under the banner of "rule of law," much of it without explicit government authorization. So when Aung San Suu Kyi—herself the (then) chair of the State Committee on Rule of Law—resorted to nationalistic rhetoric when defending Myanmar against charges of genocide in the International Court of Justice in (UN News 2019), she was arguably reflecting wider views within the country's leadership. Setting aside the specifics of Myanmar, I suggest that we can discern more universal themes within this skirmishing— particularly the struggle to insulate the law school at a national university from global engagement that could have had ramifications for domestic politics.

III. Legal Education's Knowledge Mandate

Constraining what legal scholars may do, as the civilian government did administratively in Myanmar and the military junta then converted into extra-legal brutality (Human Rights Watch 2021), is a way of curbing what Halliday terms law's "knowledge mandate": "the capacity to exert influence . . . an epistemological warrant for public influence mediated by occupational and organizational politics" (Halliday 1985: 422). He argues that this public influence derives from law's unique ability to speak publicly in both a technical and a moral register. In the case of legal education, this is also coupled with the prestige that attaches to the university—still a powerful totem in most Asian societies. When legal academics engage with external partners, beyond their core teaching and research activities, they are both exercising and expanding their "knowledge mandate."

Following Gunningham, Kagan, and Thornton (2004), we could also characterize this as legal education's "social license": the autonomy and authority to speak and engage that derives from the self-regulating privilege that is accorded to legal education institutions by state and society. Whether we think of this as a "license" or a "mandate," legal academics' freedom to exercise it is profoundly affected by the ways in which stakeholders, such as government, business, the legal profession, and transnational actors, seek to constrain or expand it.

In the United States, the United Kingdom, Australia, and much of Europe, universities willingly nurture and participate in public policy relationships and channels. They do so because this both exercises and extends their knowledge mandate. As the prestige of the institution grows, it bolsters the university's professional control over knowledge production, and it elevates individual scholars as "experts." In combination, these effects quite often translate into financial benefits, either collectively for the university or individually for a researcher. For a university sector that is perpetually underfunded, this makes external engagement important.

Halliday (1985) argues that normative professions such as law and syncretic professions such as the academy are more likely to have a broad knowledge mandate: law creates its knowledge, and claims its authority, through moral or normative discourse, and the academy draws on both scientific and normative foundations for its epistemological base. Law schools are where these two powerful professional cohorts—legal professions and academics—intersect, to help create the professional authority of university legal education.

An important caveat is that legal professionals in many places share a self-identity that mixes altruism and a commitment to ideas of justice with pragmatism about markets, self-interest, and profit maximization. This is one reason that Dezalay and Garth have depicted elite lawyers "[as] 'double agents' who maintain the legitimacy of their clients on one hand, but also stand for the independent authority of law on the other" (Munger 2012: 480). The normative orientation of legal academics can be similarly mixed or diverse. Universities, in turn, are even more normatively diverse and thus more difficult to mobilize collectively than a traditional profession such as law (at least within political systems where the legal profession enjoys a high degree of autonomy).

A further complication is that the knowledge mandate of universities is increasingly instrumentalized by the state and industry. "Engagement" with partners outside the university is now both an expected and rewarded form of work for academics in higher education systems such as those of the United Kingdom and Australia. Most recently this can be seen in the measurement of research "impact" in the United Kingdom (e.g., Jones et al. 2017) and in Australia, in the preferential funding of research in which government agencies, corporations, and/or nonprofit entities are both research partners and beneficiaries of the work (Australian Research Council 2020).

The effect has been that universities in the Anglo-Australian system self-consciously create these engagement opportunities and spaces, while government also imposes them through regulatory measures. Thus, the creation and labeling of "engagement" as a recognized form of university work also functions as a "regulatory space" (Hancher and Moran 1989) which is open to, and can be contested, by multiple actors. Law schools are particularly significant sites of contestation because both their knowledge mandate and the style of normative knowledge that they produce have ready application for political and policy purposes.

IV. Shaping Law School Engagement with Policy in Asia

Since the 1990s, Asian states from Afghanistan to Singapore have responded to globalizing influences by strengthening their universities and consciously installing new models of legal education (Miyazawa et al. 2008; Taylor 2010). These legal education reforms were often narrated as elements in national development strategies (Taylor 2010) in which the model of American-style "law schools" was often invoked as an ideal form of legal education. Instead of law being a foundational discipline for multiple careers, policymakers advocated for a more vocational "law school" in order to heighten the technical expertise of the legal profession in support of more globally exposed economies.[5] Subsequent decades, however, have seen the US model critiqued at home and abroad, as well as more variation in the institutional design of legal education throughout Asia, including a great deal of hybridity. South Korea's adoption of a limited number of exclusively graduate-level law schools, for example, was a reaction to Japan's failure to meld (then) seventy-four new US-style law schools with the legacy of undergraduate law faculties and a highly restrictive national bar exam. By contrast, Shanghai Jiao Tong University pioneered a 3+3 model of blended undergraduate and graduate legal education that targeted an elite group of high-achieving

---

[5] In Japan, the introduction of law schools initially boosted the number of graduates seeking employment as attorneys, and it simultaneously depressed the number of law graduates seeking to enter the public service.

students who would be groomed for international practice. McConnaughay and Toomey (2015) argue that the establishment of the Peking University School of Transnational Law (STL) under local champion Hai Wen, "one of China's leading development economists," and the importation of "leading U.S. professors and practitioners" as a core part of the design also marked a more fundamental turning point in the development of legal education in Asia (McConnaughay and Toomey 2015: 3). In the wake of the American Bar Association's decision not to accredit a law school outside the United States—and STL in particular—it reframed its mission to prepare students for transnational practice in which the influence of China and non-Western legal systems on trade is growing. In doing so, they chart a potential siniciza-tion of global legal education.

As more stakeholders began to focus on the national economic impor-tance of law schools, they became sites of political and regulatory compe-tition for control. Among the many issues now being contested are how law schools and their leadership conceive their knowledge mandate, and how legal academics engage with the domain of public policy. The next section looks at some modalities through which legal educators have either ex-panded their knowledge mandate or acquiesced in its constraint, and which regulatory forces and actors feature in those processes.

A. The PRC: The Case of the Disappearing Legal Clinic

As the twenty-first century dawned, Mainland China was in the throes of rapid and significant changes to its legal education system. Some of these were clearly influenced by the American legal education model (Taylor 2010), but China funded most of the restructuring of its legal education through di-rect state investment, supported by the development of a domestic ranking system and the rapid expansion of coursework master programs. Wang, Liu, and Li (2017) give a nuanced account of the drivers and effects of the inter-nationalization of China's legal education and the ways that it intersects with American legal education and knowledge production in the Anglosphere. The wide dispersal of universities in the country, however, meant that the results remain tiered and uneven: elite institutions in Beijing, Shanghai, and some provincial capitals look very different than those at the periphery.

China did not immediately follow the Japanese and Korean trajec-tory of shifting undergraduate legal education to vocational, bar-focused, graduate-level law schools. However, from 2000, it did take the developmental lead in Asia in the introduction of clinical legal education at universities, initially through the pioneering program at Wuhan, established in the 1990s (Cai 2011: 163), and then in South Central University (in Wuhan), Fudan and East China Universities in Shanghai, and Peking and Tsinghua Universities in Beijing. By 2011, there were more than 130 "legal aid clinics" attached to law schools (Cai 2011: 168). One of the drivers for the rapid expansion of legal clinics based at universities was foreign donor funding; the Ford Foundation played a catalytic role in establishing clinical legal education and funding the Committee for Chinese Clinical Legal Educators (CCCLE) to support its diffusion (Phan 2005; Liu 2008; Chapter 2, this volume). Clinical law programs were coordinated through the CCCLE and their kind and quality varied fairly dramatically with location: elite institutions such as Tsinghua, Peking, and Wuhan had much more robust programs than those at many regional law schools. Another driver was the limited funding base of the state legal aid bureau and its inability to deliver services in peri-urban and rural areas (Liebman 1999).

Clinics, as a form of legal education developed originally in the United States, take multiple forms: they can be based in a law school and function like a legal office handling certain categories of cases on a no-fee basis; they can involve selection of cases for development into public interest litigation; or they can deploy students outside the law school to promote legal awareness and basic legal knowledge such as in "Street Law" programs. All of these styles are found in China (Liu 2008). What each type of clinical experience has in common is experiential learning ("learning by doing"), usually involving a fairly close connection to the funding mechanisms and organization of state-provided legal aid, and (in the United States and US-influenced settings) a normative orientation. Many clinicians see this form of legal education and external engagement as a multifaceted mission: (1) skills formation for pre-professional students through practical, experiential learning; (2) the transformation of those students' perspectives through inculcating values such as legal ethics and a commitment to social justice (Bloch 2011) and the capacity for reflexive action; and (3) the virtuous co-option of student labor to provide legal services for the poor—a perennially understaffed and underfunded enterprise in most countries.

The centrality of students to the clinical enterprise is interesting, because students—by definition—are not legal experts. Clinical legal education, often coupled with legal aid programs, promises to create a cohort or generation of law students sensitized to the living conditions of the poor and to the limits of law in their own country. Whether clinical legal education actually delivers on that promise is an open question (Phan 2005; Liu 2008). It has been critiqued as delivering negligible results in the short term and potentially little systemic impact in the long term (Note 2007; Joyce and Winfrey 2004). The success of programs such as BABSEACLE (2021), however, suggests that there is an undiminished appetite for building and developing clinical legal education programs in South East Asia.

In China, part of the appeal of preparing students for law-related work by building their "real-world" exposure and skills is that the system postgraduation relies heavily on bureaucratic management of disputes, rather than litigation. For external actors such as donors, the normative appeal of supporting the start-up phase of clinical education in China was using students to "do an end run" around existing political and bureaucratic elites to effect what in legal development terms was part of "access to justice" or "legal empowerment" (e.g., van Rooij 2009). An early critique was that the rapid infusion of foreign money and models into China could thwart the development of indigenous institutions (Dowdle 2000) and thus contradict the "local ownership" tenet of the legal empowerment movement. In this case, Chinese state actors proved to be astute regulatory players. Clinical legal education seems to have progressed as a legal transplant of form, without the attendant American social and educational history or emancipatory political ideology.

Significantly, neither China's Ministry of Justice nor the Ministry of Education contributed funding to the clinics during their first decade of operation (Cai 2011), meaning that they were either funded by universities or used a self-funding (fee-based) model. But state actors undoubtedly calculated that it would be beneficial to have a cohort of law graduates with some exposure to practical training during law school. The Ministry of Justice might also have thought that legal service provision by the (then) relatively small number of formally credentialed lawyers in China would continue to require supplementation through government legal workers, barefoot lawyers, paralegals, and students (Fu 2009).

By the Beijing Olympics in 2008, however, the political climate for progressive lawyering had begun to chill. Scholars began to describe this as China's "turn from law" or "turn from rule of law," where the active support for using law and legal institutions to mediate social conflict was considerably decelerated (Minzner 2018). It was visibly consolidated in the Party Congress of

2012, with the election of Xi Jinping as the Party Secretary, in 2013, as PRC president and in 2018, as PRC president for life. Halliday and Liu (2016) describe in detail the fate of activist lawyers in China since this turning point, and Stern (2016) analyzes the state's political use of the bar exam as a tool for inculcating its preferred version of concepts such as "rule of law."

A direct consequence of this political shift was the disappearance of some high-profile clinics, one example being the Centre for Women's Law Studies and Legal Services affiliated with Peking University.[6] Initially disaffiliated by the university in 2010, it was closed in 2016 by government decree (Tatlow 2016). At the same time, surveillance and punishment of legal academics and legal aid activists has increased (The Guardian 2016), and public use of keywords such as "human rights" or "rule of law" is closely monitored. Eva Pils (2016) has called this "rule by fear." So, the clear implication here is that Chinese law schools do not have an unfettered ability to advance into an engagement or nascent policy space like clinical legal education, even to produce a public good, if that conflicts with the Party's fear of "empowerment" translating into social instability.

B. The Philippines: Declining to Engage

Since his election in 2016, Philippines president, Rodrigo Roa Duterte, has struggled with the concept of rule of law.[7] In May 2017, he imposed martial law across the entire southern province of Mindanao, in response to an armed taking of the city of Marawi. To the dismay of many legal scholars, the Philippine Supreme Court upheld this overreaching decree. Duterte is widely believed to have engineered the Court's removal of its own Chief Justice the following year, because she was an impediment to his disregard for legality (Deinla, Rood, and Taylor 2018).

The siege of Marawi was a traumatic event: the militants claimed to be affiliated with the Islamic State, more than 2,000 residents were killed and 600,000 were displaced by the fighting, and much of the central city was physically destroyed (Deinla 2018). The great fear of Muslim Filipinos was

---

[6] Beijing Zhongze Women's Legal Counseling Service Center (formerly the Center for Women's Law Studies and Legal Services of Peking University): http://ngochina.blogspot.com.au/2010/04/peking-university-womens-legal-aid.html.

[7] The extrajudicial killings of drug users and drug traffickers (both alleged and actual) carried out under his direction now represents the second largest number of civilians killed by their own government in South East Asia after the Cambodians annihilated by Pol Pot.

that these events would further delay their demand for self-determination, after nearly four decades of armed conflict with the government in Manila. In fact, Duterte did deliver in part on his electoral promise to conclusively resolve the conflict in Mindanao. The Bangsamoro Organic Law was signed into law in July 2018 and, because it required constitutional change, was put to a regional plebiscite in early 2019 (Tiojanco 2019). The successful vote ushered in the transitional period that will create the Bangsamoro Autonomous Region of Muslim Mindanao (BARMM) (Abuza and Lischin 2020). The Bangsamoro ("Home of the Moro") will be an Islamic law jurisdiction with considerable delegated legal authority which in a de facto way will transform the Philippines from being a unitary to a federated state. The legal and social reality, of course, is complicated: Mindanao has a high degree of ethnic, linguistic, and religious diversity, and even within the BARMM, not all population centers are majority Muslim. What the BARMM has in common with the rest of Mindanao, however, is that it is poor—if Mindanao were a country, it would be sit in the United Nations' "least-developed" band (United Nations 2020).

Law schools in the Philippines have had ample time to become engaged with the social justice issues that affect Muslim Filipinos and indigenous communities in Mindanao. Some, like the Jesuit university Ateneo de Davao, which houses the Al Qalam Institute for Islamic Identities and Dialogue in Southeast Asia, have done so. In the Mindanao State University main campus in Marawi City, even as that city's siege continued, 8,000 students returned to campus in August 2017 as an act of Muslim-Christian solidarity, retaking the university as a liberal enclave that repudiates Islamist intolerance (Straits Times 2018).

However, academics in Mindanao described the policy silence from Manila as "deafening" (Personal communication 2018a). One explanation is that decades of armed conflict have delegitimized Muslim interests among metropolitan elites. The Filipino legal establishment has tightly proscribed the visibility and the mandate of both *shari'a* as a source of law in the Philippines and Islamic legal actors as justice providers. So, for example, the Supreme Court in Manila administers *shari'a* courts and *shari'a* judges as part of the Court's operations, but does not describe either on the Court's website. The state *shari'a* courts operate exclusively in Mindanao, although Muslim Filipinos also live in Manila and other parts of the country. Only with the creation of the BARMM will the *shari'a* court jurisdiction expand beyond the family law matters and application of the Philippine Code of Personal Status.

Until 2020, a law graduate in Manila could legitimately not know that the Philippines is a pluralist legal system in which *sharia* governs the lives of nearly five million Filipinos. Although the advent of the BARMM is forcing a reconsideration of how to provide *sharia* legal services, to date Islamic legal professionals in the Philippines have been ceded minimalist qualifications through a simplified bar exam for *sharia* judges and advocates. Consequently, they lack the prestige of advocates who pass the hypercompetitive national (secular) bar exam. Few universities in the Philippines offer Islamic law as a course for credit.[8] The prestigious College of Law of the University of the Philippines appears to be the only law school in Manila to have offered Islamic law as an elective course, but not as a preparation for practice. A handful of universities in Mindanao offer Islamic law and jurisprudence courses for the purpose of taking the *sharia* bar examination. The non-state system of Islamic courts maintained by the Moro National Liberation Front (MNLF) in parallel to the state system is largely staffed with judges educated in the Middle East and North Africa. *Sharia* by its nature is a multinodal system of authority. The policy risk of not engaging with the task of developing *sharia* capability in the Philippines that is attuned to Filipino social, cultural, and political realities is that other discourses and actors are ready to fill the space.

C. Indonesia: The Scholarship Vacuum

Indonesia is a middle-income, majority Muslim country with a pluralist legal system in which nearly 4,500 universities operate more than 300 law schools: state, private, and Islamic. Consult a rankings list of universities in Asia, however, and you find that even the three universities regarded domestically as prestigious (University of Indonesia, Bandung Institute of Technology, and Gadjah Mada University) struggle to break into the top 500 band (e.g., Times Higher Education 2020). The Ministry of Research, Technology, and Higher Education estimates that of the country's 5,400 or so full professors, only 5 percent are producing internationally refereed research

---

[8] Islamic/*Shari'ah* studies are offered as a full course of study leading to a Bachelor's degree in some other universities, predominantly in Mindanao. There is an Institute of Islamic Studies based in the University of the Philippines (Diliman) that offers specialized Master's and PhD research on any topic involving Islam/ *Shari'ah* in the Philippines.

(Personal communication 2018b), which speaks to both the research culture and the structural incentives for producing, peer-reviewing, and publishing research. Law is no exception to these patterns.

The regulatory response of the Ministry has been to recredential universities through clustering and to drive forced mergers and closures, particularly of low-quality private institutions (Global Business Guide 2018). The clustering or ranking of universities is based on human resources quality, institutional quality, student activity quality, and scientific research and publication quality.

The University of Indonesia and Gadjah Mada University are generally regarded as Indonesia's leading law schools, based largely on perceptions of prestige and the profiles of faculty members. However, they are also the beneficiaries of the expansion of public universities in the postindependence period and what Sinaga argues is a lingering prejudice against private institutions that is empirically suspect (2018). Of the 393 law programs in Indonesia, 346 (or 88 percent) are private; of the 58 accredited with an "A" rating, 34 (or 58 percent) are private (Sinaga 2018: 176).

A scholarly debate has simmered across decades about the mission of the Indonesian law school—whether it should teach "pure law," whether it should serve the national interest and teach "progressive law," or whether it should have a more sociolegal, empirically informed cast (Rosenbaum 2014). Bedner (2013) also sees the formalist character of legal education in Indonesia as an impediment to both research quality and practice-readiness, which would be consistent with Chesterman's thesis (2015) about the constraining power of colonial models.

The state calls forth "engagement" from legal academics in Indonesia in at least three ways. One is the relatively recent government mandating of "community service" as part of the *tridharma perguraan tinggi*, or "three pillars" of higher education, comprising education, research, and community service (e.g., Universitas Indonesia 2020). Community service was added as a factor in the university accreditation scheme from 2017, and this is the pillar into which law school activities such as legal clinics and support for local NGOs can be fitted. Separately from this, individual faculty members from major schools are routinely tapped for policy-related service by government. In the past this often took the form of individual "consulting," and for some prominent legal academics this was a major part of their work portfolio (and income). This was structurally enabled by the prohibition on government agencies commissioning research or consulting services from other organizations, such as NGOs or universities, but this barrier was removed by procurement regulation reform in 2018 (Perpres 16/2018 2018).

The relatively new Indonesia Jentera Law School has adopted a very different model of engagement. Jentera is the private legal education part of an interlocking series of legal reform projects developed over the past twenty years or so which include the leading legal reform NGO the Centre for Legal and Policy Studies (PSHK), a foundation (YSHK), the Dan Lev Law Library, the *Jentera* law journal, and Hukum Online, an online legal information portal that is both open access and commercial. Significantly, Jentera has made democracy, anticorruption, and rule of law part of its animating values (Jakarta Post 2015) and aims to produce graduates who can contribute to public policy through evidence-based research. Of the hundreds of law schools in Indonesia, this is the only one that so clearly aspires to the kind of engagement model that we see in the United States, the United Kingdom, or Australia.

A further mode of engagement for legal academics since Indonesia's democratization in 1998 has been partnering with international donor projects, which are screened and approved by government through the National Planning Agency (BAPPENAS). Over the past twenty years, lawyers at PSHK and other legal NGOs in its network—in many cases now part of Jentera— have made themselves indispensable partners in foreign donor-funded legal assistance projects. As Dezalay and Garth have noted (2010), their alumni make up a new generation of activist lawyers who sit outside the conventional government–large law firm–public university domain, even while they maintain close relationships with each. While law schools in Indonesia have in the past been happy to accept new resources, such projects have also engendered a degree of bitterness and frustration (Bosch 2016) when a project has the effect of taking the most productive staff out of the law school, paying them a premium to work for an outside organization, and framing the law schools as "recipients" of aid, rather than as agents and genuine partners in the design and implementation of the projects (Bosch 2016; Rosenbaum 2014).

On the donor side, however, we now see considerable innovation in Indonesia. The Australian government's Knowledge Sector Initiative (KSI) has been an innovative partnership with Indonesia's National Planning Agency. The project aims to boost the capability of NGOs and nodes within universities to pursue evidence-based research that can contribute to better policymaking.[9] Policymaking here means policies that advance social

---

[9] http://www.ksi-indonesia.org/en/pages/knowledge-sector-initiative

equity. KSI adopted a genuinely iterative design for the project, which has been predominantly Indonesian in its leadership, staffing, and partnerships. Although university research centers feature as partners for KSI, it is significant that the Centre for Legal and Policy Studies (PSHK), part of the network to which the Jentera Law School belongs, is the only core legal partner in the project.[10]

D. Japan: Capture and Capitulation

We can think of Japan's adoption of US-style legal education since the mid-1990s as a slow-motion car crash being reported in stages (e.g., Saito 2006; Saegusa 2009; Taylor 2010; Tanaka 2016). The new system commenced in 2004 with (then) seventy-four newly launched graduate law schools. Part of the normative impetus for this dramatic institutional redesign was the desire on the part of some reformers to realize the post–World War II promise of a liberal vision of social justice in Japan. Lawyers were to engage in a wider range of work in support of a citizenry that had—at least statistically—less access to legal services than their Anglo-European peers. By establishing the new graduate school system and retaining law as an undergraduate discipline, a much larger cohort of law graduates would ensue (Taylor 2010). Assuming that they passed the national bar exam at rates not dissimilar to the those in the United States—about 70 percent—this would significantly expand the size of the practicing profession. A second discourse in support of the change was the need to expand the number of lawyers with new and different kinds of knowledge—particularly those able to handle transnational work (in English), and those supporting the country's industrial policy in fields such as intellectual property. So, entwined with a domestic narrative of "progress" was a clear awareness of globalizing influences and the threat they posed to an historically closed and protected legal profession (Justice System Reform Council 2001).

More than one of the newly established schools aimed to deliver a distinctive style of socially engaged and practical legal education that would have been a departure from the abstract rote-learning of the past. Some of the proposed "solutions" to this structural dependency were to hire foreign

---

[10] See for example: http://www.pshk.or.id/wp-content/uploads/2017/08/Understanding-Policy-Making-in-Indonesia-PSHK.pdf

law professors, teach courses—particularly international commercial law courses—in English, and introduce skills training through clinical education and mooting.

Fast forward to 2021 and arguably none of the reform goals has been achieved. Instead, the law schools' knowledge mandate has shrunk. A key factor here has been the choice by stakeholders such as the Japan Federation of Bar Associations, the Supreme Court, and the Ministry of Justice to retain a largely unchanged national bar exam and control the annual pass rate. In recent years this has hovered at less than 29 percent (jumping to 33 percent in 2019) for the bar taken after law school and 3.8 percent for a "preliminary bar exam" that does not require law school enrollment (Nichibenren 2020). The goal of manipulating the bar passage rates is to hold down the numbers of new entrants to the profession to less than 1,500 per annum. Aspiring law students, confronted by a system in which success rates have been declining, have voted with their feet, and this has forced the closure of just under 50 percent of the law schools established in 2004 (Breaden and Goodman 2020: 137).

The Japan Federation of Bar Associations has long argued that the high quality of domestic legal practitioners (and by extension, judges and prosecutors) in Japan can only be sustained by limiting the numbers of bar-passers through a hypercompetitive bar exam. The more sordid reality is that putting their thumbs on the scale in this way masks the precarious nature of legal practice and income outside the main commercial hubs of Tokyo and Osaka, and so maintains the illusion of a well-remunerated, prestigious profession (Nakazato et al. 2010). As a protective play, this narrative has been a regulatory triumph for the bar. Few leaders in the profession have spoken about the social injustice toward students who have paid high tuition, studied hard, and are unable to pass the bar exam through no fault of their own. For the more than 70 percent of unsuccessful candidates, there are few alternative pathways within law or business: the stigma of failure is immense.

A less-commonly reported aspect of this reform fiasco is the impact on the quality of public policy. One of the early critiques of the system change was that luring talented students into graduate law schools was counterproductive for a country that had traditionally educated bureaucrats, business people, and aspiring lawyers together in faculties of law and politics (Riles and Uchida 2009); indeed, for the first few years of the law school experiment, students did desert the national public service exam in significant numbers in order to take the bar. What the redesign did not do was to add interdisciplinary skills to this highly educated and highly subsidized (Tanaka 2016) cohort. The most successful bar-passers tend to be, not surprisingly, students who took undergraduate law and followed this up with law school. This results in the polar opposite of the type of law graduate produced in the United States or Australia, whose systems are designed to allow law graduates to build on a disciplinary background in science, social science, medicine, economics, business studies, or accounting. So when Japanese law graduates advance into public service, business, or the legal profession, they do so with a very narrow knowledge base.

A third dimension of this problem has been the sunk costs for legal academics who were tasked with establishing new, duplicative legal education institutions. This became obvious once it was clear that the national bar exam would not include international, transactional, contextual, or comparative law topics. Students naturally began to desert newly established skills or "international" courses (some of which were taught in English) and offerings such as clinical legal education. A telling irony is that the excellent Intercollegiate Negotiation and Arbitration competition established in Japan during the reform period is now contested largely by undergraduate Japanese students and international students, not by the Japanese law school students whose skills and careers it was designed to support.[11]

As a mood of crisis gradually enveloped the sector (Tanaka 2016), Japanese law school academics understood that their school's bar passage rate was existentially important; in fact, government subsidies for law schools would be tied to it (Breaden and Goodman 2020). Thus other pursuits, including research and policy engagement, needed to be subordinated to this goal. For much of the past two decades, then, producing globally competitive, peer-reviewed research, in the way that Korean universities, for example, have been able to mandate, is an aspirational but distant goal for many of Japan's legal scholars.

Over the same period, the Japanese government inserted a pump-priming "global" university competition into the higher education system, aimed at boosting international research linkages, attracting international student enrollments through educational innovation, and encouraging Japanese student mobility internationally. In theory, Japanese law schools should have been well positioned to take advantage of this initiative, not least because of the complementary evolution of their peer schools in Asia (e.g.,

---

[11] See http://www.negocom.jp/eng/.

BABSEACLE 2021). An important example is the development of regional-level collaborations in South East Asia, sponsored through the Asian Law Institute (ASLI) at the National University of Singapore (NUS), which also draws in Anglosphere law schools while positioning NUS in a powerful convening and funding role. However, because of design deficiencies of Japan's law school system, the incentives for student and staff mobility are heavily constrained—at least until the supply-side of the system is further rationalized.

V. Conclusion

This chapter has shown that the knowledge mandate for law schools in Asia, while theoretically broad in the way conceptualized by Halliday, varies in practice by location and institutional context. It also varies over time and is closely correlated with the political climate of the day, in ways that resonate with the depiction of elite lawyers tacking through shifting political winds in Dezalay and Garth's biographical narratives from Asia (2010). One way of testing such variation in knowledge mandate is to examine the way in which normative considerations shape law school policy "engagement," and what animates or constrains this engagement.

Viewed in this way, legal education is much more than a series of technical design choices: engagement with policy reveals strong normative contesta-tion in a space constituted by both state and non-state actors. Within Asia, "engagement" work can be an entry point for transnational actors who seek to influence local public policy by enrolling law schools, their staff, and their students in networks and epistemic communities that advance particular normative agendas, such as the United Nations' Sustainable Development Goals. As we saw in the case of Myanmar, agents of the state may actively resist these globalizing influences by monitoring what is being discussed in their law schools, what knowledge is being produced, and what kinds of partnerships law schools enter.

In Japan, we observe a different contestation of globalizing norms. Law schools were originally a state-sponsored design that sought to respond to Japan's lack of global competitiveness in legal services by widening the pro-fessional knowledge mandate. A coalition of domestic lawyers and state ac-tors who were focused on short-term protectionism, however, thwarted this initiative. In Indonesia, on the other hand, private sector and civil society interests have succeeded in charting an altruistic engagement path outside the stasis of the state-centric university system. These competitions for control of legal education design are consistent with Dezalay and Garth's arguments in *Asian Legal Revivals* (2010) about the ability of powerful actors in the legal system—particularly the private bar—to mobilize social capital in ways that benefit themselves.

The state also makes demands of law schools as repositories of knowledge—either by reaching in to access expertise, or by trying to design regulatory frameworks that will harness research and engagement behaviors that it deems desirable. Indonesia's Higher Education Ministry is experimenting with this kind of regulation, conscious of the engagement and impact agendas being advanced in Australian and UK higher education. Law schools and their academics are not passive in the face of such initiatives; they exert their own agency. As we saw also in the Philippines and in Indonesia, differently situated institutions are animated by different normative considerations. The degree to which law school elites are open to acknowledging alternative and pluralist sources of legal legitimacy also determines whether they can produce and contribute knowledge for policy at a time of national transformation.

These kinds of institutional design differences matter, not simply for the relative strength and prestige of law as an academic field, or as a profession when viewed at the national level (a perennial source of interest to lawyers), but more profoundly for how legal knowledge is able to be produced and deployed in the face of complex global challenges. What these experiences of Asian law school engagement show is that some regulatory relationships between public policy actors and law schools facilitate such engagement more than others. The knowledge mandate for the profession widens or narrows accordingly.

References

Abuza, Zachary and Luke Lischin (2020). "The Challenges Facing the Philippines' Bangsamoro Autonomous Region at One Year," United States Institute of Peace Special Report No. 468. June. https://www.usip.org/sites/default/files/2020-06/20200610-sr_468-the_challenges_facing_the_philippines_bangsamoro_autonomous_region_at_one_year-sr.pdf.

Australian Research Council (2020). Linkage Program. https://www.arc.gov.au/grants/linkage-program/arc-centres-excellence.

BABSEACLE (2021). Bridges Across Borders South East Asia Community Legal Education Initiative. https://www.babseacle.org.

Bedner, A.W. (2013). "Indonesian Legal Scholarship and Jurisprudence as an Obstacle for Transplanting Legal Institutions," *Hague Journal on the Rule of Law* 5(2): 253–273.

Biz Journal (2016). Houkadaigakuin, seidoushippai ga ketteiteki. . . [Graduate Law Schools: System Failure Is Definitive . . .]. https://biz-journal.jp/2016/03/post_14 199.html.

Bloch, Frank S., ed. (2011). *The Global Clinical Movement: Educating Lawyers for Social Justice.* Oxford.

Bosch, Anna (2016). "Local Actors in Donor-Funded Rule of Law Assistance in Indonesia: Owners, Partners, Agents?" Unpublished PhD dissertation. University of Washington.

Breaden, Jeremy and Goodman, Roger (2020). "MGU 2008–2018: The Law School and Other Reforms" in J. Breaden and R. Goodman, *Family-Run Universities in Japan: Sources of Inbuilt Resilience in the Face of Demographic Pressure, 1992–2030.* Oxford.

Cai, Yanmin (2011). "Global Clinical Legal Education and International Partnerships: A Chinese Legal Educator's Perspective," *Maryland Journal of International Law* 26: 159–172.

Callahan, Mary (2017). "Aung San Suu Kyi's Quiet Puritanical Vision for Myanmar," *Asia Nikkei.* March 29. https://asia.nikkei.com/Politics/Aung-San-Suu-Kyi-s-quiet-puri tanical-vision-for-Myanmar.

Cheesman, Nick (2015). *Opposing the Rule of Law.* Cambridge.

Chesterman, Simon (2015). *The Rise and Fall of Legal Education in Asia: Inhibition, Imitation, Innovation.* NUS Law Working Paper 2015/015. http://law.nus.edu.sg/wps/.

Crouch, Melissa (2017). "In Memoriam: 'Saya' U Ko Ni, Myanmar's Advocate for Constitutional Reform (March 22, 2017)," *Australian Journal of Asian Law* 17(2): Article 1, 2016. https://ssrn.com/abstract=2939411.

Deinla, Imelda (2018). "Travel Notebook: Marawi City," *The Interpreter,* Lowy Institute. https://www.lowyinstitute.org/the-interpreter/travel-notebook-marawi-city.

Deinla, Imelda and Veronica Taylor (2015). *Towards Peace: Rethinking Justice and Legal Pluralism in the Bangsamoro.* RegNet Research Paper No. 2015/63. http://ssrn.com/abstract=2553541.

Deinla, Imelda, Rood Stephen, and Veronica Taylor (2018). "Justice Removed, Justice Denied," *The Interpreter,* Lowy Institute. https://www.lowyinstitute.org/the-interpre ter/philippines-justice-removed-justice-denied.

Dezalay, Yves and Garth Bryant (2010). *Asian Legal Revivals: Lawyers in the Shadow of Empire.* Chicago.

Dowdle, Michael William (2000). "Preserving Indigenous Paradigms in an Age of Globalization: Pragmatic Strategies for the Development of Clinical Legal Aid in China," *Fordham International Law Journal* 24: 56.

FHUI (2020). *Visi dan misi* [Vision and Mission]. http://law.ui.ac.id/v3/visi-dan-misi/.

Fu, Hualing (2009). Access to Justice in China: Potentials, Limits, and Alternatives. http://ssrn.com/abstract=1474073.

Global Business Guide (2018). Education | Indonesia's Tertiary Education Sector: Aiming Higher. http://www.gbgindonesia.com/en/education/article/2018/indonesia_s_ter tiary_education_sector_aiming_higher_11849.php.

The Guardian (2016). "China Steps Up Human Rights Crackdown with Arrest of Foreign Activist," January 13. https://www.theguardian.com/world/2016/jan/13/china-human-rights-crackdown-arrest-peter-dahlin-swedish-activist.

The Guardian (2017). https://www.theguardian.com/world/2017/aug/28/aung-sang-suu-kyis-office-accuses-aid-workers-of-helping-terrorists-in-myanmar.

Gunningham, Neil, Kagan Robert A., and Thornton Dorothy (2004). "Social License and Environmental Protection: Why Businesses Go beyond Compliance," *Law & Social Inquiry* 29(2): 307–41..

Halliday, Terence C. (1985). "Knowledge Mandates: Collective Influence by Scientific, Normative and Syncretic Professions," *The British Journal of Sociology* Vol. XXXVI(3): 421–447.

Halliday Terence C. and Lucien Karpik (1998). *Lawyers and the Rise of Western Political Liberalism*. Oxford University Press.

Halliday Terence C. and Sida Liu (2016). *Criminal Defense in China: The Politics of Lawyers at Work*. Cambridge.

Hancher, L. and M. Moran (1989). "Organizing Regulatory Space," in L. Hancher and M. Moran, eds., *Capitalism, Culture and Economic Regulation*. Clarendon Press.

Human Rights Watch (2021) "Myanmar: Coup Leads to Crimes Against Humanity" 31 July. https://www.hrw.org/news/2021/07/31/myanmar-coup-leads-crimes-against-humanity#

Jakarta Post (2015). http://www.thejakartapost.com/news/2015/07/08/noted-lawyers-legal-activists-establish-anti-graft-school.html.

Jones, Molly Morgan, Cartriona Manville, and Joanna Chataway (2017). "Learning from the UK's Research Impact Assessment Exercise: A Case Study of a Retrospective Impact Assessment Exercise Questions for the Future," *Journal of Technology Transfer*. 1–25. https://doi.org/10.1007/s10961-017-9608-6.

Joyce, Arwen and Tracye Winfrey (2004). "Current Developments 2003–2004: Taming the Red Dragon: A Realistic Assessment of the ABA's Legal Reform Efforts in China," *Georgetown Journal of Legal Ethics* 17(4): 887–902.

Justice System Reform Council (2001). Recommendations of the Justice System Reform Council—For a Justice System to Support Japan in the 21st Century. June 12. http://www.kantei.go.jp/foreign/judiciary/2001/0612report.html.

Liebman, Benjamin L. (1999). "Legal Aid and Public Interest Law in China," *Texas International Law Journal* 34(2): 211–286.

Liu, Titi M. (2008). "Transmission of Public Interest Law: A Chinese Case Study," *UCLA Journal of International Law and Foreign Affairs* 13(1): 263–94.

McConnaughay, Philip and Colleen Toomey (2015). *Preparing for the Sinicization of the Western Legal Tradition: The Case of Peking University School of Transnational Law (November 20, 2015)*. Peking University School of Transnational Law Research Paper No. 16-1. https://ssrn.com/abstract=2710550 or http://dx.doi.org/10.2139/ssrn.2710550.

Minzner, Carl (2018). *End of an Era: How China's Authoritarian Revival Is Undermining Its Rise*. Oxford.

Miyazawa, Setsuo, Kay-Wah Chan, and Ilhyung Lee (2008). "The Reform of Legal Education in East Asia," *Annual Review of Law & Social Science* 4: 333–60.

Munger, Frank (2012). "Globalization through the Lens of Palace Wars: What Elite Lawyers' Careers Can and Cannot Tell Us about Globalization of Law," *Law and Social Inquiry* 37(2): 476–499.

Nakazato, Minoru, J. Mark Ramseyer, and Eric Bennett Rasmusen (2010). "The Industrial Organization of the Japanese Bar: Levels and Determinants of Attorney Income," *Journal of Empirical Legal Studies* 7(3): 460–489.

Nichibenren (2020). *Bengoshi Hakusho* [Japan Federation of Bar Associations, *Lawyer White Paper*]. https://www.nichibenren.or.jp/library/pdf/document/statistics/2019/1-3-2_2019.pdf.

Note (2007). "Adopting and Adapting: Clinical Legal Education and Access to Justice in China," *Harvard Law Review* 120(8): 2134–2155.

OHCHR (2018). A/HRC/39/64 Human Rights Council, Report of the detailed findings of the Independent International Fact-Finding Mission on Myanmar (September 10–28, 2018). https://www.ohchr.org/EN/HRBodies/HRC/Pages/NewsDetail.aspx?NewsID=23575&LangID=E.

Perpres 16/2018 (2018). Self-Management Procurement Type III (Swakelola Tipe III): Collaboration between Government and Civil Society Organization for Development Innovation. https://www.akatiga.org/language/en/swakelola-tipe-3/.

Personal Communication (2018a). Legal Academic Project Interviewee, Manila, November.

Personal Communication (2018b). Indonesian Government Official, Ministry of Research, Technology and Higher Education (as it then was), Jakarta, November.

Phan, Pamela N. (2005). "Clinical Legal Education in China: In Pursuit of a Culture of Law and a Mission of Social Justice," *Yale Human Rights and Development Law Journal* 8: 117–152.

Pils, Eva (2016). http://theasiadialogue.com/2016/02/15/rule-of-law-vs-rule-by-fear/.

Reuters (2021). "Thousans suspended at Myanmar universities as junta targets education" May 10. https://www.reuters.com/world/asia-pacific/thousands-suspended-myanmar-universities-junta-targets-education-2021-05-10/

Riles, Annelise and Takashi Uchida (2009). "Reforming Knowledge? A Socio-Legal Critique of the Legal Education Reforms in Japan," *Drexel Law Review* 1(1): 3–51.

Rosenbaum, Stephen A. (2014). "Beyond the Fakultas' Four Walls: Linking Education, Practice and the Legal Profession," *Pacific Rim Law and Policy Journal* 23(2): 1–27.

Saegusa M. (2009). "Why the Japanese Law School System Was Established: Co-optation as a Defensive Tactic in the Face of Global Pressures," *Law & Social Inquiry* 34(2): 365–398.

Saito T. (2006). "The Tragedy of Japanese Legal Education: Japanese 'American' Law Schools," *Wisconsin International Law Journal* 24(1): 197–208.

Silver, Carole, Jae-Hyup Lee, and Jeeyoon Park (2015). "What Firms Want: Investigating Globalization's Influence on the Market for Lawyers in Korea*Columbia Journal of Asian Law* 27(1): 1.

Simion, Kristina (2021). *Rule of Law Intermediaries: Brokersing Influence in Myanmar*. Cambridge.

Sinaga, V. Selvie (2018). "Private Law Schools in Indonesia: Their Development, Governance and Role in Society," *IJAPS* 14(2): 165–185.

Stern, Rachel E. (2016). "Political Reliability and the Chinese Bar Exam," *Journal of Law & Society* 43(4): 506–33.

Straits Times (2018). http://www.straitstimes.com/asia/se-asia/8000-students-return-to-marawi-campus-despite-ongoing-clashes.

Tanaka M. (2016). "Japanese Law Schools in Crisis: A Study on the Employability of Law School Graduates," *Asian Journal of Legal Education* 3(1): 38–54.

Tatlow, Didi Kirsten (2016). "China Is Said to Force Closing of Women's Legal Aid Center," *New York Times.* January 29. https://www.nytimes.com/2016/01/30/world/asia/beij ing-women-legal-aid-guo-jianmei.html.

Taylor, V.L. (2010). "Legal Education as Development," in Stacey Steele and Kathryn Taylor, eds., *Legal Education in Asia: Globalization, Change and Contexts.* Pp. 215–240. Routledge, Taylor & Francis Group.

Times Higher Education (2020). World University Rankings. https://www.timeshighered ucation.com/world-university-rankings/2020/world-ranking#.

Tiojanco, Bryan Dennis Gabito (2019). "The Philippine People Power Constitutions: Social Cohesion Through Integrated Diversity," in Jaclyn L Neo and Bui Ngoc Son, eds., *Pluralist Constitutions in Southeast Asia.* Pp. 251–282. Hart.

UN News (2019) "Aung San Suu Kyi defends Myanmar from accusations of genocide at top UN court UN News 11 December. https://news.un.org/en/story/2019/12/1053221

United Nations (2020). Least Developed Countries. https://www.un.org/development/ desa/dpad/least-developed-country-category.html.

Universitas Indonesia (2020). Long Term Plan. https://www.ui.ac.id/en/long-term-plan.html.

van Rooij, Benjamin (2009). Bringing Justice to the Poor: Bottom-Up Legal Development Cooperation. http://ssrn.com/abstract=1368185.

Wang, Zhizhou, Sida Liu, and Xueyao Li (2017). "Internationalizing Chinese Legal Education in the Early Twenty-First Century," *Journal of Legal Education* 66(2): 237–266.

7

Transnational Legal Networks and the Reshaping of Legal Education in Latin America

The Case of SELA

Javier Couso[*]

I. Introduction

Ever since the emergence of the notion of the globalization of law (Shapiro 1993), scholars have examined the globalization of legal education, an important subset of the former. Thus, there have been studies on the shifting destinations of law graduates from the Global South to universities in the Global North, to pursue LLMs and doctoral degrees in law (Lazarus-Black and Globokar 2015; Garth 2015). This is, indeed, a key aspect of the globalization of legal education, but it exhibits an important, in fact, crucial shortcoming: its reach is limited to the small elite of law graduates from the Global South who can either afford the large financial costs involving the pursuit of graduate studies in law abroad, or win the highly competitive scholarships available to do so. Due to this, a more complete analysis of the globalization of legal education needs to include other, indirect, ways in which this process unfolds. Given that the overwhelming majority of law students from the South never study in the North—but instead pursue their degrees in their home countries—the impact of global legal education is mostly experienced by students through the academics who did study abroad and then teach them. Thus, the reach of global legal education can be better comprehended by bringing to light this indirect dimension.

---

[*] It is relevant to disclose that the author has been an active member of SELA since 2001.

Javier Couso, *Transnational Legal Networks and the Reshaping of Legal Education in Latin America* In: *The Globalization of Legal Education*. Edited by: Bryant Garth & Gregory Shaffer, Oxford University Press. © Oxford University Press 2022. DOI: 10.1093/oso/9780197632314.003.0007

This process, however, is seldom a peaceful one. The existing academic elites in the Global South rarely welcome the arrival of young legal scholars bringing new approaches and understanding of law and legal education to their home countries, especially when such expertise makes obsolete that of the traditional legal academy. The newcomers are typically viewed by the "old guard" as a threat to their positions of academic power, so they resist them, dismissing their new perspectives as unsuitable to local conditions. This has happened—with an impressive regularity—throughout Latin America, especially since graduate legal studies abroad shifted from the traditional Continental European sites (where the "old guard" had been trained) to elite schools in the United States, Canada, the United Kingdom, and, most recently, Australia and New Zealand. Most Latin America legal academics returning to their home countries after completing their training at these Anglo-American global sites of legal education still face hostility and isolation.

It is in this context that transnational networks of legal academics from the North and the South come into play. Indeed, these sites do not just play the ostensible role of serving as meeting points where scholars discuss their research, but, in the case of young legal academics from the Global South, these networks allow them to share their plight with colleagues similarly situated, something which, in turn, provides them with new strategies in their struggle for recognition and academic consolidation. Not all transnational legal academic networks operate in the same way. But the potential of common patterns is always present.

While a full-fledged study of the global networks of legal academics—and their conferences and related activities—would provide valuable insights on the ways in which these organizations contribute to the globalization of both legal research and legal education, this chapter shall deal with a rather unique transnational legal network, the so-called *Seminario en Latinoamérica de Teoría Constitucional y Política* (Latin American Seminar on Constitutional and Political Theory), also known as SELA. This network—which brings together legal scholars from Latin America's most important law schools and one of the United States' most prestigious centers of legal education, Yale Law School—represents one of the most consequential networks contributing to global legal education in South America in the last twenty-five years.

II. The "Latin American Seminar on Constitutional and Political Theory" (SELA)

Every year, for the past quarter of a century, a group of around 150 influential Latin American legal scholars meet with a group of up to ten of Yale Law School's faculty for three days at a city in the region. Although SELA's name suggests that it deals only with constitutional and political theory, over the years it has expanded its scope, so that it currently covers a rather large range of legal subjects.

What makes SELA different from other legal academic networks is not the continuity that it exhibits—there are other international legal associations which are much older than SELA—but, more significantly, the tight academic community that it has created, and the role that it plays in furthering US conceptions of law and legal education throughout Latin America. This closed (by invitation only) organization has created a close-knit group, which developed a type of intellectual exchange that was rare in the region's legal academy at the time SELA was launched (in 1995). In an area of the world that has traditionally followed the Spanish, French, and German ways of doing academic work in law—with their strict hierarchies between consolidated scholars and young faculty and graduate students—SELA represents a fresh way of conducting academic debates in the Latin American legal field. It is a place where even the least known graduate student can directly refute the most prestigious scholar, armed with just the intellectual force of her argumentation. To highlight this aspect of SELA might seem rather banal to social scientists or scholars from the Anglo-American legal academia (who are used to this kind of intellectual exchange), but it is definitely not a minor shift in a region where academic hierarchies still play a role in seminar rooms of law schools and legal conferences.

The origins of SELA can be traced to 1995, soon after the sudden—and premature—death of Argentinean legal philosopher Carlos Nino. A brilliant and charismatic legal scholar, Nino divided his academic work between Yale Law School and the University of Buenos Aires, where he mentored a group of influential Argentinean legal scholars, informally known as the "Nino Boys."[1] After his passing, his close friend and colleague, Owen Fiss at Yale, envisioned with a few of his Latin American students an annual meeting

---

[1] For an analysis of Carlos Nino's role as a public intellectual, see Basombrío (2008:12).

in Nino's memory, gathering legal scholars from the region with Yale law professors.

At first, SELA started with a handful of law schools in Argentina and Chile, but, a couple of years later, expanded to other countries of the region, eventually covering most of the top law schools of Latin America. As of 2020 the participant institutions were the following: Universidad de Buenos Aires, Universidad de Palermo, Universidad de San Andrés and Universidad Torcuato di Tella (Argentina); Universidade de São Paulo, Universidade do Estado do Rio de Janeiro and Fundação Getulio Vargas-Rio de Janeiro (Brazil); Universidad de Chile, Universidad Diego Portales and Universidad Adolfo Ibáñez (Chile); Universidad de los Andes (Colombia); Universidad Nacional Autónoma de Mexico, Instituto Tecnológico Autónomo de Mexico and Centro de Investigación y Docencia Económicas (Mexico); Instituto Paraguayo de Derecho Constitucional (Paraguay); Pontificia Universidad Católica del Peru and Universidad Peruana de Ciencias Aplicadas (Perú); Universidad de Puerto Rico (Puerto Rico); Universitat Pompeu Fabra (Spain); and Yale Law School (United States).

Although a collective endeavor, it is hard to imagine that SELA would have become the strong network that it is today without the dedicated work of Owen Fiss, who, over the last quarter of a century, has been both the intellectual leader and the key organizer of SELA. Exhibiting an extraordinary commitment to this network, Fiss enrolled his colleague Robert Burt (who died in 2015) in the task of persuading other colleagues at Yale Law School to attend annual meetings in different Latin American cities during their summer holidays (since the meetings usually take place in June), not a small feat for a conference mostly held in Spanish and Portuguese, which forces English speaking attendees to follow the proceedings with the help of simultaneous translation.

A distinguished constitutional law scholar, Owen Fiss was crucial to imprint SELA's character as a place where a free, open, and rigorous deliberation takes place. In addition to Fiss, Yale law faculty who regularly attend SELA include Daniel Markovits (who has increasingly taken up Fiss's role as the leader of the network), former dean Robert Post, Carol Rose, George Priest, Reeva Siegel, Paul Kahn, Claire Priest, Cristina Rodriguez, Tom Tyler, James Silk, and Mindy Roseman. Other Yale law faculty who have participated include Harold Koh (when he served as dean), James Forman, and Muneer Ahmad, among others.

From the organizational point of view, SELA is heavily dependent on the work of Fiss and Markovits, as well as on the Yale Law School administrative team that supports them in the planning and execution of the annual conferences and the elaboration of the volume that publishes the papers delivered, Bradley Hayes and Renee DeMatteo. While in its origins the governance structure of SELA was heavily dependent on the Yale faculty, in the early 2000s a formal "Organizing Committee" was introduced. This body is integrated by a group of ten to twelve representatives of the different countries participating at SELA, as well as by the Yale law faculty most heavily involved in the organization (Fiss, Markovits, Rose, and Hayes). The Organizing Committee decides on the program of each annual meeting, as well as other organizational matters, including the acceptance of new members to the network. SELA is financed by a combination of Yale Law School's contributions and that of the approximately twenty law schools from Latin America and Spain that belong to the network (though Yale provides the bulk of the finances to make the conference possible).

III. SELA's Annual Meeting

Typically, SELA's annual meeting includes a keynote speech delivered by a scholar not belonging to the network, who is especially invited to attend (since 2016, this keynote speech is called the "Robert A. Burt Keynote Address"). The range of subject matters of the keynote includes legal and political theory, political science, sociology, economics, and even literary theory.

The annual meeting's core is a series of panels aimed at discussing papers prepared by members of the SELA network. All participants are expected to read in advance, so there is no presentation of them, but instead just some introductory remarks by a designated commentator, who starts off the debate by summarizing the main points of the papers presented and posing some questions to the authors. While in the first years of SELA the papers were commissioned by the Yale faculty, eventually they started to be selected in a competitive way by the Organizing Committee, from abstracts submitted by the members of the network.

SELA's annual meeting includes a session known as "Democracy Roundtable," devoted to the discussion of the state of constitutional democracy in the host country. For this special session, members of the country where the meeting takes place typically invite prominent politicians, journalists, social scientists, and other relevant personalities from different political outlooks to openly discuss the most pressing issues related to the state of their democratic system, before the entire SELA audience.

The conference's structure—of working only in plenaries—ensures that all the attendees have an opportunity to discuss each of the papers presented. This—rather unique—feature of SELA is particularly valuable for junior academics, since they get the chance to have a 150 legal academics commenting on their papers, including some of the most prominent Latin American legal scholars and distinguished Yale law professors. This is an extraordinary academic experience for young scholars, far removed from the scarcely attended panels of large law conferences where most junior scholars start their careers. Furthermore, the methodology of holding only plenary sessions with an audience already familiar with the papers being discussed, is not only intellectually stimulating for presenters and discussants alike, but promotes a lively "conversation" that goes for years on end within the network, something which, in turn, contributes to consolidate shared understandings about the role of law and courts in a constitutional democracy.

The paradigm that frames most of the debates taking place at a typical SELA meeting is a liberal-egalitarian one. Thus, the kind of authors most likely to be cited in the papers are Ronald Dworkin, H.L.A. Hart, John Rawls, Owen Fiss, Jeremy Waldron, Robert Alexy, Catherine Mackinnon, Reva Siegel, Carlos Nino, Jürgen Habermas, Tom Scanlon, and Thomas Nagel, as well as scores of Anglo-American and European scholars who work within that tradition. While this intellectual paradigm was overwhelming in the first years of SELA, as time passed, it has been complemented (and even challenged) by participants trained in critical legal studies, feminist jurisprudence, postcolonial and post-Marxist legal theories, and other nonliberal paradigms. Methodologically, while in its origins SELA was heavily antiformalist and with a tendency to address the topics discussed using the tools of Anglo-American analytic jurisprudence, over the last decade or so it has opened itself to the methodologies used by law and society, the public law branch of political science, and even legal anthropology. The new legal paradigms and methodological approaches have resulted from the gradual inclusion of new members trained in those intellectual traditions.

The last effort to broaden SELA's outlook came in 2016 when, in the midst of President Barack Obama's decision to improve the US relationship with Cuba, the network decided to hold its annual meeting in Havana, after having invited a delegation of Cuban legal scholars to previous meetings. This bold decision allowed SELA to start an unprecedented academic debate with Cuban academics. The engagement between a mix of liberal-egalitarians, feminists, postcolonial theorists, radical-democrats, and critical legal scholars, with orthodox Marxists professors from Cuba, added further interest to SELA.

In spite of its more eclectic membership—in terms of the political and legal philosophies they embrace—SELA remains a fundamentally liberal egalitarian organization. Due to its past trajectory, and the fact that liberal legalism remains dominant among law schools in much of the Global North and in Latin America, SELA has managed to welcome scholars embracing different paradigms and methodologies while maintaining its liberal democratic and egalitarian outlook.

IV. SELA's Ethos and Purpose

In order to better understand the evolution of SELA over the last quarter of a century, it is useful to explain its original ethos and goals, which is best captured in an account of two of its original members. In a document labeled "History of SELA" (2000), Roberto Saba and Andrés Jana had this to say about the "meaning" of SELA at its inception:

Almost twenty years ago, a group of law students from Argentina and Chile—hoping to improve the legal culture in their countries—began to look for answers to their academic needs in graduate programs offered by law schools in foreign countries, primarily in the United States (. . .). With each new student arriving in New Haven, a network of personal linkages with members of the Yale Law School faculty began to grow. A common legal language and a set of shared interests and values developed as well. It was in this context that a new idea took shape: a seminar that would create a space for reflection for the growing number of people who shared common interests (. . .). The expansion of this group was not limited to Yale Law School alumni. Rather, the circle was reaching a group of scholars who appeared to share a certain vision of law, its relation to democratic values, and the urgent need to begin a substantive intellectual discussion about legal matters. It seemed necessary, then, to generate something that would begin to create links among these scholars and strengthen the incipient continental legal community whose peculiarities made it look, in some of our countries, like a counter-cultural phenomenon. These goals explain some of the guidelines adopted by SELA from the start (...) The first of these goals was that of consolidating a community of legal dialogue. This required us to focus on the topics to be discussed, and the relationships among participants. Secondly, the seminar discussions had to reflect the intellectually honest, sharp, and critical style (...). No one would assume the role of "lecturer" or "expert professor" at the debate table. SELA would be a meeting for intellectual work, not a set of lectures. Its panels and meetings would be characterized by deep and analytic discussion among peers, rather than a reiterated formula of presentations followed by questions addressed to the speakers. The subject matters to be chosen would be about law—not about "constitutional," "commercial," "civil," or "criminal" law. The idea that law cannot be divided into boxes with clear-cut labels was fundamental to the kind of discussion we sought. All participants, regardless of their specific area of expertise, would need to be able to participate on an equal footing with regard to respect, commitment, and seriousness (...). SELA has been concerned with both substance and process. Its founders agreed that it should seek to deepen understanding of complex theoretical issues, model a more discussion-oriented form of intellectual discourse than is the norm in Latin America, and create a venue for the formation of a professional community. SELA reaches out to the current generation of scholars and public intellectuals. (...) In just a few years, SELA has become an intellectual center of gravity in Latin America (...). "Now we write, discuss, and hear each other in a different way," says Martín Böhmer '90 LLM and JSD candidate. "We share a common definition of a winning argument, of a quality paper or presentation, of a fruitful discussion," he adds. Participants speak, too, of "a rich intellectual space" where their community can renew and extend itself. For many, it is perhaps the only space where they can come together with scholars from different countries and institutions to work in a common enterprise.[2]

As this revealing passage suggests, SELA started with a strong sense of a mission. The purpose was nothing short of attempting a cultural shift in Latin America's legal academy. This would be achieved through the gradual construction of a community of scholars sharing a "common language," "a

[2] See Saba and Jana (2000).

certain vision of law," and an "intellectual style" characterized by sharp, analytical, and horizontal debates. Finally, SELA was expected to become a meeting point that will bring together scholars from different countries of the region sharing the above-stated conceptions. Thus, the network was expected to help their members confront the hierarchical, parochial, and formalistic traditional legal discourse then prevailing in Latin America. The purpose of exercising influence in the legal, judicial, and political affairs of their own countries was also an explicit goal of the network.

The timing of the launching of SELA could not have been more appropriate. In the mid-1990s, Latin America's legal academy was undergoing a radical change in its outlook, particularly in the domain of public law (Couso 2010; López Medina 2004). In parallel with the processes of democratic transition that most countries of the region were undergoing, and in the midst of the strong criticism of the way the judiciaries—and more broadly, the legal systems—had behaved during the wave of brutal military dictatorships in the preceding decades (Hilbink 2007; Correa Sutil 1999), a new generation of legal scholars was starting to challenge the old one. The most common criticism issued by the new generation against the judiciary and the legal academy was its "formalism." By this, they meant the mechanical application of statutory law, even in cases where it led to utter violation of important constitutional values (with the material injustice that came with it). In addition, they challenged the existing legal orthodoxy in the region, with its traditional understanding of law, for its provincialism, reflected particularly in the resistance of the courts and the traditional legal academy to embrace international human rights law and, especially, the decisions of the Inter-American Human Rights System. Most original SELA members shared the notion that courts can be important actors on behalf of social justice through an active enforcement of the constitutional principle of substantive equality.

A final common theme that contributed to SELA's original cohesion, was the strong indictment shared by its members of the way legal education and research was being conducted in Latin America at the time. SELA's launching (in 1995) coincided with the constitution of the first fully professional academic communities in Argentina, Chile, Peru, and Colombia.[3] By academic community, I mean the substitution of the traditional organization of the Latin American law school (which was typically based on teaching by prestigious litigants and lawyers on an hourly basis, using legal treatises written

---

[3] Brazil, Mexico, and Puerto Rico already had such academic communities.

by themselves in their spare time) for a legal academy made of scholars devoted to full-time teaching and research, as happens in the legal academy of most of the Global North. Thus, in addition to a common understandings of the nature and role of law and courts in a constitutional democracy, as well as the relevance of international human rights, there was a very tangible element that united SELA members, that is, the notion that there was an important "struggle" to replace what was seen as an obsolete—and deeply flawed—legal academy with a more professional and modern one.

SELA provided a significant "refuge" for scores of Latin American junior scholars who had gotten their LLMs and SJDs in the United States and other former colonies of the United Kingdom, and who were confronting the traditional legal academy in their home countries. Once a year, these young scholars could gather at SELA not just to catch up with the latest theoretical developments in law but, as significantly, to share their academic experiences with like-minded scholars of the region, and devise strategies to succeed in changing the way legal teaching and research was done in the region.

As time passed, and the members of SELA started to succeed in their consolidation at their respective countries' academic institutions, the network managed to remain relevant—and to even expand its influence in the region—thanks to its openness to different legal paradigms and methodologies (even some that are at odds with the liberal-egalitarian legalism that was SELA's original seal). The bulk of the members who attend the network nonetheless continue to adhere to the liberal-egalitarian legalism that was dominant in its early years, but in dialogue with the other perspectives and methodologies on law and legal education now present in the network, a feature of SELA which makes it rather rare in the—mostly compartimentalized—world of the legal academy.

At this point, is pertinent to inquire how SELA compares to other transnational legal academic networks operating in Latin America, given that there are a number of other transnational legal entities working in the region, which also contribute to shape prevailing ideas about law and legal education. This is no place to attempt to offer a complete list or taxonomy of all of them. However, we can point to some of the most significant networks operating in the region in order to compare them with SELA.

There are both traditional and new scholarly networks that implicate Latin American teaching and scholarship. The traditional global legal associations are the International Association of Constitutional Law, the International Academy of Comparative Law, and the International Association of Law Schools, which have Latin American chapters and, occasionally, hold meetings in Latin America. More recently, two transnational initiatives have more purposely aimed to shape legal research and legal education in the region. One is the Latin America's Ius Constitutionale Commune project (von Bogdandy 2015), led by Professor Armin von Bogdandy of the Max Plank Institute for Comparative Public Law (at Heidelberg). It has been promoting for almost a decade a common understanding of the values and principles that its supporters think can lead to a "transformative" constitutional law in Latin America, based on the jurisprudence issued by the Inter-American Court of Human Rights, as well as other liberal-egalitarian doctrinal sources. This operation, however, is organized in such a way that prevents the constitution of an enduring network. The other is the International Society of Public Law (an outgrowth of the prestigious International Journal of Constitutional Law, I·CON). This latter network could, in time, develop another interesting site for Latin American legal scholars imbued with the scholarly values of Anglo-American law, but it is too soon to know if it will foster the kind of cross-regional intellectual exchange that has characterized SELA.

The contrast between SELA and these other global networks of legal scholars operating in Latin America helps us better understand the unique nature of SELA. As opposed to the regional chapters of the international legal associations noted in this chapter, SELA is not defined by a specific legal discipline or a specific research project. Furthermore, as opposed to these other legal networks, SELA is by invitation only and is thus not open to any scholar who wishes to associate herself with it. For all the shortcomings of this last feature of SELA, it crucially contributed to creating the close-knit community it generated, something which, in turn, helped this network shape legal education in Latin America in ways that not even the International Association of Law Schools managed to do.

V. Conclusion

Whenever one deals with the flow of legal ideas from the United States to Latin America, the shadow of the Law and Development movement rapidly appears on the horizon. Perhaps due to the fact that it was the first postcolonial attempt by the United States to shape the legal field in Latin America, when a similar initiative is analyzed the question of whether or not it represents a re-enactment of the Law and Development movement immediately comes to mind. Is SELA similar to the Law and Development movement? Does it represent another instance of legal imperialism?

There are a number of features of Yale's Latin American Seminar on Constitutional and Political Theory that makes the comparison with the Law and Development movement plausible. As in the case of the latter, SELA has been a way to transmit US legal values and ideas to Latin America. It also involves a link between top Latin American law schools and prestigious academic institutions in the United States. In both cases a sense of mission was at the core of the enterprise (a mission involving the "modernization" of the legal field in Latin America). But, at this point, the similarities end since, to start with a key element, in the case of SELA the enterprise has been a successful one. Indeed, as opposed to the spectacular failure of the Law and Development" movement (Gardner 1980; Trubek and Galanter 1974), SELA has managed—in a persistent and gradual way—to contribute to reshape Latin America's legal academy, as well as to propagate the values of liberal legalism in the region. Furthermore, its capacity to adapt to changing global and regional circumstances and, in particular, its ability to absorb new paradigms and methodological perspectives, has ensured its survival for a quarter of a century.

Putting aside the comparison with the Law and Development movement, what distinguishes SELA from other forms of exportation of US law and legal education to countries of the Global South is the less targeted, more horizontal, and almost communitarian way in which SELA has operated. Indeed, marked from its beginning by strong personal relationships, the above-mentioned features of this network seem to have been critical for its capacity to grow and reach most of Latin America's top law schools without losing its intellectual appeal.

It is difficult to demonstrate—in a scientific way—that SELA has been an important factor in the consolidation of a US-style of legal academic work in Latin America, but there are strong indicia that it has contributed significantly. At the very least, one can point to the disproportionate number of presidents of universities and deans of law schools, justices of supreme and constitutional courts, and highly influential legal scholars who have been members of SELA to support this claim.

References

Basombrío, Cristina (2008). "Intelectuales y poder: la influencia de Carlos Nino en la presidencia de Alfonsín," in *Temas de Historia Argentina y Americana*. Vol. XXII (Enero-Junio) Pp. 15–51. Pontificia Universidad Católica Argentina.

Correa Sutil, Jorge (1999). "La Cenicienta se Queda en la Fiesta. El Poder Judicial Chileno en la Década de los 90," in P. Drake and I. Jaksic, eds., *El Modelo Chileno, Democracia y Desarrollo en los Noventa*. Pp. 281–315. LOM Ediciones.

Couso, Javier (2010). "The transformation of constitutional discourse and the judicialization of politics in Latin America," in J. Couso, A. Huneeus, and R. Sieder, eds., *Cultures of Legality: Judicialization and Political Activism in Latin America*. Pp. 141–160. Cambridge University Press.

Gardner, James A. (1980). *Legal Imperialism: American Lawyers and Foreign Aid in Latin America*. University of Wisconsin Press.

Garth, B. (2015). "Notes Toward an Understanding of the U.S. Market in Foreign LL.M. Students: From the British Empire and the Inns of Court to the U.S. LL.M," *Indiana Journal of Global Legal Studies* 22(1): 67–79 (December 1).

Hilbink, Lisa (2007). *Judges beyond Politics in Democracy and Dictatorship: Lessons from Chile*. Cambridge University Press.

Jana, Andrés and Roberto Saba (2000). History of SELA. https://law.yale.edu/centers-workshops/yale-law-school-latin-american-legal-studies/sela/history-sela.

Lazarus-Black, Mindie and Julie Globokar (2015). "Foreign Attorneys in U.S. LL.M. Programs: Who's In, Who's Out, and Who They Are," *Indiana Journal of Global Legal Studies* 22(1): 3–65.

López Medina, Diego (2004). *Teoría Impura del Derecho*. Legis.

Shapiro, Martin (1993). "The Globalization of Law," *Indiana Journal of Global Legal Studies* 1(1): 37–64.

Trubek, David M. and Marc Galanter (1974). "Scholars in Self-Estrangement: Some Reflections on the Crisis in Law and Development," *Wisconsin Law Review* 1974(4): 1062–1101.

von Bogdandy, Armin (2015). "Ius Constitutionale Commune en América Latina: Una mirada a un constitucionalismo transformador," *Revista Derecho del Estado* 34: 3–50 (July).

PART III

GLOBAL LAW SCHOOLS

8

The Unstoppable Force, the Immovable Object

Challenges for Structuring a Cosmopolitan Legal Education in Brazil

Oscar Vilhena Vieira and José Garcez Ghirardi

I. Globalization, Return to Democratic Rule, and the Need for Innovative Legal Professionals in Brazil

I had said, that some of our crew left their country on account of being ruined by law; that I had already explained the meaning of the word; but he was at a loss how it should come to pass, that the law, which was intended for every man's preservation, should be any man's ruin. Therefore he desired to be further satisfied what I meant by law, and the dispensers thereof, according to the present practice in my own country.

—*Gulliver's Travels* (1956), Book IV, Chapter V

Democratization and globalization have posed unique challenges for many emerging countries as they have pressed them to find suitable answers to competing imperatives. On the one hand, the fast-paced changes in the global economy have pushed them to rapidly adjust to a radically transformed international marketplace. On the other, they have had to cope with mounting internal demands for broader individual rights and social equality (Scherer-Warren 2006; Rossana Rocha Reis 2012; Ventura et al. 2010). Failure on the first task could mean falling even further behind developed countries; failure on the second could create the risk of grave social unrest. Balancing this dual constraint of economic efficiency and social fairness has proven a particularly difficult act to perform.

Oscar Vilhena Vieira and José Garcez Ghirardi, *The Unstoppable Force, the Immovable Object* In: *The Globalization of Legal Education*. Edited by: Bryant Garth & Gregory Shaffer, Oxford University Press. © Oxford University Press 2022. DOI: 10.1093/oso/9780197632314.003.0008

Law has played a major role in the effort by these countries to cope with this tension. This is hardly surprising. The faster patterns of social and economic interaction changed and diversified, the more legal institutions and norms appeared instrumental in the quest for some degree of certainty and standardization both for intra- and international transactions (Gessner and Cem Budak 1998).

As an international arena, globalization has been largely perceived as involving a *globalization of legal rules and governance,* that is to say, as an attempt to establish a *global law* framework capable of sustaining and fostering the free flow of capital, goods, and services (though not necessarily people). As Halliday and Osinsky (2006) observe:

> Although often invisible and taken for granted, law is heavily implicated in the process of globalization. Economic globalization cannot be understood apart from global business regulation and the legal construction of the markets on which it increasingly depends. Cultural globalization cannot be explained without attention to intellectual property rights institutionalized in law and global governance regimes. The globalization of protections for vulnerable populations cannot be comprehended without tracing the impact of international criminal and humanitarian law or international tribunals. Global contestation over the institutions of democracy and state building cannot be meaningful unless considered in relation to constitutionalism.

At the national level, legal reform was at the heart of the attempt by many emerging countries to enhance the political liberties of their citizens (Rudra 2005). In Brazil, since the return to democratic rule and the enactment of the 1988 Constitution, the language of rights has become a chief vehicle in the struggle against social disparity.

A vast array of new social, environmental, and consumer rights, coupled with policies to increase access to justice, has enhanced the relevance of law in everyday Brazilian life (Vieira 2008). New institutions have been created or perfected (e.g., Public Defender's and Public Prosecutor's Offices) to give citizens more efficient legal means to demand the enforcement of rights and to oversee the conduct of public officials. The explosion of litigation in areas such as consumer law, the intensive use of strategic litigation for public interest causes, and even the trials for corruption of high-profile public figures testifies to the new centrality of legal institutions in Brazil over the last decades.

The transformed economic dynamics of the country in the twenty-first century further amplified the importance of law, as the new scenario both required and sprung from new legal institutiones (exemplified by regulatory agencies and new consumer codes) (Grinover 2009). Courts have become key players in this process, frequently seeking to adjust, through innovative readings, old legal norms to new sociopolitical realities (Vieira 2008b). Similar stories could be told about other nations in the Global South (Botha 2013).

Due to this vast and complex set of changes both within and without national borders, emerging countries have become hard-pressed to rapidly "import" and form law professionals capable of tackling and designing novel solutions to unprecedented, intricate problems. The first option consisted not only in opening the national market for international legal services but also in sending a massive number of elite young lawyers to attend LLM programs and obtain professional experience abroad. The latter option spurred a debate over legal education. It gained momentum in some developing nations, generating a stream of academic writing on the topic (Cunha et al. 2018). Alongside this theoretical debate, a number of concrete attempts have been made to answer the need of educating global lawyers (Gingerich et al. 2017).

In Brazil, a pioneering experience has been that of FGV Direito SP, founded in 2002 (Ambrosini et al. 2010). Its story aptly illustrates the difficulties to implement a new paradigm for legal education in an emerging South. It also suggests that any successful attempt at reform in this area depends on the institution's ability to strike a politically workable, educationally sensible balance between global demands and local realities, between new and traditional paradigms (Cunha et al. 2018). Thus, FGV Direito SP's project can be understood only against the background of its relation to the traditional law schools and legal culture still hegemonic in the country.

II. Traditional Legal Education and Political Perspectives in Brazil

A man slowly goes by. A dog slowly goes by.
A donkey slowly goes by. Slowly . . . the windows stare.
Gosh, what miserable life.
Any little town.

—Carlos Drummond de Andrade (2013)

Attempts to alter the way law is taught and researched are, in any country, quite different a task from efforts to change, say, the teaching of engineering or medicine. Law is inextricably linked to political power: it is a prime tool for shaping and perpetuating social hierarchies and compromises; its workings affect every aspect of public and private life; it is the backbone of political societies, markets, and the foundation of political regimes.

Once proposals of new ways to teach law necessarily entail new ways of thinking about law, of understanding its social role and practical functioning, they represent a potential risk to the social settlements from which they arise. They are, hence, bound to be met with a type of resistance which, far from being merely academic or methodological, bespeaks deeply seated and profoundly consequential political disagreement.

Law schools are the key arena in which this political contest is fought. As Dezalay and Garth (2012 5) observe:

> [L]aw is at the core of the processes that structure, produce and reproduce the field of power. More concretely, the key to the position of law is its relationship to two sets of more or less closely connected institutions—the faculty of law and the state. The faculties of law serve central roles in the reproduction of knowledge, governing elites, and the hierarchies among elites and expertises. Efforts to transform the faculties of law . . . inevitably touch the relatively fragile fabric of power, legitimacy, and domination embedded in the basic structures of those faculties.

Faculties of law are thus the loci where the crucially important social imaginary concerning law is primarily formed and reinforced. Law professors do not simply expose legal concepts: they define what law is or should be, they state the social purpose it serves or should serve. Curricula and teaching methodologies are not neutral elements but ideological tools to naturalize some readings of norms, interpretation, and legal institutions while silencing others.[1] Thus, any transformative project for legal education is a proposal to lay bare the non-neutral nature of traditional models and

---

[1] As Duncan Kennedy points out in a well-known piece: "much of what happens [in law schools] is the inculcation through a formal curriculum and the classroom experience of a set of political attitudes toward the economy and society in general, toward law, and toward the possibilities of life in the profession" (1982: 595).

ultimately advocates changes in law itself. Innovative proposals for legal education represent, in critical ways, a challenge to the often unstated social arrangements implicit in the traditional teaching model. This is certainly true in Brazil, as a brief overview of the origins of its law schools will help understand.

The first Brazilian law schools were created in 1827 by imperial decree to provide the newly independent country with a much-needed legal bureaucracy (Abreu 2019). It would indeed be awkward for the young nation to keep on having its justices and government officials trained in Coimbra (as it had customarily been done) after having broken away from Portugal in 1822 (Fávero 2006). The state needed to prove capable of educating its own legal and political elite.

These two components—dependence of the state and bureaucratic vocation—would have long-lasting effects on the way law would be taught in the country. As the prime necessity was that of forming personnel apt to perform various administrative tasks—not necessarily legal in nature—the initial curricula was rather extensive, including subjects such as economics and politics (Vieira 2012). Law schools aimed at providing students with as much information as possible on every aspect of law in the hope that, later on, this vast amount of information would help them to sufficiently occupy different positions in government.

In spite of changes over the years, this initial design imprinted on Brazilian legal education an enduring propensity to be encyclopedic, with courses usually closely following the structure of the major codes. Typically, such courses were oblivious to practical applications as alumni were expected to learn to solve problems when they started practicing (Trubek 2011). Almost two centuries later, both these aspects (all-encompassing curricula, internship as prime locus for practical knowledge) are still emblematic of mainstream Brazilian legal education.

Beyond the impact that the goal of forming state bureaucrats had on curricula and teaching priorities, the vicinity to power which characterized law schools also importantly affected their institutional dynamics. Not unlike the English Inns of Court (Ghirardi 2012), Brazilian law schools were primarily loci for networking and jockeying for advantageous positions in government. The classroom was understandably deemed secondary to the camaraderie in the school's courtyard or in the nearby bars; allegiances thus formed were essential for future professional success (Guy 1990).

For the same reason, technical legal expertise was less important than political acumen, as the ability to ingratiate oneself to the right colleagues was key to success in a country where legal and political elites were virtually identical. Students who prioritized lessons and books over socializing were often ridiculed as *rábulas*, a derogatory term used to designate petty-minded lawyers (Falcão 1998). The devaluation of the classroom and the primacy of social networking over academic debate became another hallmark of Brazilian legal education.

In this environment, professors were likewise praised according to their standing on the public stage. More often than not, it was their success outside the academy that validated their position as scholars. Higher court justices, state ministers, and secretaries, alongside the most successful and prestigious private lawyers of the day, were considered natural professors to an institution that aimed at preparing students for government office (Gardner 1980). They were often worshipped by a crowd of students eager to obtain exactly the kind of successes these masters had achieved.

In line with this cult of personality, the glossing of canonical, authoritative authors was a popular everyday practice. In a markedly hierarchical society, *who* was saying it was frequently more important than *what* was being said. Not unusually, the *canonical author* being quoted was the very professor delivering the class, as the imperial decree which created the first law schools had encouraged professors to write the textbooks for their own courses.[2] A *magister dixit* ethos became deeply entrenched in Brazilian law schools. The selection of new professors, in tandem with this practice, seemed to depend more on personal allegiances than on academic achievement.

Since those times, it has been customary for young scholars in Brazilian law schools to start their teaching careers in the same institution where they have graduated, a practice strongly discouraged in other countries. Needless

---

[2] "Art. 7 - The Lenses will choose the compendiums of their profession, or arrange them, not existing already, as long as the doctrines are in agreement with the system sworn by the Nation. These compendia, once approved by the Congregation, will serve interim; submitting to the approval of the General Assembly, and the Government will have them printed and supplied to the schools, and their authors will be given the exclusive privilege of the work for ten years." Art. 7 de Agosto 11, 1827, Collecção das leis do Imperio do Brazil, available at http://www2.camara.leg.br/atividade-legislative/legislacao/publicacoes/doimperio/colecao2.html (Braz.) (our translation) [Original text: "Art. 7.º - Os Lentes farão a escolha dos compêndios da sua profissão, ou os arranjarão, não existindo já feitos, contanto que as doutrinas estejam de acordo com o sistema jurado pela Nação. Estes compêndios, depois de aprovados pela Congregação, servirão interinamente; submetendo-se porém à aprovação da Assembléia Geral, e o Governo os fará imprimir e fornecer às escolas, competindo aos seus autores o privilégio exclusivo da obra, por dez anos."] (Rio de Janeiro, 21 de agosto de 1827. Foi publicada esta Carta de Lei nesta Chancelaria-mor do Império do Brasil).

to say, this greatly increases the risk of nepotism and endogeneity (formal selection processes notwithstanding) due to the personal links candidates and professors inevitably develop through the educational process. This personal dimension, in turn, has contributed to lessening the importance of technical legal mastery and academic skills as a means to gain access to a teaching career in law compared to the building of useful political connections.

The working together of these elements—devaluation of classroom work and technical legal skills; prevalence of *magister dixit* over scholarly debates; political prestige as the basis for academic reputation—would become characteristic of Brazilian legal education. Over time, as the rise of industrialization and urbanization profoundly reshaped the agrarian society, and for which the first law schools emerged, these elements would come under increasing criticism. They started being seen as the source of what was more and more perceived as the dismal quality of legal education in the country. There was widespread consensus that substantial changes in the social, political, and economic matrices of the country had not affected the teaching of law in the now more numerous schools.

As early as 1955, Professor San Thiago Dantas delivered a caustic denunciation of the obsolescence of Brazilian legal education (Vieira 2012). His commencement speech at the *Faculdade Nacional de Direito* is a shrewd critique of the disconnect between the training students received at university and the tasks they needed to perform. In 1986, José Eduardo Faria, professor at one of the most prestigious law schools in the country, would take up and accentuate Dantas's criticism. His *A Reforma do Ensino Jurídico* (The Reform of Legal Education) (Faria 1986) deplores the gap between the traditional model—marked by emphasis on formalism, teacher-centered pedagogy, lecturing, and parochialism—and concludes that Brazilian legal education has become blatantly incompatible with the country's new context, both in economic and political terms.

Some attempts to modernize law schools appeared in the 1960s and 1970s—of which the Center for Study and Research in Legal Education (Centro de Estudos e Pesquisas no Ensino do Direito), also known as CEPED, is the most emblematic example (Gardner 1980). These attempts aimed at altering the paradigms for both the teaching and researching of law. These efforts were, however, incapable of understanding and dialoguing with the Brazilian legal community. Even some of the most preeminent participants of this movement believe it was misled in crucial ways, as David Trubek and Marc Galanter discuss in *Scholars in Self-Estrangement* (1974) and James

A. Gardner in *Legal Imperialism* (1980). These authors criticize, above all, what they saw as a noncritical, culturally blind effort to export those legal models deemed paradigmatic by powerful countries.

A couple of more endogenous efforts to modernize legal education should also be noted. In the 1980s, Pontifical Catholic University of São Paulo School of Law reduced the number of students per class and introduced mandatory student-presented seminars with problem-solving methods in most of its courses. Such changes illustrate the broader movement of legal education reform which, as Gardner (1980: 83–84) argues, had been taking place in Latin America since the 1960s. Around the same time, a number of key theoretical legal scholars started challenging legal formalism and the authoritarian legal system. This movement known as Alternative Law led by Roberto Lyra Filho in 1983 from the University of Brasília Law School, resembles the origins of the Critical Legal Studies Movement in the U.S. Despite their undeniable relevance and impact over legal thinking, these attempts at change remained, for the most part, peripheral to the everyday life of legal teaching. In most law schools, lecturing continued to be the rule, as did the tacit understanding that the skills needed for actual, effective lawyering should be learned outside the university (Vieira 2012).

To make matters worse, some governmental policies for higher education proved seriously ill-advised. In the 1990s, the (correct) diagnosis that access to Brazil's university system was all but impossible to a huge percentage of the population led the government to lessen the hurdles for opening new institutions. This resulted in an exponential growth in the number of institutions: from 165 law schools in 1995, to 505 in 2001, to 1,308 in 2015.[3] The government's expectation that a large number of schools would lead to competition, and competition, to better quality education, tragically never materialized. The result of this uncontrolled massification process was a further downgrading of the already gravely dysfunctional legal education system in the country.

The fact that Dantas's main arguments could still be sensibly restated by Vieira many decades later bears testimony to the resistance of the traditional legal education model: "The longevity of the . . . traditional models, which have only partially been modernized, with the updating of curricula and

---

[3] According to the National Institute of Educational Studies and Research (INEP)'s data, in 2000 there were 442 graduate law courses. In 2015, this number raised to 1,172, considering both online and presential courses. INEP, SINOPSES ESTATÍSTICAS DA EDUCAÇÃO SUPERIOR—GRADUAÇÃO, http://portal.inep.gov.br/web/guest/sinopses-estatisticas-da-educacao-superior.

acceptance of a handful methodological changes . . . is impressive. To a certain degree, they confirm Douglas North's contention that once an institution is established, it becomes very difficult to change its nature" (Vieira 2012).

Created to destabilize institutional inertia and to bridge the gap between legal research, the classroom, and Brazilian demands for updated legal thinking and legal expertise, FGV Direito SP embraced the challenge to create a new law school in this congested market (Cunha et al. 2018: 247–263). It has done so based, on the evidence that the country lacked both an autonomous legal academy, buffered from the interests of the legal profession, and a new generation of professionals capable of aptly responding to the needs arising from globalization and from the social changes which importantly transformed the country since the return to democratic rule.

In this new context, Brazil could no longer ignore the need for an institution able to host independent legal research, open to empirical enquiry and to the designing of solutions to complex practical problems. There were new demands from a legal profession that had to respond to a more complex, globalized, and entrepreneurial context, both in the private and public spheres.

Moreover, Brazil, at that time, made a bid to become a more active global player. This entailed a demand for institutional protagonism, since globalization is also about institutional competition. A country aiming to play a larger role in the globalization process has to develop a legal culture and legal institutions conducive to its ambition. The process of implementing this ambitious project within a conservative educational system, a bureaucratic and traditional legal environment, and a deeply unequal society would necessarily face important challenges.

III. Three Main Challenges Attached to Offering Global-Oriented Legal Education in Brazil

It was against this uninspiring background that the project of FGV Direito SP took shape. FGV Direito SP's new curriculum and novel methodology spring, thus, from this bold commitment to providing Brazil with the legal professionals it needs to grow and to overcome social disparity in the context of a globalized world. As a result, a number of new subjects have been created and taught for the first time as mandatory undergraduate courses in Brazil. Their names (e.g., Crime and Society; Regulation and Development;

Corporate Procedural Law; Law and Economics; Global Law; Law and Development; Law and Arts) bespeak the determination to think and present law in its dynamic relationship with other areas of knowledge and practice. Unlike the customary practice in Brazilian universities, FGV Direito SP does not see law as a more or less self-contained reality, to be learned in its entirety and then applied to the world. It suggests that law is rather an ever-changing, conflictual object that is defined as it relates to other dimensions of social practice.

A new curriculum alone would do little to change legal education, however, if not coupled with a new methodological approach to the teaching of law. Therefore, apart from moving away from the letter-of-the law, statute-commentary syllabuses which characterize traditional legal teaching, FGV Direito SP implemented a student-centered methodology designed to foster problem-solving abilities and to lead students to think critically about law. The reasons for adopting this new methodology, however, are well beyond sheer pedagogical concerns.

The traditional lecture method adopted in most Brazilian law schools deserves criticism not only because it presents the law as a somewhat static, fixed reality to be memorized and learned before it can be put to use. FGV Direito SP's opposition to it, as already pointed out, is rooted in the belief that it critically reinforces a hierarchical pattern of relationship which has been a long, problematic component of Brazilian society. It reinforces the notion that knowledge and truth are above, held by those in positions of power and prestige. It implicitly requires from students an attitude of passive acceptance and silent obedience, as they are not proficient, nor educated enough, to have the right to genuinely question their masters.

The political innuendo of such a tradition, especially in a country like Brazil, is clear enough. It would be hard to overstate the impact on our national story of government practices that mirror exactly the concept of authority implicit in this form of teaching and of legal teaching in particular, something which makes matters even more dangerous. It helps buttress a notion of law as a prerogative for a privileged few, something from which the ordinary person is understandably detached and ignorant.

Therefore, the methodological changes advocated by and brought about by FGV Direito SP represent more than a new way of teaching the law. Together with the efforts to become an international reference in legal research, these changes embody a new way of thinking about the law, about the country and about each citizen's right and duty to make his or her voice heard and to contribute to creating a more just Brazilian society. They reflect the core mission of the Getulio Vargas Foundation, which is "to contribute to the social and economic development of the country, to the enhancement of national ethical standards, to a shared and responsible governance and to the strengthening of Brazil's international position" (FGV 2017).

This new approach to law has been hailed, in Brazil and Latin America, as a much-needed break with the past and as a blueprint for future projects. FGV Direito SP and a few other Latin America law schools are engaged in educating a distinct, intellectual, new generation of lawyers and legal scholars capable of effectively taking part in designing complex business models, in solving social inequality problems, and in improving government practices.

And this is for good reason. Legal professionals in Brazil are today much more exposed to the impact of a globalized world than they were just ten years ago. They will probably be even more exposed a decade from today. Globalization is becoming increasingly complex, blurring traditional frontiers in the way it reshuffles global and local realities. Brazil has been acutely affected by these transnational processes (Shaffer 2012: 229–264).

The country's main trading partner is no longer North America but China. More intense, commercially meaningful relations with China, Arab countries, and Latin American neighbors have entailed changes that command a renewing of the way Brazilian legal professionals shape their professional practice (Cunha et al. 2018). More and more, it is paramount that they understand law's intricate connections with areas such as the economy, the corporate world, and international politics. Nor can they any longer avoid a deep understanding of the relationship between different legal regimes, their norms and practices.

The country has become more active in the discussion of themes impacting global issues—for example, international trade, environmental regulation, global warming, and human rights. This requires both the capacity to understand the intricacies of international regulation and the skills to design and analyze legally effective proposals. This holds true both for the broader international arena and for the more specific context of Latin American realities.

As already mentioned, globalized-capitalism today is not a system of free competition among corporations in the international arena. States and, therefore, law are an integral part of this competition for development. They are partners of (or obstacles to) entrepreneurs, since they regulate activities, offer incentives, or put up barriers to their activities. This can only be achieved if adequate legal tools are in place and if they are effective in implementing policies. The need for a body of legal professionals capable of designing and operating such tools is, thus, of prime strategic importance.

Besides adopting a new curriculum, as research and teaching methodologies, FGV Direito SP develops four specific strategies to structure a more cosmopolitan environment for legal research and education:

1. The first strategy, in place since the foundation of FGV Direito SP, was the decision *to attract professors and researchers with some international experience.* Today, all members of the full-time faculty have concluded their LLMs, PhDs, or post-PhDs abroad. Faculty selection processes are open to foreign academics. A recent junior faculty initiative, combined with a post-PhD program, was launched in 2016 to attract foreign academics to São Paulo. These initiatives aim to provide both comparative and global legal perspectives as an ordinary element of teaching and research.

2. The second initiative is *the Global Law Program, by which FGV Direito SP receives international senior scholars* for short periods to offer courses both to Brazilian students and exchange program students. Courses are normally offered in English and accompanied by a faculty member. This program has received seventy-six professors since 2009. Besides amplifying the exposure of students to global and comparative law teaching experiences, the Global Law Program was also designed to foment academic encounters that are fructifying in joint research projects.

The Global Law Program is also engaged in *promoting the exchange of students.* Since 2009, FGV Direito SP has sent 159 students abroad, which means around 20 percent of the student body, and has hosted 137 foreign students. This movement occurred mostly within the network of schools with which the school has agreements or with Law School Global League affiliates. At this moment, a major fundraising effort is being done to permit students with different economic backgrounds to take part in the exchange program.

3. The *Law School Global League is a result of an original joint effort between FGV Direito SP and Tilburg University Law School.* The primary objective, since the beginning, was to aggregate law

schools around the globe that are strongly committed to globalize their programs and initiatives. The idea was to structure a more horizontal arena to discuss the challenges and promote legal education in a more connected and globalized world. Today, the Global League counts twenty-four members, distributed among all continents. The League carries out its mission by promoting four main activities: an annual dean's meeting; a summer course; an academic conference; and the hosting of four research groups in the fields of human rights, new technologies and the law, business, and anticorruption.

4. A fourth strategy is directed to *improve legal research in a context of expansion of global scholarship*. Legal research in emerging academic communities can become influenced and even captured by theoretical lineages, subjects, interests, and questions formulated mostly in the Global North academia. The aim to engage in a more cosmopolitan academic dialogue requires not just openness but also knowledge, excellence, and specific training to participate in global research networks and research agendas. The challenge is to engage in this global debate without losing the perspective from where one is and the issues one is supposed to confront.

In addition to these initiatives, which have by themselves strongly impacted the capacity of our academic community, FGV Direito SP is profoundly committed to fomenting research driven to address complex institutional, social, and economic issues that affect not only the Brazilian society but also other emerging countries. The FGV Fund for Applied Research, and the several centers focused on applied research, is an institutional effort to produce research that dialogues with the international debate without losing sight of local challenges. In this vein, FGV Direito SP also created a specific seminar to support its professors' efforts to publish and engage in international academic dialogue.

IV. Three Traps: Legal Colonialism, Academic Solipsism, and Elitism

[W]hat happens when a new work of art is created is something that happens simultaneously to all the works of art which preceded it. [...]

The existing order is complete before the new work arrives; for order to persist after the supervention of novelty, the whole existing order must be, if ever so slightly, altered; and so the relations, proportions, values of each work of art toward the whole are readjusted; and this is conformity between the old and the new.

—T.S. Eliot (2018)

T.S. Eliot's remarks on innovation in literature have become famous as they seemed to felicitously synthesize the broader dynamics of innovation and tradition. They seem to suggest that any new social practice or institution depends, in order to be conceivable and become viable, on a meaningful dialogue with the order it purports to transform. This dialogue is indeed inevitable, for the very assessment that things need to be changed, discarded, or preserved is founded on a shared understanding of what is at stake (Taylor 2008).

That is why sharp divides between *traditional* and *innovative* tend to be misleading and, often, counterproductive. They are misleading because they hint at an absolute break not observable in social practices, where a substantial degree of continuity is a condition, not an impairment, to change (MacIntyre 2014). Even extraordinary revolutionary breakups could not have been successful without resource to many elements of the order they openly contested.

In more ordinary social change, what occurs is a dialectic clash between rival or contesting viewpoints and attitudes which keep on sharing, nevertheless, a good amount of common ground. That is why the result of such transition processes is usually not an *all or nothing, old or new* affair but, as Eliot points out, a broad readjustment of practices and a resignifying of the social institutions disputed.

Proposals for innovating law schools fall into this category of social contention and must, therefore, find a way to negotiate their way with the tradition it aims to alter and with the social groups that act as gatekeepers. This general trend gets complicated when translated to the specific setting of the Global South. In these countries, a project aimed at offering global-oriented legal education in an emerging power, apart from negotiating with traditional competitors, has to attempt to avoid falling into the traps of *legal colonialism, academic solipsism,* and *social elitism.* Each of them represents one aspect of the challenge of building a positive dialogue between the global and the local in the Global South.

A. Legal Colonialism

Legal colonialism is a chapter in the much broader debate on cultural exchanges and ideological imperialism (Smith 2013). From this perspective, the creation of a less parochial legal education experience in the Global South runs the permanent risk of being seen, at best, as an attempt to merely transplant US/European models to a regional context (Berkowitz et al. 2004). At worst, it may be perceived as a spearhead to the agenda of North cultural dominance.

In different degrees and at different times, both types of criticism have emerged in Brazil. The latter arose mainly in the 1960s, when pioneering efforts to renew Brazilian legal education, sponsored by American agencies, had as a background a climate of violent political polarization between left- and right-wing groups.[4] The former was noticeable at the beginning of this century and was linked to the legal community's reaction to FGV Direito SP's project (Ambrosini et al. 2010). With varying levels of cogency, these arguments still represent a powerful rhetorical strategy in a country again bitterly politically divided and severely split over the desirable national attitude in face of globalization.

Proposals for renewing legal education have to take this criticism seriously. New forms of lawyering and new understandings of law are indices of broader ideological constructs and, therefore, not value-neutral (Dezalay and Garth 2002: 81). Naively incorporating them to the curricula would indeed risk just replicating, in the country, models hegemonic in the Global North. Ignoring or denying such risk would be foolish and dangerous.

The antidote to that is not, however, ignoring the emergence of a new global dynamics for law and shutting oneself in some imaginary form of legal nationalism. Refusing to consider changes is as deleterious as accepting them unquestioningly. Critics of the *ideological bias* of new forms of legal education in a global context are often slower to recognize their own ideological biases. If it is true that all educational change is ideologically motivated, so is educational conservatism.

---

[4] To illustrate this state of affairs, we can mention two events: (1) At least 150,000 people attended the "Central do Brasil" rally, in which then president João Goulart called for political and social reforms, including: rent control, nationalization of oil refineries, and redistribution of lands; (2) in response, six days after the rally and indicating the polarized political atmosphere, the "Marcha da Família com Deus pela Liberdade" (March of the Family with God for Liberty) was organized. This event represented the conservative interests and sectors of society (see Bandeira 2010).

In Brazil, these ideological confrontations over legal institutions are set in a very peculiar social framework, which Roberto Schwarz has discussed in detail. According to Schwarz, Brazilian nineteenth-century elite found a way to create a compromise between bourgeois liberalism, in discourse, and slave work, in practice, which had profound effects in the social functioning of the country:

> The bourgeois, enlightened, and European criterion, according to which caprice is a weakness, is no more or less real or "Brazilian" than the criterion that emanates from our nonbourgeois social relations, in which the element of personal, arbitrary will is prominent; [. . .] Modeled on the practical interest of a single social class that is as linked to bourgeois precepts as to the discretionary, arbitrary aspect of slavery and clientelism, the two evaluations existed and were backed up by the guarantee of experience and necessity. In other words, more real than the conflict was the accommodation between them, incongruous but advantageous, one of the marks of Brazil's "monstrous" inscription in the contemporary scene (Schwarz 2001: 27).

The debate over innovation in legal education must then strive to avoid the twin snares of naïve transplanting and naïve preserving and face the difficulties attached to producing a much-needed institutional *aggiornamento* in a large country in the Global South.

The best path to take seems that of being clear about the choices one is making and explicit about the reasons for making them. The workings of international financial markets, organizations and agencies, the problems of refugees, environmental hazards, and terrorism affect the country and pressure its legal and political institutions to respond to them. These problems will not go away simply by being ignored, nor will Brazil's capacity to handle them be improved if no action is taken.

In the international arena, these problems have been shaped and dealt with, from a legal viewpoint, by instruments and dynamics mirroring, unsurprisingly, those of the Global North powers leading the globalization process (Kofman et al. 1996). This hegemony is hardly surprising and has been described and discussed at length. Acknowledging that this is so does not signify automatically subscribing to this model. On the contrary, playing a relevant role in this scenario without passively submitting to it or accepting it requires mastering such viewpoints and instruments.

A proposal for positively changing legal education in Brazil needs, therefore, to reorient legal research to be at the same time more empirical and critical than traditional formalist scholarship, and to educate students to be capable of critically reading the new *global law* scenario. They have to be taught the rules currently shaping the game so that they can operate, question, and eventually contribute to shaping these rules. A refusal to learn or teach the grammar in which global transactions are made denies the country the much-needed skills of being able to question it.

This critical stance coupled with in-depth understanding of the working of the system and its implications is the best method to correct the danger of legal colonialism. By bringing to the open the inextricable connections between legal education and political and ideological allegiances, the creation of a new model of thinking about law burdens both its supporters and critics with the responsibility of offering clear arguments in defense of their respective positions. And this is, in itself, a major contribution to improving the quality of legal education in the country.

B. Academic Solipsism

The second trap to be avoided is that of *academic solipsism*, that is to say, that of becoming isolated in one's own institutional culture. By adopting distinct research and teaching methodologies, which challenge established patterns, the new educational experience may lack the capacity to insert itself as an effectively innovative force in a more traditional national legal setting. As many of its key features (e.g., curriculum, methodologies, institutional design) do not find counterparts in the existing law schools, there is a real risk of this type of academic isolationism.

A critical stance is a powerful factor in avoiding this trap. FGV's project was that of creating *a new law school in Brazil*, a formula in which both the novelty (*new* law school) and the place (*in Brazil*) are equally important (Dezalay and Garth 2012: 178–179). That is to say, the reform proposed is one that wishes to make sense within the legal culture of the country, a goal that cannot be achieved without permanent dialogue with existing models.

The critical approach to the new methodologies and perspectives necessarily involves an understanding of their points of contact with all the elements of the hegemonic forms of legal education. By identifying such points of convergence, the new project helpfully makes explicit the points of divergence and allows for a very profitable debate on the rationale underneath both models.

The new perspective embodied by FGV Direito SP, and the estrangement it caused, represents an opportunity for a highly desirable plurality in Brazilian legal education. It brings to light the fact that in a healthy democracy, law will and should be perceived differently by different groups. The alternatives that the new curriculum and methodology bring forth offer a prime opportunity for traditional practices to make their case anew. It allows for advocates of traditional methods to explain more clearly why, in their view, such methods still make sense in changed national and international contexts.

FGV Direito SP's experience has shown that this dialogue has started to occur in Brazil and that methodological solipsism is being slowly overcome. Even though there are numerous examples of resistance, and criticism against a more problem-oriented, interdisciplinary, and globalized approach to law, a new dialogue has begun. The academic exchange with more progressive sectors of traditional law schools has increased, mostly in the fields of teaching methodologies and curriculum reforms.[5] The awareness of the divergence between models, and of the reasons for it, has meant that Brazilian students interested in law, for the first time, have a real option when deciding which university to pursue. It is no longer, as before, a choice between good quality and bad quality law schools (which is not a choice at all), but between competing ways of conceptualizing law and its institutions.

The dialogue with the profession, and society at large, has been easier. Both public and private practices are more open to innovation, since they daily have to face the challenges coming from the processes of democratization and globalization, which are difficult to respond with the traditional legal tool box. Evidence of this kind of dialogue is the large number of research and courses done in partnership between FGV and the public sector. It is also important to mention the growing competition for FGV's students by law firms (Dezalay and Garth 2002: 183). Finally, it is worth highlighting a disproportional presence of FGV presence in the public debate. The risk of

---

[5] In this sense, FGV has been deeply engaged, offering winter and summer courses on teacher training on active and student-centered methodologies and online courses. FGV DIREITO SP, http://direitosp.fgv.br/sites/direitosp.fgv.br/files/arquivos/edital-curso_de_inverno_de_formacao_docente_em_ensino_juridico_0.pdf. In addition, FGV has been organizing events and seminars on the topic, such as the lecture "Do we still need the classroom?" *Ainda precisamos da sala de aula?*, FGV DIREITO SP, http://direitosp.fgv.br/evento/ainda-precisamos-sala-de-aula; as well as the event "Legal Education on debate: initiatives that make a difference." *Ensino Jurídico em debate: iniciativas que fazem a diferença*, FGV DIREITO SP, http://direitosp.fgv.br/evento/ensino-juridico-debate-iniciativas-fazem-diferenca.

solipsism has therefore been softened by the commitment of the school and its community to focus on issues of pressing importance for Brazilian society at large, and not only for the economic sectors that are beneficiaries of the globalization process.

C. Elitism

Social elitism is perhaps the most difficult trap to overcome by any law school offering global-oriented, sophisticated legal education. In face of the country's deep and widespread inequality, there is a danger that educational experiences aiming at global excellence may contribute, in spite of their original aims and potential merits, to deepen the gap between those who have and those who do not have the means to access such experiences, as the gap between those who have acquired and have not acquired this global-oriented legal education.

This risk becomes greater given the high costs involved in any project promising prime-quality education. Top-quality research and teaching are known to demand substantial funding as they involve, apart from stipends to attract talented faculty, significant resources to support core academic activities (e.g., updating of library, sponsoring of international events, modernizing of equipment). If this is true in any country, it becomes much more problematic in Brazil, where around 97 percent of the population earns no more than five times the meager minimum wage.[6]

This problem of exclusionary costs has remained less visible for a long time in Brazilian higher education, including law schools. It has, however, always existed. The most prestigious universities in the country are, with a handful of exceptions, public institutions with tuition being paid for by all taxpayers, not by the students who attend them. Historically, access to these institutions has been possible almost exclusively to top-middle and upper-class families, who could afford to send their children to expensive private primary and secondary schools (Dezalay and Garth 2002: 293). Less fortunate students had to attend private institutions, mostly low-priced and of very low quality.

---

[6] According to the Brazilian Institute of Geography and Statistics (IBGE), around 22 percent of the Brazilian population earns a maximum of two times the minimum wage, and 75 percent earns between two to three times the minimum wage. *Vamos conhecer o Brasil*, INSTITUTO BRASILEIRO DE GEOGRAFIA E ESTATISTICA, https://7a12.ibge.gov.br/vamos-conhecero-brasil/nosso-povo/trabalho-e-rendimento.html.

Through this regressive model of "free" public university education, the country has been able to promote and protect one of the most persistent and profound levels of inequality, among democracies. In the last decade, several programs of affirmative action are repositioning, for the good, the role of public universities (Dos Santos et al. 2014).

Thus, a project that intends to offer top-quality education that lessens, instead of widens, the gap between haves and have-nots has a formidable problem in its hands. In the case of FGV Direito SP, efforts have been made to create a system of scholarships, loans, and private donations, unfamiliar to Brazilian universities, to become a more inclusive environment. Grants from private donors and a pioneering program of endowment (spontaneously funded by alumni, students, faculty, and staff) have made the school slightly more accessible to talented students regardless of their income.[7] It was also necessary to adjust the selection process so it became less elitist. A program of active search for students from diverse backgrounds, mostly at public high schools, was implemented to achieve a more diverse community. The efforts are obviously insufficient to overcome the structural inequalities that forged Brazilian society for centuries, needing therefore to be constantly reviewed and enlarged, so as to open space for a larger audience.

The importance of these strategies surpasses its financial dimension. They bring to the fore the thorny issue of how to allocate resources for higher education in a country where access even to lower levels of schooling is still problematic. An alternative selection and financing model implemented by a private institution makes more urgent the need for debating the matter and requires more sophisticated arguments from critics and supporters alike.

V. Conclusion

Seen from a comprehensive viewpoint, the challenges of avoiding *legal colonialism*, *academic solipsism*, and *social elitism* point to a varied set of

---

[7] According to the FGV website, around 30 percent of students benefit from refundable scholarships programs, *Bolsas de* Estudos, FGV DIREITO SP, http://direitosp.fgv.br/bolsas-de-estudo. Further, ten students benefit from a nonrefundable scholarship "Bolsas de Estudos da Presidência," which fully or partially exempts the student from paying tuition fees. In addition, there has been an increasing number of students that benefit from the Program Endowment Direito GV, funded by legal and natural persons. The program started in 2012, with just one student receiving a R$1000 monthly scholarship to cover indirect student and living costs. In 2014, the number had jumped to twelve scholarships. *Resultados*, ENDOWMENT DIREITOGV, http://edireitogv.com.br/transparencia/res ultados.

problems (such as social and economic disparities, state inefficiency, scarcity of credit) that beset societies in the Global South, their national individual traits notwithstanding. They also suggest that any relevant legal education project entails ruptures and new ways of thinking and acting that extend far beyond the educational field. These ruptures and new ways embody complex ethical and political choices.

The way a law school responds to such challenges and choices is what ultimately defines it as an institution. Legal education, as already noted, is far from neutral. It directly and crucially impacts the idea and practice of justice in any country, and they are elemental to sustaining and perfecting democracy and of designing a fairer social landscape.

That is why, all the important innovations it brought about notwithstanding, one trait of FGV Direito SP's project stands out as radically novel in the Brazilian landscape: its courage to make explicit the political nature of legal debates. The teaching and researching of law, as well as the methodologies used to carry out these tasks, are inevitably linked to specific agendas. This fact is not a problem for serious academic work; it is the very condition for it.

By boldly bringing this dimension to the fore, FGV Direito SP has made it very difficult for traditional discourses on the neutrality of legal teaching to remain credible. Traditional and new law schools are now pressed—by their students, faculty, and professionals—to justify their options and choices, to clarify their goals, and to explain the rationale underlying their operations. This is a major contribution which, arguably, will help change much more than legal education. The School's project and social policies demand and foster, within and without its walls, an ethic of debate and dialogue elemental to building a better country.

References

Abreu, Sérgio França Adorno de (2019). *Os aprendizes do poder: o bacharelismo liberal na política brasileira*. São Paulo: Edusp.

Ambrosini, Diego Rafael, Natasha Schmitt Caccia Salinas, and A. Angarita (2010). *Construção de um sonho, Direito GV: inovação, métodos, pesquisa, docência*. Escola de Direito de São Paulo da Fundação Getúlio Vargas.

Bandeira, Luiz and Alberto Moniz (2006). *O Governo João Goulart: As lutas sociais no Brasil*. Revan.

Berkowitz, Daniel, Katharina Pistor, and Jean-François Richard (2003). "The Transplant Effect," *Comparative Law and Economics. The American Journal of Comparative Law* 51 (1): 163–203.

Botha, Henk (2013). "Of Selves and Others: A Reply to Conrado Hübner Mendes," in Vieira, Oscar V. Upendra Baxi, and Frans Viljoen eds., *Transformative Constitutionalism: Comparing the Apex Courts of Brazil, India and South Africa.* Pp. 65–74 Pretoria University Law Press.

Carlos Drumond de Andrade (2013). *Alguma Poesia: Uma cidadezinha qualquer.* Companhia das Letras.

Cunha, Luciana Gross et al. (2018). *The Brazilian Legal Profession in the Age of Globalization the Rise of the Corporate Legal Sector and Its Impact on Lawyers and Society.* Cambridge University Press.

Dezalay, Yves and Bryant Garth (2002). *The Internationalization of Palace Wars: Lawyers, Economists, and the Contest to Transform Latin American States.* University of Chicago Press.

Dezalay, Yves and Bryant Garth (2012). *Lawyers and the Construction of Transnational Justice.* Routledge.

Dos Santos, Sales Augusto, and Laurance Hallewell (2014). "Affirmative Action and Political Dispute in Today's Brazilian Academe," *Latin American Perspectives* 41(5): 141–156.

Eliot, T.S. (2018). *The Sacred Wood: Essays on Poetry and Criticism.* Boston: Charles River Editors.

Falcão, Joaquim (1998). *Lawyers in Society: The Civil Law World.* Beard Books. Washington DC: University of California.

Faria, José Eduardo (1986). *A Reforma do Ensino Jurídico.* Revista Crítica de Ciências Sociais.

Fávero, Maria de Lourdes de Albuquerque (2006). "A universidade no Brasil: das origens à Reforma Universitária de 1968," *Educar Em Revist.* 28: 17–36.

Fundação Getúlio Vargas (2017). About FGV. Accessed November 16, 2017. http://www.cies-uni.org/en/brazil/about.

Gardner, James A. (1980). *Legal Imperialism: American Lawyers and Foreign Aid in Latin America.* University of Wisconsin Press.

Gessner, Volkmar, and Ali C. Budak (1998). *Emerging Legal Certainty: Empirical Studies on the Globalization of Law.* Ashgate

Ghirardi, José G. (2012). "A Praça Pública, a Sala de Aula: Representações do Professor de Direito no Brasil," in Evandro M. de Carvalho et al., *Representações do Professor de Direito.* Pp. 25–36. Curitiba: CRV.

Gingerich, Jonathan et al. (2017). "The Anatomy of Legal Recruitment in India: Tracing the Tracks of Globalization," in Wilkins, David B., Vikramaditya S. Khanna and David Trubek eds., *The Indian Legal Profession in the Age of Globalization.* Pp. 548–577. Cambridge University Press.

Grinover, Ada P. (2009). "Brasil," *Os ANAIS da Academia Americana de Ciências Políticas e Sociais* 622(1): 63–67. Sage: UK. doi: 10.1177 / 0002716208328446.

Guy, John (1990). *Tudor England.* Oxford University Press.

Halliday, Terence C, and Pavel Osinsky (2006). "Globalization of Law," *Annual Review of Sociology* 32: 447–470.

Jewel, Lucille A. (2008). "Bourdieu and American Legal Education: How Law Schools Reproduce Social Stratification and Class Hierarchy," *Buffalo Law Review* 56(4): 1155–224.

Kennedy, Duncan (1982). "Legal Education and the Reproduction of Hierarchy," *Journal of Legal Education* 32(4): 591–615.

Kofman, Eleonore and Gillian Youngs (1996). *Globalization: Theory and Practice*. Pinter.

MacIntyre, Alasdair C. (2014). *After Virtue: A Study in Moral Theory*. Bloomsbury.

Rossana Rocha Reis (2012). O direito à terra como um direito humano: a luta pela reforma agrária e o movimento de direitos humanos no Brasil. CEDEC. http://www.scielo.br/scielo.php?script=sci_arttext&pid=S0102-64452012000200004.

Rudra, Nita (2005). "Globalization and the Strengthening of Democracy in the Developing World," *American Journal of Political Science* 49(4): 704–730.

Scherer-Warren, Ilse (2006). "Das Mobilizações às Redes De Movimentos Sociais," *Sociedade e Estado* 21(1): 109–130.

Schwarz, Roberto and John Gledson (2001). *A Master on the Periphery of Capitalism Machado de Assis*. Duke University Press.

Shaffer, Gregory C. (2012). "Transnational Legal Process and State Change," *Law & Social Inquiry* 37(2): 229–264.

Shaffer, Gregory C. (2014). *Transnational Legal Ordering and State Change*. Cambridge: Cambridge University Press.

Shapiro, Martin and Alec Stone Sweet (2004). *On Law, Politics and Judicialization*. Oxford University Press.

Smith, Linda Tuhiwai (2013). *Decolonizing Methodologies: Research and Indigenous Peoples*. 1st ed. London: Zed Books.

Swift, Jonathan (1956). *Gulliver's Travels; The Tale of a Tub; and the Battle of the Books, Etc.* Oxford University Press.

Taylor, Charles (2008). *Modern Social Imaginaries*. W. Ross MacDonald School Resource Services Library.

Trubek, David M. (2011). *Reforming Legal Education in Brazil: From the Ceped Experiment to the Law Schools at the Getulio Vargas Foundation*. University of Wisconsin. Legal Stud. Research Paper No. 1180. https://ssrn.com/abstract=1970244.

Ventura, M, L Simas, V.L.E Pepe, and F.R Schramm (2010). "Judicializaçãoo Da Saúde, Acesso à Justiça E a Efetividade Do Direito à Saúde," *Physis* 20(1): 77–100.

Vieira, Oscar V. (2008). "Public Interest Law: A Brazilian Perspective," *UCLA Journal of International & Foreign Affairs* 13(1): 219–261.

Vieira, Oscar V. (2008b). "Supremocracia," *8 Revista Direito GV* 441. http://www.scielo.br/pdf/rdgv/v4n2/a05v4n2.pdf.

Vieira, Oscar V. (2012). "Desafios do Ensino Jurídico Num Mundo em Transição: O Projeto da Direito FGV," *Revista de Direito Administrativo*, Rio de Janeiro 261: 375–382.

Vieira, Oscar V., Upendra Baxi, and Frans Viljoen (2013). *Transformative Constitutionalism: Comparing the Apex Courts of Brazil, India and South Africa*.

Wilkins, David B., Vikramaditya Khanna, and David M. Trubek (2018). *The Indian Legal Profession in the Age of Globalization: The Rise of the Corporate Legal Sector and Its Impact on Lawyers and Society*. Cambridge: Cambridge University Press.

9

Isolation and Globalization

The Dawn of Legal Education in Bhutan

*David S. Law**

I. Introduction

On July 31, 2017, the first twenty-five students enrolled in Bhutan's first law school held their first day of classes. The Jigme Singye Wangchuck School of Law (JSW), named for the much beloved and now-retired fourth King of Bhutan, is currently housed in a temporary campus adjacent to a resort in the hills overlooking the capital city of Thimphu (the "hills," in this case, happen to be the Himalayas) while a permanent campus undergoes construction a short ride from the country's sole international airport in Paro.

To imagine JSW as a one-room schoolhouse would be inaccurate because it has, in fact, two classrooms. Neither has air conditioning, and the lower classroom is cooler, so as the morning progresses, the classes migrate downhill. The Himalayan climate is temperate in the summer, but traditional Bhutanese dress is required of students and faculty alike in the classroom (and in other public buildings), and this garb—a robe-like *gho* with knee-high socks for men, a dress-like *kira* for women—can get rather warm.

Tradition and modernity coexist cheek by jowl at JSW. The *gho* and *kira* are paired with ID cards and lanyards that give the students the appearance of junior government officials (which, in reality, many if not most of them will be). Courtesy of an anonymous donor, every student carries to every class an Acer laptop running Chrome OS, which gives the school's information technology (IT) administrators maximal control and the ability to push software updates and course materials to students automatically. The crack

* A version of this chapter first appeared in volume 9 of the *Yonsei Law Journal*. I am indebted to Nima Dorji and Michael Peil for their generous feedback, guidance, and hospitality; to the organizers of the UC Irvine symposium on the globalization of legal education—Bryant Garth, Anthea Roberts, and Greg Shaffer—and to Jed Kroncke for invaluable comments and suggestions.

David S. Law, *Isolation and Globalization* In: *The Globalization of Legal Education.* Edited by: Bryant Garth & Gregory Shaffer, Oxford University Press. © Oxford University Press 2022. DOI: 10.1093/oso/9780197632314.003.0009

IT team has also wrangled one of the most reliable broadband connections in the country for JSW's exclusive use. All students take the same classes, which end every day with a vegetarian lunch. Students and faculty alike serve themselves out of giant cauldrons and wash their own dishes on the way out. Separate dormitories house JSW's inaugural class of thirteen female and twelve male students, all fresh out of high school, with a second class of thirteen women and five men on its way. The student handbook forbids sexual behavior on campus.

In its first year of operation, the total population of the law school consisted of fourteen full-time faculty, sixteen administrators, and the twenty-five students who make up the first-year class. With a single class of first-year students, its annual budget is under US$500,000. The only course of study JSW currently offers is a five-year undergraduate LLB program. At full strength, the school will have approximately thirty administrators, twenty-five faculty, a total enrollment of 125 students, and an annual operating budget of roughly US$1.2 million. The annual intake of students is not expected to grow; the result will be a very favorable student-faculty ratio of better than 6:1. Class size has been designed to match ongoing demand, which JSW officials are confident can be calculated with precision based on the hiring needs of relevant government agencies and limited private-sector employers. The degree of central planning in Bhutan enables JSW leadership to predict legal employment opportunities up to a decade in advance, particularly in the public sector: each ministry can project exactly how many people it will hire and when.

JSW owns a bus that ferries the students into town for shopping trips to the market and on field trips on the weekends. With a population of roughly 150,000, Thimphu is the largest city in Bhutan by some margin, but there are still no chain stores, fast-food restaurants, or even traffic lights. The resulting character and charm of Thimphu reflect not only its small size and its stage of economic development but also a highly ambivalent attitude toward globalization. Withdrawal from the outside world has partly been a natural byproduct of Bhutan's location in the Himalayas and the inherent inaccessibility of much of the country. But it has also served as a self-preservation strategy for a tiny country of less than one million people trapped between India and China, the two most populous countries in the world.

Against this backdrop, the establishment of Bhutan's first law school feels in many ways like a radical break with the past. JSW is unapologetically outward looking and up to date. Technologically savvy, globally networked, and intent on internationalizing the training of its students, it is the antithesis of the "hermit kingdom" stereotype. The school also defies all economic logic. With free tuition for all, a five-year interdisciplinary and experiential curriculum, and a student-faculty ratio to rival Yale Law School, JSW is structurally designed to lose money. The creation of a cosmopolitan, cost-intensive law school deep in the Himalayas, in one of the world's most tradition-conscious and least affluent countries, is rife with incongruities.

And yet, in other ways, the creation of JSW is deeply unsurprising. Its design and development express both global trends and national imperatives. For reasons that are not difficult to fathom, Bhutan has always feared for its continued existence. Withdrawal from the outside world has been one strategy for securing the autonomy and survival of the nation. But these goals are also served by the establishment of institutions that give the nation control over the training of its own elites. In the context of a country like Bhutan, legal education doubles as a form of nation building. The strategy may have evolved, but the goals remain the same.

The account that follows relies primarily on interviews and discussions conducted in Bhutan in the summer of 2017 with numerous scholars, administrators, judges, and government officials, all of whom were extraordinarily cooperative and generous with their time—even by the high standards of Bhutanese hospitality—but for reasons of confidentiality cannot be identified. Except as indicated otherwise, direct quotations are drawn from these interviews.

II. Three Impressions: Isolation, Tradition, Anxiety

The first impression that Bhutan makes on visitors is jarring—literally so. Planes land hard at the airport in Paro because the runway is short. Modern jet aircraft (such as the five narrow-body A319 aircraft collectively owned by Bhutan's two airlines) push the outermost limit of what the country's only international airport can accommodate. The thin mountain air and the short runway, which has already been extended as far as the surrounding mountains and river will permit, barely allow for an A319; wide-body jets are out of the question. Given the mountainous terrain, there are few places to put an airstrip within a reasonable distance of the capital. But building an airstrip that was too short to accommodate a 727 also had the effect, for many years, of perpetuating a certain degree of isolation.

The second impression is of a country that remains deeply enamored of its royal family. A giant portrait of the fifth king with his wife and son faces the tarmac and is the very first sight to greet visitors; several more portraits gaze down upon immigration and baggage claim. This trend continues in every building and every home. Love of royalty in Thailand pales by comparison. On paper, the country transitioned to a "Democratic Constitutional Monarchy" with its adoption of a new constitution in 2008 (Dorji and Peil 2022; Law 2017: 232–233), but popular sentiment tells a different story. The magnitude of affection for the monarchy is difficult to convey. Suffice it to say that avoiding the likeness of the current king or his father (after whom JSW is named) is akin to avoiding the sight of the American flag in Texas: it cannot be done.

What one does *not* see at Paro airport—at least, not anymore—is equally telling. There was, until recently, a prominently visible sign from "DANTAK" welcoming visitors to Bhutan. Dantak is the name of the long-running project under which the Border Roads Organisation, an offshoot of the Indian army, has built most of Bhutan's roads. The relationship between India and Bhutan is intimate and complex. Bhutan depends heavily on its southern neighbor for trade and foreign aid. India underwrites much of Bhutan's infrastructure—such as the construction of JSW's permanent campus—and its influence has become a source of local sensitivity. Local vigilantes took it upon themselves to tear down the sign; more recently, Bhutanese officials took the less drastic but still revealing step of having Dantak's name painted over.

This brings us to the third impression that Bhutan makes: it is a country that fears engulfment by its gargantuan neighbors and clings to its distinctiveness as a matter of self-preservation. Isolation, caution toward outsiders, and cultivation of national identity have served as defense mechanisms against overbearing neighbors. Enclosed on all sides by China and India, the tiny Bhutanese community chose, in effect, to hide in the mountains. China's annexation of Tibet in 1951—and persistent rumors that Mao himself referred to Bhutan as one of Tibet's "five fingers," which must one day "rejoin" Tibet—were not reassuring.[1]

---

[1] Mao Zedong is reputed to have said: "Xizang [Tibet] is China's right hand's palm, which is detached from its five fingers of Ladakh, Nepal, Sikkim, Bhutan, and Arunachal. As all of these five are either occupied by, or under the influence of India, it is China's responsibility to 'liberate' the five to be rejoined with Xizang [Tibet]" (Bhattacharyya 2017). Whether Mao (or China's leadership) ever expressed such sentiments is a matter of dispute (Atwill 2018: 76; Bradsher 1959: 750, 752).

In the aftermath of Tibet's annexation, Bhutan closed its border with China, and India's prime minister paid a well-timed visit to offer help in protecting the kingdom's borders. The resulting friendship treaty formally ceded control of Bhutan's foreign policy to India for several decades, and the border with China remains closed to this day. But the relationship with India—Bhutan's first-ever diplomatic relationship—also began the process of opening the country to the rest of the world. In the early 1960s, the Indian prime minister laid the foundation for Bhutan's first-ever road. It would be several more years before most Bhutanese would lay eyes for the first time upon an automobile.

Roughly a decade later, in 1974, India annexed the neighboring kingdom of Sikkim, and the protection offered by India began to look like a mixed blessing indeed. Many in Bhutan saw parallels between their own situation and that of the Sikkimese, who had arguably made themselves vulnerable to annexation by allowing themselves to become a minority in their own country. The Lhotsampa—southern Bhutanese residents of Nepali descent—became a focus of such anxieties. Restrictive citizenship laws in place since 1958 have made it difficult for many Lhotshampa to normalize their status, but the 1988 census nevertheless revealed that roughly one-quarter of the population of Bhutan was ethnically Nepali (Dorji and Peil 2022). Bhutan's otherwise idyllic image was sullied by a violent uprising of the Lhotsampa in the early 1990s amidst mass emigration, forced expulsions, and allegations of other rights violations by the government. The treatment of the Lhotsampa remains a sensitive topic in Bhutan.

At this point, the Bhutanese could certainly be forgiven for wanting to retreat into the mountains once again. The external environment remains treacherous. At the very moment that JSW was welcoming its first class in Thimphu, Indian and Chinese troops were hurling rocks at each other a few hours away in Doklam (Kumar 2020: 90). Little could be more unnerving than the prospect of war between India and China on one's own soil. But hiding is no longer an option.

The natural enemy of self-imposed isolation is globalization, meaning the lowering of barriers—natural, legal, political, and otherwise—to transnational interaction. Bhutan has not escaped globalization, although that is not for lack of trying. The government did not allow television or internet access until 1999. Mobile phone service was only introduced in 2004. Throughout the twentieth century, communication for most Bhutanese meant either sending a letter (which would take one or two weeks to reach from one end of the country to the other) or visiting a nearby military base and using its wireless communications capabilities. The advent of technologies such as satellite TV receivers that could be hidden in one's yard meant, however, that outside influence was coming to Bhutan one way or the other. The end of Bhutan's self-imposed isolation from global information flows has less to do with any newfound embrace of globalization or belief in the value of open markets and open borders than with a realization that technological change makes resistance futile, and that the nation is better served by dealing with change on its own terms than trying to ignore it altogether.

JSW is, in many ways, a microcosm of Bhutan's efforts to navigate a dilemma that is familiar to many developing countries. Bhutan is torn between two competing demands—the need for outside assistance and the need for autonomy. On the one hand, it is profoundly dependent on foreign assistance to achieve its development goals or even to balance its books from year to year. Thus, for example, outsiders have been essential to the creation and design of JSW at every step of the way, from the hiring and training of faculty, to the design of the curriculum, to the construction of the campus.

On the other hand, Bhutanese policy is focused intently on maintaining local control of the development process and bolstering national identity and autonomy. JSW is perfectly consistent with these goals: the establishment of a school that can supply the country with elite lawyers, judges, and bureaucrats—and shape their thinking from day one—is tantamount to the creation of national infrastructure that diminishes Bhutan's reliance on India and India's influence over Bhutan. In legal education as in other domains, the challenge for Bhutan is to find ways of obtaining outside help while not only preserving but enhancing local ownership and identity.

III. The History of Bhutan's First Law School

In a country with a population of less than 900,000, there are at most 350 people with legal training in the whole country. Roughly half serve in the judiciary, and of the remainder, the majority are civil servants. There are probably fewer than fifty practicing lawyers in the entire country or one lawyer for every 20,000 people. Not surprisingly, legal fees are astronomical by Bhutanese standards, and the UN Development Programme has taken the position that Bhutan is in urgent need of lawyers.

Prior to the opening of JSW in 2017, those Bhutanese wishing to study law had no choice but to go abroad, which in practice overwhelmingly meant India. Upon their return to Bhutan, law graduates complete a one-year, government-run conversion course to "Bhutanize" their legal training. Graduates of the course earn a Post Graduate Diploma in National Law (PGDNL) and are eligible to sit for the Royal Civil Service Examination, which is the gateway to the most prestigious jobs in the country such as positions in the judiciary and Attorney General's office. JSW is slated to assume responsibility for the conversion course, which has more than doubled in enrollment over the last decade to roughly sixty students per year but is projected to decline in popularity as JSW's main degree program begins to siphon off domestic demand.

A major force behind the creation of JSW was the US-based multinational law firm White & Case, thanks largely to its willingness and ability to bankroll the development of a law school in an obscure, mountainous corner of the world. The firm's initial involvement is said to have stemmed from contact between the then head of Bhutan's Royal Education Council (subsequently named ambassador to Kuwait) and a White & Case lawyer based in Germany who visited Bhutan and reported favorably on the need and opportunity for creation of a law school to the chair of the firm, Hugh Verrier.

Bhutan's current king, Jigme Khesar Namgyel Wangchuck (not to be confused with his father and predecessor, Jigme Singye Wangchuck, after whom the law school is named), invited Verrier to his coronation in 2008. Verrier, in turn, committed White & Case to assist Bhutan on a pro bono basis in a variety of ways, which eventually included support for the establishment of JSW. The firm dispatched Lou O'Neill, of counsel and coordinator of the firm's global pro bono efforts, to Bhutan for three months in 2009 to perform a needs assessment. On the basis of that assessment, White & Case prepared a lengthy report that recommended, among other things, the establishment of a law school in due course.

Other would-be advisors from abroad sounded a less encouraging note. Faculty at Stanford Law School counseled against the creation of a free-standing law school, especially one that would be targeted solely at a small market of Bhutanese students while at the same time disconnected from Bhutan's existing universities and thus unable to leverage a broader set of resources. They argued that it would be more cost-effective to continue sending students to India and elsewhere for study, and to invest in supplementing and improving that foreign training rather than replacing it.

The king favored an immediate start on the establishment of a law school and assigned responsibility for the task to his younger sister, Princess Sonam Dechan Wangchuck, a Stanford graduate and LLM graduate of Harvard Law School, who also spearheads a number of other initiatives relating to the justice sector, such as creation of a bar association. Thereafter, O'Neill returned to Bhutan almost every year to work with the Royal Education Council and help lay the groundwork for the creation of JSW.

The initial planning process took four years. The luminaries on the planning group used this time to think about curricular design and canvass all stakeholders, ranging from members of parliament to prospective employers. With the benefit of a clean slate, they were able to explore foundational questions and options that are usually foreclosed. What should be taught? What do people need from lawyers? In what ways should Bhutanese lawyers be different from, say, Indian lawyers or Singaporean lawyers? And so forth.

In their discussions, they were fortunate to have not only the luxury of time to think about the curriculum but also freedom from exogenous requirements as to what must be taught, or concerns about revenue, or even the job market for law graduates. The relatively underdeveloped legal profession and institutional environment also meant that they did not need to deal with many of the stakeholders that might otherwise stand in the way of optimal pedagogical design. For example, they did not have to address the demands of the bar association or bar exam because neither exists yet in Bhutan.

The result has been a law school that is distinctive, if not also progressive, by international standards. JSW charges students no tuition or fees. Indeed, it is not even willing to fine students for violating its code of conduct. Such policies reflect the overarching goals of enhancing access to the legal profession and producing a bench and bar that mirror Bhutanese society, not just the Bhutanese elite. The curriculum is unusual by Asian standards: it is deeply interdisciplinary and incorporates heavy doses of compulsory experiential learning and alternative dispute resolution, with an eye to producing well-rounded judges and civil servants as well as practice-ready private attorneys.

The creation of JSW—or, as it was known in the planning stages, the Royal Institute of Law—soon demanded the hiring of key personnel, especially administrators and specialists in legal education capable of making granular decisions, hiring faculty and staff, and implementing high-level policies decided at the planning stage. By late 2012, Princess Sonam Dechan and White

& Case were ready to pull the trigger on hiring JSW's senior leadership. Given that much of the point of creating a Bhutanese law school was to ensure that the school would have a strongly Bhutanese identity, the new school would need to have a Bhutanese face. But it would also need the specialized knowledge and skills in legal education and the actual operation of a law school that, by definition, were lacking in Bhutan.

Given these conflicting needs, the unsurprising outcome was the eventual selection of a Bhutanese dean and a foreign vice dean. The dean, Sangay Dorjee, is a Bhutanese government administrator with no law background but previous experience at the Ministry of Labor and, most recently, the Royal Education Council (the main vehicle of the early planning stages). The vice dean, Michael Peil, had been approached by White & Case while serving as associate dean for international programs at Washington University School of Law. Both were initially recruited in 2013—Dorjee as project director, Peil as foreign consultant—and were subsequently tapped in 2016 to lead the school they had helped to plan.

Formal establishment of JSW as a legal entity occurred in 2015 with the king's issuance of a royal charter, which is arguably constitutional in the sense that it is entrenched (it can only be amended by royal decree, not legislation) and confers power upon a governing body to enact statutes and regulations pertaining to JSW's operation. The charter establishes JSW as an "autonomous" entity, which makes it almost unique among higher education institutions. Bhutan's other higher education institutions were consolidated under the aegis of the Royal University of Bhutan (RUB) in 2000, with the exception of JSW and the medical school. RUB reportedly was not keen to absorb either a law school or a medical school, both of which it considered outside its core competence.

The content and, indeed, the mere existence of the royal charter accord JSW a degree of privilege. The fact that it possesses its own charter gives JSW a basis for asserting its independence from the civil service, which is the largest employer in Bhutan and will in all likelihood be the largest consumer of JSW graduates. Other language in the charter guarantees JSW academic freedom, for the purpose of enabling it to serve as a nonpartisan, apolitical engine for improvement of law. Institutional autonomy is further reinforced by the explicit guarantee of adequate government funding found in Article 1(3) of the charter, which provides that "[t]he State shall make adequate financial provisions for the sustainable operation of the law school." JSW's mandate under the royal charter explicitly includes both research and teaching: the official objectives of the school are to "provide legal education, facilitate research in law and related fields, [and] promote cultural enrichment and traditional values" (Royal Charter 2015, art. 2). Of particular interest to comparative law scholars is the fact that the charter explicitly affirms and acknowledges the value of comparative legal scholarship and pedagogy (*id.*, pmbl.).

In terms of organizational structure, the charter provides that the king appoints the president of JSW (namely, Princess Sonam Dechan), and it packs the school's "highest governing authority," the eleven-member Governing Council, with a variety of luminaries. Pursuant to the charter, the Governing Council is chaired by the Chief Justice of Bhutan and also includes the Attorney General, the Secretary of the Ministry of Education, a member of the Bar Council (which does not yet exist as of this writing), the dean, one representative elected by the faculty (at present, the vice dean), one representative elected by the students, and up to three additional members appointed by the president (currently including a representative of the Royal Civil Service Commission, a member of His Majesty's Secretariat, and the Secretary of the Ministry of Finance). Although the charter does not spell out the relationship between the Council and the president, it is hard to imagine the Council telling the princess what to do.

IV. Curriculum

With respect to the design of the curriculum, the planning process confronted a number of fundamental and interdependent design questions. What kind of degree would JSW confer? What would be the duration of studies? What courses would the school require? The broader the desired scope of substantive coverage, the longer the course of study would need to be and the higher the cost. The answer to these questions would need to be consistent with Bhutanese development policies, resource availability, and the needs and interests of relevant stakeholders.

The curricular advisory committee convened by the princess made a point of evaluating a range of foreign models. These included:

(1) Australia or Singapore (a four-year undergraduate LLB, with the option of a second graduate-level degree);

(2) the EU single-degree model (a single three-year first degree in law);

(3) the Bologna Process model (a three-year first degree, followed by an optional two-year graduate degree);

(4) India's post-1985 National Law School model (a five-year combined BA/LLB undergraduate program); and,

(5) the US model (a three-year graduate degree in law).

Notwithstanding its growing traction in other parts of Asia (Law 2015: 1015–1020), the American model was quickly and decisively rejected. The stated reasoning behind the rejection was twofold. First, a graduate-only model of legal education was wasteful from the perspective of Bhutan's human resources development strategy, which prioritizes the most efficient acquisition of essential skills over investment in nonessential breadth of training. It was viewed as an inefficient use of scarce resources to equip students with two different skill sets—one at the undergraduate level, the other at the graduate level—only one of which would ordinarily be used. While additional breadth of training might be needed in some cases, it was deemed more efficient simply to send selected individuals to India for the extra training than to invest in giving all lawyers training in an additional field.

The key decision makers settled initially on a five-year undergraduate program resembling India's National Law School model.[2] Several explanations were offered for this choice (and a desire to emulate India was not one of them). First, a longer course of study gives JSW the opportunity to "do what we really want in terms of inputs": it creates space both for training practice-ready graduates, and for making a JSW education "uniquely Bhutanese" by giving students the time and opportunity to imbibe their "rich culture and traditions." Second, a five-year degree program would align at least somewhat with the Bologna Process, which calls for participating states (mostly in Europe) to facilitate student and labor mobility by standardizing their higher-education credentials. Under the Bologna Process, universities are to offer a three-year first-degree followed by an optional two-year second degree, meaning that five years of study in the same field leads to both an undergraduate and a graduate degree (such as an LLB and an LLM).

In the end, JSW's Governing Council settled upon the combination of an undergraduate law degree (LLB) and a postgraduate diploma in national law (PGDNL), which is the same diploma awarded to graduates of the one-year

---

[2] As recently as 2018, the JSW website indicated that graduates would receive both a BA and an LLB, in line with the Indian model.

conversion course. This combination does not precisely duplicate the Indian model, in that JSW does not award a second undergraduate degree. Nor, however, does it track the Bologna Process model, as the five-year course of study is indivisible and does not lead to a graduate degree. JSW is also developing an LLM program that is likely to be targeted at foreign students with an interest in Bhutan.

The first three years of the curriculum consist entirely of compulsory courses. Over their fourth and fifth years, students take a total of four electives and engage in experiential learning. For comparative purposes, the defining characteristics of the curriculum are (1) its interdisciplinarity, (2) its emphasis on practical skills, and (3) its simultaneous and competing tendencies toward both internationalization and Bhutanization.

The interdisciplinary and practical dimensions of the curriculum are interrelated and justified by the country's need to train elite civil servants as well as practicing attorneys. Discussions with stakeholders during the planning process established the starting point that, unlike leading US law schools, Bhutan's sole law school cannot afford to produce lawyers who are merely "book smart," then expect them to learn the rest on the job—in part because opportunities for on-the-job training scarcely exist in a country that lacks a well-developed legal profession in the first place. JSW graduates must hit the ground running, and in many cases, they must also be prepared to occupy positions of public trust from day one.

The resulting curriculum is in some ways reminiscent of what Oxford calls "PPE"—a course of study so ubiquitous among British political elites that it has been dubbed "the degree that runs Britain"[3]—and aims to acquaint the future elites of Bhutan with a smattering of the following:

(1) Economics, to help them draft agreements and advise businesses;
(2) Political science, because they are future elite civil servants and/or members of parliament; and
(3) Philosophy (in addition to mandatory coursework in Buddhist philosophy more specifically), for a variety of reasons. First, philosophy is akin to a "national sport" in Bhutan and thus an essential part of any educated person's upbringing. Second, it is viewed as a form of ethical training that lawyers ought to possess. The palace is wary, and perhaps rightly so, of the idea of lawyers who lack a strong ethical foundation.

---

[3] PPE is short for Philosophy, Politics, and Economics (Beckett 2017: 25).

In due time, it will almost certainly fall upon JSW graduates to give life and meaning to the 2008 constitution. To place silver-tongued lawyers with excellent communication skills and poor ethical mooring in control of the nation's nascent legal and political infrastructure is considered dangerous.

There is ample preparation for private practice as well, in the form of:

(1) two semesters of moot court (one in English, one in Dzongkha);
(2) three semesters of legal research and writing;
(3) two semesters of mandatory live-client clinical experience;
(4) a mandatory course in law practice management (in addition to the professional responsibility course familiar to US law students); and,
(5) a tenth and final semester consisting wholly of a mandatory full-time externship (off campus, if not overseas, with a goal of landing international placements to the greatest extent possible).

Befitting a tiny, far-from-autarkic country that speaks the global lingua franca of law and business, the curriculum also exposes students to a healthy dose of international and comparative law. Indeed, as noted previously, JSW's royal charter explicitly affirms the importance and value of comparative approaches to law. International law and international commercial law are both compulsory. By contrast, unlike many American law schools, JSW offers no course explicitly entitled "Comparative Law." But its absence most definitely does not signal a lack of commitment to comparative law.

There is more than one way of introducing comparative law into the curriculum. One approach is to wall off the comparative study of law in a dedicated, specially labeled course or two, which is the American approach (or, more accurately, the approach among those American law schools that offer comparative training at all). Doing so runs the risk of implying, however, that comparative law is a distinct enterprise that can be segregated from the study of the core legal subjects that are tested on bar exams, and that core legal subjects need not be approached in a comparative manner. The second approach is to treat comparative legal analysis as a basic skill that all lawyers should possess, and to integrate and promote it throughout the curriculum.

The JSW curriculum adopts the latter approach. The absence of a dedicated "Comparative Law" course is indicative of how comparative approaches pervade the overall curriculum, to the point that comparative law cannot be segregated or disentangled from everything else that JSW students learn. For example, Constitutional Law is designed as a two-semester course, the idea being that students will spend the first semester studying constitutional law from a comparative perspective, which will equip them with the comparative skills and substantive framework to approach domestic constitutional law in the second semester in an informed and sophisticated way. Likewise, other core courses such as torts, contracts, and jurisprudence are all comparative by design. The curricular design signals implicitly that the comparative and the domestic are of equal importance and, indeed, that the comparative is a prerequisite to the study of the domestic rather than an addendum.

Last but definitely not least, from the Bhutanese perspective, are the (many) aspects of the curriculum that give it a uniquely Bhutanese flavor. There is widespread agreement on the desirability of a law school that meets international standards (and thus can credibly claim to produce world-class lawyers ready for transnational practice) yet is also local and unique (and thus satisfies the nation-building imperative). The desire to avoid choosing the global over the local (or vice versa), and instead to fashion a curriculum that is simultaneously globalized and localized, is not difficult to understand.

The problem is that these goals seem facially contradictory. How can a curriculum be both global and local? In other words, how can a country like Bhutan have its cake and eat it too? In theory, the desire for legal education that is both globalized and localized would appear to set up an intractable conflict. By definition, what is local in character cannot also be international and vice versa. Some aspects of local and global practice seem difficult to reconcile. For example, whereas Bhutan has a long-standing tradition of relatively consensual, community-based mediation, the dominant model of legal education at the international level emphasizes and valorizes formalized, courtroom-centered dispute resolution. Likewise, tort law has never been a part of local practice, as Bhutan has traditionally lacked the very concept of tort law. But it is difficult to imagine that a twenty-first-century law school, operating in accordance with international standards and expectations, could fail to offer tort law altogether.

In practice, however, JSW has not experienced much of a quandary. The solution has involved little more than a tolerance for juxtaposition and bricolage and—not least of all—a willingness to adopt a longer program of study. To the extent that there is an international or global version of some subject on the curricular wish list, JSW has been happy to embrace that version. And to the extent that there is not, JSW has been happy to develop unique offerings of its own. Rather than choosing between the global and the local, JSW has chosen both. In other words, the solution to the dilemma has simply been to spend more money.

The importance attached to the Bhutanization of the curriculum highlights the nation-building imperatives behind the creation and financing of a costly, labor-intensive law school from scratch in lieu of continued outsourcing to India. Highly Bhutanese elements of the curriculum include:

(1) A compulsory course entitled "Law and Gross National Happiness." The question of what is uniquely Bhutanese is in practice almost synonymous with the question of what advances Gross National Happiness, or GNH for short. The concept of GNH traces its origins to a casual comment by the fourth king (the eponymous JSW) in response to a question from an Indian reporter, circa 1974. Asked about Bhutan's gross national product—a comparative metric that obviously does not favor a tiny country of less than one million people— the fourth king responded that Bhutan does "not believe in Gross National Product. Because Gross National Happiness is more important." The concept of GNH has since become a source of national pride as well as national identity (if not also a national obsession that surfaces even in graffiti). It is now entrenched in Bhutan's constitution as an official goal of the state.[4] Fleshing out the concept of GNH and using it as a basis for exploring competing constitutional conceptions of the aims of the state promise to be a cottage industry for Bhutanese constitutional law and have the potential to become Bhutan's trademark contribution to the field of comparative constitutional law.

(2) A compulsory upper-year course on "law, religion, and culture" (in addition to Dzongkha language, legal history, and Buddhist philosophy courses). An important contributor to GNH is the sense of identity and belonging that comes with the celebration and cultivation of heritage and tradition.

(3) The designation of environmental law as a compulsory second-year course. The importance attached by JSW to environmental law mirrors the attachment of the country as a whole to environmentalism, which

---

[4] "The State shall strive to promote those conditions that will enable the pursuit of Gross National Happiness" (Constitution of the Kingdom of Bhutan 2008, art. 9(2)).

is in turn a direct manifestation of GNH, because GNH demands environmental protection and sustainability (among many other things).

(4) A course entitled "Penal Code & Restorative Justice," rather than "Criminal Law," because the framing of the course should reflect the fact that social harmony is another important dimension of GNH.

(5) A "Human Rights and Human Duties" course—soon to be retitled "Human Dignity"—which is akin to a sociology course animated by a combination of conventional human rights ideology and a Bhutanese emphasis on social responsibility.

(6) Five semesters of compulsory Dzongkha, because Dzongkha is Bhutan's official language (and thus the language of the courts) and a matter of national heritage.

The need for Dzongkha instruction is real and illustrates the nation-building aspects of JSW. Most Bhutanese lawyers have only limited ability to work professionally in Dzongkha, notwithstanding its official status, because they studied law in India and, in the best-case scenario, might have gone on to obtain an LLM from Australia, the United States, or the United Kingdom. Under any plausible educational scenario, the only legal vocabulary they will have acquired is in English. Thus, for example, even justices of the Bhutanese Supreme Court have been known to write their opinions in English, then turn them over to others for translation into Dzongkha, with the result that the justices themselves may be taken by surprise at something in the unfamiliar, but controlling, Dzongkha version.

The difficulty of working in Dzongkha is aggravated by the fact that, compared to English, Dzongkha is a language with a relatively small vocabulary and has not historically been applied in legal contexts, with the result that many legal terms do not already have clearly established Dzongkha equivalents. For this reason, the Supreme Court's Secretariat had a specialist in Dzongkha who spent fifteen years developing an indigenous Dzongkha legal vocabulary that rises above the level of mere transliteration. He was responsible for determining, for example, which Dzongkha word would be adopted as the term of art for "contract." It was part of his job to appear before an official committee on the Dzongkha language to argue in favor of his translation choices (for example, by pointing out that the term had previously been used in an analogous context). JSW poached this very person from the Supreme Court to teach its Dzongkha courses.

(7) Eighteen units of instruction in Buddhist philosophy.

The obligation imposed by the Royal Charter upon JSW to promote "cultural enrichment and traditional values" has been interpreted as calling upon JSW to provide instruction in both Dzongkha (Bhutan's official language) and Buddhist philosophy. The Bhutanese Constitution explicitly provides that "religion remains separate from politics," but also specifies that "Buddhism is the spiritual heritage of Bhutan." Because Buddhism is part of the nation's heritage, its advancement promotes GNH.

(8) A two-semester alternative dispute resolution course that has deliberately been christened "Appropriate Dispute Resolution" to reflect Bhutan's deeply rooted tradition of community-based mediation.

The American, Bhutanese, and Indian National Law School curricula all share in common a high degree of interdisciplinarity by Asian standards. The significant clinical and externship components are points of differentiation from the Indian model and similarity to the American model. So too is the extensive four-week orientation program for incoming students, which is deliberately modeled on the orientation courses that US law schools mandate for foreign LLM students.

Pedagogy at JSW is, like Bhutanese law itself, an eclectic mix: it reflects the heterogeneity of the faculty and ranges from lecturing (in philosophy), to almost fully Socratic instruction (in torts), to simulation and experiential learning (in contracts), with little effort at uniformity.

V. Faculty

The job description for all faculty is the "three-legged stool" familiar to US academics—namely, research, teaching, and administration. As in the United States, there is no specialization so far in terms of orientation toward teaching and research (in terms of either individual faculty focusing on one or other, or formally differentiated career tracks for teaching faculty and research faculty). Moreover, the leadership at JSW anticipates that it will always be the only law school in Bhutan and will consequently remain free of competitive pressure (from rankings, research assessment exercises, and so forth) that might force a shift in one direction or the other.

Of the fourteen full-time faculty, ten are Bhutanese and four are from the United States. At the time of the law school's launch, they were complemented by visiting faculty from the University of Vienna, and by two short-term visitors from the United States who obtained Fulbright grants to provide temporary assistance with student skills training and pedagogy. The expansion plans for the faculty call for the hiring of two more faculty to cover mandatory courses in Dzongkha (Bhutan's official language) and property law.

JSW's Bhutanese overseers are conflicted as to the desired mix of local and foreign faculty. On the one hand, in an ideal world, they would probably prefer to rely mostly or wholly on Bhutanese faculty. As one official explained, Bhutan is still "to a certain extent . . . a feudal society with hierarchy" that "doesn't want western professors with western ideas. . . . At the end of the day, we are still a monarchy. There are certain etiquettes and customs we follow that must continue. We are very passionate about our culture, our traditions, our unique identity."

On the other hand, the Bhutanese realize as a practical matter that full localization of the faculty is a "dream" that "will never happen," and they would be "very happy" to take a gradualist approach with a "half-and-half" mix. First, they realize that they are unlikely to cover all of their teaching needs with only local faculty, especially in the short term. Although JSW has already hired almost of its permanent faculty, it is temporarily short-handed because many of the Bhutanese faculty are currently overseas, or will soon be sent overseas, to obtain advanced degrees. Most of the Bhutanese faculty hold five-year undergraduate law degrees from India and are hired with the understanding that they will be sent overseas for further training. Second, visiting foreign faculty are viewed as an intellectual resource and a source of enrichment for the Bhutanese faculty. As the Chief Justice (and chair of the Governing Council) observes: "Experts will bring their own knowledge; we will have our own knowledge. We can marry the two together."

A. Faculty Training

JSW's goal is for all of its Bhutanese faculty to possess at least an LLM or master's degree in addition to the usual undergraduate degree in law from India. The local faculty are sent abroad to obtain LLM degrees from various countries in the English-speaking world, mainly the United States and Australia. Funding for this overseas study comes from a combination of scholarship aid (in the form of full-tuition scholarships) and foreign aid (to cover travel and living expenses), much of which has been provided by the Austrian government. Of the ten Bhutanese faculty, four are US-trained (with LLM degrees from George Washington University (GW) and Lewis & Clark); a Master's in Legal Studies from Washington University in St. Louis, and an MS in Philosophy from Fordham); three are Australian-trained (with LLM degrees from Sydney, UNSW, and Canberra); and one who already holds an LLM is pursuing a PhD in law at the University of Victoria in Canada.

GW's appearance on the list is no fluke but instead reflects a long-standing presence in Bhutan established by its former associate dean for international and comparative studies, Susan Karamanian, who secured an informal and semi-exclusive arrangement for GW to accept a judge from Bhutan each year into the LLM program on a full-tuition scholarship. With Karamanian's recent departure from GW, the door opened for Washington University in St. Louis (the former affiliation of JSW's vice dean, as well as the current affiliation of the author) to offer the Bhutanese judiciary a similar arrangement.

B. Faculty Recruitment

Hiring key personnel for a country's first-ever law school runs into a "chicken-and-egg" problem: a law school must be created because the country lacks lawyers, but the creation of a law school requires the recruitment of lawyers. A country that has never had a law school is likely to find legal scholars in short supply. Lateral hiring is not an option because there are no other law schools. Experienced law school administrators do not exist, while those capable of running a law school are in high demand for other positions; a small country has only so many elites to go around. Another complicating factor is that the Bhutanese are, by some accounts, not especially keen on teaching as a profession. A partial solution was to hire foreign faculty, but heavy reliance on foreign faculty was not viewed as a desirable long-term solution. The scarcity of Bhutanese candidates led JSW to adopt an approach of hiring people with the potential to teach law, then investing in the training they would need to actually teach law by sending them abroad (as described previously).

For domestic candidates, the mechanics of the hiring process are similar to what happens elsewhere. At the start of each year, JSW identifies its needs, and the dean appoints a faculty selection committee, which puts out an "informal call" for prospective applicants. (An informal call suffices in lieu of formal advertisement because, as one administrator notes, "we know all the lawyers in Bhutan.") Existing faculty in roughly the relevant area of interest take the candidate to lunch, which serves as a de facto initial interview. The names of promising candidates then go to the committee, which interviews finalists. Finally, candidates give a job talk to the full academic council. The job talks diverge from traditional job talks in the US sense because no papers are presented (and that is because no one in Bhutan has any academic papers), but, otherwise, it comes close in form: thirty to forty-five minutes of substantive presentation are followed by a question-and-answer session.

The hiring of JSW's initial four international faculty members was, by comparison, "relatively easy." Two (husband and wife) were proactively recruited by JSW with the help of White & Case. For the other two (also husband and wife), the process bore a greater resemblance to an "international NGO" search than a law faculty recruitment process. Vacancies were advertised through "PIL Net, AALS, everything." In total, JSW fielded sixty applicants from twenty countries, at all levels of seniority. With the exception of two francophone applicants, all were native English speakers. The applicants ranged from very junior candidates to nearly retired or retired practitioners wanting to use JSW as a springboard into law teaching (and to run the law school "like a little law firm"). Now that the school is already established, any hiring of further international faculty is likely to follow a process similar to that for domestic candidates (with the substitution of videoconferencing for the lunch and in-person job talk).

The applicant pool for clinical positions is distinctive. A typical candidate is a lawyer from the United States or possibly India, in his or her forties, who has been teaching short courses at a variety of law schools and is hoping to exit legal practice by parlaying that prior experience into a permanent position somewhere. The mere fact that a position is clinical in nature "automatically self-selects for Americans" because the United States has the longest and most extensive experience with clinical legal education. The majority of the candidates are Americans with prior clinical teaching experience whose interest has perhaps been piqued by somewhat romanticizing and patronizing media coverage that portrays JSW as the pet project of Americans venturing abroad like modern-day missionaries to modernize (or globalize, or Americanize—take your pick) an adorably tiny and oddball hermit kingdom (Kielburger and Marc 2015; Schultz 2016). Most of the remaining applicants are Indian practitioners with some law-teaching experience (which is unsurprising, given the size and proximity of the labor pool). The Indian applicants typically offer in their applications to teach other courses if not hired for a clinical position.

VI. Admissions

Traditionally, Bhutanese students know where they will end up based entirely on their academic performance in grade twelve. The top students in the country are called to Thimphu by the Department of Adult and Higher Education (DAHE) and choose in order of their nationwide ranking from a list of available foreign scholarships. Students must either decide on the spot or go to the back of the line and choose from whatever is left after everyone else has picked. Number one typically picks a Fulbright scholarship, which is then crossed off the list, while numbers two and three usually snap up the Australian equivalent. The next few take spots in India. Once the eighty or so foreign scholarships are gone, another four hundred students accept places in Sherubtse College (the "Harvard of Bhutan"); another eight hundred or so choose the College of Science and Technology, also in Bhutan; and so on, until all slots are filled.

JSW's approach to admissions departs significantly from this system. First, as a new institution, it has treated affirmative outreach as a necessity. JSW faculty and staff personally visit all of Bhutan's fifty-eight high schools, which represents considerable effort. Notwithstanding Bhutan's small size— roughly half the size of Indiana—domestic travel between most points is grueling. There is no rail system, airports are few and far between (and not always operational), and the winding mountain roads are arduous and often in poor condition, to the point that a journey of thirty miles can easily take the better part of a day. JSW is then presented to potential students as a challenge: "This will be the hardest thing you've ever done."

Second, JSW devised a unique admissions process that combines elements of the global and the local. High school grades are weighted only 30 percent rather than 100 percent. Standardized test scores—discussed later—count for 45 percent. Finally, interviews count for the last 25 percent. From JSW's first-ever pool of applicants, fifty candidates were shortlisted for interviews based on a combination of their grades and standardized test scores. The inaugural class of twenty-five students was filled over the course of three rounds.

The standardized test in question is a version of the LSAT designed specifically for Bhutan. It is called, simply, the "Bhutan-LSAT" and was developed by the creators of the regular LSAT, the US-based Law School Admission Council (LSAC). Applicants are urged to familiarize themselves with the format of the test and sample materials available on JSW's admissions web page, but they are also told that there is no real way of studying for this test. The Bhutan-LSAT is a microcosm of Bhutan's approach to the choice between global and local approaches: whenever possible, it chooses both. In legal education as in other areas, Bhutan is characterized by a contradictory desire for institutions that are global (and thus credibility-building) yet also local (and thus identity-building). What better way to do so than a bespoke version of a foreign-made test?

Third, JSW pursued an unorthodox interview strategy. In the run-up to the admission of its inaugural class, JSW was taken by surprise when DAHE unexpectedly accelerated its schedule by two weeks due to holidays. This gave JSW a total of four days to plan its strategy. Knowing that the top students were already in Thimphu to attend the DAHE interviews, JSW reconstructed DAHE's rankings and spent two days interviewing candidates in roughly that order at the rate of ten or eleven candidates per day, before the DAHE interviews began. Its stated rationale was to give students a backup in case they preferred not to take a risk on a new and untested institution. Unlike DAHE, JSW gave students two weeks to decide, on the view that "we don't want you unless you want to be here." As a strategic matter, however, waiting to conduct interviews until students had already accepted foreign scholarship offers from DAHE on the spot would have likely decimated JSW's prospects for recruiting the very best students.

This approach bore fruit. For JSW's inaugural class, six of the top twenty-five students in the country accepted admissions offers from JSW, including the presumptive Fulbright recipient at the very top of the list. At the same time, however, over half of the students admitted by JSW would not have qualified for the most elite scholarships offered by DAHE. In response to JSW's decision to interview the top candidates first, DAHE has taken the view that it will still fill every available scholarship slot, and that JSW's entry merely means more satisfied students and families.

VII. International Influences

As a minuscule developing country wedged between two superpowers, Bhutan faces its fair share of challenges, but, in the area of legal education, it has enjoyed a rare advantage—namely, a blank slate. The lack of existing domestic institutions, combined with the mature state of foreign institutions, presented a best-case scenario for a fully rational and deliberative approach to the design of a legal education system that reflects best practices. On the one hand, they were relatively unconstrained by path dependence and historical accident. On the other hand, they faced a wealth of existing systems from which they could learn and draw inspiration.

Conscious choice among competing models has indeed played a significant role in the design of JSW. Relevant design considerations have included dissatisfaction with the most obvious model—the Indian system—as well as a degree of sensitivity to Indian influence. Even under such favorable conditions, however, conscious design cannot account fully for the particular manner in which JSW has developed. Its design has inevitably also reflected a combination of resource constraints, human foibles, and sheer happenstance.

The architects of JSW set out very deliberately to canvass the entire world for the best possible ideas and practices. At one level, globalization facilitated this task by placing an entire world of experience at their disposal. At another level, however, globalization made the task impossible. The bigger and more complex the world, and the more models from which to choose, the harder it becomes for decision makers to make optimal choices based on command of all relevant information. Which models manage to capture their attention, and which models do not, can reflect the quirks of personal acquaintance, or foreign aid, or sheer luck.

In this situation, the architects of JSW could not help but behave like everyone else. To some degree, they fell back on personal knowledge and personal networks, and they were constrained by the fact that funding was, and remains, in short supply. The funding environment played a critical role in determining what models and influences would find traction in Bhutan. Those with money to offer at the outset wielded disproportionate influence that has embedded itself in the form of first-mover advantage. Upstream involvement early in the process shows strong signs of translating into lasting impact with the help of path dependence.

Financial constraints and lack of existing infrastructure leave Bhutan little practical choice but to seek international partners in developing its legal education system. And in Bhutan, international support has historically meant reliance on India, which accounts for over two-thirds of all foreign aid received by Bhutan as well as nearly 80 percent of all imports and 90 percent of all exports (Chaudhury 2018; Ramachandran 2018). Acceptance of the inevitability and desirability of an extremely close relationship with India coexists with ambivalence toward the scope and degree of Indian assistance. Diversification of the country's international partnerships and sources of support is a key element of Bhutanese development and nation-building strategy.

These dynamics have been evident in the creation of JSW. Through the 1960s and 1970s, the vast majority of skilled professionals in Bhutan—from doctors and accountants to teachers and civil servants—hailed from India. The existence of a domestic law school is intended to reduce the country's reliance on India for human capital. Nation-building goals are inseparable from educational goals: in the words of one JSW official, "no matter how benign or generous" India may be, "if Bhutan doesn't have its own experts and resources, Bhutan will cease to exist in any meaningful way." Matters such as the design of the curriculum and the choice of international partners reflect deliberation not only over how best to design a system of legal education but also how to advance Bhutan's development, distinctiveness, and self-preservation as a state.

A variety of law schools from around the world have expressed interest in partnering with JSW but usually for the purpose of student exchange. The stereotypical approach is to seek a memorandum of understanding that can be collected "like a trophy" and trumpeted in brochures to students as another overseas study opportunity, without much real engagement or commitment of resources. It is not difficult to see why schools elsewhere might value opportunities for their students (and perhaps also their faculty) to spend time in a hermit kingdom that they have read about in the *New York Times* (Schultz 2016).

Partnerships of this variety hold little obvious benefit for JSW. As the only law school in the country, it has no need to compete for students by offering study-abroad programs, and in any event, overseas travel and living expenses are prohibitively costly for most Bhutanese students. At the same time, an incoming flow of foreign students would burden a developing institution without the administrative apparatus needed to accommodate a regular flow of visitors. JSW lacks the manpower to handle multiple institutional relationships, particularly at a time when key personnel are themselves pursuing advanced studies abroad. By comparison, the kind of partner most valuable to JSW—namely, those willing to bear the cost of hosting and training JSW faculty—has been scarce.

Expressed in national terms, the two biggest outside players in shaping Bhutan's new legal education system thus far have probably been the United States and Austria, in that order. India's influence is significant yet difficult to unpack. On the one hand, the Bhutanese have no desire to simply imitate the Indian model. On the other hand, there are strong practical reasons to pursue compatibility with the Indian system, and the actual result bears more than a passing resemblance to the Indian model.

A. India

Aversion to the Indian model of legal education reflects not only sensitivity about excessive Indian influence in general but also dissatisfaction with Indian legal education in particular. In light of the fact that all of Bhutan's current lawyers and judges were at least partly trained in India, it may seem striking that Indian legal education is held in low regard, but, in this case, familiarity has bred contempt. The term used to describe traditional Indian pedagogy is "chalk and talk": an instructor stands at a chalkboard and speaks from "dusty yellow notes" that have barely changed in decades. India's elite National Law Schools sought to address these ills in the late 1990s with a significantly revamped and interdisciplinary curriculum that expanded the course of study from three to five years, but they are still afflicted by what one graduate described as "low-paid, bad instructors."

Notwithstanding this aversion to the Indian model of legal education, the reality is that India has played a massive role in the development of Bhutanese legal education and will continue to do so for years to come. JSW is, like Bhutan more generally, dependent on India for infrastructure of both the tangible and intangible varieties. In a literal sense, India is building legal education in Bhutan by funding the construction of the new permanent JSW campus in Paro. More importantly, however, all of Bhutan's existing lawyers and judges received some or all of their legal training in India. Thus, given JSW's emphasis on recruiting local faculty as heavily as possible, Indian legal education will continue to be a formative intellectual influence on Bhutanese law faculty for years to come.

It is probably no coincidence that the JSW curriculum resembles that of India's National Law Schools in key respects, including its length, its interdisciplinarity, and its dual-degree character. The notion that JSW has modeled its curriculum on an Indian model does not sit well in Bhutan; the preferred narrative is that JSW has followed the Bologna Process model, which also calls for a similar curriculum. Ironically, however, the logic behind the Bologna Process—which is essentially a regional harmonization project—suggests that Bhutan should be pursuing harmonization not with faraway Europe but with its own neighbor India, an overwhelmingly important trading partner and source of human capital that already shares an open border with Bhutan.[5]

B. The United States

The United States is a major source of key personnel, funding, technical assistance, scholarships, and inspiration for Bhutanese legal education. The support that comes from the United States is fundamentally unlike the support that comes from various European countries, however, in that it has primarily taken the form of uncoordinated private initiative rather than systematic and strategic governmental sponsorship.[6] Indeed, American actors have on occasion pursued competing objectives and given conflicting advice. For example, while White & Case was recommending the establishment of a law school and providing crucial financial and technical assistance for the launch of JSW, advisors from Stanford Law School were arguing against the creation of a law school—especially a freestanding one.

Many a law school might value the bragging rights of having a partnership with Bhutan's first law school, but the partnerships that have actually materialized share two common threads. The first is a personal connection of some kind. Stanford Law School's early involvement, for example, was attributable to the fact that Princess Sonam Dechan had attended Stanford as

---

[5] Bhutan's second largest city, Phuntsoling, and the adjoining Indian city of Jaigaon are separated by an open gate through which Bhutanese and Indians pass freely.

[6] Although there is no Fulbright scholarship specifically earmarked for Bhutan, the Fulbright Scholars program has provided financial support for Americans to teach on a temporary basis at JSW, and it remains free to entertain further Bhutanese requests.

an undergraduate (and was not the only member of the royal family to do so). GW's substantial footprint in the Bhutanese judiciary stemmed from an encounter between former Chief Justice Sonam Tobgye and an American Bar Association administrator who, in turn, introduced the Chief Justice to Susan Karamanian at GW. Likewise, Washington University's role in educating JSW faculty and Bhutanese judges is attributable to connections between faculty at JSW and Washington University.

The second common thread is a willingness to commit resources that the Bhutanese themselves want. For example, Stanford expressed interest in student exchange and also offered in-kind assistance in the form of faculty and student manpower to help write Bhutanese legal textbooks and advice on how to build a cost-effective legal education system. Ultimately, however, the strategic advice foundered on the Bhutanese view of JSW as part of a nation-building strategy, while the teaching materials were never adopted. It was also unlikely that a brand-new institution gearing up to teach its own inaugural class would commit the resources needed to deal with foreign students (much less the expectations that American law students in particular bring to the table). By contrast, other schools such as GW, Washington University in St. Louis, and Lewis & Clark enjoyed fortuitous connections with JSW and have since endeared themselves simply by offering scholarships to Bhutanese scholars and judges. Given the extent to which the upper ranks of the Bhutanese judiciary are already populated by GW graduates, such scholarship schemes seem likely to pay reputational dividends in the long term.

At the intangible level, American influence is now embedded in JSW's pedagogy and curriculum in self-perpetuating ways. JSW's heavy dose of clinical education, in particular, seems likely to ensure ongoing demand for the kind of faculty who are more prevalent in the United States than in Europe or elsewhere in Asia. Given the role that personal connections and networks have played thus far in JSW's development, the existence of a continuing faculty pipeline from the United States to Bhutan suggests that American influence will remain considerable, albeit unsystematic and uncoordinated.

C. Austria

The Austrian government has invested heavily and deliberately in Bhutan. The Austrian Development Agency (ADA), which maintains an office in Thimphu, has funneled both financial and in-kind support to JSW, although its enthusiasm has fluctuated. JSW has also made initial contact with Eurasia-Pacific Uninet, an international network of research institutions that is led and financed by Austria, with the goal of exploring potential funding and research collaboration opportunities.

The in-kind support from Austria takes the form of exchanges with the University of Vienna that occur on terms highly favorable to JSW. As ADA funding is conditional upon identification of a suitable partner institution in Austria, ADA paid for JSW officials to conduct a fact-finding visit to Austria. Relevant considerations for JSW included the partner institution's willingness to invest resources and ability to offer courses in English. Whereas the University of Salzburg scored poorly on both dimensions, the University of Vienna seized the opportunity. Pursuant to a memorandum of understanding, the University of Vienna has hosted JSW faculty as visitors and sent its own faculty to JSW to cover areas of teaching need identified by JSW (which thus far has meant courses in human dignity and political science), all at its own expense.

More extensive collaboration with the Austrians is hindered by a factor absent from dealings with the United States or India—namely, the language barrier. Because Austrian faculty offer most of their courses in German, the range of courses that they can cover for JSW is limited. Likewise, the language barrier limits Bhutanese desire and need for instruction in Austria.

D. Other Countries

Other actual or prospective sources of support include Canada, Singapore, and Germany. Canada is, like the United States, a suitable and desirable locale for Bhutanese faculty as well as judges to obtain advanced training. A Dalhousie LLM sits on the Bhutanese Supreme Court, while the University of Victoria's law school has enrolled JSW's constitutional law professor in its PhD program and will conduct additional scholarly exchange with Bhutan thanks to a governmental scholarship scheme, the Queen Elizabeth II Diamond Jubilee Advance Scholars program. Canadian involvement thus combines elements of the American and European approaches: like the American approach, it is driven by the initiative of specific individuals and institutions, but like the European approach, it enjoys governmental backing.

Waiting in the wings is National University of Singapore, which has offered to be of assistance and thus far has sent a lawyering skills specialist to conduct training sessions for JSW faculty. Another potential player is Germany. Although its impact has thus far been minimal, Germany's well-known academic exchange service, the Deutscher Akademischer Austausch Dienst (DAAD) (Law and Chang 2011: 577 n.267), is fielding a fact-finding mission to Bhutan. While DAAD has the organization and wherewithal to fund bilateral faculty exchanges and scholarships for JSW faculty, the Germans ultimately face the same constraint as the Austrians—namely, any support or training that they provide must be in English, which limits the available options.

VIII. Conclusion

The dawn of legal education in Bhutan poses something of a paradox. Dwarfed by mammoth neighbors on all sides and consequently fearful of absorption, Bhutan has long resorted to withdrawal, insularity, and cultivation of a distinctive identity as national survival strategies. Yet this tiny developing country that has for centuries made a point of isolating itself from the rest of the world for the sake of its own survival has now embraced a resource-intensive model of legal education that relies heavily in both design and execution on international advisors and sponsors. The adoption of a globalized model of legal education by the so-called hermit kingdom makes for a striking juxtaposition of isolation and globalization, if not a degree of incoherence or outright contradiction. Nevertheless, the decision is open to a combination of political, cultural, and functional explanations.

The most obvious and important explanation for the existence of JSW is political: the creation of a domestic system of legal education is explicitly part of an overall nation-building strategy. JSW may not be cost-effective or self-sustaining, but for a country in Bhutan's vulnerable position, it is understandable that nation building might be given priority over penny-pinching. Law being the lifeblood and the language of the state, a domestic institution that enables Bhutan to produce its own legal experts is both a form of infrastructure and a way of promoting national self-sufficiency and distinctiveness. And in reality, JSW has in fact functioned as a site of production for national identity. Among other things, it is quite literally an institutional locus for the invention of a national language: Dzongkha as a legal language is being invented through the process of being taught at JSW.

To say that nation-building goals motivated the creation of JSW, however, begs the question of why the Bhutanese concluded that these goals called for the establishment of a full-blown, freestanding law school (as opposed to, say, a series of add-on courses designed and offered by an existing university). From a cultural or sociological perspective, this policy choice might be said to demonstrate the irresistible pull of what sociologists have called "world culture"—namely, a common set of understandings and expectations concerning what countries must do in order to thrive and win acceptance (Meyer et al. 1997: 166–168). On this view, national development and educational policies tend to be "enactments of conventionalized scripts" that nation-states learn to follow as members of "world society" (*id.*, 159, 149–150, 155). Putting aside any functional justifications, a law school may simply be something that every country is supposed to have—an essential accoutrement of any self-respecting and respectable nation. A national law school is arguably a "trapping of statehood, like an anthem or flag or paper money" (Law 2016: 56). In other words, Bhutanese state sponsorship of a law school may be understood at least partly as a form of norm-driven behavior. The logic of globalization is not strictly economic; it is also normative and cultural. To view JSW as a mere national vanity project is to discount the power and ubiquity of the norms in question.

Functional considerations, in turn, help to explain JSW's heavy reliance on foreign models. It seems neither realistic nor sensible for any country today to construct a wholly unique system of legal education from scratch. Such an undertaking would be not only costly but also maladaptive: at a time of increasing economic globalization, an idiosyncratic form of training and credentialing only makes it harder for lawyers to operate transnationally. All of this holds especially true for a tiny, developing country like Bhutan. In the absence of raw materials for constructing a system of law or legal education that could plausibly be described as autochthonous, resistance to foreign models is not an option, and necessity is the mother of imitation. The case of legal education in Bhutan illustrates the extent to which globalization is often not a matter of choice but of necessity.

A critical question from the Bhutanese perspective is whether and to what extent these choices might compromise the country's distinctive identity and traditions and thus undermine the very goals that they are intended to achieve. By definition, national identity and traditions cannot be mere echoes of a global template. Is there a natural and unavoidable tension, if not contradiction, between identity building and globalization? Or can Bhutan enjoy the best of both worlds, in the form of a law school that advances a distinctive national identity yet also commands the international acceptance and prestige that come with the adoption of global standards and practices?

To some extent, Bhutan has been able to have its cake and eat it too because the pursuit of a globalized model of legal education still leaves room for choice. Globalization cannot be reduced to imitation and harmonization; it also involves competition and pluralism (Law 2008: 1334–1335). The "global" does not speak with a unified voice in Bhutan: from India to Austria to the United States, the influences are disparate, and the process of integrating and reconciling them has scarcely begun. The world of legal education offers a buffet of options, which has enabled Bhutan to diversify the range of influences at work. From a nation-building perspective, embracing a diverse mix of countervailing influences is a perfectly plausible strategy for avoiding excessive influence from a particular direction (in this case, India).

Globalization is also consistent with a degree of localization. "Glocalization"—the adaptation of global phenomena to local conditions— is not a contradiction in terms but rather a widespread phenomenon (Robertson 1995: 28–29). If even McDonald's—the epitome of all that critics of globalization love to hate—makes a point of customizing its offerings from one country to the next, the legal education industry can surely do the same. Reliance on foreign models has not prevented JSW from supplementing its curriculum with courses built to address local needs and interests. By choosing to shoulder the cost of an elaborate, resource-intensive curriculum, Bhutan has avoided a zero-sum choice between a law school that is distinctively Bhutanese and a law school that is compatible with the outside world. Not all dilemmas can be solved with money, but some can—at least until the money runs out. The resulting pastiche of foreign and local elements may not be fully coherent or original, but it is certainly different.

References

Atwill, David (2018). *Islamic Shangri-La: Inter-Asian Relations and Lhasa's Muslim Communities, 1600 to 1960*. University of California Press.

Beckett, Andy (2017). "The Degree that Runs Britain," *The Guardian*. February 23.

Bhattacharyya, Abhijit (2017). "China's Bhutan Push to Fulfill Mao's Old Dream," *Asian Age*. June 27. https://perma.cc/8ST8-XLTP.

Bradsher, Henry (1969). "Tibet Struggles to Survive," *Foreign Affairs*. July.

Chaudhury, Dipanjan Roy (2018). "Bhutan May Receive More Financial Assistance," *The Economic Times*. October 22. Accessed June 23, 2020. https://perma.cc/EVN5-99P7.

Constitution of the Kingdom of Bhutan (2008). https://www.constituteproject.org/constitution/Bhutan_2008.pdf?lang=en

Dorji, Nima and Michael Peil (2022). "Bhutan," in David S. Law et al., eds., *Oxford Handbook of Constitutional Law in Asia*. Forthcoming.

Kielburger, Craig and Marc Kielburger (2018). "The Unique Law School Coming Soon to Happy-Centric Bhutan," *The Huffington Post*. June 2. Accessed June 23, 2020. https://perma.cc/U9FY-F8KG.

Kumar, Suneel (2020). "China's Revisionism Versus India's Status Quoism: Strategies and Counter-strategies of Rivals in Doklam Standoff," *Jadavpur Journal of International Relations* 24(1): 73–100.

Law, David (2017). "Alternatives to Liberal Constitutional Democracy," *Maryland Law Review* 77(1): 223–243.

Law, David (2016). "Constitutional Archetypes," *Texas Law Review* 95(2): 153–244 (December).

Law, David (2008). "Globalization and the Future of Constitutional Rights," *Northwestern University Law Review* 102(3): 1277–1350.

Law, David (2015). "Judicial Comparativism and Judicial Diplomacy," *University of Pennsylvania Law Review* 163(4): 927–1036 (March).

Law, David and Wen-Chen Chang (2011). "The Limits of Global Judicial Dialogue," *Washington Law Review* 86(3): 523–578 (October).

Meyer, John et al. (1997). "World Society and the Nation-State," *American Journal of Sociology* 103(1): 144–181.

Ramachandran, Sudha (2018). "Can Bhutan's New Government Avoid Doklam 2.0?," *The Diplomat*. October 29. Accessed June 23, 2020. https://perma.cc/8BPG-ZRVF.

Robertson, Roland (1995). "Glocalization: Time-Space and Homogeneity-Heterogeneity," in Mike Featherstone et al., eds., *Global Modernities*. Pp. 25–44. London: Sage.

Royal Charter (2015). The Government of Bhutan. February 21. Accessed June 24, 2020. https://perma.cc/3AMN-VSP9.

Schultz, Kai (2016). "A Law School in a Kingdom of Buddhism," *New York Times*. October 9, at A6.

10

China and the Globalization of Legal Education

A Look into the Future

Philip J. McConnaughay and Colleen B. Toomey

When someone asks where Peking University's School of Transnational Law (STL) is located, it is tempting to reply, "in the future." In many respects, this answer would be correct.

STL's physical location is Shenzhen, China, renowned as China's "Silicon Valley" and arguably the world's leading center of innovation and finance. Just forty years ago, Shenzhen was a small agricultural and fishing community with a population of barely 50,000. Its transformation began in 1980, when Deng Xiaoping declared the city China's first "Special Economic Zone," intended to lead reform and the "opening" of China to the West. Between 1980 and 2016, Shenzhen's GDP in real terms grew at an average annual rate of 22 percent, the highest in China, and the city transformed first from an economy based on agriculture to one based on manufacturing, and then from manufacturing to one based on technological innovation and services. Today, Shenzhen's population is approaching twenty million, and it is home to such world-leading technology and financial services giants as Tencent, Huawei, Ping An, DJI Drones, BGI, BYD, and ZTE.

Shenzhen is Hong Kong's closest Mainland neighbor, only minutes to the north. Both are located at the mouth of China's Pearl River Delta, where the Pearl River empties into the Shenzhen Bay and the South China Sea. The nine major Mainland cities of the Delta—Guangzhou, Shenzhen, Dongguan, Zhaoqing, Foshan, Huizhou, Jiangmen, Zhongshan, and Zhuhai—are interconnected by a massive infrastructure of modern roads, rail, telecommunications, energy, and water. A new forty-eight-kilometer bridge and tunnel system soon will connect Hong Kong and Macau and Zhuhai, thereby completing the interconnection of the entire Delta via highway. The World

Philip J. McConnaughay and Colleen B. Toomey, *China and the Globalization of Legal Education* In: *The Globalization of Legal Education*. Edited by: Bryant Garth & Gregory Shaffer, Oxford University Press. © Oxford University Press 2022. DOI: 10.1093/oso/9780197632314.003.0010

Bank recognizes the Pearl River Delta as the world's largest and most populous single metropolitan area (World Bank Press Release 2015), an evolving "Megacity" expected to reach a population of eighty million as a result of "the most rapid urban expansion in human history" (The Guardian 2017; Satellite Images 2017).

The economic integration of Shenzhen and Hong Kong, and ultimately of the entire Pearl River Delta, seems inevitable. The multi-trillion dollar joint Shenzhen–Hong Kong financial services area known as "Qianhai," touted as China's "Wall Street," already has more than 125,000 registered businesses, with an additional several hundred firms from around the world registering each week (Yiu 2017). A similarly ambitious joint project, the "Lok Ma Chau Loop Innovation and Technology Park," in the disputed Shenzhen–Hong Kong border region, will continue to expand the high-tech incubation capacity of the region (Khan and Curran 2017). Exchange between Shenzhen and Hong Kong is advancing as if it already is a single integrated economy.

Shenzhen and the Pearl River Delta also serve as a principal gateway for China's "Belt and Road Initiative," a massive revival and expansion of the trans-Eurasian "Silk Road." The Belt and Road Initiative reflects China's desire for deeper economic engagement with nations to its west—essentially all of Central, South, and Southeast Asia, Eurasia, and East Africa—as well as a foreign policy strategy for the twenty-first century. The Initiative includes a China-led US$1.3 trillion investment in an infrastructure of roads, high-speed rail, telecommunications, pipelines, and ports interconnecting China with all of Central, South, and Southeast Asia, Eurasia, and East Africa. The Belt and Road Initiative has been called the "new face of globalization" (Brinza 2017).

These developments have had a profound impact on STL's approach to legal education. STL began as an "experiment" of sorts, established in 2007 by special authorization of China's State Council to offer China's only American law Juris Doctor (JD) program.[1] The law school's original objective was accreditation by the American Bar Association (ABA), similar to US law schools. When this possibility evaporated with the ABA's 2012 decision not to extend its accrediting authority beyond the United States and Puerto

---

[1] State Council Circular X.W.B. [2007] No. 46. Technically, the State Council authorized Peking University to establish and award an *International Fa Lv Shuo Shi*, or literally, an "international Juris Master degree." The Juris Master, or "JM," is a recognized postbaccalaureate professional degree in law in China. The authorization of an *International Fa Lv Shuo Shi* was understood to mean an American-style Juris Doctor degree. STL's JD curriculum is taught entirely in English.

Rico, STL had to reconsider its mission. There was no question about the law school continuing a top JD program substantially compliant with ABA Standards, but we also desired to expand STL's educational mission to better reflect the extraordinary developments under way in Shenzhen and the Delta and our dedication to the creation of a *Chinese* legal profession every bit as capable and competitive as those of the most advanced Western nations, especially the United States and the United Kingdom.

Initially, our redirected focus was STL's China law Juris Master (JM) curriculum, which originally had been added to the JD program only in order to comply with domestic regulatory concerns, not as a strategically important educational objective in its own right.[2] We enlisted the assistance of one of China's foremost scholars of civil law and legal education, Professor GE Yunsong of Peking University, to help revise the content and teaching method of STL's China law curriculum in ways designed to achieve professionalism and skills acquisition objectives similar to those of our JD curriculum. The revisions recognize that China law and civil codes, although based largely on the civil law codes of Germany, in fact reflect a host of customary, communist, Soviet, American, and other influences. The changes dramatically elevated the importance of STL's China law curriculum in relation to our JD curriculum in a way that is directly analogous to the juxtaposed legal traditions of Shenzhen and Hong Kong.

In fact, the ongoing economic integration of Shenzhen and Hong Kong is providing observable examples for incorporation into STL's dual degree program of the direct interface of Chinese and common law traditions, and perhaps a preview of their joint evolution. China purposefully is experimenting with the emerging legal regime in Qianhai in order to determine the legal rules and practices most conducive to economic exchange between parties from such fundamentally different legal traditions. Qianhai courts, for example, include both Mainland and Hong Kong judges. A special Qianhai agency is charged with identifying foreign laws that may provide useful guidance in the evolution of China's legal regime for multinational exchange. The Shenzhen and Hong Kong stock exchanges are linking with the prospect of a more unified regulatory regime. The South China Arbitration Commission

---

[2] Even though the State Council's authorization of an *International Fa Lv Shuo Shi* was understood to refer to an American-style JD, there was some concern within Peking University that a JD could not be awarded without an accompanying, officially recognized, Juris Master (*Fa Lv Shuo Shi*). STL's Mainland Chinese students, consequently, are required to take both curriculums. STL's JM curriculum is taught largely in Chinese.

is creating new panels of arbitrators and rules of procedure designed especially for multilegal system disputes. And so on.

China's Belt and Road Initiative is accompanied by similar efforts to create a transnational legal infrastructure most conducive to successful exchange between China and Belt and Road countries, except that China–Belt and Road exchange, unlike Shenzhen–Hong Kong exchange, often will involve parties exclusively from non-Western legal traditions, or at least from mixed legal traditions. The new China International Commercial Court (CICC) in Shenzhen and the Shenzhen Court of International Arbitration both have undertaken procedural adjustments designed specifically to accommodate mixed legal tradition dispute resolution.

It is not clear what new transnational commercial and legal rules and practices will emerge from the economic integration of Shenzhen and Hong Kong and from China's growing exchange with Belt and Road countries. What is clear, however, is that new practices and principles will emerge, that they will be heavily influenced by Chinese and other non-Western traditions, and that they likely will preview parallel developments throughout China and worldwide as China's global influence continues to grow.

To be sure, the Western legal tradition—common law and civil law as practiced in Anglo-European countries—will not simply recede into insignificance. International trade with the United States, the European Union, the United Kingdom, Canada, and Australia likely will continue to grow, and along with it, the continuing influence of the Western legal tradition. But China's engagement with the non-Western world, especially Africa and Belt and Road countries, is challenging as never before prevailing assumptions of a global convergence of law around the Western legal tradition, perhaps foreshadowing, as Harold Berman predicted, the formation of a new legal tradition "in which a multicultural East and West and North and South [begin] to forge a new tradition of world law" (Berman 2000: 763).

Legal education must prepare a new generation of lawyers capable of anticipating and contending with these developments. This chapter examines the unique educational program of Peking University School of Transnational Law as one approach to this challenge. Section I briefly revisits the original purpose and goals of STL and the ABA decision that prevented their achievement. Section II examines STL's pivot to its China law curriculum, and the influence STL's approach to China law education is having on legal education in China and Asia generally. Section III explores the likely influence of Shenzhen–Hong Kong integration, legal developments in the Greater

Pearl River Delta, and China's Belt and Road Initiative on STL's program of legal education and on legal education globally. Finally, Section IV briefly examines some of the advantages and challenges STL enjoys and confronts as an academic unit of a Chinese university.

I. STL in the Beginning

China and Shenzhen recognized early on that sustainable economic development in Shenzhen and the Pearl River Delta turns in part of the presence of research universities sufficient to contribute to an educated workforce and technological innovation. The idea was to achieve the same "cluster" of leading universities and scientists, businesses, and supportive government policies that contributed to the rise of California's Silicon Valley, Boston's Route 128, Austin, Texas, and other technology hubs in the United States. Among the early research university targets were three of China's best—Peking University (PKU), Tsinghua University, and Harbin Institute of Technology (HIT). All three eventually agreed to establish campuses in Shenzhen, and the government of Shenzhen provided a several-thousand-acre prime location "University Town" campus for them to share.

One of the early chancellors of PKU's "Shenzhen Graduate School" was Professor Hai Wen, a celebrated developmental economist who had been integral in the establishment of PKU's acclaimed National School of Development in Beijing. It was Hai Wen's idea to establish a law school on PKU's Shenzhen campus, one that would be unique in China. It would offer an American JD, in English; be competitive academically with the very best US law schools; and charge tuition and fees that would be dramatically lower than those a growing number of Chinese graduate students were paying for US-based legal education. The graduates of PKU's elite Shenzhen law school, moreover, would enjoy identical professional opportunities. The goal was for STL graduates to "walk out and work for Paul Hastings, Akin Gump and other similar firms" (Lehman 2012).

In 2007, PKU and Chancellor Hai Wen succeeded in achieving the authorization of China's State Council to establish such an American JD program in China. They recruited former Cornell University president and dean of the University of Michigan Law School, Jeffrey Lehman, to serve as STL's Founding Dean. In 2008, Peking University School of Transnational Law admitted its first students. STL's singular inaugural ambition, apart from providing an exceptional JD curriculum on par with the best American law schools and placing its graduates in leading American law firms, was full accreditation by the American Bar Association. What better confirmation could there be for elite prospective employers that STL graduates had succeeded in a program every bit as rigorous and demanding as the best American law schools?[3]

Accordingly, Founding Dean Lehman undertook to create a law school that conformed to ABA Standards. The JD curriculum was taught largely by visiting scholars recruited from the very best US law schools—Harvard, Stanford, NYU, Chicago, Michigan—together with US practitioners who were among the profession's most esteemed, including two former ABA presidents. The academic calendar consisted of six five-week modules specially designed to accommodate the periodic short-term visits that were the only visits feasible for these groups. The law school recruited a small resident faculty of similarly distinguished scholars and practitioners that included Americans who would be persuasive to the ABA.[4] Guest lectures by leading US jurists and government officials supplemented the regular curriculum in order to "acculturate" STL students to the actual workings of the US government and judiciary.

Despite STL's newness, recruiting top Chinese students with sufficient English proficiency was not an especially difficult challenge. Peking University, or "Bei-da," as it is known in Chinese,[5] is China's first and most renowned comprehensive research university, commonly regarded as one of the leading universities in the world. Becoming a PKU student is the aspiration of millions of young Chinese, whose English proficiency has risen steadily with mandatory English language study in elementary and secondary school and with greater access to television and the internet. Consequently, STL is fortunate in its ability to attract students with the capacity to meet the demands of an intensive JD curriculum taught in English.

The combination of leading US professors and practitioners teaching top Chinese law students worked exactly as planned. Visiting US professors

---

[3] This objective was consistent with the growing "Americanization" of legal education worldwide. Japan and South Korea recently had announced the establishment of postbaccalaureate JD degrees, as had universities in Australia, Canada, Hong Kong, Singapore, India, and the Philippines, with other nations contemplating similar moves (Lubbers 2010; Kim 2012; Silver 2014).

[4] STL's inaugural resident faculty included a former Deputy Director of the ABA's Section on Legal Education, two leading practitioners who were former clerks on the US Supreme Court, and two internationally renowned scholars.

[5] "Beida" is colloquial for Peking University, representing the combination of the first syllables of "Beijing" (Bei) and "Daxue," or university (da).

spoke compellingly of the comparability of STL to their home law schools, and leading US practitioners expressed similar enthusiasm when comparing STL students to their young American associates. Harvard Law Professor Charles Ogletree observed, "The students [at STL] are absolutely remarkable. . . . I am convinced that the young people I taught there would be exceptional American lawyers." United States District Judge Ellen Segal Huvelle reported, "I found that the students at STL demonstrated a keen appreciation for and understanding of the culture, values and ethics of the American legal system. If anything, they demonstrated far more enthusiasm for embracing our legal system than U.S. law students exhibit." Former ABA President Robert Hirschon said, "The STL students [I teach] discuss the same hypotheticals and read the same course book as students at the University of Michigan and University of Virginia. I can state . . . without reservation that the students I teach at STL have a similar level of appreciation and understanding of the culture, values and ethics of the American legal system as [the] foreign [law] students I teach in the United States" (ABA Accreditation Comments 2012). The government of Shenzhen contributed to the enthusiasm by agreeing to fund a new signature building for the law school designed by the leading architectural firm Kohn Pederson Fox (KPF) of New York.

Lehman took full advantage of the momentum and on October 15, 2010, wrote to the ABA to announce that, if the ABA were to adopt the recommendation of a Special ABA Committee barely two months earlier that the ABA extend its accreditation regime to law schools located outside of the United States, STL would seek ABA approval.[6] Support soared among the American scholars, practitioners, and jurists who taught at STL and among the US law firms and legal services companies operating in China. "I'm very confident STL will get ABA accreditation," declared the global legal strategist for Thompson West, which is responsible for the worldwide marketing of the legal database *Westlaw*. "The Chinese students specializing in American law will help maintain the growth of international trade. . . . This means more jobs, transactions and opportunities." The head of Akin Gump's Beijing office

---

[6] On June 10, 2010, the ABA Council of the Section of Legal Education and Admissions to the Bar appointed a "Special Committee on Foreign Law Schools Seeking Approval under ABA Standards," whose July 19, 2010, Report recommended, inter alia, that the Council proceed with the accreditation of law schools outside US borders that meet ABA Standards, provided "that the curriculum is primarily focused on U.S. law, the instruction is primarily in English, and the faculty are primarily J.D. graduates of ABA approved law schools." *Report of Special Committee on Foreign Law Schools Seeking Approval under ABA Standards*, July 19, 2010.

explained, "For us it is important because we depend on Chinese lawyers, most of whom have had to go to the U.S. and get a graduate law degree" (Mendoza 2009).

Unfortunately for STL, the Special Committee's recommendation coincided with an unprecedented downturn in the US markets for legal services and legal education (Wald 2010). As a result, barely a month following the recommendation that the ABA begin accrediting foreign law schools, US lawyers and law deans began writing the ABA to express their strong opposition. One practitioner wrote: "This is an absurd inquiry that I adamantly oppose. . . . The American market already is saturated with lawyers. . . . We don't need more lawyers, we need less" (Grogin letter, ABA Accreditation Comments 2012). Deans, faculty, and students of US law schools objected to the potential impact of foreign law school accreditation on US-based LLM programs, on the US legal services job market, and on the perceived value of a JD degree. To be sure, these groups also expressed concerns that transcended rank protectionism—for example, about foreign law schools being unable to "acculturate" students to "American values" and about the potential dilution of ABA accreditation resources—but protectionism seemed at the core of opposition that was growing almost as rapidly as the US markets for legal services and legal education at the time were shrinking (ABA Accreditation Comments 2012).

The overwhelming perception in the United States seemed to be that STL's mission was (1) to flood the American market for legal services with US bar-eligible Chinese lawyers while (2) depriving American law schools of foreign applicants by educating them *in* China at far less cost than they would have paid to attend law school in the United States. Lost in all the protectionist noise was the more realistic probability that STL would *expand* the worldwide market for American legal services by promoting the adoption of American conventions of law practice abroad.

Almost two years to the day following the Special Committee's recommendation, the Council of the ABA Section of Legal Education and Admissions to the Bar voted 15 to 0, with two abstentions, *not* to proceed with the accreditation of foreign law schools. Professor John Flood of the University of Westminster (London) expressed the prevailing view: "[The] decision was driven by . . . practitioners in the U.S. who are intimidated by foreigners taking American jobs against a backdrop of a shrinking legal market" (Favate 2012).

Most observers, including many within Peking University, viewed the Council's decision as the death knell for the School of Transnational Law.

Founding Dean Lehman did not: "Freed from any need to worry about the American Bar Association," he declared, "STL [would] now be able to focus in a more single-minded manner on the ultimate question: what kinds of education will best prepare professionals to serve a world in which the processes of globalization—economic, social and political—are likely to continue accelerating in the decades to come?" (Lehman 2014).

II. STL's Pivot to China

STL began as a JD-only law school; it initially did not offer a China law Juris Master curriculum. Moreover, although STL commenced a China law Juris Master program shortly following its establishment, this was due to a regulatory complication that jeopardized the award of a JD degree without an accompanying JM, not to an affirmative desire to offer a JM curriculum. STL's start-up priority remained a superior JD program. The JM curriculum was of secondary importance, scheduled largely in hours-long classes over weekends taught by visiting professors, with only one Chinese professor in residence during STL's first few years.

This is no longer the case. In the immediate aftermath of the ABA's decision, STL identified as a strategic priority enriching our China law curriculum with resident professors and with the goal of professional skills acquisition comparable to STL's JD program.[7] The objective is for STL students to acquire with respect to China law practice the same skills STL's JD program seeks to instill: rigorous analytical thinking, the ability to see all sides of an issue, the ability to solve complex problems creatively, and the ability to persuade, both orally and in writing.

Legal education at other Chinese law schools, however, does not yet provide a model to which STL might aspire in this regard. Legal education in China still is largely theoretical and provided via one-way lecturing to large numbers of students, often hundreds at a time. The study of law is not based on the case method, classes are not interactive, the acquisition of professional skills is not a priority, and the overall academic rigor of most law programs

---

[7] Founding Dean Lehman left STL to become Founding Vice Chancellor of NYU Shanghai shortly following the ABA's 2012 decision. Philip McConnaughay became dean in 2013. McConnaughay had been dean of Penn State Law, Founding Dean of Penn State's School of International Affairs, a professor of law at the University of Illinois, Urbana-Champaign, and a partner of Morrison & Foerster, resident in Hong Kong and Tokyo. McConnaughay led STL's pivot to China and the rest of the non-West.

is not high (Weidong 2004). In a very real way, the reform of STL's China law curriculum is creating a new model of JM legal education for China.

To be sure, there are intrinsic obstacles to achieving learning outcomes in China law JM curriculums that are similar to the intended outcomes of American law JD curriculums. Most Chinese codes are of Germanic origin, and the different objectives of German and common law legal education are well known. "[T]he basic approach of modern German legal science [is] seeking to arrange all legal material of a given branch of law in the form of a logically consistent system which is organized around a few key . . . general principles of law, from which all concrete legal norms can be logically deduced" (Grote 2005: 167). "In Germany, the statute—*des Gesetz*—is *the* fundamental concept of all law" (Maxeiner 2007: 556). Legal problem-solving in a private law context proceeds according to a highly prescribed, logical, step-by-step methodology (Wolff 2004: 22–23), rarely influenced by political, economic, and social considerations (Grote 2005: 177–178).

"Lawyers [educated] in a common law tradition," in contrast, "[are] much more skeptical of the idea of law as an internally consistent system of rules" (Grote 2005: 164). "United States [statutory] legislation is rarely [as] comprehensive or systematic [as in civil law countries]. Nor is the theory of statutory interpretation [as] refined [or as prescriptive]" (Grote 2005: 180). Political, economic, and social considerations, moreover, often are central to arguments seeking to influence the judicial interpretation of law.

Consequently, simply transplanting to a China law JM curriculum the methods of instruction that have been so successful in American law JD curriculums—the case study method; smaller, interactive class sessions with Socratic questioning of students; and an increased emphasis on experiential learning—is not necessarily useful in the study of civil law codes.

Nonetheless, even though most Chinese codes are of Germanic origin, much Chinese legislation, in fact, lies somewhere in between German "legal certainty" and American "legal indeterminacy" (Maxeiner 2007: 541–542). Chinese legislation reflects "the influence of [multiple] different legal traditions and cannot simply be regarded as belonging to any of the 'traditional' legal families; [China is a] 'mixed jurisdiction'" (Li, Li and Hu 2017; Wolff 2004: 38). Moreover, "mainland Chinese statutory law is not always as clear as one would wish and [some] areas of law are not yet codified at all" (Wolff 2004: 47).

As a result, Germany's precise "step-by-step" methodology for solving private law problems is not alone sufficient for China legal education and law practice. China's statutes, jurisprudence, and legal scholarship are far less developed than Germany's; interpretation and argument are critical to the development of Chinese law (Ge Yunsong, September 9, 2015, email message to authors). At the same time, because China *is* a comprehensive code-based system and not a common law system of judge-made law in combination with statutes, a methodology for the proper application of statutes clearly is critical for China legal education and law practice.

STL China law professors attempt to achieve both of these pedagogical objectives by *combining* (1) a German-style case study method that insists upon a rigorous step-by-step methodology of statutory application with (2) intense interpersonal classroom exchange and Socratic questioning designed to expose ambiguities and omissions in statutory language, elicit alternative interpretations, and identify possible economic, social, and policy bases of various interpretations. Case study represents a significant advance in Chinese legal education, made possible only with the recent advent of published judicial judgments (Xinhua News 2013). As one STL professor explains, "The case method necessitates the transition of classroom teaching from traditional knowledge-based lecturing to more interactive teaching. Interactive teaching sometimes seems less efficient, but it can be more effective in terms of helping students understand the complexity and subtlety of legal issues and legal thinking. [In this way], case study urges the students to focus on developing fundamental skills of critical reading and writing and professional skills of analyzing facts and interpreting rules" (STL Professor Mao Shaowei, September 9, 2015, email to authors).

Of course, interactive classes based on the case method function well only up to a certain size, and they consequently tend to be appreciably more expensive for a university to provide than classes of one-way lectures to hundreds of students. But the return for students is high. Students appreciate the difference early on (STL student essays on file with authors):

> *The study of . . . law is something new and unfamiliar to me, unlike any schooling I've ever been through before. The professors use the Socratic method here; they call on you, ask you a question, and you answer it. At first, I thought it was inefficient—why didn't they just give a lecture? But I soon learned that it was not just a matter of efficiency, but a way to educate yourself. Through professors' questions, you learn to teach yourself. And through this method of questioning, answering, questioning, answering, they seek to develop in you the ability to analyze. . . . [STL] professors train the mind.*

The most attractive part of STL for me is [the] teaching method, which is concentrated on motivated thinking instead of forced feeding. . . . Professors will not say yes or no to any answer; they ask students to think in wider and deeper ways.

[T]he Socratic Method . . . left me with the deepest impression. I got a better understanding of the differences between STL and traditional Chinese law schools—initiative [and] critical thinking are greatly emphasized at STL. Although it is true that the four years of learning at STL will be challenging and demanding, [I have learned] that studying law can be interesting and thrilling.

The reform of STL's China law curriculum represents a major step toward the realization of a *Chinese* legal profession on par with those of the most advanced Western countries. STL's dual degree program provides the additional platform for an entirely new level of legal services with respect to transnational matters.

III. The Influence of Shenzhen and the Rest of the Non-West

The next stage in the evolution of STL's program of legal education is focusing on the possibility of blending elements of our common law and China law curriculums in light of parallel developments both regionally and internationally. For this we are drawing guidance from developments in the ongoing economic integration of Shenzhen and Hong Kong, including specifically China's experimentation with blended and new legal mechanisms and institutions in joint Shenzhen–Hong Kong projects such as the Qianhai services industry area and the Lok Ma Chau Loop Technology Park. Both are likely to preview eventual legal developments throughout China and influence transnational legal developments throughout the world.

The Shenzhen half of the Shenzhen–Hong Kong equation, of course, is at once both an economic miracle and mystery. Conventional economic theory holds that economic growth depends on the effective enforcement of agreements and judicial protection of clear property rights (North 1991: 477; Qiao and Upham 2017: 4). Shenzhen has neither, at least in the sense of a fully developed body of commercial and property law, mature regulatory institutions, a reliable and professional judiciary, or an established legal profession. Each of these remains nascent, barely existing as of the early 1990s.[8]

Yet Shenzhen's phenomenal economic growth and expansion has occurred and continues to forge ahead despite this "deficiency." Shenzhen's 2018 GDP growth, for example, was 8.8 percent, outpacing Hong Kong and Singapore and leading all other Mainland Chinese cities (Hua 2019). Shenzhen also continues to invest in R&D at a rate that exceeds that of most other cities and nations: in excess of 4 percent of GDP annually (He and Gan SCMP 2016). The World Intellectual Property Organization's (WIPO's) Global Innovation Index (GII) announced in June 2017 that Shenzhen–Hong Kong had surpassed California's Silicon Valley (Shenzhen Daily 2017). The Economist has declared Shenzhen "one of the world's most innovative cities," noting that Shenzhen alone accounts for more high-quality international patents than either Great Britain or France, and that Shenzhen alone is responsible for nearly 50 percent of the international patents filed from China annually (The Economist 2017).

The only significant caveat sounded by observers of Shenzhen's phenomenal growth and government officials alike is the need to develop the legal framework essential to sustain the economic miracle.[9]

Hong Kong's economic history is strikingly similar to Shenzhen's in fundamental respects, but also strikingly different. Like Shenzhen, Hong Kong transformed from a small fishing village at the edge of the South China Sea into a world-leading center of finance and increasingly fintech. Unlike Shenzhen, Hong Kong's economic ascendancy was accompanied by the transplantation and contemporaneous development of a mature British legal system commonly regarded as the principal explanation of Hong Kong's economic success.

---

[8] It was only in the 1990s that the PRC Lawyers Law began requiring a university degree to qualify for the National Judicial (i.e., Bar) Exam, and the Judges Law and Public Procurators Law did the same for judges and prosecutors. Even then, legal training/education was not required, nor is it yet. Although the last decade has seen tremendous strides forward in the professionalization of all three groups, each also still has a high representation of individuals not qualified by training or experience for membership. See, e.g., "Susan Finder Deconstructs the Chinese Court System," July 3, 2017, The New Lens International Edition, Reuters, https://international.thenewslens.com/article/72415 (regarding the ongoing professionalization of the Chinese judiciary).

[9] Former Shenzhen Mayor and Party Secretary Xu Qin observed, "The earlier the city improves its legal environment, the more likely it is we will secure a sustained competitive advantage." See http://www.wantinews.com/news-6242221. This observation is not new. The mutual dependence of economic modernization and legal modernization was a cornerstone of Deng Xiaoping's vision for Shenzhen when the city was designated China's first Special Economic Zone (Delmas-Marty 2003).

Whereas Hong Kong's rule of law tradition, body of commercial laws, courts, regulatory institutions, and legal profession are among the most fully developed, sophisticated, and reliable in the world, Shenzhen's and the rest of the Pearl River Delta's, although making strides toward professionalization, reliability and independence, are among the least developed.

China's openness to experimenting with laws and legal institutions in Shenzhen suggests that the region's eventual legal infrastructure likely will blend Chinese and Western characteristics. This is perhaps best illustrated by developments already underway in Qianhai, the multi-trillion dollar joint "Shenzhen-Hong Kong Modern Service Industry Cooperation Zone" touted as China's answer to Wall Street (Qianhai, http://www.szqh.com.cn). For example, Qianhai's "Benchmark Chambers International," which is supported by Shenzhen's Justice Bureau, is charged with identifying foreign laws that might be instructive for the future legal framework of Qianhai and the Pearl River Delta (http://www.bcisz.org/eng/). The new Shenzhen-based First Circuit of the Supreme People's Court is exploring the implications of using Hong Kong commercial law as applicable law for contracts made in Qianhai. The Shenzhen Intermediate People's Court for Qianhai includes Hong Kong citizens on the panels of judges ("juries") hearing Hong Kong–related cases (Liu and Li 2018). Shenzhen's South China International Economic Trade and Arbitration Commission has split from CIETAC, in part, to ensure its flexibility and responsiveness to the unique legal environment and multinational disputes characteristic of Qianhai and the rest of the Pearl River Delta. Guangdong Province has received special dispensation from the national government to permit Mainland and Hong Kong law firms and lawyers to form partnerships that are not permitted elsewhere in China (Guangdong Pilot Scheme), and the Hong Kong Law Society has published a study pertaining to the role of Hong Kong solicitors in the development of the legal profession in Qianhai (Law Society Working Paper).

Examples of how China and Western legal and commercial traditions might blend are suggested by recent field research regarding contract practices, real property transactions, and dispute resolution in major China markets, especially Shenzhen and the Pearl River Delta. Without delving deeply into any of these studies, it seems clear that, even though Chinese commercial practices governed traditionally by relational considerations, or *guanxi*, have moved on a massive scale to more formal mechanisms of exchange, including impersonal written contracts, relational considerations continue to play an important role in the articulation, performance, and governance of the contracts and transactions. Chen, Deakin, Siems, and Wang (2017: 20 and 25–27) found this in their report of the attitudes of market participants in their examination of the relationship between contract, corporate, and financial law and recent economic growth in China; Qiao and Upham (2017: 35–37) report similar findings in their examination of China's and Shenzhen's markets for real property transactions; and Ali (2010) reports an ongoing gulf between Asian party commercial dispute resolution preferences and those of parties from Western legal traditions.

These findings expose the complex cross-cultural and cross-legal system challenges that lawyers and law students confront in determining how to successfully bridge commercial traditions in which law and specific contract terms are determinative of performance and outcomes in one (i.e., "legal predictability"), but subordinate to relational values and practices in the other. To illustrate, even though China and Western commercial practices seemingly are converging around the use of written contracts, it may be that *reducing* the highly detailed and prescriptive nature of contracts as practiced in the West (i.e., reducing "legal predictability") is necessary for *enhanced commercial stability* in transactions involving parties from Chinese or other relational traditions. Contract terms in these transactions might incorporate relational principles as affirmative duties that substitute for specific terms; perhaps, as an example, imposing a duty to adjust in good faith to evolving or unforeseen circumstances instead of substituting prescribed outcomes for circumstances or situations yet to occur. Contractual choice of law clauses might specify principles of equity as applicable law instead of or in addition to identifying a precise body of law. Successful dispute resolution clauses might require more flexible procedures or more elastic notions of impartiality so that mediation and arbitration may be blended more easily with the same decision maker. And so forth (McConnaughay 2001: n.82 at 447).

China's infrastructure investment in and emphasis on exchange within a new "Belt and Road" market—for which Shenzhen and Qianhai have been designated points of strategic support[10]—add a further level of complexity to possible new legal mechanisms of international exchange. The Belt and Road Initiative has two principal components: an overland Silk Road Economic "Belt" and sea-based Maritime Silk "Road." The land-based portion includes five principal economic corridors: (1) China-Mongolia-Russia;

---

[10] "Qianhai-Shekou New Plan Charted," July 17, 2017, *Shenzhen Daily*. Shenzhen alone aims for over US$165 billion in trade with Belt and Road countries by 2020. "China's Economic Powerhouse Shenzhen Banks on R&D to Bring It to New Heights," January 31, 2016, *South China Morning Post*.

(2) China-Indochina; (3) China-Myanmar-Bangladesh-India; (4) China-Pakistan; and (5) China–Central Asia–West Asia. The maritime route extends from China through Southeast Asia, coastal South Asia, the Arabian Peninsula, East Africa, and into the Mediterranean. Significantly, Belt and Road countries, overwhelmingly, have non-Western or mixed legal traditions, often civil or common law codes adopted during periods of colonization or modernization, but also strong—and extant—religious (e.g., Islamic), Soviet/communist, and customary law traditions.[11]

China is undertaking legal infrastructure development efforts in relation to the Belt and Road Initiative that are intended to help ensure a transnational legal infrastructure capable of supporting sustainable economic exchange. The China International Commercial Court (CICC), for example, was established, in part, to help address growing demand for dispute resolution services involving Belt and Road Initiative transactions (Finder 2018); the International Chamber of Commerce Belt and Road Arbitration Commission was established for similar reasons (Bermingham 2018). Qianhai's Benchmark Chambers International (BCI), the same agency charged with identifying foreign laws that might be instructive for the future legal framework of Qianhai and the Pearl River Delta, also has been charged with researching the different legal systems and practices in Belt and Road countries with respect to foreign trade, investment, engineering contracts, intellectual property, labor exporting, taxes, and foreign exchange controls and customs. BCI's executive director, Xiao Jingyi, explained, "The project will be the first Chinese-language legal repository to focus on [legal] information from the Belt and Road countries. It is another major exploration for [China's] rule of law innovation" (Shenzhen Daily 2017).[12]

The deepening relationships between China and Belt and Road countries portend significant non-Western influence on the development of

---

[11] The normative "gap" in non-Western nations between Western-style commercial codes and legal institutions, on the one hand, and actual legal and commercial practices, on the other, is well documented. See McConnaughay 2001: 427, n.113 and 455–456; Potter 1995: 2; and Shaw 1980: 318 ("work is just now beginning on the study of how traditional Asian legal systems met and often persisted under the 'Westernizing' reforms demanded by the treaty powers"). See https://www.cia.gov/library/publications/the-world-factbook/fields/2100.html for a US-generated list of national legal systems.

[12] The Hon. Rimsky Yuen, Hong Kong Secretary of Justice, Hong Kong Law Society, has noted the efforts of the Law Society to contribute to the development of a transnational legal infrastructure for Belt and Road exchange (May 12, 2017): "The joint efforts of providing robust legal services to the B&R economies will contribute to the building of a transnational legal order, which will in turn promote the rule of law at the international level, and thus ultimately contribute to human advancement."

commercial and legal practices and principles, both within the region and globally. The same is true of China's global economic ascension and several parallel developments, such as the growth of legal professions in countries with non-Western or mixed legal traditions and growing worldwide commercial exchange among non-Western diasporas. Collectively, these developments suggest an inevitable upending of prevailing assumptions of a global convergence of law around the Western legal tradition in favor of far greater legal diversity or a convergence of an entirely different nature.[13]

At STL, we are addressing the legal education implications of these developments in several ways. First, we are endeavoring to add depth to our curriculum with respect to the legal systems of major Belt and Road countries, and with respect to transactions and commercial dispute resolution involving non-Western parties. One course focuses on commercial dispute resolution and arbitration involving Chinese-African transactions. Another surveys Islamic law and traditions. Another by a visiting Kazakh scholar surveyed the legal systems of members of the Commonwealth of Independent States, or CIS (Armenia, Belarus, Kazakhstan, Moldova, Russia, Tajikistan, Turkmenistan, Ukraine, and Uzbekistan). Another explores Supreme People's Court initiatives with respect to Chinese judicial reform and the establishment of courts and rules of choice of law with expertise pertaining to Belt and Road and other international transactions. And so forth.

Second, we are recruiting scholars to our resident faculty whose research focus is new and emerging mechanisms of transnational governance, such as the multinational networks of public, private, national, and international actors that are producing transnational norms and regulatory structures

---

[13] As Martin Jacques predicts in his epic study, *When China Rules the World*, 560 (2012), "With the rise of China, Western universalism will cease to be universal—and its values and outlook will become steadily less influential. [T]he West will be obliged to learn from and incorporate some of [China's] insights and features. . . . [A global] Western-style rule of law . . . is by no means proven." Former Australian Prime Minister Kevin Rudd made a similar point in his March 5, 2018, Commencement Address at West Point: "China will soon replace the United States as the world's largest economy. China will begin to challenge US regional but not global military dominance. China is also creating its own new multilateral institutions outside the UN framework, such as the AIIB. China also continues to expand its strategic and economic reach across Europe and Asia. And Xi Jinping has made plain he does not see China's role as simply replicating the current US-led liberal international order for the future. . . . China leaves open what future changes it may make to the international rules-based system in the future. The desirability of having a form of rules-based system, rather than simple chaos, lies deep within Chinese political consciousness. . . . But it is important to remember that 'order', the alternative to 'chaos', will not necessarily be an American order." http://kevinrudd.com/blog/2018/03/05/kevin-rudd-speaks-to-the-us-military-academy-west-point-understanding-chinas-rise-under-ji-xinping/.

independently of national government action with respect to such matters of transnational concern as climate change, technology transfer, food safety, energy, and natural resource protection.

Finally, we are encouraging faculty to include within existing courses perspectives of particular importance to Belt and Road exchange. Major regional and international law firms have been doing the same (Cremer 2016).

IV. Some Advantages and Challenges of Being Part of a Chinese University

Establishing STL was a bold move by China and Peking University, with great potential for Chinese legal education and the development of a sophisticated Chinese legal profession. STL is fundamentally different from any other law school in China: an American/Common Law JD curriculum, an innovative approach to China law education, and a demanding professional orientation at a postbaccalaureate level. These characteristics clearly are a significant step beyond China's undergraduate approach to the study of law as a social science and its fledgling graduate professional Juris Masters programs (to be distinguished from the excellent academic-track LLM and PhD programs in law at a few leading Chinese universities).

In many ways, the experiment of STL has paid off: demand for admission is extremely high among China's top university graduates, having grown exponentially with increasing awareness of STL, and the professional placement of STL graduates has been exceptional. Nearly 100 percent of each of STL's six graduating classes have secured positions by graduation with leading Chinese and multinational law firms (Jun He, Fangda Partners, King & Wood Mallesons, Skadden Arps, Wilmer Hale, Kirkland & Ellis, Morrison Foerster, Paul Weiss, Herbert Smith, Freshfields, etc.), leading Chinese and multinational companies and financial institutions (Huawei, General Electric, Tencent, Ping An, Baidu, etc.), leading state-owned enterprises and government offices (Sinopec Corporation, China Development Bank, Citic Securities, China Railways International, Foreign Ministry, CIETAC, multiple Provincial Governments and Procuratorates, etc.), and leading international organizations, NGOs, and public interest groups (UNHCR, Asia Development Bank, etc.). STL graduates who aspire to an academic career have been admitted to Yale, Harvard, Stanford, Chicago, Sciences Po, the College of Europe, and other elite universities for PhDs.

Interest in STL's unique approach to China law education is high among other China law schools, and parallel developments, whether emulation or not, are increasingly frequent. International interest in STL also is high. The European Law Faculties Association requested a presentation about STL at their 2015 annual meeting, as did the prestigious 2016 St. Petersburg, Russia, International Legal Forum. STL also has a steady stream of visitors from US law schools, the US judiciary, and US- and UK-based law firms.

But there are challenges, too. STL's potential contributions to China are constrained by unrealized aspects of the experiment. The principal short-coming is a lack of administrative adjustment necessary to accommodate such a fundamentally different approach to legal education; it is as if the university decided to undertake the bold experiment of STL without considering the necessity of changing preexisting rules designed to ensure conformance to the old model.

For example, the study of law in China traditionally has been regarded as a social science, subject to the same academic rules and thesis requirements as arts and sciences disciplines that result in graduate research degrees. This results in governing academic rules that are different from and sometimes in conflict with those with which a professional degree law program must comply, just as it would in the United States if universities insisted that their law schools conform to graduate school rules instead of to ABA standards and professional licensing requirements.

Occasionally, this difference can cut to the heart of the faculty and decanal responsibilities and prerogatives essential to the integrity and design of a professional degree curriculum, especially one intended to conform to American and other international professional licensing standards. Usually, we have been able to work out a solution when the tension threatens core law school values, but both the university and China's Ministry of Education clearly will have to consider moving toward greater discipline-specific discretion and standards if they wish to pursue professional degree programs on par with those of the United States and other Western nations.

Another example of STL's somewhat ill fit with preexisting policies has to do with strict central government control over graduate school admissions: the Ministry of Education controls by quotas allocated to all Chinese universities the total number of Mainland Chinese students they may admit into particular degree categories—Bachelor's, Master's, and PhD. Traditionally, the better the university, the lower the quota, thereby ensuring highly selective admissions among the best universities and spreading top students among universities the Ministry has targeted for elite status. Each university then has discretion in how it allocates its quotas among its various disciplines and programs. Centrally determined subquotas also may apply, as in Master's programs when the Ministry dictates that no more than 50 percent of the overall quota may be applicants who have earned "exemptions" from the National Graduate School Entrance Exam;[14] the remainder must gain admission by meeting or exceeding the particular university's or program's "cut score" on the National Exam.

Some discretion in admissions criteria remains insofar as more students typically earn eligibility for admission to a particular program than the program's quota will permit, thus requiring the program to establish criteria for selecting among the qualified applicants, but the quota allocations themselves tend to be inflexible.

It is difficult to quarrel with an admissions practice grounded in merit and administered by the Ministry of Education, along with other policies, in ways that have succeeded in the rapid elevation of the quality and stature of so many Chinese universities.[15] Yet, the centralized admissions process and quota system do disadvantage STL (and sometimes other China graduate school programs) in two significant ways.

First, talented PRC students educated at leading universities abroad lose out on the opportunity to gain admission to elite Chinese graduate schools by earning an "exemption" from the National Graduate School Admissions Exam, which can be awarded only by domestic universities. They consequently must take the exam if they wish to apply for admission; yet, they feel underprepared for the exam due to their years and education abroad (e.g., one of the core topics tested on the exam is Chinese political theory). This deters many highly qualified PRC students from seeking graduate school admission in China. This is especially disappointing to STL given the level of English proficiency STL's JD curriculum requires and the growing interest

---

[14] Undergraduates who place among the top few graduates of leading universities may earn "exemptions" from the National Graduate School Entrance Exam and gain admission solely on the basis of their "exempt" status.

[15] See, e.g., https://www.timeshighereducation.com/world-university-rankings/china-a-rapidly-evolving-university-system, and https://www.weforum.org/agenda/2017/06/universities-best-reputation-china-times-higher-2017/. See also January 24, 2017, Notice of Ministry of Education, Ministry of Finance and National Development and Reform Commission on Issuing (Interim) Methods of Facilitating the Development of World-class Universities and World-class Disciplines. Some do complain, however, that the National Graduate School Admissions Exam is not always administered fairly, with geographic and other differences reflecting attempts at favoritism or cheating. See, e.g., http://www.aacrao.org/resources/resources-detail-view/national-graduate-school-entrance-examination-in-china--lower-numbers--fraud-operation-in-harbin.

in STL among academically gifted, English-proficient PRC students who studied at top universities outside of China.

Second, in combination with STL's comparatively low tuition (also subject to government control), the quota system affects STL's economic viability insofar as our student population is both much lower than demand among highly qualified applicants and much lower than necessary to meet the cost of a program that is dependent on a sizeable contingent of expatriate professors and administrators earning salaries competitive with those of top public US law schools.[16]

There are additional challenges resulting from China's central regulation of higher education, which tends toward "one size fits all" and in which universities only recently have been granted partial autonomy over their practices and policies (Yi and Yang 2014) with individual disciplines enjoying even less autonomy but still hoping for some. Hopefully, this situation reflects simply a developmental challenge likely to improve with time and experience.

We also contend with textbook import delays and restrictions (including occasional book censorship and bans) and China's infamous "Great Firewall" of internet regulation, but we have been reasonably successful without official interference in developing "workarounds" that meet our educational program and faculty research needs. Nonetheless, these sorts of governmental controls over content clearly present troubling issues for higher education in China and obstacles to conforming to basic international standards regarding access to information essential for research and scholarship.[17]

Finally, although STL has not encountered any overt interference with the content of our program of legal education or classroom discussions, which include deep explorations of all topics typical of top US law schools (including US constitutional rights and liberties and international human rights, often with identical visiting faculty), recent developments elsewhere within the university are not equally respectful of Peking University's tradition of academic freedom.[18]

---

[16] Highly restrictive staffing quotas that are applied uniformly across disciplines also impede appropriate investment in discipline-specific objectives, such as development (i.e., fund-raising) staff for units, such as law, for which industry- or government-funded research is not prevalent.

[17] See, e.g., "How Can Scholars Tackle the Rise of Chinese Censorship in the West?," January 5, 2018, *Times of Higher Education*; "Chinese Power May Lead to Global Academic Censorship Crisis," December 7, 2017, *Times of Higher Education*; "Sage Is Latest Publisher to Warn of Chinese Censorship Pressure," November 23, 2017, *The Financial Times*; "Outcry as Latest Global Publisher Bows to Chinese Censorship Pressure," November 8, 2017, *The Financial Times*.

[18] See, e.g., "Backlash Sparked Over Pressure to Stop China Student #MeToo," April 25, 2018, *The Washington Post* (https://www.washingtonpost.com/world/asia_pacific/outrage-in-china-over-pressure-on-student-to-stop-activism/2018/04/25/a6523ba0-4853-11e8-8082-105a446d19b8_st

V. Conclusion

Peking University School of Transnational Law began as an American law school in China, a transplant reflective of the growing worldwide appetite for American legal education and perhaps as well of an assumption that law everywhere eventually will converge around the Western legal tradition. When STL's ambition of ABA approval evaporated with the ABA's decision not to extend its accreditation jurisdiction beyond the United States, STL was forced to take a fresh look at its purpose and mission. We did not need to look far. The mixing of legal traditions underway in China's Pearl River Delta challenges more sharply than ever before both of the assumptions upon which STL was founded, as does China's growing global influence and the promise of China's Belt and Road Initiative. These developments compel a rethinking of legal education, whether American, Chinese, or other. This is the task to which STL turned. We preserved STL's American law JD curriculum but dramatically elevated the importance of STL's China law curriculum and introduced new methods of instruction likely to influence the teaching and exploration of China law and legal traditions everywhere. Additionally, we increasingly blend these two curriculums in ways reflective of the blending of Western and non-Western legal traditions under way in China and throughout the non-West. STL is attempting to prepare its graduates for the day, as Harold Berman predicted, "in which a multicultural East and West and North and South [begin] to forge a new tradition of world law." This is why, when we are asked where STL is located, it is tempting to reply, "in the future."

References

ABA Accreditation Comments (2012). https://www.lawcrossing.com/employers/arti cle/8037/ABA-Accreditation-of-Foreign-Law-Schools/ and http://apps.americanbar. org/legaled/accreditation/Comments%20on%20Accreditation%20of%20Foreign%20 Schools.html.

Ali, Shahla F. (2010). *Resolving Disputes in the Asia-Pacific Region: International Arbitration and Mediation in East Asia and the West*. Routledge.

ory.html?noredirect=on&utm_term=.85cc88467c3f); "Public Outcry After China Campus #MeToo Activist Pressured into Silence," April 24, 2018, *Reuters World News*; "#MeToo Meets China's Censors and Students Learn a Tough Lesson," April 23, 2018, *The Wall Street Journal*; and "Peking University Student to School: Stop Trying to Gag Me on Rape Case!," April 23, 2018, *supchina SINICA* (https:// supchina.com/2018/04/23/beida-student-to-school-stop-trying-to-gag-me-on-rape-case/).

Au-Yeung, Allen and Cedric Sam (2015). "Three Cities, One Bridge," *South China Morning Post.* November 19.

Berman, Harold (2000). "The Western Legal Tradition in Millennial Perspective: Past and Future," *Louisiana Law Review* 60: 739, 763.

Bermingham, Finbarr (2018). "ICC Launches Belt and Road Arbitration Commission," *Global Trade Review.* March 8. https://www.gtreview.com/news/asia/icc-launches-belt-and-road-arbitration-commission/.

Brinza, Andreea (2017). "Is China's Belt and Road Ready to Be the New Face of Globalisation?," *South China Morning Post.* May 15.

Chen, Ding, Simon Deakin, Mathias M. Siems, and Boya Wang (2017). *Law, Trust and Institutional Change in China: Evidence from Qualitative Fieldwork*, University of Cambridge Legal Studies Research Paper Series, Journal of Corporate Legal Studies 15(10): 20 and 25–27 (February).

Cremer, John (2016). "Law Firms Gear Up to Serve Clients Tackling Issues Surrounding Belt and Road Initiative," *South China Morning Post.* November 1.

Delmas-Marty, Mareille (2003). "Present Day China and the Rule of Law," *Chinese Journal of International Law 2: 11.* Oxford University Press. http://chinesejil.oxfordjournals.org/content/2/1/11.full.pdf.

The Economist (2017). "Welcome to Silicon Delta: Shenzhen Is a Hothouse of Innovation." April 12.

Favate, Sam (2012). "ABA Council Votes Against Accrediting Foreign Law Schools," *The Wall Street Journal Law Blog.* August 7. http://blogs.wsj.com/law/2012/08/07/aba-council-votes-against-accrediting-foreign-law-schools/.

Finder, Susan (2017). "Susan Finder Deconstructs the Chinese Court System," *The New Lens International Edition, Reuters.* July 3. https://international.thenewslens.com/article/72415.

Finder, Susan (2018). "Update on China's International Commercial Court," *Supreme People's Court Monitor.* March 11. https://supremepeoplescourtmonitor.com/2018/03/11/update-on-chinas-international-commercial-court/.

Grote, Rainer (2005). "Comparative Law and Teaching Law Through the Case Method in the Civil Law Tradition—A German Perspective," *University of Detroit Mercy Law Review* 82: 163, 167.

Guangdong Pilot Scheme (2014). Guangdong Provincial Department of Justice Pilot Scheme on Affiliation Between Hong Kong Law Firm and Mainland Law Firm which Organize as Joint Venture Partnership, Guangdong Provisional Government.

The Guardian (2017). "The Great Leap Forward: China's Pearl River Delta." January 25.

He Huifeng and Nectar Gan (2016). "China's Economic Powerhouse Shenzhen Banks on R&D to Bring It to Greater Heights," *South China Morning Post.* January 31.

Hua, Chai (2019). "Shenzhen Surpasses HK in GDP," *China Daily.* February 28. https://www.chinadaily.com.cn/a/201902/28/WS5c7720fda3106c65c34ebd70.html.

Jacques, Martin (2012). *When China Rules the World.* Penguin Books.

Khan, Natasha and Edna Curran (2017). "Hong Kong Cozies Up to Shenzhen to Create Future," *Bloomberg News.* June 11. https://www.bloomberg.com/news/articles/2017-06-11/hong-kong-cozies-up-to-shenzhen.

Kim, Rosa (2012). The "Americanization" of Legal Education in South Korea: Challenges and Opportunities. http://ssrn.com/abstract=2012667.

Lau, Chris (2015). "Circuit Court, Jury Break New Ground," *South China Morning Post.* January 29.

Law Society Working Paper (2012). *The Development of the Legal Profession in Qianhai*. The Law Society of Hong Kong. Working Paper on Qianhai Project. http://www.legco. gov.hk/yr12-13/english/panels/ajls/papers/aj0326cb4-540-1-e.pdf.

Lehman, Jeffrey S. (2012). "The Peking University School of Transnational Law: What? Where? Why?," Address to The Council of International Affairs of the New York City Bar Association, 3. January 31. (on file with authors).

Lehman, Jeffrey S. (2014). "Transnational Legal Education in the 21st Century: Two Steps Forward, One Step Back," *The Senobu Foundation Distinguished Lecture*, Tokyo. March 16. (on file with authors).

Li Xueyao, Li Yiran, and Hu Jiaxiang (2017). "Globalisation and Innovative Study: Legal Education in China," in Andrew Harding, Jiaxiang Hu, and Maartje De Visser, eds., *From Imitation to Innovation: Legal Education in Asia*. Pp. 251–275. Brill Nijhoff

Liu, Z. and J. Li (2018). "The Rule of Law Experiment in China's Pilot Free Trade Zones: The Problems and Prospects of Introducing Hong Kong Law into Guangdong," *Hague Journal on the Rule Law* 10: 341–364.

Lubbers, Jeffrey S. (2010). Japan's Legal Education Reforms from an American Law Professor's Perspective, 15–18. http://ssrn.com/abstract=1552094.

Maxeiner, James R. (2007). "Legal Uncertainty: A European Alternative to American Legal Indeterminacy?," *Tulane Journal of International & Comparative Law* 5: 541, 556.

McConnaughay, Philip J. (2001). "Rethinking the Role of Law and Contracts in East-West Commercial Relationships," Virgina Journal of International Law 1: 427, n.82 at 447.

McConnaughay, Philip and Colleen Toomey (2017). "Preparing for the Sinicization of the Western Legal Tradition: The Case of Peking University School of Transnational Law," in Andrew Harding, Jiaxiang Hu, and Maartje De Visser, eds., *From Imitation to Innovation: Legal Education in Asia*. Pp. 223–250. Brill Nijhoff.

Mendoza, Jaime (2009). "China Legal," *U.S.-China Today*, University of Southern California, July 31, quoting Chang Wang.

North, Douglass (1991). "*Institutions, Ideology and Economic Performance*," *Cato Journal* 11: 477–487, at 477.

Qianhai. http://www.szqh.com.cn.

Qiao, Shitong and Frank K. Upham (2017). "China's Changing Property Law Landscape," in Michele Graziadei and Lionel Smith, eds., *Comparative Property Law*. Pp. 311–332. Elgar.

Potter, Pitman B. (1995). *Foreign Business Law in China*. P. 2. The 1990 Institute.

Satellite Images (2017). "China's Fastest Growing Cities," *The Guardian*. March 21. https://www.theguardian.com/cities/2017/mar/21/timelapse-satellite-images-china-fastest-growing-cities.

Shaw, William (1980). "Traditional Korean Law and its Relation to China," in Jerome Alan Cohen, ed., *Essays on China's Legal Tradition*. Pp. 302, 318. Princeton University Press.

Shenzhen Daily (2014). "Center Set-Up in City to Help Identify Foreign Laws." May 22.

Shenzhen Daily (2017). "Polices from Belt and Road Countries to Be Compiled," (quoting Xiao Jingyi). March 22.

Shenzhen Daily (2017). "SZ-HK Overtakes Silicon Valley." June 23.

Silver, Carole (2014). "Globalization and the Monopoly of ABA-Approved Law Schools: Missed Opportunities or Dodged Bullets," *Fordham Law Review* 82: 2869, 2871, and 2878–2879.

Wald, Eli (2010). "Foreword: The Great Recession and the Legal Profession, in the Economic Downturn and the Legal Profession," *Fordham Law Review* (5)78: 2051–2066. http://ir.lawnet.fordham.edu/flr/vol78/iss5/1.

Weidong, Ji (2004). "Legal Education in China: A Great Leap Forward in Professionalism," *Kobe University Law Review* 39: 1, 12–13.

Wolff, Lutz-Christian (2004). "Structural Problem Solving: German Methodology from a Comparative Perspective," *Legal Education Review* 14: 19, 22–23.

World Bank Press Release (2015). World Bank Press Release. January 26. http://www.worldbank.org/en/news/press-release/2015/01/26/world-bank-report-provides-new-data-to-help-ensure-urban-growth-benefits-the-poor.

Xinhua News (2013). "Chinese Courts to Publish Judgments Online," *China Daily.* November 28. https://www.chinadaily.com.cn/china/2013-11/27/content_17136289.htm.

Yi, Mei and Rui Yang (2014). "Governance Reforms in Higher Education: A Study of China," *UNESCO, International Institute for Education Planning.* http://unesdoc.unesco.org/images/0023/002318/231858e.pdf.

Yiu, Enoch (2017). "Number of Firms Registered in Qianhai up 68 Percent, But Small Players Can't Get a Look In," *South China Morning Post.* February 8.

11

Who Wants the Global Law School?

Kevin E. Davis and Xinyi Zhang[*]

I. Introduction

Judging from the academic literature, US legal educators and their supporters all want to build global law schools (Backer 2009: 54; Clark 1998; Maxeiner 2008; Sexton 1996).[1] The impetus comes from globalization; in other words, the impetus comes from increased flows of goods, services, people, and information across international borders. The conventional wisdom is that as globalization progresses, the practice of law becomes increasingly likely to involve transactions or disputes with cross-border dimensions. Lawyers increasingly will be called upon to represent parties involved in matters such as issuing sovereign bonds, building hydroelectric projects, merging with or acquiring firms with multinational operations, maintaining global supply chains, adopting children from overseas, or advocating for human rights in foreign countries. The increased prevalence of transnational legal practice will, in turn, increase the demand for students who have been prepared for that kind of practice by being educated about transnational law.

The presumption in much of the literature is that if law schools build a global law school, students will come (Barrett, Jr. 1997b: 856). The process by which students decide whether, and to what extent, to participate in the globalization of legal education has received relatively little attention. However, understanding that process is critical because students clearly have choices; they choose whether to attend law school, which law school to attend, and,

[*] We are grateful to Ava Haghighi for excellent research assistance and to Amy Wilson, Benedict Kingsbury, Siqi Tu, Benjamin Van Rooij, the editors of this volume, and participants in the conference on Globalization of Legal Education for helpful comments. Kevin Davis gratefully acknowledges support from the Filomen D'Agostino and Max E. Greenberg Faculty Research Fund at NYU School of Law. The views expressed in this chapter are those of the individual authors and do not necessarily represent the views of New York University or the NYU School of Law.
[1] Most of the articles cited here are aspirational. We suspect that relatively few US law schools have made significant efforts to offer the kinds of training recommended in this literature.

Kevin E. Davis and Xinyi Zhang, *Who Wants the Global Law School?* In: *The Globalization of Legal Education*. Edited by: Bryant Garth & Gregory Shaffer, Oxford University Press. © Oxford University Press 2022.
DOI: 10.1093/oso/9780197632314.003.0011

in many cases, whether to take advantage of opportunities to study transnational law.

Underlying the standard view is a relatively simplistic understanding of how students make decisions about legal education. According to that understanding, students value alternative forms of legal education based primarily on how they impact their opportunities to practice law after they graduate (Grossman 1996: 942). For example, students will value the opportunity to study Latin American law if they believe it will help them to land the job they covet in a large law firm's Latin American practice group.

In the standard model, the demand for educational opportunities is a derived demand, meaning it is determined entirely by the demand for some other good or opportunity; in this case, postgraduation professional opportunities (Shah 2010: 843). This is an unwarranted oversimplification. The gap between this theory and the reality of how students decide which educational opportunities to pursue offers plenty of room for law schools to stumble in their efforts to attract students to programs on transnational law.

We believe that demand for educational opportunities, and particularly demand for opportunities that form only part of an expensive postgraduate degree program, is shaped by a complex set of psychological and social factors. Career concerns are not necessarily the most important of those factors. This insight is widely accepted in studies of higher education that focus on undergraduates, but has had limited impact in the literature on US legal education (Garth 2015; Krishnan and Dias 2015; Silver and Ballakrishnen 2018). Understanding those factors, as well as the overall decision-making processes in which they play a role, is of both academic and practical value. Shedding light on the process by which law students decide whether to pursue transnational educational opportunities promises not only to contribute to the literature on higher education but also to help law schools develop programs in transnational law that students find compelling.

We illustrate this argument by using a case study of a set of semester-long study abroad programs in which we were both directly involved; an initiative known as "NYU Law Abroad." It was launched by New York University School of Law (NYU Law) in spring 2014 (New York University School of Law 2013). NYU Law Abroad was explicitly designed to respond to changes in legal practice caused by globalization. The programs were optional, not mandatory, for NYU JD students. Consequently, as members of the team responsible for implementing the program, we were immediately forced to confront the challenge of inducing students to choose to participate. This experience demonstrated that impact on postgraduation career opportunities was not necessarily the most important factor in students' decision-making.

The next section of this chapter discusses the view that demand for transnational legal education is a derived demand driven by globalization. The third section draws on sociological theories and research in higher education to present an alternative view; namely, that demand in this context is a construct of psychological and social as well as economic factors. The fourth section describes NYU Law Abroad, including both the supply-side factors that led the law school to create the program and the demand it triggered among students. The fifth section concludes.

II. Derived Demand

The derived demand theory is premised on the idea that globalization is a persistent trend which generates demand for lawyers who are capable of appreciating the legal consequences of transnational activities (Barrett, Jr. 1997a: 983). This leads to demand for lawyers familiar with the laws of multiple jurisdictions, which in turn generates demand for multijural legal education; that is to say, demand for training in the laws of multiple jurisdictions (Davis and Trebilcock 2006). We will examine each of the steps in this process in turn.

A. Globalization and the Demand for Transnational Legal Services

It is uncontroversial that cross-border flows of capital, goods, services, people, and information require supporting legal services (Barrett, Jr. 1997a). Those legal services typically take one of two forms: advice on the legal consequences of particular transactions (Ali 2013: 250), which might include advice on different ways of structuring a transaction to achieve the same purpose, and assistance in resolving disputes about transactions which have already occurred (Barrett, Jr. 1997a: 989–990). The tasks are connected because understanding the legal consequences of a particular course of action involves anticipating the sorts of disputes it is likely to generate and how those disputes will be resolved. Both tasks require understanding all of the laws applicable to the transaction or dispute in question.

Until recently, all forms of globalization—international flows of capital, services, people, goods, and data—were increasing steadily (Law 2008: 1301; Thomas 2000: 1476; Trachtman 2010: 296). In that context it was reasonable to conjecture that demand for the associated legal services was increasing apace. Since the financial crisis of 2008, however, the trend line has frayed. Worldwide volumes of trade in goods and services, as well as foreign direct investment, have declined overall, although some flows, such as computer services and tourism, have increased (Loungani et al. 2017; World Bank Group n.d. a-e). At the same time, Brexit and the Trump administration's support for economic nationalism have cast a political cloud over the entire globalization project (The Economist 2017). In this more complex world, it is difficult to sustain a blanket assumption that further globalization is inevitable and will drive steadily increasing demand for legal services.

Even if it is too soon to sound the death knell for globalization, and the volume of cross-border transactions and disputes actually increases over time, there need not be a proportional increase in the demand for legal services. Some cross-border transactions and disputes demand more advice from lawyers than others. For example, international sales of goods between most countries are so routine that information about how to structure transactions to achieve predictable legal effects is widely available, even to people without legal training—countless entrepreneurs around the world figure out how to import goods from China without legal advice. The situation is different for transactions that are unusual, or where the applicable legal principles change frequently or are not widely accessible. A sale of advanced computer equipment from a US entity to an Iranian one might be a good example because the sale must comply with legislation implementing US sanctions on Iran. There are similar variations in the extent to which lawyers are involved in other types of international transactions. The financing and construction of a one-of-a-kind international pipeline in Central Asia is likely to require more legal assistance than financing and building a warehouse in Mexico. In short, different forms of globalization—different volumes and types of transnational activities—generate different levels of demand for legal services.

B. Demand for Multijural Lawyers

If globalization does generate demand for lawyers, there is an open question as to what kinds of lawyers will be able to satisfy that demand. Some proponents of the global law school suggest that lawyers who work on transnational transactions or disputes have to be familiar with the laws of all the jurisdictions implicated (Backer 2009: 83; Drumbl 1998; Sánchez 1997: 641). Different levels of familiarity might be required. At one end of the spectrum is the lawyer who is familiar with the law of only one jurisdiction, the monojural lawyer. At the other end of the spectrum is the lawyer who is equally capable of practicing the laws of all the relevant jurisdictions, the perfectly bijural or multijural lawyer (Bowers 2002). In between are lawyers with varying levels of familiarity with the different jurisdictions' laws.

It is not obvious that effective transnational lawyers must be familiar with the laws of all the jurisdictions implicated in a matter. The middle ground between perfectly monojural and perfectly multijural lawyers includes people who are not necessarily familiar with the specific features of the legal systems implicated in a matter, but who are also familiar with the general issues that arise in transnational settings. Imagine, for example, a Canadian lawyer who is only capable of offering advice on Quebec law. By virtue of his or her training or experience in transactions or disputes involving Canada's common-law provinces, that lawyer might appreciate the potential differences between legal systems and have a sense of what questions to ask foreign lawyers, even in a transaction involving, say, New York law and Chinese law. That general familiarity with transnational legal issues might allow the lawyer to be more effective than a purely monojural lawyer in a variety of cross-border transactions (Valcke 2004).

The clients who demand multijural lawyers may also want lawyers who are multilingual (Melitz 2008; Isphording and Otten 2013). In many cross-border matters either the parties speak different languages or the applicable laws are written in different languages. Lawyers involved in these cases benefit from being able to communicate in the relevant languages because they can avoid the costs of translation. Similarly, when the parties come from different cultural backgrounds, lawyers who can negotiate different cultural norms without intermediaries will avoid unnecessary costs, frictions, and misunderstandings (Silver 2013: 459–462, 470). In this sense, linguistic and cultural skills are what economists call complements to multijural legal skills, meaning their presence enhances the demand for the services of multijural lawyers.

Cross-border matters do not automatically generate demand for multijural lawyers. In the first place, not all cross-border transactions involve multiple legal systems. Some cross-border transactions are conducted between jurisdictions that have chosen to harmonize their laws. This is most obvious within the European Union, where many subjects are governed by European law rather than the law of one of the member states. At the global level, the best example of harmonization is probably the UN Convention on Contracts for the International Sales of Goods, which provides a common set of rules to govern international sales of goods (United Nations Convention on Contracts for the International Sale of Goods 1980). In addition, in the case of many commercial transactions, the parties have the option of choosing the applicable law, and it is common for them to choose a *legal lingua franca*, meaning a set of norms that are accessible to all kinds of otherwise monojural lawyers (Davis and Trebilcock 2006: 190–196, 201). A good example of these kinds of substantive norms is the UNIDROIT *Principles of International Commercial Contracts* (International Institute for the Unification of Private Law [UNIDROIT] 2010). Meanwhile, on the procedural side, the rules promulgated to govern commercial arbitration before major arbitral institutions are designed to be accessible to lawyers from all sorts of jurisdictions (i.e., procedural *legal lingua franca*).

Here is a second reason why cross-border matters might not require the assistance of multijural lawyers: teams of monojural lawyers might be effective substitutes for multijural lawyers (Davis and Trebilcock 2006: 190, 200–201). For example, instead of turning to lawyers licensed to practice in both New York and Mexico for advice on a cross-border acquisition, the parties might call upon multinational law firms which can staff the matter with monojural lawyers based in New York and Mexico City. The choice between a multijural lawyer and a team of monojural lawyers is likely to involve trade-offs. Monojural lawyers have the advantage of specializing in the laws of a single jurisdiction. However, they face of the disadvantage of having to coordinate with one another in ways that involve translating legal concepts from one system (e.g., *amparo* or equitable lien) into terms used in another system. A multijural lawyer, or even a team of multijural lawyers, may be less specialized but can avoid the need for legal translation.

C. Derived Demand for Multijural Legal Education

According to the derived demand theory, if globalization generates demand for multijural lawyers, then prospective students will demand multijural legal training from law schools. That is to say, training that covers more than domestic law and *legal lingua franca*. Demand for bijural training should be particularly strong among law students who expect to be able to offer related linguistic and cultural skills. That training can take several different forms, since there are many different ways in which a school might arrange for its students to learn about foreign and transnational law (Backer 2009: 49–112).

The most extreme approach involves complete and prolonged immersion, and usually leads to some sort of dual degree. In this model, students are required to travel physically to the foreign jurisdiction to be taught by local faculty alongside local students for long enough to be capable of practicing at the same level as a monojural local lawyer. At the other end of the spectrum are short courses in transnational or comparative law taught as part of a law school's regular curriculum by its regular faculty and designed to provide only general knowledge about foreign and transnational law rather than specific knowledge about any particular legal system. In between are study abroad programs that offer varying amounts of exposure to local faculty, students, and practitioners.

The demand for more and less immersive experiences will depend in part on the level of demand for training in foreign languages and cultures. A US student who wants to provide advice on Chinese law and also negotiate agreements with Chinese business executives in their native tongue is more likely to want an immersive experience in China than a student who simply wants to be able to work effectively with (English-speaking) lawyers in the Beijing office of her or his law firm.

The derived demand theory admits at least two main caveats to the prediction that increased globalization will lead to increased demand for multijural training from law schools. The first caveat is that demand for multijural training from law schools will be limited by the extent to which students can obtain equivalent or better training elsewhere. If, for instance, students expect to learn how to practice transnational law on the job after graduation, then there will be little demand for law schools to provide similar learning opportunities. In fact, large law firms with offices in multiple locations sometimes permit lawyers to spend short stints in foreign offices. In principle, that kind of on-the-job training in multijural legal practice might be superior to training in law school.

There is a second obvious caveat to the derived demand theory. Even if derived demand for multijural lawyers is a factor that explains demand for multijural training, it may not be the only factor. Potential employers look for many attributes in law students, and multijural training is only one of them.

Factors such as raw intellect, doctrinal knowledge, familiarity with clients' operations, interests, and aspirations are also important. Law schools offer a bundle of opportunities to law students, and the demand for any single component of the bundle will depend heavily on what else is on offer. Students may show little interest in multijural training if it interferes with their ability to take courses that allow them to earn high grades, learn US legal doctrine, or take interdisciplinary courses that boost their understanding of business or politics.

D. Evidence of Derived Demand for Multijural Legal Education

There is little doubt that the derived demand theory explains at least a portion of the demand for multijural legal education. The best evidence comes from studies of students who pursue LLM degrees at US law schools. The relevant literature makes it clear that economic motivations are critical for those students. For instance, in a series of surveys of the classes of 1996, 1998, and 2000, 82 percent of respondents indicated that "expansion of professional opportunities in home country" was an important motivation for pursuing a US LLM. Meanwhile, 51 percent listed "desire to improve English skills" (Silver and Ballakrishnen 2018). The derived demand theory is also consistent with data which show that the leading destinations for students who move internationally to study law are the United States, the United Kingdom, France, and Germany (Roberts 2017: 62–72). These countries historically have accounted for significant amounts of international trade and investment (along with China, Japan, and the Netherlands) (World Trade Organization 2017: 48–49, 53; United Nations Conference on Trade and Development 2017: 8) and, in the case of the first three countries, offered training in legal and linguistic lingua franca (Garth 2015).

III. A Theory of Constructed Demand

A. Limitations of Derived Demand

The derived demand theory reflects an economist's way of understanding educational decision-making. Economists tend to presume that the principal determinants of variations in demand—both across individuals and over time—are economic variables such as stocks of human capital, relative prices, and incomes, and that preferences can safely be treated as similar across people and stable over time (Stigler and Becker 1977). The derived demand theory adheres to this approach by focusing on growth in demand for multijural lawyers—which, in turn, should drive up the prices they can command for their services—as the principal determinant of how law students' decisions to pursue multijural training will vary over time. To be clear, however, the theory acknowledges that the level of demand at any given point in time also will be determined by economic or social constraints, such as limited financial resources, or familial obligations, that limit students' mobility and prevent them from pursuing opportunities to study abroad.

This theory rests on several important assumptions, namely: employers are well informed about students' capabilities when they make decisions about whether to hire them; students are rational, reasonably well-informed actors who choose educational programs to achieve the best possible career outcomes, evaluated according to a set of well-ordered preferences that are stable over time and relatively consistent across individuals; and more specifically, the career preferences of US law students favor postgraduation employment with either private law firms that offer high earnings prospects, or high-profile governmental, intergovernmental, or nongovernmental organizations.

Virtually all of the assumptions that underlie this approach to educational choice are contestable. Employers may not be well informed about students' capabilities. Students may not be well informed about their educational options and how pursuing different options will impact their careers. Students may not make educational decisions based on reasoned consideration of the consequences. They may also not have stable well-defined preferences over different outcomes. And, to the extent students do account for the consequences of the decisions, they may not weigh career consequences very heavily.

The assumption that employers are well informed is particularly easy to challenge in the law school context. In many US law schools, most opportunities for multijural training take the form of optional courses offered after the first year of a three-year degree (Backer 2009: 76–82). However, many law firms hire students at the beginning of their second year of law school, on the basis of grades from the first year. Strictly speaking, those students are only being hired to work at the law firm for the summer following their second year of law school. In practice, however, the vast majority of students who work at law firms during their summer break receive offers of permanent employment (National Association for Law Placement [NALP] 2017: 29). If a firm decides not to extend an offer of permanent employment to a student employed for the summer, it is likely to be because of their performance at the law firm rather than because of anything they have done or not done in law school (Yale University Law School 2017). The upshot is that law firms frequently hire law students before they know whether the student has pursued opportunities for multijural legal training. Furthermore, even if an employer does know what opportunities a student has pursued, they might have a hard time determining what skills the student has acquired as a result.

There is also an open question as to whether students have good information about the value of multijural training. There is no obvious source for information about the state of demand for various types of legal training. No single employer has an incentive to produce much information of this sort. Individual lawyers may be able to pass this information on to students in direct communications, but not that many law students have this kind of personal relationship with practicing lawyers who have direct knowledge of opportunities to work on transnational problems. Consequently, the information available to students is likely to depend on what is provided at the initiative of law school faculty and staff.

The economists' assumption that people make decisions based on rational assessments of the consequences has come under attack from social scientists in other disciplines. Psychologists suggest that decision-making is distorted by innate personality traits and cognitive biases, as well as our limited cognitive capacity in the face of complex decisions that require analysis of large amounts of information (Ajzen 1991; Rabin 1998). Some social scientists go so far as to suggest that individuals' actions are largely determined by normative rules embedded in social structures that are beyond their control. French sociologist Pierre Bourdieu occupies a middle ground with an influential theory which posits that human actions are rarely "decisions" of reason based on conscious, rational calculation with purposive goals, nor are they determined by cultural or material mechanisms external and superior to the individuals (Bourdieu 1985: 11–24; Bourdieu 1996; Bourdieu 1986: 46–58; Bourdieu 1990; Bourdieu and Wacquant 1989; Bourdieu 1989). Rather, human actions follow an economic logic that is constitutive of practices "most appropriate to achieve the objectives inscribed in the logic of a particular field at the lowest costs" which, socially and historically constructed, "can be defined in relation to all kinds of functions," with the maximization of economic interests being only one of them. Since Bourdieu's theory has been influential in studies of education, we will use the next couple of paragraphs to outline its key components.

According to Bourdieu, social practices are engaged in by agents who operate in specific "fields" (e.g., the religious field, the political field, the artistic field, the scientific field, the legal field), holding various amounts and forms of accumulated resources known as "capital" (economic, cultural, social, or symbolic), guided by a set of internalized dispositions he calls "habitus." Habitus is a "structuring mechanism" that operates within agents as a repertoire of thoughts, perceptions, expressions, and actions that make possible an infinite capacity to achieve diversified tasks, but with limits set by historically and socially bounded conditions. It also includes internalized beliefs about what is possible and impossible, and senses of inclusion and exclusion, from the social position in which an individual is situated. Habitus is shaped disproportionately by early socialization, which is regulated by an individual's class or group origin. In turn, individual agents and, more generally, members of social groups, actively reproduce and constitute a social world that is in accordance with the objective social structures (of distinctions and hierarchy) in which they reside. Agents draw on habitus and their stocks of capital as they formulate strategies to compete for power and authority in any given field. As a result, the practices they select often reproduce inequalities and preexisting patterns of inclusion and exclusion.[2]

Bourdieu's theory challenges not only the assumption that decisions are based entirely on conscious calculation but also the assumption that they can be explained primarily by reference to stable preferences over economic outcomes. Bourdieu rejects reducing the historically variant, socially constituted notion of "interest" to a constant propensity to seek monetary or material gain. Individuals and groups are motivated by desire to establish status and domination (aka the power to distinguish), which is not only achieved through accumulation of economic capital but also through command over cultural embodiments and signals (cultural capital), possession of a network of durable, institutionalized relationships that provide its own members the backing of the collectively owned resources (social capital), and honor or

---

[2] However, it is important to note that Bourdieu also points out the creative, inventive aspects of habitus and thus does not negate agency. It predisposes individuals to certain practices but does not predetermine that. Bourdieu thinks that while habitus leads to the reproduction of the social conditions, it does so in a relatively unpredictable way.

prestige that are collectively recognized in the field (symbolic capital). The efficacy of each form of capital is subject to the logic of the field, in which agents struggle for not only the monopoly of the capital that is effective but also for the power to command "conversion rates" between different forms of capital. Within this framework, according to Bourdieu, interest is "a socially constituted concern for, and desire to play, given social games" in which agents compete for distinctions. Therefore, preferences for certain outcomes, whose differences are rooted in relation to the unequal amount of capital endowed with different social class/group, would only make sense in response to the historically arbitrary value assigned to certain practices in a given field. In that, preferences are socially and historically constructed, rather than constant and static. This approach also allows for the possibility that students' preferences might be mutable, susceptible to influence from authority figures and peers.

Following this logic, then, we can challenge the assumption that when law students consider the consequences of their educational decisions they focus primarily on career outcomes, measured primarily in terms of monetary earnings. In the educational context, where intellectual curiosity and cultural competence are valued, students might choose a particular course of study (in this case, multijural training) as an end in itself. Through the working of habitus, these considerations might often come "naturally" to students, rather than in a linear, systematic manner. At the same time, the likelihood of taking this course of study is mediated by the students' prior socialization and the extent to which their outlook aligns with those who are around them in school.

B. An Alternative to Derived Demand

Given the limitations of the derived demand theory, we propose to explore whether an alternative theory of educational decision-making helps to understand law students' decisions about whether and to which extent to pursue opportunities for multijural training. The derived demand theory presents demand as the virtually automatic product of mathematical operations on data from the market for multijural lawyers, taking the distribution of economic capital into account. Drawing insights from Bourdieu, we instead characterize demand as a complex social process that not only includes economic calculations but also involves the interplay between the non-economic capital and dispositions that students bring with them to law school, in part as a result of their social class and status, the socialization that takes place while they are in law school in the course of interactions with peers and faculty, and historically contingent conceptions of status and power. We call this alternative theory of demand for educational opportunities, "constructed demand" to suggest that demand is constructed from a variety of factors.

Research on college choice as well as undergraduate student interests in studying abroad provides empirical grounds for the constructed demand model. Students' educational choices are explained to some extent by economic variables such as individuals' initial stock of human capital, measured by academic preparation and achievement, and access to resources required to pursue expensive opportunities (often measured by family income and financial aid) (Paulsen 2001; Perna 2006). Taken as a whole, however, the literature suggests that both college choice and students' interest in studying abroad are shaped by a complex interplay of factors such as socioeconomic status, gender, race and ethnicity, cultural and social capital, and organizational environment (McDonough 1997; Stevens 2009; Salisbury et al. 2009; Salisbury et al. 2010; Salisbury et al. 2011; Goldstein 2006; Stroud 2010; Simon and Ainsworth 2012).

Similarly, in the literature on demand for legal education there are hints that demand might be shaped by factors besides the career opportunities opened up by cross-border transactions or disputes. The data on international flows of students toward countries such as the United States, the United Kingdom, and Germany are consistent with the idea that students' choices are motivated by desires for status or intellectual growth, and not just economic benefits (Garth 2015; Krishnan and Dias 2015). Meanwhile, at the level of individual students, many Indian lawyers pursue US LLMs even though, for reasons specific to the Indian market for legal services, they expect the degree to have little impact on their career prospects. Silver and Ballakrishnen claim that, "for the most part, the degree is more of a chance to have a 'break year' where [the Indian students] can be intellectually engaged further before returning to the 'real' careers" (Silver and Ballakrishnen 2018).

In a similar vein, Lazarus-Black and Globokar find that many students trained outside the United States were motivated to pursue LLMs at US law schools by interests in "advancing human rights, improving peoples' social welfare, ensuring fair business practices, and serving as a resource in their country of origin to advance law in new directions" (Lazarus-Black and

Globokar 2015: 50). Relatedly, students from Latin America, Africa, Asia, and the former Soviet Union cited perceptions that the United States was more "legally developed" in certain areas of law than their home nations as reasons to value US legal education (Lazarus-Black and Globokar 2015: 37). There is no obvious way in which the demand for lawyers to pursue these sorts of socially oriented careers is connected to the volume of cross-border transactions or disputes. However, even for lawyers hoping to pursue careers in social justice, certain aspects of US law serve as legal lingua franca. Consequently, if there is relatively high demand overseas for, say, human rights lawyers with knowledge of US civil rights law, then the derived demand theory would predict high demand for US LLM degrees specializing in human rights law. At the same time, the perception of the superiority of US law might reflect more than just an objective assessment of US legal hegemony. As Bryant Garth argues, in certain parts of the world and in certain segments of society, perceptions of the status of US law and affinity for Western ideals might reflect a history of US imperialism and ideological influence (Garth 2015).

IV. NYU Law Abroad

To explore the value of derived demand and constructed demand in explaining law students' decisions to study abroad we present a case study of NYU Law's study abroad programs. NYU Law Abroad makes for a good case study because it represents the product of an exceptionally large investment in multijural training, at least by the standards of US law schools. At the same time, the programs are optional, not mandatory, which means that students' decisions about whether to participate can be used to draw inferences about demand for multijural training (New York University School of Law 2017b). The derived demand theory predicts that a program like NYU Law Abroad ought to have attracted significant numbers of students interested in improving their career prospects. At the same time, the distinctive features of Law Abroad and our relationship to the programs limit the value of this case study.

First, US JD students are not representative of all potential law students. Because many aspects of US law serve as *legal lingua franca*, and the English language is a bona fide lingua franca, the derived demand theory predicts that US JDs will have relatively low levels of interest in multijural training. A cleaner test of the theory would cover students whose home countries' laws and language are less widely used in international business, that is, cases in which the derived demand theory predicts that there will be relatively strong demand for multijural training. Accordingly, our study should be read alongside analyses of demand from students who are not originally from the United States, such as those surveyed by Silver and Ballakrishnen (Silver and Ballakrishnen 2018).

Second, NYU Law's experience might not be representative of experiences at other US law schools. NYU Law is a highly ranked national law school located in the heart of New York City, one of the most cosmopolitan cities in the world and in close proximity to many potential employers that engage in transnational legal work. As a result, NYU's JD students operate in a very different cultural environment and face different employment opportunities from students at many other law schools. They also may be more mobile, on average, than students at regional law schools (since many of them have already demonstrated the ability to move in order to be at a national school). In addition, NYU Law has made an exceptionally large investment in multijural legal education, including but not limited to NYU Law Abroad (Adcock 2015). We suspect that the magnitude of that investment has had opposing effects on demand for NYU Law Abroad. On the one hand, it has probably attracted an unusually internationally oriented student body to NYU. On the other hand, it has given them an unusually large array of alternative ways of obtaining multijural training.

Finally, a third limitation on the value of this case study stems from the fact that we were both personally involved in the creation and operation of these programs. Consequently, we cannot claim to be objective observers.[3] At the same time, our unique perspective on NYU Law Abroad gives us access to information that would be relatively difficult for other researchers to uncover. Moreover, our subjective beliefs about this program may themselves be useful data for other researchers.

---

[3] For instance, because of the constraints imposed by our positions, we do not offer much beyond publicly available information about the supply side of the Law Abroad initiative, i.e., the factors that led NYU Law to launch the programs.

A. Background

NYU Law has been in the vanguard of efforts to globalize legal education in the United States for at least twenty years (Adcock 2015). A transformative moment in the history of NYU Law was the establishment of the Global Law School Program, later renamed the Hauser Global Law School (Sexton 1996: 330–333; Dorsen 2001: 332; Sexton 2001a; Sexton 2001b). The creation of the Global Law School was led by then dean of the law school, John Sexton, and supported by a major donation from a pair of wealthy philanthropists, Rita and Gus Hauser. The Global Law School Program consisted of three main components:

1. Global Faculty. A set of faculty recruited from around the world who would be invited to teach repeatedly at the NYU campus in New York.
2. Global Scholars Program. A scholarship program for foreign graduate students.
3. Curriculum and research. Support for curricular innovations and research from "a transnational perspective."

John Sexton explicitly justified the Global Law School Program as a response to globalization. Interestingly, in published writings he emphasized the connection between globalization and law reform, suggesting that the twenty-first century would demand lawyers capable of bringing insights from multiple legal systems to bear on common or transnational problems. He was particularly interested in making NYU attractive to foreign students planning to work overseas.

By the end of the first decade of the twenty-first century, NYU Law was no longer the only global law school in the US (Yale University Law School n.d.). Other top-ranked US law schools had expanded their numbers of visiting faculty and many US law schools expanded LLM programs aimed at students from overseas. In addition, there was a broad consensus in the US legal academy around the need to adopt a transnational perspective on curriculum design and academic research (Chesterman 2009; Lewis 2009; White 2007: 1287).

At the same time, the larger university to which the law school belonged had also evolved. After serving fourteen years as dean of the law school, John Sexton was appointed president of New York University (New York University School of Law n.d.a). He almost immediately expanded NYU's network of overseas facilities for hosting New York–based students studying abroad. He also launched an ambitious plan to build two new campuses overseas, one in Abu Dhabi and the other in Shanghai. The resulting institution is known as the Global Network University, with three main "portal" campuses (New York, Abu Dhabi, and Shanghai) and smaller facilities at ten other overseas sites (plus one in Washington, D.C.) (New York University n.d.b).[4]

NYU Law initially had little to do with the central university's overseas sites. Its flagship JD program consisted exclusively of courses offered at the New York campus, with the only exceptions being semester-long exchange programs at select foreign institutions (New York University 2010). The Global Law School attempted to offer a transnational legal education, but mainly in New York. The Global Law School was designed "to bring the world to NYU," not "to bring NYU to the world" (Adcock 2015: 16, 19).

This all changed with the advent of the programs now known as NYU Law Abroad, which allow NYU Law students to study for a semester in NYU facilities in one of three locations: Buenos Aires, Paris, and Shanghai. Students abroad are charged the same tuition and fees that they would pay in New York. The programs are aimed primarily at NYU Law's 3L JD students, but 2Ls and, as of spring 2016, LLM students, are also permitted to enroll.[5]

NYU Law Abroad was created at the recommendation of a committee of the law school's board of trustees ("the Strategy Committee") charged with exploring how changes in the legal profession should affect the JD program (New York University School of Law 2013). Most of the Strategy Committee's recommendation focused on enhancing the value of the third year of the JD degree. Among other things, the Strategy Committee recommended that the Law School better prepare its graduates for practice in an increasingly globalized world. The Strategy Committee wrote:

The increasingly global nature of law practice, in areas ranging from climate change to commerce and war crimes to taxes, demands lawyers able to work across jurisdictional and cultural boundaries. And, despite English being one of the world's dominant languages, knowledge of local languages

---

[4] As of fall 2017, the foreign sites were located in Accra, Ghana; Berlin, Germany; Buenos Aires, Argentina; Florence, Italy; London, England; Madrid, Spain; Paris, France; Prague, the Czech Republic; Sydney, Australia; and Tel Aviv, Israel.

[5] "The program is designed primarily for third year NYU law students; exceptions for other NYU Law students will be considered on a case-by-case basis, with permission of the Vice Dean and the faculty program directors" (New York University n.d.a). As of fall 2017, only one LLM student has ever enrolled in Law Abroad.

is more critical as more litigation, M&A work, and other transactions take associates all over the world and require them to deal with regulators and local counsel in foreign jurisdictions. Existing study-abroad programs offered by law schools (including NYU), offer valuable opportunities for study of foreign law, but NYU Law School can improve on current offerings—and distinguish itself and its graduates—by developing a more ambitious, integrated program that combines language training, cultural education, and foreign practice opportunity (through internships and clinics) with formal course study in other countries. NYU Law School faculty, working in collaboration with overseas partners, are well positioned to design a program that will prepare students for global legal practice (New York University School of Law 2012: 3–4).

The Strategy Committee's report makes no reference to evidence of demand from students for additional opportunities to study abroad. On the contrary, it notes that "only a small number of students take advantage of [NYU's existing] exchange programs."

NYU Law Abroad was launched in fall 2012, and the first cohort of students went overseas in January 2014. The program offers students less immersion in the local legal culture than a dual degree or even a traditional exchange program, but more immersion than any program that could be offered in the United States. On the one hand, the entire program—including the curriculum—is designed and administered by NYU Law, the classes take place in buildings occupied full-time by NYU (the central university), and the classes are all taught in English. On the other hand, all the courses are taught by faculty from the relevant region, students from local law schools participate in most of the classes (free of charge), and each site offers language courses in French, Spanish, and Mandarin, respectively. In addition, in Buenos Aires and Paris, students can enroll in a limited number of courses at local law schools as exchange students, including courses offered in Spanish and French. In Buenos Aires and Paris, students have the option of participating in a clinical course that allows them to work on public interest matters involving clients from the region. The structure of the program is flexible enough to accommodate courses that cover foreign law, as opposed to comparative or transnational law, in varying levels of detail.[6]

---

[6] Since the focus of this essay is student demand, we will not detail the process by which the curriculum is developed. Suffice to say, the process involves significant consultation between faculty based

The NYU Law Abroad sites were designed to accommodate either sixteen (Paris) or twenty-five (Buenos Aires and Shanghai) students, reflecting the fact that the programs were intended to induce a meaningful portion of NYU Law's roughly 1,300 JD students (roughly 420 per class) to study overseas.[7] This ruled out relying on exchange programs or dual-degree programs. Exchange programs are almost invariably structured so that they do not involve any extra tuition charges to the students (New York University School of Law n.d.b). Accordingly, the participating schools try to maintain a balance between the number of incoming and outgoing students. Typically, an exchange program is capped at two to five students per year. NYU Law is one of the most selective law schools in the United States, and it also has one of the largest student bodies (U.S. News & World Report n.d.). It would be difficult for a school like NYU Law to find suitable exchange partners that could both accommodate a significant portion of NYU Law's student body and send an equivalent number of suitably qualified students. As for dual degree programs, they typically require at least one additional year of study[8] and, in the case of programs in non-English-speaking jurisdictions, fluency in a foreign language. Few US law students are sufficiently interested in studying abroad to incur the cost of additional year of schooling. Plus, a relatively small number of students are fluent in a foreign language.

The NYU Law Abroad programs change from year to year. The curriculum of each site is reviewed and adjusted yearly based on teaching evaluations from the students, faculty availability, and indications of substantial student interest in certain topics. In addition, logistical improvements related to scheduling and programming are made in response to student feedback.[9]

Since the purpose of this case study is to analyze student interest in NYU Law Abroad, it is important for us to explain how students enter the

---

in New York and those based overseas. Nor do we discuss the ways in which Law Abroad has been used to support the development of international research networks.

[7] The number of students allowed in the Paris program (initially 14, now 16) is lower than that in Buenos Aires and Shanghai (25) because NYU Law's partner institution in Paris limits the number of foreign students they can enroll.

[8] This is partly because of American Bar Association rules that limit the number of credits taken overseas that can be counted toward the JD degree (American Bar Association 2016).

[9] During the period covered by this chapter, Law Abroad was administered primarily by two full-time administrators (including Zhang) based in New York who reported to a vice dean (Davis). Each program has a New York–based faculty director. In the case of Buenos Aires there is also an onsite faculty director. Additional support is provided as needed by onsite staff employed by the central university. In addition to supporting students and faculty, the administrative staff of Law Abroad work on ensuring compliance with American Bar Association regulations, agreements with local partners, and local laws.

program. This begins with recruitment. NYU Law Abroad is a prominent part of the information aimed at prospective students. The program has a dedicated page on the law school's website (New York University School of Law 2017b), which includes not only information about the application process and curriculum but also video testimonials from previous participants. Presentations to JD students who have been admitted to NYU Law but who have not yet matriculated routinely include mentions of NYU Law Abroad. As for matriculated students, each fall there is a panel discussion of opportunities to work and study abroad, which includes both faculty and students. Separate panels are organized early in the spring to present information about individual sites. Videos of the panels are posted online. The panels and the opening of the application periods are advertised on digital billboards around the law school.

The majority of students apply to study abroad in the spring before the year they intend to go abroad. For example, students who intend to go abroad in spring 2020 apply in spring 2019. There is a second round of applications at the beginning of the fall semester for programs that have spots remaining. Traditionally, only a handful of students join in the fall. At the time of application, students do not know what adjustments will be made to the programs during the semester they are going abroad. Similarly, students are not provided detailed information about facilities and immigration requirements until after they are enrolled in the program.[10]

The spring application process permits students to apply simultaneously to multiple NYU Law Abroad and exchange programs, but they must rank them in order of preference. As part of the application process, students are asked to submit a law school transcript, a curriculum vitae, and a five-hundred-word "plan of study" that addresses how their application satisfies the stated criteria for selection. Those criteria comprise the following:

- The academic or professional reasons stated for the particular study abroad program;
- The extent to which the plan fits in with the student's overall academic and/or professional objectives, including courses already taken;
- Whether the student plans to coordinate the proposed program with work or research during the preceding or following summer;

[10] We have no reason to believe that information about logistical limits of the program (e.g., convoluted student visa application processes or changes limiting people entering China on a student visa to a single entry) systematically causes students to withdraw.

- Student's proficiency in and efforts to learn the language of the program site/host country;
- Familiarity with the region; and
- Evidence of preparedness for study abroad (New York University School of Law 2017a).

Students are selected by the faculty directors of the respective programs. In addition to the explicitly stated criteria for selection, there is a preference for students who appear to be on track to secure employment after graduation. Or perhaps more accurately, there is a bias against students who are not on track. This mainly affects applicants in their penultimate year of law school who have not yet secured employment for the coming summer (i.e., the summer prior to their final year of law school) since a summer job is usually an important step toward postgraduation employment. The reason for this is that NYU Law, like other US law schools, is very concerned about maintaining a high overall rate of postgraduation employment for its JD students. Accordingly, the law school is not enthusiastic about allowing students who are likely to be searching for a job during their final semester of law school to participate in NYU Law Abroad or exchange programs.

Student interest in NYU Law Abroad was relatively low in its first year of operation, but over the course of the next three years, enrollment in the Buenos Aires and Paris programs stabilized at or near their full capacities. Interest in Shanghai was consistently lower, and in the fourth year, the Shanghai program was suspended because enrollment was too low to make it viable.

B. Evidence of Derived Demand

There is some evidence that interest in NYU Law Abroad is shaped by students who believe that participation will be valuable in their future careers. Over its first four years of operation, about 21 percent of the students who participated in NYU Law Abroad listed career interests as a rationale for applying. In addition, the program consistently attracts students who are interested in international business transactions and international arbitration. Enrollment in courses that focus on dispute resolution and cross-border transactions has been stable across all NYU Law Abroad sites, while enrollment in the public interest clinics offered in Paris and Buenos Aires has been more variable.

At first glance, the relatively low level of interest in the Shanghai program is difficult to reconcile with the derived demand theory. China represents a larger proportion of global trade and investment than South America (European Union n.d.; World Trade Organization 2017: 13), and thus the demand for training in Chinese law ought to be relatively high. We will return to this puzzle later on. For now, we only note that differences in students' linguistic skills arguably help to resolve the puzzle. The derived demand theory suggests that perceived demand for multijural lawyers will lead to demand for legally oriented language training, at least among students who expect to be able to become reasonably capable in the relevant language. Consistent with this hypothesis, students applying to NYU Law Abroad have shown consistent interest in language courses. In fact, the desire to acquire or improve language skills is the single most cited rationale for application among students who participated in NYU Law Abroad (mentioned by 23 percent of the students). Actual enrollment in language courses varies based on whether or not the levels of instruction that are made possible within the program match students' existing language abilities. Students also have opted out of language courses because they have found the workload to be too heavy, in combination with the law courses they are taking. However, students whose needs for language training cannot be met fully within a program often actively seek out alternative methods of language training, such as private tutoring and language exchanges with local students.

The derived demand theory predicts that demand for training in any foreign legal system or foreign language will be strongest among students who expect to be capable of functioning in the relevant foreign language. The differences in demand for Paris, Buenos Aires, and Shanghai, respectively, are consistent with this prediction. NYU Law Abroad programs are too short to permit anyone to become fully functional in a completely new foreign language. This means that students who focus on the career benefits of language training are most likely to choose programs that enable them to become more competent in a foreign language in which they expect to be able to function, at least eventually. We observe some calculation on the students' end in assessing their investment and return in language learning when deciding whether or not to study in each site. There are more students who have some level of familiarity with French and Spanish than those who are familiar with Mandarin, as typical American law students have more opportunities to study French and Spanish in their pre-law education. In addition, students who have no prior familiarity with any of the languages mentioned above may still be more likely to choose to learn French and Spanish because those two languages share a common alphabet with English, which make them relatively easy for an English speaker to learn.

In 2016, we solicited postgraduation feedback from the first two cohorts of students who participated in the Law Abroad program in 2014 and 2015. We specifically asked about the longer-term impact of the program, especially with regard to their professional development. Respondents noted that the program was critical for them to improve language skills (especially in Paris and Buenos Aries) and gain knowledge of foreign legal systems and cultures. A handful of respondents indicated that the experience played a direct role in helping them secure a job. Some mentioned that the topic came up frequently in job interviews after law school. More commonly, students reported that their experiences abroad were well received by employers. Their enhanced knowledge of foreign legal systems and cultures gave them a professional edge in comparison to fellow recent graduates at their law firms, often increasing their chances to be selected to work on cases related to foreign clients. A few thought that the program enhanced their professional network and opened the door to new career opportunities abroad. Some alumni of the program reported that their pursuit of a nontraditional law school experience became a signifier of their problem-solving skills and ability to think outside the box among employers.

We present alumni feedback as evidence for derived demand with a few caveats. First, the response rate of the alumni feedback was low (37.1 percent for Buenos Aires, 46.2 percent for Paris, and 22.7 percent for Shanghai). It is therefore hard to tell if the reported experience can be generalizable to the entire group. Second, students may have overstated the professional benefits given the fact that the survey specifically asked them to detail this aspect. Third, those who had a more positive experience during and after the program may have been more likely to provide feedback. Given the selection bias, we were unable to determine whether the reported linguistic and professional benefits were objectively obtained through participating in the program or were simply part of a "self-fulfilled prophecy" that students were conditioned to believe in.

C. Evidence of Constructed Demand

Although some features of the NYU Law Abroad case are consistent with the derived demand theory, many are not.

The most obvious inconsistency is that as a result of the program's structure, students would not expect participation in NYU Law Abroad to contribute to their prospects of securing postgraduation employment, at least not in an immediately tangible way. Recall that NYU Law Abroad participants study abroad in either their 2L or 3L spring semester. This means that most students have secured summer associate positions, which often lead to full-time jobs after graduation (in the case of 2Ls) or full-time jobs (in the case of 3Ls), before they study abroad. In other words, at the time students apply for these employment opportunities, they are not able to show employers that they have completed any potentially valuable coursework abroad. While students may mention their intentions to participate in NYU Law Abroad to potential employers during interviews, they can only do so in a limited way as they would not yet be able to describe or show what they have learned abroad. Therefore, for many students the basic structure of NYU Law Abroad rules out the possibility that their decisions to participate will be based on immediate impact on their careers. The same will be true of any optional study abroad program that takes place after the third semester of law school. We do not want to overstate this point, however, because a nontrivial minority of potential participants in NYU Law Abroad can reasonably anticipate that they will be searching for employment shortly after completing the program. For some potential applicants this will be because they have not yet found a summer position. For some, their summer position may not be the kind that is likely to lead to postgraduation employment, as is common among students who work in government or for public interest organizations. Still, other students may anticipate changing employers shortly after graduation.

In addition, employers care about other factors besides participation in NYU Law Abroad. We know, for example, that employers value good grades. Therefore, in addition to the fact that most employers do not see transcripts that indicate participation in NYU Law Abroad when making hiring decisions, in the rare case they do, the number of good grades is likely to outweigh the impact of NYU Law Abroad courses.

Students' self-reported reasons for participating in NYU Law Abroad and choosing among the three sites also belie the claim that impact on career outcomes is a dominant factor in their decision-making. As Table 11.1

Table 11.1. Application Rationales Cited by Participants in NYU Law Abroad*

Application Rationales	AY 2013–2014	AY 2014–2015	AY 2015–2016
Desire to improve language skills	25%	20%	28%
Career interest in international law and/or working abroad	24%	19%	23%
Interest in gaining exposure to different legal systems	20%	13%	2%
Interest in study abroad and cultural immersion	18%	21%	15%
Location-specific	13%	28%	32%

*Data in this table are collected through annual program evaluations completed by the participants in the program. This is an open-ended question and the categories are the result of careful readings of student responses.

shows, a majority of students who participated in NYU Law Abroad cited reasons besides career considerations or language training as rationales. At the application stage students tend to emphasize professional and academic reasons for studying abroad. However, we can also draw on information from postprogram reviews and informal conversations. Program alumni consistently recognized personal benefits they gained from the program, such as cultural immersion and making close friends. We know, in addition, that some students choose to study abroad in attempts to diversify their law school experience. For many 3L students that choose to study abroad, the fact that they have already secured employment means that they can afford to "take more risks" and pursue a nontraditional law school experience before graduating. Many also see participating in NYU Law Abroad as the "last chance" they have to be able to live in and travel around a different part of the world *for fun*. Thus, students' demand for the program is not only based on expectations of the benefits in their future career but also from anticipation of the undesirable aspects of that career.

To the extent that participation in Law Abroad is motivated by career benefits, those benefits seem to take the form of "symbolic capital" that students hope to use to distinguish themselves from their peers. They do not necessarily need the experience, but they can draw on it when circumstances arise: for example, as "talking points" in interviews and in chit-chats with partners to build networks and rapport (as mentioned in the alumni survey). The value of this kind of symbolic capital need not be tightly correlated with the volume of multijural legal work.

The "fun" aspect of the program is greatly mediated by peer influence. First, students' impressions of the program are influenced, sometimes quite significantly, by the experiences of those who have already participated in the program. If they have friends who enjoyed the program, they are more likely to consider participating themselves. Second, students are more likely to participate in the program if their friends are also considering to do so. The prospect of living and traveling with friends abroad is attractive. Conversely, students have voiced reluctance over spending time away from their friends for a full semester, especially if that is the final semester they have at the law school.

Friends are not the only determinants of the fun factor associated with studying abroad. Students' general beliefs about the sites' locations also seem to matter. At one point the law school asked prospective students to record their immediate impressions of each city. For Buenos Aires and Paris, the responses were rife with words like "lights," "music," "wine," "dance," "culture," and "romantic." For Shanghai, the associations were, overall, noticeably less positive: "big," "noisy," "crowded," "business," and "pollution." We believe, but cannot prove, that these sorts of ideas contributed to students' perceptions of the relative value of studying in each place. We would expect them to determine, for instance, which places were regarded as "strange" and "uncomfortable" as opposed to "exotic" or "exciting." This would explain the relatively low levels of interest in studying in Shanghai.

The clustering of student interests in "fun" and "romantic" places that is either European (Paris) or signals clear European influence (Buenos Aires) is reminiscent of a much older story of study abroad in the United States. Historically, through the late nineteenth century and during the twentieth century, sending their children on a "Grand Tour" to Europe was popular among wealthy American families as a way for their children to "absorb and assimilate in to high European culture" (Lewin 2009).[11] Although students who participated in the Law Abroad program never explicitly claim their affinity for "high European culture," we believe that at least some part of their preference for Paris and Buenos Aires stems from assumptions and beliefs that are historically and socially associated with the romantic ideals of the Grand Tour rather than based upon rational analysis of available data.

---

[11] Lewin also suggests that the idea of the Grand Tour continues to influence study abroad practices in the United States.

We also suspect but cannot prove that students' interest in NYU Law Abroad programs has been influenced by their interactions with faculty members. Faculty involved in the administration of NYU Law Abroad programs regularly promoted the programs to students with whom they had relationships. Faculty who were skeptical of the program sometimes discouraged students from participating. This means that demand for the programs was influenced to some extent by the wide array of factors that determined the patterns of relationships between faculty members and 1L or 2L students. These include whether faculty involved in NYU Law Abroad teach large courses typically taken in the first three semesters of law school, alignment of the student and the faculty's academic interests, and even personalities.

Students who rely on the general reputation of study abroad locations or cues and advice from peers or faculty to make decisions about studying abroad may be responding rationally to information overload. NYU law students have over three hundred courses to choose from, as well as fellowships, clinics, journals, and year-long dual-degree programs. Faced with this enormous array of choices and pressed by deadlines, it may be rational for students to turn to heuristics such as general reputation or recommendations from peers or faculty.

Finally, an interesting feature of the students who enrolled in NYU Law Abroad is that students from minority ethnic groups were slightly overrepresented relative to the population of the law school (Law School Survey of Student Engagement 2004).[12] This observation might be consistent with the derived demand theory. It may be that minorities were more likely to possess the linguistic or cultural skills that complement multijural training. Another possibility, however, is that NYU Law Abroad tends to attract students who are predisposed toward travel and exploration, and those dispositions tend to emerge in immigrants or children of immigrants, or perhaps in members of disadvantaged minority groups.[13]

In light of the above, we are convinced that it is misleading to characterize students' decisions to participate in NYU Law Abroad as the products of rational calculations of the potential impacts on their post-law school careers.

---

[12] This finding is consistent with data from the 2004 Law School Survey of Student Engagement (finding that Asian/Pacific, foreign national, joint degree, and transfer students are more likely than other students to participate in a study abroad program).

[13] Interestingly, minority students are historically underrepresented among American undergraduate students who study abroad (NAFSA n.d.). Therefore, it is worth investigating characteristics of minority students who enter elite law schools.

Those decisions are better characterized as rational, or at least reasonable, efforts to achieve both career and non-career-related outcomes that are shaped by students' predispositions, what they do and do not know or think they know, their social positions, and their personal histories.

V. Conclusion

Commentators regularly justify initiatives to provide opportunities for US law students to study overseas on the grounds that they will satisfy demand from students who want multijural training in order to improve their career prospects. Such commentators embrace what we have called the derived demand theory. However, there are important reasons to doubt that demand for multijural lawyers is the only, or even the most important, explanation of demand from law students for multijural training while in law school. There are plausible reasons to doubt whether employers take this kind of training into account when making hiring decisions, that students weigh career outcomes highly when making decisions about which opportunities to pursue as part of a law school degree, or even that students' decisions involve any careful, calculated analysis. These possibilities suggest that demand for multijural training might not simply be derived from demand for multijural lawyers, but might instead by constructed from a larger set of factors, including the kinds of contingent historical and social factors that Bourdieu emphasizes in his theoretical model.

Our case study of NYU Law Abroad supports the claim that demand for at least one set of study abroad programs is based on more than just perceptions of employers' demand for multijural lawyers. Some NYU JDs' interest in studying abroad has been driven, to some extent, by perceptions that multijural training, in combination with language training, would make them more appealing to employers. But potential impact on their careers was only one of several factors in students' decisions. Other factors include the desire to have fun, influences from their peers, and ideas about the appeal of the locations of the study abroad sites. These non-career-related factors are in turn shaped by changing historical and social circumstances, such as students' earlier socialization, the extent to which study abroad experience is valued by the social group they are in, and geopolitical conditions.

These findings may be useful to law schools trying to decide whether and what kinds of study abroad opportunities to offer their students. If nothing else, the findings highlight the potential value of certain recruitment techniques, such as testimonials from peers and dissemination of information about the "fun" aspects of programs along with information about opportunities for intellectual and professional development. More generally, these findings suggest that law schools ought to pay close attention to the non-career-oriented factors that might influence their students' educational decision-making at any given moment in time and try to respond accordingly. This is likely to involve coordination between several parts of the law school's academic and administrative staff, including faculty, career advisors, counselors, and members of the communications team.

Our finding about the limited influence of derived demand at NYU Law also hints at an intriguing challenge for all law schools, even keeping in mind the distinctive features of NYU Law and NYU Law Abroad. Should law schools offer opportunities that maximize students' abilities to work as multijural lawyers if students value other kinds of opportunities? If not, should they give students the opportunities they want, even if those opportunities do not necessarily enhance the students' capabilities after graduation? In other words, should the global law school be designed to serve the needs of the legal profession, the interests of students, or perhaps some other set of interests? This important question is likely to bedevil law schools for years to come.

References

Adcock, Thomas (2015). "Going Global," *NYU Law Magazine.* 2015: 16–19. http://blogs.law.nyu.edu/magazine/2015/going-global/.

Ajzen, Icek (1991). "The Theory of Planned Behavior," *Organizational Behavior and Human Decision Processes* 50(2): 179–211.

Ali, Farida (2013). "Globalizing the U.S. Law School Curriculum: How Should Legal Educators Respond?," *International Journal of Legal Information* 41(3): 249–282.

American Bar Association (2016). *ABA Standards and Rules of Procedure for Approval of Law Schools 2016–2017, Criteria for Accepting Credit for Student Study at a Foreign Institution, Section I(c)(1).*

Backer, Larry Catá (2009). "Internationalizing the American Law School Curriculum (in Light of the Carnegie Foundation's Report)," in Jan Klabbers and Mortimer Sellers, eds., *The Internationalization of Law and Legal Education.* Pp. 49–112. Springer.

Barrett, Jr., John A. (1997). "International Legal Education in the United States: Being Educated for Domestic Practice While Living in a Global Society," *American University Journal of International Law and Policy* 12(6): 975–1013.

Barrett, Jr., John A. (1997). "International Legal Education in U.S. Law Schools: Plenty of Offerings, But Too Few Students," *International Law* 31(3): 845–867.

Bourdieu, Pierre (1985). "The Genesis of the Concepts of Habitus and Field," *Sociocriticism* 2(2): 11–24.

Bourdieu, Pierre (1986). "The Forms of Capital," in J.E. Richardson, ed., *Handbook of Theory and Research for the Sociology of Higher Education*. Pp. 46–58. Translated by Richard Nice. Greenword Press.

Bourdieu, Pierre (1989). "Social Space and Symbolic Power," *Sociological Theory* 7(1): 14–25.

Bourdieu, Pierre (1990). *The Logic of Practice*. Translated by Richard Nice. Stanford University Press.

Bourdieu, Pierre (1996). *Distinction: A Social Critique of the Judgment of Taste*. Translated by Richard Nice. Routledge.

Bourdieu, Pierre and Loïc J.D. Wacquant (1989). *An Invitation to Reflexive Sociology*. University of Chicago Press.

Bowers, James W. (2002). "The Elementary Economics of Bijuralism: A First Cut," *Journal of Legal Education* 52(1–2): 68–74.

Chesterman, Simon (2009). "The Evolution of Legal Education: Internationalization, Transnationalization, Globalization," *German Law Journal* 10(7): 877–888.

Clark, David S. (1998). "Transnational Legal Practice: The Need for Global Law Schools," *American Journal of Comparative Law* 46(Supplement 1): 261–274.

Davis, Kevin E. and Michael J. Trebilcock (2006). "The Demand for Bijural Education in Canada," in Albert Breton and Michael Trebilcock, eds., *Bijuralism: An Economic Approach*. Pp. 173–210. Ashgate Publishing.

Dorsen, Norman (2001). "Achieving International Cooperation: NYU's Global Law School Program," *Journal of Legal Education* 51(3): 332–337.

Drumbl, Mark A. (1998). "Amalgam in the Americas: A Law School Curriculum for Free Markets and Open Borders," *San Diego Law Review* 35(4): 1053–1090.

The Economist (2016). "League of Nationalists." Accessed June 25, 2020. https://www.economist.com/news/international/21710276-all-around-world-nationalists-are-gaining-ground-why-league-nationalists.

European Union (n.d.). Eurostat—International Trade in Goods, European Union. http://ec.europa.eu/eurostat/statistics-explained/index.php/International_trade_in_goods.

Garth, Bryant (2015). "Notes Toward an Understanding of the U.S. Market in Foreign LL.M. Students: From the British Empire and the Inns of Court to the U.S. LL.M.," *Indiana Journal of Global Legal Studies* 22(1): 67–79.

Goldstein, Susan B. (2006). "Predictors of U.S. College Students' Participation in Study Abroad Programs: A Longitudinal Study," *International Journal of Intercultural Relations* 30(4): 507–521.

Grossman, Claudio (1996). "Projecting the Washington College of Law into the Future," *American University Law Review* 45(4): 937–945.

International Institute for the Unification of Private Law [UNIDROIT] (2010). UNIDROIT Principles of International Commercial Contracts, art. 1.6(2).

Isphording, Ingo Eduard and Sebastian Otten (2013). "The Costs of Babylon—Linguistic Distance in Applied Economics," *Review of International Economics* 21(2): 354–369.

Krishnan, Jayanth K. and Vitor M. Dias (2015). "The Aspiring and Globalizing Graduate Law Student: A Comment on the Lazarus-Black and Globokar LL.M. Study," *Indiana Journal of Global Legal Studies* 22(1): 81–93.

Law, David S. (2008). "Globalization and the Future of Constitutional Rights," *Northwestern University Law Review* 102(3): 1277–1349.

Law School Survey of Student Engagement (2004). "2004 Annual Survey Results," *Student Engagement in Law Schools: A First Look*. https://lssse.indiana.edu/wp-content/uploads/2016/01/LSSSE-2004-Annual-Survey-Results.pdf

Lazarus-Black, Mindie and Julie Globokar (2015). "Foreign Attorneys in U.S. LL.M. Programs: Who's In, Who's Out, and Who They Are," *Indiana Journal of Global Legal Studies* 22(1): 3–65.

Lewin, Ross (2009). "Introduction: The Quest for Global Citizenship Through Study Abroad," in Ross Lewin, ed., *The Handbook of Practice and Research in Study Abroad*. Pp. xiii–xxii. Routledge.

Lewis, Margaret K. (2009). "International Law Takes Center Stage in Legal Education," *The National Law Journal*. September 7. LexisNexis.

Loungani, Prakash, Saurabh Mishra, Chris Papageorgiou, and Ke Wang (2017). *World Trade in Services: Evidence from a New Dataset*, International Monetary Fund, Working Paper No. 17/77, 34, fig. 16.

Maxeiner, James R. (2008). "Learning from Others: Sustaining the Internationalization and Globalization of U.S. Law School Curriculum," *Fordham International Law Journal* 32(1): 32–54.

McDonough, Patricia M. (1997). *Choosing Colleges: How Social Class and Schools Structure Opportunity*. State University of New York Press.

Melitz, Jacques (2008). "Language and Foreign Trade," *European Economic Review* 52(4): 667–699.

NAFSA (n.d.). Trends in U.S. Study Abroad. http://www.nafsa.org/Policy_and_Advocacy/Policy_Resources/Policy_Trends_and_Data/Trends_in_U_S__Study_Abroad/.

National Association for Law Placement [NALP] (2017). *Perspectives on 2016 Law Student Recruiting*. Washington DC: National Association for Law Placement, Inc.

New York University (2010). Global Network University Reflection. Accessed June 26, 2020. https://www.nyu.edu/about/leadership-university-administration/office-of-the-president-emeritus/communications/global-network-university-reflection.html.

New York University (n.d.). Global Programs and Research. Accessed June 26, 2020. https://www.nyu.edu/about/leadership-university-administration/office-of-the-president/office-of-the-provost/global-programs.html.

New York University School of Law (n.d.). Before You Apply, New York University School of Law. Accessed November 14, 2017. https://www.law.nyu.edu/global/globalopportunities/nyulawabroad/before.

New York University School of Law (2012). *Board of Trustees Strategy Committee Report and Recommendations* (October). New York: New York University School of Law. http://www.law.nyu.edu/sites/default/files/ECM_PRO_073917.pdf

New York University School of Law (2013). NYU Law Announces Ambitious New Study-Abroad Program as Part of Curricular Enhancements Emphasizing Focused Study in Third Year. Accessed June 24, 2020. http://www.law.nyu.edu/news/nyu_law_announces_study-abroad_program_curricular_enhancements_third_year.

New York University School of Law (2017). Application Procedure. Accessed November 17, 2017. http://www.law.nyu.edu/global/globalopportunities/nyulawabroad/application.

New York University School of Law (2017). NYU Law Abroad. Accessed June 26, 2020. http://www.law.nyu.edu/global/globalopportunities/nyulawabroad.

New York University School of Law (n.d.). John Sexton: Biography. Accessed November 14, 2017. https://its.law.nyu.edu/facultyprofiles/index.cfm?fuseaction=profile.overv iew&personid=20281.

New York University School of Law (n.d.). Prospective Exchange Students: General Information. Accessed November 14, 2017. http://www.law.nyu.edu/global/globalop portunities/incomingexchangestudents.

Paulsen, Michael B. (2001). "The Economics of Human Capital and Investment in Higher Education," in Michael B. Paulsen and John C. Smart, eds., *The Finance of Higher Education: Theory, Research, Policy & Practice*. Pp. 55–94. Agathon Press.

Perna, Laura W. (2006). "Studying College Access and Choice: A Proposed Conceptual Model," in John C. Smart, ed., *Higher Education: Handbook of Theory and Research*, vol. 21. Pp. 99–157. Springer.

Rabin, Matthew (1998). "Psychology and Economics," *Journal of Economic Literature* 36(1): 11–46.

Roberts, Anthea (2017). *Is International Law International?* Oxford University Press.

Salisbury, Mark H. et al. (2009). "Going Global: Understanding the Choice Process of the Intent to Study Abroad," *Research in Higher Education* 50(2): 119–143.

Salisbury, Mark H. et al. (2010). "To See the World or Stay at Home: Applying an Integrated Student Choice Model to Explore the Gender Gap in the Intent to Study Abroad," *Research in Higher Education* 51(7): 615–640.

Salisbury, Mark H. et al. (2011). "Why Do All the Study Abroad Students Look Alike? Applying an Integrated Student Choice Model to Explore Differences in the Factors that Influence White and Minority Students' Intent to Study Abroad," *Research in Higher Education* 52(2): 123–150.

Sánchez, Gloria M. (1997). "A Paradigm Shift in Legal Education: Preparing Law Students for the Twenty-First Century: Teaching Foreign Law, Culture, and Legal Language of the Major U.S. American Trading Partners," *San Diego Law Review* 34(2): 635–679.

Sexton, John Edward (1996). "The Global Law School Program at New York University," *Journal of Legal Education* 46(3): 329–335.

Sexton, John Edward (2001). "Curricular Responses to Globalization," *Penn State International Law Review* 20(1): 15–18.

Sexton, John Edward (2001). "Out of the Box Thinking About the Training of Lawyers in the Next Millennium," *University of Toledo Law Review* 33(1): 189–202.

Shah, Maulik (2010). "The Legal Education Bubble: How Law Schools Should Respond to Changes in the Legal Market," *Georgetown Journal of Legal Ethics* 23(3): 843–58.

Silver, Carole. 2013. "Getting Real About Globalization and Legal Education: Potential and Perspectives for the U.S.," *Stanford Law and Policy Review* 24(2): 457–501.

Silver, Carole and Swethaa S. Ballakrishnen (2018). "Sticky Floors, Springboards, Stairways & Slow Escalators: Mobility Pathways and Preferences of International Students in U.S. Law Schools," *University of California Irvine Journal of International, Transnational, and Comparative Law* 3: 39–70.

Simon, Jennifer and James W. Ainsworth (2012). "Race and Socioeconomic Status Differences in Study Abroad Participation: The Role of Habitus, Social Networks, and Cultural Capital," *ISRN Education*. 2012. Article ID 413896. http://www.hindawi.com/ journals/isrn/2012/413896/.

Stevens, Mitchell L. (2009). *Creating a Class: College Admissions and the Education of Elites*. Harvard University Press.

Stigler, George J. and Gary S. Becker (1977). "De Gustibus Non Est Disputandum," *American Economic Review* 67(2): 76–90.

Stroud, April H. (2010) "Who Plans (Not) to Study Abroad? An Examination of U.S. Student Intent," *Journal of Studies in International Education* 14(5): 491–507.

Thomas, Chantal (2000). "Globalization and the Reproduction of Hierarchy," *University of California Davis Law Review* 33(4): 1451–1501.

Trachtman, Joel P. (2010). "The International Law of Financial Crisis?," *American Society of International Law Proceedings* 104: 295–299.

United Nations Conference on Trade and Development (2017). *World Investment Report 2017*.

United Nations Convention on Contracts for the International Sale of Goods, U.N. Doc. A/CONF 97/19 (April 11, 1980).

U.S. News & World Report (n.d.). "Find the Best Law Schools." https://www.usnews.com/best-graduate-schools/top-law-schools.

Valcke, Catherine (2004). "Global Law Teaching," *Journal of Legal Education* 54(2): 160–182.

White, James P. (2007). "A Look at Legal Education: The Globalization of American Legal Education," *Indiana Law Journal* 82(5): 1285–1292.

World Bank Group (n.d.). Exports of Goods and Services (% of GDP). Accessed February 8, 2018. https://data.worldbank.org/indicator/NE.EXP.GNFS.ZS.

World Bank Group (n.d.). Foreign Direct Investment, Net Inflows (BoP, Current US$). Accessed February 8, 2018. https://data.worldbank.org/indicator/BX.KLT.DINV.CD.WD.

World Bank Group (n.d.). Foreign Direct Investment, Net Outflows (BoP, Current US$). Accessed February 8, 2018. https://data.worldbank.org/indicator/BM.KLT.DINV.CD.WD.

World Bank Group (n.d.). International Tourism, Expenditures (% of Total Imports). Accessed February 8, 2018. https://data.worldbank.org/indicator/ST.INT.XPND.MP.ZS.

World Bank Group (n.d.). International Tourism, Receipts (% of Total Exports). Accessed February 8, 2018. https://data.worldbank.org/indicator/ST.INT.RCPT.XP.ZS.

World Trade Organization (2017). *World Trade Statistical Review 2017*.

Yale University Law School (2017). What to Do When You Don't Get an Offer from Your Summer Employer. https://law.yale.edu/student-life/career-development/students/career-guides-advice/what-do-when-you-dont-get-offer (webpage no longer accessible).

Yale University Law School (n.d.). International Law. Accessed December 1, 2017. https://law.yale.edu/study-law-yale/areas-study/international-law.

12

"Have Law Books, Computer, Simulations—Will Travel"

The Transnationalization of (Some of) the Law Professoriate

*Carrie Menkel-Meadow**

After graduating from Brandeis in 1975, I decided to study with the masters of Middle Eastern Studies—the British. I enrolled at St. Antony's College, Oxford University, where I took a master's degree in the history and politics of the modern Middle East. St. Anthony's was everything I hoped for by way of formal education, but I learned as much in the dining room as in the classroom. As the center of Middle Eastern studies in England, St. Antony's attracted the very best students from the Arab world and Israel . . . I learned to be a good listener, though, and there was plenty to listen to.

—From Beirut to Jerusalem, Thomas L. Friedman (1989, 6–7)

I. Introduction: The Peripatetic Law Professor and Her Data Sources

This chapter chronicles the "transnationalization" of some of the law professoriate. In a book about empirical studies of the globalization of legal

* Thanks to audiences at the University of California Irvine conference on the Globalization of Legal Education, Sept. 8–9, 2017; the Center for Transnational Legal Studies Tenth Anniversary Conference at the University of Toronto, June 21–22, 2018; the conference on Research on Legal Education at the University of New South Wales, Dec. 3–5, 2017; and conference on Challenges to Legal Education in a Globalized World at Haifa University, May 21–25, 2018, for comments on various versions of this chapter. Thank you to Silvia Faerman, Orna Rabinovich-Einy, Victor V. Ramraj, Bryant Garth, Alain Verbeke, Chiara Besso, Loukas Mistelis, Katherine Lynch, Franz Werro, Joel Lee, and Robert Meadow, some of my fellow travelers in my legal education journeys. Thanks to Lynda Bui and Alex Cadena for editorial and research assistance.

Carrie Menkel-Meadow, *"Have Law Books, Computer, Simulations—Will Travel"* In: *The Globalization of Legal Education*. Edited by: Bryant Garth & Gregory Shaffer, Oxford University Press. © Oxford University Press 2022. DOI: 10.1093/oso/9780197632314.003.0012 education, this chapter is empirical in the sense of my own participant observations from teaching in over two dozen countries, teaching law students, and interacting with law faculty, from all over the world. My point is simple—to the extent that both faculty and students can study law in more than one country, in more than one legal system, their knowledge of the world and their ability to be well-educated professionals can be transformed by "transnational" legal knowledge. "Globalization" of legal education can occur domestically by study of international law in one's own country, but to be truly "transnational" in my view, education must occur outside of one's own home. Transnational legal education is more than "legal"—it must be cultural as well. Or, as my sociolegal discipline puts it—Law in Context![1] Or as I prefer, Law in Many Contexts!

This chapter is offered in celebration of the tenth anniversary of the Center for Transnational Legal Studies (CTLS). CTLS (conceived at Georgetown University, by then dean Alex Aleinikoff and a committee on international legal education on which I served (see https://www.law.georgetown.edu/ctls/), is a program of legal education for students from over twenty different countries, who study together, where no one is "home," in London, and are taught by professors from different institutions, educated in many different legal systems—civil, common, religious (e.g., *shari'a*) and hybrid systems of law, on many different subjects.

This chapter also reflects on some of my own experiences of teaching in twenty-six different countries, on five continents (whether as full-time, part-time, or visiting faculty) and in several of the United States' largest LLM programs (with foreign students, e.g., Georgetown and Harvard), and is also based on interviews with both students and faculty in those programs. Over the last few decades I have taught in a variety of regional legal education programs (e.g., INCAE (Instituto Centroamericano de Administración de Empresas in Central America),[2] Erasmus in Europe, National University of Singapore (Chen-Han 2017; Chesterman 2008), and in a variety of law school summer programs, both American and international, that include students and faculty from different countries. I have also participated in

---

[1] As first imagined by William Twining and others, Cambridge University Press has long published a series of Law-in-Context texts, combining legal doctrine with sociolegal and cultural materials. See, e.g., Twining 2000; Roberts, and Palmer 2020.

[2] INCAE has two campuses, one in Managua, Nicaragua, and the other in San Jose, Costa Rica. I have taught several times on both campuses. Students come from all over Central American and a few South American countries to study in executive education format for MBA or LLM equivalents, using Harvard Case Study methods and, for me, active clinical simulation and role-play education.

or directed several programs to teach law professors how to teach (particularly how to add "experiential" learning to the more common diet of didactic lecture (Wilson 2009),[3] in places as diverse as China, the United Kingdom, Mexico, Israel (see Menkel-Meadow and Nutenko 2009; Munin and Efron 2017), and Norway). I have also been retained to evaluate legal education programs in a wide variety of countries by universities, accrediting bodies, and private foundations and funders. Finally, I have been part of several initiatives to bring transnational and international legal education into required programs in American law schools (e.g., "Week One: Law in a Global Context" at Georgetown, and the now required first-year course in International Legal Analysis at the University of California, Irvine (Menkel-Meadow 2011), which spawned the school-wide student initiative, the Global Justice Summit, see section IV.[4]

"Transnational" legal education now takes many forms—study abroad programs for students, during full semesters or years, summer programs, faculty exchanges, graduate law programs (including LLM, SJD, and PhD), formal appointments of "Global" faculty either visiting or shared between several universities,[5] distinguished practitioner visits,[6] externships in legal institutions both within and outside of a student's home country,[7] and a wide array of international, transnational, and comparative law courses in both

---

[3] I participated in 2007–2009 in a program developed by Tsinghua University and Temple University to teach Chinese law professors how to teach experientially, in conventional law classes (an antidote to replication of either Socratic American models or didactic lecture of Europe). I have taught with these methods in courses on five continents and have observed the popular uptake of more active learning in a variety of law school settings, see work of Joel Lee and Helena Whelan Bridges at NUS, Alain Verbeke in Belgium, Holland, and Portugal, the LLM program in Dispute Resolution at the University of Hong Kong (Katherine Lynch, Shahla Ali), and some of the new clinical programs in Argentina and Chile, see discussion of GAJE below, *infra* note 41.

[4] For other efforts to encourage mandatory international law study, see United Nations General Assembly Resolution 44/23 announcing 1990 as the "decade of international law" and encouraging the teaching of public international law; Institut de Droit International 1997; Ali 2013.

[5] NYU was probably the first law school in the United States to have a formal "Global law professor" designation, but "foreign" visitors from one nation to another for lecturing is as old as the original European universities in Bologna, Paris, Leuven, and other of the first European law faculties. "Visiting" law lecturers in the old days were actually more able to "travel" without computers and simulations, but with Latin or other common languages for the elite educated. For modern accounts of transnational legal education programs, see, e.g., Roberts 2022 (Chapter 14, this volume); Jamin and Van Caenegem 2016; Gane and Huang 2016.

[6] Former Supreme Court and international court justices, such as Aahron Barack (Israel), Richard Goldstone (South Africa), Michael Kirby (Australia), and Albie Sacks (South Africa) are frequent visiting law professors in many law faculties in the United States and Europe.

[7] In the Southwestern–Universidad de Buenos Aires summer program in which I taught for many summers, students fluent in Spanish were able to extern in the Argentine Supreme Court, as well as with judges, prosecutors, and some private attorneys. There is nothing like being "inside" another legal system (at all of its levels) to educate law students about how law is administered in different political and legal contexts.

public and private law subjects, including mandatory courses in international law in some schools and now including international law clinics (e.g., human rights).

Modern law students can study law from a comparative and theoretical perspective, in classes, as well as by immersion in a particular job, with international and transnational border-crossing practices. The increasing number of international venues for lawmaking, interpretation, and enforcement (from international, national, regional courts, hybrid arbitral bodies (e.g., International Center for the Settlement of Investment Disputes) to multinational legislative bodies; e.g., the European Parliament, and now transnational administrative governance (see, e.g., Halliday and Shaffer 2014; Krisch, Kingsbury, and Stewart 2005)) allows students to see legal norms being created, negotiated, adjudicated, and somewhat differentially enforced.

For me, the basic theme has been for students to understand the concepts and applications of legal pluralism in which legal problems are situated in different contexts and countries, often with both formal and informal choices of law and choices of venues (Berman 2007; Michaels 2009; Merry 1988), preferably through study away from one's own legal home. Transnational law is a complex system of potentially applicable norms, rules, and practices, which are enacted in law offices, private negotiations, public diplomacy, private mediation, or arbitration settings, and in a wide variety of regional and international formal tribunals. Unlike most national systems, ordered by vertical hierarchies of laws and institutions, the transnational world is more varied, horizontal, and complex with both overlapping and also potentially conflicting rulings.[8] There is no Supreme Court of the World to smooth out conflicting interpretations—the International Court of Justice is a court of limited and voluntary jurisdiction of disputes between states, not able to deal

---

[8] As a theoretical (and empirical) matter transnational legal and sociolegal scholars debate whether there is too much "fragmentation" (or, as some have argued, too much "assemblage" or "bricolage" without definitive legal ordering, Sassen 2006, or whether the increase in various forms of both hard and soft law lead to a denser set of legal norms, providing more, rather than less, global governance, see, e.g., Halliday and Shaffer 2014; Abbott and Snidal 2000; Shaffer and Pollack 2010; Ahdieh 2004). Both scholars and students experience these large jurisprudential issues better, in my view, when engaged in truly transnational (and subject-matter diversity) legal education. Ideally, the modern transnational law student will study this question in different locations to actually experience the issues. Consider, for example, the difference in treatment of American civil rights claims (in a federal system) from human rights violation claims in a nation in the European Union (with the doctrine of "margin of appreciation"). I teach the "veiling" issues from the varied treatment in different countries as an illustration of modern pluralistic complexity, see R (Begum) v. Headteacher and Governors of Denbigh High School, (2006) UKHL 15; S.A.S. v. France, 2014 Eur. Ct. H.R. 695 (2014); Ferrari and Pastorelli 2013.

with many actors in the modern world—individuals, groups, subnational, and transnational entities (think both multinational corporations and terrorist groups). While no single legal system, including the formal international/regional courts and tribunals (now over twenty-six of them (Alter 2014; Shany 2014)) can provide a single international legal order, the multiplicity of institutions, tribunals, rule systems, codes, dispute processes, and soft law now present a staggering set of norms and processes to regulate both domestic and border crossing activity. We are all legal pluralists now.

True transnational legal education will depend on many competencies—intellectual and analytic, yes, but also interpersonal cultural competencies, language skills (see Raume and Pinto 2012), and the ability to negotiate collaboratively with those whose value systems may be different. Ironically, graduates of cosmopolitan transnational legal programs may have more commonalities with each other in their elite statuses than they may have with their own countrymen.[9] At the same time, modern communication technologies may also make distance learning (many countries now have on line master of law programs) possible to increase access to such education, and, as some hope, thereby "democratize" legal education (Aleinikoff 2007).

Like Thomas Friedman, I have learned much by listening to others—both faculty and students—from different legal cultures, and I hope I have contributed to the transnationalization of legal education by introducing a wide variety of teaching modalities and concepts in universities and legal programs hungry to diversify teaching from didactic lectures, and to incorporate the knowledge bases of an increasingly diverse global student body that often migrates from one system to another in preparation for being a well-educated modern transnational lawyer. Whether or not students, professors, or lawyers actually practice or teach in different jurisdictions, there is no question that all legal work is now affected by laws, legal institutions, and legal cultures that cross boundaries, comprising a new form of "transnational legal studies" (Menkel-Meadow 2011; Aleinikoff 2007, 2006; Sugarman and Sherr 2001; Chesterman 2009; Zumbansen 2000). Again, like Thomas Friedman's graduate education at Oxford, my hope has been that when people from different cultures study together and break bread together (not to mention, drink at pubs, or go dancing together, or yes, even marrying each other[10]),

---

[9] For arguments about the growing cosmopolitan elite status of international lawyers, see, e.g., Dezalay and Garth 1988.

[10] I have been following many of the international romances that have begun at CTLS or other transnational programs in which I have taught! To the extent that legal licenses are still nationally based, this presents a huge problem for internationally diverse lawyer partners.

they will learn more than the "law on the books" and will come to see both the commonalities and differences in their legal systems.[11]

Law and legal rules are chosen, not given (except in some colonial and religious-based legal systems) and so learning about how different groups of societies choose solutions to particular social and legal problems can only be enhanced, in my view, by study of different choices made in different legal systems. And, as noted by scholars such as William Twining (law) and Anthony Giddens (sociology), law is increasingly pervasive in all aspects of social life, including the local. "Globalization is the intensification of world-wide social relations which link distant localities in such a way that local happenings are shaped by events occurring many miles away and vice versa" (Giddens 1990). A good modern legal education, must, in my view be trans-national, including the local,[12] national, *inter-national* (the law of states relations), and *trans-national* (all the legal rules and legal institutions that affect transactions, disputes, and relations of people, services, and products that cross national boundaries) (Twining 2009). Law professors who learn and teach in different countries can enhance their own transnational knowledge, even in a field, like law, which remains state/sovereignty-based.[13]

At both theoretical and practical levels, truly transnational legal education raises questions about legal hegemony, diffusion, and transplantation of legal ideas, practices, and power. While earlier generations (Galanter and Trubek 1974) and critical legal studies scholars (see, e.g., Kennedy 2006) (I am a member of both of these groups) eventually came to decry the export of American ideas (whether "neo-liberal economics" (Dezalay and Garth 2002; Mattei and Nader 2008) or American constitutional ideas and interpretations (Choudry 2006)) and newer scholars continue to document the one-way flows of legal "transplantation" (Watson 1993; LeGrand 1997), education,

---

[11] For a thoughtful analysis of the different locations or venues for actual legal education (including the formal and informal interactional, especially in diverse student bodies), see Israel, Skead, Heath, Hewitt, Galloway, and Steel 2017.

[12] Saskia Sassen and Scott Bollens, among others, have argued that the city is the best place from which to study the interactions of the local, national, and international. See, e.g., Bollens 2012; Sassen 2006.

[13] Anthea Roberts has documented that most of the law professoriate is limited in its training, with the vast majority of law professors earning their degrees from a single jurisdiction, see Roberts 2022 (Chapter 14, this volume). In my recent experience, however, there is a growing diversity of legal training and nationalities in many of the world's leading universities. As examples consider some places where I have taught: Queen Mary Commercial Law Center (Italians, Greeks, Dutch, and many other nationals of international experience on the faculty); also in the United Kingdom, King's College of Law Faculty, Oxford, Cambridge, UCL; and in Asia, National University of Singapore, University of Hong Kong, and now some of the new Chinese and Japanese law schools, see, e.g., McConnaughay and Toomey 2022 (Chapter 10, this volume).

and interpretation (Nicola 2018; Roberts 2017), others of us see increasing influence of non-American sources and interpretations of law (Barak 2002; Law and Versteeg 2012). True transnational legal education should induce a form of humility about any one way of "solving" legal problems and an openness to other legal configurations and interpretations (see Menkel-Meadow 2011) (e.g., most notably, as examples, the increasing influence of the Canadian Charter of Human Rights, the South African Constitution, and decisions of the European Court of Human Rights on interpretations of legal rights outside of the United States).[14] True transnational and comparative legal education allows professors to challenge the received wisdom of their own legal educations, often formed within single legal systems, establishing a sort of intellectual hegemony in their minds and legal education practices, and when well-practiced, allows both students and professors from different legal environments to learn from each other.

II. Some Illustrations from CTLS and Points Beyond

The Center for Transnational Legal Studies was founded in 2008 by Georgetown University and ten other law schools: King's College (United Kingdom), Melbourne (Australia), Frei Universitat (Germany), ESADE (Spain), Hebrew University (Israel), Fribourg (Switzerland), Universidad di Sao Paulo (Brazil), University of Torino (Italy), University of Toronto (Canada), National University of Singapore (and later joined by universities from Mexico, Chile, Korea, Colombia, Portugal, the Netherlands, New Zealand, India, China, and Russia). Students attend for either one semester or a full year and are taught by faculty from participating schools. There are usually between 150 and 175 students a year in the program, and all students receive a "Certificate in Transnational Legal Studies" and credit for their work in their home institutions. Given the credit allocations, most students take four courses per semester while in attendance (getting academic credit for the required core course, the transnational colloquium, and the Global Practice Exercise). Each semester a rich and different set of courses is offered, depending on faculty expertise, while an effort is made to balance private law offerings (e.g., international business transactions, comparative corporate

---

[14] For an elaboration of different models of consideration of "outside" sources of legal interpretation, see Jackson 2010; Breyer 2015.

governance, international commercial arbitration) with public law offerings (e.g., human rights, humanitarian law, international organizations, comparative constitutionalism, emergencies law, refugee and immigration law), and some "mixed" or interdisciplinary theory or policy courses (e.g., language rights, trade policy, intellectual property policy, transnational health policy, international dispute resolution).

In original design, each course was to be taught by at least two professors from different legal systems (common-civil law or "mixed" systems, e.g. Israel, Canada[15]) to offer an explicit comparative approach to all subjects.[16] The design has not always been feasible in practice, but efforts are made to infuse all courses with comparative content. Several core aspects of the program include an introductory "Global Practice Exercise" of a week of intensive study and "practice" of some global legal problem (e.g., international arbitration or criminal extradition) in diverse groups of students, a "Core" course of introduction to transnational and comparative law concepts, which has varied from theoretical, jurisprudential, and philosophical treatments to comparative law study of discrete legal problems (e.g., privacy policy, migration, contracts, torts) and a sociolegal approach to cultural variations in law (Jessup 1956; Koh 2006, 1996; Darian-Smith 2016), and a mandatory seminar/colloquium of exposure to the new and leading scholarship of participating faculty and other transnational legal scholars.

I was on the Georgetown committee that helped conceptualize the program and wrote the first Global Practice Exercise (a transnational employment problem, providing choice of law, venue, and dispute resolution tribunals issues). To date, about 1,200 students and 125 faculty from participating schools (about 20) from around the globe have participated in the program. CTLS has also sponsored several academic conferences and dedicated lecture programs on transnational legal education, international criminal law, language rights, international migration, privacy, contract law, human rights, and other subjects. The program has also encouraged (some, but not enough in my view) joint scholarly projects (see, e.g., Arjona, Jamal, Menkel-Meadow, Ramrai, and Satiro 2012; Luban and Mezey 2014). Faculty in residence have participated in book groups, seminars, and informal intellectual

---

[15] The University of Victoria has just begun a "transsystemic" program of Canadian and indigenous law, see JD/JID (common law–indigenous law) degree: https://www.uvic.ca/law/about/indigenous/jid/index.php.

[16] Or what one law professor has labeled "Transsystemic Legal Education" (Strauss 2006).

discussion or "salons" on a variety of topics (e.g., teaching to a culturally diverse student body).

The program began in the fall of 2009, with the first Global Practice Exercise, with small groups of nationally diverse students engaging in reading fact situations, legal authorities from different systems, an employment contract, and the rules of courts and international arbitral tribunals. In small groups, all students worked in English, although for some students, English was their second, third, fourth, or even fifth language. One of my students, who was working in his fourth language, was concerned about how he was going to make a ten-minute closing argument to an international arbitration panel, when he had never spoken English out loud to such a large audience and had never engaged in a moot exercise in his own traditional European university. I counseled him, and he gave the best (more creative and most cogent) argument in the group. I kept in touch with him—years later he completed an LLM at Harvard (with, as it turned out, two other CTLS students in his class)—and he is now a young lawyer in an international practice in his own country. I have volunteered to be his reference for life, and he continues to follow my own work in his country and in my legal scholarship as we continue our mutual transnational legal studies.

At the end of the Global Practice Exercise (an intense week of classes, lectures, student performances, and some writing) the program celebrates with a party in Regent's Park and eventually the students peel off in groups to sleep, find their families, or go on to party. Imagine this teacher's delight when a group of intense German and Israeli students asked if I would accompany them to continue their substantive argument about how the Global Practice Exercise should actually be handled in a multijurisdictional setting. Some of these students knew that I was the daughter of Holocaust refugees, so consider how the intense engagement of a new generation of Germans and Israelis together forging relationships that would move on to transnational contacts in the future made my heart sing. Yes, both I and Thomas Friedman know that personal relationships are not enough to prevent war, or hostile relationships and stereotyping, but for us peace-and-justice seeking legal educators, this is still a momentous start and reframing of the world order at the individual level (Slaughter 2004).

Transnational legal education can work in many ways, however, and we optimistic transnationalists should know that we cannot control how people learn to think when opened to new materials and information. On my return to the first year of CTLS some months later I was in conversation with several students who had studied with our inaugural director, distinguished civil libertarian and litigator for human rights, Professor David Cole (and Professor Colm O'Cinneide of the University College of London law faculty) in a course on Comparative Approaches to Counterterrorism and Human Rights. A group of students from European universities who, like their professors, were strongly opposed to torture in counterterrorism efforts, told me they had changed their mind about the appropriate uses of some forms of torture when they listened to the stories of their Israeli classmates (all of whom had likely served in the Israeli Defense Forces before attending law school). As Thomas Friedman says, learning by dining and living together can be as dramatic and influential as formal education. Such learning cannot be predicted to go in any one direction.

The "Core" course or Introduction to Transnational and Comparative Law has been an exciting intellectual challenge for discussion among faculty from different legal systems and viewpoints. In my own year of teaching with my colleague Franz Werro (jointly appointed at Georgetown and the University of Fribourg), we debated whether there was such a viable concept as "transnational law," as I argued that such processes as commercial arbitration exist in transnational "space" with its own transnational *lex mercatoria*, legitimation, and justifications (Paulsson 2013; Gaillard 2010; Schultz 2014), and Professor Werro argued there could be no law unmoored from formal state institutions (Roberts 2005; Teubner 1997). Arbitration enforcement, for example, depends on international treaties—for example, the New York Convention on the Recognition and Enforcement of Foreign Arbitral Awards (1956) and the Washington Convention (1965) on International Investment Arbitration, both of which, in turn, depend on national courts to resolve disputes about recognition, enforcement, or vacatur. But, most private commercial international arbitration occurs in private hearings, based on transborder contracts, with rules of procedure chosen by the parties, and derived from rules of private arbitral tribunals. Party consent, not formal legal command, is the mantra of this form of international dispute resolution. Other professors who teach this course must jointly reconcile different jurisprudential approaches or choose different subject areas to develop comparative law perspectives on how legal pluralism operates across systems. We also used several experiential exercises, such as having students draft transnational privacy regulations, negotiate a language policy for the program, and debate the advantages and disadvantages of using foreign sources in legal decisions and the merits or disadvantages of requiring "consideration" for contract formation (difference in Anglo-American and civil code jurisdictions). Different core course teachers have emphasized different issues, including colonialism and imperialism in lawmaking, alternative legal systems, both in process (ADR, indigenous processes) and substance (*shari'a* law), code versus common law, different legal remedies in different systems, "crimmigration," in the transnational context, disputes about the role of law in ameliorating poverty and injustice, and whether "globalization" is a good development or not (see, e.g., Sornarajah 2011, 2015; Riddich 2006: 203).

In one of my favorite student encounters in this course, a student (from Melbourne and now a practicing lawyer in Australia and my friend, as well as mentee) queried us to consider whether the international rules and customs of dueling (before international courts and tribunals existed) could be considered a form of transnational legal ordering (see Yarn 2000). He also got me to focus on art theft as a transnational legal issue, and CTLS has now offered a course on the subject.[17] For many students in this course, engagement with issues of the "law in action" or sociolegal approaches to law, as well as theoretical and philosophy of law questions, were a departure from their more conventional doctrinal courses at home. In some iterations of the core course, explicit instruction on the sociology of the globalization of the legal profession is also provided (see Sokol 2007; Silver 2000; Terry 2008).

Students are also required to participate in faculty colloquia as scholars present and query each other on the latest issues in international and transnational law, outside of conventional course categories, including such issues as whether there is convergence or divergence in legal doctrinal development in the various legal harmonization projects (in contract, personal injury, and other private law subjects), as well as challenges faced in such transborder problems as counterterrorism and human rights, privacy, antitrust regulation, international trade, and the laws of war and peace. Outside speakers also present cutting-edge practice issues from different areas of law (international criminal law, environmental law, discrimination law, human rights with proportionality and "margins of appreciation" doctrine, and international business transaction issues).

The program has also sponsored international legal film nights, viewing films dealing with different legal proceedings, humanitarian and war films, human rights films,[18] and films about legal scandals (such as Enron) to

---

[17] Taught by Prof. Christian Ambruster of Germany.
[18] For a partial filmography, see Menkel-Meadow 2016.

enliven discussions of variable state treatment of such issues as human rights, corporate social responsibility, financial regulation, antitrust, and migration policy. An international audience of faculty and students makes such film-viewing a wonderful opportunity for comparative dialogue and exchange.

In a location such as London, education in the classroom is supplemented with class field trips to courts (e.g., UK Supreme Court, the International Court of Justice and the International Criminal Court in The Hague, the International Court of Sport in Lausanne, ordinary criminal and civil courts), tribunals (labor and employment and other specialty sites of adjudication), mediation and arbitration proceedings (London Court of International Arbitration and the International Chamber of Commerce Arbitration Court in Paris), and various public hearings. In one of the most creative courses offered at CTLS, Helena Whalen-Bridge of Singapore taught a course in comparative advocacy[19] by having students study and then "moot" different kinds of hearings in different kinds of courts and tribunals in different countries at different levels of adjudication. When I was on the faculty at CTLS, I was able to sit on the bench of three different UK courts as a guest of sitting judges[20] and to experience being an English judge in both jury (criminal) and judge (civil) proceedings, with my students in attendance for private briefings on comparative judicial decision-making. In recent years, students have been provided with programs on career development for transnational lawyers and some opportunities to work in legal settings.

As another illustration from the extended CTLS family,[21] consider a course on transnational law taught at National University of Singapore by my CTLS colleague, Victor V. Ramraj. In the first class (in which I participated as a student), Professor Ramraj asked his students to draw on a world map patterns of world trade in different centuries. (He was working on a scholarly project on the British East India Company (Bose and Ramraj forthcoming)). In a multinational class of students, Asian students could plot the Silk Road and Asian sea routes but had little to no knowledge of what I could do—plot the three (western) continent slave trade of the seventeenth and eighteenth

---

[19] Comparative Legal Argument and Narrative. See Whalen-Bridge 2016.

[20] Thank you to judges John Toulmin, Nick Madge, and Carlos Dabezias. Thanks also to Justice Brenda Hale for arranging tours of the UK Supreme Court and for presenting to our students on the issues of judging on a high court, as did US Supreme Court Justice Ruth Bader Ginsburg (in 2010).

[21] CTLS faculty now constitute a large transnational extended family, as do student alums. CTLS faculty have taught not only at the "mothership" in London but also have visited at the partner schools. I have taught full courses at the Universities of Toronto, Torino, Fribourg, Melbourne, and Singapore, and have lectured at Hebrew University, King's College, Diego Portales, UNAM, and several of the "non-partner" affiliates.

centuries. When our student-drawn maps could be combined over time and place, we had a much richer (and multicultural) understanding of just how old and varied transnational trade (and its customs, rules, and practices) were. Note, as well, that the departure from professorial didactic lecturing encouraged group discussion and student participation in learning both history and law. Globalization is not new—it is as old as many ancient civilizations; it is just now easier for those of us affected by it to study together and share ideas about its consequences and possible legal regulation.

III. Comparisons to Other Forms of Global Legal Education

Both before and after my participation in CTLS, I have taught in a wide variety of other countries in full semester or shorter form Visiting Professor appointments. As a faculty member at Georgetown and a Visiting Professor at Harvard, Stanford, and other universities, I have also been able to interact with visiting professors from many other countries, and, over the last twenty years, to teach hundreds of foreign LLM students.[22] I have taught in regional programs, such as INCAE in Nicaragua and Costa Rica (which offers an LLM equivalent program over a 1–2 year period with short course residencies[23]),

---

[22] For many years I taught the Civil Procedure and Dispute Resolution section of Georgetown's Foundations of American Law program, a program open to foreign LLM students attending the United States' most prestigious law schools. This program is held for over a month in Washington, D.C., for students beginning LLM studies at about ten different universities. In addition to instruction in basic US law first-year subjects, students attend field trips to various levels of courts in Washington, including the Supreme Court and have social encounters with judges, lawyers, professors, and other law students. It is through this program that I have made dozens of lifetime friendships with foreign lawyers. Others, like Peter Strauss, who ran Columbia's LLM program for decades, or William Alford at Harvard, have similar experiences of an "extended family" of former students. After teaching at Harvard in 2001, my Harvard LLM students insisted on taking me out for dinner in New York after September 11, 2001, so we could talk about what had happened (many of them were working in New York law firms) and hug each other for reassurance.

[23] *Instituto Centroamericano de Administración de Empresas*, INCAE (Central American Institute of Business Administration), originally founded during the Alliance for Progress under the Kennedy administration, now has affiliations with Harvard (for an MBA modeled on Harvard Business School case studies) and Georgetown (for an executive LLM program in Law). I have taught in this program four times, using a "case" (and simulation) method to teach mediation, negotiation, arbitration, and informal dispute resolution, using materials from the United States and Central and South America. For a while I could teach in Spanish, but more often I work with translators, with whom I meet before the program to educate them about technical terms and concepts. My knowledge of Spanish is helpful to check the technical accuracy of translated legal terms. The INCAE program provided another interesting take on legal education. Some of the students were "sponsored" in scholarships by their employers, law firms, banks, governmental agencies, or other large organizations, and were required to submit papers after each course segment on how they would use what they had learned in that segment. While not all legal learning should be immediately usable, this form of academic

at Erasmus in Europe (which allows European first degree law students to study in other countries, making such classes diverse in nationality[24]), and in programs jointly sponsored by particular institutions to allow teaching in different venues and with students from different countries. Professor Franz Werro managed a joint Georgetown-Fribourg program of courses in the summer months that included students from over fifteen countries—some comparative (tort and privacy law) and some international (commercial arbitration). The latter course was co-taught by myself and Pierre Tercier, then the president of the International Chamber of Commerce Court of Arbitration, and met at locations in Switzerland, as well as the Paris office of the ICC. Global education, at its best, included simulations and preparation for an arbitration, interviews, and guest lectures from participants and administrators of international arbitration, and two professors with training in different systems and with some different views about leading issues in the field (Menkel-Meadow 2008).

Similarly, for many years I taught in a multischool, multinational (Argentina, the United States, Brazil) summer program in Buenos Aires, sponsored by Southwestern Law School in the United States, with participation of the University of Buenos Aires and the University of Salvador, administered by Professor Silvia Faerman. Co-teaching with my colleague Bryant Garth and French sociologist of law, Yves Dezalay, we focused, in this multinational environment, on sociolegal analysis of "neo-liberalism" and legal transplants in the study of "globalization" in South America.[25]

---

accountability and "education-for-use" is now reflected domestically as legal education regulators (e.g., ABA in the United States, new proposals in the United Kingdom) seek to demand more transparency in learning goals, outcomes, and measurement of competencies.

[24] I taught Feminist Legal Theory to a group of Erasmus students in Switzerland. With seven countries represented in the group, and legal differences in the legality of prostitution (some by nation, others by province or canton, as in Switzerland), we had quite spirited discussions about whether prostitution should be legalized. Only those from Anglo countries (the United Kingdom and the United States) seemed totally opposed to some forms of legalization and regulation (as opposed to students from Switzerland, Germany, Italy, the Netherlands, and Spain). One of my earliest comparative law memories is walking with my German-born father through the red-light district in Amsterdam (in the 1960s) and seeing how different nations and cultures differed so much from my own.

[25] To illustrate that globalization is not unidirectional, one can note that it was Argentina that led to McDonald's developing "sit-down" McCafes in many parts of the world. In a wonderful café society like Argentina, take-out coffee would not do! On a more somber note, globalization can also be observed in Argentina (and Chile) as the US College of the Americas military training was used to train military to effectuate "disappearances" during the dictatorships in the 1970s and 1980s in those countries (as well as in Paraguay, Brazil, and Uruguay). Though South Africa's Truth and Reconciliation Commission is probably most known to Americans, it was, in fact, South and Central Americans who first formed both truth and reconciliation commissions and bodies. See Hayner 2001; Dorfman 1991.

In other venues I have taught more conventional classes: international commercial arbitration, mediation, negotiation, legal ethics, and international dispute resolution in Italy, England, Singapore, Belgium, Chile, Paraguay, Canada, Australia, France, Hong Kong, and Israel, among others, but always with experiential, simulation, and role play components, often quite unusual in countries more used to large didactic lectures for undergraduate first degree law students. My students in International Dispute Resolution participate in multinational disarmament treaty negotiations, commercial mediation and arbitration sessions, legal and contract drafting exercises, and dispute system design exercises (e.g., creating processes for transitional justice or constitutional conventions).

In Australia, the University of Melbourne operates a unique master of law program that includes non-lawyers who may earn a degree by taking a wide variety of legal and policy courses in the law faculty. In Melbourne, I taught a wonderful group of students—who were mostly already formed professionals, from Australia, China, Indonesia, Malaysia, Cambodia, and New Guinea—the relatively new subject of "Dispute System Design," in which over a six-month period each student completed a project of designing a dispute system and a writing a paper and, where possible, tried to implement their plan. Students worked on such projects as managing disputes in the use of wind farms, developing a dispute resolution program for banks dealing with the mortgage foreclosure crisis, developing dispute systems for trade tariffs in Indonesia, creating a dispute system for abused children, their social workers, and the legal system, and creating a program for retired military claimants in a benefits program, among others. Most movingly for me, a transitional justice scholar, I was able to keep in touch, for several years, with a survivor of the Khmer Rouge regime, who was studying the effectiveness of the Extraordinary Courts in adjudicating claims for that atrocity, in which most of his family perished.[26]

As a scholar who works on transitional justice issues, the ability to teach in so many countries that have suffered atrocities, civil wars, genocides, and postconflict violence and regeneration or some reconciliation is priceless. As I watch other scholars parachute in for a few days to do interviews with lawyers, victims, prosecutors, judges, and advocates, or to live in one place long enough to do archival, as well as interview, work, it has been

---

[26] Sadly, since I taught that course I have been to Cambodia and have seen the effectiveness of the Court is quite abysmal. See White 2017.

extraordinary for me to be able to teach and work with students and local faculty (and their families) who have experienced both harms and efforts to either prosecute or reconcile those harms, especially for me in Paraguay, Brazil, Argentina, Chile (Menkel-Meadow 2015), Israel (Menkel-Meadow and Nutenko 2009), Northern Ireland, and Germany,[27] and also in jurisdictions now struggling to achieve different kinds of democracy and new governance systems: Singapore (see Tushnet 2015) and Hong Kong. The ability to learn from students, to live, for more than a few weeks or even months, within another country, from the place of actually working in the legal culture allows a "behind the doors" view of the operation of legal institutions and also an ability to see how laypeople process those legal developments. To be able to do so in a variety of different countries has permitted me a rare form of comparative legal knowledge.[28]

For students, the most common form of transnational legal education is the pursuit of a first degree in one's own country, followed by a second (LLM (Silver 2002, 2006, 2010, 2012a; Garth 2015; Hupper 2015, 2008, 2007; Kim 2016)) or third (SJD or PhD) degree in another country, except for an increasing number of students who now may dabble in transnational education by taking a semester or summer abroad. Initially both LLMs and doctoral degrees in law were intended primarily for those seeking academic positions. Now the LLM may have an additional "credentializing" effect in the competition for legal employment, and some LLM programs now offer important substantive specializations for practitioners, for example, in taxation, national security, dispute resolution, corporate governance, and international business (Silver 2012b; Ballakrishnen 2012).[29] For American law schools, the LLM has become a major source of revenue and has become highly professionalized.[30]

[27] My experience in China is quite different. Efforts to "deal" with the Cultural Revolution are still quite controversial, see recent novel, Thien 2016.

[28] At the same time I will confess that over the years as I have attempted to write a book on comparative transitional justice, I am unable to complete the work as conditions on the ground change and I feel an "outsider" cannot fully capture what is happening. With Israel, in particular, where I teach and work on peace issues, I have a rule: if one hasn't been there in six months, one's knowledge is probably flawed and dated.

[29] For some analysis of the impact of internationally trained or "influenced" lawyers are on their own legal regimes, see Dezalay and Garth 2011, 2012.

[30] The International Legal Education Abroad Association is now a group of LLM administrators which meets to share information about recruitment, admissions, curriculum, placement, and social and financial support, see ILEAC, https://www.Translegal.com. Its most recent conference at American University Washington College of Law met in February 2018 and attracted administrators of LLM programs from the United States and many other countries. NAFSA (the major organization for international study abroad programs in higher education in the United States) has also been

The major law schools in the United States, Europe, and now Asia have working partnerships with many other law programs to allow (first degree) students to study for a limited period of time abroad.[31] Even without a formal degree program, these experiences still are important broadening exercises as long as there is real enrollment in "regular" courses in such schools. The many programs (summer and otherwise) that simply move an American faculty and student group to another country (Georgetown had such a program for many years in Florence, Italy, in which I taught, and many schools do summer programs of their own students in foreign locales (London, Oxford, Paris, Rome, Israel)) do not really offer a *transnational legal education* experience, even if the dislocation and move to another legal culture may teach something about the differences in legal cultures.[32] Recent efforts to bring "American style" legal education (three-year postgraduate JD) to Japan, China, Korea, and Australia are another form of "transnationalizing" legal education, in content and method of legal study, if not necessarily diversification of the student body. The various experiments to do this are being intensively studied and are meeting with very mixed results (Wang, Liu, and Li 2017; Rosen 2017).[33]

We are just beginning to study the internationalization of legal education through both first degree and graduate law programs, through the prodigious work of Carol Silver (Chapter 15, this volume), Laurel Terry, Anthea Roberts (Chapter 14, this volume), and others, but much of this work notes that "foreign" students in any law program are often ghettoized in separate courses, often with adjunct or part-time faculty and are not really fully integrated with each other (as is the case at CTLS and other programs where no one is "home"). When I taught at Harvard Law School over a decade ago, Harvard had commissioned McKinsey Consulting to evaluate their LLM and foreign student programs, and as a result, when I arrived to teach there in 2001, every JD class (except for the first-year courses) was required to set aside a

---

sponsoring programs on Global Legal Education, see https://www.nafsa.org/Programs_and_Events/Global_Learning_Colloquia/Legal/NAFSA_Global_Learning_Colloquium_on_Legal_Education/.

[31] See, e.g., programs with SciencesPo in Paris, Leiden, and Amsterdam in the Netherlands, University College London, Bucerius in Germany, Di Tella in Argentina, National University of Singapore, and international law programs of NYU sited in Paris, Buenos Aires, and China.

[32] Think about how much Americans learned about Italian criminal procedure as they watched the developments in the criminal prosecutions of Amanda Knox (for murder) or Marian True (for expropriation of ancient art on behalf of the Getty Museum), see Eakin 2010.

[33] For some analysis of efforts to replicate American style practical or clinical education, see Godwin and Wu 2017.

certain number of spots for foreign students. The effect of this was, at least for me, quite telling. My American and foreign LLM students bonded and have remained in contact with each other and with me across many borders for many years. What was most interesting was that I allowed students (both Americans and "foreigners") to negotiate in other than English, as I had enough ability in language comprehension to observe and give feedback in at least French and Spanish. This truly allowed "transnational" culture to enter the American law classroom and provided a wonderful opportunity to teach the importance of language facility and accurate translation in multinational business and diplomatic negotiations.[34] When I returned to Georgetown from Harvard I began to set aside seats in all my classes for foreign LLMs or SJDs. Over my years at Georgetown, my ADR classes were all microcosms of the United Nations (well, not enough students from Africa, but otherwise quite diverse!). And, as has been true for many American law professors who teach foreign students (and future leaders), I formed relationships that resulted in legal consultation projects with lawyers, universities, and governments abroad.[35]

While the United States has been a major destination for graduate law students in modern times, this was not always so. South American lawyers studied in Spain, France, and Germany for decades; the Japanese in Germany; many Asian students (Singapore, Hong Kong, China, India) and Australians and Canadians in the United Kingdom; and Africans[36] in France, Germany, the United Kingdom, Belgium, and the Netherlands, depending on the particular colonial imprints on the development of legal systems, some of which have broken with colonial institutions, and others which have developed more pluralistically to include both the old colonial legacies and newer commitments in law and legal institutions (i.e., South Africa). Recent developments in the world economy (e.g., the 2008 economic crisis), changing political alignments (e.g., Brexit), and immigration policies (e.g.,

---

[34] Think about the significance of international legal language and translation abilities as we consider what "de-nuclearization" might mean in different languages and legal and political cultures! (This word is not recognized in my spelling checker!).

[35] Much has been written about the nomadic American professors who have consulted on new constitutions and other legal reforms following the fall of the Berlin Wall or the economic liberalization policies in China and other parts of Asia, as well as the earlier law and development movement, see Trubek and Galanter 1974; Trubek and Santos 2006.

[36] The legal systems of much of South America are based on the French (not Spanish) civil code (due to Napoleonic influences); the Japanese legal system has been based on the German civil code; and other "post-colonial" legal systems are often a mix of their imperialist-colonial rulers, indigenous legal orders, and modern constitutions and legal systems, see Glenn 2010; Clark, Merryman, and Haley 2010.

President Donald Trump's "travel ban" on movement from some countries[37]) are leading to changes in the demographics of transnational law study. While the greatest number of graduate law students in the United States are now coming from China, Korea, and Canada, European students from the continent are more likely to study in each other's law faculties or in the United Kingdom (where attempts to assess the effects of Brexit are ongoing).[38] Students from Muslim or *sharia*-based nations are now studying Islamic finance and law in new centers of study in the United Kingdom and other new Middle Eastern specialty programs in Doha or Dubai.[39]

Law students who study in regions with regional legal or economic systems (the European Union, ASEAN, and Mercosur) are more likely to have transnational legal education in their own law faculties (e.g., mandatory study of EU law) or to seek training and certificate programs in other countries within their own region. The "uptake" of various educational reforms (experiential, practical, clinical, and service learning, mandatory international law courses) in law study has been variable in different law faculties around the world. For example, although the United States pioneered clinical education, many of the law schools in Australia now, in my view, surpass the United States in the diversity of their educational experiences (e.g., clinical programs in "rural" law (Mundy, Kennedy, and Neilsen 2018) and indigenous law programs (see Sarat and Sheingold 2001)[40]).

The most creative law school I have witnessed is the law school at CIDE in Mexico City, which combines full-time professors, practitioners, experiential and research instruction for all students, and interdisciplinarity in all of its courses (see Menkel-Meadow 2007).[41] Founded in the early 2000s, CIDE, as a public school, is dedicated to joint learning with students being active in every class, instruction in research methods, and participation in national legal research projects, diversity from different regions of Mexico, and

---

[37] *Trump v. Hawaii*, 138 S. Ct. 2392 (2018) (latest version of "travel ban" from Libya, Syria, Yemen, Somalia, Iran, Iraq, Venezuela, North Korea sustained by US Supreme Court).

[38] At a briefing I attended in London, just after Brexit, British higher education officials predicted that the top universities (Oxbridge, UCL, LSE) would continue to have many foreign students but that if migration and student visa policies changed after negotiation of the "new" Euro relationship, other universities might suffer (in the sense of fewer students, less revenue, and decreased diversity of student bodies). Meeting at UCL, June 2016.

[39] Islamic finance law programs also exist at Harvard Law School and many British universities. See, e.g., SOAS, Queen Mary Commercial Law Program, School of Law.

[40] See University of New South Wales, West Australia, etc., and Global Alliance for Justice Education (GAJE) for International Association of Clinical teachers, https://www.gaje.org, now publishing the *International Journal of Clinical Education* (edited in the United Kingdom).

[41] Centro de Investigacion y Docencia Economicas, Estudios Juridicos, https://www.cide.edu.

a variety of pedagogic innovations (e.g., internet simulations with students from other countries).[42] Though many claim that the Langdellian method of Socratic and case study instruction in the United States has been the most profound influence on legal education in modern history, my experience has been to witness a great variety of innovations in legal education in many other parts of the world.

IV. Assessing Impacts?

In looking at the many varieties of "globalized" or "internationalized" legal education, with very little rigorous comparative data or studies,[43] it is difficult to come to definitive qualitative or quantitative conclusions about what is most effective, what is learned, or even what the long-term effects or impacts of these programs are for both the students in them and the faculty who teach them. For me, this chapter reflects a qualitative argument that learning law in different contexts, with different legal systems, diverse student bodies, and diversely trained faculty, in locations other than one's home, must be a qualitative good in our controversially globalizing world.[44]

The "effects" which I can name and should be the subject of further rigorous empirical study are those on curriculum and pedagogy, research and scholarship, cultural understanding (legal humility and cultural competence), and what I would call "institutional sensitivity, innovation and competence." Such effects may be different for the professoriate and for students (e.g., for those who seek only social networking or the "foreign party" experience), and so rigorous study of the effects of truly transnational legal education must focus on both groups and ideally, over time (an "after the J.D./LLM/LLM/SJD/International" project?[45]).

---

[42] In 2003–2004, I was a consultant to the Hewlett Foundation to evaluate this program and recommended it as model of legal education innovation for the rest of the world.

[43] Carole Silver and Laurel Terry are two American exceptions to this statement, as in many different ways they are studying both international legal education and the development of the internationalized legal profession.

[44] Globalization remains a controversial topic in economic, see, e.g., Stieglitz 2002, as well as cultural developments, as does its assessment in legal developments and legal education, see, e.g., Trubek, Dezalay, Buchanan, and Davis 1994; Nesiah 2013; Silver 2013; Thomas, Aleinikoff, Alford, and Weiler 2007.

[45] See the longitudinal "After the J.D. Project," an unprecedented decades-long study of a cohort of American law students, now lawyers, conducted by the American Bar Foundation and researchers; Dinovitzer, Garth, Sander, Sterling, and Wilder 2004.

A. Curriculum and Pedagogy

When professors travel and teach abroad with different modalities and legal education structures they should be learning to "take in" as well as "give out." The intercultural legal dialogues and debates that have produced many different versions of CTLS "core" course curricula have also transformed the way that many of the faculty have brought their learning home (Pillard, Cole, Sornarajah, and Werro 2012). Many law schools now require some form of international or transnational law courses, and for many of us those courses now include not only more conventional public international law subjects but also private international law, regional law, sociolegal approaches to law, legal pluralism, and comparative law.

At the University of California Irvine, where we now require a course in "International Legal Analysis" in the first year, variations on that course include transnational litigation, legal pluralism, globalization theory, as well as treatment of public international law organizations and concrete transnational problems (trade, human rights, transitional justice, and international criminal law) to instill in our students a sense of the complexity of legal pluralism and many different ways to interpret law in a globalized setting. For several years I led a collaboration of our first year International Legal Analysis teachers to involve the whole first-year class in a shorter version of Georgetown's Week One. My colleague Christopher Whytock and I developed a problem based on the complex, multijurisdictional, and multitribunal problem of the *Chevron v. Ecuador* litigation (see, e.g., Whytock 2013) to introduce first-year students to treaties, different dispute processes, enforcement issues, forum selection, and legal pluralism in sources of law. All of our students, across sections, worked together in small groups to write short papers and, eventually, to negotiate and argue different aspects of the international problem. Since this exercise used multiple teaching modalities and experiential components, it sparked high student participation and motivation in learning about transnational legal issues. In the last two years, international law issues presented by our new political administration have deepened student interest and motivation for such study and exercises in class.

As a result of my own transnational teaching experiences and the spirit of our new law school's focus on the public interest, I have been the faculty director for the last nine years of our student-initiated Global Justice Summit. Since all first-year students study international legal issues and are concerned about "world justice" or the sociology-based "World Society" movement, they were motivated to create a student participation learning program that would be a "moot," but not of conventional appellate court arguments. So for the last nine years, we have created a new fictionalized fact situation each year requiring the negotiation and then drafting of either a new constitution for a new nation, or a treaty (for environmental, migration, or war and peace issues). Students are assigned to roles as country representatives or NGOs, often with detailed individual instructions, and after workshops in negotiation, complex multiparty negotiation, comparative constitutionalism, or international substantive issues (e.g., environmental or transitional justice), they spend a full weekend in real time negotiating and drafting the relevant documents. This program now provides academic credit for those who write either substantive or process reflective papers, following the exercise, and the program is always supplemented with substantive lectures by experts in the relevant field. In one year we had two professors from other countries, experts in comparative constitutionalism, lecture on their own experiences in constitution drafting (South Africa and Iraq) and over 150 students participated in the drafting of a new constitution for a fictional, post–Hunger Games–like country (see generally Collins 2010). Recently, we have focused on international environmental and migration problems and international disputes over areas like the South China Sea and the Ukraine-Crimea international law issues.

Similarly, many of my CTLS colleagues have returned to their home schools to revise their own subject-matter courses to reflect different legal cultural perspectives, especially for those who taught transsystemically or who audited each other's courses. During my faculty directorship year at CTLS, I audited or attended over half of our courses, including those on Shari'a Law, Critiques of International Investment Law, Language Rights, Comparative Emergencies Law, and Humanitarian Law. Virtually all of my international law courses have been affected by my participation in such multisystemically taught courses. Others of my colleagues attended my own simulation-based courses (e.g., International Dispute Resolution), and I have been fortunate to observe first-hand the innovations from such teaching transported to many law schools outside of the United States. I have now taught versions of my Negotiation, Mediation, and Dispute Resolution classes in law faculties around the world, and have been able to mentor and train a new generation of law professors in other countries.

Although I am aware of no systematic study of changing curricular requirements in international legal education generally, it would be useful for someone to undertake a longitudinal study of the transformation of legal curricula within all legal systems. For example, I have observed European programs come to require EU Law in a diet of otherwise clearly demarked "public" or "private" law subjects. Other innovations I have observed or participated in are a new mandatory course in mediation at KU Leuven, more practice-based learning, externships, and service learning in the United Kingdom, and the Netherlands; new clinical programs in Chile and Argentina (including representation of survivors of the military dictatorships in continuing prosecutions and the development of new causes of action, e.g., lawsuits questioning governmental services in shanty towns, and claims of "looks/beauty" discrimination); and the addition of more participatory skills courses (e.g., negotiation) and finance and business subjects in law programs in France and Singapore. As law itself becomes more "internationalized," whether through harmonization, transplantation, or regulatory processes, we could and should be looking at how new legal developments are reflected (or not) in new pedagogies. Issues like internet contracting, online dispute resolution, uses of artificial intelligence or "algorithmic justice,"[46] and international migration now lend themselves to transnational coordination and study. Institutions of transnational legal study should be at the forefront of international legal problem-solving. I have long suggested that all law schools, domestic and transnational, should provide for "capstone" problem-solving seminars in which advanced students work together across disciplines and legal systems to take on the modern challenges of our world: migration, technology (Pagallo 2018), poverty, health and disease, hate speech (see, e.g., Chemerinsky and Gillman 2017; Kaye 2018; Waldron 2012), religious freedom, discrimination, and peace promotion (see Luban 2020). Students at CTLS suggest that international human rights has become the most salient aspect of transnational legal study, demonstrating the possibility of a transnational legal order with both transnational and domestic effects.[47]

---

[46] I am a participant in the yearly International Online Dispute Resolution Forum, which presents and studies new development in online dispute resolution programs in both the private sector and in court systems throughout the world. The European Union has mandated the development of online dispute resolution for consumer disputes in the European Union. See Menkel-Meadow 2016.

[47] Student alumni panel at Tenth Anniversary Conference of Center for Transnational Legal Studies, University of Toronto, June 22, 2018 (reporting on a survey conducted of CTLS students). Students reported that whatever their chosen fields of practice, transnational legal education at CTLS has proven relevant in almost all aspects of their work, including solvency, banking, project

B. Research and Scholarship

With the increased number of international legal scholarly conferences (e.g., my intellectual home, the Law and Society Association, has been holding international meetings for over twenty years, and the Onati Center for Socio-legal Studies (Spain) has hosted many conferences of international and comparative sociolegal issues), and peripatetic law professors working in many different countries, we are observing an increase in collaborative and comparative legal scholarship. Many prominent scholars collaborate on legal harmonization projects for the International Law Commission–UN, the European Union, American Law Institute, the Institut de Droit, the Acquis Group, and other multinational law reform groups, while others collaborate on scholarly and theory-based projects.[48] A smaller, but very important group of scholars collaborate on comparative empirical projects to study both socio-legal phenomena in comparative settings (e.g., the work of my current colleagues Bryant Garth (Dezalay and Garth 1988, 2022, 2011, 2012) and Gregory Shaffer (Halliday and Shaffer 2014), and my former colleague Richard Abel (Abel and Lewis 1989, a large comparative project on the legal profession) (see also Katvan, Silver, Ziv, and Sherr 2017), as well as the impact of particular legal reforms (e.g., the diffusion of "alternative dispute resolution" in legal systems around the world (see Ali 2018; Steffek, Unberauth, Genn, Greger, and Menkel-Meadow 2013; Creutzfeldt 2018; Sweet and Grisel 2017) and comparative constitutional developments (Ginsburg and Dixon 2014)). Recent international conferences have also focused on empirical assessment of legal education itself.[49] The proliferation of international journals[50] makes dissemination of international, comparative, and transnational scholarship quite easy, especially in the new age of open access and electronic journals.

---

investment, corporate law, as well as international contracting and actual human rights work in transnational tribunals, as well as domestic.

[48] The outpouring of large legal anthologies on comparative law subjects by Oxford, Cambridge, Elgar, Routledge, and Taylor & Francis publishers now brings together in volumes, if not physical space, legal scholars from across the globe to compare and contrast ongoing legal developments in a wide range of subject matters. See, e.g., Bussani and Mattei 2013; Palmer, Roberts, and Moscati 2018.

[49] See International Conference on Research on Legal Education, hosted by the University of New South Wales, December 2017.

[50] I was co-editor, with Michael Freeman, of UCL of the *International Journal of Law in Context (Cambridge University Press)* for over ten years, a journal that focused on international interdisciplinary studies of law and legal institutions.

C. Cultural Competency or "Capability"

If there is one particularly outstanding aspect of transnational legal education it has to be the kind of social, as well as intellectual, interactions contemplated by Thomas Friedman and others. Substantive learning is, of course, what we promise and advertise, but the ability to learn from, speak with, and understand those from different national, ethnic, and legal cultures is really the heart of good transnational programs which occur "away" from home. The fact that this is so important a goal of such programs does not mean it is easy. At CTLS, for example, diversity among the students is far greater than that of the faculty, as many of the students are not original "nationals" of the countries from which they come, and there are more schools represented in the student body than any one semester of teachers (some of whom are also not of the "nationality" of their home schools). The diverse mix of backgrounds and intellectual orientations presents great opportunities for learning but also challenges of human communication and understanding. To appropriate the term of Amartya Sen's concept of the human "capability" approach (Sen 1993, 1999, 2006; Menkel-Meadow, Ramraj, and Thiruvengadam 2020), I like to think that good multicultural programs can teach, model, and explore the notion of developing "cultural capability"—the idea that one can be aware of, sensitive to, and able to "work with" or "within" situations of cultural "difference."

Modern social and legal theory has contributed to a "post-colonial" sensitivity to directions of influence. We no longer totally accept the "rightness" of "laid down" civil codes or legal institutions of the past, or the "superiority" of particular groups over others (at least in theory, if not in worldwide practice!). We now aspire to learn from everyone—social pluralism produces legal pluralism. Most of our legal systems prohibit various forms of discrimination, and many of us live in demographically and economically diverse societies. Nevertheless, providing both a "safe" and "rigorous" place for encountering, analyzing, and dealing with differences is difficult (see, e.g., Menkel-Meadow 2018), and yet may be facilitated by programs like CTLS where there are, in fact, so many differences to contend with—legally, socially, and culturally.[51]

Several of us at CTLS and in my other international encounters have spent much time talking with each other, looking for and preparing materials

---

[51] See, e.g., Lee 2009, for a thoughtful example of how to deal with both "stereotypic" notions of culture and working through them for greater complexity and layers of human understanding.

on "cross-cultural" teaching. American universities now often require some kind of diversity and inclusion training for both students and faculty. We have been less successful with formalizing such work in legal exchange programs.[52] It would also be extremely useful to interview and study students, over time, who attend such programs. Have they developed more broad-minded views of differences from themselves or do some "contact" encounters increase stereotyping?[53]

D. Institutional Sensitivity, Competence, and Innovation

The founding of CTLS ten years ago was an effort to create a totally new institution—a place for transnational, comparative, and international legal study, without a "home" institution. Although many institutions came together to found and fund this program, the idea was that teaching, and, eventually administration, would be shared by all the institutions participating to create something different from, and "free-standing" from, more conventional law schools. Do we know if CTLS has succeeded? We have student evaluations that have largely been very positive over the years and many faculty who return for more than one tour of duty. But CTLS will move physically this year to join King's College's facilities in London, so the question of whether it will retain its own individual identity is real. We have not, as far as I know, conducted ongoing studies of our students or faculties to chart their development and learning from the program beyond their first year of participation. My anecdotal experience is that those who have studied at CTLS are much more likely to seek legal work in international institutions and transnational practices around the world, but this could clearly be the effect of self-selection into the program in the first place. At many of our member schools, admission to CTLS is highly competitive and controlled by the

---

[52] Our first administrative director of CTLS, Scott Foster of Georgetown, recruited an excellent cross-cultural education expert to orient our students at CTLS. I often wondered why our faculty was not required to attend as well. Since that time (2009), my many colleagues at CTLS and in my other law faculties have spent much time discussing such issues. There are the international education associations mentioned above that do specialize in such training, but international legal education, I think still requires its own particularized form of cultural competency training, see, e.g., the Cross-Cultural Competency Certification program of the International Mediation Institute, https://www.imimediation.org, and the *Journal of Studies in International Education* (NAFSA) for some resources.

[53] The "contact" hypothesis in sociology, political science, psychology, and peace studies suggests that positive contacts must be structured to facilitate tolerance. Gordon Allport is credited with developing this theory, Allport 1954; see also https://www.facinghistory.org.

home institution; at Georgetown that has been less true. Unlike a nationally based law school, CTLS cannot promise placement services, though physical presence in the United Kingdom (and at least for a little while longer, in the European Union) allows students some access to work opportunities in countries other than their homes.

Other institutions I have worked in, like NU Singapore, have had formal alliances with other law schools (NYU and Yale) so that institutions can collaborate on curriculum, faculty selection, degree requirements, and student services,[54] but free-standing programs (like some summer abroad programs) or one-off exchange programs for students and faculty may not provide the institutional support and cultural sensitivity to make the experience as rich and successful as it should be. Administration of foreign LLM and SJD programs are being professionalized at most major institutions in the United States and in many parts of the rest of the world (the United Kingdom, Netherlands, Australia, Japan, to name a few). We should be collectivizing our knowledge about many things:

1. Are we providing excellent transnational education substantively?
2. Are we facilitating rigorous intellectual and social encounters?
3. Are we contributing to the development of positive legal reforms, internationally, and within particular regions and nations (e.g., access to justice, human rights, reduction of poverty, public health, good governance, reduction in corruption, general human well-being)?
4. How do we promote mutual transnational legal understanding?
5. Are we having any more "permanent" impact on our students? On their home institutions? On ourselves as faculty?
6. Are we producing new legal or social knowledge with our international and comparative encounters?
7. What are the "legal needs" of the world that we are addressing? What should we be focusing on?
8. What lasting effects, if any, can there be from single semester, year, or summer introduction to the variability of legal and social arrangements?

---

[54] Student counseling services have become more complex in recent years everywhere, but the particular needs of student counseling and management in international settings can be compounded by cultural disorientation, language issues, visas, mental health issues, physical health, thefts and other criminal activity, accidents, drinking, drugs, and sexual assault issues (all of which I have witnessed in one place or another).

I am a committed transnational educator who is also a committed "contextualist." How we structure legal education will vary with the legal systems we are engaged with, and with the theorists, practitioners, and students that work with us. Not everyone can be "transnationalized" in the same or uniform way. Different nations, law schools, and individuals will have differentiated goals about what they are trying to accomplish with respect to substantive legal outcomes and the processes by which they are enacted. As we know from past encounters with "law and . . . . (development, colonialism and intellectual imperialism)," ambitious and perhaps hegemonic projects (e.g., democracy building and good governance, not to mention economic development and promotion of particular legal or economic systems) will be subject to economic and political factors beyond our control as educators and scholars. Yet what I am still certain of, in the current era, troubling though it is for the flourishing of transnational cooperation, is that innovation and influence in law, in education, in culture, and, yes, even in politics, travels in multiple directions now. The diversity and growth in transnational legal programs now on offer are promoting a "globalization of legal education" that in my view (and I suspect yours and Thomas Friedman's too), is, in fact, a qualitative good.

References

Abbott, Kenneth W. and Douglas Snidal (2000). "Hard and Soft Law in International Governance," *International Organization* 54(3): 421–456.

Abel, Richard and Philip Lewis (1989). *Lawyers in Society: Comparative Theories.* University of California Press.

Ahdieh, Robert (2004). "Between Dialogue and Decree: International Review of National Courts," *New York University Law Review* 79(6): 2029–2163.

Aleinikoff, T. Alexander (2007). "Remarks on the Globalization of the American Law School," *Proceedings American Society of International Law* 101: 184–186.

Aleinikoff, T. Alexander (2006). "Law in a Global Context: Georgetown's Innovative First Year Program," *Penn State International Law Review* 24(4): 825–827.

Ali, Farida (2013). "Globalizing the U.S. Law School Curriculum: How Should Legal Educators Respond," *International Journal of Legal Information* 41(3): 249–282.

Ali, Shahla (2018). *Court Mediation Reform.* Edward Elgar Publishing.

Allport, Gordon (1954). *The Nature of Prejudice.* Addison-Wesley.

Alter, Karen (2014). *The New Terrain of International Law: Courts, Politics and Rights.* Princeton University Press.

Arjona, Cesar, Arif Jamal, Carrie Menkel-Meadow, Victor Ramraj, and Francisco Satiro (2012). "Senses of Sen: Reflections on Amartya Sen's Ideas of Justice," *International Journal of Law in Context* 8: 155–178.

Ballakrishnen, Swethaa (2012). "Homeward Bound: What Does a Global Legal Education Offer the Indian Returnees?," *Fordham Law Review* 80(6): 2441–2480.

Barak, Aharon (2002). "A Judge on Judging: The Role of a Supreme Court in a Democracy," *Harvard Law Review* 116(1): 19–162.

Berman, Paul Schiff (2007). "Global Legal Pluralism," *Southern California Law Review* 80(6): 1155–1238.

Bollens, Scott A. (2012). *City and Soul in Divided Societies*. Routledge.

Bose, Neilesh and Victor V. Ramraj (Forthcoming). *Sources of Legal Authority in the Pre-Modern State Era: The British East India Company, 1600–1757.*

Breyer, Stephen (2015). *The Court and the World: American Law and the New Global Realities*. Vintage.

Bussani, Mauro and Ugo Mattei, eds. (2013). *The Cambridge Companion to Comparative Law*. Cambridgee, UK.

Chemerinsky, Erwin and Howard Gillman (2017). *Free Speech on Campus*. Yale University Press.

Cheng-Han, Tan (2017). "NUS Law in the Noughties: Becoming 'Asia's Global Law School,'" *Singapore Journal of Legal Studies* 76: 215–238.

Chesterman, Simon (2009). "The Evolution of Legal Education: Internationalization, Transnationalization, Globalization," *German Law Journal* 10(6–7): 877–888.

Chesterman, Simon (2008). "The Globalization of Legal Education," *Singapore Journal of Legal Studies* 67: 58–67.

Choudry, Sujit, ed. (2006). *The Migration of Constitutional Ideas*. Cambridge University Press.

Clark, David, John Merryman, and John Haley (2010). *Comparative Law: Historical Development of the Civil Law Tradition in Europe, Latin America, and East Asia.* LexisNexis.

Collins, Suzanne (2010). *The Hunger Games*. Scholastic Press.

Creutzfeldt, Naomi (2018). *Ombudsmen and ADR: A Comparative Study of Informal Justice in Europe*. Palgrave Macmillan.

Darian-Smith, Eve (2016). "The Crisis in Legal Education: Embracing Ethnographic Approaches to Law," *Transnational Legal Theory* 7(2): 1–29.

Dezalay, Yves and Bryant Garth (2002). *The Internationalization of Palace Wars: Lawyers, Economists and the Contest to Transform Latin American States*. University of Chicago Press.

Dezalay, Yves and Bryant Garth (1988). *Dealing in Virtue: International Commercial Arbitration and the Construction of a Transnational Legal Order*. University of Chicago Press.

Dezalay, Yves and Bryant Garth (2012). *Lawyers and the Construction of Transnational Justice*. Routledge.

Dezalay, Yves and Bryant Garth (2011). *Lawyers and the Rule of Law in an Era of Globalization*. Routledge.

Dinovitzer, Ronit, Bryant Garth, Richard Sander, Joyce Sterling, and Gita Z. Wilder (2004). *After the JD: First Results of a National Study of Legal Careers*. NALP Foundation for Law Career Research and Education.

Dorfman, Ariel (1991). *Death and the Maiden*. Penguin Press, NY.

Eakin, Hugh (2010). "Marian True on Her Trial and Ordeal," *The New Yorker*. October 14.

Ferrari, Alessandro and Sabrina Pastorelli (2013). *The Burqa Affair Across Europe: Between Public and Private Space*. Routledge.

Gaillard, Emmanuel (2010). *Legal Theory of International Arbitration*. Martinus Nijhoff.

Galanter, Mark and David Trubek (1974). "Scholars in Self-Estrangement: Some Reflections on the Crisis in Law and Development Studies," *Wisconsin Law Review* 1974(4): 1062–1102.

Gane, Christopher and Robin Hui Huang, eds. (2016). *Legal Education in the Global Context: Opportunities and Challenges*. Ashgate Publishing.

Garth, Bryant (2015). "Notes Toward an Understanding of the U.S. Market in Foreign LL.M. Students: From the British Empire and the Inns of Court to the U.S. LL.M.," *Indiana Journal of Global Legal Studies* 22(1): 67–79.

Giddens, Anthony (1990). *The Consequences of Modernity*. Stanford University Press.

Ginsburg, Tom and Rosalind Dixon (2014). *Comparative Constitutional Law*. Edward Elgar.

Glenn, H. Patrick (2010). *Legal Traditions of the World*. Oxford University Press.

Godwin, Andrew and Richard Wai-sang Wu (2017). "Legal Education, Practice Skills, and Pathways to Admission: A Comparative Analysis of Singapore, Hong Kong and Australia," *Journal of Legal Education* 66(2): 212–36.

Halliday, Terence and Gregory Shaffer, eds. (2014). *Transnational Legal Orders*. Cambridge University Press.

Hayner, Priscilla (2001). *Unspeakable Truths*. Routledge.

Heins, Marjorie (2018). *Ironies and Complications of Free Speech*. New York—self-published; available on Kindle.

Hupper, Gail (2015). "Educational Ambivalence: The Rise of a Foreign-Student Doctorate in Law," *New England Law Review* 49(3): 319–447.

Hupper, Gail (2008). "The Academic Doctorate in Law: A Vehicle for Legal Transplants," *Journal of Legal Education* 58(2): 413–54.

Hupper, Gail (2007). "The Rise of an Academic Doctorate in Law: Origins Through World War II," *American Journal of Legal History* 49(1): 1–60.

Israel, Mark, Natalie Skead, Mary Heath, Anne Hewitt, Kate Galloway, and Alex Steel (2017). "Fostering 'Quiet Inclusion,' Interaction and Diversity in the Australian Law Classroom," *Journal of Legal Education* 66(2): 332–356.

Jackson, Vicki (2010). *Constitutional Engagement in a Transnational Era*. Oxford University Press.

Jamin, Christopher and William van Caenegem, eds. (2016). *The Internationalisation of Legal Education*. Springer International Publishing.

Jessup, Philip (1956). *Transnational Law*. New Haven: Yale University Press.

Katvan, Eyal, Carole Silver, Neta Ziv, and Avrom Sherr (2017). *Too Many Lawyers? The Future of the Legal Profession*. Routledge.

Kaye, David (2018). "How to Fix Social Media Without Censorship," *Commentary, Reuters*. June 20. https://www.reuters.com/article/us-kaye-media-commentary/com mentary-how-to-fix-social-media-without-censorship-idUSKBN1JF34H.

Kennedy, Duncan (2006). "Three Globalizations of Law and Legal Thought: 1850–2000," in David Trubek and Alvaro Santos, eds., *The New Law and Economic Development: A Critical Appraisal*. Pp. 19–73. Cambridge University Press.

Kim, Jongyoung (2016). "Global Cultural Capital and Global Positional Competition: International Graduate Students' Transnational Occupational Trajectories," *British Journal of Sociology of Education* 37(1): 30–50.

Koh, Harold (1996). "The 1994 Roscoe Pound Lecture: Transnational Legal Process," *Nebraska Law Review* 75(1): 181–207.

Koh, Harold (2006). "'Why Transnational Law Matters.' Keynote AALS Keynote on Integrating Transnational Perspectives in the First Year Curriculum, January 3–7, 2006," *Penn State International Law Review* 24(4): 745–753.

Krisch, Nico, Benedict Kingsbury, and Richard Stewart (2005). "The Emergence of Global Administrative Law," *Law and Contemporary Problems* 68(3): 15–62.

Law, David S. and Mila Versteeg (2012). "The Declining Influence of the American Constitution," *New York University Law Review* 87(3): 762–858.

Lee, Joel (2009). "Asian Culture—A Definitional Challenge," in Joel Lee and Teh Hwee Hwee, eds., *An Asian Perspective on Mediation.* Pp. 54–61. Singapore: Academy Publishing.

LeGrand, Pierre (1997). "The Impossibility of Legal Transplants," *Maastricht Journal of European and Comparative Law* 4(2): 111–124.

Luban, David (2020). "Responsibility to Humanity and Threats to Peace: An Essay on Sovereignty," *Berkeley Journal of International Law* 38(2): 185–239.

Luban, David and Naomi Mezey (2014). "Introduction: Law After Babel," *Special Issue on Law and Language, Kings College Law Journal* 25: 223–230.

Macdonald, Ronald (1997). "The Teaching of Public and Private International Law," *Institut de Droit International* 10: 1–4. http://www.justitiaetpace.org/idiE/resolutio nsE/1997_str_01_en.PDF.

Mattei, Ugo and Laura Nader (2008). *Plunder: When the Rule of Law Is Illegal.* Blackwell Publishing.

McConnaughay, Philip J. and Colleen B. Toomey (2022). "China and the Globalization of Legal Education: A Look into the Future," in Bryant Garth and Gregory Shaffer, eds., *The Globalization of Legal Education: A Critical Study.*

Menkel-Meadow, Carrie (2008). "Are Cross-Cultural Ethics Standards Possible or Desirable in International Arbitration?," in Peter Gauch, Franz Werro, and Pascal Pichonnaz, eds., *Mélanges en l'honneur de Pierre Tercier.* Pp. 888–904. Schulthess.

Menkel-Meadow, Carrie (2016). "In the Land of Blood and Honey: What's Fair or Just in Love and War Crimes? Lessons for Transitional Justice," in Caroline Joan S. Picart, Michael Hviid Jacobsen, and Cecil Greek, eds., *Framing Law and Crime: An Interdisciplinary Anthology.* Pp. 105–133. Rowman and Littlefield.

Menkel-Meadow, Carrie (2016). "Is ODR ADR? Reflections of an ADR Founder," International Journal of On*line Dispute Resolution* 3: 4.

Menkel-Meadow, Carrie (2015). "Process Pluralism in Transitional/Restorative Justice: Lessons from Dispute Resolution for Cultural Variations in Goals beyond Rule of Law and Democracy Development (Argentina and Chile)," *International Journal of Conflict Engagement and Resolution* 3(1): 3–32.

Menkel-Meadow, Carrie (2007). "Taking Law and . . . Really Seriously: Before, During and After 'The Law,'" *Vanderbilt Law Review* 60(2): 555–595.

Menkel-Meadow, Carrie (2011). "Why and How to Study Transnational Law," *University of California, Irvine Law Review* 1(1): 97–29.

Menkel-Meadow, Carrie (2018). "Why We Can't 'Just All Get Along': Dysfunction in the Polity and Conflict Resolution and What We Might Do About It," *Journal of Dispute Resolution* 2018(1): 5–25.

Menkel-Meadow, Carrie and Irena Nutenko (2009). "The Next Generation: Creating a New Peace Process in the Middle East," *Negotiation Journal* 25(4): 567–584.

Menkel-Meadow, Carrie, Victor Ramraj, and Arun K. Thiruvengadam, eds. (2020). *Amartya Sen and Law.* Routledge.

Merry, Sally Engel (1988). "Legal Pluralism," *Law and Society Review* 22(5): 869–896.

Michaels, Ralf (2009). "Global Legal Pluralism," *Annual Review of Law and Social Science* 5: 243–262.

Mundy, Trish, Amanda Kennedy, and Jennifer Neilsen, eds. (2018). *The Place of Practice: Lawyering in Rural and Regional.* Federation Press.

Munin, Nellie and Yael Efron (2017). "Role-Playing Brings Theory to Life in a Multi-Cultural Learning Environment," *Journal of Legal Education* 66(2): 309–331.

Nesiah, Vasuki (2013). "A Flat Earth for Lawyers Without Borders: Rethinking Current Approaches to the Globalization of Legal Education," *Drexel Law Review* 5(2): 371–390.

Nicola, Fernanda (2018). *The Global Diffusion of U.S. Legal Thought: Changing Influence, National Security, and Legal Education in Crisis.* Edward Elgar.

Pagallo, Ugo (2018). *Comparatists, Philosophers, and Programmers: On the Past and Future of Transnational Legal Education.* Paper presented at 10th Anniversary Conference of CTLS. June 22.

Palmer, Michael, Marion Roberts, and Maria Moscati, eds. (2020). *Research Handbook on Comparative Dispute Resolution.* Edward Elgar.

Paulsson, Jan (2013). *The Idea of Arbitration.* Oxford University Press.

Pillard, Nina, David Cole, M. Sornarajah, and Franz Werro (2012). "Why Transnational Legal Education," Center for Transnational Legal Studies Pamphlet.

Raume, Denise and Meital Pinto (2012). "Philosophy of Language Policy," in Bernard Spolsky, ed., *The Cambridge Handbook of Language Policy.* Pp. 37–59. Cambridge University Press.

Riddich, Kerry (2006). "The Future of Law and Development: Second Generation Reforms and the Incorporation of the Social," in David M. Trubek and Alvaro Santos, eds., *The New Law and Economic Development: A Critical Appraisal.* Pp. 203–252. Cambridge University Press; Cambridge UK.

Roberts, Anthea (2022). "Cross-Border Student Flows and the Construction of International Law as a Transnational Legal Field," in Bryant Garth and Gregory Shaffer, eds., *The Globalization of Legal Education: A Critical Study..*

Roberts, Anthea (2017). *Is International Law International?* Oxford University Press.

Roberts, Simon (2005). "After Government? On Representing Law Without the State," *Modern Law Review* 68(1): 1–24.

Roberts, Simon and Michael Palmer (2020). *Dispute Processes: ADR and the Primary Forms of Decision Making.* Cambridge University Press. 3d ed.

Rosen, Dan (2017). "Japan's Law School System: The Sorrow and the Pity," *Journal of Legal Education* 66(2): 267–288.

Sarat, Austin and Stuart Sheingold (2001). *Cause Lawyering and the State in a Global Era.* Oxford University Press.

Sassen, Saskia (2006). *Territory, Authority, Rights: From Medieval to Global Assemblages.* Princeton University Press.

Schultz, Thomas (2014). *Transnational Legality: Stateless Law and International Arbitration.* Oxford University Press.

Sen, Amartya (1993). "Capability and Well-Being," in Martha Nussbaum and Amartya Sen, eds., *The Quality of Life.* Pp. 30–52. Clarendon Press.

Sen, Amartya (1999). *Development and Freedom.* Anchor Press.

Sen, Amartya (2006). *Identity and Violence.* W.W. Norton.

Shaffer, Gregory and Mark A. Pollack (2010). "Hard vs. Soft Law: Alternatives, Complements and Antagonists in International Governance," *Minnesota Law Review* 94(3): 706–799.

Shany, Yuval (2014). *Assessing the Effectiveness of International Courts.* Oxford University Press.

Silver, Carole (2012). "Coping with the Consequences of 'Too Many Lawyers': Securing the Place of International Graduate Students," *International Journal of the Legal Profession* 19(2–3): 227–245.

Silver, Carole (2013). "Getting Real About Globalization and Legal Education: Potential and Perspectives for the U.S.," *Stanford Law & Policy Review* 24(2): 457–501.

Silver, Carole (2006). "Internationalizing U.S. Legal Education; A Report on the Education of Transnational Lawyers," *Cardozo Journal of International and Comparative Law* 14(1): 143–76.

Silver, Carole (2012a). "States Side Story: Career Paths of International LL.M. Students, or 'I Like to Be in America,'" *Fordham Law Review* 80(6): 2383–2440.

Silver, Carole (2002). "The Case of the Foreign Lawyer: Internationalizing the U.S. Legal Profession," *Fordham International Law Journal* 25(5): 1039–1084.

Silver, Carole (2000). "The Case of the Foreign Lawyer: Internationalizing the U.S. Legal Profession," *Law and Policy in International Business* 31(4): 1093–1150.

Silver, Carole (2010). "The Variable Value of U.S. Legal Education in the Global Legal Services Market," *Georgetown Journal of Legal Ethics* 24(1): 1–57.

Slaughter, Anne Marie (2004). *A New World Order.* Princeton University Press.

Sokol, D. Daniel (2007). "Globalization of Law Firms: A Survey of the Literature and a Research Agenda for Further Study," *Indiana Journal of Global Legal Studies* 14(1): 5–28.

Sornarajah, M. (2011). "Why 'No' to Transnational Legal Studies," in Cornelia T.L. Pillard et al., eds., *Why Transnational Legal Education*. Pp. 20–25. Center for Transnational Legal Studies.

Sornarajah, M. (2015). *Resistance and Change in the International Law on Foreign Investment.* Cambridge University Press.

Steffek, Felix, Hannes Unberauth, Hazel Genn, Reinhard Greger, and Carrie Menkel-Meadow (2013). *Regulating Dispute Resolution.* Hart Publishing.

Stieglitz, Joseph (2002). *Globalization and Its Discontents.* W.W. Norton & Company.

Strauss, Peter (2006). "Transsystemia—Are We Approaching a New Langdellian Moment? Is McGill Leading the Way?," *Journal of Legal Education* 56(2): 161–171.

Sugarman, David and Avrom Sherr (2001). "Globalisation and Legal Education," *International Journal of the Legal Profession* 8(1): 5–10.

Sweet, Alec Stone and Florian Grisel (2017). *The Evolution of International Arbitration: Judicialization, Governance, Legitimacy.* Oxford University Press.

Terry, Laurel (2008). "The Legal World Is Flat: Globalization and Its Effect on Lawyers Practicing in Non-Global Law Firms," *Northwestern Journal of International Law and Business* 28(3): 527–60.

Teubner, Gunther, ed. (1997). *Global Law Without a State.* Taylor & Francis.

Thien, Madeleine (2016). *Do Not Say We Have Nothing.* W.W. Norton & Company.

Thomas, Chantal, Alex Aleinikoff, William Alford, and Joseph Weiler (2007). "The Globalization of the American Law School," *Proceedings of the Annual Meeting* (American Society of International Law) 101: 183–199.

Trubek, David M. and Alvaro Santos, eds. (2006). *The New Law and Economic Development: A Critical Appraisal.* Cambridge University Press.

Trubek, David M., Yves Dezalay, Ruth Buchanan, and John R. Davis (1994). "Global Restructuring and the Law: Studies of the Internationalization of Legal Fields and the Creation of Transitional Arenas," *Case Western Reserve Law Review* 44(1): 407–498.

Tushnet, Mark (2015). "Authoritarian Constitutionalism," *Cornell Law Review* 100(1): 391-.

Twining, William462. *General Jurisprudence: Understanding Law from a Global Perspective*. Cambridge University Press.

Twining, William (2000). *Globalization & Legal Theory*. Cambridge University Press.

Waldron, Jeremy (2012). *The Harm in Hate Speech*. Harvard University Press.

Wang, Zhizhou, Sida Liu, and Xueyao Li (2017). "Internationalizing Chinese Legal Education in the Early Twenty-First Century," *Journal of Legal Education* 66(2): 237–66.

Watson, Alan (1993). *Legal Transplants: An Approach to Comparative Law*. University of Georgia Press. 2d ed.

Whalen-Bridge, Helena (2016). *Legal Skills in Transnational Legal Education*. Paper presented at Doing Transnational Legal Education, June 18, 2016, Center for Transnational Legal Studies, King's College School of Law, United Kingdom.

White, Cheryl S. (2017). *Bridging Divides in Transitional Justice: The Extraordinary Chambers in the Courts of Cambodia*. Intersentia.

Whytock, Christopher (2013). "Some Cautionary Notes on the 'Chevronization' of Transnational Litigation," *Stanford Journal of Complex Litigation* 1(2): 467–486.

Wilson, Richard (2009). "Western Europe: Last Hold Out in Worldwide Acceptance of Clinical Legal Education," *German Law Journal* 10(6–7): 823–846.

Yarn, Douglas H. (2000). "The Attorney as Duelist's Friend: Lessons From the Code Duello," *Case Western Reserve Law Review* 51: 69.

Zumbansen, Peter (2012). "Defining the Space of Transnational Law: Legal Theory, Global Governance and Legal Pluralism," *Transnational Law and Contemporary Problems* 21(2): 305–336.

PART IV

TRANSNATIONAL FLOWS OF STUDENTS, FACULTY, AND JUDGES IN THE CONSTITUTION OF LEGAL FIELDS

13

Who Rules the World?

The Educational Capital of the International Judiciary

Mikael Rask Madsen

The creation of a global structure of international courts has been an ongoing project throughout the twentieth century and well into the twenty-first. It was—and is—part of a more general endeavor of creating an international community governed by law. While the proliferation of international courts has been described elsewhere (Alter 2014; Kingsbury, Krisch, and Stewart 2005; Koskenniemi and Leino 2002; Romano 1999), we know surprisingly little about who are the actual judges sitting at the helm of contemporary judicialized international law and ruling (on) the world? What has once been termed the "invisible college of international lawyers" (Schachter 1977) remains to a large extent invisible to this day. But it is now a much larger college as the proliferation of international courts has resulted in a corresponding multiplication of the number of international judges. Today more than three hundred men and women hold the office of international judge (Swigart and Terris 2014). Most are found in Europe at the two regional courts of the Court of Justice of the European Union and the European Court of Human Rights, but many other regional and global courts also employ a significant number of international judges. Besides some mainly descriptive studies of the international judiciary (Swigart and Terris 2014), we have very little analysis of who these people are and what commonalities they have, notably in terms of education, knowledge, and know-how (see, however, Cohen 2010; Cohen and Madsen 2007; Vauchez 2007).

[*] The statistical analysis included in this chapter has been facilitated by the help of Troels Kjeldberg, a visualization expert at iCourts, and Ioannis Panagis, computer scientist at iCourts. This research is funded by the Danish National Research Foundation Grant no. DNRF105 and conducted under the auspices of iCourts. Thanks to the participants at the Conference on The Globalization of Legal Education: A Critical Study, University of California, Irvine School of Law, September 8–9, 2017.

Mikael Rask Madsen, *Who Rules the World?* In: *The Globalization of Legal Education.*
Edited by: Bryant Garth & Gregory Shaffer, Oxford University Press. © Oxford University Press 2022.
DOI: 10.1093/oso/9780197632314.003.0013

In a previous work, in collaboration with Niilo Kauppi, I argued that the expanding international judiciary is increasingly taking the form of what we coined a transnational power elite (Kauppi and Madsen 2013b; Madsen 2014). We understand a transnational power elite as a transnational grouping which is not simply powerful due to its institutional affiliation but also by its collective transnational capital in terms of knowledge and know-how of global governance, as well as its connectedness to key national and international legal-political sites. Thinking in terms of transnational power elites—instead of relying on an institutionalist understanding—provides a different access point for analyzing thinking about global governance (Kauppi and Madsen 2014). Moreover, by approaching the international judiciary as a transnational power elite, the fallacy of institutional analysis can be avoided; that is, it is not the institutions as such, in this case international courts, that are seen as governing the world but the transnational power elites constituting and instituting them. The basic argument is therefore the following: in order to make intelligible the power and interest of global legal governance, it is necessary to invert the common logic of inquiry of international institutional analysis by asking not only which organizations and rules govern, but who governs those organizations and rules. In the case of international courts, that involves in particular an analysis of judges.[1]

This chapter builds on this earlier research and logic of inquiry. The guiding research question therefore is the extent to which international judges are indeed such transnational elites that have both the knowledge and connections marking such a social group. Or alternatively, whether they are more localized players connecting to more national or regional sites of knowledge and law and politics. The present analysis is, however, limited in two ways. It does not address the larger social spaces created around international courts and their agents. The focus is instead on a more limited set of agents, namely, international judges. To speak to the larger project of a critical study of the globalization of legal education, the analysis is further limited to a study of mainly the educational capital of the international judiciary. While this is obviously a limitation to the analysis, the focus on educational capital (Bourdieu 1996b) is nevertheless helpful for drawing up a general picture of the international judiciary and its relative cosmopolitan profile. In its most basic sense, educational capital is an institutionalized form of cultural

---

[1] International courts are obviously not run by international judges alone. Other important agents of international courts are, for example, registrars and other more bureaucratic actors. For the purpose of this study, however, we only look into the narrower category of international judges.

capital that confers a set of unique properties on the holder of such capital (Bourdieu 2011). In the case of judges, who virtually all have law degrees, the unique property is the capacity to speak law and determine its contents—what sometimes is referred to as legal capital (Dezalay and Madsen 2012). Since practically all agents analyzed in this study have that capital, it is not analytically fruitful to focus on legal-educational capital as such. What is interesting, however, is the relative internationalization of the international judiciary in terms of education: Are international judges national legal champs promoted to international tasks? Or, alternatively, are they internationally trained and thereby part of a more cosmopolitan segment of the legal profession?[2]

The empirical analysis included in this study presents unique new data that has been collected with the goal of, among other things, unpacking the educational profile of the international judiciary. More specifically, the chapter conducts a comparative analysis of the judges at nine international courts based in Africa, Europe, Latin America, and the Caribbean. These courts operate in different legal subject matters. Three are human rights courts: the European Court of Human Rights (ECtHR), the Inter-American Court of Human Rights (IACtHR), and the African Court of Human and Peoples' Rights (AF). Three are regional economic courts: the Court of Justice of the European Union (CJEU), the East African Court of Justice (EACJ), and the Caribbean Court of Justice (CCJ). Three are courts with global reach: the International Court of Justice (ICJ), the World Trade Organization's Appellate Body (WTO AB), and the International Criminal Court (ICC). As explained in detail in the subsections of the empirical study, the analysis compares these nine international courts in a set of different dimensions with the goal of identifying similarities and differences based on region, nationality of judges, age, frequency of studies abroad, and attendance of elite universities.

The analysis proceeds the following way. In the first section, I briefly discuss the object of inquiry and some common ways of approaching it—and how the present study compares to the state of the art. I also provide a short introduction to the data set and its sources. Then follows the empirical study.

---

[2] A similar line of inquiry has been pursued in a set of publications by Bryant Garth and Yves Dezalay that explores legal elites, ranging from international arbitrations to national statesmen, and how their positioning between national and the international legal and political fields create a particular transnational legal power. See, e.g., Dezalay, Yves, and Bryant Garth. 2010. *Asian Legal Revivals: Lawyers in the Shadow of Empire*. Chicago: University of Chicago Press.

In the first section of the empirical study, the chapter explores *how international* the international judges actually are in terms of education. The section explores this question using both aggregated and disaggregated data on the nine international courts included in this study. The second empirical section asks *how elitist* international judges are when measured against their education and the educational institutions that they frequently attend. This section also explores the extent to which international judges have doctoral degrees. The chapter concludes with a general discussion of the relative cosmopolitanism of the international judiciary and its implications.

I. Studying the International Judiciary

The first truly international court, the Permanent Court of International Justice (PCIJ), was set up in 1922 under the auspices of the League of Nations. After an initial period of significant activity in the 1920s—a mere jazz age of international law—the situation became more difficult in the 1930s as the court increasingly faced the rising tensions between major European powers. The PCIJ was eventually suspended when World War II broke out. Yet it was resurrected in 1946 as the ICJ and as the principal organ of the new United Nations, itself in part a continuation of the defunct League of Nations. The PCIJ also impacted the idea of the international judiciary in a less visible yet equally important way. Of particular interest here are the many debates documented in the *travaux préparatoires* about who could—or should—be appointed as judges to rule on matters involving sovereign states. A set of preexisting professional groupings emphasized their respective qualifications in this regard. International law professors found themselves to be particularly competent, in part due to their long commitment to creating international courts and institutions. Diplomats also saw themselves as fit for the task ahead, and even the obvious choice for the new job. And, finally, judges—at this time in history implying only national judges—found themselves to have the right set of skills (Madsen 2016). The first bench of the PCIJ was a compromise between these competing professional groupings: "three judges, three legal advisers and five professors" (Spiermann 2013: 140). This caused some consternation among diplomats, but the dominant group of law professors turned out to be good at striking a balance between legal development and political sensitivity. Some forty years later, a group of European judges dominated by law professors at the ECtHR would similarly demonstrate their skills in "legal diplomacy" (Madsen 2011a). Current cases before international courts also suggest that the job of judging international affairs involve both law and political sensitivity (for example, Alter 2001; Shaffer, Elsig, and Puig 2016). This raises the fundamental question of whether the international judiciary is influenced by a form of path dependency derived from its original post–World War I configuration.

Existing studies of international judges generally confirm that the international judiciary is still influenced by these original dynamics. According to one study, by 2006 there were 215 international judges, coming from 86 different countries (Terris, Romano, and Swigart 2007: 17). Of these 215 judges, 136 were European—most were British and French. Most interesting is, however, the fact that the professional profile of the judges generally has followed the path of the PCIJ: 40 percent were mainly legal academics, 33 percent had pursued careers as judges, and 27 percent had been civil servants of various kind. By 2012, the number of judges had climbed to 304 distributed among 21 international courts (Swigart and Terris 2014: 621). One hundred eleven different nationalities were represented, notably by a growth in international courts in Africa. According to these scholars, 26 percent had a judicial background, 21 percent a civil servant background, and 19 percent came from legal academia. The rest came from private practice or combinations of these categories (Swigart and Terris 2014: 621).

I have in previous publications challenged these categorizations as producing a too one-dimensional portrait of international judges as being either professors, civil servants, or judges (Madsen 2014). In-depth studies of single courts suggests that a crucial feature of many international judges is long and complex careers revolving in and out of these categories, as well as other professional jobs, notably in policy expertise and politics. A telling example is the first bench of the ECtHR. It was made up of elite legal academics— some 80 percent had a doctoral degree—who had worked in or had real access to a number of other relevant spheres of law and politics (Madsen 2011b: 48). Moreover, the study suggests that these actors were not quite as "denationalized" as critics of international courts often argue. They were instead very often powerful domestic actors who had been promoted to international posts due to important national careers and who maintained deep connections to their home states. In other words, although they were international when sitting at the ECtHR, they were in practice first and foremost prestigious senior lawyers in their domestic fields.

All these existing studies have mainly assessed the international judiciary by using different professional categories. This chapter seeks a different assessment in terms of education. Turning to the educational capital of international judges provides a different but also complementary way of addressing these questions related to the configuration of the international judiciary. International judges are generally perceived as holding elite positions within the international legal profession. The question is what role education and particularly commonalities in education play in the formation of this elite group. If we accept that education is an access point to the legal market rather than an end in itself, the question is whether international legal education, notably from prestigious international universities, abounds in the CVs of international judges. Or, alternatively, do the top national universities provide the pathway to the position of international judge? A third hypothesis could be that the selection of international judges is simply not influenced by their educational profile. Existing data from the cited studies give some tentative answers to this question. Tetris et al. observe in 2007 that the world's most prestigious universities, including Oxford, Cambridge, London, and Paris in Europe, and Harvard, Yale, and Columbia in the United States, had trained (as a primary or secondary degree) close to a quarter of all international judges—the majority being trained in the United Kingdom (Terris, Romano, and Swigart 2007: 18). They also indicate that judges originating from the developing world might be more likely to have pursued studies abroad.

This study tests these hypotheses against the backdrop of new data on the education of all judges appointed to the nine international courts included in the data set. More specifically, we have drawn up a list of all judges appointed to these nine courts since their inception and then collected data on the judges' individual education. We have also collected a number of other variables, but these are not used in this analysis. Since some courts have been in operation for many decades, for example, the ICJ, the ECtHR, and the CJEU, these courts contribute to the data set with a relatively high number of judges. Also, a few international judges have held positions at multiple international courts. In those cases, they are counted for each appointment to an international court. In practice, a judge with multiple appointments is a very rare occurrence and without statistical significance. The total number of judges included in the data set is 504.

Using data on the place of birth of individual judges, we have coded their education as being national or international in terms of whether they have studied at home or abroad. In the empirical analysis, we also, in some instances, include the name of the universities where they received their degree in order to identify universities that have educated many international judges. The data are also coded in such a way that we can identify gender, nationality, and the international court where they work or have worked. Moreover, based on nationality or the location of the international court where they have been employed, we can test for regional and subregional differences with regard to education. We have also included data on the year of appointment to the relevant international courts in order to be able to identify different historical patterns.

The data has generally been collected by using a host of sources, including the yearbooks of international courts, the "Who Is Who" of a number of countries, and various online sources such as newspapers, home pages, and LinkedIn accounts. The information is generally cross-checked against multiple sources when possible. In some instances, we have not been able to detect the place of study. Of the 504 judges included in the data set, we are lacking information about the university issuing the degree in the cases of 52 judges; that is, in roughly 10 percent of the cases we lack that specific information, but we have still been able to find data indicating whether they studied abroad or not. However, in the bigger picture of this study, we deem these limitations in the data to be statistically insignificant.

II. How International Are International Judges? Studying at Home or Abroad?

Some scholars of globalization have argued that globalization is driven by a global class. Samuel Huntington, for example, identifies as a key feature of global elites that they are denationalized and instead what he terms "Davos Men"; that is, they are internationalists who pose a threat to the coherence of the nation-state and, specifically in Huntington's analysis, the "American Creed" (Huntington 2005). Another author, David Rothkopf is even more radical and argues that a global "superclass" has emerged (Rothkopf 2008). This new class, comprising some 6,000 individuals, according to the author, is defined by the fact that their connections to one another are more important than their connections to their home countries. These are just some examples of literature highly critical of what it presents as the rise of a class of globalizers with scant respect for the culture and interests of their countries of origin (see broader literature review in Kauppi and Madsen 2013a).

The critique of denationalized globalizers is also very well known to students of international courts and international judges. International courts have repeatedly been accused of living in an artificial international legal bubble, far away from the complexities of national societies and politics, and without a sense of obligation toward their home states (for example, Flogaitis, Zwart, and Fraser 2013; Popelier, Lambrecht, and Lemmens 2016). The assumption is often that such globalizers have mutual affiliations that have been formed already during their education. Aspiring judicial globalizers—as other members of this alleged global class—are assumed to meet and connect at elitist educational institutions in much the same way as the old British elite mingled at, for example, Eton and Oxford in earlier days. It is, of course, an empirical question whether this is at all the case, and one we explore in the following.

Figure 13.1 examines the extent to which international judges have studied at home or abroad. Studying abroad is defined as having taken a university degree from a country other than one's home country. The statistics on home/abroad in Figure 13.1 are split into three time periods: (1) before 1970, (2) 1970–1990; (3) after 1990. The rationale for this periodization is that international courts up until 1970 were a very limited phenomenon at the international level, with the ICJ and, in Europe, with the two regional courts of the ECJ and the ECtHR.[3] In the subsequent period—1970–1990—a number of other regional courts were established in Latin America and Europe. In the third period, after 1990, there was a significant increase in the number of regional courts in Latin America and Africa, as well as through the creation of new global courts in Europe (Alter 2012). Figure 13.1 presents the findings for all courts included in the data set in two visualizations of the number of international judges having received degrees abroad or at home: Figure 13.1a provides simple descriptive statistics; Figure 13.1b visualizes the findings as stacked bar charts.

What is most striking from Figures 13.1a and 13.1b is the relatively small percentage of international judges who have actually studied abroad. Before the 1990s, only one out of five international judges had studied abroad. After

---

[3] Please note that we have not included data on the judges of the predecessor of the ICJ, the PCIJ. Our data therefore starts in 1946.

	Before 1970	**1970 to 1990**	**After 1990**
Abroad	20.33%	19.35%	31.71%
Home	79.67%	80.65%	68.29%

Figure 13.1a. Location of Education Home/Abroad—All Courts

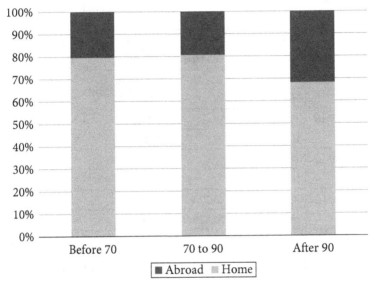

Figure 13.1b. Location of Education Home/Abroad—All Courts

1990, the number climbs to close to a third. Considering these findings, it is questionable that international judges form close-knit international groupings at the time of their education. That said, it does not exclude that they possibly create other more indirect bonds in terms of, for instance, studying very similar subjects but at different institutions, or being introduced to similar moral or political ideas (Roberts 2017). Our data set cannot detect that, however.

Figure 13.2 disaggregates these numbers in order to identify whether some international courts are more "international" than others in terms of the educational background of the judges. Figure 13.2 uses the same periodization as Figure 13.1 but disaggregates the data so that the percentages of each court is visible. In Figure 13.2a, the data are presented as simple descriptive data and in Figure 13.2b as stacked bar charts.

Court	Education Location	Before 1970	1970 to 1990	After 1990
AF	Abroad			28.26%
	Home			71.74%
CCJ	Abroad			73.33%
	Home			26.67%
EACJ	Abroad			57.14%
	Home			42.86%
ECJ	Abroad	0.00%	21.05%	19.39%
	Home	100.00%	78.95%	80.61%
ECtHR	Abroad	22.50%	12.94%	24.78%
	Home	77.50%	87.06%	75.22%
IACHR	Abroad		11.11%	12.77%
	Home		88.89%	87.23%
ICC	Abroad			47.06%
	Home			52.94%
ICJ	Abroad	23.19%	27.63%	33.64%
	Home	76.81%	72.37%	66.36%
WTO	Abroad			44.78%
	Home			55.22%

Figure 13.2a. Location of Education Home/Abroad—Individual Courts/ Periods

What is apparent from Figures 13.2a and 13.2b is that there are significant differences between the individual courts with regard to how many judges have studied abroad. Also, it is clear that the extent to which international judges have studied abroad increases significantly in the third period (after 1990). This increase in studies abroad is largely a result of the educational trajectories of judges at non-European international courts, notably in Africa (EACJ) and the Caribbean (CCJ). New global courts such as the WTO AB and the ICC also generally have more judges who have studied abroad.

We can better identify these patterns by differentiating the international courts according to the location of the courts. Figure 13.3 distinguishes between European courts (ECJ and ECtHR), courts in the Americas and Caribbean (IACtHR and CCJ), in Africa (EACJ and AF), and global courts (ICC, ICJ, WTO AB), the latter marked "international" in the figure. As in

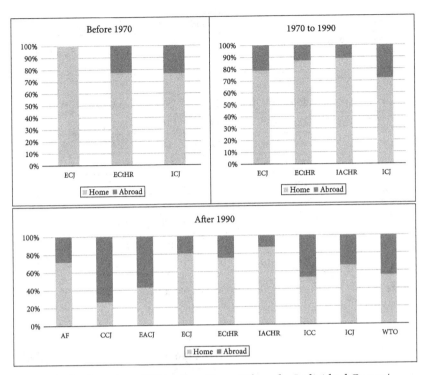

Figure 13.2b. Location of Education: Home/Abroad—Individual Courts/ Periods

the previous analyses, in Figure 13.3a we present the simple descriptive statistics, and in Figure 13.3b we use stacked bar charts. In Figure 13.3b we only include the two last periods (1970–1990 and after 1990).

Figure 13.3 underscores the findings of Figure 13.2, namely, that international courts in Africa are the most international in terms of the judges having studied abroad. This is probably to a large extent the result of the unavailability of advanced degrees in those countries and to the attractiveness of degrees from abroad in the local job market (Roberts 2017). The global courts, probably as a consequence of increased influence of non-Western judges, are also increasingly internationalized in terms of the education of the judges.

A final assessment of the relative internationalization of international judges in terms of education can be done by differentiating the international courts not according to location or specific court as in the previous figures, but by looking into the subject matters in which these courts specialize. In

Period	Continent	Abroad	Home	Abroad	Home
Before 1970	Europe	9	45	17%	83%
	Americas	0	0		
	Africa	0	0		
	International	16	53	23%	77%
1970 to 1990	Europe	19	104	15%	85%
	Americas	2	16	11%	89%
	Africa	0	0		
	International	2	55	4%	96%
After 1990	Europe	75	249	23%	77%
	Americas	17	45	27%	73%
	Africa	37	51	42%	58%
	International	99	146	40%	60%

Figure 13.3a. Education Home/Abroad by Location of Court/Time

our data set, we can locate three courts in the area of regional human rights (ECtHR, IACtHR, and AF), three in regional economic law (ECJ, EACJ, and CCJ), and three in global matters (ICJ, ICC, and WTO AB). Figure 13.4 provides first the simplified statistics (Figure 13.4a) and then a visualization using stacked bar charts (Figure 13.4b) with regard to these three types of courts in terms of subject area.

In these aggregated numbers of each of the three subject areas of international courts, we find that the least internationalized area is international human rights. Interestingly, this area of international law makes the most direct claim to universality of international law, but it is nevertheless the least internationalized in terms of the education of the judges who end up ruling on matters of international human rights at international courts. One plausible explanation is that the member states drawing up the list of candidates for positions at international courts in the area of human rights are well aware that the universalizing discourse on international human rights might be countered by the appointment of judges who are more trained in national ways of understanding human rights. A recent study of the ECtHR confirms this explanation, arguing that the way in which the member states recently have sought to counter the Europeanizing tendencies of the ECtHR has been by promoting national judges to the international bench. Such appointment strategies, it appears, tacitly ensure that knowledge and know-how of

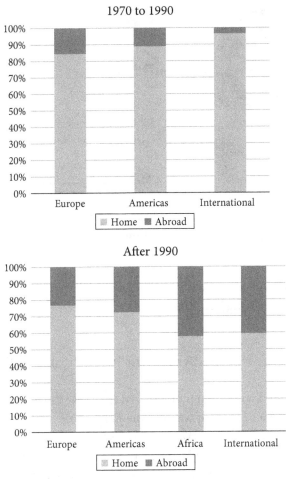

Figure 13.3b. Education Home/Abroad By Location of Court/Time

	Abroad	Home
Economic	30.98%	69.02%
Global	36.26%	63.74%
Human rights	22.16%	77.84%

Figure 13.4a. Education Home/Abroad Subject Area of Court

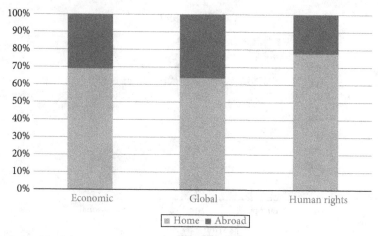

Figure 13.4b. Education Home/Abroad Subject Area of Court

national legal systems are both available and likely to influence the outlook of the system at large (Madsen 2015).

III. Elite Universities and the International Judiciary

This chapter has so far mainly presented data that differentiated international courts with regard to whether the judges employed by those courts have studied abroad or not. We have, however, not addressed whether they have studied in some particular areas of the world or at some specific universities when they pursue their studies. This section seeks to answer that question by providing data on the universities that most frequently have issued degrees to international judges. Using this data, we seek to visualize, on a world map, the center(s) of global legal education for international judges. Finally, we test for the prevalence of advanced degrees in terms of doctoral degrees and whether the pursuit of advanced degrees can explain patterns of relative internationalization of judges at international courts.

As noted previously, it is often assumed that globalization is driven by a certain class of people who are educated at the same universities and thereby bestowed with intersubjective ideas about politics, economics, and law. Historically, universities have played a major role in the reproduction of elites as, for example, documented in numerous studies of the Ivy League in the United States, Oxbridge in the United Kingdom, or the *grandes écoles* in

France (Bourdieu 1996b; Hartmann 2000; Lillard and Gerner 1999; Mullen 2009). Law faculties or law schools are often highlighted as particularly elitist sites of education—however, not always because of academic rigor but more often because of the social connections which can be acquired at those establishments (Dahrendorf 1969). For the purpose of this analysis, it is, however, not relevant whether elite law schools provide rigorous training or good social connections. The main goal is to identify whether there are single institutions or clusters of institutions that have trained a significant number of international judges.

Using our data set on international judges, Figure 13.5 calculates the top ten universities that have educated the most international judges. The assessment is made by adding up the total number of degrees issued by each university to persons who have been appointed to the international courts included in this study.

To scholars of elite international legal education, this top-ten list comes with few surprises. Indeed, some of the best-known international elite universities in the United Kingdom, the United States, and France appear on the list. Considering the general European dominance with regard to international courts and probably international law more generally, it is also unsurprising that European elite universities are represented with four out of the

University Top-10 Descending	Total
University of Cambridge	38
University of London	33
Harvard University	25
University of Paris	24
University of Oxford	19
Columbia University	14
Yale University	11
University of Madrid	10
University of Bonn	10
New York University	10

Figure 13.5. The Top-10 Universities in the Education of International Judges

top five institutions on the list. Among the positions from six to ten, we do find some surprises, notably the University of Bonn. We have no particular explanation for the place of Bonn University except that its location close to the Benelux countries has made it attractive for more students and that it is generally well respected in Germany for legal education. Other major German universities are also repeat players but cannot be seen in Figure 13.5, which includes only the ten highest scoring universities. But because of the decentralized profile of German higher education, quite a few universities (Frankfurt, Heidelberg, Berlin, Hamburg, and Munich) are the producers of degrees for international judges. Less surprising is that the University of Madrid also appears on the list, considering its attraction for Latin American students pursuing advanced degrees in law in Spanish. The remainder of the universities (Yale, Colombia, and NYU) are all well-known institutions of international elite education in law, also in the field of international law. Their lower position on the list probably most of all reflects that there are only a limited number of US international judges.

Comparing the set of identified universities, notably the list of universities with a score of more than ten, and the rest of universities that have trained international judges, we can visualize the landscape of educating international judges using the tool of (so-called) heat maps. This allows us to visualize where the "heat is on" in terms of the higher education of international judges. Figure 13.6a presents the heat map of the entire world in this regard.

It is apparent from Figure 13.6a that a small cluster of universities around the Paris-London axis and surroundings and the traditional US East Coast

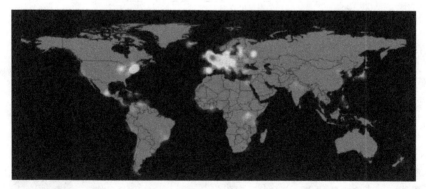

Figure 13.6a. Heat Map of Major Educational Institution of the International Judiciary

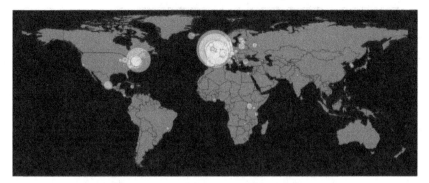

Figure 13.6b. Major Educational Institution of the International Judiciary

legal educational establishment are the leading producers of international judges. To further identify these patterns, Figure 13.6b uses a different visualization technique that in addition to coloring the location of major universities also adds circles relative to the number of graduates of that institution. In addition, labels have been added for the top universities in this regard.

Both Figure 13.6a and Figure 13.6b highlight the centrality of the same few educational institutions to the training of international judges. A few additional institutions of relevance, however, can be observed using this visualization, notably the National Autonomous University of Mexico and Moscow State University. The former, it appears from the data set, has trained a number of Latin American judges; the latter has catered to East European judges, particularly from neighboring countries of the former Soviet Union. Another circle worth noting is in Kampala, Uganda, where a number of African judges have received training.

The statistics presented in Figures 13.5 and 13.6 do not distinguish between whether the judge has pursued regular degrees or advanced degrees in this regard. The existing studies of international judges cited generally suggest that there is a relative high number of holders of doctoral degrees among international judges. In what follows, we first detect the total number of doctors among international judges in the data set and then see if we can identify particular patterns in this regard with respect to the international courts included in the analysis. As a doctoral degree, we have included a set of postgraduate degrees that lead to the title "doctor," including PhD, LLD, and JD. However, a JD degree is not considered a doctoral degree in this context as it is a law degree more similar to a European *candidatus/candidata juris*. In Figures 13.7a and 13.7b, judges without doctoral degrees are not

Period	No. of Doctoral Degrees	Total No. of Judges	Percentage
Before 1970	44	70	62.9%
1970 to 1990	67	123	54.5%
After 1990	192	356	53.9%

Figure 13.7a. Number of Doctoral Degrees and Number of Judges per Period

	Before 1970	1970 to 1990	After 1990
AF	0.0%	0.0%	26.3%
EACJ	0.0%	0.0%	16.7%
ECJ	44.4%	45.5%	57.1%
ECtHR	82.6%	70.6%	64.6%
IACHR	0.0%	41.7%	51.9%
ICC	0.0%	0.0%	40.6%
ICJ	55.3%	42.1%	48.8%
WTO	0.0%	0.0%	87.0%

Figure 13.7b. Percentage of Doctoral Degrees at Individual Courts per Period

considered. As a consequence, the CCJ is not included in the figures as none of its judges have received doctoral degrees.[4]

Figure 13.7 provides the statistics on the relative frequency of doctoral degrees among international judges. Figure 13.7a first provides the general picture of the frequency of doctoral degrees among international judges in absolute numbers and in percentage terms across three time periods. Figure 13.7b distinguishes different international courts in this regard and provides the percentage of judges with doctoral degrees at the individual courts.

Figures 13.7a and 13.7b make an interesting finding, namely, that international judges, when compared to the legal profession at large, have a disproportionately high number of individuals with doctoral degrees. Although the average figure has been declining since the first period (Figure 13.7a), the current number is close to 54 percent, which is a high number when compared to the legal profession at large. Only legal academia as an institution can compete with that number. Among courts, the only other major national court

---

[4] We also exclude from the analysis honorary doctoral degrees.

that comes to mind that has a similar high percentage of judges with doctoral degrees is the German Constitutional Court (*Bundesverfassungsgericht*), which has a 100 percent score of doctoral degrees in its First Senate and 75 percent in its Second Senate.[5] Other major supreme courts do not come close to these numbers. However, as Figure 13.7b illustrates, there is also noticeable variation among the courts in this regard. The two African courts included in the study have the lowest total number with doctoral degrees. At the other end of the continuum, we find the WTO AB, which has close to 90 percent. The ECtHR, which started out with 80 percent of the judges holding doctoral degrees, has now dropped to 65 percent. Overall, around 50 percent of the judges hold doctoral degrees in the courts included in this study.

Figures 13.8a and 13.8b identify patterns with regard to each of the courts studied as concerns whether the holders of doctoral degrees have studied

		Before 1970		1970 to 1990		After 1990	
Court		No.	%	No.	%	No.	%
AF	Abroad					3	60.00%
	Home					2	40.00%
EACJ	Abroad					2	66.67%
	Home					1	33.33%
ECJ	Abroad	0	0.00%	2	20.00%	5	15.63%
	Home	4	100.00%	8	80.00%	27	84.38%
ECtHR	Abroad	6	31.58%	9	25.00%	17	20.24%
	Home	13	68.42%	27	75.00%	67	79.76%
IACHR	Abroad			1	20.00%	3	21.43%
	Home			4	80.00%	11	78.57%
ICC	Abroad					7	53.85%
	Home					6	46.15%
ICJ	Abroad	4	19.05%	4	25.00%	8	38.10%
	Home	17	80.95%	12	75.00%	13	61.90%
WTO	Abroad						50.00%
	Home						50.00%

Figure 13.8a. Location of Education of Doctoral Degrees per Court and Period

[5] For details, see http://www.bundesverfassungsgericht.de/DE/Homepage/homepage_node.html.

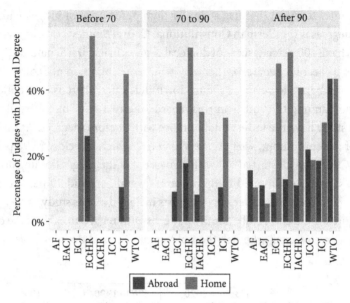

Figure 13.8b. Judges with Doctoral Degrees per Period and Court and Location of Degree

abroad or at home. Figure 13.8a provides the simple statistics of the percentage of holders of doctoral degrees who have studied abroad or at home, as well as the total number. (Note that judges without doctoral degrees are not included in Figure 13.8a). Figure 13.8b presents the percentage of judges with doctoral degrees in relation to the total number of judges, split between degrees awarded at home and abroad.

As it appears from these statistics, there is noticeable variation among the courts studied with regard to the location of the institutions that have awarded the doctoral degrees to international judges. Compared with the analysis presented in Figures 13.2 and 13.3 about the frequency of studies abroad, the pattern with respect to doctoral degrees is rather similar. Most judges with doctoral degrees received from abroad are found at African courts (AF and EACJ) and at new global courts (ICC and WTO AB). However, the number of doctoral degrees among African judges is, as shown, the lowest in the total data set when excluding the CCJ. The regional courts in Europe (ECJ and ECtHR) and Latin America (IACtHR) stand out as the least international in this regard. It is well known that at least until recently, the value of domestic doctoral degrees in law was generally very high, notably in Europe; and in some European countries, notably the larger ones, higher than foreign doctoral degrees. This underlying logic is probably reflected in the patterns seen with regard to the two European courts. It is possible that the same is the case with regard to the IACtHR in terms of the valorization of domestic degrees. Moreover, it is likely that governments' choices when identifying candidates for regional international courts are influenced—deliberately or not—by considerations of knowledge of domestic law. All things equal, domestic doctoral degrees are more likely to focus on nationally informed questions than degrees from abroad. But this remains speculative and cannot be supported by the data set used in this analysis.

IV. Discussion and Conclusion

The number of international courts has proliferated over the past two decades, resulting in a multiplication of the number of international judges. Currently, more than three hundred men and women hold the office of international judge. A fair share of these judges is found at the two mega regional courts of the CJEU and the ECtHR, but many other regional and global courts now also employ a significant number of international judges. Scholarship on international courts has generally been marked by institutionalist approaches. This has provided very little insight into who the men and women are who decide important cases in international human rights, international economic law, and international criminal law, and, for example, draw up the boundaries of states. This chapter unpacks the international judiciary by a comparative analysis of nine international courts based in Africa, Europe, Latin America, and the Caribbean in order to provide a more precise picture of this alleged global class of judges.

The chapter has more precisely addressed two related questions in this regard by examining the educational backgrounds of international judges. First, *how international* judges are in practice as measured by their educational background. Second, whether international judges belong to an international elite in terms of having studied at the same international elite legal educational institutions. To answer those two questions, the chapter first conducted a number of statistical analyses of the general educational profile of international courts, as well as variations among them related to their location and their putative subject-matter jurisdiction. The study, secondly, identified the role of elite universities in the production and reproduction of international judges, as well as the frequency of international judges with doctoral degrees, another marker of distinction of this professional group.

Generally, and perhaps counter to popular intuition, we can observe that international judges are predominantly trained at domestic institutions of higher education. This is particularly true for European international courts, while African and Caribbean international courts employ more internationally trained judges. Global courts, particularly the new ones established since 1990 (WTO AB and ICC), also feature a larger proportion of internationally trained judges. In fact, the general patterns of internationalization of their education are similar to students in general, including students of international law (Roberts 2017). International judges, however, stand out with regard to the frequency of doctoral degrees among them as compared to the legal profession at large. More historical studies of international courts note that international judges, since the PCIJ, have included many academics or semi-academic lawyers. This in part accounts for the high frequency of doctoral degrees. Another explanation is that doctoral degrees function as a marker of distinction when appointing international judges. The holders of doctoral degrees have, in other words, a slight competitive advantage over other jurists in the competition for seats on the international bench.

The general conclusion of this study is that international judges hardly form a detached or denationalized elite when looking into their educational profile. In fact, the data and analysis presented suggest that international judges tend to be educationally embedded in national legal fields. This finding seems to confirm earlier studies of global legal elites that have similarly emphasized how international lawyers make large parts of their careers in domestic fields (Bourdieu 1996a; Jarle Christensen 2016). What is highlighted by such studies, as well as the present one, is that the international sphere of law to a large extent is a continuation of domestic forms of reproducing elites (Dezalay and Madsen 2012). The different patterns observed in this study between, for example, Europe and Africa are in fact not differing from the regional models of producing elites. While European elites typically pursue elite education in their top national universities, African elites are more likely to go abroad. The case of the CCJ with its extreme internationalization is clearly a case in point in this regard.

Education is, of course, only one way of assessing the social construction of the international judiciary. To get a fuller picture, one will also have to study the longer professional trajectories of the relevant agent. What such studies tend to find is that international judges have multiple engagements across relevant social fields. In many cases, these agents are quite embedded in national legal fields—both educationally and professionally—but they are not limited by these boundaries, a typical trait of elites anywhere. To understand the real power of international courts, it is therefore necessary to also look beyond the institutionally delineated category of judges and include in the analysis the broader transnational professional constituencies emerging around these institutions and practices. It is in fact precisely the rise of this broader complex of legal power and power elites, in which international judges play a key part, that has made international courts prominent features of global governance.

References

Alter, Karen (2001). *Establishing the Supremacy of European Law: The Making of an International Rule of Law in Europe.* Oxford University Press.

Alter, Karen J. (2012). "The Global Spread of European Style International Courts," *West European Politics* 35(1): 135–154.

Alter, Karen J. (2014). *The New Terrain of International Law: Courts, Politics, Rights.* Princeton University Press.

Bourdieu, Pierre (1996a). "Foreword," in Yves Dezalay and Bryant Garth, eds., *Dealing in Virtue: International Commercial Arbitration and the Construction of a Transnational Legal Order.* Pp. vii–viii. University of Chicago Press.

Bourdieu, Pierre (1996b). *The State Nobility: Elite Schools in the Field of Power.* Stanford University Press.

Bourdieu, Pierre (2011). "The Forms of Capital (1986)," in Imre Szeman and Timothy Kaposy, eds., *Cultural Theory: An Anthology.* Pp. 81–93. Blackwell.

Cohen, Antonin (2010). "'Dix personnages majestueux en longue robe amarante': La formation de la cour de justice des communautés européennes," *Revue française de science politique* 60(2): 227–246.

Cohen, Antonin and Mikael Rask Madsen (2007). "Cold War Law: Legal Entrepreneurs and the Emergence of a European Legal Field (1945–1965)," in Volkmar Gessner and David Nelken, eds., *European Ways of Law: Towards a European Sociology of Law.* Pp. 175–202. Hart Publishing.

Dahrendorf, Ralf (1969). "Law Faculties and the German Upper Class," in Wilhelm Aubert, ed., *The Sociology of Law.* Pp. 294–309. Penguin.

Dezalay, Yves and Bryant Garth (2010). *Asian Legal Revivals: Lawyers in the Shadow of Empire.* University of Chicago Press.

Dezalay, Yves and Mikael R. Madsen (2012). "The Force of Law and Lawyers: Pierre Bourdieu and the Reflexive Sociology of Law," *Annual Review of Law and Social Science* 8: 433–452.

Flogaitis, Spyridon, Tom Zwart, and Julie Fraser, eds. (2013). *The European Court of Human Rights and Its Discontents: Turning Criticism into Strength.* Edward Elgar.

Hartmann, Michael (2000). "Class-Specific Habitus and the Social Reproduction of the Business Elite in Germany and France," *The Sociological Review* 48(2): 241–261.

Huntington, Samuel P. (2005). *Who Are We?: America's Great Debate*. Free Press.

Jarle Christensen, Mikkel (2016). "International Prosecution and National Bureaucracy: The Contest to Define International Practices Within the Danish Prosecution Service," *Law & Social Inquiry*. 43(1): 152–181.

Kauppi, Niilo and Mikael Rask Madsen (2013a). "Transnational Power Elites: The New Professionals of Governance, Law and Security," in Niilo Kauppi and Mikael R. Madsen, eds., *Transnational Power Elites: The New Professionals of Governance, Law and Security*. Pp. 1–16. Routledge.

Kauppi, Niilo and Mikael Rask Madsen, eds. (2013b). *Transnational Power Elites: The New Professionals of Governance, Law and Security*. Routledge.

Kauppi, Niilo and Mikael Rask Madsen (2014). "Fields of Global Governance: How Transnational Power Elites Can Make Global Governance Intelligible," *International Political Sociology* 8(3): 324–330.

Kingsbury, Benedict, Nico Krisch, and Richard B. Stewart (2005). "The Emergence of Global Administrative Law," *Law and Contemporary Problems* 68(15): 15–61.

Koskenniemi, Martti and Päivi Leino (2002). "Fragmentation of International Law? Postmodern Anxieties," *Leiden Journal of International Law* 15(03): 553–579.

Lillard, Dean and Jennifer Gerner (1999). "Getting to the Ivy League: How Family Composition Affects College Choice," *The Journal of Higher Education* 70(6): 706–730.

Madsen, Mikael R. (2014). "The International Judiciary as Transnational Power Elite," *International Political Sociology* 8(3): 332–334.

Madsen, Mikael Rask (2011a). "Legal Diplomacy—Law, Politics and the Genesis of Postwar European Human Rights," in Stefan Ludwig Hoffmann, ed., *Human Rights in the Twentieth Century: A Critical History*. Pp. 62–81. Cambridge University Press.

Madsen, Mikael Rask (2011b). "The Protracted Institutionalisation of the Strasbourg Court: From Legal Diplomacy to Integrationist Jurisprudence," in Mikael Rask Madsen and Jonas Christoffersen, eds., *The European Court of Human Rights between Law and Politics*. Pp. 43–60. Oxford University Press.

Madsen, Mikael Rask (2015). "The Legitimization Strategies of International Courts: The Case of the European Court of Human Rights," in Michal Bobek, ed., *Selecting Europe's Judges*. Pp. 259–278. Oxford University Press.

Madsen, Mikael Rask (2016). "Judicial Globalization: The Proliferation of International Courts," in Sabino Cassese, ed., *Research Handbook on Global Administrative Law*. Pp. 282–302. Edward Elgar.

Mullen, Ann L. (2009). "Elite Destinations: Pathways to Attending an Ivy League University," *British Journal of Sociology of Education* 30(1): 15–27.

Popelier, Patricia, Sarah Lambrecht, and Koon Lemmens, eds. (2016). *Criticism of the European Court of Human Rights—Shifting the Convention System: Counter-dynamics at the National Level*. Intersentia.

Roberts, Anthea (2017). *Is International Law International?* Oxford University Press.

Romano, Cesare P.R. (1999). "The Proliferation of International Tribunals: Piecing Together the Puzzle," *NYU Journal of International Law and Politics* 31(4): 709–751.

Rothkopf, David (2008). *Superclass: The Global Power Elite and the World They Are Making*. Farrar, Straus and Giroux.

Schachter, Oscar (1977). "Invisible College of International Lawyers," *Northwestern University Law Review* 72: 217–226.

Shaffer, Gregory C., Manfred Elsig, and Sergio Puig (2016). "The Extensive (but Fragile) Authority of the WTO Appellate Body," *Law & Contemporary Problems* 19(1): 237–273.

Spiermann, Ole (2013). "The Legacy of the Permanent Court of International Justice: On Judges and Scholars, and Also on Bishops and Clowns," in Christian J. Tams and Malgosia Fitzmaurice, eds., *Legacies of the Permanent Court of International Justice*. Pp. 399–413. Nijhoff.

Swigart, Leigh and Daniel Terris (2014). "Who Are International Judges?," in Cesare P.R. Romano, J. Karen Alter, and Yuval Shany, eds., *The Oxford Handbook of International Adjudication*. Pp. 619–638. Oxford University Press.

Terris, Daniel, Cesare P.R. Romano, and Leigh Swigart (2007). *The International Judge: An Introduction to the Men and Women Who Decide the World's Cases*. Oxford University Press.

Vauchez, Antoine (2007). "Une élite d'intermédiaires: Genèse d'un capital juridique européen (1950–1970)," *Actes de la recherche en sciences sociales* 1(166–167): 54–65.

14

Cross-Border Student Flows and the Construction of International Law as a Transnational Legal Field

Anthea Roberts[*]

How does the global flow of students shape the production and diffusion of knowledge in international law as a transnational legal field? Education plays a crucial role in shaping individuals' approaches and networks (incoming influences) and represents a meaningful form of soft power through which academics in some states are able to diffuse ideas, materials, and approaches across borders (outgoing spheres of influence). However, what are the patterns that reflect, and forces that shape, whether individuals from certain states are likely to cross borders to undertake tertiary studies? And, if they do undertake transnational study, where do they go? And how might these patterns influence the construction of transnational fields, such as international law?[1]

When asked to reflect on the professional community of international lawyers, Oscar Schachter memorably called it an "invisible college" whose members were "dispersed throughout the world" yet "engaged in a continuous process of communication and collaboration." Schachter pointed to a number of factors in reaching this conclusion, including the "transnational movement of professors and students" (Schachter 1977: 217). International lawyers have long been taken with Schachter's description of their professional community. However, as I argue in *Is International Law International?*, it might be better to understand the transnational field of international law as

[*] This chapter is based on a modified version of Chapter 3 from ANTHEA ROBERTS, IS INTERNATIONAL LAW INTERNATIONAL? (2017).
[1] When I refer to "international law" and "international lawyers," I am referring to the field of public international law and to international lawyers who have a specialty in public international law, rather than to lawyers who engage in comparative law or transnational contracting and dispute resolution more generally.

Anthea Roberts, *Cross-Border Student Flows and the Construction of International Law as a Transnational Legal Field*
In: *The Globalization of Legal Education.* Edited by: Bryant Garth & Gregory Shaffer, Oxford University Press.
© Oxford University Press 2022. DOI: 10.1093/oso/9780197632314.003.0014

comprising a "divisible college" of international lawyers marked by patterns of difference and dominance (Roberts 2017: 1–2).

International law academics in different states often have distinct profiles based on where they studied, whom they teach, which languages they use, what and where they publish, and how they engage with practice. Rather than a single community, the field consists of separate—though overlapping—communities, often demonstrating distinct approaches, reference points, hierarchies, areas of expertise, and spheres of influence. This chapter examines the role of transnational legal education in this process. It considers what implications can be drawn from the existence (or otherwise) of transnational educational experiences of students and academics,[2] with a particular focus on students who cross borders to complete a law degree and the educational backgrounds of international law professors at elite universities in the five permanent members of the UN Security Council.[3]

I argue that the patterns that can be observed in these transnational flows reflect and reinforce certain nationalizing, denationalizing, and Westernizing influences that characterize the field of international law.[4] When students study law in only their own state, they are more likely to develop a nationalized approach to international law, though this depends in part on the state in which they study. When students cross borders to study international law, this has a denationalizing effect on them as they are exposed to another national approach to international law and a different community of international law professors and students. However, because students typically move toward core, Western states, transnational legal education often introduces or reconfirms a Western orientation. As many of these students return home to practice or teach after their studies, these movements create pathways for ideas, approaches, and materials to move from core states to periphery and semiperiphery ones.

---

[2] There can be many experiences that can add to the level of internationalization of students and faculty, including exchange programs at the student level, visiting positions at the faculty level, and work in foreign firms or international organizations. Completing a more holistic account of these influences was beyond the scope of this chapter, though some scholars have attempted it with respect to individual academies like the US legal academy, see, e.g., Scoville and Markovic (2016), and I tracked some other nationalizing and denationalizing influences in Roberts (2017: Chapter 3). Although it presents only one piece of a broader puzzle, it is worth focusing on law degrees given that they represent a particularly important and visible socializing process within the professional formation of international lawyers and one that typically occurs at a relatively formative stage of a lawyer's intellectual development and career.

[3] For an explanation of why I chose these states and universities for my book, and how I selected the academics to study from these states, see Roberts (2017: Chapters 1–2 and app. A).

[4] For an explanation of these terms, see Roberts (2017: Chapter 2.IV).

The asymmetrical movements of students from the periphery and semiperiphery toward the core, and ideas and materials radiating from the core toward the periphery and semiperiphery, play an important role in producing the unequal and divisible colleges of international law. These educational patterns reflect and reinforce some of the hierarchies and inequalities that characterize the international legal field more generally, including the disproportionate power of legal elites in core states to define the "international" in their own image and to transpose their national ideas, materials, and approaches onto the international plane. These patterns of difference and dominance are central to understanding the construction of international law as a transnational legal field and are at odds with the self-image of universality that the field likes to project (Roberts 2017: Chapter 1).

This chapter focuses on how these asymmetrical transnational educational dynamics play out with respect to the field of public international law. However, it would be worth others exploring to what extent the same or different patterns appear in other legal and nonlegal fields, particularly those that aspire to being global, international, transnational, or comparative, such as transnational corporate law, comparative constitutional law, international relations, world history, and economics.[5] It may well be that the more "international" a field becomes, the more it dollarizes on particular currency, reflecting and reinforcing certain hierarchical relationships that inhibit heterogeneity (Dezalay and Garth 2002: 44–47). These patterns of diversity and difference, and hierarchy and heterogeneity, also create a template for understanding the construction of transnational legal orders (Halliday and Shaffer 2015).

I. Transnational Student Flows

No comprehensive data is available on the transnational flow of law students, let alone on students who cross borders to study international law. But the UN Educational, Scientific and Cultural Organization (UNESCO) has compiled reasonably comprehensive data about cross-border flows of tertiary

---

[5] For instance, it might be that students from semiperiphery civil law states who wish to work in large international law firms would place particular emphasis on studying in the United States, whereas those who wish to enter the legal academy may still privilege studying in a core state that shares the same legal family and/or language as their state of origin.

students in general,[6] along with more specific data about cross-border flows of law students into around thirty-five (mainly European and Organisation for Economic Co-operation and Development (OECD)) states.[7] This section deals with each in turn.

A. Cross-Border Flows of Students in General

Broadly speaking, the global flow of students and ideas to date appears to have been shaped by two asymmetrical dynamics. First, students are more likely to move from peripheral and semiperipheral states toward core states, and from non-Western states to Western ones, than the other way around. The symbolic capital associated with undertaking further legal education differs markedly among states because enhanced status is generally associated with movement toward the core rather than away from it. This means that, when it comes to the transnational movement of students, some states function primarily as host states ("importer states"), while others function predominantly as sender states ("exporter states"). This can be seen in Table 14.1, which sets out the top ten importer and exporter states.

Australia and South Africa represent good examples of these core–periphery and Western/non-Western dynamics because they are regional educational hubs that evidence a clear disparity between where their students come from (mainly non-Western states) and where their students go (mainly Western states) (see Figures 14.1 to 14.4).[8]

Second, the transnational flow of ideas and materials is asymmetrical in the opposite direction: legal concepts and materials, like textbooks and case law, are more likely to move from core states to peripheral and semiperipheral ones, and from Western states to non-Western ones, than vice versa. This asymmetrical diffusion results from the hierarchical nature of

[6] UNESCO collects data on all "internationally mobile students" who "have [physically] crossed a national or territorial border for the purpose of education and are now enrolled outside their country of origin." See UNESCO (2017b). Internationally mobile students are a subgroup of "foreign students," a category that includes all noncitizen students in the country, including those who have permanent residency. *Id.* These data cover only students who pursue a higher education degree or diploma outside their country of origin, excluding students who are under short-term, for-credit study and exchange programs that last less than a full academic year. *Id.*

[7] This information was provided by e-mail by Chiao-Ling Chen, UNESCO, but is not available on the UNESCO website.

[8] All of the figures are taken from Roberts (2017), and are based on the UNESCO website data.

Table 14.1. Top Ten Importer and Exporter States of International Students

Country	Population (millions) in 2017	Outgoing Int'l Student[a]	Incoming Int'l Student[b]	Top Five Destination Countries[c]	Top Five Source Countries[d]
Australia	25	12,026	294,438	US, New Zealand, UK, Germany, Canada	China, India, Malaysia, Vietnam, Nepal
China	1,385	801,187	123,127	US, Australia, UK, Japan, Canada	No data
France	67	80,635	235,123	Belgium, UK, Canada, Switzerland, Germany	China, Morocco, Algeria, Tunisia, Senegal
Germany	83	116,342	228,756	Austria, Netherlands, UK, Switzerland, US	China, Russia, India, Austria, France
India	1,320	255,030	41,993	US, Australia, UK, New Zealand, Canada	Nepal, Afghanistan, Bhutan, Nigeria, Malaysia
Italy	61	56,712	90,419	UK, Austria, France, Germany, Switzerland	China, Albania, Romania, Iran, Greece
Japan	127	30,179	132,685	US, UK, Germany, Australia, France	China, South Korea, Vietnam, Nepal, Indonesia
Kazakhstan	18	77,965	12,533	Russia, Kyrgyzstan, US, Turkey, UK	Uzbekistan, India, China, Kyrgyzstan, Russia
Korea, Rep.	51	108,047	54,540	US, Japan, Australia, UK, Canada	China, Vietnam, Mongolia, US, Japan
Malaysia	32	64,480	60,244	UK, Australia, US, Egypt, Jordan	Bangladesh, Indonesia, China, Nigeria, Iran

Table 14.1. *Continued*

Country	Population (millions) in 2017	Outgoing Int'l Student[a]	Incoming Int'l Student[b]	Top Five Destination Countries[c]	Top Five Source Countries[d]
Nigeria	194	75,539	No data	UK, Ghana, US, Malaysia, Ukraine	No data
Russia	147	56,328	226,431	Germany, Czechia, US, UK, France	Kazakhstan, Ukraine, Belarus, Turkmenistan, Uzbekistan
Saudi Arabia	33	86,486	73,077	US, UK, Canada, Australia, Jordan	Yemen, Syrian Arab Republic, Egypt, Palestine, Pakistan
United Kingdom	65	31,078	428,724	US, France, Netherlands, Germany, Australia	China, India, Nigeria, Malaysia, US
United States	326	67,665	907,251	UK, Canada, Grenada, Germany, France	China, India, South Korea, Saudi Arabia, Canada

[a] See UNESCO (2017a). These figures were extracted on Oct. 23, 2017 and are for 2016.

[b] *Id.* These figures are for 2015, except the United Kingdom, France, and Japan (collectively for 2014), and Kazakhstan (2016).

[c] These destination states were taken from the summary page for each state UNESCO website on Oct. 23, 2017. The website did not clarify from which year these figures were drawn.

[d] *Id.*

student-teacher relationships—where diffusion works better from teacher to student, and from student to student, than from student to teacher—and from the tendency of foreign students who study law abroad to return home to teach or practice rather than to stay where they undertook foreign study.

Within these broad patterns, students often move within groupings of states that are bound together by a common language, colonial history, and membership in the same legal family. The UNESCO data shows the significance of native languages in the global flow of students, whether it be students traveling from francophone states in Africa and Asia to study in France, or students from Belarus, Kazakhstan, Kyrgyzstan, Tajikistan, Ukraine, and

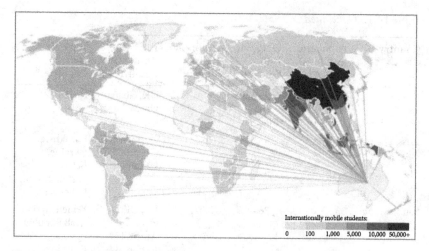

Figure 14.1. Australian Inbound Flow of International Students

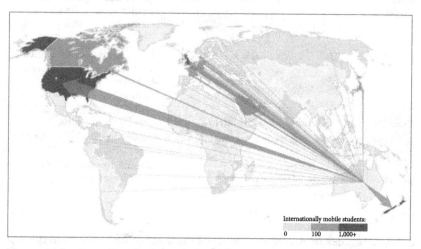

Figure 14.2. Australian Outbound Flow of International Students

Uzbekistan choosing to head to Russia. Student flows are often concentrated within legal families and, in particular, along ex-colonial pathways.[9] These influences are evident in regression analyses,[10] but they can also be seen in

[9] For instance, the pattern of students seeking to study in their former colonial master seems to be weaker for many states in South America, such as Brazil and Argentina vis-à-vis Portugal and Spain, respectively.

[10] On the basis of regression analysis of UNESCO statistics from previous years, Holger Spamann found that more than twice as many students from any state studying abroad select a state of the same

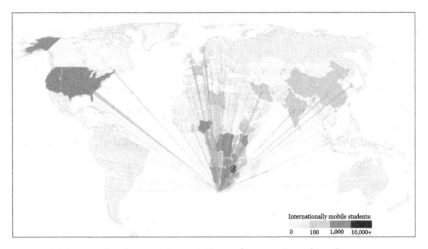

Figure 14.3. South African Inbound Flow of International Students

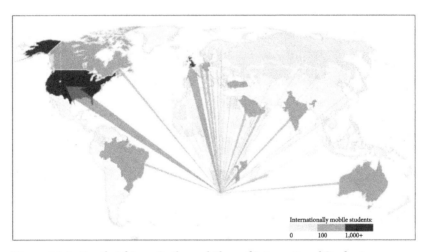

Figure 14.4. South African Outbound Flow of International Students

the pattern of attendance of students from Nigeria (a common law, former UK colony) and Mauritania (a civil law, former French colony) (see Figures 14.5 and 14.6).

legal family rather than a state in a different legal family. When the attraction of host countries was held fixed, students from former colonies were twenty-five times more likely to study in a university of their former colonial power than elsewhere (Spamann 2009: 1851).

Despite the influence of native languages and legal families, the educational institutions of core English-speaking states exhibit an especially far-reaching pull. English represents the closest thing to an educational lingua franca. The top three importers of foreign students are English-speaking, common law states (the United States, the United Kingdom, and Australia), and together they host 35 percent of international students worldwide (UNESCO 2017c). Many students from non-English-speaking, non-common-law states study in these states. English-language programs are

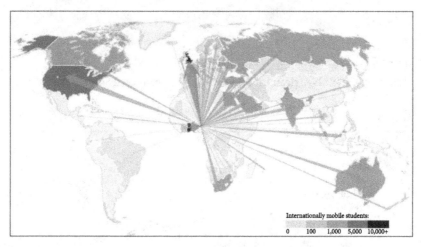

Figure 14.5. Outbound Flow of International Students from Nigeria

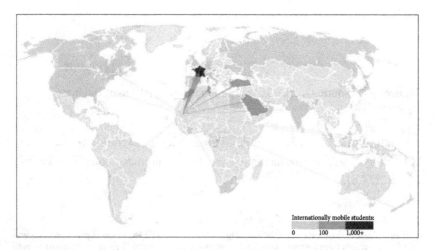

Figure 14.6. Outbound Flow of International Students from Mauritania

also becoming more common in non-English speaking states like China, Germany, the Netherlands, and Switzerland, which are seeking to attract foreign students.

Taken together, these trends demonstrate that there are multiple cores and peripheries—an anglophone core, a francophone core, a russophone core, and so forth. Each core state has its own semiperipheral or peripheral states, though the apex of each core differs in height. France forms an apex for studies within the francophone world and for students from civil law states. Russia forms an apex for studies within russophone Eurasian states, though the relationship is changing for states like Ukraine that are reorienting toward the West. All in all, fewer students travel to Russia to study than to France, which in turn is fewer than the number of students traveling to the United Kingdom and the United States to study. This means that there are not just hierarchies within particular core–periphery dynamics but also among different core states. However, these patterns are subject to change over time. Changes in the magnitude and orientation of student flows often also track changes in the political and social orientation of sending and receiving states and in the broader geopolitical and economic context. These changes can be illustrated by the student flows, both generally and from particular states, toward the Soviet Union (USSR) and Russia in pre- and post-Soviet times.[11] These shifts can also be seen in the relative decline of the Western dominance of transnational education with the global share of students being taught in the core Western states shrinking significantly over the last few decades at the same time as various regional hubs, like Singapore and South Africa, have increased their market share. UNESCO data shows that North America and Western Europe hosted 63 percent of the global international students in 1999, while only 55 percent by 2015. That market share began to increase in other regions, such as East Asia and the Pacific, where it grew from 14 percent in 1999 to over 20 percent by 2010, and Eastern Europe where it grew from 7 percent in 1999 to 12 percent in 2015 (UNESCO 2017c). Additionally, the election of President Donald Trump in the United States, with his anti-immigration rhetoric and Muslim travel ban, and the United Kingdom's Brexit vote to leave the European Union, have also resulted in dropping foreign student application numbers.[12]

---

[11] For more details, see Roberts (2017: Chapter 3.I).
[12] See Saul (2017); Strauss (2017); Sellgren (2017); Walker and Warrell (2017); Weale (2016).

As one example of the movement of key non-Western powers to build up their transnational student numbers, China's government is increasing its funding to elite universities with the aim of moving up the global rankings and attracting five hundred thousand foreign students per year by 2020 (Dong 2010; Xing and Chen 2011). Top Chinese law schools are beginning to offer LLM programs in English designed to attract students from around the world.[13] The Chinese government is offering tens of thousands of scholarships to Chinese universities to foreign students, scholars, and diplomats,[14] including a significant number to individuals coming from Africa (Shambaugh 2014: 110; Marks 2007: 2). These efforts represent an attempt by China to build up its soft power by sensitizing foreign students to Chinese views, customs, and preferences, and to cultivate professional and personal networks that will carry on into the future (Shambaugh 2014: 241–245; Jia 2010).[15]

B. The Globalization of Legal Education

One cannot assume that the patterns that characterize transnational flows of students in general will necessarily apply to cross-border flows of law students in particular, let alone to those who study international law. Despite the lack of full data about transnational flows of law students, the following may be surmised on the basis of the available information.

First, it would be reasonable to assume that the general data on student flows considerably underestimates the role of native languages and shared legal families in the global flow of law students (Spamann 2009: 1851). Unlike many subjects, such as medicine, economics, finance, engineering, and computer science, law is still very local or national in its orientation or, at a minimum, legal knowledge tends to be very specific to legal families. Success in legal studies also relies strongly on language skills. Thus, we should expect to see multiple core–periphery relationships in legal education based on

---

[13] For instance, China University of Political Science and Law, Wuhan University, Xiamen University, and Law School of Shanghai Jiao Tong University have all introduced English-language LLM and/or PhD programs, often with a focus on international or Chinese law, which are designed to attract international students. See, e.g., School of Law, Xiamen University (2016); China University of Political Science and Law (2016); Koguan Law School (2013); Wuhan University (2016).

[14] See China Scholarship Council (2017).

[15] Other attempts by China to build its soft power include support for Confucius Institutes in many universities throughout the world. See Mattis (2012).

language and legal families. This suggestion conforms to descriptions of the first two waves of globalization of legal thought which occurred first through colonization and then through legal educational routes following ex-colonial pathways (Kennedy 2006: 19).

Second, it would be reasonable to expect broad movement toward core, English-speaking states, most notably the United States and the United Kingdom, in view of the general importance of these states as educational destinations, the emergence of English as the educational and business global lingua franca, and the dominance of US and UK firms in the market of "global" law firms. Carole Silver has undertaken the most extensive studies on this topic in the United States, primarily focusing on the growing size and significance of US Master of Laws (LLM) programs. More than 110 US law schools now offer LLM programs, which cater almost entirely to foreign students, and some schools are finding that their JD programs are beginning to attract higher numbers of foreign students (Silver and Ballakrishnen, Chapter 15; Silver and Ballakrishnen 2018: 67; Silver 2012: 2404–2405; Silver 2006).

UNESCO has collected data on international students studying law in around thirty-five states for the period 2008–2012, which is reproduced in Table 14.2 and followed by a bar chart in Figure 14.7 of the most popular of these states for foreign students studying law. This data is somewhat problematic as not all states record information in the same way.[16] Nonetheless, the limited available data reveals a clear anglophone core, based primarily on the United Kingdom and the United States, and a francophone core.

France and the United Kingdom benefit from two crosscurrents in global student flows. First, both are ex-colonial powers that forcibly exported their legal system and language to numerous states. Thus, more than half of all foreign students studying in France were from francophone Africa (Marshall 2013). Although France did not colonize states in Latin America, the civil codes that were exported there by Spain and Portugal were derived from the French and German codes, so students from Latin America often travel to France and Germany for further study (though many are now increasingly turning to the United States and the United Kingdom). Second, both

---

[16] In particular, some states, like France, reported statistics for "foreign" students studying law (that is, including foreign nationals who are permanent residents), whereas other states, like the United States and the United Kingdom, reported on "international" students (that is, excluding students who are nationals or permanent residents). The number of foreign students is likely to be higher than the number of international students, which skews the statistics in favor of France.

Table 14.2. Foreign and International Students Studying Law in Select States (Roberts 2017)

Country	Def'n of Int'l Student[a]	2008	2009	2010	2011	2012	Average
France	F	20,005	20,505	21,300	22,040	21,636	21,097
United Kingdom	N	16,504	18,006	18,961	19,826	20,729	18,805
United States	N	6,464	6,766	7,014	7,268	7,584	7,019
Germany	N	6,318	6,497	6,544	N/A	5,615	6,243
Australia	N	2,979	3,418	3,704	3,606	3,628	3,467
Austria	N	2,770	3,184	3,952	4,090	3,286	3,456
Italy	F	1,811	1,538	1,133	4,088	4,238	2,561
Switzerland	N	1,635	1,712	1,817	1,931	1,953	1,809
Greece	F	N/A	N/A	N/A	1,379	N/A	1,379
Czech Republic	F	999	1,081	1,154	1,026	896	1,031
Malaysia		N/A	1,112	884	705	N/A	900
Portugal	N	787	661	822	N/A	1,279	887
Belgium	N	761	390	1,081	1,030	1,048	862
New Zealand	N	998	902	855	768	768	858
Netherlands	N	871	470	743	N/A	N/A	694
Turkey	F	512	496	530	678	934	630
Canada	N	515	546	609	696	N/A	591
Slovak Republic	N	264	432	581	806	816	579
Romania		N/A	N/A	511	488	536	511
Poland	F	N/A	287	N/A	428	433	382
South Korea	F	N/A	N/A	N/A	N/A	380	380
Sweden	N	354	370	358	381	333	359
Lithuania		303	300	310	353	359	325
Norway	N	306	363	282	308	322	316
Hungary	N	284	329	314	314	301	308
Luxembourg		215	N/A	312	N/A	N/A	263
Bulgaria		211	234	231	211	220	221
Chile	N	314	N/A	252	35	61	165
Estonia	N	129	135	133	N/A	148	136
Slovenia	N	32	410	33	38	39	110
Latvia		127	105	81	89	106	101
Denmark	N	28	41	84	99	107	71

Table 14.2. *Continued*

Country	Def'n of Int'l Student[a]	2008	2009	2010	2011	2012	Average
Cyprus		8	22	19	38	201	57
Finland	N	50	43	42	42	70	49
Israel		N/A	N/A	33	63	N/A	48
Iceland	N	29	44	51	57	N/A	45
Malta		71	62	N/A	13	12	39

[a] N = nonresident students, F = foreign students. The data covers international students enrolled in full-degree programs. Where the data was not provided, this column is left blank.

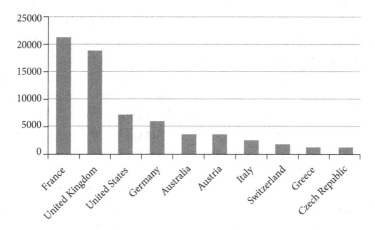

Figure 14.7. Foreign and International Students Studying Law in Select States (Roberts 2017)

are located in Europe, where cross-border flows of students are notably high because of schemes like the Erasmus program. It remains to be seen how Brexit will change these patterns in the medium to long term, but university applications from Europe to the United Kingdom are already down given factors such as uncertainty over fees and scholarships (Weale 2016).

The United States is often assumed to be the leading destination for legal studies, in terms of both numbers and prestige. For instance, Mathilde Cohen has explained that "[t]op students tend to study abroad for their Master's degrees. Common-law jurisdictions, particularly the United States, are the most popular destination" (2016: 508). "The dominance of US legal education in training legal talent for the global economy is one of the most notable developments in recent decades," Sida Liu has argued (2013: 686). David Clark supported his assertion that "American legal education . . . has the highest prestige of any legal education in the world" by pointing to the "large number of foreign lawyers who enroll for further education in the United States, more than those who study in any other foreign country" (2009: 1061).

US law schools may be the most prestigious according to international rankings, but the UNESCO data indicates that the number of foreign law students studying in the United States (an average of 7,019 per year from 2008 to 2012) is apparently a good deal lower than the average for France (21,097 per year) and the United Kingdom (18,805 per year), and only slightly higher than for Germany (6,243 per year) (Roberts 2017: 66). In the United States, international students studying law make up 1 percent of the total number of international students, compared with 5 percent in the United Kingdom and 8 percent in France. Many factors may contribute to this result, including how selective degree programs are and how much they cost. The number of foreign students US law schools admit will probably increase, including into their JD programs, because of declines in domestic applications.[17] However, on the flip side, foreign student application numbers have also dropped since Trump's election (Saul 2017).

Although law students frequently move toward the core to study, most end up returning home to work (Liu 2013: 685–686; Goldhaber 2005). As a result, transnational legal studies do not create as significant a brain drain as is true in some other fields. In the United States, "stay rates" seem to be considerably lower for law than for fields like science and engineering (Silver 2012: 2396–2398, 2433; Silver 2005: 899). The number of foreign-educated lawyers taking the New York bar examination has increased, even though only a fraction of these lawyers intend to stay and practice in the United States and an even smaller percentage end up staying (Silver 2005: 906–907). In some states, such as China, qualifying for the New York bar functions as a signal of excellence and may be a prerequisite for employment by international law firms or major multinational companies. In the United Kingdom, completing a UK

---

[17] US law schools are currently facing a crisis given a drastic drop in the number of law school applications. As fewer Americans apply for JDs, many law schools may seek to retain tuition dollars by admitting more foreign JD and LLM students. See Clark (2009: 1050–1051); Edley (2012: 329); Robel (2012); Bronner (2013).

LLM is not sufficient to entitle students to be admitted to practice. In France, even though many foreign students come to study law, very few go on to successful careers at the French bar or in the French academy.

C. Implications for the Divisible College

What implications might follow from these global and law-specific student flows for the construction of international law as a transnational legal field? First, the core–periphery and Western/non-Western dynamics affect which persons are likely to study law in one state only (nationalizing influence) or more than one state (denationalizing influence) and where they are apt to go (Westernizing influence).

Those who start their education in core states may be unlikely to study law in other states in ways that denationalize their approach to law or diversify their perspective by making them cross a geopolitical, language, or legal family divide. Such students typically receive few incentives to travel to the semiperiphery or periphery to complete further legal study because doing so is not associated with enhanced symbolic capital and heightened career prospects. Accordingly, if stepping outside one's national context to view international law from a different vantage point is a formative part of being an international lawyer and understanding diverse approaches to the field (Murray and Drolshammer 2000: 517), lawyers from these states may be the least likely to gain these sorts of denationalizing experiences. On the other hand, these lawyers are more likely to experience diversity within the classroom if they study at one of the universities with a significant number of foreign students.

By contrast, students from semiperipheral or peripheral states are less likely to experience a diversity of student nationalities within their home classrooms. But these students have greater incentives than students from core states to attain the denationalizing awareness of studying law in more than one state because obtaining foreign law degrees is typically associated with increased social capital in the form of higher levels of prestige and enhanced job prospects.[18] Of course, because not all students will have the

---

[18] On the meaning of social capital in general, see Bourdieu and Wacquant (1992: 119); Bourdieu (1987: 812). On the relevance of social capital in transnational student flows, see Silver (2012: 2386–2387).

means to study abroad, this opportunity might be more open to students with private funds or scholarship opportunities. Moreover, achieving the potential status increase associated with foreign study typically requires that these students travel toward the core rather than laterally or away from it.

The typical direction of travel means that the degree of diversification students undergoes from studying abroad will depend in part on the state in which they begin their legal training. Australian students have incentives to study abroad and thus denationalize, but they flock to the United Kingdom and the United States, so that on the whole they do not noticeably diversify by crossing a geopolitical, language, or legal family divide. Students from China, in contrast, are likely to study in places like the United States and the United Kingdom (because of the movement toward English and the common law) or France and Germany (because the Chinese legal code draws significantly on the Japanese one, which is based on the German civil code), meaning that they are apt to denationalize and diversify on geopolitical, language, and sometimes legal family grounds.

The direction of these movements may confirm or introduce a Westernizing influence. Students from Western states who seek further legal training typically go to other Western states, which confirms or reinforces their Western orientation. Students from non-Western states who seek further law degrees often go to Western states, which introduces a Western orientation. Still, these students will not necessarily accept everything they learn in Western environments. For instance, some scholars noted that the Chinese government encouraged its lawyers to study abroad in Western states precisely so that these lawyers would be well equipped to understand Western approaches and schooled in the techniques that might enable China to beat some of these Western states at their own game. There are also exceptions to the movement toward Western states, such as movement from one non-Western state to another non-Western state, like students who transfer from a russophone semiperipheral state to study in Russia itself or from China to study in Japan. But, in terms of overall trends, law students engaging in transnational study generally progress toward the core and toward the West, while Western students do not commonly leave the West.

Second, the asymmetric nature of these student flows means that legal academics at elite schools in core states are prone to be highly influential in constituting the transnational field of international law. Elite schools have proved to have great impact on domestic legal markets. For example, a study on the American legal academy found that the vast majority of US legal academics had obtained their law degrees from Harvard or Yale, and thus these two institutions were able to "infect" the broader academy with their intellectual ideas through the placement of their students as academics in other schools (Katz et al. 2011: 84). These student flows suggest that a similar phenomenon occurs in international law, though on a global scale, as international law academics and practitioners often complete part of their legal education at a handful of elite law schools in a small number of core states (Twining 2009: 282–283).

This phenomenon has also been observed with respect to international judges (Madsen, Chapter 12). A 2006 study of all sitting international judges found that many had studied at a handful of elite schools, particularly in the United Kingdom, the United States, and France (Terris et al. 2007: 17–18; Hernandez 2014: 133–134; Hernandez 2012: 192 n.41).[19] The media have highlighted the role played by elite schools in relatively few states in the creation of the international law field.[20] The importance of credentialing in core, typically Western, states has also been observed in other transnational legal fields, such as arbitration. In international commercial arbitration, Yves Dezalay and Bryant Garth have noted that the crucial difference between successful Third World arbitrators and their First World counterparts is that national stature is not enough (1996: 25–26). An arbitrator from the periphery must find ways of gaining access to and credibility with the center, such as by completing graduate studies at elite universities in core states. Similarly, Sergio Puig found that most elite investment treaty arbitrators are Western, but that the backgrounds of frequently appointed non-Western arbitrators confirm the importance of obtaining a law degree from elite UK, US, or French schools (Puig 2014: 405).

Third, the asymmetric student flows are likely to contribute to the asymmetric diffusion of legal ideas and materials. As noted, although law students frequently move toward the core to study, most end up going home to work (Liu 2013: 685–686; Goldhaber 2005). These reverse flows are meaningful because where people study and the ideas and sources they are exposed to

---

[19] For more information, see Hernandez (2012: Chapter 2.III.B).

[20] For instance, according to an article by Christopher Schuetze in the *New York Times*, although the field of public international law is gradually spreading globally, a handful of universities in the United States and Europe hold disproportionate sway when it comes to training the international law elite. See Schuetze (2014). The article described a handful of universities in England and the United States as leading the way, citing reasons such as stellar brands; wealthy endowments; renowned faculties; and ready access to fellowships, internships, and development opportunities. These universities also create benchmarking standards as their degrees are easier for others to evaluate than degrees from thousands of universities across the world. *Id.*

often affect their subsequent choices in scholarship and practice (Twining 2009: 280).

Noteworthy examples of such influence can be cited, such as the "Chicago Boys" from Chile who studied economics at the University of Chicago before returning home to introduce their neoliberal learning into President Augusto Pinochet's government (Dezalay and Garth 2002: 44–47; Valdés 1995). Similar observations have been made in domestic contexts. For instance, one explanation given for why US lawyers advising businesses about selecting a state of incorporation usually choose either Delaware or their home state is that they typically know little about the laws of other states (Carney et al. 2012: 129–130; Daines 2002: 1581; Romano 1985: 273). Most US law schools teach only the law of their home state and Delaware corporate law, whereas elite law schools usually focus on Delaware law rather than the law of the state where they are based, and casebooks tend to contain more Delaware cases than cases from any other state.[21]

Diffusion studies show that legal ideas and materials typically move in the opposite direction to transnational student flows. In corporate law, for example, Holger Spamann has found that diffusion of legal materials—including statutes, case law, and textbooks—occurs mainly within legal family trees and along ex-colonial lines (Spamann 2009: 1876). Students moved primarily within legal families and from peripheral and semiperipheral states (former colonies) to core states (former colonial masters). By contrast, legal sources moved in the opposite direction. The textbooks of core states contained few references to legal materials from other legal systems. The textbooks of peripheral and semiperipheral countries contained numerous references to foreign case law, which came predominantly from core countries and especially from those within the same legal family tree.

The effect of interstate educational hierarchies on the transnational flow of ideas is often reinforced by the interpersonal hierarchy established by the teacher–student relationship. The diffusion of ideas works best in a downward direction, traveling from teacher to student. The teacher stands in front of the classroom and shares his or her views with the students. The teacher sets the intellectual agenda by prescribing the textbook and readings that are to be discussed. Students come to learn and are also tested on their understanding by the teacher, which gives students an incentive to try to understand what

---

[21] For explanations based on other factors, such as the importance of precedent and the corporate law expertise of Delaware courts, see generally Kamar (1998); see also Black (1990); Coates (2012); Eisenberg (1989); Fisch (2000); Sanga (2014).

the teacher wants the students to know and what the teacher thinks about the materials.

Diffusion also works relatively well in a horizontal direction, from student to student. Students may listen to each other in the classroom and interact outside the classroom, creating a network of peer contacts (Silver 2012: 2406). Studies of technological diffusion found that peer-to-peer interactions are particularly useful in encouraging someone to adopt new ideas (Coleman et al. 1995: 68). But there may be limits to the transfer of ideas in this way. Various studies have suggested that international students typically forge bonds with other international students, rather than with domestic students (Itsoukalas 2008: 131; Fincher and Shaw 2009; Waters and Brooks 2011: 574). For instance, Silver's work on US law schools suggests that a strong divide separates the JD students (who are primarily American) and the LLM students (who are primarily foreign) (2006: 168–170; 2012: 2407).[22] Thus, diffusion of ideas may often work better within each group than between groups.[23]

Diffusion of ideas is likely to work less well in an upward direction, from student to teacher. In some states, such as China, France, and Russia, law professors primarily lecture without engaging in class discussion or encouraging questions.[24] This scenario offers little opportunity for student-to-teacher transfers of ideas. In other states, such as the United States, professors often involve their students in a Socratic dialogue, allowing for more room for two-way communication and reciprocal learning. Even there, however, a student will typically hear his or her professor speak far more than a professor will hear a given student speak. And professors have fewer incentives to try to get inside the heads of their students, as they are the ones who set the exams that students take, rather than the other way around.

---

[22] Experiences may also differ between US law schools. Some law schools put JDs and LLMs in separate classes or place them on different curves within the same class. Others put them in the same classes and on the same curve, while others go further and have programs to facilitate interaction, such as a buddy JD/LLM system. See, e.g., Boston College Law School (2016).

[23] This seems to be particularly prevalent when domestic and international students are typically enrolled in different programs, like the JD or Bachelor of Laws and LLM or PhD programs. Where domestic and international students are combined within a single degree, the opportunities for them to mix, share insights, and develop networks with each other are greatly increased. For instance, some UK legal academics commented that they saw a much larger disconnect between undergraduate and graduate law students than between domestic and foreign law students who were in the same programs. *Source:* E-mail on file with author, sources nondisclosed for confidentiality.

[24] For more discussions on the traditional method of teaching international law in China, see Qizhi (2016); see also Gao (2002: 224).

Upward diffusion is possible, notably when dealing with LLM and Doctor of Philosophy (PhD) students or in small and interactive classroom settings. Nevertheless, downward and lateral diffusion are likely to be more common. This observation means that, in terms of the diffusion of ideas, where a state's students go to study is frequently a more important indicator of where individuals from that state will look to find ideas than where their foreign students come from. If Taiwanese judges study law in Germany, they are more likely to end up citing German precedents than German judges or law professors are to cite Taiwanese precedents on account of having had Taiwanese students in their classrooms. Generally, what one learns in a foreign environment as a student likely leaves a deeper impression on one's intellectual makeup than what one learns as a teacher by having foreign students in the classroom.

The asymmetric movement of students and lawyers means that the diffusion of legal ideas and materials is more likely to proceed from core to peripheral states, and from Western to non-Western states, than the other way around. These dynamics also help to explain how localisms from core states may come to be globalized and to define what is understood by "global" approaches. For instance, Liu observed that increasing numbers of international law students have entered UK and US law schools to receive "global" legal education (Liu 2013: 678), and John Flood explained that many young lawyers from around the world now find it essential to obtain an LLM degree at a major UK or US law school so as to be "conversant with global legal techniques" (Flood 2007: 54; Flood 1999: 140–144; Silver 2002: 1040). In this way, the national approaches of some states are able to assert disproportionate influence in defining the "international."

II. Educational Backgrounds of Professors

In a report on the internationalization of legal education, the proportion of academics who had received degrees from other jurisdictions was viewed as a primary indicator of internationalization (Jamin and Van Caenegem 2016: 7), yet rates of foreign legal education vary considerably among states. In my book, I examined the educational backgrounds of the international law academics at the five most elite universities in the five permanent members of the Security Council.[25] I also added Australia in order to show some

---

[25] As noted above, the method for selecting these universities and international law academics is set out in Roberts (2017: Chapters 1–2 and app. A). One point to note about this selection is that, where

core–periphery, ex-colonial dynamics between Australia and the United Kingdom. Based on this information, it seems that, at least when it comes to international law academics' own educational backgrounds, this sort of transnational movement is much more prevalent in some academies than others. Educational migration also tends to follow predictable patterns that reflect and reinforce certain nationalizing, denationalizing, and Westernizing influences that shape international law as a transnational legal field.

A. Tracking Educational Diversity

Some law professors have studied law in two or more states, whereas others have only studied law in a single state. I refer to the first set of professors as exhibiting "educational diversity," because they are subject to some denationalizing educational influences, even if these are only limited. At least to date, educational diversity has originated in two main ways. First, future professors study law in their home country and then complete graduate legal education in another state before returning home to teach. I refer to this as "outbound diversity" because it stems from outward travel by domestic lawyers (Roberts 2017: 72–73). Second, future professors study law in their home country and then complete graduate legal education in a second state before going on to teach law in that second state or a third state. I refer to this as "inbound diversity" because it stems from the entry of foreign lawyers into a specific legal academy (Roberts 2017: 73).

Table 14.3 shows the results for the international law academics from the elite universities of the five permanent members of the UN Security Council plus Australia with respect to educational diversity and inbound diversity. (I included Australia in order to show some of the core–periphery dynamics between Australia and the United Kingdom.) The first column provides the percentage of international law academics that hold law degrees from more than one state (educational diversity). These figures confirm that some legal

available, I relied upon country and world rankings of law schools. However, these rankings play a much more significant role in some states than others and often do not account for other factors that might affect students' selection of law schools, such as a desire to practice in a particular location after graduation or the law school's location in a particularly desirable area. I also relied upon rankings of law schools in general, not of law schools specializing in international law in particular. This means that, for instance, the US rankings did not include New York University, which falls outside the top five law schools on general rankings despite ranking first with respect to international law.

Table 14.3. Educational Diversity of Academics in the Study

Country	Educational Diversity: Percentage of academics with law degrees from more than one state	Inbound Diversity: Percentage of academics with a first law degree from another state
Australia	73	20
China	41	4
France	7	5
Russia	8	0[a]
United Kingdom	77	74
United States	32	32

[a] I treated degrees from the USSR as being degrees from Russia, even if they were obtained in places that now form other ex-Soviet states, like Ukraine.

systems are very nationalized in terms of the legal education of their international law academics (Russia and France), some are highly denationalized (the United Kingdom and Australia), and some fall in between (the United States and China).

The second column reflects the percentage of international law academics who received their first law degree in a state other than the state where they are teaching (inbound diversity). At least to date, the location of academics' first law degree has typically been a relatively good indicator of their nationality; having received a first law degree from a foreign state often signals that academics are not now or were not originally nationals of the place where they are teaching. The educational diversity exhibited in core states like the United States and the United Kingdom primarily resulted from inbound diversity, whereas the educational diversity exhibited in China and Australia primarily resulted from outbound diversity. The United Kingdom is an outlier with respect to its extremely high rate of inbound diversity.

B. Explaining Educational Diversity

Whether legal elites in a given state tend to study law abroad and, if so, where they go largely depends on perceptions of social capital in those states. Aspiring legal academics will have an incentive to study law in multiple states if foreign qualifications are valued by the academy that they are seeking to enter. In terms of the direction of these flows, status increases typically correspond with moves toward states with more highly ranked educational institutions, which often means core, Western states.

1. Lack of Educational Diversity: Russia and France

The international law academies in both Russia and France exhibited low levels of educational diversity. In Russia, all of the academics had earned two or three law degrees, but almost all of them had obtained all of those degrees in Russia. In less than a handful of cases, an academic had completed a first law degree in Russia, followed by a foreign LLM (in the United Kingdom or Germany), and followed by a PhD in Russia. This lack of educational diversity is not surprising for academics who trained during the Soviet era when it was often not possible to study abroad. But no drastic movement in this regard appears to apply to the younger generations of international law professors appointed to these universities. This reality partly reflects how recently Russia opened up to the world after the collapse of the Soviet Union in 1991 and how long systemic changes require to take hold. It may also reflect the fact that younger lawyers who study abroad do not end up returning to join the Russian international law academy. In addition, none of the Russian international lawyers had completed their first law degree outside of Russia.

Discussions with Russian academics indicate that implicit hierarchies and language constraints mostly explain the low levels of foreign study to date. Russian students could study in other Russian-speaking states but, as Russia would consider itself to be at the core of this language and the constellation of post-Soviet states, these students have little incentive to do so. This outcome fits with patterns from the general student flows where students from other Russian-speaking states (like Belarus, Kazakhstan, Kyrgyzstan, Tajikistan, Ukraine, and other countries in the Commonwealth of Independent States) are much more inclined to study in Russia than the reverse. As for studying in a foreign language, since most domestic universities teach only in Russian, they do not prepare students well for studying abroad. In response to federal regulations, Russian law schools require all students to complete one language course.[26] Most students study English, German, or French, with English being the most popular. But this language instruction tends to consist of single courses rather than integrated study in other courses or the

---

[26] The standard says in Paragraph 5.1 that a graduate must have necessary skills for professional communication in a foreign language, and in Paragraph 6.3, that the program of study should include the mandatory coursework in "Foreign language in the field of jurisprudence" (Order of the Ministry 2010).

curriculum in general. Only a handful of Russian law schools teach courses in English.[27] There are few opportunities to practice foreign languages because most of the teaching materials are in Russian, few foreign academics teach in Russia, and many of the foreign students are Russian speakers from former Soviet states.

Two other factors are also at play. First, even though it has been twenty years since the end of the Cold War, the isolation of Russia from the West means that the senior generation has few links with international lawyers in Western states, which has made it more difficult to create pathways of connection for the younger generation (Roberts 2017: 75). Second, in terms of academic incentives, although a foreign Master's degree is readily understood within the Russian university framework, it is not clear what a foreign PhD or JSD (Doctor of Juridical Science) equates to in Russian credentials, which matters because an academic must hold a doctorate that is recognized in Russia in order to supervise PhD students in Russian universities (Roberts 2017: 75). After the Master's, Russian scholars usually seek a Candidate of Sciences degree, which involves writing a significant thesis. To become a full professor, a Doctor of Sciences degree is often (though not always) required. Russian doctorates are typically awarded at a much more senior stage than when a Western scholar would usually be awarded a PhD or JSD, so the two are not clearly equivalent (Roberts 2017: 75). This disparity creates a disincentive for studying abroad at the PhD level, as the qualification is not readily understood within the Russian system in the absence of an Agreement on Mutual Recognition of Academic Degrees.

Movements are afoot to change the relative isolation of Russian students from global higher education. Two in particular are worth highlighting. First, in 1993, the government announced a national scholarship scheme to support talented students and postgraduate students wishing to study abroad, which has gained in popularity over time (Directive of the President 1993: 3451; Order of the Ministry 2016). Other schemes to encourage foreign higher education have been introduced, though many do not cover legal studies (Presidential Decree 2013: 7147). Second, international mooting competitions, like the Jessup Moot Court Competition, are becoming popular in Russia, leading to a new generation of Russian international law students whose members are familiar with non-Russian sources

---

[27] These include the Higher School of Economics, Moscow State Institute of International Relations, the Peoples' Friendship University, the Russian Foreign Trade Academy, and Saint Petersburg State University.

of international law, especially English textbooks like those written by Ian Brownlie, Malcolm Shaw, and Lassa Oppenheim, and case law of international tribunals (Issaeva 2013: 3).

These developments are essential to creating a more globally integrated body of well-trained, more denationalized legal professionals. Yet few of these individuals return to Russia and, when they do, they often work in law firms or nongovernmental organizations rather than join the Russian legal academy. After all, Russian academia pays poorly and some young Russians complain that the existing international law academy is insular. According to one young Russian international lawyer who studied abroad, some members of the current generation are becoming more denationalized, but the Old Guard retains control at the universities:

> The scene at universities is still dominated by old guards, professors conditioned by the Soviet system. They serve as heads of departments and as such have significant influence over hiring decisions (both professors and PhD students) and curricula for international law courses. They serve as editors of textbooks co-written by professors of the department. They ensure that much of the Soviet legacy remains in the textbooks.[28]

It may be, then, that denationalizing influences are growing in the younger generation, but these will inevitably need time to seep into the broader culture, and the process may be still slower in the academy.

In France, all of the academics included in the study had received two or, more commonly, three law degrees, and most of these degrees were French. Only a few had earned a first law degree in France, followed by an LLM in the United States, followed by a PhD in France. One had pursued a doctor of juridical science (SJD) in the United States. As with Russia, language barriers and implied hierarchies appear to play an explanatory role. Not only is it easier for most French scholars to study in French than in other languages, but also France would consider itself to be at the apex of the French-language and French-speaking civil law states, negating any substantial incentive to engage in further study at universities in francophone Africa or Asia or elsewhere in French-speaking Europe. In addition, French academics who study in the United Kingdom and the United States must deal with the language

---

[28] Source: e-mail on file with author.

difference and shift from a civil law system to a common law one, which is difficult and makes the experience potentially less relevant in their local market. Accordingly, even though French students in general (not necessarily law students) seem to study abroad at a high rate that does not appear to hold true for French international law professors.[29]

Recruitment processes are also part of the picture. No differentiation is made between the process for hiring academics in French law and hiring academics who specialize in international law. The selection committee is all French and, to be hired at an entry-level position, a would-be professor must have completed a PhD in law in France and demonstrate proficiency in French. These requirements generally have the effect of ruling out academics not trained exclusively or primarily in France and creating an incentive to privilege domestic rather than foreign educational experiences.

The main exception to this nationalized French approach is offered by the newer-style Sciences Po Law School (Sciences Po), one of the graduate schools of the Paris Institute of Political Studies, which has made a splash within the French academy. Christophe Jamin, Sciences Po's dean, explained that the idea was to break from the traditional French mold by being more interdisciplinary and internationalized (Jamin 2012: 263–267). Sciences Po embraces social science perspectives instead of spurning them in the name of doctrinalism and the autonomy of law. It employs some foreign professors and others with foreign training; it admits an extremely international student body; it teaches an increasing number of classes in English; and its students generally spend at least one year studying abroad. Several professors in the study who received foreign LLMs or PhDs/JSDs now hold positions at Sciences Po.[30]

[29] Some academics noted that some French legal scholars go to study in Quebec, where they have the advantage of learning in French about a mixed civil and common law system. However, this pathway was not well trodden within the group of academics examined in this study. E-mail on file with author. Similarly, when it comes to EU law, it may be that some French law professors choose to study in other states with well-respected EU law programs, such as Italy and Belgium, but French law professors tend to teach either international law or European law, so the profile of such academics was not checked for the purposes of this research.

[30] The law school also relies much more heavily on professors who come from practice than the leading French law schools, reportedly having twenty full-time faculty to two hundred adjunct practitioners. Sciences Po also has a number of foreign professors who teach in English and French. See Jamin (2014).

2. Intermediate Educational Diversity: China and the United States

In China, 41 percent of the international law academics received at least one law degree outside the country, which typically resulted from outbound rather than inbound diversity (that is, scholars completing an LLB in China followed by an LLM or PhD outside China).[31] Similar observations about educational diversity have been made about the training of most personnel at the Ministry of Foreign Affairs (Shambaugh 2014: 67) and some elite Chinese law firms.[32] Foreign legal education seems to be most prevalent within the younger generation, suggesting that educational diversity is increasing over time. Of the academics who studied abroad, their educational destinations included Australia, Canada, Germany, Japan, South Korea, Switzerland, the United Kingdom, and the United States. Therefore, these academics not only experienced denationalizing influences but also typically diversified by crossing geopolitical, language, and sometimes legal family divides in their foreign study.

Many factors help to explain these trends. The Chinese government actively encourages its nationals to study or spend time abroad by, for instance, offering scholarships or providing funding to help pay for the costs associated with studying or visiting educational institutions in other states (Roberts 2017: 78). Another important factor facilitating this educational diversity is that many Chinese students know foreign languages, particularly English, and many Chinese universities bring in foreign professors to teach courses in foreign languages, mainly English (Roberts 2017: 78). Implicit hierarchies also play a role. Instead of privileging domestic legal training, Chinese universities prize international experience, principally in the form of higher degrees (like LLMs, PhDs, JSDs, and SJDs) from elite schools in core Western states; they often treat such degrees as a stronger marker of quality and expertise than local ones. (The educational diversity of China's top legal scholars is also paving the way for the appointment of a growing number of Chinese legal scholars, in both international law and other specialties, to law schools in a variety of states throughout the world.[33])

---

[31] This pattern is consistent with observations about Chinese international lawyers and academics. See Hua (2004: 49).

[32] According to one Chinese scholar, some of the top Chinese law firms are now reportedly requiring Chinese students to have completed an LLM at Oxbridge or a top-fourteen US law school in order to be hired. E-mail on file with author.

[33] See, e.g., Phil Chan (Macquarie University), Henry Gao (Singapore Management University), Wenhua Shan (University of New South Wales), Julia Ya Qin (Wayne State University), Jiangyu Wang (National University of Singapore), Dongsheng Zang (University of Washington), and Angela Huyue Zhang (King's College).

Modern legal education in China remains of relatively recent origin, which helps to explain the tendency to look to and privilege foreign legal education. This tendency results in part from the lasting effects of the Cultural Revolution (1966–1976), which destroyed the former Chinese legal system. From 4,144 law students and 857 graduating law students in China in 1965, the numbers dropped to 410 law students and 49 graduating law students in 1976 (Weiguo 2000).[34] It was not until the late 1970s that Chinese universities began to recruit students by a national entrance examination. Since then, the number of law schools and law students has multiplied, rising sixfold in the last fifteen years alone (Minzner 2013: 336; Haicong 2009: 57). By 2006, China could boast over six hundred law schools and over three hundred thousand law students (Irish 2007: 250; Minzner 2013: 349).

Foreign education in general, and the study of international and transnational law in particular, is encouraged by the government in the interest of better equipping its lawyers to protect China's national interests. For instance, in December 2011, the PRC Ministry of Education and Central Politics and the Law Commission released the Central Politics and Law Commission Opinion on the Implication of the Program for Legal Elite Education, which states five aims, including: "Cultivat[ing] legal elites with different specialties: the emphasis of the Program is to cultivate legal professionals who are proficient in different areas of practice. In order to make a breakthrough, the priority is to cultivate international law professionals who have knowledge of international laws and can participate in international affairs in order to protect national interests" (Ministry of Education 2011). To achieve these goals, the government declared the intention to establish roughly twenty educational institutions specializing in international and transnational law and to set up a foundation to support study abroad by law school students and legal academics (Ministry of Education 2011). According to a 2016 study, international law is now also taught at more than six hundred Chinese universities and nearly twenty universities and research institutes may grant doctoral degrees in international law (Qizhi 2016).

In the United States, the vast majority of law professors obtain an undergraduate degree in a nonlegal subject and then a graduate degree in law. Some complete a Master's degree or PhD in another subject, mostly in the United States but often in the United Kingdom. Yet they rarely complete a second

---

[34] For example, in 1957, only 385 graduated from politics and law programs (National Bureau of Statistics of China 1983: 521–522).

law degree at all, like a PhD in law or a JSD/SJD, let alone doing so outside the United States, partly because of language difficulties and implied hierarchies. Limited foreign language skills prevent most US legal academics from studying in places like France and Germany. Within the English-speaking world, they find little incentive to study law abroad in states like Australia owing to implied hierarchies. Even though the greatest educational movement from the United States is to the United Kingdom, most elite US universities view themselves as superior to the elite UK universities. As the United States sits at the core, little prestige is associated with seeking educational degrees outside the country (Jamin and van Caenegem 2016: 7).

Two law-specific factors are also at play. The fact that US academics complete nonlegal degrees in the United Kingdom, but not legal ones, partly reflects the timing of foreign study and the perception of US legal scholars that the enterprise they are engaged in is different from that of their foreign peers. Most US legal academics who studied abroad did so between graduating from college and attending law school in the United States. This route is standard for those on prestigious scholarships, such as the Rhodes and Marshall awards. As a result, these academics are much more inclined to pursue Master's and PhD programs in nonlaw subjects, such as economics and international relations, than to embark on legal degrees. Legal realism also took hold in the United States in a way that has made the US legal academy deeply skeptical about the value of legal reasoning (Posner 1987). One consequence is that US legal academics typically dismiss European legal training and scholarship as doctrinal and formalist in comparison with the more realist and interdisciplinary approach they celebrate in their native legal training and scholarship.

Almost no US law academics who acquire their first law degree in the United States seek an additional law degree, let alone one in a foreign state (Roberts 2017: 80). Some market factors help to drive this result. In the United States, unlike many states, law is a postgraduate degree so that US law students have fewer incentives to undertake additional legal study in another state. PhDs are becoming more common in nonlegal subjects, like economics, history, and sociology, but not in law.[35] This development reflects the value that the US legal academic market places on becoming interdisciplinary over becoming internationalized. Increasingly, aspiring US law professors are spending one or two years as a visiting assistant professor at a

---

[35] But see Yale Law School (2016).

domestic law school before entering the US market. This route may function as a partial substitute for further legal study, but there are clear rewards to be gained by penetrating the networks that help secure an entry-level teaching position.

This nationalized educational profile describes the majority trend in US law schools, where 68 percent of the academics in this study evidenced no educational diversity. However, a minority trend has emerged in the last few decades at some of the elite schools, though it is not clear that this trend applies to US law schools more generally. Some 32 percent of the US international law academics at the elite schools in this study received their first law degree outside the United States, often before completing a second or third law degree in the United States or elsewhere. As a result, almost all of the diversity of education in the US law academy comes from inbound rather than outbound diversity, which reflects the United States' status as a core state. Some US professors seek to internationalize their perspective later in their legal careers through experiences such as being a senior Fulbright Scholar in a foreign country. But the well-trodden educational pathways to a US tenure track job are almost exclusively domestic, especially when dealing with legal education.

3. Significant Educational Diversity: The United Kingdom and Australia

In the United Kingdom and Australia, almost all of the academics held two or three law degrees and the vast majority received those degrees from at least two countries (77 percent in the United Kingdom and 73 percent in Australia). This finding accords with a recent study of the internationalization of legal education that concludes that the UK legal academy is one of the most internationalized in the world (Platsas and Marrani 2016: 299–300). Still, while both states score highly in terms of diversity of legal education, they present very different models of denationalization. The United Kingdom evidences strong inbound diversity, whereas Australia evidences strong outbound diversity. This dichotomy reflects the core–periphery dynamics between these states.

In terms of inbound diversity, 74 percent of the UK international law academics in the study received their first law degree outside the United Kingdom (Roberts 2017: 81). Thus, most of these UK international law academics are likely to be (or, at least, are likely to have been) foreign nationals. A considerable number of these foreign-trained academics came from Australia, but they also hailed from Austria, Canada, Germany,

Greece, Ireland, Italy, Latvia, the Netherlands, Nigeria, the United States, and Zambia. Many received their LLMs in the United Kingdom, but others received them in Australia, Canada, Germany, the Netherlands, South Africa, Switzerland, the United States, and Zambia. Most of them received their PhDs in the United Kingdom, but PhDs or the equivalents were also awarded by Australia, Austria, France, Germany, Italy, Switzerland, and the United States. These findings reflect the tremendous—and highly unusual—educational diversity of the UK legal academy (Roberts 2017; Platsas and Marrani 2016: 304).

The United Kingdom therefore represents an exception to the general asymmetric patterns of core states, which feature highly internationalized student bodies but relatively nationalized faculties. It is unclear what has made the UK legal academy so open to hiring foreign-trained academics. As the head of the Commonwealth legal empire, the UK law profession has developed strong connections with lawyers in many states throughout the world, and a significant amount of educational and professional movement has always taken place within the Commonwealth. European integration, which has seen the movement of lawyers and law students within Europe, adds to this phenomenon. Whether as a cause or an effect, UK law firms have traditionally hired large numbers of foreign-trained lawyers, particularly at midlevel positions. But the internationalization of the UK legal academy also seems to be driven by certain financial pressures and opportunities.

In terms of financial pressures, since academics are not well paid in the United Kingdom, gifted UK nationals have few incentives to enter the academy. To remain globally competitive, UK universities have responded by opening up the recruitment process to international applicants. As UK universities are some of the best-ranked in the world, foreign-trained academics are motivated to work at elite UK law schools. Moreover, because the UK academic recruitment process is both competitive and internationally open, some of the best British-trained international law academics end up at very good regional schools rather than the most elite schools. The United Kingdom has also been a magnet for internationally minded legal academics from other states that have traditionally been more domestically oriented, like Germany.

In terms of financial opportunities, UK universities admit a high percentage of foreign law students, particularly in their lucrative LLM programs (Roberts 2017: 82). UK universities charge one fee for domestic and EU students and another, much higher, fee for international students. For instance, in 2012–2013, an MPhil in law at Oxford University cost £3,828 for domestic and EU students and £13,200 for international students (University of Oxford 2018).[36] This differential makes international students attractive to the UK universities as a major source of revenue. International and transnational offerings are popular with LLMs thanks to their transportable nature, which has enabled UK universities to hire more academics with these backgrounds and for these academics to assume a relatively central role in the law schools. The UK situation contrasts with the US market where a large proportion of the international students complete the LLM degree in order to take the New York bar and those who have not completed a first law degree in a common law jurisdiction are required to study many US subjects, which are usually taught by US-trained professors.

For their part, Australian international law academics typically received their first law degree from Australia, which is on the Western semiperiphery, and then moved toward core countries, most commonly the United Kingdom and the United States, to complete their second and third law degrees (Roberts 2017: 82). Around 80 percent of Australian international law academics received their first law degree in Australia, which leaves 20 percent who were originally educated in foreign states. Those who originally studied law outside Australia attended schools in Brazil, Canada, Germany, Japan, New Zealand, the United Kingdom, and the United States. Around 73 percent of the academics received law degrees in two or more states, the most common pattern being for the academic to have completed the first law degree in Australia, followed by an LLM and/or a PhD in a foreign state. The high rate of outbound educational diversity has a lot to do with the position of Australia on the semiperiphery, which encourages its academics to look outward and to value the external. Australia is also a relatively affluent state with many available scholarship schemes for foreign study, mostly in the United Kingdom and, to a lesser extent, the United States.

The Australian international lawyers in this study tended to flock to like-minded or relatively similar states when pursuing LLMs and PhDs. The perspective of these international lawyers is likely to be denationalized to some extent in virtue of having studied abroad, but it is still probably Westernized and not subject to the diversifying influence of crossing a geopolitical, linguistic, or legal family divide. Australian international law academics thus

---

[36] This is unlike the US model where high fees, often around US$50,000, are charged to domestic and international students alike.

commonly experience semiperipheral-to-core diversification, but otherwise are not highly diversified. The relative consistency of their educational migratory patterns also suggests that the Australian legal academy is less radically diversified than the UK legal academy.

C. Implications for the Divisible College

How might the existence of educational diversity in international law professors, and whether this diversity comes about primarily from inbound or outbound diversity, affect the construction of the divisible college of international lawyers?

First, the lack or existence of educational diversity may have a nationalizing or denationalizing effect. If academics have studied law only in the place where they teach, the experience is likely to have a nationalizing effect. They may be more likely to have learned international law with an emphasis on the domestic case law and practices of that state, to have been exposed to the views of international law academics from that state, and to have developed national networks. There is a greater probability that they were a national of that state and that they learned in an environment where they were surrounded by other nationals of that state. They may be less apt to have had the sorts of dislocating experiences that would make them aware of their own national assumptions, lenses, and biases when approaching international law.

By contrast, if academics have studied law in multiple countries, this experience may have a denationalizing effect. These academics are more likely to have studied domestic case law and practices in relation to the international law of more than one state, to have been exposed to academic work from different states, and to have developed transnational, rather than just national, networks. There is a greater chance that they will have been a national minority within the classroom or encountered students or teachers from diverse states with distinct national perspectives. All of these dislocating experiences may tend to make them aware of their own and others' national assumptions, lenses, and biases when approaching international law, providing them with a firsthand experience of the comparative international law phenomenon.

Anne Peters, a German international law scholar, has written about the espousal by international legal scholars of positions that can be linked to prior education in their domestic legal system and that serve the national interest, which she refers to as "epistemic nationalism" (2007: 721). She does not argue that scholars should completely detach themselves from their education and cultural context, which she concedes would be impossible and unnecessary, but that they should make a conscious effort to internalize the perspectives of their "others" (Peters 2007: 721; Marxen et al. 2015: 4 n.2). One way to become aware of one's national biases, and to see the world through other eyes, is to study international law in more than one state.

Nationalizing and denationalizing effects may have more impact at the wholesale than the retail level. Academics who individually had a wholly national experience of learning international law may still become quite internationalized if they work in an academy that is largely composed of academics that come from or have studied in multiple states. But the nationalizing effect is likely to be intensified when the international legal community in a state is predominantly made up of academics that have studied law only in that state, as is the case in Russia and France. There seems to be a greater probability that these communities will produce relatively self-contained dialogues about international law and thereby reinforce the divisible college of international lawyers.

This sort of self-contained community is exemplified by Russia. Lauri Mälksoo has observed that international law scholars in Russia are often, first and foremost, Russian international law scholars in the sense that they tend to be "linguistically and network-wise relatively distinct and separated from international law scholars in the West" (Mälksoo 2015: 87). Russian international law scholars form a separate epistemological community that is tied together by common language, history, and geography, resulting in a fairly "self-contained" international law dialogue with roots in the Soviet government's isolationist attitudes that created a parallel world to the West. This reality was stark in Russian debates about Crimea following its 2014 annexation by, or reunification with, Russia (Roberts 2017: 84).

Second, the lack or existence of educational diversity may affect the sources and approaches that scholars use when identifying and analyzing international law. In comparative law, diversity of legal education is linked with greater comfort in dealing with foreign legal materials in general, and in encouraging recourse to legal materials from the state where the foreign study took place. For instance, Justice Gérard La Forest of the Canadian Supreme Court has noted a "definite link" between the use of US precedents by his colleagues on the court and the training of those justices in the United States (1994: 213). Likewise, Justice Claire L'Heureux-Dubé of the same court has explained that judges, lawyers, and academics who go abroad for parts of their education naturally turn for inspiration and comparison to those jurisdictions whose ideas are already familiar to them (1998: 20).

Beyond the level of anecdote, this link is beginning to be explored more systematically. For instance, David Law and Wen-Chen Chan are studying the connection between a diversity of legal education and the willingness of justices on supreme or constitutional courts in various countries to draw on comparative law (Law and Chan 2011: 571). Law has demonstrated that whether the judges of the Japanese Supreme Court, the Korean Constitutional Court, the Taiwanese Constitutional Court, and the US Supreme Court are likely to draw on comparative law in deciding cases correlates with the commonness of foreign legal education in those systems, as indicated by the diversity of legal education of judges, law clerks, and constitutional law academics at elite schools in those states (see Table 14.4) (Law 2015: 1035).

Conversely, lack of educational migration may also produce tangible consequences. In discussing the parochialism of the US Supreme Court in its choice of authorities, Law and Chan reason that "American judges are not to be blamed if their own vision ends at the water's edge. They are simply products of the system that created them" (Law and Chan 2011: 576). As long as US law school faculties do not place a premium on hiring scholars with foreign or comparative law expertise or training their own students in foreign law, today's US law clerks and tomorrow's US judges and law professors will neither seek nor possess foreign or comparative training. Law and Chan argue that the day that US law students prize a degree in comparative law or a foreign law degree as a stepping-stone to a US Supreme Court clerkship or a teaching position in a US law school is the day that judicial comparativism will become truly institutionalized (Law and Chan 2011: 576; Roberts 2017: 85).

Specific emigrational patterns also have a palpable effect because lawyers and academics are more inclined to draw on materials from the foreign jurisdiction in which they trained. In Law and Chan's study of the Taiwanese Constitutional Court, they found a strong relationship between the educational backgrounds of the justices and the sources of foreign law that they cited. Judges with German law degrees accounted for 87 percent of citations to German precedents and 60 percent of the citations to German constitutional or statutory provisions. Judges with some US legal training were responsible for 62 percent of citations to American precedent (Law 2015: 980; Law and Chan 2011: 558). These correlations are not difficult to explain: in

Table 14.4. Diversity of Legal Education in Japan, South Korea, Taiwan, and the United States (Law 2015: 1035)

	Japan	South Korea	Taiwan	United States
Foreign-trained justices	2/15 US: 2	4/9 US: 3 Germany: 1	11/15 Germany: 7 US: 4 Japan: 2 China: 1	None
Foreign law usage by parties and/or their attorneys	Low	Law firms tend to hire foreign law experts for cases that receive oral argument (i.e., high-profile cases)	Low	Low
Foreign-trained clerks	Roughly half, including at least one German-trained and one French-trained clerk	(1) Around 60% of clerks have foreign training (2) Additional researchers are hired specifically for their expertise in foreign law (3) Research Institute personnel all have foreign training	Most	None
Foreign-trained constitutional scholars at elite law schools	University of Tokyo: 1/4 (25%) Keio Law School: 2/4 (50%) Waseda Law School: 2/4 (50%)	Seoul National University: 6/6 (100%) Korea University: 5/6 (83%) Yonsei University: 5/5 (100%)	National Taiwan University: 8/8 (100%)	Harvard: 2/28 (7%) Stanford: 1/16 (6%) Yale: 2/19 (11%)

Taiwan, as elsewhere, judges are more likely to cite what they know than what they do not know (Law 2015: 980).

Similar observations have been made about the Americanization of legal education in Israel, which has been described as a modern form of "legal colonialism" (Sandberg 2010: 1, 2). Many Israeli faculty members gain a postgraduate education in American law schools and, as a result, have imported research and teaching practices, as well as theories and values, from US law schools to Israeli ones. This exposure affects Israeli legal scholarship: it tends to focus more on universal issues and less on local ones; the perceived value of doctrinal work is waning while the prestige of theoretical and interdisciplinary work is rising; the main language of legal academic discourse is English; and US content and materials are heavily featured. It also seems to extend beyond scholarship, influencing the way legal issues and cases are approached in Israeli society and courts (Sandberg 2010: 13–23).[37]

These patterns suggest that scholars who have studied law only in one state and work in a highly nationalized environment may be more likely to cite sources, such as case law and academic commentary, from that state. Because Russian and French scholars have typically studied law only in Russia and France, they may tend to cite a high proportion of Russian and French materials, respectively. Similarly, because many US international law academics have studied law only in the United States, they may be predisposed to rely primarily on US cases, practice, and academic commentary. By contrast, because Chinese and Australian international law academics evidence a high degree of outbound educational diversity, these academics may be inclined to draw on materials and ideas from elsewhere, including first and foremost the states in which they studied.

The asymmetries of these educational movements mean that usually this sort of diffusion is primarily one-way rather than fully reciprocal. Chinese international law academics who have studied in the United States, the United Kingdom, and France are likely to be better placed to understand the perspectives of those states and to draw on materials and ideas from those states than the other way around. This circumstance may contribute to the field's Western orientation because it means that Western materials experience greater diffusion than non-Western materials and are more apt to constitute the field's common language. In the longer term, however, the lack of knowledge in Western international law academies about Chinese and other non-Western approaches and materials will become more problematic as China and other non-Western states grow in power.

Third, educational migration patterns might suggest some movement toward English common law approaches as a legal, global lingua franca. Although no large-scale data is available on this point, the educational

---

[37] Giving examples of the influence of (1) *Brown v. Board of Education*, 347 U.S. 483 (1954), on Israel policy with regard to allocation of land resources to minorities in a Jewish state; (2) US theories concerning indigenous people and distributive justice on the privatization of agricultural land in Israel; and (3) American theories of distributive justice and social responsibility on the attitude of the Israeli legal world to land expropriations.

backgrounds of many successful international lawyers suggest that students who originally studied law in a non-English-speaking civil law state and then acquire further legal training in an English-speaking common law state are more common than the reverse. Many students who engage in transnational legal study stay within their language and legal family. But, to the extent that some traverse these lines, they appear to favor somewhat asymmetric movement toward English-speaking common law states (Jamin and van Caenegem 2016: 7). In some cases, students complete their first law degree in a common law state and then an LLM or PhD in schools like Leiden University in the Netherlands, the Graduate Institute of International and Development Studies in Switzerland, and the European University Institute in Italy, but these institutions tend to be highly internationalized by virtue of their professors rather than steeped in civil law approaches.

These asymmetric patterns could be expected to affect what emerges as the lingua franca of international lawyers. For example, Colin Picker argues that international law evidences a mixed common law/civil law heritage, but that the balance between the two influences has shifted over time. Whereas international law was originally much more like civil law, it has shifted in the last sixty years to become more like the common law (Picker 2008: 1104–1106; Picker 2009b: 162). In studying this drift in the context of the World Trade Organization, Picker identifies one explanatory factor as the large number of officials, practitioners, and scholars in the field who have pursued legal studies in common law states, including many civil-law-trained students who undertook postgraduate legal studies in common law systems (Picker 2009a: 133–134). Even when law students have not attended common law universities themselves, their lecturers and advisors will often have studied or spent considerable time at such universities.

In the nineteenth and early twentieth centuries, universities in civil law states played a far more prominent role in Western legal education and thought (Glendon et al. 2014: 56–57; Clark 2009: 1060 n.165; Kennedy 2006: 24). The emergence of English as the global lingua franca is a critical factor in developing and sustaining legal cultures, and English is closely associated with the common law. Thus, Picker claims that the ever-increasing role of English in international law suggests that the influence of common law legal cultural characteristics will continue and possibly expand (Picker 2012: 42–44). This process tends to be exacerbated by the linguistic insularity of most native English speakers.

Fourth, states at the core of their language and legal family often evidence a clear asymmetry: for the most part, they are relatively internationalized in terms of their student bodies, but much more nationalized in terms of the education of their own professors. This pattern seems to be largely true of Russia, France, and, to a somewhat lesser extent, the United States. Such asymmetry means that they generally evidence a greater degree of international output than international input; these academics are well placed to diffuse some of their ideas to an international audience through their teacher–student relationships (output), but they are subject to relatively national influences in terms of determining their own approaches (input). This asymmetry is consequential because diffusion is more likely to occur in a downward and lateral direction than in an upward direction (Roberts 2017: 89).

The exception to this pattern is the United Kingdom, the only core state in the study to evidence double internationalization: a radically internationalized student body and international law academy. The international law academy is also internationalized through inbound diversity, with academics from a wide range of other countries, including many non-English-speaking and civil law states. Double internationalization helps to make the UK legal academy a fertile place for the development of international law because it brings together international lawyers from a broad variety of states as both students and teachers. The common language of these professors and students is the "international" and "transnational" rather than the "national" because not even the professors have a national legal tradition in common.

The UK academy's double internationalization, coupled with the leading role of London in international law practice and its proximity to other centers of international law like The Hague, makes it well suited for an outsized influence on shaping the construction of international law as a transnational legal field. It becomes a true meeting place for "the international"—a melting pot of internationalization on both input and output levels. Of course, this diversity is not perfect. For example, the profile of inbound diversity shows that few international law academics at the elite schools come from non-Western states. Yet, compared with those in the other states in the study, UK international law academics may enjoy more internationally diverse professional networks, which could well encourage them to draw upon legal developments and sources from a much wider range of states than their peers in many other states.

Nevertheless, these profiles and patterns are dynamic. Whether or not the unusual internationalization of the UK legal academy continues to the same degree following Brexit remains to be seen. There are already reports of international and foreign academics not applying to, or leaving, the UK academy in the wake of the United Kingdom's Brexit vote. The Brexit vote has also put into doubt significant European research funding for UK universities, and UK universities have started to fall within international rankings within recent years (Adams 2017).[38] All of these changes may affect the relative openness and attractiveness of the UK legal academy to foreign scholars, as well as the opportunities and incentives to focus on international, transnational, and European scholarship (Weale and O'Carroll 2017; Pells 2017). At least for now, however, the UK international law academy is extremely internationalized, subject to potentially shifting patterns going forward.

Finally, although this section tracks educational patterns of the international law academics at the top five law schools in each state, some of these states include other universities that specialize in international law whose patterns may differ from those norms. The best example of this is New York University (NYU), the top-ranked law school for international law in the United States (U.S. News & World Report 2017), which is strikingly more denationalized than its sister schools on a variety of measures (Roberts 2017: Chapter 5.I.A.). This difference can be seen by comparing the statistics for NYU's international law faculty with those for the international law faculties at the other elite US law schools. For the NYU international law faculty, 78 percent completed their first law degree outside the United States, compared with 32 percent for the other elite US law schools. Moreover, 67 percent of the NYU international lawyers exhibited educational diversity in their law degrees, compared with 32 percent for the other elite US law schools.[39]

The international law group at NYU is atypical in the US law academy. Some of the academics have backgrounds that would look more at home in the UK academy. Others are US-trained, though have often done much of their publishing in peer-reviewed journals, which is more common in Europe than the United States. Indeed, writing for the twenty-year celebration of the first edition of the *European Journal of International Law*, Martti Koskenniemi noted ironically that "[t]he European Journal has since then become one of the more interesting publications in the field and New York

---

[38] But see Pells (2017).
[39] These figures represent the regular NYU international law faculty, not the more diverse visiting faculty that forms part of the Hauser Global Law School Program.

University has come to be regarded as the home of the world's most prestigious European law school" (Koskenniemi 2009: 18). The character of NYU is particularly significant in the US market given the high number of foreign LLMs that NYU teaches each year. However, even though NYU is more internationalized than its counterparts, the diversity of its regular faculty nonetheless largely derives from its inclusion of international law academics trained in other Western states, including Australia, New Zealand, the United Kingdom, and Israel, suggesting both denationalizing but also Westernizing influences.

III. Conclusion

When one looks at transnational movement of law students and law professors, what appears are hierarchical patterns and unequal core–periphery dynamics. Students from core, Western states rarely study law outside the West, while elite law students from outside this core are attracted to studying in core Western states because of the social capital associated with such moves. This results in an asymmetrical movement of students followed by an asymmetrical movement of ideas, materials, and approaches in the reverse direction. As I explore more fully in my book, these inequalities appear not just in legal education but also in many areas of international law, from the cases that international law textbooks cite to the nationality and educational profiles of top international arbitrators and counsel before the International Court of Justice (Roberts 2017: Chapters 3.IV, 4.IV, and 5.III).

Transnational legal education may make the international law field more "international" in one sense, but it reproduces and likely exacerbates certain forms of dominance and inequality in a way that belies the field's claim to universality in another sense. It is this latter point that leads to the questioning of whether international law really is international. What versions of international law are adopted in the academies of each core state, which are then radiated out to their semiperiphery and periphery states, is beyond the scope of this chapter and is more fully discussed in my book (Roberts 2017: Chapters 1, 4–6). However, these hierarchical and asymmetrical transnational flows of students and ideas, materials, and approaches have much to tell us about the sociology of the globalization of knowledge in general, and of law and international law in particular.

References

Adams, Richard (2017). "UK Universities Fall Down Global League Tables After Budget Cuts," *The Guardian*. June 7.

Black, Bernard S. (1990). "Is Corporate Law Trivial?: A Political and Economic Analysis," *Northwestern University Law Review* 84(2): 542–597.

Boston College Law School (2016). LLM Program. Accessed December 27. https://www.bc.edu/bc-web/schools/law/admission-aid/llm-program.html.

Bourdieu, Pierre (1987). "The Force of Law: Toward a Sociology of the Juridical Field," *Hastings Law Journal* 38(5): 805–853.

Bourdieu, Pierre and Loïc J.D. Wacquant (1992). *An Invitation to Reflexive Sociology*. University of Chicago Press.

Bronner, Ethan (2013). "Law School's Applications Fall as Costs Rise and Jobs Are Cut," *New York Times*. January 30.

Carney, William J. et al. (2012). "Lawyers, Ignorance, and the Dominance of Delaware Corporate Law," *Harvard Business Law Review* 2: 123–151.

China Scholarship Council (2017). Introduction to Chinese Government Scholarships. February 14. http://www.csc.edu.cn/laihua/scholarshipdetailen.aspx?cid=97&id=2070.

China University of Political Science and Law (2016). LLM in International Law. Accessed December 28, 2016. http://www.lawschoolchina.com/llm.

Clark, David S. (2009). "American Law Schools in the Age of Globalization: A Comparative Perspective," *Rutgers Law Review* 61(4): 1037–1078.

Coates IV, John C. (2012). "Managing Disputes Through Contract: Evidence from M&A," *Harvard Business Law Review* 2: 295–343.

Cohen, Mathilde (2016). "On the Linguistic Design of Multinational Courts: The French Capture," *International Journal of Constitutional Law* 14(2): 498–517.

Coleman, James S. et al. (1966). *Medical Innovation: Diffusion of a Medical Drug Among Doctors*. Bobbs-Merrill Company.

Daines, Robert (2002). "The Incorporation Choices of IPO Firms," *New York University Law Review* 77(6): 1559–1611.

Dezalay, Yves and Bryant Garth (2002). *The Internationalization of Palace Wars: Lawyers, Economists, and the Contest to Transform Latin American States*. University of Chicago Press.

Dezalay, Yves and Bryant Garth (1996). *Dealing in Virtue: International Commercial Arbitration and the Construction of a Transnational Legal Order*. University of Chicago Press.

Directive of the President of the Russian Federation on Scholarships of the President of the Russian Federation [trans. from Russian] (1993). Собрание актов Президента и Правительства Российской Федерации [Collection of Acts of the President and Government of the Russian Federation], No. 37.

Dong, Liu (2010). "Universities to Rival West's in 25 Yrs: Report," *Global Times*. February 4.

Edley, Christopher (2012). "Fiat Flux: Evolving Purposes and Ideals of the Great American Public Law School," *California Law Review* 100(2): 313–330.

Eisenberg, Melvin Aron (1989). "The Structure of Corporation Law," *Columbia Law Review* 89(7): 1461–1525.

Fincher, Ruth and Kate Shaw (2009). "The Unintended Segregation of Transnational Students in Central Melbourne," *Environment and Planning* 41(8): 1884–1902.

Fisch, Jill E. (2000). "The Peculiar Role of the Delaware Courts in the Competition for Corporate Charters," *University of Cincinnati Law Review* 68(4): 1061–1100.

Flood, John (1999). "Legal Education, Globalization, and the New Imperialism," in Fiona Cownie, ed., *The Law School—Global Issues, Local Questions.* Pp. 127–158. Taylor & Francis.

Flood, John (2007). "Lawyers as Sanctifiers: The Role of Elite Law Firms in International Business Transactions," *Indiana Journal of Global Legal Studies* 14(1): 35–66.

Gao, Lingyun (2002). "What Makes a Lawyer in China? The Chinese Legal Education System After China's Entry into the WTO," *Willamette Journal of International Law and Dispute Resolution* 10: 197–238.

Glendon, Mary Ann, Paulo G. Carozza, and Colin Picker, eds. (2014). *Comparative Legal Traditions: Texts, Materials and Cases on Western Law.* West Academic Publishing. 4th ed.

Goldhaber, Michael D. (2005). "They Rule the World: One-Year LL.M. Programs at U.S. Law Schools Are on the Rise Again, Attracting Fledgling Power Brokers from Around the World," *The American Lawyer.* September 14.

Haicong, Zuo (2009). "Legal Education in China: Present and Future," *Oklahoma City University Law Review* 34(1): 51–58.

Halliday, Terence C. and Gregory Shaffer, eds. (2015). *Transnational Legal Orders.* Cambridge University Press.

Hernández, Gleider I. (2012). "Impartiality and Bias at the International Court of Justice," *Cambridge Journal of International Law and Justice* 1(3): 183–207.

Hernández, Gleider I. (2014). *The International Court of Justice and the Judicial Function.* Oxford University Press.

Hua, He (2004). "Zhongguo Jindai Guoji Faxue de Dansheng yu Chengzhang [The Birth and Growth of International Law in Modern China]," *Faxue Jia [Jurist]* 4: 49.

Irish, Charles F. (2007). "Reflections on the Evolution of Law and Legal Education in China and Vietnam," *Wisconsin International Law Journal* 25: 243–254.

Issaeva, Maria (2013). "Twelfth Anniversary of Russia's Participation in the Jessup Competition: A View from Behind the Curtain," *Международное правосудие [International Justice]* 3(7).

Itsoukalas, Ioannis (2008). "The Double Life of Erasmus Students," in Mike Byram and Fred Dervin, eds., *Students, Staff and Academic Mobility in Higher Education.* Pp. 131–152. Cambridge Scholars Publisher.

Jamin, Christophe (2012). *La Cuisine du Droit.* LGDJ.

Jamin, Christophe (2014). Interview with Antoine Garapon, host. "Où en est l'enseignement du droit?," Esprit de Justice (Podcast), *France Culture Radio.* September 25. http://www.franceculture.fr/emission-esprit-de-justice-ou-en-est-l-enseignem ent-du-droit-2014-09-25.

Jamin, Christophe and William van Caenegem (2016). "The Internationalisation of Legal Education: General Report for the Vienna Congress of the International Academy of Comparative Law, 20–26 July 2014," in Christophe Jamin and William van Caenegem, eds., *The Internationalisation of Legal Education.* Pp. 3–36. Springer International Publishing.

Jia, Chen (2010). "Class Act Promotes Global 'Soft Power,'" *China Daily.* November 11.

Kamar, Ehud (1998). "A Regulatory Competition Theory of Indeterminacy in Corporate Law," *Columbia Law Review* 98(8): 1908–1959.

Katz, Daniel et al. (2011). "Reproduction of Hierarchy? A Social Network Analysis of the American Law Professoriate," *Journal Legal Education* 61(1): 76–103.

Kennedy, Duncan (2006). "Three Globalizations of Law and Legal Thought: 1850–2000," in David Trubek and Alvaro Santos, eds., *The New Law and Economic Development: A Critical Appraisal.* Pp. 95–173. Cambridge University Press.

KoGuan Law School of Shanghai Jiao Tong University (2013). L.L.M. Program. Last modified November 21, 2013. http://law.sjtu.edu.cn/International/Article120102.aspx.

Koskenniemi, Martti (2009). "The Politics of International Law—20 Years Later," *European Journal of International Law* 20(1): 7–19.

L'Heureux-Dubé, Claire (1998). "The Importance of Dialogue: Globalization and the International Impact of the Rehnquist Court," *Tulsa Law Review* 34(1): 15–40.

La Forest, Gérard V. (1994). "The Use of American Precedents in Canadian Courts," *Maine Law Review* 46(2): 211–220.

Law, David S. (2015). "Judicial Comparativism and Judicial Diplomacy," *University of Pennsylvania Law Review* 163(4): 927–1036.

Law, David S. and Wen-Chen Chang (2011). "The Limits of Global Judicial Dialogue," *Washington Law Review* 86(3): 523–577.

Liu, Sida (2013). "The Legal Profession as a Social Process: A Theory on Lawyers and Globalization," *Law and Social Inquiry* 38(3): 670–693.

Mälksoo, Lauri (2015). *Russian Approaches to International Law.* Oxford University Press.

Marks, Stephen (2007). "Introduction," in Firoze Manji and Stephen Marks, eds., *African Perspectives on China in Africa.* Pp. 1–14. Pambazuka Press.

Marshall, Jane (2013). "International Mobility of African Students—Report," *University World News.* July 6.

Marxsen, Christian et al. (2015). "Introduction to Symposium: The Incorporation of Crimea by the Russian Federation in the Light of International Law," *Zeitschrift für ausländisches öffentliches Recht und Völkerrecht* [*Heidelberg Journal of International Law*] 75(1): 3–5.

Mattis, Peter (2012). "Reexamining the Confucian Institutes," *Diplomat.* August 2.

Ministry of Education (2011). Jiaoyubu, Zhongyang Zhengfa Weiyuanhui Guanyu Shishi Zhuoyue Falü Rencai Jiaoyu Peiyang Jihua de Ruogan Yijian [Several Opinions of the Ministry of Education and the Central Politics and Law Commission of the Communist Party of China on Implementing the Plan for Educating and Training Outstanding Legal Talents], Xinhua. December 23.

Minzner, Carl F. (2013). "The Rise and Fall of Chinese Legal Education," *Fordham International Law Journal* 36(2): 335–395.

Murray, Peter and Jens Drolshammer (2000). "The Education and Training of a New International Lawyer," *European Journal of Law Reform* 2(4): 505–543.

National Bureau of Statistics of China (1983). *1983 Statistical Yearbook of China.* China Statistics Press.

Order of the Ministry of Education and Science of the Russian Federation on Enforcing Federal Educational Standard of Higher Professional Education in the Field of Jurisprudence (qualification (degree) "bachelor" [trans. from Russian] (2010). Бюллетень нормативных актов федеральных органов исполнительной власти [Bulletin of Legal Acts of Federal Executive Authorities], No. 26.

Order of the Ministry of Education and Science of the Russian Federation on Scholarship Holders of the President of the Russian Federation for Education Abroad in 2016–17 Academic Year [trans. from Russian], approved by the Deputy Minister of the Ministry of Education and Science of the Russian Federation. 2016. No. 653. 2015. http://gzgu.ru/doc/in-student/2015/653.pdf.

Pells, Rachael (2017). "Brexit Exodus: EU Academics 'Already Pulling Out' of UK Universities, MPs Warned," *Independent*. January 25.

Pells, Rachael (2017). "UK Universities Dominate Global Rankings for First Time Despite Brexit Reputation Fears," *Independent*. September 5.

Peters, Anne (2007). "Die Zukunft der Völkerrechtswissenschaft: Wider den epistemischen Nationalismus [The Future of Public International Law Scholarship: Against Epistemic Nationalism]," *Zeitschrift für ausländisches öffentliches Recht und Völkerrecht* [*Heidelberg Journal of International Law*] 67: 721–776.

Picker, Colin B. (2008). "International Law's Mixed Heritage: A Common/Civil Law Jurisdiction," *Vanderbilt Journal of Transnational Law* 41(4): 1083–1140.

Picker, Colin B. (2009). "A Framework for Comparative Analyses of International Law and its Institutions: Using the Example of the World Trade Organization," in *Comparative Law and Hybrid Legal Traditions*. Pp. 125–126. Schulthess & Co.

Picker, Colin B. (2009). "Beyond the Usual Suspects: Application of the Mixed Jurisdiction Jurisprudence to International Law and Beyond," *Journal of Comparative Law* 3(1): 160–177.

Picker, Colin (2012). "The Value of Comparative and Legal Cultural Analyses of International Economic Law." Unpublished PhD thesis. University of New South Wales (on file with UNSW Library).

Platsas, Antonios E. and David Marrani (2016). "On the Evolving and Dynamic Nature of UK Legal Education," in Christophe Jamin and William van Caenegem, eds., *The Internationalisation of Legal Education*. Pp. 299–310. Springer International Publishing.

Posner, Richard A. (1987). "The Decline of Law as an Autonomous Discipline: 1962–1987," *Harvard Law Review* 100(4): 761–780.

Presidential Decree of the Russian Federation on Measures to Strengthen the Professional Potential of the Russian Federation [trans. from Russian] (2013). Собрание законодательства Российской Федерации [Russian Collection of Legislation], No. 52 (Vol. II).

Puig, Sergio (2014). "Social Capital in the Arbitration Market," *European Journal of International Law* 25(2): 387–424.

Qizhi, Wu (2016). 国际法教学与人才培养的现状分析与建议—基于师生调查问卷形成的分析报告 [International Law Teaching and Training—Analysis and Suggestions Based on a Survey Study of Students and Teachers]. http://mp.weixin.qq.com/.

Robel, Lauren K. (2012). "Association of American Law Schools Presidential Address 2012," *Association of American Law Schools*. https://www.aals.org/services/presidents-messages/presidential-address-2012/.

Roberts, Anthea (2017). *Is International Law International?* Oxford University Press.

Rogers, Everett M. (2010). *Diffusion of Innovations*. Free Press. 4th ed.

Romano, Roberta (1985). "Law as a Product: Some Pieces of the Incorporation Puzzle," *Journal of Law, Economics, and Organization* 1(2): 225–283.

Sandberg, Haim (2010). "Legal Colonialism—Americanization of Legal Education in Israel," *Global Jurist* 10(2): Article 6.

Sanga, Sarath (2014). "Choice of Law: An Empirical Analysis," *Journal of Empirical Legal Studies* 11(4): 894–928.

Saul, Stephanie (2017). "Amid 'Trump Effect' Fear, 40% of Colleges See Dip in Foreign Applicant," *New York Times*. March 16.

Schachter, Oscar (1977). "The Invisible College of International Lawyers," *Northwestern University Law Review* 72(2): 217–226.

School of Law, Xiamen University (2016). "Curriculum of LLM Program 2016–2017 Spring Semester." September 30. http://law.xmu.edu.cn/en/page/Curriculum.

Schuetze, Christopher F. (2014). "A Bigger World of International Law," *New York Times*. October 6.

Scoville, Ryan and Milan Markovic (2016). "How Cosmopolitan are International Law Professors?," *Michigan Journal of International Law* 38(1): 119–135.

Sellgren, Katherine (2017). "UK University Applications Fall by 4%, UCAS Figures Show," *BBC News*. July 13.

Shambaugh, David (2014). *China Goes Global: The Partial Power*. Oxford University Press.

Silver, Carole (2002). "The Case of the Foreign Lawyer: Internationalizing the U.S. Legal Profession," *Fordham International Law Journal* 25(5): 1039–1084.

Silver, Carole (2005). "Winners and Losers in the Globalization of Legal Services: Offshoring the Market for Foreign Lawyers," *Virginia Journal of International Law* 45(4): 897–934.

Silver, Carole (2006). "Internationalizing Legal Education: A Report on the Education of Transnational Lawyers," *Cardozo Journal of International and Comparative Law* 14: 143–175.

Silver, Carole (2012). "States Side Story: Career Paths of International LL.M. Students, or 'I Like to Be in America,'" *Fordham Law Review* 80(6): 2383–2440.

Silver, Carole and Ballakrishnen, Swethaa (2018). "Sticky floors, springboards, stairways & slow escalators Mobility Pathways and Preferences of International Students in U.S. Law Schools," *UC Irvine Journal of International, Transactional, and Comparative Law.* 3:39.

Silver, Carole, and Swethaa S. Ballakrishnen (2022), "International Law Student Mobility in Context: Understanding Variations in Sticky Floors, Springboards, Stairways and Slow Escalators, Chapter 15 this volume.

Spamann, Holger (2009). "Contemporary Legal Transplants: Legal Families and the Diffusion of (Corporate) Law," *Brigham Young University Law Review* 2009(6): 1813–1878.

Strauss, Valerie (2017). "Why U.S. Colleges and Universities Are Worried About a Drop in International Student Applications," *Washington Post*. July 13.

Terris, Daniel et al. (2007). *The International Judge: An Introduction to the Men and Women Who Decide the World's Cases*. Brandeis University Press.

Twining, William (2009). *General Jurisprudence: Understanding Law from a Global Perspective*. Cambridge University Press.

UNESCO Institute for Statistics (2017). Data for the Sustainable Development of Goals. Accessed November 17, 2017. http://uis.unesco.org/en/.

UNESCO Institute for Statistics (2017). Glossary. Accessed August 17, 2017. http://uis.unesco.org/en/glossary.

UNESCO Institute for Statistics (2017). International Student Mobility in Tertiary Education. Accessed October 23, 2017. https://data.uis.unesco.org.

University of Oxford (2018). Tuition Fees from 2012/13 Onwards. Accessed January 27, 2018. http://www.ox.ac.uk/students/fees-funding/fees/rates.

U.S. News and World Report (2017). Best International Law Programs. https://www.usn ews.com/best-graduate-schools/top-law-schools/international-law-rankings.

Valdés, Juan Gabriel (1995). *Pinochet's Economists: The Chicago School in Chile.* Cambridge University Press.

Walker, Owen and Helen Warrell (2017). "UK University Applications Down for First Time Since 2012," *Financial Times.* July 13.

Waters, Johanna and Rachel Brooks (2011). "'Vive la Différence?': The 'International' Experiences of UK Students Overseas," *Population, Space and Place* 17: 567–578.

Weale, Sally (2016). "UK University Applications from EU Down by 9%, Says UCAS," *The Guardian.* October 26.

Weale, Sally and Lisa O'Carroll (2017). "Brexit Brain Drain Threatens UK Universities, MPs Warn," *The Guardian.* April 25.

Weiguo, Wang (2000). *A Brief Introduction to the Legal Education in China*, Paper presented at the Conference of International Legal Educators, 24–27 May 2000, Florence, Italy. https://www.aals.org/2000international/english-/chinaintro.htm.

Wuhan University (2016). Popular Programs. Accessed December 28, 2016. http://admiss ion.whu.edu.cn/courses_rec.html.

Xing, Li and Chen Jia (2011). "China Offers Scholarships," *China Daily.* July 22.

Yale Law School (2016). Ph.D. Program. Accessed December 31, 2016. https://www.law. yale.edu/studying-law-yale/degree-programs/graduate-programs/PhD-program.

15

International Law Student Mobility in Context

Understanding Variations in Sticky Floors, Springboards, Stairways, and Slow Escalators

*Carole Silver and Swethaa S. Ballakrishnen**

Over the last few decades, international students increasingly have been recognized as central actors in discussions about the globalization of law, and, in particular, as transformative actors in the processes of legal education. Legal education in this regard reflects the trend of internationalization in higher education generally. For example, in 2004, Philip Altbach suggested that there were about two million students worldwide who studied outside their home countries and that this figure likely would rise to about eight million by the year 2025, with a continuing majority population from Asian countries coming to the United States (Altbach 2004: 19).[1] Despite recent changes in

* Silver acknowledges support from the Northwestern University Pritzker School of Law Faculty Research Program. Ballakrishnen acknowledges the structural support of the American Bar Foundation and the funding support from Access Lex for various stages of this research. Silver also acknowledges the data contributions by Neil G. Ruiz, obtained through a Freedom of Information Act request by Ruiz while he was Senior Policy Analyst and Associate Fellow of The Brookings Institution. We are indebted to the law schools that supported our work by facilitating access to their international students, and to unnamed key informants at those and other law schools; in addition, we are especially grateful to the international students and graduate alumni who shared their experiences so generously with us. For invaluable research assistance, we thank Northwestern Pritzker Law graduates Shinong Wang and Injune Park and UC Irvine Law students Widad Diab and Sydney Martin. For comments on earlier versions of this work, we thank Bryant Garth, Sida Liu, Beth Mertz, Gregory Shaffer, and the participants at The Globalization of Legal Education: A Critical Study (Sept. 2017), Law & Society Association annual meeting (June 2017), Legal Education in Crisis? (March 2017), After the JD and Future Research (Nov. 2016), Metrics, Diversity and Law (May 2016), International Legal Ethics Conference (July 2016), University of Wisconsin East Asian Legal Studies Center (Feb. 2016), and the Global Legal Skills Conference (May 2015).

[1] The United States was the largest host country and home to more than a quarter of the world's international students (which is more students than the United Kingdom, Germany, and France combined) (Altbach 2004: 20). Altbach described the flow of students in the early 2000s as being dominated by Asia: "The large majority of foreign students in the United States come from developing

Carole Silver and Swethaa S. Ballakrishnen, *International Law Student Mobility in Context* In: *The Globalization of Legal Education*. Edited by: Bryant Garth & Gregory Shaffer, Oxford University Press. © Oxford University Press 2022.
DOI: 10.1093/oso/9780197632314.003.0015

transnational flows and financial orders that might well impact these trends,[2] international student mobility generally has followed Altbach's predictions: a half decade ago (2016–17), for instance, the number of international students in the United States was more than one million, with 68 percent of all these students originating from Asia.[3] And while international student enrollment during the pandemic and the concurrent political and economic conditions dropped significantly, enrollment of new international students in the fall of 2021 suggests that international enrollment in higher education, for the most part, may rebound and perhaps even grow (Martel 2021).

Despite these overarching trends, traditionally there have been other important variations in the demographic characteristics of international

and newly industrializing countries, with 55 percent from Asia. (The top five countries sending scholars to the United States are India. China, South Korea, Japan, and Taiwan)" (Altbach 2004: 20). For a focus on Asia, see Altbach (2013: 143–147). See also Bhandari and Lefébure (2015: 143).

[2] As with much of the findings in this chapter, which was edited during various stages of the COVID19 pandemic, the actual nature of these trends and their impacts on student mobility remains a moving target. The "big Asia" story in particular was impacted by a range of laws and policies that erupted in response to the unprecedented global pandemic. In early June 2020, for example, the United States placed new restrictions for Chinese students with military ties. See Elizabeth Redden, *Inside Higher Ed.* May 29, 2020. At one point in the editing process of the chapter, the United States Immigration and Customs Enforcement (ICE) Agency modified temporary exceptions that were in place for the spring and summer 2020 semesters, which had allowed international students to take classes virtually during the COVID-19 pandemic. This requirement for students to enroll in classes that had "in class activities" to maintain their status followed the decision of multiple schools to stay online and observe public health advisories during the pandemic. News reports speculated that one million foreign students risked being frozen out of American colleges, costing them close to $41 billion in lost revenues. See Jessica Dickler and Julia Hollingsworth, *CNBC News*, July 7, 2020. Although we expect these policies to have certain lasting impacts in higher education flows and policies (trends we hope to keep track of and study), this chapter does not deal with its complexities. We mention this to especially frame the import of this research.

[3] Overall, in 2017 there were more than 4.6 million students studying outside of their home countries, representing slightly more than half of Altbach's estimate for 2025 at approximately the midway point in the period on which he focused (IIE 2017). This is but one set of statistics that highlight the demographic transformation in global higher education and, given the context of an increasingly global workforce, this premium on international education is not surprising (IIE, *Open Doors*, 2017). This was the second year when more than one million international students studied in the United States (IIE, *Open Doors*, 2017). The proportion of students coming from Asia increased by 6.5 percent over the previous year; the three top sending countries in 2016–2017 were China, India, and South Korea, which accounted for 55.2 percent of all international students in the US International Students Places of Origin (IIE 2018). Altbach was not the only scholar to predict this trajectory for international students and their concentration from Asian countries. For example, Laurel Terry's more recent research on World Trade Organization data reports that "[b]etween 1999 and 2007, the number of international students doubled from 1.75 million to nearly 3 million," with more than one-third of these students from Asia (Terry 2011: 305, 307, quoting Council for Trade in Services, Background Note by the Secretariat: Education Services). Of these, "North America and Western Europe are still 'top destinations' for globally mobile students." And other similar data (for 2009 and 2010) confirm that this is a trend of US dominance in the global education market (IIE 2011). The numbers since then have, despite some alterations produced by the ever raging pandemic and its political and economic conditions, continued to, for the most part, rise.

students. For example, the numbers of international students who pursue higher education outside of their home countries are not evenly represented across all educational departments and technical fields (Institute of International Education "IIE", *Fast Facts* 2017; IIE, *Fast Facts* 2010; Fischer 2010).[4] Recent data on international student enrollment[5] reflect that engineering and business (including management) account for the top and largest share of international student enrollment.[6] The larger category of STEM fields, which includes engineering, math and computer science, and physical and life sciences, accounted for 44 percent of all international student enrollment in the United States in 2016–2017 (IIE, *Fast Facts* 2017).[7] In comparison, enrollment in the social sciences, humanities, and legal studies and law enforcement was approximately 8 percent, 2 percent, and 1 percent, respectively (IIE, *Fast Facts* 2017). Of course, given the scope of the number of international students that the United States admits each year, this is not a small sum (15,306 students in legal studies and law enforcement, for example) (IIE, *Fast Facts* 2017; Turner 2015). The rationale for the relatively low numbers in transnational legal education is fairly straightforward: seen as a nontransferable and highly jurisdictional training, legal practice remained domestic[8] for

[4] See IIE, *Fast Facts* (2017), reporting on thirteen fields of study; IIE, *Fast Facts* (2010), see also Fischer, reviewing the 2008–2009 rates of international student enrollment (2010).

[5] The IIE reports that recently, social science has enrolled more students than the physical and life sciences. Compare 2017 *Fast Facts* (reporting 83,046 students in social sciences in 2016–2017 compared to 76,838 in physical and life sciences), with 2010 *Fast Facts* (reporting 61,285 students in physical and life sciences in 2009–2010 compared to 59.865 in social sciences).

[6] Engineering's position in this hierarchy is unsurprising for a range of reasons, and reflects the assets of the sciences generally. First, the sophisticated levels of training available in the United States, along with the investment necessary for equipment and laboratories, especially at tertiary levels of higher education, have been relatively scarce in the home countries of many international students. Second, training in technical subjects, including science and engineering, also is highly transferable; because knowledge in the sciences is not limited by jurisdictional applicability, training in one country transfers valued skill sets irrespective of work and life choices made after the completion of the course. Third, because of this sophistication and applicability, international training offers steep labor market benefits for its recipients—both in the host as well as the home country. Thus, not only do these graduate level degrees offer an "in" into a Western lifestyle, they also translate to superior labor market benefits for students who return to their home countries (Lowell and Findlay 2001). For another model of how these superior labor market benefits transfer in the home country context, see Saxenian's description of "brain circulation," which describes how Chinese and Indian-born engineers transfer Western technical and institutional know-how to their home countries (2005: 35).

[7] Two-thirds of foreign students pursuing a bachelor's or higher degree are in science, technology, engineering, mathematics (STEM), or business, management, and marketing fields (Ruiz 2014).

[8] While LLM programs have been in operation for many decades, prior to the 1990s they were seen as primarily a credentialing system for foreign-trained lawyers who wanted an American education before pursuing academic careers in their own country (Hupper 2015: 319; Hupper 2008: 413; Hupper 2007: 1; Silver 2000: 1095). In contrast, the LLM as a degree that has interested practitioners and academics alike is a more recent phenomenon that coincided with the emergence of global legal and business markets (Silver and Freed 2006: 23).

the most part until the mid-1990s, when it slowly began to be more inclusive to external entrants.[9]

In particular, the LLM degree (which is the standard master's training in law that approximately three-quarters of law schools in the United States offer for international students[10]) has changed the way legal training is perceived by suppliers and consumers of this education.[11] From the US law school's perspective, in addition to the obvious financial benefits,[12] the inclusion of international students signals an internationalization of the school's educational atmosphere and experience.[13] On the other hand, from the perspective of the incoming students, changes in the world market for legal services have created a new environment in which an international legal education has practical value and demand.[14]

[9] A study of the Harvard Law School's graduate population shows that numbers of LLM students steadily have increased since the mid-1990s in the one graduate school program studied (Ballakrishnen 2008). The only other time these enrollments were of even comparable magnitude was in the post–World War II phase, when a steady number of international government officers and tax professionals were sent to HLS for a specialized tax LLM (Ballakrishnen 2008).

[10] Silver's (2002: 1039) research on LLMs in the United States provides some insight into the number of schools that offer these programs, as well as the number of students enrolled in them. Using data collected from the websites of individual law schools, she records that "[i]n 1999, at least sixty-eight U.S. law schools offered some sort of graduate degree available to foreign lawyers," and "[m]ore than half of these programs [were] available exclusively to foreign lawyers" (Silver 2002: 1043). By 2004, 102 law schools offered graduate programs open to foreign law graduates, more than half of which were exclusively for foreign lawyers (Silver, *Internationalizing*, 2006: 147). By 2016, the number of schools supporting at least one LLM program open to foreign law graduates had increased to 154, based on a review of law school websites (records on file with Silver).

[11] The literature on students who come to the United States for a master's program in law deals with the consequences of this dynamic both for the institutional and the individual actors, as well as the implications this has for the broader legal profession (Silver 2009; Silver, *Internationalizing*, 2006: 146, reviewing why international students come to the United States for an LLM).

[12] LLM programs are financially important for US law schools because the schools can charge full tuition without worrying about the credential of the students for the purpose of national rankings (e.g., U.S. News & World Report). This is true even though schools take seriously the benefits to the general community and student learning that arise from the presence of international students in law school graduate programs (Silver, *Internationalizing*, 2006: 155; Silver 2012: 228; Tolbert 2016).

[13] Law schools have a growing interest in expanding their student population to include international students. Further, many schools have made dedicated efforts to create a community for their international students. Increasingly, law schools have described the benefits of actively assimilating the incoming international graduate students not only to offer a world-class education to them but also to offer a broader experience for American students in the classroom. For a short commentary on the advantages of integrating LLMs in American classrooms, see Robel (2006: 799).

[14] This practical value and demand has not been universal, and it is one example of the variability in these returns that we seek to explore in this chapter. Earlier research has shown that the advantage of global education and credentialing depends on the country in which these lawyers are practicing. For example, in work on US legal education and the global legal services market, Carole Silver argues that this is related to various factors, including liberalization structures, institutional limitations, and the resultant extent to which local and global law is necessary to be primed. In countries like Germany, where law firms long have embraced international work and local legal education is imperative even for cross-national practice, for example, having an LLM is more of a differentiator in the market than a sorter (Silver 2001: 21–28, "But with the strength of the state exam score as a guiding signal, the PhD and LLM are limited to supporting rather than determinative roles in the German

But while a small number when juxtaposed against the larger influx of international students in all fields and levels of education, the 1 percent figure representing students who come to the United States for higher education in law is significant for our purposes (IIE, *Fast Facts* 2017; *Fast Facts* 2010).[15] In the 2013–2014 academic year, for example, the American Bar Association Section of Legal Education and Admissions to the Bar reported enrollment for all ABA-approved law schools in all degree programs at nearly 140,000 students (not a small number!) (American Bar Association 2013).[16] By the fall of 2016, this number had dropped to just below 125,000, reflecting a decrease in the Juris Doctor (JD) population, which was offset somewhat by an increase in enrollment in post-JD and non-JD programs (American Bar Association 2016).[17] While the largest segment of international students studying law in the United States is enrolled in graduate programs (identified as "post-JD" by the ABA, and including the LLM), there has been a concurrent rise in the number of international students who wish to pursue a more mainstream US law degree, that is, the JD. In recent research, we show that while certainly not a seamless assimilation, the percentage of international students in mainstream JD programs not only has increased substantially in the last decade but also has surpassed other domestic minority groups in certain instances, and this is particularly the case in law schools ranked at the top of the *U.S. News* rankings (Ballakrishnen and Silver 2019).[18]

hiring market"). On the other hand, in new markets, US legal education may be more of a necessity than mere icing on the cake (Silver 2001: 41). See also Roberts and Koskenniemi, describing flows of international students studying law in the context of various influences, including language and legal family (2017: 61–67).

[15] IIE defines "international student" as "anyone studying at an institution of higher education in the United States on a temporary visa that allows for academic coursework. These include primarily holders of F (student) visas and J (exchange visitor) visas. For the purposes of *Open Doors* (2018), students at institutions other than accredited colleges and universities are not counted (i.e. secondary schools or vocational schools). Individuals who have permanent residency or a separate work visa are not counted."

[16] 128,641 enrolled full-/part-time JD students at 202 ABA-approved law schools and 11,132 non-JD students, including post-JD (which includes LLM and SJD students), postbaccalaureate and non-JD online (reported Jan. 18, 2014).

[17] 110,951 enrolled full-/part-time JD students at 206 ABA-approved law schools and 13,667 non-JD students, including post-JD and postbaccalaureate(American Bar Association 2016).

[18] See Ballakrishnen and Silver, describing the increasing proportion of law schools with larger populations of nonresident aliens than Black, Asian, or Latinx students: "NRAs [non-resident aliens] comprised a larger proportion of the student body than Black students at half of the Top Twenty law schools in 2017, up from just ten percent in 2011 (2019). Growth in the number of Top Twenty schools with more NRAs than Asians/Asian-American (from 0% to 30 %) and Latinx students (from 15% to 45%) also was substantial during this period . . ." (references omitted) (Ballakrishnen and Silver 2019).

In this strain of work tracing these students and their mobility contexts, we suggest that these changing demographics of international student participation in US legal education are important at the individual level in terms of identity creation and that their mobility both into and within law schools can be theorized in four kinds of metaphorical pathways: *sticky floors, springboards, stairways,* and *slow escalators* (Ballakrishnen and Silver 2019; Silver and Ballakrishnen 2020). In this chapter, we use these four metaphorical categories to further expand on the ways in which students find different sources of persuasion and pushback as they navigate their respective paths within law schools. We suggest that these mobility pathways are important because they give us a way of making sense of the factors shaping students' preferences, including the relative importance of access to resources before (e.g., language, immigration status, prior work experience) and after (e.g., training opportunities, lawyer regulation and licensing at home and abroad) the desired degree. Our main argument, building on earlier work, is that context matters across time, across different local contexts[19] and, importantly, across different levels of analysis (Ballakrishnen 2012: 2441; Bhandari 2015; Silver 2012: 2384; Silver 2001: 3). Particularly, while student decisions are molded at different stages by the particularities of their specific positional advantages and constraints, they also are embedded within a range of institutional limitations and structural opportunities that are constantly in a state of flux. Although our data cannot speak to career trajectories over time, they can—and do—reveal the importance of the interactions between these factors at the individual and institutional levels. Ultimate choices (and, as we argue, tracks) that students seem to "make" often are larger reflections of a range of interactions between each of these constraints and capacities. Considering these mobility patterns in relation to the metaphorical categories we offer also enables us, as we show in the following, to visualize the larger potential this case of international JD students can offer for theories of malleable social capital and recursive transnationalism (Ballakrishnen 2012: 2441; Garth 2015; Halliday and Carruthers 2007; Halliday 2009: 263; Kim 2016: 1135).

---

[19] See Bhandari (2015), providing a review of the impact of Asia's sending potential and the relevance of its local dynamics.

I. Trends in International Legal Education

The rise of the United States as an important site for educating international lawyers occurred roughly in tandem with the ascendance of US law firms in the global market for legal services and during a period when US higher education also increasingly was valorized (Ruiz 2014).[20] The position of US legal education draws from and reflects the interplay between and among these factors and the respective forces in local contexts contributing to this intersection. In this section, we trace the development and changing demographics of international law students' participation in US legal education. Our description here is necessarily general and aims at linking the fluidity of patterns of students' participation to institutional forces at work within various sending countries and the United States, and across education and legal market contexts.

The presence of international students in US law schools is not a new phenomenon. For most of the post–World War II era, international scholars interested in academic careers enrolled in US law schools to pursue a doctoral degree, commonly known as the Doctor of Juridical Sciences (SJD), and since the 1970s, they essentially have comprised the main group interested in the SJD (Hupper 2007: 1; Hupper 2008: 413; Hupper 2015: 319). But the SJD was limited as a receptor, both because of resource constraints exerted on potential candidates in their home countries (e.g., national funding for these programs, opportunities for returnees), and as a result of parallel resource constraints in the United States (e.g., limited funding for graduate study at this level, lack of faculty resources for supervising and mentoring SJD students). Partly as a result, the more common home for international law students grew to be the classroom-focused postgraduate Master of Laws (LLM) degree program. Early on, in the 1930s, according to Gail Hupper (2008: 51), LLM programs were developed as a sort of consolation prize for students who did not complete their SJD. At that time, the LLM included characteristics of a degree intended to be earned by scholars, including a thesis as a common graduation requirement. But as legal practice became more remunerative and prestigious around the world, international lawyers and law graduates could throw off the pretense of scholarship and justify pursuit of a graduate degree on other grounds. Recall that the 1980s and early

---

[20] "The United States is the preeminent global hub for academic training. In the 2012–2013 academic year the United States hosted a record 819,644 international students, 21 percent of all students studying abroad worldwide" (Ruiz 2014).

1990s was a period of significant global expansion for US-based law firms and their clients (Silver 2000: 147). By the 1990s, when US law schools experienced a period of growth in their LLM degree programs, international law graduates were thinking about how to make themselves attractive to what we now think of as global law firms.

By the early 2000s, approximately 40 percent of all ABA-approved law schools offered at least one LLM program open to international law graduates, with some schools offering multiple of these programs organized around various substantive specialties, for example (Silver, *Internationalizing* 2006: 147). According to the ABA, enrollment in post-JD programs approximately doubled during the ten years beginning in the mid-1990s, and during that period the proportion of international students in this group went from comprising about 40 percent of all LLM students to nearly 60 percent of them.[21] Importantly, during this phase of global legal education, the signal of the LLM was to convey a readiness for interaction beyond home country borders, and it served as a mechanism to distinguish its holder from others at home whose experience was limited to the local context (Ballakrishnen and Silver 2019; Silver 2001). The LLM was considered by both students who pursued it and by their employers as preparation for working with US-based clients and organizations and perhaps clients from other countries as well. As an Argentinian lawyer explained his thinking in 1995 about pursuing an LLM:

> And then, at the same time there were a lot of factors like, the U.S. was getting bigger and bigger in terms of economy in Argentina, and . . . it was more and more important to have English. And uh, a lot of investors from the U.S. were coming to Argentina. And uh, I realized that it was a very important matter for me because I wanted to have like, you know, like U.S. clients and the only [way] I could do it was like studying their law, like the U.S. law and talking good English.[22]

But even among the group of LLM graduates from the late 1990s and early 2000s, some wanted more than the credential from their LLM experience

---

[21] The ABA reported 1996 enrollment in post-JD programs as 2,630, and as 4,060 in 2004 (ABA reports on file with Silver).

[22] 170-99. Interviews with international law students and graduates, and with their employers and law firm hiring partners practicing with elite national and international law firms, were conducted as part of Silver's ongoing research exploring globalization, legal education, and the legal profession. The year of the interview is indicated after the hyphen (i.e., this interview was conducted in 1999).

Motivation	Proportion of Respondents indicating this as important
Expansion of professional opportunities in home country	82%
Interest in a particular area of law	54%
Desire to improve English skills	51%
Career advancement	39%
Desire to live in the United States	39%
Influence of colleagues/friends who had an LLM	29%
Path to a job in the United States	29%
Family considerations	21%
Necessity for US bar exam	16%

Figure 15.1. Motivations for Pursuing US LLM, Respondents from Graduating Classes of 1996, 1998, and 2000

(Silver 2005: 897).[23] Responses to a survey of LLMs who graduated in 1996, 1998, and 2000 that included a question about their motivations for pursuing the LLM (Figure 15.1) indicate that, for certain students, the LLM was considered a path to something else (Silver 2009; Silver 2001).[24] Variation keyed to home country environments as well as to factors such as career contexts, among others (Silver 2001; Silver, *Internationalizing* 2006: 158). Students in private firms and corporate positions from Japan and South Korea, for example, were interested in the LLM's bar eligibility status (Ginsburg 2004: 440; Kim 2009; Lee 2007: 231; Moon n.d.; Oh 2005: 530; Silver et al. 2015: 3; Seong-Hyun 2011: 217). A Korean LLM explained that "[i]n Korea, LLM value is first, American license—bar exam. LLM is a process to get license." (I73-03). A Japanese LLM reported on the norm for her employer being that "[a]ll employees have passed the New York bar, and all take it after their LLMs!" (I74-03). Other students, typically from Europe, hoped for a

---

[23] See Silver (2005: 897), describing international LLM students' interest in gaining practice experience in the United States following their LLM graduation.

[24] See Silver (2009), describing the survey and results. The data reported in Figure 15.1 was collected as part of a larger study of the careers of US LLM graduates (Silver: 2002). See also Lazarus-Black (2017: 467), describing international students' reasons for pursuing an LLM in the United States as including "professional and career advancement . . . ; personal reasons, such as marriage to a U.S. citizen . . . ; a desire to pursue intellectual questions . . . ; interest in a field of law that they described as 'underdeveloped' in their home country. . . . improving their proficiency in English, learning about U.S. society, extending work-related networks, and developing friendships. Most of the [50 interviewed international students] . . . gave multiple reasons for wanting to study in the U.S."

practice experience—long or short term—in the United States.[25] This was challenging for a variety of reasons, since there remained an ill-hidden favoritism by the law schools for their JD students, spearheaded by the weight ascribed to employment outcomes for JD graduates by *U.S. News* (Espeland and Sauder 2016: 119).[26] There was (and arguably still is) no countervailing force that pressed the interests of LLMs with regard to law school career services offices. One LLM graduate (115-06) described the job search as:

> [D]ifficult because of the way the LLM process works, because essential[ly] you're supposed to wait until all the firms fill their JD slots and then, if they have anything, then they will come and look for you. You know, it's hard, because how do you know? Because firms like [Firm Name] met with all of [the LLMs] and they were very positive. They were like yeah, yeah, but they are not allowed to recruit LLMs before they recruit JDs. . . . Oh, because . . . you know, a LLM is second best to JDs always.

Others echoed this frustration with the recruiting process generally in law firms, as well as with career services offices.[27]

---

[25] The survey of LLM graduates from the years 1996, 1998, and 2000 found, for example, that students from Europe (EU and non-EU) comprised the largest group (approximately 38%) of LLM graduates who remained in the United States at least several years after graduating (Silver, 2012: 2400, Table 5). Students' thinking about staying in the United States to work often changed over the course of their LLM year. For example, a 1998 LLM graduate from Germany described the evolution of her thinking about trying to remain in the United States for a period of practice after graduation: "My anticipation was I wanted to spend my year there and then go back home to Germany and hopefully be good enough to start in one of those big international law firms and then maybe get an overseas assignment or something that way. That was the initial plan. And then when I came to [SCHOOL NAME] . . . I immediately said, you know, one year is really passing by too quickly. I mean I already haven't seen how fast the first semester passes and knowing that graduation was May, I, at that point already couldn't see myself going home already in May. And I said, what I want to do at all possible is try and maybe find work and stay for another half year or year." I19-07. A Belgian 1996 LLM graduate was determined to stay in the United States from his first day, explaining, "I always remember when, my first day in [U.S. CITY] and it was my first time in [U.S. CITY] actually. I arrived quite late at night and then, in the morning, because of the jet lag, I woke up very early and I saw . . . I saw the sun going up and people jogging . . . and I said to myself okay I'm going to stay here for the rest of my life. . . . And I kept this thought for quite some time. And that is why I wanted badly to stay in the U.S. after the LLM." I31-08.

[26] See generally, Espeland and Sauder (2016: 119), referring to the consequences for LLM programs of *U.S. News*' exclusive focus on JD programs.

[27] A French LLM graduate's comment reflected her personal experience regarding competitiveness of an LLM: "I didn't get any summer internships, because of course law firms were looking for JD graduates who were gonna work as associates. . . . And I thought with my LLM I could compete against them, and maybe work potentially as an associate. . . . I really did not realize, it took me a long-time to realize I am not going to be hired as an associate with a French JD and an U.S. LLM." I26-07. An LLM graduate from Venezuela (class of 2000) noted: "I have to say that the office of career services at [LAW SCHOOL] as well as the Graduate Program staff emphasized to the graduate students that the job opportunities available were mostly for JDs and that the help that they could offer was limited because of that." S111. An Austrian 2000 graduate commented: "I am very happy with my current job,

While much remains the same for LLM students today as it was ten or even twenty years ago, in some respects things are quite different, reflecting changes in students' home country contexts as well as in the environments they hope to join or return to. Students' motivations for pursuing an LLM offer an example. On one hand, students talk about the LLM as advancing their career opportunities,[28] helping them strengthen their English language skills, and in gaining the cultural exposure that comes with living outside of their home countries[29]—all motivations for pursuing an LLM that were expressed by the LLMs who graduated between 1996 and 2000. On the other hand, while many of these factors remain relevant, LLMs today also increasingly describe the degree as a means to another end—whether the bar, a US-based practice experience, or both—that *itself* is necessary in order for the LLM credential to serve as a mark of distinction in the student's home country.[30] A Chinese LLM student (C50-15) referred to this in the context of describing a summer internship. In explaining that the position did not involve compensation (a common feature of some of these opportunities for international students following visa conditions), she said: "I don't care [about being paid]. . . . It's not a big problem. It's part time. For LLMs, the most important thing is to get U.S. experience, to help us get a permanent job later. And passing the bar––after passing the bar."

however, I would like to point out that career services at [LAW SCHOOL] were absolutely lousy and entirely focussed [sic] on placing JDs." S132. (S indicates survey response).

See also Mindie Lazarus-Black (2017: 462), describing international LLM students as experiencing different job opportunities reflecting home country differences.

[28] A student from China explained that she came for the LLM "for a boost. I don't know if I'm typical or not, but my life, in terms of study, is like going up steps. So, it's like small city in China, and then larger city, and then Beijing, and then the next step, the United States. It's just a step up a bit. I think that would get me a . . . not an advantage but a broader perspective about the business, the subject, so as to be better for my first job." C52-15.

[29] A Chinese LLM explained that she had three goals: "1. Opportunity to stay here [in the United States], 2. English skill, writing and speaking because I know language is so important in the legal field, and 3. I've never studied or lived abroad alone for a long time. So I want to know how it feels. I wanted to do this in high school, [or] to go to college in the U.S. But I didn't make it. So it's a dream in my mind, I have to make it." C50-15.

[30] Two 2017 LLM graduates from China explained the importance of the bar exam in the context of discussing how students select courses (students are identified by interview number): "C067-17: I want to speak for, I think, most of Chinese students when they are picking the class. I think the first thing that they're concerned about is the bar requirement, right? C068-17: Yeah, that's true. It's like your routine. You'll get an LM [sic] degree, and then sit for the bar, and get a license. [*Laugh*] C067-17: So, I think the most important guidance for them is the bar exam requirement." A Russian LLM (class of 2014) explained her frustration with the lack of job opportunities in the United States for LLM graduates: "I have looked into every way to find even a low-paying or unpaid job." C04-15.

The law schools continued building and growing LLM programs, and today nearly 80 percent of all law schools offer at least one post-JD degree program for international law graduates, reflecting an approximate doubling of the law schools offering such a program over the last ten years.[31] The number of students enrolled in post-JD programs also has increased substantially, more than doubling between 2004 and 2016 to just under 10,000 students.[32] Of course, the market dynamics that have produced (and continue to produce) this rise in international students are not stagnant or fully predictable. For example, over the course of this period, changes in immigration policy, regulatory restrictions, market conditions, or, as is more recently the case, public health crises might—and have[33]—impact(ed) international student enrollments more generally. And while it is not possible to determine exactly what proportion of post-JD student enrollment is comprised of international law graduates (because the ABA does not mandate reporting of this figure by law schools), all indications suggest that the lion's share of growth in post-JD enrollment traditionally was fueled by international students.[34]

---

[31] Research conducted by Silver and her research assistant in the spring of 2016 involving a review of individual law school websites showed that 78 percent of ABA-approved law schools supported at least one LLM program in which international law graduates could enroll. It is relatively common for law schools to offer multiple of such degree programs. Northwestern Pritzker School of Law is an example. It offers a general LLM program for international law graduates. It also offers an LLM in human rights, and one in tax; both of these are open to domestic JD graduates as well as to international law graduates. In addition, it offers four executive LLM degree programs based in different parts of the world, and each of these is aimed exclusively at international law graduates. While Northwestern might be at the high end of the spectrum on number and type of LLM degree programs for international law graduates, consider the example of the University of Southern California Gould School of Law, a newer entrant to the group of law schools offering graduate degrees for international law graduates. USC offers an on-campus LLM and an online LLM, a two-year LLM, and a Masters in Comparative Law degree aimed at international LLM graduates interested in additional US legal education (*Degrees*, n.d.).

[32] The ABA reported enrollment in 2016 of 9,866 students in post-JD programs, which includes LLMs and SJD degrees, as well as Master of Common Law programs (*2016 JD/Non-JD Enrollment Data*, n.d.).

[33] At the initial time of our writing, the COVID-19 pandemic had not yet begun. Over the course of revising and rethinking our work, there has been speculation on the ways in which international student enrollments would be impacted by the pandemic and, as with other parts of this story, many of the factors framing these experiences are very much still—and likely to remain—in flux. Still, we think this focus and speculation highlight an important way in which to think about these students' trajectories and the fragility in our capacities to predict their futures. More generally, about international student enrollment predictions and fragility in this context, see, e.g., Dickerson (2020). On the fragility of international students in law schools in the face of the pandemic, see, e.g., Seron (2020). On the impact that it might have on law schools, more generally, see Spivey (2020). For the budget impact the declining enrollment of international students in these schools, see, e.g., the reporting on Law.com, available at https://www.law.com/2020/04/15/due-to-covid-19-fewer-international-students-could-hit-law-schools-hard/ (last visited July 10, 2020).

[34] IIE's data also is generally consistent with this (IIE, *Fields of Study 2014–2016*, n.d.).

Top-20 Ranked Law Schools			Schools Outside of the Top-20 Ranking	
	All JD Students	Percentage of JDs who are NRAs	All JD Students	Percentage of JDs who are NRAs
2011	19,213	4.13%	1,27,717	1.42%
2012	18,928	4.35%	1,20,576	1.60%
2013	18,530	5.28%	1,10,269	1.81%
2014	18,361	5.75%	1,01,484	2.14%
2015	18,038	6.81%	95,869	2.52%
2016	18,021	6.85%	93,074	2.47%
2017	17,898	7.64%	92,298	2.48%

Tracing the New Internationals: JD Enrollment Patterns and the Big Asia Story

Figure 15.2. Nonresident Alien JD Students in Law Schools in Top-20 and Non-Top-20 Ranked Law Schools, 2011 and 2017

At the same time, despite what future demographic patterns might be, there has been an increasing trend of international students not being contained in non-JD programs. Particularly in the last half decade, there has been growth in the proportion of international students enrolling in US JD programs, too (Figure 15.2). While the numbers and proportions remain small, they are not insignificant, particularly in law schools highly ranked by *U.S. News* (Ballakrishnen and Silver 2019). Overall, as a percentage of all JDs in all ABA-approved law schools, international students (defined by the ABA based on their nonresident alien status) increased from 1.78 percent of the JD student body in 2011 to 3.32 percent in 2017. Figure 15.2 highlights the difference between law schools within and outside of the top twenty of the *U.S. News* rankings with regard to the relative participation of international students who are nonresident aliens, which is the way international students are reported by law schools in required disclosure to the American Bar Association.[35] Relatedly, and as discussed in other work, nonresident aliens are becoming a significant segment of diverse populations in certain law

[35] These data are reported by the law schools based on students' visa status, so they capture an element of international identity that may not entirely reflect students' sense of their own identity. The nonresident alien figures are reported in law school Standard 509 reports, and available for individual law schools and the annual aggregate group (American Bar Association, J.D. Enrollment and Ethnicity 2011; 2016). On international identity, see Ballakrishnen and Silver (2009). On how the Top-20 category is defined, see Ballakrishnen and Silver (2019) at n. 6.

schools where they are more numerous than Black, Asian, or Latinx students. For example, there were more nonresident aliens than Black students at half of the top twenty law schools in 2017, up from only 10 percent in 2011 (Ballakrishnen and Silver 2019, Table 3).

To better understand the interplay of global and local factors shaping students' decisions, it is helpful to consider data offering an overview of the relationship among home country, degree program, schools, and international enrollment in US law schools. To that end, we draw on a data set comprised of information taken from US visa approvals for international students enrolled in institutions of higher education and studying law for the period 2008 through 2012.[36] These data illustrate the "big Asia" story as well as differences between the LLM and JD enrollment (Ruiz 2014). During the five-year period of 2008–2012, F-1 visas were approved for nearly 20,000 (19,161) students studying law.[37] The vast majority of the visas were granted to students for master's level degrees: 82 percent of all of the records analyzed

[36] These data were obtained from Neil Ruiz, who obtained them through a FOIA request while he was Senior Policy Analyst and Associate Fellow at The Brookings Institution (Ruiz 2014). In his writing about the data, Ruiz described his source as a "new database on foreign student visa approvals from 2001 to 2012." The data reflect approvals of F-1 visas, which Ruiz describes as "the most common visa issued to foreigners studying in a full-time academic program. Students must be accepted by an approved school, document they have sufficient funds to cover 12 months of expenses and demonstrate academic preparedness to succeed in the program" (Ruiz 2014: 3). For a discussion of limitations of the visa data, see Ruiz (2019: 6). However, in this chapter, the data analyzed are limited as follows: First, details regarding only the years 2008–2012 were shared by Ruiz. Second, in response to our request for information on law students, Ruiz shared only visa approvals for students studying law as defined by the Classification of Instructional Programs (CIP) code, referenced in the I-20 form (Ruiz 2014: 7). The field of law is defined as "Legal Professions and Studies" (National Center for Education Statistics, n.d.). The data were cleaned to exclude records for students who had enrolled in (1) universities that had no law school, and (2) law schools that are not accredited by the ABA. In addition, with regard to the master's level analysis, records for students enrolled in law schools that did not support a master's program for international law graduates (determined by reference to the law school website and to ABA records) also were excluded. Omitting these from the analysis resulted in excluding records for 31 doctoral level students and 107 master's level students. Generally, the CIP codes indicate that the program of "law" includes both the JD (for example, the code 22.0101 is defined as "[a] program that prepares individuals for the independent professional practice of law, for taking state and national bar examinations, and for advanced research in jurisprudence. Includes instruction in the theory and practice of the legal system, including the statutory, administrative, and judicial components of civil and criminal law") and a master's degree (for example, the code 22.0202 is for "Programs for Foreign Lawyers," and the code 22.0203 covers "American/U.S. Law/ Legal Studies/Jurisprudence"). Note that in this chapter, we describe data characterizing students in a doctoral-level program as JD students, consistent with the CIP definition. Finally, we note the likelihood that the data are overinclusive in certain ways that we could not counter through cleaning and analysis, and Ruiz was unable to make a more refined cut in order to address these concerns.

[37] See Ruiz (2014) as well as Ballakrishnen and Silver (2019), regarding limitations of the data presented here.

LLM/Master's Level	% of Total Master's Sent by Country	JD/Doctoral Level	% of Total JD Sent by Country
China	22.68%	Canada	25.02%
South Korea	7.93%	China	19.33%
Japan	6.81%	South Korea	15.91%
Brazil	4.20%	Taiwan	2.98%
India	4.15%	United Kingdom	2.44%
Germany	3.55%	India	2.38%
France	3.52%	Brazil	2.26%
Taiwan	3.34%	France	2.17%
Thailand	3.30%	Saudi Arabia	1.88%
Saudi Arabia	2.95%	Italy	1.61%
Total % represented	62.43%	Total % represented	75.98%

Figure 15.3. Top Sending Countries with Visa Approvals to Pursue Legal Studies, 2008–2012

were for students in master's level programs, which includes the LLM.[38] Only 18 percent of the records were for students pursuing a JD.[39]

International JD students, according to these data, were most likely to be Canadian, Chinese, or South Korean (Figure 15.3). These three sending countries together accounted for approximately 60 percent of all international JDs (Figure 15.3). Canada's dominance in the JD group likely reflects, at least in part, the proximate ease of migration to the United States and the small number of law schools in Canada; for students who do not gain admission to one of Canada's top law schools, the United States offers an additional and larger pool of schools with prestigious reputations.[40] In addition, for Canadians as well as international students generally, beginning compensation levels at US-based "Big Law" private firms are another attraction (Chambers Student 2016).

[38] See Ruiz (2014) as well as Ballakrishnen and Silver (2019), regarding the CIP definition for master's level degrees as including "Program for Foreign Lawyers."

[39] See Ballakrishnen and Silver (2019), regarding defining doctoral-level programs as a JD according to the CIP code.

[40] A JD graduate interviewee from Canada explained, "I applied to law school at probably four or five of the Canadian universities. . . . After I didn't get accepted to any of those, then I started looking across the border. I applied to, I think, three schools in the U.S." I046-15.

In contrast to the JD group, for the LLM/master's population, ten countries rather than three account for just over 60 percent of the LLMs (Figure 15.3). At the same time, the three largest sending countries for the master's group still comprise a significant force, accounting for almost 40 percent (37.42 percent) of all international graduate (master's) level students. This contrast between the LLM population and the very focused domination of home countries found in the JD group reflects the inherent international characteristic of the LLM degree program itself. It is known as a degree for international law graduates, and this international aspect of its identity is described as being a push factor for international students who choose the JD as an alternative law school path.[41]

Asia has dominated as a sending region for the aggregate population of international students studying in the United States, without regard to field of study, as mentioned earlier and as evidenced by data from *IIE*, which reported that in 2016–2017, students from Asia accounted for 68 percent of all international students in the United States for higher education.[42] In the field of law, visa approvals data indicate that Asia (using IIE's country classifications) accounted for approximately 50.5 percent of all students in the combined master's and doctorate level degree programs (International Institute of Education, Places of Origin 2015/16; Places of Origin 2016/17; National Center for Education Statistics, n.d.). The biggest Asian sending countries for legal studies, according to these data, were China, South Korea, and Japan, which together account for over one-third of the total number of visa approvals for international students to study law in both degree levels, combined.[43] And while there are differences between the JD and master's

[41] See Ballakrishnen and Silver (2019), describing the distancing international JD students attempt from the LLM, including, for example, one student who described the inherent advantages of the JD program over the classic LLM route that other international students might take: "Notice that there are not many international students, especially Chinese students, in JD program. But there are many in LLM program. But actually as an LLM student, you cannot, like, practice law. I'm not sure if I understand it right, you cannot practice law or, like, you are ineligible to take the Bar exam, or so. . . . And I think the JD program sounds more interesting to me than the LLM program.") (I015-17 at 11).
[42] Students from East Asia accounted for approximately 43 percent of all international students (China is by far the biggest sending country of this group, followed by Korea, Taiwan and Japan (in that order)) (IIE, Places of Origin 2016/2017). India sent slightly more than half the number of Chinese students (186,267 students in 2016–2017) (IIE, *Places of Origin*, 2016/2017). Vietnam also was an important sending country from Asia (sending 22,438 students in 2016–2017) (IIE, *Places of Origin*, 2016/2017).
[43] For the aggregate group of international students studying all subjects in the United States, IIE reported that the top three sending countries are China, India, and South Korea (IIE, *Places of Origin*, 2016/2017). India falls to fourth place in the law-focused group, just above Taiwan (IIE, *Places of Origin*, 2016/2017). For information on the visa data describing students studying law in the United States, see IIE, *Places of Origin* (2016/2017).

level groups with regard to the identity and significance of Asian sending countries, China and South Korea figure most prominently among Asian countries in both populations and together account for the largest group of international JD students (Canada is the single most significant sending country).[44] Much has been written about higher education and legal education in these two countries, which suggests why they are the most important Asian feeder countries for US law schools, including the reform of the legal education regime in South Korea, the strength of US and UK law firms in China's market, and their preference for US law school credentials—the latter, related in part at least, to China's regulatory approach to foreign law firms (Ballakrishnen and Silver 2019; Ballakrishnen and Silver 2020; Liu 2008: 771; Silver 2001: 33–53; Silver 2002).[45] Moreover, a US JD, at least, may serve as a proxy for assessing a law graduate's comfort and expertise for practicing in an English-speaking environment.

Our earlier research explains that the trends in the degree programs are hardly universal and vary significantly in relation to factors across levels of analysis (Ballakrishnen and Silver 2019, 2020). As we argue in this chapter, once dissected along the four pathways for mobility that we propose following, many of these interrelated factors could further be categorized along the lines of their global and local coordinates, as well. We turn to these pathways next.

II. Mobile Pathways: Sticky Floors, Springboards, Stairways, and Slow Escalators

The dilution of the LLM as a credential proved a frustration for students that limited their prospects. For some, this was a functional limitation: LLM graduates were stymied by the refusal of most US jurisdictions at the time to recognize the degree as leading to bar eligibility (Lazarus-Black 2017: 480; Silver 2003: 491; Silver and Freed 2006). This caused problems for graduates who wanted to work in states other than New York and California (the two major jurisdictions where, historically, the LLM could satisfy US legal

---

[44] See *supra* note 39, for a description of the visa data and its limitations.

[45] Keep in mind that these categories of home country are not necessarily mutually exclusive, based on interviews conducted with international JD students for earlier research (Ballakrishnen and Silver 2019; Ballakrishnen and Silver 2018). The Canadian group also may include Asian immigrants to Canada, which was the case for several of our interviewees.

education conditions for bar admission), and, instead, motivated them to pursue a JD. A South African LLM (120-09) explained these considerations as leading him to return to his US law school for a JD:

> I got a head hunter in DC, and I started looking around for another position, and then she thought of financial services at other firms, and got a lot of interest from [Law Firm name]. . . . [U]nfortunately about the same time it was 9/11, and that caused everything to dip. And where litigation would have been okay, the financial markets took a dive, and there were no new mutual fund issuances, which had driven a lot of the profits or the practice group for a long-time at [Law Firm name], so the market was down, and, um, there was less interest in the area. They sent, [Law Firm name] sent me to [City] where they had more of a need, to interview there. And I had discussion with a partner, but again it would have required, they were talking about me, because of the Bar issues, [State] had the same Bar issues that [State] has, that you've got to re-qualify by getting, I would have had to sat for the [State] Bar, and I would have had to done a few, a couple of more courses. So after having gone all through that already, and already got my Bars, I was not keen. So I started seriously thinking about what to do, and I decided to go back to [LLM law school name] to get my JD.

Still, while bar eligibility was important, many respondents found the jump from an LLM to a JD useful even beyond this functional distinction. For example, a Filipino lawyer (172-01) who earned an LLM in 2001 and later returned for a JD described his thinking about the LLM as follows:

> For one thing it was a very common practice to pursue graduate legal studies . . . in the U.S. . . . . On top of that I wanted to enhance my credentials. I saw it [the LLM] as a way to enrich my personality. I thought that being exposed to a more international community would help me not only as a lawyer but as a person.

This is generally consistent with the students who described the LLM as break year with intellectual engagement (Ballakrishnen 2012: 2441). Other students (e.g., C02-14) have described the LLM as a "field test" for the JD. A Chinese student (C09-15) who did an LLM first and then transferred into the JD program at her law school (JD class of 2016), for example, explained that she initially hedged her bets in her decision about which degree to pursue:

> So I think I can do LLM first and see if I really like it. 'Cause you know, like, JD is really a big commitment. . . . either in terms of time or money. So I think it's a good thing for me to do LLM and see if I really like, I can, you know, figure out how to do a JD afterwards. . . . If I don't like it, I can just go back.

At least for those who had studied law at home before coming to the United States, the decision to pursue the JD was seen as a way to distinguish oneself in a market that had begun to saddle the LLM with a distinct, unshakeable international tag (Ballakrishnen and Silver 2019).[46] As another recent Chinese JD graduate (C06-15) who earned her first law degree in China explained, her decision about which US law degree program to pursue was predicated on the distinct advantages the JD offered when compared to the LLM:

> Well, because the Chinese, there are so many students pursuing the LLM degrees in China. I mean there are plenty of students going . . . all over the United States to get their LLM degree. And I thought by the time I graduate from United States with my LLM degree, get back to China, maybe I am not so competitive. But JD degree, well, I mean I say will guarantee my ability to pursue my legal career.

But in addition, the decision to pursue a JD also was described as a way to more thoroughly prepare for practice in the United States. A recent Mexican graduate (C25-15) who also had earned a first degree in law in his home country, for example, described his decision about which degree to pursue as related to his career goals as well as to differences in the curricular framework for the LLM and JD:

> So I thought the JD was a better fit for me because I wanted to start from the very basics . . . of the U.S. legal system, and then go up from there, instead of my first course being about taxation and bankruptcy or something very

---

[46] See Ballakrishnen and Silver (2019), describing efforts of international JD students to distance themselves from international LLMs.

specific. And I also wanted to practice in the U.S.—and I thought JD was a better venue for that.

For other students, the path to the JD was more direct, usually following a home country undergraduate degree in a field other than law. For these international students without a law background, the LLM was not an available option; the decision to pursue the JD was part of the deliberation about where and what to study next. One student's reasoning, for example, included thinking that a US JD will distinguish her from her Hong Kong classmates, give her a credential that is recognized at home as well as abroad, and signal quality while positioning her for more choices in her career.[47] She had the option to earn a JD in Hong Kong (where law also is offered as an undergraduate course of study) but had decided instead to start her legal education in the United States directly at the graduate level.

Finally, there were international students whose first degree was earned in the United States. For these students, applying for a US JD felt like an extension of their undergraduate degree. While they described opportunities in their home countries, there was no suggestion that these opportunities would have been seriously considered by them, personally, as equivalent to pursuing a JD in the United States. A recent JD graduate (C64-17) originally from China explained:

> I won't have the chance to study law back in China, just because I did my undergrad here. China has a undergrad law degree, and I don't think the quality of the education for a graduate law degree in China without a bachelor background would be the same. And a JD degree, in my view, is way more valuable than a graduate degree in law in China.

Similarly, a Korean student (C19-15) explained why she did not seriously consider returning to Korea for law school, despite there being a graduate law school system in place:

---

[47] "And at that time I was thinking, do I want to stay in Hong Kong for a legal education [with] a ton . . . of other people? So a lot of my friends, they attend LLB in Hong Kong, so they already have their law degree and their undergraduate study. And Hong Kong also provided JD programs as well, but I was thinking, you know, I received my undergrad location in kind of the best university in Hong Kong and I know how this education is like. And also if I receive a JD degree in the States I can always go back to Hong Kong if I want, because they really welcome to American JD. So, and if I'm lucky enough, I can stay in the U.S. So going to, to pursuing a JD degree in the U.S. gives me more choices, and also I think that U.S. has the best legal education so that's why I want to come here." C47-15.

> I heard that classes were harder [in Korea], . . . because I don't know any of the difficult vocab or anything. . . . I don't feel comfortable doing like reading comprehension in Korean. . . . So I didn't feel comfortable about taking [the] Korean [version of the] LSAT. . . . And the Korean legal system is not as strong as the one in the U.S., the legal market's not doing well. So I didn't think about going to a Korean law school.

For both women, the reputation of the US system of legal education and of the US legal system itself, compared to those in their home countries, influenced their decision to remain in the United States for law school. At least as important, though, was that their assessment of opportunities for pursuing legal education at home involved the prospect of uncomfortable compromises, which were made even more acute because both were able to earn their law degrees from top-ranked US law schools.

Together, these varied experiences suggest the kinds of new trajectories and hybrid tracks to global legal education. They also help reveal that the rise of international JDs has not been the product of a single kind of mobility process. For many international students, there were choices to be made about where they would pursue their law degree (e.g., in the United States or in their home country), what kind of credential made sense for their own personal and professional aspirations (e.g., JD vs. LLM vs. SJD), and the eventual cost-benefit analysis of opportunities these respective paths might offer. Even for those who *did* choose to pursue a JD, the paths varied: some transferred to a JD from an LLM at the same school; for others, the LLM led to a JD at another, more prestigious law school. And among those who started directly in the JD program, not all JDs were equal, and a JD in one school could serve as a steppingstone for a transfer to a JD program in a school with a more internationally recognized reputation. In all, the path to the JD for many of these students was hardly straightforward, and the circuitous routes pursued by them offer new ways of thinking about both the journey and its embedded expectations.

To make sense of these various trajectories, this chapter employs the imagery developed in our earlier work of four pathways to illuminate certain broad categories within which they fall (Silver and Ballakrishnen 2020). The *first* of these pathway categories employs what mobility scholars have referred to as the "sticky floor." The sticky floor effect is traditionally employed to characterize a declining wage gap across a given distribution, that is, larger wage gaps at lower quintiles of distribution and lower wage gaps at the top of a distribution. Theoretically, it suggests that those who are most disadvantaged at the individual level (i.e., at the lower quintiles of distribution) also are further disadvantaged by the structures within which they are embedded (i.e., larger wage gaps) (Chi and Li 2008; Deshpande and Sharma 2016; Jain and Mukherji 2010: 23; Tesch et al. 1995).[48] In our employment of the metaphor, the stickiness further stifles students who already are at a disadvantage, and "the floor" prevents students from getting off the ground despite their desire to move to the next step, whether that involves enrolling in an LLM or JD degree program, transferring to a more prestigious school, or pursuing a specific kind of job opportunity. Although selection considerations curtail our data from theorizing about these categories fully, we can imagine that this stickiness might involve a range of factors including language, financial resources, seniority in their home country, and personal considerations and responsibilities. They are not in the "path to JD" diagram (Figure 15.4), but they remain an important data point for consideration, signaling an "in-waiting" cohort of international students that might be the next group to saturate the LLM market, especially as those positioned just above them move their aspirations from an LLM to a JD track. An example of a student on the sticky floors pathway, who recently got "un-stuck," is a Chinese lawyer (C70-17) who had wanted to pursue a US LLM in the early 2000s but remained in China for more than ten years, working in several corporate counsel positions. Upon finally gaining admission to an LLM program at an elite US law school, he reported that he had decided against the JD for now, at least, because "time is against" him.

The *second* kind of pathway offers a sort of springboard for students. Unlike sticky floors, springboards are poised to afford mobility. Springboards can lead to many different opportunities and positions (e.g., other kinds of advanced graduate degrees or policy jobs that are advantaged by, *but do not require*, a law degree[49]), but the common theme in our conceptualization of this metaphor is that they serve as a platform for movement to *pivot* or change direction at the individual level. This characterization rests on the degree not being an end in itself; neither is our focus here on its utility for substantive reasons. Instead, for those for whom global legal education acts

---

[48] Labor economists usually use this metaphor for explaining gender and other kinds of wage gaps across contexts.

[49] Recent research shows that there is some anxiety around this idea of being employed in law-adjacent or "JD advantaged" jobs. Although this important implication might have extensions for international students, the data itself does not include an analysis on their behalf. See Carle 2020.

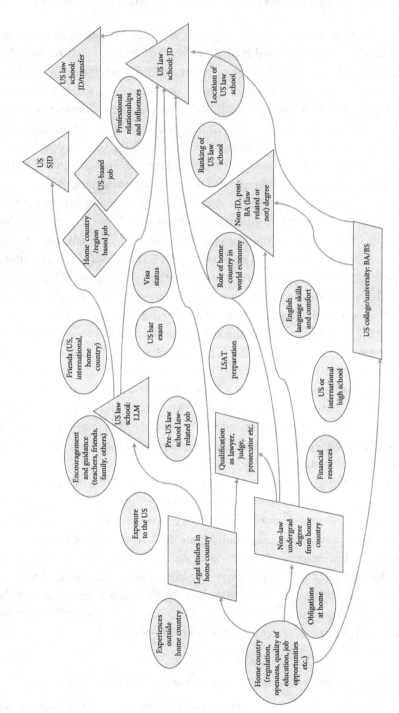

Figure 15.4. Pathways of International Students

as a springboard, the motivation to pursue the credential might be personal, a function of factors beyond the credential itself, or a "halo" advantage that allows them access to paths beyond the springboard. Springboard-ers are not likely to jump to the JD, but not because they fail to see the value in it per se. Rather, the JD has no value for *them* (and, as we discuss in the following two strategies of *stairway* and *slow escalators*, that would require more intention) (Garth and Sterling 2018: 123).[50] For example, LLM graduates described the LLM as enabling them to realize that they did not want to be a lawyer after all, and chose instead to pursue an entirely different career (e.g., S120, a film producer), or, rather than preparing them for work in a particular jurisdiction—whether the United States, their home country, or a third country—it positioned them for a career with an international tribunal (S233). Global legal education for them might be a sufficient signal to help them catapult to where they want to go, and the limitations of the LLM are not problematic for them (Garth and Sterling 2018: 123). Further, springboard-ers may not have resources to invest in legal education beyond the opportunity that the springboard offers them, making this, therefore, their one shot at their personal (and/or professional) pivot.

A *third* kind of pathway category that we identify is the stairway—a more direct mobility pathway from one kind of program to another, or one kind of school to another. The structure itself offers a chance for students to access and move from their own individual starting point (perhaps a nonlaw degree in the United States or an LLM, for example) to a definite goal— be it, for example, a mainstream US law degree, a law degree from a certain kind of school, or a specific kind of career upon graduation. For each such student, their individual path might vary and different individual levels of agility and energy (metaphorically) may result in differing starting points, directions, speeds, and, overall, different experiences and trajectories. Movement on this pathway—from an LLM to a JD, from one school to another with a wider reputation, or into a JD from another field, for example—might reflect previous international experiences, exposure, and socialization specifically to the United States, and experience on the stairway itself,[51] among other factors. But importantly, in this imagery, the individual agency and ambition to traverse this pathway is key. Students have a clear

---

[50] See Garth and Sterling (2018: 123), characterizing legal career paths as on- and off-Broadway.
[51] For another use of the stairway metaphor in the context of students' gains in higher education, see Paige et al. (2017).

intention to be on a given path, whether it be to stay in the United States, to go back to their home country, or to open up even more geographical positions for play in their future career trajectory.[52] And the stairway is seen as the mechanism from which they can get from their current position to their imagined future position.

Yet, at the same time, no pathway is just about the institutional blueprint it offers. Within the same "stair," international students may take seemingly identical steps with very different consequences; even for those from the same home country who enroll in the same US law school, differences in skills, advantages, and responsibilities may mediate the paths very differently. It is to explain this variation despite being in what professes to be a linear path to one's goals and its actual outcome, that we offer a *fourth* pathway: the *slow, crowded escalator*. We use this fourth metaphor to highlight the importance of the path itself over individual goals, ambitions, and determination. Much like the stairway, escalators offer an institutional metaphor, but unlike the stairway where individual characteristics are key (i.e., in the internal logic of the metaphor, speed, agility, energy), the escalator is more about the pace and structure of the *path itself*. The metaphor offers special nuance for the understanding of this kind of mobility: escalators take people in a uniform direction, from a common starting point. They might seem perfectly functional, advantageous even for someone who is not able to (or even just not inclined to) take the stairs. And they may seem somewhat egalitarian— in that everyone is going at the same set speed. However, this set pace is mired with its own limitations. For one, a set pace might be —and, especially from the perspective of someone who might have high individual ability and agility—a relatively slow pace. Second, the path might not be what it first offered to be. For example, there might be people in front of you who do not know the rules—they might stand on a walking side of the escalator and block your path, so what you thought was a faster path could be experienced as frustratingly slower. Further, at first glance, it may seem easier than what is involved in navigating a stairway, for example,

---

[52] For example, it was common for interviewees, especially students from Asia, to describe engaging in a continuous assessment of how their JD degree, their law school and even their coursework would be perceived at home because of the possibility that they will want to move home in the future. A Korean student explained, "eventually [we] want to go back Korea, the school name matters a lot and that's why we transferred to [name of law school]." C19-15. Another Korean student commented on the importance of being a transaction lawyer based on the JD because he could not be licensed in Korea: "And when you go back to Korea, you can only do transactional, obviously. . . . So I think that influences a lot of people." C18-15.

reflecting advantages of class, home country, and similar factors that may lead to entry to the escalator. But even here, the path may be frustrating as well as slow: students may have trouble fitting in, or finding friends and communities that make their journey sustainable. Finally, to extend the metaphor even further, students on this pathway may also experience regular maintenance issues—from routine administrative burdens[53] to the emotional pressure of the law school and job market experiences that present real difficulties for many international students, despite their having taken the escalator (Ballakrishnen and Silver 2019). Together, we use these extensions to the metaphor here to flesh out the possible nuances to a relatively simple argument: the path to a JD may initially be visualized as a superior path, one that will make students achieve their imagined goals much faster than if they had taken the stairs. The logic of the escalator depends on a trust that the transportation system itself functions as a teleporter of mobility. But students might be disappointed with how much they can do while on the escalator, and how much more the pathway can do for them overall.

III. Glocal Trends: Local Contexts, Global Repercussions

This discussion of transportation systems is aimed at highlighting the hurdles and constraints that are part of the experiences and paths of international students. The pathways and mechanisms are not mutually exclusive, and a student's journey may reflect all four over the course of their education and career. And despite the challenges, students generally perceive the value in their choices, which is evidenced by the rise in international enrollment. But while no path is doomed, none is smooth sailing, either. Although there has been an increase in international student enrollment in US law schools, without the institutions to supportively house international students both during their degree and after, their rise still is riddled with obstacles.

Further still, the rise in enrollment is not a static individual-dependent trend alone: country-level variation in professional regulation and, in turn, valuation of the US degree, has been central for dictating these patterns. In other work, we have shown how specific local contexts long have been

---

[53] See Ballakrishnen and Silver (2019), describing administrative burdens of being an international student.

important in predicting and preparing students for international careers, offering important insights into student motivations for pursuing degrees as well as the postgraduate valorization and transferability of these degrees. For some students, the decision to earn an LLM, for example, was a way to help themselves stand out in their home country (Bhandari 2015; Silver and Ballakrishnen 2020; Silver 2007: 74).[54] A graduate from Mexico from the early 2000s, now with a private law firm that serves local, foreign, and international clients, explained that having the LLM was useful for—and increasingly, demanded by—the industry clientele because it signaled a certain kind of exposure to American culture.[55]

But the valuing of global credentials within local contexts was hardly universal, much less uniform. Other work has highlighted the contextual and interactional nature of cultural capital associated with international credentials. In his study of academic and corporate careers that drew upon a graduate degree in the United States, Jongyoung Kim explains that "the same cultural capital plays out very differently depending on national contexts. In Korea, the U.S. professional degree functions as global cultural capital for the cosmopolitan elite, while in the United States it works as an entrance ticket to corporations and academe" (Kim 2016). Similarly, Bryant Garth's description of the comments of an economics graduate illustrates the point:

A Brazilian student some years ago made a striking comment about this process, referring to an economics student from Brazil at the University of Chicago. When the student is at the airport in São Paulo on the way to Chicago, the economics student noted, he is at the top of the hierarchy in Brazil. As soon as he lands in the United States, he goes right to the bottom of the U.S. hierarchy. If he needs extra money, he or his spouse may only take whatever jobs an undocumented person can take (Garth 2015: 74–75).

Ballakrishnen, in their study of Indian LLM graduate returnees, finds that "the value of the [LLM] credential fluctuates depending on the receiver of the

---

[54] A German LLM graduate, for example, commented: "[T]here are lots of lawyers in Germany . . . and so it's quite important to have something where you can distinguish yourself from at least a lot of the other lawyers, so I thought I actually need something more than just the [German] university degree to tell prospective employers." I39-08.

[55] "Clients love it if you have the LLM, and they love it even more if you pass the bar in the U.S. The Industry—law—is starting to require the LLM . . . I think they [clients] feel more comfortable when speaking to a guy who's been exposed to American culture. Your laws are more rigid, so they think you understand what's at stake when you're doing a deal. They feel more comfortable that you know what the consequences are." I71-03.

information" (Ballakrishnen 2012: 2471). This can involve interpretation by other lawyers, for example, who may or may not have studied in the United States, or by a client with little insight into the subtleties of professional credentials. The theoretical suggestion this offers is that, across contexts, there are macro and micro level forces at play in determining the value of US legal education as a "marker of professional hierarchy" (Ballakrishnen 2012: 2457).

For those who wish to gain access to the US legal services market (an option that was not always open to earlier LLM cohorts and is challenging today, as well), getting an LLM is a passport of sorts.[56] But with the globalized demands of legal services markets, the advantage of the LLM is not limited to those who practice law in the United States.[57] Returning LLMs gain advantages in their home countries both because of the practical advantages the LLM offers (training in relevant and governing law, including national and international, exposure to new networks, etc.), as well as its signaling "halo" advantages, which come from being associated with an international law school from a high status country.[58] In addition to these core functional factors that affect their outcomes in the workplace, returnees can attain numerous other parallel advantages that are "functional" at the personal level, such as using the LLM to create contacts and networks with a global legal community and even locally,[59] and drawing language and cultural capital from this association.

Even so, the nature and interaction of these rewards to credential varies. Past research has shown that different factors at the individual[60] and institutional

---

[56] For a broad review of the expectations and potential payoffs students have from this program, see Silver, reviewing why international students come to the United States for an LLM (2006: 147).

[57] Silver's early research shows that the LLM is commonly a condition for partnership or for access to certain jobs and firms outside of the United States, typically relevant to LLMs who return, at some point, to their home countries (2006: 147). This is particularly important in the case of certain countries, including certain jurisdictions in Latin America where the LLM is particularly valorized (Silver, Internationalizing 2006: 156).

[58] This signaling is not always one that has similar access for all LLM candidates who stay. And many international law graduates return to their home countries and gain advantages with their employers and existing networks as a direct result of their LLM (Silver 2001; Silver 2012: 2383–2384; Ballakrishnen 2012: 2445).

[59] An example of the creation of local contacts was described by a Chinese student, initially an LLM but now returning to the United States for a JD, who reported that he obtained a job in China with a top internationally focused Chinese law firm (for the period between the LLM and JD) through a contact he made in his LLM program with a lawyer who had been counsel in the Chinese firm. C02-17.

[60] For a review of how students with different credentials fare (in this case, students with LLMs versus JDs in the US law firm market), see Silver (2005: 907–914).

levels[61] alter the kind of advantages that the LLM offers. Further, a key part of this analysis is recognizing the environment in which this credential is being used as capital.[62] The most common example is the distinction between a US LLM and a JD credential within the organizational context. While the LLM can indeed be a powerful degree in certain circumstances, we know that both students and recruiters treat it differently than a US JD degree.[63]

Similarly, research reveals other ways in which the context of the LLM's use affects its value, including Silver's research illustrating the difference US-LLM-educated graduates have in the appraisal of their credential depending on the home country to which they return.[64] Still, most practical extensions are limited in that they only consider the rewards for graduates returning to countries with some sort of a strong global presence affecting the legal profession.

IV. Discussion

Contrary to accounts from even a decade ago, the globalization of law and legal institutions is no longer a neglected field of study (Halliday and Carruthers 2007: 1135).[65] Still, following from its definition, much of the theory of transnational legal ordering has been restricted mainly to testing legal "orders."[66] Global legal education does not fit within the strict definition of a transnational legal order since it is not routinely expressed in recognizable *legal* form; nor does it obviously derive its institutionalization from concurrent norm-making and -shaping across three (transnational, national, local) levels (Halliday and Shaffer 2015: 3). However, legal education can

---

[61] One example of this institutional level advantage has been the valorization of the LLM credential differently in different organizations within the same country (Silver, *Internationalizing* 2006; Silver 2001).

[62] This conception of the LLM as "capital" that can be valorized in specific environments is borrowed, broadly, from the work of Dezalay and Garth (1997: 109), which frames law and lawyers in terms of social capital. We thank them for useful comments on earlier work that helped conceptualize this extension to the original argument.

[63] In concurrent work we are analyzing data on international JD students in American law schools—data that can speak to this separation of the two degrees as considered from the perspective of the students (Ballakrishnen and Silver 2019: 647–678; Ballakrishnen and Silver 2018; Silver 2001).

[64] See Silver (2001: 21–54), explaining how the value of this education is variable depending on the host country context (in this case, China and Germany).

[65] See, e.g., Rajah (2015), Wilkins, Khanna, and Trubek (2017), and Dezalay and Garth (2011).

[66] For evidence of what a transnational legal order could look like, see Dezalay and Garth (1997: 109). For further theorizing, including ways in which transnational legal ordering can be extended, see Halliday and Shaffer (2015).

socialize students to think as lawyers in particular ways and can indirectly affect their practice subsequently, especially if they perform the function of brokers by practicing law domestically and transnationally.[67] They can, through practice, become conduits for the flow of transnational legal norms and legal practices, such as drafting particular kinds of documents. Naturally, as we noted previously, this impact will be a function of the context of the country to which they return—or turn. But we find the spirit of the transnational legal ordering framework useful as we think through the implications of the mapped paths and trends for students and the important window it offers to reveal the ways in which local and global actors emerge and interact. We especially appreciate the synergies of this against the wealth of transnational recursivity theory, which demonstrates the interrelated nature of understanding global legal orders as a function of interactions—with and without alignment or fit—between local and global norms.[68] Transnational legal ordering theory, for example, offers that "national and local resistance can be a catalyst that compels recursive global and transnational law making because it increases the likelihood that powerful actors will be compelled, in their own self-interest in order to ensure greater effectiveness, to negotiate rather than impose norms" (Halliday and Carruthers 2007: 1135). The credential of an American legal education was variable and negotiable following exactly these interactive dynamics of the local and the global. Local variations remained important for headlining global trends and the difference in different kinds of valorization shaped the import of the credential itself.[69]

To extend this theory of contextual referencing to the previous social capital argument, it is necessary to push the "context" of the host country further. Thus, in contrast to the literature on how LLM advantages transfer to countries where there are deep-rooted functional advantages to having a US law degree (either as a requirement for practice or as a key distinctive credential in influencing labor market outcomes), for instance, Ballakrishnen's previous work has examined how having an LLM plays out in host nations like India

---

[67] There are several examples of transnational practice that these students may engage in and the hybrid implications this may have in changing the legal fields—and orders—locally and globally. For example, see Merry (2006: 38–51). Similarly, Halliday and Carruthers (2007) discuss the importance of brokers more generally as conduits for the flow of transnational legal norms in local jurisdictions.

[68] See Halliday and Carruthers (2007), setting up the main frameworks for understanding recursivity of law in transnational contexts.

[69] See discussion in *supra* note 14, regarding variation in the strength of professional capital represented by an LLM, between different countries.

that have a "closed"[70] market for international legal services (Ballakrishnen 2012: 2441). India's case is unique in terms of the legal profession, in that it is a quasi-protectionist host country that has been more restrictive with opening its legal market than its Asian counterparts.[71] The formal regulatory resistance[72] to opening the legal market, along with the broadening stratification of the domestic Indian profession, has created institutional and organizational[73] cultures in which American legal credentialing is not afforded a particularly uniform favor. Ballakrishnen's research suggests that while some graduates find resonance and validation in certain interactions, for the most part the degree is more of a chance to have a "break year" where they can be intellectually engaged further before returning to their "real" careers. Students do not expect the LLM or these experiences to have much—if any—direct impact on their career prospects when they return. And when it does impact their life, it usually is primed in unpredictable ways (for example, a partner might mention a "Harvard educated" junior to clients in passing to

[70] We refer to the Indian market as "closed" here (and going forward) because while technically restrictive of foreign legal practitioners and organizations, the regulatory mechanisms that control this osmosis have been manipulated in different ways to informally allow for diffusion of international legal practice within the Indian legal market (Ballakrishnen 2020).

[71] The Indian economy, like other similarly developing economies, traditionally has been closed. In 1991, the liberalization reforms opened some sectors for global commerce, which directly impacted the nature and scope of international transactional work that came into the country. The legal profession, however, stays securely closed. The statutory restriction against the practice of law by non-Indian lawyers is a fairly blanket restriction, and there has been some debate as to what this means (*Lawyers Collective v. Bar Council of India* (2009)). Ballakrishnen (2009) has argued elsewhere that this lack of clear explanation for what the phrase "practice of law" means—e.g., the practice of "any" law, the practice of "any law in India," and/or the "practice of law in India"—is what enables India to be selectively liberal.

[72] Not only is the Indian legal market currently closed to the entry of foreign players, there is no reason to believe it will open anytime soon (Ganz 2010). However, there has recently been some movement on the possibility of UK-based law firms entering the Indian legal market (Baxter 2011). Still the pressures against such entry, given the Indian regulatory temperament, make the possibility of opening the Indian legal market doubtful. For a recent interview with the president of the Society of Indian Law Firms, in which he reiterates this stand about being "happy with the existing arrangements" of not having foreign lawyers, see Bar and Bench (2011). See Saluja (2017), reporting that the Law Minister has requested a proposal on entrance of foreign law firms. In March 2018, however, the Indian Supreme Court ruled that while foreign law firms cannot be allowed entry into the country without an amendment to the Advocates Act of 1962, foreign lawyers *can* visit India on a "casual" "fly in fly out" basis and advise on foreign laws and international commercial arbitration, the later, subject to rules by the Bar Council of India (*Bar Council of India v. A.K. Balaji and Others* (2015)).

[73] Ballakrishnen's research on Indian LLMs draws from two main qualitative samples: a 2007–2008 study on students and recent alumni at Harvard Law School (n = 14), and a 2011 study on LLM students (n = 9) and LLM returnees (n = 19) from a range of other US law schools (2012, 2441). These data revealed that most workplaces did not give credit for an LLM year and fewer offer advantages as a reward to the credential. While there are a few firms that offer financial assistance (in the form of loans) to employees who want to pursue a graduate degree in law overseas, the year is still "written off" when the student returns to the firm.

help create rapport, but it will not be the basis of promotion or increasing the lawyer's salary) (Ballakrishnen 2012: 2441). It is this indirect halo advantage that many Indian students who continue to explore US LLM options have, that stands in contrast to returnees to countries where a US LLM (or a foreign degree generally) is set up to have traditional functional credentialing benefits for its returnees.[74]

Our use of the Indian case is only illustrative, and examples from other countries may show a more direct advantage, such as in Korea, where even before liberalization of the legal market, outward-facing global law firms had been developed by Korean lawyers and utilized LLM graduates as their "global" representatives (Silver, Lee, and Park 2015: 1–3). Differences in the rewards upon return remain important as we consider the reasons why students might be making choices to pursue other international law degree options. Indeed, these differences may also relate to an association with a particular law school over and above the more general appeal of the United States as being the source of the degree. Essentially, if host country organizational and institutional factors are crucial to determining how the LLM is mined as a credential, what happens to this American legal degree in countries where the United States does not have a structured legal presence?[75] The extensions of this research question remain relevant in the case of all international higher education markets where students' returnee prospects are crucial to their decision-making processes.

Tracing the paths of international law students reveals as much about what is on the pathways map (Figure 15.4) as what is not depicted there. The map highlights the various choices made deliberately by students in pursuing global legal education in the United States and ultimately in their post-graduation jobs, as well as factors shaping their opportunities. Each of the turning points or connectors, depicted by arrows, is malleable, responding to the various forces (some of which are described in the oval shapes on the

[74] The term "functional benefits" is used here (and hereinafter) to refer to both the broader functional gains attached to international education like prestige, immigration prospects, and better returns in the labor market (e.g., promotions, raise in pay, etc.), as well as LLM-specific functional gains like language training and LLM-specific rewards that are typically available upon return to other home countries. These "specific rewards" could be, as in the case of China, a requirement to enter the domestic branch of an international law firm, or, as in the case of Germany, direct signaling of distinctive benefits. See Silver (2002: 1039–1043; *Internationalizing*, 2006), offering a review of LLM advantages more generally. See also Robel (2006: 797–799), providing a more detailed explanation of the China/Germany comparison.

[75] The current formal regulation in India that governs lawyers (The Advocates Act) does not allow the practice of law by non-Indian lawyers. Even if there is a decoupling of this in practice, the regulation is suggestive of the formal resistance to the Americanization of these markets. For institutional decoupling more generally, see Meyer and Rowan (1977: 340).

map) supporting, motivating, challenging, and/or barricading pursuit of a next step. These next steps may appear rather obvious in hierarchy, but the hierarchy itself is neither fixed nor static, and it depends on a range of diverse resources available for it from the environments it is embedded within. Instead, in the context of global legal education, interpretation of that hierarchy requires a consideration of several factors, including home country and context, the relative position of the United States and any relevant third countries, and a comprehensive understanding of the various actors and institutions that shape what is construed as most valuable and attractive. The choice of whether and how to pursue US legal education occurs in the midst of a contest of sorts, for recognition and preference. It is a moving target, where one can imagine the four path mechanisms interacting in complex, confusing, and perhaps even dangerous ways.

To understand the variations in global recursive scripts, transportation imagery offers a good metaphor: where people go depends on where they start, what connections they make during their journeys, and what choices they make at different points in the process. But at the same time, this is not simply about choice at the individual level. It also matters who else is traveling with you, who is ahead of you and giving you way to move forward, and who is pressuring you to get off and walk a different path. And further still, the path may become meaningless over time. Temporality—that is, when students graduated from their programs, the state of the market the year they graduated, the kinds of opportunity structures that are available to them at graduation, five years after, ten years after, and so forth—all these could offer variations to life and career trajectories of these students. And they are important to consider especially because they are factors that students and graduates have no control over. And these factors remain even more relevant in the case of the three-year JD program (often longer still when students transferred from other kinds of programs), where the variable viability of the market that would absorb them when they graduated remains even more unpredictable.

From the students' perspective—which is the mainstay of this chapter—there are distinct changes about these preferences from even a decade ago. We show in other work the ways in which this rise in the international student population within law schools, while important, does not involve a single seamless monochromatic category (Ballakrishnen and Silver 2019). Instead of this meta category of "international student," what was more important was micro differences that shaped the ways in which students navigated these spaces.

From a demand perspective, the entry of international students is subject to a range of push and pull factors. Law schools court international students through various mechanisms, and these students comprise an increasingly important population because of the decline of domestic applicants to law school. Moreover, related resource constraints strain law schools' efforts to meet, much less exceed, the competition for students, student opportunities during and after law school, support for students during law school and a school's reputation in the larger community that may demand more and varied activities and outreach. It is clear that international students have become an important population for many, if not most, US law schools based on the rise in the number of schools with at least one dedicated LLM program (to nearly 80 percent in 2016) and the related enrollment growth during this period when the size (i.e., headcount) of post-JD programs more than doubled. While law schools do not report the proportion of post-JD students who are international, we estimate this figure well above the halfway mark, and the visa data set generally is consistent with such an estimate. Moreover, as JD programs have shrunk, this emphasis on post- and non-JD enrollment, with its heavily international population, puts pressure on law schools to adjust their conception of the typical law student, with repercussions for faculty and the allocation of resources, at a minimum (Silver 2013: 533–560; Silver, *Internationalizing* 2006: 227). In 2016, for example, close to half of all graduating students (all degree programs, combined) at Washington University in St. Louis School of Law were international.[76]

Relatedly, while international students contribute substantially financially[77] and otherwise to law schools and to higher education generally,

---

[76] For example, Washington University School of Law conferred degrees in May 2016 on "228 JDs, 173 LLMs, 2 JSDs, and 11 MLS degrees." *WashU Law Celebrates Commencement 2016*, WASH. UNIV. SCH. OF LAW, http://law.wustl.edu/news/pages.aspx?id=10736 (last visited August 16, 2017). According to the Law School's Standard 509 Report, twenty-three JD degrees were awarded to nonresident aliens. *See Washington University 2016 Standard 509 Information Report*, WASH. UNIV. SCH. OF LAW, 2016, https://www.abarequireddisclosures.org/Disclosure509.aspx (select "2016" and "Washington University"). Assuming for the sake of discussion only that all of the LLMs and SJDs were international students and that none of the other JDs or MSLs were international (all in all, relatively conservative assumptions), approximately 48 percent of all degrees awarded in 2016 were awarded to international students.

[77] International students' (in all fields and not limited to law) spending in all fifty states contributed more than US$30 billion to the US economy in 2014, according to the US Department of Commerce. Additional breakdowns of the economic impact of international students by host state are available from NAFSA, which conducts a detailed regional, state, and congressional district analysis on the economic benefits of spending by international students and their dependents to the US economy, using Open Doors data combined with calculations of the local tuition and cost of living rates (NAFSA, n.d.).

competition for them is intense. Given the heightened stake of Asia and Asian students in international higher education, the United States cannot afford to equivocate. As of 2014, China and India remained the largest sending nations to the three countries[78] that are most competitive to the United States for international higher education students: the United Kingdom,[79] Canada,[80] and Australia.[81] India, in particular, holds the demographic advantage of being the world's youngest population—making it an important site for education policymakers.[82]

At the same time, these ramifications are hardly one-sided. The influx of international students into these new spaces is moderated by institutional factors, but they also are responsible for the co-creation of others that affect the institution. For example, from the law schools' perspective, the impulses and aesthetics that shape the curation of a law school cohort depend on many factors, including the differences that characterize international students who participate in an LLM or JD program, and what it means to have diversity (of home country; gender, race, and ethnicity; background experience and global exposure; among other factors) within the international student community. Yet, significantly, at the same time, with this influx, what it

---

[78] For a list of countries with significant investment in international higher education, see *The Guardian* (2015).

[79] Approximately 18 percent of all students in UK higher education came from other countries in 2012–2013, according to the Higher Education Statistics Agency (HESA). OECD (2013) statistics show that the United Kingdom attracts a large proportion of international students globally, with a market share of around 13 percent in 2011, second only to the United States, with 16.5 percent (HESA 2014). Chinese students were the largest group of international students studying in the United Kingdom from 2012 to 2013, making up almost a fifth of the total, according to data released by HESA this year. Indian students were the second largest group, comprising 5.3 percent of international students, despite their number declining by around 25 percent since 2011–2012, according to the Higher Education Funding Council for England, coinciding with visa changes (HESA 2014; OECD 2013; Sinhal 2014). For more data on the higher education numbers in the United Kingdom, see *International Student Statistics: UK Higher Education*, UKCISA, Nov. 29, 2015.

[80] Just between 2012 and 2013, international student enrollment in Canada rose by 84 percent. Even so, Canada's student enrollment is less than half of the United Kingdom's, at about 8 percent of all postsecondary enrollment. Of these, almost half of all students are from India, China, and South Korea (32.42 percent of all international students are from China, 10.79 percent are from India, and 6.23 percent from South Korea). For more details, see Canada Bureau for International Education (2015).

[81] Australia attracts even more international students from Asia—for obvious proximity reasons—than the United States, the United Kingdom, and Canada; the top ten sending countries to Australia all are from Asia. However, India and China again remain the two most prominent sending countries overall across general sectors (university, vocational, etc.). For monthly detailed reports with breakdowns by sector for 2014, see Australian Government Department of Education and Training (2014).

[82] "India, Asia's third largest economy, is projected to add 300 million people to its workforce over the next 2 decades—the equivalent of the entire United States (U.S.) population. And all this growth will be among the youth, India's huge 'demographic dividend' that will need to be educated" (Bhandari 2015; Goodman 2015).

means to be diverse has changed, as has what a global legal education means to an international student, and neither is understood as a universal or static idea. For instance, as law schools increasingly diversify their degree program offerings (including new master's programs for nonlaw graduates, substantively and experientially focused curricula, distance learning, and executive education, for example), the variety of ways in which being successful in recruiting international students matters also has proliferated. This is complicated by the challenge of understanding motivations for enrollment that reflect only home country and legal market considerations, and the nuance involved in gauging how an expanding set of programs can reach new student pools, in diverse professions and job markets, stages of career, and with varying resources. At the same time, law schools grapple with the tension of various conceptions and presentations of diversity, including how to make diversity look good for different audiences. *U.S. News'* consideration of diversity, for example, does not recognize international students in its analysis; this, along with the exclusive focus on the JD program, has enabled the LLM to function as an international enclave. But as international students increasingly shift toward the JD, these once-clear lines and depictions of diversity may blur.

From the perspective of sending countries, the enthusiasm for global legal education may reflect a fluidity regarding the characteristics, experiences, and skills associated with power, status, and access. In earlier research, Silver showed that while the more globally mobile German legal market viewed the LLM as an additional currency, it was never seen as the only legitimizing factor for a local lawyer. On the other hand, the more nascent Chinese legal services market looked to US-oriented signals more strictly and in turn, the value of the LLM in the Chinese context gained sanctity. She argued that in Germany, because of the relatively long tradition of working at an international level, language and US connections are not novel (Silver 2001: 54–55). Similarly, Ballakrishnen's early research referenced a range of different halo and functional reasons a US legal education was useful to returnees. In contrast to Indian students who were unlikely to reap functional benefits from a US LLM, for an LLM student returning to China to work for a domestic firm, "trying out the Bar" was useful (because it would give her "extra points— but no penalty" to clear it), and it was an "unwritten rule" that individuals with LLMs, especially those from a "top school," were more likely to have stronger promotion prospects on return, even though the US degree was not substantially useful in navigating their domestic legal system (Ballakrishnen 2012: 2445).

At the same time, beyond these inter-country differences in valorization, there are variations between countries across time. Societies are not static in this regard, as evidenced in the shifting landscape of home countries of international students enrolling in higher education in the United States over the last twenty to twenty-five years. During this period, the number of students from Europe has remained relatively constant,[83] but their proportion in the group of all international students in the United States has dropped by half, from a high of 20 percent to their current standing at just under 10 percent. This is due in large part to the rise of Asian and, to a lesser extent and recently, of Middle Eastern students (O'Malley 2014). But equally important is that the way students from Asia are participating has shifted, at least in law, from a marginal role institutionally to one that may more deeply puncture existing hierarchies. This shift is made possible by larger trends that position families to provide financial support, among other things. Rajika Bhandari (2015) explained these forces in the context of higher education generally:

> Unprecedented economic growth has driven major social and demographic change and institutional reform and, in most countries, has brought about greater stability. The advent of a large middle class, coupled with openness and market reforms driven by economic imperatives, has contributed to greater interconnectedness among Asian states and between them and the rest of the world. . . . These dynamics are also reflected in the landscape of higher education, especially at a time when economic growth in many rapidly developing Asian economies is linked to knowledge production, advanced skills, and the rising demand for higher education.

Even postgraduation, expanded opportunities to work in the United States—if they materialize—may reverberate against legal practice at home, since the option of returning is attractive as long as it offers comparable responsibility and opportunity to graduates' US-based career options. Generally, the draw to return home serves as an important factor, too, stemming from family considerations to increasingly exciting professional opportunities.[84] Moreover, at the same time, the presence of more international

---

[83] European students went from 73,489 in 1994–1995 to a high of 91,915 in 2015–2016 (IIE, *All Places of Origin*, 1949/50–1999/00; IIE, *Leading Places of Origin*, 2014/15– 2015/16).

[84] "U.S.-trained Chinese-born talent is becoming a key force in driving Chinese companies' global expansion and the country's efforts to dominate next-generation technologies like artificial intelligence and machine learning. Where college graduates once coveted a prestigious overseas job and foreign citizenship, many today gravitate toward career opportunities at home, where venture

JDs likely will challenge the already flagging efforts of US law firms to address diversity by pressing for recognition; this comes at a time when there is growing awareness of the failure of these firms to embrace Asian American lawyers, much less lawyers whose home countries are part of the Asia-Pacific region (Chung et al. 2017).[85]

Even as they are predicated on receiving country logics, home country dynamics also change the ways in which countries send or plan to send candidates abroad. For instance, at the same time that China has been sending students to the United States for the LLM and JD, it also has been internationalizing its own faculties (Gooch 2012).[86] One way in which this has occurred is by hiring American law graduates to teach in China (along with law graduates from other jurisdictions outside of China).[87] These faculty members contribute to the preparation of students in formal and informal ways, including by their analysis of the culture and hierarchy of US legal education and the legal profession. While initially constrained in adjunct or visiting statuses, they now are being integrated into mainstream roles at certain law faculties.[88] The addition of Americans, among other international faculty, to law faculties outside of the United States, is both a reflection and response to global legal education and globalization of the market for legal services (see Roberts, Chapter 14, this volume) marking a step in the iterative process of interpreting the hierarchies framing what it means to be local and global.

V. Conclusion

For students from other countries US legal education has, until recently, meant the LLM. The addition of the JD as an alternative path reflects several changes, including the inflation of the credential (the LLM is simply "not enough"); how it is valued is a flexible, mutable process that varies across specific inter- and intra-country contexts (Silver 2001; Ballakrishnen

capital is now plentiful and the government dangles financial incentives for cutting-edge research" (Bloomberg News 2018).

[85] "Asian Americans have the highest ratio of associates to partners of any racial or ethnic group, and this has been true for more than a decade" (Chung et al. 2017).

[86] See Gooch (2012), describing a general trend of hiring foreigners among Chinese universities.

[87] The Peking University School of Transnational Law faculty consistently has included American legal academics, see, e.g., Peking University, *Visiting Faculty* (n.d.).

[88] See, e.g., Peking University Law School, *Joseph L. Pratt* (n.d.).

2012: 2441). The variations in sending countries sketched previously in the description of the data set on visa approvals illustrate an increasing awareness by students from China and South Korea, at least, that the opportunities offered after a JD differ from those attached to the LLM. Of course, it remains to be seen if all of these patterns of mobility might have been fundamentally changed by the disruption of the global pandemic and its resultant market and movement dynamics, especially within these two countries and the United States. Still to the extent the future is predicated in some ways by the period that preceded it, we expect that the variations in law schools will continue to provide important differences to international students. Factors like the *U.S. News* ranking as well as location (e.g., whether the school is proximate to a major legal market or not) and predictability of job prospects will remain attractive features to international cohorts.[89] At the same time, we expect that malleability of credential, the assumption of risk, and the possibility of making imagined communities with their peers will matter. Moreover, students also will face choices of investing in educational trajectories that might look different—following the range of virtual/hybrid options that different schools have adopted over the last few years. To the extent that students are choosing to move into (and from) these globally interdependent and fragile markets, we expect their decisions will continue to be influenced by the diversity of students and others in the law school, university, networks,[90] and larger community—in which significant populations from the same home country may be perceived as either supportive or constraining, or both. These variations in support environments and the resources that they can extend to different cohorts of individuals embedded within them are important to consider. Still, these data offer only an initial exploration of their possible future permutations. While we can suggest nuance to the range of student experiences, without long-term data on their career paths and alumni decisions, we cannot offer details about the extent of its impact. It is our hope that future research will consider the importance of this cohort as a significant data point to unpack the wealth of its surrounding contextual variations.

---

[89] For example, the proportion of students who take first postgraduation jobs in firms in the Big Law category is one factor cited by certain international students as an important attribute in light of the students' desires to shape their careers to preserve and create opportunities to move to their home country/region in the future. C02-17.

[90] In separate research undertaken in collaboration with Anthony Paik and Steven Boutcher, we are exploring the social networks of law school students through a multi-method, longitudinal study of students in both the JD and LLM programs. The study, Diverse Student Experiences in Law School Study, is funded by AccessLex Institute, award number FY1907UG001 (PIs: Paik, Silver, Boutcher, and Ballakrishnen). See Paik, Ballakrishnen, Silver, Boutcher, and Whitworth for a discussion of international law students' social networks.

References

All Places of Origin: 1949/50–1999/00 (n.d.). *Institute of International Education.* https://www.iie.org/Research-and-Insights/Open-Doors/Data/International-Students/Places-of-Origin/All-Places-of-Origin/1950-2000.

Altbach, Philip G. (2004). "Higher Education Crosses Borders," *Change Magazine* 36(2): 18–24.

Altbach, Philip G. (2013). "The Asian Higher Education Century?," *International Higher Education* 59: 143–147. https://doi.org/10.6017/ihe.2010.59.8493.

American Bar Association (2013). 2013 Fall Non-JD Enrollment. https://www.americanbar.org/content/dam/aba/administrative/legal_education_and_admissions_to_the_bar/statistics/2013_fall_jd_nonjd_enrollment.xlsx: https://www.american bar.org/content/dam/aba/administrative/legal_education_and_admissions_to_the_bar/statistics/2013_fall_jd_nonjd_enrollment.xlsx, 2013.

American Bar Association (2016). "2016 JD/Non-JD Enrollment Data," *Statistics Archives.* https://www.americanbar.org/content/dam/aba/administrative/legal_education_and_admissions_to_the_bar/statistics/2016_jd_non_jd_enrollment.xlsx.

American Bar Association (2016). 2016 Fall Non-JD Enrollment. https://www.american bar. org/content/dam/aba/administrative/legal_education_and_admissions_to_the_bar/statistics/2016_jd_non_jd_enrollment.xlsx:, https://www.americanbar. org/content/dam/aba/administrative/legal_education_and_admissions_to_the_bar/statistics/2016_jd_non_jd_enrollment.xlsx.

American Bar Association (n.d.). "J.D. Enrollment and Ethnicity," *Standard 509 Disclosure.* http://www.abarequireddisclosures.org/.

Associate Professor Joseph L. Pratt (n.d.). Peking University Law School. http://en.law.pku.edu.cn/faculty/faculty1/48131.htm.

Ballakrishnen, Swethaa S. (2008). "Hari and Kumar Go to HLS." (unpublished LL.M. thesis, Harvard Law School) (on file with author).

Ballakrishnen, Swethaa S. (2012). "Homeward Bound: What Does a Global Legal Education Offer the Indian Returnees?," *Fordham Law Review* 80(6): 2441–2480.

Ballakrishnen, Swethaa S. (2009). *Lawful Entry: A Preliminary Framework for Understanding the Liberalization Prospects of the Indian Legal Market.* (on file with author).

Ballakrishnen, Swethaa S. (2020). "India: Present and Future: A Revised Sociological Portrait," in Hilary Sommerlad, Richard L. Abel, Ole Hammerslev, and Ulrike Schultz, eds., *Lawyers in the 21st Century.* Pp. 713–33. Hart Publishing.

Ballakrishnen, Swethaa S. and Carole Silver (2019). "A New Minority? International JD Students in US Law Schools," *Law & Social Inquiry* 44(3): 647–678. https://doi.org/10.1017/lsi.2018.12.

Ballakrishnen, Swethaa S. and Carole Silver (2020). "Language, Culture, and the Culture of Language: International JD students in U.S. Law Schools," in Meera Deo, Mindie Lazarus-Black, and Elizabeth Mertz, eds., Power, *Legal Education, and Law School Cultures.* Pp. 191–223. Routledge.

Bar & Bench (2011). "Conversation with Lalit Bhasin Managing Partner Bhasin & Co." November 22. https://www.barandbench.com/interviews/conversation-lalit-bhasin-managing-partner-bhasin-amp-co.

Bar Council of India v. A.K. Balaji and Others (Indian Supreme Court 2015). Civil Appeal Nos. 7875–7879.

Baxter, Brian (2011). "India Leaves Door Ajar for U.K. Firms," *The Am Law Daily*. September 29. http://amlawdaily.typepad.com/amlawdaily/2011/09/india-foreign-firms.html.

Bhandari, Rajika (2015). "Asia's Stake in 21st Century Higher Education," *Institute of International Education (blog)*. August. https://www.iie.org/Learn/Blog/2015/08/2015-August-Asias-Transformation-And-The-Role-Of-International-Higher-Education.

Bhandari, Rajika and Alessia Lefébure (2015). "Asia: The Next Higher Education Superpower?," *IIE and AIFS Foundation* 143.

Bloomberg News (2018). "Chinese Workers Abandon Silicon Valley for Riches Back Home." January 10. https://www.bloomberg.com/news/articles/2018-01.

Carle, Susan D (2020). "The Current Anxiety About JD Advantage Jobs: An Analysis," *San Diego Law Review*. 57: 675.

Carole Silver, Jae-Hyup Lee, and Jeeyoon Park (2015). "What Firms Want: Investigating Globalization's Influence on the Market for Lawyers in Korea," *Columbia Journal of Asian Law* 1(20).

Chi, Wei and Bo Li (2008). "Glass Ceiling or Sticky Floor? Examining the Gender Earnings Differential across the Earnings Distribution in Urban China, 1987–2004," *Journal of Comparative Economics* 36(2): 243–263. https://doi.org/10.1016/j.jce.2007.12.001.

Chung, Eric, Samuel Dong, Xiaonan April Hu, Christine Kwon, and Goodwin Liu (2017). "A Portrait of Asian Americans in the Law," *Yale Law School and National Asian Pacific American Bar Association*. https://static1.squarespace.com/static/59556778e58c62c7db3fbe84/t/596cf0638419c2e5a0dc5766/1500311662008/170716_PortraitProject_SinglePages.pdf.

Degrees (2018). *USC Gould*. Accessed February 28, 2018. http://gould.usc.edu/academics/degrees/.

Deshpande, Ashwini and Smriti Sharma (2016). "Disadvantage and Discrimination in Self-Employment: Caste Gaps in Earnings in Indian Small Businesses," *Small Business Economics* 46(2): 325–346. https://doi.org/10.1007/s11187-015-9687-4.

Dezalay, Yves and Bryant Garth (1997). "Law, Lawyers and Social Capital: 'Rule of Law' versus Relational Capitalism," *Social & Legal Studies* 6(1): 109–141. https://doi.org/10.1177/096466399700600105.

Dezalay, Yves and Bryant Garth, eds. (2011). *Lawyers and the Rule of Law in an Era of Globalization*. Routledge.

Dickerson, Caitlin (2020). "My World Is Shattering: Foreign Students Stranded by the Coronavirus," *New York Times*. April 26.

Education at a Glance 2013: OECD Indicators (2013). *OECD*. http://dx.doi.org/10.1787/eag-2013-en.

Espeland, Wendy Nelson and Michael Sauder (2016). "Rankings at the Top: Inside the Dean's Office" in *Engines of Anxiety: Academic Rankings, Reputation, and Accountability*. Pp. 100-133. Russell Sage Foundation.

Facts & Figures (2015). *Canada Bureau for International Education*. November 29. https://cbie.ca/media/facts-and-figures/.

Fast Facts 2010 (2010). *Institute of International Education*. https://www.iie.org/Research-and-Insights/Open-Doors/Fact-Sheets-and-Infographics/Fast-Facts.

Fast Facts 2017 (2017). *Institute of International Education*. https://www.iie.org/Research-and-Insights/Open-Doors/Fact-Sheets-and-Infographics/Fast-Facts.

Fields of Study 2014–2016 (2018). *Institute of International Education*. Accessed March 31, 2018. https://www.iie.org/research-and-insights/open-doors/data/international-students/fields-of-study.

Findlay, Allan and B. Lindsay Lowell (2001). "Migration of Highly Skilled Persons from Developing Countries: Impact and Policy Responses," *International Migration Papers* 44: 8.

Fischer, Karin (2010). "Foreign-Student Enrollment in U.S. Rise Despite Global Recession," *The Chronicle of Higher Education.* July 8. http://www.chronicle.com/arti cle/Foreign-Student-Enrollments-in/66214/.

Ganz, Kian (2010). "India Legal Market to Stay Closed, Edwards Angell Partner Says," *Bloomberg.com.* November 9. http://www.bloomberg.com/news/2010-11-10/india-legal-market-to-stay-closed-until-2015-edwards-angell-partner-says.html.

Garth, Bryant (2015). "Notes Toward an Understanding of the U.S. Market in Foreign LL.M. Students: From the British Empire and the Inns of Court to the U.S. LL.M.," *Indiana Journal of Global Legal Studies* 22(1): 67–75. https://doi.org/10.2979/indjgloleg stu.22.1.67.

Garth, Bryant G. and Joyce Sterling (2018). "Diversity, Hierarchy, and Fit in Legal Careers: Insights from Fifteen Years of Qualitative Interviews," *Georgetown Journal of Legal Ethics* 31(1): 123–74.

Ginsburg, Tom (2004). "Transforming Legal Education in Japan and Korea," *Pennsylvania State International Law Review* 22(3): 433–440.

Gooch, Liz (2012). "Chinese Universities Send Big Signals to Foreigners," *New York Times.* March 11. https://www.nytimes.com/2012/03/12/world/asia/12iht-educlede12.html.

Goodman, Allan E. (2015). "A Passage to India," *Institute of International Education (blog).* October. https://www.iie.org/Learn/Blog/2015/10/2015-October-A-Passage-To-India.

The Guardian (2015). "Top 20 Countries for International Students." November 10. http://www.theguardian .com/higher-education-network/blog/2014/jul/17/top-20-countries-international-students.

Halliday, Terence (2009). "Recursivity of Global Normmaking: A Sociolegal Agenda," *Annual Review of Law and Social Science* 5: 263–289. https://doi.org/10.1146/annurev.lawsocsci.093008.131606.

Halliday, Terence and Bruce Carruthers (2007). "The Recursivity of Law: Global Norm Making and National Lawmaking in the Globalization of Corporate Insolvency Regimes," *American Journal of Sociology* 112(4): 1135–1202. https://doi.org/10.1086/507855.

Halliday, Terence C. and Gregory Shaffer (2015). *Transnational Legal Orders.* Cambridge University Press.

Hupper, Gail J. (2015). "Educational Ambivalence: The Rise of a Foreign-Student Doctorate in Law," *New England Law Review* 49(3): 319–47.

Hupper, Gail J. (2008). "The Academic Doctorate in Law: A Vehicle for Legal Transplants?," *Journal of Legal Education* 58(3): 413–454.

Hupper, Gail J. (2007). "The Rise of an Academic Doctorate in Law: Origins Through World War II," *Journal of Legal History* 49(1): 1–60.

International Student Data (2014). *Australian Government Department of Education and Training.* https:// internationaleducation.gov.au/research/International-Student-Data/Pages/InternationalStudentData 2014.aspx#Detailed_Monthly.

International Student Economic Value Tool (2017). *NAFSA.* Accessed November 18, 2017. http://www.nafsa.org/Policy _and_Advocacy/Policy_Resources/Policy_Trends_and_Data/NAFSA_International_Student_Economic_Value_Tool/.

Jail, Neera and Shoma Mukherji (2010). "The Perception of 'Glass Ceiling' in Indian Organizations: An Exploratory Study," *South Asian Journal of Management* 17(1): 23.

Kim, Jongyoung (2016). "Global Cultural Capital and Global Positional Competition: International Graduate Students' Transnational Occupational Trajectories," *British Journal of Sociology of Education* 37(1): 30–50. https://doi.org/10.1080/01425692.2015.1096189.

Lawyers Collective v. Bar Council of India (2009). Writ Petition No. 1526/1995.

Lazarus-Black, Mindie (2017). "The Voice of the Stranger: Foreign LL.M. Students' Experiences of Culture, Law and Pedagogy in U.S. Law Schools," in James A.R. Nafziger, ed., *Comparative Law and Anthropology*. Pp. 462–477. Edward Elgar Publishing.

Leading Places of Origin: 2014/15–2015/16 (n.d.). *Institute of International Education*. https://opendoorsdata.org/data/international-students/leading-places-of-origin/

Lee, Kuk Woon (2007). "Corporate Lawyers in Korea: An Analysis of the 'Big 4' Law Firms in Seoul," in Dai-Kwon Choi and Kahei Rokumoto, eds., *Judicial System Transformation in the Globalizing World: Korea and Japan*. Pp. 219–50. Seoul National University Press.

Liu, Sida (2008). "Globalization as Boundary-Blurring: International and Local Law Firms in China's Corporate Law Market," *Law & Society Review* 42(4): 771–804. https://doi.org/10.1111/j.1540-5893.2008.00358.x.

Martel, Mirka (2021). IIE Fall 2021 International Student Enrollment Snapshot, https://www.iie.org/en/Research-and-Insights/Publications/Fall-2021-International-Student-Enrollment-Snapshot.

Merry, Sally Engle (2006). "Transnational Human Rights and Local Activism: Mapping the Middle," *American Anthropologist* 108(1): 38–51. https://doi.org/10.1525/aa.2006.108.1.38.

Meyer, John W. and Brian Rowan (1977). "Institutionalized Organizations: Formal Structure as Myth and Ceremony," *American Journal of Sociology* 83(2): 340–363. https://doi.org/10.1086/226550.

Moon, Jaewan (unpublished manuscript). Impact of Globalization on Korean Legal Profession (on file with author).

National Center for Education Statistics (2018). Classification of Instructional Programs. Accessed March 31, 2018. https://nces.ed.gov/ipeds/cipcode/cipdetail.aspx?y=55.

Oh, Soogeun (2005). "Globalization in Legal Education of Korea," *Journal of Legal Education* 55(4): 525–530.

O'Malley, Brendan (2014). "Middle East Swells International Student Growth in US," *University World News*. November 20. https://www.universityworldnews.com/post.php?story=2014112021585741.

Open Doors (2011). *Institute of International Education*. https://www.iie.org/Research-and-Insights/Open-Doors/Fact-Sheets-and-Infographics/Fast-Facts.

Open Doors 2017 Report (2017). *Institute of International Education*. https://www.iie.org/Why-IIE/Announcements/2017/11/2017-11-13-Open-Doors-Data.

Open Doors FAQ (2018). *Institute of International Education*. Accessed April 26, 2018. https://www.iie.org/Research-and-Insights/Open-Doors/Frequently-Asked-Questions.

Paige, Susan Mary, Amrita A. Wall, Joseph J. Marren, Brian Dubenion, and Amy Rockwell (2017). *The Learning Community Experience in Higher Education: High-Impact Practice for Student Retention*. Routledge, Taylor & Francis Group.

Paik, Anthony, Carole Silver, Steven Boutcher, and Swethaa Ballakrishnen. Diverse Student Experiences in Law School Study (research funded by AccessLex Institute, award number FY1907UG001).

Paik, Anthony, Swethaa Ballakrishnen, Carole Silver, Steven Boutcher, and Tanya Whitworth, *Diverse Disconnectedness: Homophily, Social Capital Inequality and Student Experiences in Law School* (under submission 2021).

Places of Origin, 2015/2016–2016/2017 (n.d.). Open Doors Report on International Educational Exchange, *Institute of International Education*. https://www.iie.org/Research-and-Insights/Open-Doors/Data/International -Students/Places-of-Origin.

Places of Origin, 2016/2017 (n.d.). Open Doors Report on International Educational Exchange, *Institute of International Education*. https://www.iie.org/Research-and-Insights/Open-Doors/Data/International -Students/Places-of-Origin.

Project Atlas Infographics (2017). *Institute of International Education*. https://www.iie.org/Research-and-Insights /Open-Doors/Fact-Sheets-and-Infographics/Infographics.

Rajah, Jothie (2015). "'Rule of Law' as Transnational Legal Order," in Terence C. Halliday and Gregory Shaffer, eds., *Transnational Legal Orders*. Pp. 340–73. Cambridge University Press.

Research and Insights (2018). *Institute of International Education*. https://www.iie.org/Research-and-Insights/Open-Doors/Data /International-Students/Places-of-Origin.

Robel, Lauren K. (2006). "Opening Our Classrooms Effectively to Foreign Graduate Students," *Pennsylvania State International Law Review* 24: 797–799.

Roberts, Anthea and Martti Koskenniemi (2017). "Is International Law International?," *Oxford Scholarship Online* 61–67. https://doi.org/10.1093/oso/9780190696412.001.0001.

Roberts, Anthea (2022). "Cross-Border Student Flows and the Construction of International Law as a Transnational Legal Field," in Bryant Garth and Gregory Shaffer, eds., *The Globalization of Legal Education: A Critical Study*.

Ruiz, Neil G. (2014). "The Geography of Foreign Students in U.S. Higher Education: Origins and Destinations," *Brookings*. August 29. https://www.brookings.edu/interactives/the-geography-of-foreign-students-in-u-s-higher-education-origins-and-destinations/.

The Salary Wars of 2016: Huge Pay Rises in New York This Summer Forced the City to Play Along (2016). *Chambers Student*. October. http://www.chambersstudent.co.uk/where-to-start /newsletter/law-firm-pay-rises-in-2016.

Saluja, Pallavi (2017). "BCI, SILF, BAI Buy Time to Submit Proposals on Entry of Foreign Law Firms," *Bar and Bench—Indian Legal News*. July 28. https://barandbench.com/foreign-law-firms-bci-silf-bai-law-ministry/.

Saxenian, Annalee (2005). "From Brain Drain to Brain Circulation: Transnational Communities and Regional Upgrading in India and China," *Studies in Comparative International Development* 40(2): 35–61. https://doi.org/10.1007/bf02686293.

Seong-Hyun, Kim (2011). "The Democratization and Internationalization of the Korean Legal Field," in Yves Dezalay and Bryant Garth, eds., *Lawyers and the Rule of Law in an Era of Globalization*. Pp. 217–38. Routledge.

Seron, Carine (2020). "The Law School's Brutal Response to COVID-19," *Harvard Crimson*. April 2. https://www.thecrimson.com/article/2020/4/2/seron-law-school-brutal-response-coronavirus/.

Silver, Carole (2012). "Coping with the Consequences of 'Too Many Lawyers': Securing the Place of International Graduate Law Students," *International Journal of the Legal Profession* 19(2–3): 227–245. https://doi.org/10.1080/09695958.2013.769439.

Silver, Carole (2000). "Globalization and the U.S. Market in Legal Services—Shifting Identities," *Journal of Law and Policy in International Business* 31(4): 1093–1095.

Silver, Carole (2013). "Holding Onto 'Too Many Lawyers': Bringing International Graduate Students to the Front of the Class," *Oñati Socio-Legal Series* 3: 533–560.

Silver, Carole (2006). "Internationalizing U.S. Legal Education: A Report on the Education of Transnational Lawyers," *Cardozo Journal of International and Comparative Law* 14(1): 143–227. https://doi.org/10.2139/ssrn.829744.

Silver, Carole (2007). "Local Matters: Internationalizing Strategies for U.S. Law Firms," *Indiana Journal of Global Legal Studies* 14(1): 67–74. https://doi.org/10.2979/gls.2007.14.1.67.

Silver, Carole (2009). "LSAC Research Report Series: Agents of Globalization in Law: Phase 1," *The Law School Admission Council*. https://www.lsac.org/data-research/research/agents-globalization-law-phase-1-gr-09-01.

Silver, Carole (2003). "Regulatory Mismatch in the International Market for Legal Services," *Journal of International Law and Business* 23(3): 487–491. https://doi.org/10.2139/ssrn.408340.

Silver, Carole (2012). "States Side Story: Career Paths of International LLM Students, or 'I Like to Be in America,'" *Fordham Law Review* 80(6): 2383–2384.

Silver, Carole (2002). "The Case of the Foreign Lawyer: Internationalizing the U.S. Legal Profession," *Fordham International Law Journal* 25: 1039–1043. https://doi.org/10.2139/ssrn.287873.

Silver, Carole (2001). "The Variable Value of U.S. Legal Education in the Global Legal Services Market," *Georgetown Journal of Legal Ethics* 24(1): 1–54.

Silver, Carole (2005). "Winners and Losers in the Globalization of Legal Services: Situating the Market for Foreign Lawyers," *Virginia Journal of International Law* 45(4): 897–908.

Silver, Carole and Swethaa S. Ballakrishnen (2018). "Sticky Floors, Springboards, Stairways & Slow Escalators: Mobility Pathways and Preferences of International Students in U.S. Law Schools," *UC Irvine Journal of International, Transnational and Comparative Law* 3: 39–70.

Silver, Carole and Mayer Freed (2006). "Translating the U.S. LLM Experience: The Need for a Comprehensive Examination," *Northwestern Law Review Colloquy* 101: 23.

Silver, Carole, Jae-Hyup Lee, and Jeeyoon Park (2015). "What Firms Want: Investigating Globalization's Influence on the Market for Lawyers in Korea," *Columbia Journal of Asian Law* 27: 1–3. https://doi.org/10.2139/ssrn.2618034.

Sinhal, Kounteya (2014). "Student Visa Rules Tightened By UK Govt," *The Times of India*. July 29. https://timesofindia.indiatimes.com/home/education/news/Student-visa-rules-tightened-by-UK-govt/articleshow/39243701.cms.

Spivey, Mike (2020). "How Will COVID-19 Impact Law Schools as the Summer Progresses?," *Above the Law*. March 27. https://abovethelaw.com/2020/03/how-will-covid-19-impact-law-schools-as-the-summer-progresses/.

Students in Higher Education 2012/13 (2014). *HESA*. February 1. https://www.hesa.ac.uk/data-and-analysis/publications/students-2012-13.

Terry, Laurel (2011). "International Students and Global Mobility in Higher Education," *Michigan State Law Review* 2011(2): 305–307. https://doi.org/10.1057/9780230117143.

Tesch, Bonnie J., Helen M. Wood, Amy L. Helwig, and Ann Butler Nattinger (1995). "Promotion of Women Physicians in Academic Medicine. Glass Ceiling or Sticky Floor?," *JAMA: The Journal of the American Medical Association* 273(13): 1022–1025. https://doi.org/10.1001/jama.273.13.1022.

Tolbert, Pamela S. (2017). "Wendy Nelson Espeland and Michael Sauder: Engines of Anxiety: Academic Rankings, Reputation, and Accountability," *Administrative Science Quarterly* 63(1): NP5–NP7. https://doi.org/10.1177/0001839217731341.

Turner, Cory (2015). "U.S. Colleges See a Big Bump in International Students," *NPR*. November 18. https://www.npr.org/sections/ed/2015/11/18/456353089/u-s-colleges-see-a-big-bump-in-international-students.

Visiting Faculty (2018). Peking University. Accessed January 28, 2018. http://newsen.pku.edu.cn/Employment/ForeignExperts/VisitingFacultyatPKU/.

Index

For the benefit of digital users, indexed terms that span two pages (e.g., 52–53) may, on occasion, appear on only one of those pages.

Note: Tables and figures are indicated by *t* and *f* following the page number

Abel, Richard, 389
academic solipsism, 265–72
Accra African Union Workshop (1972), 137
Addis Ababa Convention (2014), 145–46
additional law degrees, 456–58
Administrative Law Research Group, 111
Advisory Committee on Legal Education and Conduct (England), 169–70
African Court of Human and Peoples' Rights (AF), 405, 412–13, 422–23
African National Congress, 160–62, 163
African Scholarship Program of U.S. Universities, 133n.11
African transnationalized education
  in colonial Africa, 127–29
  decolonization during Cold War, 129–36
  developmental university in, 129–36
  Ford Foundation and, 99, 132–33, 135
  globalization of legal education, 126, 143, 145–46
  impoverishment of, 137–41
  introduction to, 32, 34–35, 124–26
  in precolonial Africa, 127
  regionalization in, 124–25, 145–47
  summary of, 148
  in twenty-first century, 141–47
Agreement on Mutual Recognition of Academic Degrees, 452
Al-Azhar in Cairo, 127
Alexy, Robert, 243
Al Qalam Institute for Islamic Identities and Dialogue in Southeast Asia, 225
Altbach, Philip, 476–77
Alternative Law movement, 260

American Bar Association (ABA), 51–52, 67–68, 94, 220–21, 312–15, 480
Americanization of legal education, 3–4, 313n.3, 464–65
American Society of International Law, 88
Americas Watch, 103
Andrade, Carlos Drummond de, 255
anglophone core in transnational flow of students, 437
anti-communism internationalization, 83
anti-imperial empire, 13–14
Anti-Rightist Movement in China, 22–23, 30
apartheid in South African higher education, 35–36, 158, 164–67
Argentine Centro de Estudios Legales y Sociales, 102
Arusha Agreement (1981), 145–46
Asian Law Institute (ASLI), 231–32
Asian legal education
  engagement dimension of law school, 213–14, 219–32
  globalization and, 215
  in Indonesia, 40–41, 226–29
  introduction to, 39–40, 68, 213–15
  in Japan, 229–32
  knowledge mandate, 218–20
  in Philippines, 224–26
  restructuring of Chinese legal education, 221–24
  summary of, 232–33
  Yangon University, 215–18
Asian Legal Revivals (Dezalay, Garth), 232–33
Association of Law Societies (ALS), 167
Association of South East Asian Nations (ASEAN), 217–18

asymmetric student flows, 444–48
Atlantic Charter, 166
Attorneys, Notaries and Conveyancers
    Admission Act (1934) (South
    Africa), 162
Aung San Suu Kyi, 216, 217, 218
Australian Department of Foreign Affairs
    and Trade (DFAT), 215–16
Australian legal education, 219, 291, 434f,
    436f, 444, 460–61
Austrian Development Agency
    (ADA), 302–3
Austrian funding for Bhutanese legal
    education, 302–3
authoritarianism/authoritarian
    regimes, 16, 21–22, 23, 25–26, 41–42,
    168, 260
avant garde global schools, 53
"avocat d'affaires" (business lawyer), 5

BABSEACLE program, 222–23
Baccalaureus Juris (B Juris), 165
Baccalaureus Procurationis (B Proc), 165
Bachelor of Laws. *See* LLB
Bainbridge, John, 99
Bangsamoro Autonomous
    Region of Muslim Mindanao
    (BARMM), 224–25
Bangsamoro Organic Law, 224–25
Bantu education policy, 164
Bantustan University of Zululand, 178
Bar Council in India, 197
Basheer, Shamnad, 193
Baxi, Pratiksha, 207–8
Baxi, Upendra, 191, 198–99, 207–8
Bedford Stuyvesant Restoration
    Corporation, 103
Beijing Conference, 114
Beijing Olympics (2008), 223–24
Belt and Road Initiative (China), 50–51,
    52–54, 311–12, 322–25
Benchmark Chambers International
    (BCI), 323
Berman, Harold, 185
Berresford, Susan, 114–15
Bhagwati, P. N., 196–97
Bhandari, Rajika, 512
Bhutanese Constitution, 292

Bhutanese legal education. *See also* Jigme
    Singye Wangchuck School of Law
Austrian funding for, 302–3
aversion to Indian model of legal
    education, 300–1
curriculum, 285–92
first law school, 281–85
global funding for, 303–4
globalization and, 280–81, 306
impressions of isolation, tradition, and
    anxiety, 278–81
introduction to, 48–50, 276–78
LLB in, 49, 277, 286–87
summary of, 304–6
US funding for, 301–2
Bhutan-LSAT, 297
"Big Law" private firms in US, 490
"Big Seven" law firms in India, 195–96
bijural legal education, 338–39
bilingual contracts, 53
biotechnology law, 53
black law students
    in South Africa, 35–36, 162–64, 170–
    71, 178–79
    in US, 67–68, 489–90
Black Lawyers Association (BLA), 168–69
Bogdandy, Armin von, 247–48
Böhmer, Martín, 244–45
Bologna Process, 286, 301
Bosnian war, 114
Bourdieu, Pierre, 342–44
Brahmins in India, 13
brain drain, 138, 145–46, 199, 205, 442–43
Brand, Johannes, 159–60
Brazilian cosmopolitan legal education.
    See also Fundação
        Getulio Vargas Law School
        in São Paulo
    challenges to, 261–72
    globalization and, 253–55, 263–65
    introduction to, 44–48
    LLM in, 255
    summary of, 272–73
    tradition legal education, 255–61
Brexit vote in UK, 437, 439–41
British East India Company, 377–78
British Inter-University Council for
        Higher Education Overseas, 132–33

British law in Cape Colony, 159
Brown, Dyke, 93
Brownlie, Ian, 452–53
Bucerius, Gerd, 5
Bucerius Law School, 5, 6–7, 22
Buddism studies, 292
Budlender, Geoff, 105
Bundy, McGeorge, 94–95, 100, 101
business law, 17, 22–23, 176, 187
Byse, Clark, 89

Cairo University, 130n.5
Cambridge University, 11–12, 194
Canadian Charter of Human
    Rights, 371–72
canon law, 10–11
Caribbean Court of Justice (CCJ), 405,
    412–13, 422–23, 424
Carnegie Corporation of New
    York, 132–33
Carnegie Endowment for International
    Peace, 96–97
Catholic University of Valparaiso, 98
Catholic Vicariate of Solidarity, 102
Cavers, David, 86–87
Center for Policy Research in New
    Delhi, 206
Center for Study and Research in Legal
    Education (Centro de Estudos e
    Pesquisas no Ensino do Direito)
    (CEPED), 259–60
Center for Transnational Law in
    London, 25, 27
Center for Transnational Legal Studies
    (CTLS), 57, 367, 372–78, 386–
    88, 390–93
Centre for Applied Legal Studies
    (CALS), 104
Centre for Legal and Policy Studies
    (PSHK), 228–29
Centre for the Study of Law and
    Governance, 207–8
Centre for Women's Law Studies and Legal
    Services (Peking University), 224
Centro de Investigación y Docencia
    Económicas (Mexico), 241
Chan, Wen-Chen, 463–64
Chandrachud, Dhananjaya Yashwant, 201

Chaskalson, Arthur, 105
Chevron v. Ecuador, 386
Childers, Erskine, 115
Chilean legal education, 30, 81
China
    Anti-Rightist Movement in, 22–23, 30
    Belt and Road Initiative, 50–51, 52–54,
        311–12, 322–25
    Cultural Revolution in, 30, 32, 110
    as emergent power, 16, 21–22, 70–71
China Centre for American Law
    Study, 108
China International Commercial Court
    (CICC), 323
China International Economic Trade
    and Arbitration Commission
    (CIETAC), 321
Chinese Academy of Social Sciences
    (CASS), 108, 111
Chinese globalization of legal
    education. See also Peking
    University School of
    Transnational Law
    clinical education movement, 30–31, 40
    educational diversity of, 455–56
    Ford Foundation and, 107–13
    introduction to, 50–54
    Juris Master curriculum, 316–19
    LLB in, 52, 53–54, 70, 455
    LLM in, 325, 438
    New York bar examination
        and, 442–43
    restructuring of, 221–24
    scholarships for, 64
    studying abroad, 444
    support for, 124–25
Chinese University of Hong Kong (CUHK
    LAW), 4
Christopher, Warren, 21
civil law studies, 64–65, 67, 244–
    45, 465–66
civil rights and Ford Foundation, 80–81,
    94, 99–100, 101–7, 102f, 113
civil society groups/organizations, 213–14
Clark, David, 441–42
CLEPR (Council of Legal Education for
    Professional Responsibility), 94, 99–
    100, 104–5, 109

clinical legal education, 9, 30–31, 40, 41–42, 94, 104–6, 112, 221–23, 229–30, 302, 384
COEPR (Council on Education in Professional Responsibility), 94
Cohen, Mathilde, 441–42
Cold War era, 16, 21, 33, 114, 129–36, 186
Cole, Bob, 116
Cole, David, 374–75
college choice research, 345
College of Law of the University of the Philippines, 226
College of Science and Technology in Bhutan, 296
colonialism
    in Africa, 127–29
    in Asia, 215
    in Brazil, 265–69
    in India, 189–99
    in lawmaking, 375–76
    legal colonialism, 265–69
    models of power, 40–41
Columbia University, 96, 160–62
Columbia University Law School, 30–31, 95–96, 103, 109–10, 116
commercial arbitration, 8–9, 337–38, 372–73, 375–76, 378–80, 445
commercialisation of African legal education, 140
Committee for Chinese Clinical Legal Educators (CCCLE), 112, 221–22
Committee on International Legal Studies, 86
Committee on World Peace through Law, 96
Common Law Admission Test, 193
common law-studies, 67, 310–11, 465–66
communism, 29–30, 31, 95–96
comparative constitutional law, 89, 290, 372–73, 386–87, 389, 430
comparative law
    in Bhutan, 284–85, 288–89
    in Chinese legal education, 110–11
    educational diversity and, 462–63
    in Global Law Program, 264
    integration of, 8, 339
    in transnational legal education, 368–69, 373, 375–76, 386

"Comparative Law" course, 288–89
comparative sociology of legal professions, 19–23
conservatism in legal profession, 190–91
constitutional democracy, 242–43, 246–47
constructed demand theory, 340–46, 356–60, 357t
Cornell University, 194, 312–13
corporate elites, 18
corporate law firms
    access to, 187
    curriculum designs for, 16–17
    elite of, 199, 202–3
    globalization and, 3–4
    Indian legal education reforms, 189–90
    legal revolution of, 47
    rise of, 5, 186
    spread of, 19–20
    traditional legal oligarchies and, 22
Corpus Juris of Roman Law, 10–11
cosmopolitan academic dialogues, 46
cosmopolitan elite, 24, 370n.9, 502
Council of Higher Education, 36
Council on Foreign Relations, 94–95
Council on Higher Education (CHE), 174–76
Court of Justice of the European Union (CJEU), 403, 405
COVID19 pandemic, 477n.2, 487n.33
criminal law studies, 31, 86, 244–45, 291, 373–74, 376, 423
Critical Legal Studies Movement, 260
cross-border flow of students, 431–38, 432t, 434f, 435f, 436f, See also transnational flow of students
cross-cultural dispute resolution, 53
cross-cultural teaching, 390–91
cultural globalization, 17–18, 254
Cultural Revolution in China, 30, 32, 110
cultural rights, 18–19, 80–81
Curriculum Committee for the American Association of Law Schools, 99–100
Cutler, Lloyd, 105

Dag Hammarskjöld Foundation, 115
Daines, Rob, 8
Dantas, San Thiago, 259, 260–61
Davis, Kenneth Culp, 95–96

debt crisis, 34, 137, 140
decolonization, 96–97, 129–36,
    158, 177–78
Delaware corporate law, 446
Delhi University, 99, 192, 201
DeMatteo, Renee, 242
democracy
    Brazilian cosmopolitan legal education
        and, 253
    constitutional democracy, 242–
        43, 246–47
    movement in South Korea, 23
    South African globalization and, 168
    in South Korea, 23
Democracy Roundtable in SELA's annual
    meeting, 242–43
denationalizing effects, 410, 443, 453, 461
Denning Report, 134
Department of Adult and Higher
    Education (DAHE), 296, 297
Department of Justice (South
    Africa), 169–70
dependency theory, 34, 137–38
derived demand theory
    alternative to, 344–46
    globalization and, 335–36
    limitations of, 340–44
    multijural lawyers, 336–38
    multijural legal education, 338–40
    in NYU Law Abroad, 353–55
    transnational legal education, 335–46
Dershowitz, Alan, 108
Deutscher Akademischer Austausch
    Dienst (DAAD), 303–4
developmental university in
    Africa, 129–36
development movement, 22, 24–25,
    135, 248–49
Dezalay, Yves, 379, 445
Dickson Poon School of Law (King's
    College London), 7, 22
Die Zeit, 5
differentiated academic systems, 145
diffusion from student to student, 447–48
divisible college of international lawyers,
    428–29, 443–48, 461–69
doctoral degrees of international judiciary,
    419–23, 420f, 421f, 422f

doctor of juridical science (SJD), 191, 247,
    382–83, 453–54, 482–83
donor states, 28, 138
donors to African legal education, 140–
    41, 143
Dorjee, Sangay, 284
double internationalization, 467
Douglas Aircraft Company, 83
downward diffusion, 448
Duarte, Rodrigo Roa, 224–25
Duke University, 88
Dworkin, Ronald, 243

East African Court of Justice (EACJ), 405,
    412–13, 422–23
economic globalization, 18, 50–51, 53,
    254, 305
economic liberalization, 192, 195–96,
    197, 204
economic nationalism, 336
economic rights, 80–81
The Economist, 320
educational diversity
    Australian legal education, 460–61
    Chinese globalization of legal
        education, 455–56
    divisible college and, 461–69
    French lack of, 453–54
    inbound diversity, 449–50, 455, 458–
        59, 467
    Japanese legal education, 464t
    outbound diversity, 65–66, 449, 450,
        455, 458, 460, 461, 465
    Russian lack of, 451–53, 462
    South Korean legal education, 464t
    Taiwanese legal education, 464t
    transnational flow of students, 443–44,
        449–69, 450t
    United Kingdom legal
        education, 458–60
    United States legal education, 456–
        58, 464t
educational reforms, 7, 14, 30, 70
education background of
    professors, 448–69
"Education for Democracy" (Ford
    Foundation), 89–90
Edwards, Randle, 109–10

Egyptian Society of International Law, 89
e-journals, 14–15
e-libraries, 14–15
elite international legal education, 416–23,
    417f, 418f, 445
elite law, 21, 89, 95, 107
elite law firms, 52
elite law schools, 5, 29–30, 34, 47–48, 51,
    55, 65, 87, 90, 117, 147, 416–17, 444–
    46, 469
engaged teaching, 6–7, 14, 38
engagement dimension of law school,
    213–14, 219–32
English Bar, 33–34
English-language programs, 436–37
English law, 11–12
environmental rights law, 254, 263
epistemic dependency, 32, 140
epistemic nationalism, 461–62
Erasmus program, 439–41
ESADE (Spain), 57–58, 372–73
European business schools, 24
European Court of Human Rights
    (ECtHR), 61–62, 371–72, 403, 405,
    407, 410, 412–13, 414–16, 420–21
European Court of Justice (ECJ), 410,
    412–13, 422–23
European Journal of International
    Law, 468–69
European University Institute in
    Italy, 465–66
evidence-based research, 41, 228–29
exclusionary costs in higher
    education, 271–72
experiential learning, 49, 222, 283, 287,
    292, 317, 367–68
Extension of University Education Act
    (1959), 163–64

Faculty of Law at Universitas
    Indonesia, 213
Faerman, Silvia, 379
family capital for law school, 201–2, 204
Faria, José Eduardo, 259
Farnsworth, E. Allan, 95–96
#FeesMustFall movement, 37, 177
feminist jurisprudence, 42–43
Filho, Ary Oswaldo Mattos, 15–16, 46–47

Filho, Roberto Lyra, 260
financial crisis (2008), 336
financialization, 22, 37, 186, 209
Financial Times, 24
Fiss, Owen, 42, 240–42, 243
Ford, Henry, II, 82–83
Ford Foundation
    African transnationalized education,
        132–33, 135
    civil rights and, 80–81, 94, 99–100, 101–
        7, 102f, 113
    funding legal studies, 87–90,
        90f, 115–16
    human rights and civil rights, 101–
        7, 102f
    Indian legal education reforms, 88–89,
        116, 190, 191, 198–99, 204
    internationalization strategy
        of, 83, 101
    international justice development,
        80–82, 82f
    international organizations and, 114–15
    introduction to, 24, 28, 29–44
    legal education and institutions, 107–13
    legal education as expertise for social
        change, 93–100
    role in legal education, 82–115, 91f,
        92f, 98f
    strategic philanthropy, 79–80
    summary of, 115–17
    transnational legal ordering, 69
foreign language skills, 456–57
Frank, Jerome, 94
Frankfurter, Felix, 95
free tuition and living expenses, 138–
    39, 277–78
Frei Universitat, 57–58, 372–73
French civil law, 127
French lack of educational
    diversity, 453–54
French law, 12, 453–54
Fribourg (Switzerland), 57–58, 372–73
Friedman, Thomas L., 59, 366, 370–71,
    374–75, 390
From Beirut to Jerusalem (Friedman), 59
FT ranking, 24
Fulbright scholarship, 164, 293, 296,
    297, 458

Fundação Getulio Vargas Law School in São Paulo (FGV DIREITO SP)
  academic solipsism, 265–72
  creation of, 260–61, 269
  Global Law School Program, 55–56, 264–65
  goal-oriented legal education of, 261–65
  historical perspective on, 44–48, 255
  introduction to, 6–7, 9, 15–16, 25, 26, 28–29, 44
  legal colonialism, 265–69
  social elitism, 265–72
Fundação Getulio Vargas-Rio de Janeiro (Brazil), 241
Fund for Free Expression, 103
funding legal studies, 87–90, 90f

Gadjah Mada University, 227
Gaither, Rowan (Gaither report), 83–84, 85
Galanter, Marc, 259–60
Gandhi, Indira, 116, 190–91
Gardner, James, 97
Garth, Bryant, 379, 389, 445
Geithner, Peter, 110
Gellhorn, Walter, 109–10
gender bias in legal education, 189
General Council of the Bar (GCB), 167
geographies of connection, 158–59
Georgetown Center for Transnational Legal Studies in London, 28–29
Georgetown Law School, 57–58
Georgetown University, 57, 95–96, 372–73
George Washington University, 50
German Constitutional Court (Bundesverfassungsgericht), 420–21
German legal education, 12–13, 28, 317–18, 345, 442
Getulio Vargas Foundation, 262–63
Giddens, Anthony, 371
GLEE project (Globalization, Lawyers and Emerging Economies), 7
global flow of students. See transnational flow of students
Global Innovation Index (GII), 320
globalization of legal education. See also Chinese globalization of legal education

in Africa, 126, 143, 145–46
Asian legal education, 215
Bhutanese legal education, 280–81, 306
Brazilian cosmopolitan legal education, 253–55, 263–65
comparative sociology of legal professions, 19–23
critical study of, 404–5
cultural globalization, 17–18, 254
denationalized globalizers, 410
economic globalization and, 18, 50–51, 53, 254, 305
general themes of, 23–27
global law schools, 44–60
historical perspectives, 10–16
impact on legal practice, 334–35
Indian legal education reforms, 189
for international judges, 409–23
introduction to, 3–10, 28–69
legal education reform and, 29–44
shifts in education policy, 125
in South Africa, 157–58, 160–62, 173–80
by study of international law, 366–67, 371
summary of, 69–72
theoretical approaches, 16–23
transnational flow of students, 126, 438–43, 440t, 441f
transnational legal education, 335–36, 378–85
transnational legal ordering/orders, 17–19
global job preparation, 7
Global Justice Summit, 386–87
global law school, 7–8, 44–60
Global Law School Program, 55–56, 264–65, 348–53
Global North, 26, 43–44, 145, 148, 246–47, 238, 268
Global Practice Exercise, 373–74
Global South, 18–19, 26, 255, 266–67, 238, 268
goal-oriented legal education, 261–65
good governance, 59–60, 140–41, 144, 203, 206, 392, 393
Government Law College (GLC) (India), 38, 55, 192, 202

Graduate Institute of International
  and Development Studies in
  Switzerland, 465–66
grantmaking, 79, 80–82, 82*f*, 85*f*, 106*f*
Great Depression, 93
Grey, Whitmore, 108
Gross National Happiness (GNH), 48–
  49, 290–91

Habermas, Jürgen, 243
habitus in legal studies, 57, 343
Hague Academy of International
  Law, 96–97
Hahlo, H. R., 162–63
Hai Wen, 50–51, 220–21, 312
Harbin Institute of Technology (HIT), 312
harmonization of teaching in African legal
  education, 145–46
Hart, H.L.A., 243
Harvard Law School, 85–86, 164,
  201, 382–83
Harvard Law School's East Asian Legal
  Studies program, 109
Harvard University, 6–7, 89, 201, 206
Hauser Global Law School, 348
Hayes, Bradley, 242
Heald, Henry, 100
Hebrew University, 57–58, 372–73
Helsinki Watch, 103
Hidayatullah, M., 191
hierarchies in the legal profession, 20–21
Higher Education Ministry
  (Indonesia), 233
Hirschon, Robert, 313–14
historically black universities, 157–58,
  170, 178
historically white universities, 157–58
"History of SELA" (Saba, Jana), 244–46
Hoffman, Paul, 82–84, 85
Hong Kong law faculties, 54
Hong Kong's rule of law tradition, 321
Hoover Commissions, 93
Hukum Online, 228
human capital theory, 138
human rights and Ford Foundation, 80,
  101–7, 102*f*
human rights law, 8–9, 31, 47, 263
Human Rights Watch, 103

Humboldt, Alexander von, 36
Huntington, Samuel, 409–10
Hutchins, Robert Maynard, 85

imperialism in lawmaking, 14, 44, 47, 136,
  248, 267, 345–46, 375–76, 393
inbound diversity, 449–50, 455, 458–
  59, 467
Independent Institute of Education, 172
Indiana University School of Law, 95–96
Indian Institutes of Technology (IIT),
  190, 194
Indian Law Institute, 89, 99
Indian legal aristocracy, 190
Indian legal education reforms
  the bar in, 199–209
  Bhutanese aversion to, 300–1
  Ford Foundation and, 88–89, 116, 190,
    191, 198–99, 204
  impact of colonialism, 189–99
  international mobility and, 504–13
  introduction to, 37–39, 49, 185–89
  Jawaharlal Nehru University in New
    Delhi, 207–8
  Jindal Global Law School, 6–7, 22, 38,
    54, 198–99, 206–7
  LLB in, 192, 201, 207
  summary of, 209–10
Indian nationalist movement, 32, 127–28
Indian Supreme Court, 191
indigenous lawyers, 129
Indonesia Jentera Law School, 40–41, 228
Indonesian legal education, 40–41, 226–
  29. *See also* Asian legal education
Indonesia's National Planning
  Agency, 228–29
information and communication
  technology (ICT), 140–41, 276–77
Inns of Court, 11–12, 32, 45, 128, 129
Institute for Air and Space Law, 96
institutional *aggiornamento*, 268
institutional autonomy, 284–85
Instituto Paraguayo de Derecho
  Constitucional (Paraguay), 241
Instituto Tecnológico Autónomo de
  Mexico, 241
intellectual property law, 53, 229, 254,
  323, 372–73

interactive classes, 53, 317, 318, 448
Inter-American Court of Human Rights
  (IACtHR), 247–48, 405, 412–
  13, 422–23
Inter-American Legal Services
  Association, 106
Intercollegiate Negotiation and
  Arbitration competition, 231
interdisciplinary research, 5, 7, 46, 209–10
International Academy of Comparative
  Law, 247–48
International Affairs program, 115
International Association of
  Constitutional Law, 247–48
International Association of Law
  Schools, 247–48
International Chamber of Commerce
  Court of Arbitration, 378–79
international commercial arbitration
  education, 8–9, 31, 372–73, 380, 445
International Court of Justice (ICJ), 369–
  70, 405, 410, 412–13
International Criminal Court (ICC),
  405, 412–13
international criminal law studies, 31,
  373–74, 376, 386, 423
International Development Law Advisory
  Service, 101
international economic law education,
  8–9, 423
international financial institutions (IFIs),
  34, 138–39, 140–41
international human rights law, 15–16,
  246, 388
International Institute for the Unification
  of Private Law (UNIDROIT), 337–38
internationalist elite, 24
internationalization of international
  judiciary study, 409–16, 411f, 412f,
  413f, 414f, 415f, 416f
internationalization of legal education
  in Africa, 143–46
  anti-communism
    internationalization, 83
  education background of
    professors, 448–69
  Ford Foundation strategy of, 83, 101
  in India, 203

in student exchange, 6–7
studies on, 382–83
*International Journal of Constitutional
  Law,* 247–48
international judiciary
  doctoral degrees of, 419–23, 420f,
    421f, 422f
  elite international legal education for,
    416–23, 417f, 418f, 445
  globalization of legal education
    for, 409–23
  internationalization of, 409–16, 411f,
    412f, 413f, 414f, 415f, 416f
  introduction to, 403–6
  study of, 406–9
  summary of, 423–25
international law student mobility, 476–79
International Legal Center (ILC), 96–
  99, 101
international legal education
  glocal trends, 501–4
  in India, 504–13
  introduction to, 476–81
  law student mobility, 476–79
  mobile pathways, 492–501, 498f
  slow, crowded escalator to, 500–1
  springboards to, 497–99
  stairway to, 499–501
  sticky floor effect in, 496–97
  summary of, 504–14
  trends in, 482–92, 484f, 488f, 490f
international organizations, 16–17, 114–
  15. *See also* Ford Foundation
international sensibility, 29–30, 90
International Society of Public
  Law, 247–48
international trade law, 31, 263
"invisible college" of international
  law, 28–29
Islamic law education, 127. *See also*
  Indonesian legal education
Israel, Americanization of legal education
  in, 464–65
Italian City States, 10–11
Ius Constitutionale Commune
  project, 247–48
Ivy League universities, 188, 416–17
Iyer, Krishna, 191–92

Jana, Andrés, 244–46
Japanese legal education
  educational diversity of, 464t
  introduction to, 41–42
  JD degrees, 25–26, 52
  US-Japanese university student
    exchange, 86–87, 229–32
Japanese Supreme Court, 463
Japan Federation of Bar Associations, 230
Javanese elite in Indonesia, 13
Jawaharlal Nehru University in New Delhi
    (JNU), 207–8
Jentera law journal, 228
Jessup Moot Court Competition, 452–53
Jigme Singye Wangchuck School of
    Law (JSW)
  admission to, 296–97
  curriculum, 285–92
  faculty of, 292–96
  faculty recruitment, 294–96
  faculty training, 293–94
  history of, 281–85
  international influences, 298–304
  introduction to, 28–29, 48–50, 276–78
  summary of, 304–6
Jindal, Naveen, 38
Jindal Global Law School, 6–7, 22, 38, 54,
    198–99, 206–7, 209–10
Johnson, Lyndon, 94–95
Judicial Research and Training Institute in
    Korea, 23, 188
Juris Doctor (JD) degree, 3, 9, 23, 310, 325,
    439, 480, 487–501
Juris Master (JM) degree, 3, 52, 54, 316–
    19, 441–42
"Justice Vision 2000" (South Africa), 169

Kamola, Isaac, 123
kanun (secular law), 127n.1
Karamanian, Susan, 294, 301–2
Kennedy, John F., 94–95
Kentridge, Felicia, 105
Kentridge, Sydney, 105
Khamepe, Sisi, 164
King's College, 57–58, 372–73
King's Counsel, 12
"knowledge to policy" engagement,
    40, 214

KoGuan Law School in Shanghai, 4, 6–
    7, 22
Kohn Pederson Fox (KPF), 313–14
Korean Constitutional Court, 463
Koskenniemi, Martti, 468–69
Krishnan, Jay, 192–93, 194–95
Kumar, Raj, 206

La Forest, Gérard, 462–63
laissez-faire policy on higher
    education, 163–64
Lasswell, Harold, 84
lateral diffusion, 448
Latin American Law School, 246–47
Latin American legal education
  Ford Foundation and, 104, 106
  global student flows, 439–41
  introduction to, 42–43
Law, David, 463–64
Law and Development movement, 248–49
"law and development" movement in
    Africa, 135
Law and Social Sciences Research
    Network (LASSnet), 207–8
Law Dean at National University of
    Singapore, 4–5
Law Dean at the Singapore Management
    School, 4–5
Law School Global League, 46
Law Society, 160–62, 173
lawyer-citizen, 90
League of Nations, 405–6
Lee Kwan Yew, 11–12
legal colonialism, 265–69
legal education. See also globalization of
    legal education
  clinical legal education, 9, 30–31, 40,
    41–42, 94, 104–6, 112, 221–23, 229–
    30, 302, 384
  as expertise for social change, 93–100
  Ford Foundation and, 87–90, 90f, 93–
    100, 107–13
  gender bias in, 189
  marked diversification of, 173–74
  monojural legal education, 336–39
  multijural legal education, 336–
    40, 346–60
  multilingualism in learning, 178–79

as problem solving, 98–99
Legal Education in Crisis summit
    (2013), 174–76
legal education reform. *See also* Indian
    legal education reforms
    introduction to, 14, 18–20, 21
    transnational legal ordering/orders and,
        23–27, 69–72
    transnational processes in, 29–44
legal formalism, 46, 245–46, 260
legal imperialism, 14, 44, 47, 136, 248, 267,
    345–46, 375–76, 393
legal indeterminacy, 317
legal pluralism, 59–60, 369–70, 375–76,
    386, 390
Legal Research and Training Institute in
    Japan, 188
Legal Resources Centre (LRC), 104
Lehman, Jeffrey, 51, 312–13
Leiden University in the
    Netherlands, 465–66
L'Heureux-Dubé, Claire, 462–63
liberal-egalitarian legalism, 42–43, 243–
    44, 247–48
Liu, Sida, 441–42
LLB (Bachelor of Laws)
    in Bhutan, 49, 277, 286–87
    in China, 52, 53–54, 70, 455
    in India, 192, 201, 207
    in South Africa, 160, 162–63, 165, 168–
        79, 174*f*
LLM (Master of Laws)
    in Australia, 291
    in Brazil, 255
    in China, 325, 438
    development of, 482–83, 487, 491
    impact on perception of legal
        training, 479
    international legal education pathways
        to, 492–513
    motivation for pursuing, 483–86, 484*f*
    SELA and, 247
    in South Africa, 170–71, 171*f*, 173–
        74, 174*f*
    specializations for practitioners, 381
    in the United States, 57, 66–69, 345–46,
        374, 382–83, 392, 439, 501–13
Lowell, Lawrence, 95

Mackinnon, Catherine, 243
"magic circle" law firms, 203
magister dixit ethos, 258–59
management education, 79–80
Mandela, Nelson, 35–36, 105, 162–63, 168
Mandelker, Daniel, 95–96
Mangena, Alfred, 160–62
Manjapra, Kris, 11
Mao Zedong, 279
Marcovits, Daniel, 241–42
marginalization in South African legal
    education, 157–58, 162–63
marked diversification of legal
    education, 173–74
market liberalization, 14–15, 22n.2
Marshall Plan, 82–83
Marxism, 108
Master of Laws. *See* LLM
Mauritanian cross-border flow of
    students, 436*f*
Max Plank Institute for Comparative
    Public Law, 247–48
McDougal, Myres, 84
McGill University, 96
McKinsey Consulting, 382–83
Melbourne Law School, 5
Menon, Madhava, 116, 191–92
meritocracy, 71, 190
Millennium Development Goals, 140–41
Mindanao State University, 225
Ministry of Education (Bhutan), 285
Ministry of Education (China), 326, 327
Ministry of Education (Myanmar), 216–17
Ministry of Justice (Japan), 230
Ministry of Research, Technology,
    and Higher Education
    (Indonesia), 226–27
Mody, Zia, 196–97
Monash University of Australia, 172
Monnet, Jean, 82–83
monojural legal education, 336–39
Moro National Liberation Front
    (MNLF), 226
Morris, Herbert, 95–96
Moscow State University, 62, 419
Msimang, Richard, 160–62
multijural legal education, 336–40, 346–60
multilingualism in learning, 178–79

multinational corporations, 16–17
multinationalization, 143–44
multinational law firms, 282, 325, 338
Muslim-Christian solidarity, 225
Myanmar legal profession, 215–18

Nagel, Thomas, 243
Nagoya University, 215–16
Nariman, Fali Sam, 201
Nariman, Rohinnton Fali, 201
National Association of Democratic
    Lawyers (NADEL), 168–69
National Autonomous University of
    Mexico (UNAM), 62, 419
National Consultative Forum, 169
National Graduate School Entrance
    Exam, 326–27
national identity, 49, 130–31, 279, 281,
    290, 304, 305–6
nationalizing effects, 461, 462
National Law School, 116
National Law School of India University
    (NLSIU), 191–92, 193, 194–95, 197–98
National Law Schools in India, 25–26, 37–
    39, 49–50, 197–200, 204, 205, 286
National League for Democracy (NLD),
    216, 217–18
National Legal Aid and Defender
    Association, 93–94
National Planning Agency
    (BAPPENAS), 228
National Research Foundation
    (NRF), 172–73
National University of Singapore (NUS),
    57–58, 215–16, 231–32, 303–
    4, 372–73
native languages in transnational flow of
    students, 433–35
Nehru, Jawaharlal, 11–12, 190
neoliberalism, 22, 34, 46–47, 126, 146–47,
    186, 379
New Deal, 94
New York bar examination, 442–43
New York Convention on the Recognition
    and Enforcement of Foreign Arbitral
    Awards, 375–76
New York Law School, 4
New York Times, 299

New York University (NYU), 468–69
New York University School of Law
    (NYU), 7–8, 28–29, 54–57, 334–35.
    See also NYU Law Abroad
Ngcobo, Sandile, 164
Nigerian cross-border flow of
    students, 436f
Nino, Carlos, 42, 240–41, 243
Nokwe, Duma, 163
non-governmental organizations (NGOs),
    71–72, 140, 228
nonlegal degrees, 456–57
non-resident alien students, 67–68
normative diffusion, 18
North, Douglas, 260–61
Northwestern University, 116
NYU Law Abroad
    background on, 346–60
    constructed demand in, 356–60, 357t
    derived demand in, 353–55
    introduction to, 334–35
    summary, 360–61

Obama, Barack, 243–44
Ogletree, Charles, 313–14
Onati Center for Socio-legal Studies
    (Spain), 389
O'Neill, Lou, 282
Oppenheim, Lassa, 452–53
Organisation for Economic Co-operation
    and Development (OECD), 430–31
outbound diversity, 65–66, 449, 450, 455,
    458, 460, 461, 465
Oxford University, 6–7, 11–12, 160–62,
    194, 206, 215–16, 459–60

pan-African initiatives, 125
parliamentary sovereignty
    doctrine, 165–66
Parsi elite in Mumbai, 199
participatory education, 7
peer-to-peer interactions, 447
Peil, Michael, 50
Peking University (PKU), 224, 312
Peking University School of Transnational
    Law (STL)
    China law Juris Master
        curriculum, 316–19

establishment of, 220–21, 312–16
impact on Chinese legal
    education, 325–28
introduction to, 28–29, 50–54, 308–12
location of, 308
Shenzhen-Hong Kong projects, 319–25
summary, 329
Permanent Court of International Justice
    (PCIJ), 61, 405–7, 424
Peters, Anne, 461–62
Philippine legal education, 224–26
Philippine Supreme Court, 224
Philosophy, Politics, and Economics.
    See PPE
Picker, Colin, 466
Pincus, William, 93–94, 102–3, 104–5
Pinochet, Augusto, 446
planetary military-fiscal-scientific-
    agricultural-industrial complex, 11
Pontifical Catholic University of São Paulo
    School of Law, 260
Pontificia Universidad Católica del
    Peru, 241
positivism, 35–36, 159–60, 165–66, 168
post-Cold War globalization, 14–15, 24–25
Post Graduate Diploma in National Law
    (PGDNL), 282
postgraduation employment, 353
PPE (Philosophy, Politics, and
    Economics), 287–88
Pravin Gandhi School of Law, 192
*Principles of International Commercial
    Contracts* (UNIDROIT), 337–38
privatisation of African legal
    education, 140
progressive law studies, 40–41
protectionism, 232–33, 315, 505–7
Protestant Reformation, 185
public interest litigation, 37, 129, 191, 192,
    196–97, 200, 222
Puig, Sergio, 445
pure *vs.* progressive law, 227

Qualification of Legal Practitioners
    Amendment Act (1997), 170
Queen Elizabeth II Diamond Jubilee
    Advance Scholars program, 303
Queen's Counsel (QC), 12, 208

rábulas, defined, 258
racial discrimination in South Africa, legal
    education, 162–64
racial oppression in South Africa, 157–58
Radiation Laboratory at MIT, 83
Ramraj, Victor V., 377–78
Rand Corporation, 83
Rawls, John, 243
Reagan, Ronald, 103
Reforma do Ensino Jurídico (The Reform of
    Legal Education) (Faria), 259
regionalization in African legal education,
    124–25, 145–47
#RhodesMustFall movement, 37, 177
Rhodes scholarships, 35–36, 38–39, 160–
    62, 206
rigorous analytic thinking, 53
"Rise Era" in comparative constitutional
    law, 89
Rockefeller Archive Center, 81
Rockefeller Foundation, 83, 132–33
Roman civil law, 10–11
Roman-Dutch law, 158–59, 160
Rosenberg, Maurice, 95–96
Rothkopf, David, 409–10
Royal Civil Service Examination, 282
Royal Education Council (Bhutan), 282,
    283, 284
Royal University of Bhutan (RUB), 284
rule of law
    in China, 223–24, 323
    donor projects addressing, 40
    in Hong Kong, 321
    in Indonesia, 228
    in legal education, 8–9, 13–14, 95–96
    in Philippines, 224
    in Yangon University, 215–18
Russian lack of educational diversity, 451–
    53, 462
russophone core in transnational flow of
    students, 437
Rwandan war, 114

Saba, Roberto, 244–46
SAILER program (Staffing of African
    Institutions of Legal Education and
    Research), 33, 99, 135–36
Scanlon, Tom, 243

Schachter, Oscar, 108, 428–29
scholarship vacuum in Indonesia, 226–29
Scholars in Self-Estrangement (Trubek, Galanter), 259–60
Sciences Po Law School (Sciences Po), 5, 6–7, 454
Security Sector Reform (SSR), 215–16
segregated legal education system in South Africa, 164
SELA network in Latin America
  annual meeting, 242–44
  ethos and purpose, 244–48
  introduction to, 25, 26, 27, 28, 42–44, 238–39
  overview of, 240–42
  summary of, 248–49
self-conscious legal globalization, 3–4
self-designated global law schools, 8–9
semiperipheral hand, 11
Sen, Amartya, 390
Sengupta, Arghya, 206
Senior Judges Training Center, 111
Sexton, John, 348
Shaffer, Gregory, 389
Shanghai Jiao Tong University, 220–21
shari'a influences in law, 127, 225–26
Shaw, Malcolm, 452–53
Shenzhen-Hong Kong projects, 319–25
Sherubtse College in Bhutan, 296
Shri Ram College of Commerce, 201
Shroff, Pallavi, 196–97
Sidel, Mark, 110
Siegel, Reva, 243
Silver, Carole, 439
Singh, Manmohan, 192–93
social capital, 10–11
social change, 30, 93–100, 266
social education, 33, 131–32
social elitism, 265–73
social justice
  in Brazil, 254
  Ford Foundation and, 80, 81, 82*f*, 85*f*, 98*f*, 103, 109–10, 111, 112–13, 114–16, 117
  in Japan, 229
  lack in Philippine legal education, 224–26
  in legal education, 174–75, 222

  in Philippines, 225
  public interest law, 35–36
  SELA network in Latin America, 43–44, 246
  in South Africa, 147, 179–80
  in US, 345–46
social license in legal education, 218–19
social organization, 18
social pluralism, 59–60, 390
social rights, 22–23, 25, 80–81, 254
Society of Law Teachers, 167
socioeconomic status, 18–19, 345
Socratic instruction, 49
South African Constitution, 371–72
South African Law Deans Association (SALDA), 174–75
South African legal education
  apartheid era, 35–36, 158, 164–67
  black law students in, 35–36, 162–64, 170–71, 178–79
  cross-border flow of students, 435*f*
  Ford Foundation and, 104–6, 113
  globalization impact on, 157–58, 160–62, 173–80
  introduction to, 28, 35–37, 157–58
  LLB in, 160, 162–63, 165, 168–79, 174*f*
  LLM in, 170–71, 171*f*, 173–79, 174*f*
  origins of, 158–67
  post-apartheid era, 168–73
  summary of, 179–80
South Asian legal education, 104
South China Arbitration Commission, 310–11
South Korean legal education
  democracy movement in, 23
  educational diversity of, 464*t*
  introduction to, 41–42
  JD degrees in, 25–26, 52
Southwestern Law School, 379
Sovietology in the United States, 82–83
Soviet Union, 437
Spaeth, Carl, 88–89
Spamann, Holger, 446
St. Stephen's College in New Delhi, 201
Stanford Law School, 88–89, 301–2
Stanford University, 8, 50
Stevens, Robert, 33–34
Stone, Victor, 95–96

strategic philanthropy, 79–80
"Street Law" programs, 222
structural adjustment policies
    (SAPs), 138–39
structural sociology, 27
student-centered methodology, 46, 262
student exchange programs, 6–7, 86–87,
    299, 302
Study Commission on US Policy Toward
    Southern Africa, 104
Support for International Legal Studies, 87
Supreme Court (Japan), 230
Sutton, Frank, 108

Taiwanese Constitutional Court, 463
Taiwanese legal education, 464t
Tananarive Conference on the
    Development of Higher Education in
    Africa (1962), 130–31, 132–33
Third World, 130
Thomas, Franklin, 103, 104
traditional legal oligarchies, 22
transformative constitutionalism, 36,
    158, 177
transnational flow of students
    asymmetric student flows, 444–48
    cross-border flow of students, 368–69,
        431–38, 432t, 434f, 435f, 436f
    data on, 430–48
    divisible college of international
        lawyers, 428–29, 443–48, 461–69
    educational diversity, 443–44, 449–
        69, 450t
    education background of
        professors, 448–69
    globalization of legal education, 126,
        438–43, 440t, 441f
    introduction to, 428–30
    native languages significance, 433–35
    summary of, 469
transnationalization. See also African
    transnationalized education
    Brazilian cosmopolitan legal
        education, 263
    introduction to, 3, 9–10
    in legal education reform, 29–44
    transnational legal ordering/orders
        and, 17–19

transnationalization of (some) law
    professoriate
    assessing impact of, 385–93
    Center for Transnational Legal
        Studies and, 367, 372–78, 386–
        88, 390–93
    cultural competency, 390–91
    curriculum and pedagogy, 386–88
    global transnational legal
        education, 378–85
    introduction to, 366–72
    research and scholarship, 389
transnational legal education
    constructed demand theory, 340–46,
        356–60, 357t
    derived demand theory, 335–46
    globalization and, 335–36, 378–85
    introduction to, 333–35
    multijural lawyers, 336–38
    multijural legal education, 338–
        40, 346–60
    NYU Law Abroad, 334–35, 360–61
    rankings and, 15
    summary, 360–61
transnational legal ordering/orders
    introduction to, 24
    judges, professors, and students, 61–69
    legal education reform, 23–27, 69–72
    overview of, 17–19, 21–22
transnational lex mercatoria, 375–76
transnational nongovernmental
    organizations (NGOs), 16–17
transnational optimism, 26, 60, 70–71
transnational organizations, 16–17
transnational power elite, 61, 404–5
travaux préparatoires, 406–7
tridharma perguruan tinggi (three pillars)
    of higher education, 227–28
Trubek, David, 259–60
Trump, Donald, 437
Truth and Reconciliation Commission of
    South Africa, 167
Tsinghua University, 312
Twining, William, 33–34, 371

U Ko Ni, 216
UN Convention on Contracts for the
    International Sales of Goods, 337–38

UN Declaration on Universal Human
  Rights, 166
UN Development Programme, 281
UN Educational, Scientific and Cultural
  Organization (UNESCO)
  African legal education, 130, 137–38,
    142–43, 145
  legal education promotion, 33, 34
  transnational flow of students, 430–31,
    433–35, 439, 442
United Kingdom (UK) legal education
  curriculum in Africa, 133–35
  educational diversity of, 458–60
  global student flows, 439–41
  international flow of students
    toward, 345
  introduction to, 33–34
  New York bar examination and, 442–43
  number of foreign law students, 442
  public policy relationships, 219
United States Agency for International
  Development (USAID), 132–33
United States (US) law, 14–15, 31, 88
United States (US) legal education. See
    also NYU Law Abroad
  approach to, 189
  ascendency of, 186
  black law students, 67–68, 489–90
  Delaware corporate law, 446
  district court in, 13–14
  educational diversity of, 456–58, 464t
  funding for Bhutanese legal
    education, 301–2
  hegemony, 21, 31
  international students in, 345–46, 482–
    83, 490–92, 501–4
  introduction to, 52–60
  Ivy League universities, 188, 416–17
  JD degrees, 66–69
  law professor salaries, 187
  legal education reform, 14
  LLM in, 57, 66–69, 345–46, 374, 382–
    83, 392, 439, 501–13
  popularity of, 441–42
  public policy relationships, 219
  transnational processes, 64–69
  US-Japanese university student
    exchange, 86–87, 229–32

Universidad Adolfo Ibáñez (Chile), 241
Universidad de Buenos Aires, 241
Universidad de Chile, 241
Universidad de los Andes (Colombia), 241
Universidad de Palermo, 241
Universidad de Puerto Rico (Puerto
  Rico), 241
Universidad de San Andrés, 241
Universidad Diego Portales, 241
Universidad di São Paulo, 57–58,
  241, 372–73
Universidade do Estado do Rio de
  Janeiro, 241
Universidad Nacional Autónoma de
  Mexico, 241
Universidad Peruana de Ciencias
  Aplicadas (Peru), 241
Universidad Torcuato di Tella
  (Argentina), 241
Universitat Pompeu Fabra (Spain), 241
Universities of Chile and Concepcion, 98
University of Bologna, 10–11
University of Bonn, 417–18
University of Brasilia Law School, 260
University of Buenos Aires, 240–41, 379
University of California, Berkeley, 116,
  191, 194
University of California, Irvine, 386
University of California at Los Angeles,
  95–96, 194
University of California Law School, 83
University of Cape Town (UCT), 159–62
University of Chicago, 94, 446
University of Chicago Law School, 97
University of Delhi, 89, 191, 201, 202
University of Fort Hare, 178
University of Illinois, 95–96
University of Indonesia, 227
University of Melbourne, 380
University of Michigan Law School,
  51, 312–13
University of Minnesota Law
  School, 95–96
University of Mumbai, 192
University of Natal-Durban, 102–3
University of Salvador, 379
University of São Paulo (USP), 47–48
University of Stellenbosch, 160

University of Sydney, 6–7
University of the Witwatersrand (Wits), 160, 162–63, 167
University of Torino, 57–58, 372–73
University of Toronto, 57–58, 372–73
University of Vienna, 293, 303
University of Washington, 215–16
University of Zululand, 164
UN Security Council, 449–50
UN Sustainable Development Goal (SDG), 215–16, 232
upward diffusion, 447–48
Urquhart, Brian, 115
U.S. News law school rankings, 480
US business schools, 24
US-China Committee for Legal Education Exchange (CLEEC), 104, 109, 111, 112–13
US Supreme Court, 95, 463

Verrier, Hugh, 282
Vidhi Centre for Legal Policy, 205–6
Vieira, Oscar Vilhena, 44, 46–47
Vietnam War, 136

W.A. Franke Global Law Program, 8
Walter Sisulu University (WSU), 178
Wan E'Xiang, 112
Wangchuck, Jigme Khesar Namgyel, 282
Wangchuck, Sonam Dechan, 50, 283–84, 301–2

Washington University School of Law, 284
Werro, Franz, 375–76
West, Thompson, 314–15
Whalen-Bridge, Helen, 377
Whelan, John, 95–96
White & Case law firm, 282, 283–84, 295, 301
Whytock, Christopher, 386
Wilkins, David, 7
W.K. Kellogg Foundation, 132–33
World Bank, 27, 34, 138–39, 142–43
World Intellectual Property Organization (WIPO), 320
World School of Law, 86
World Trade Organization, 7–8, 21, 31, 466
World Trade Organization's Appellate Body (WTO AB), 405, 412–13, 420–21, 422–23
Wuhan University, 109

Xiao Jingyi, 323
Xi Jinping, 223–24

Yale Law School, 42, 84, 94, 240–41
Yale's Latin American Seminar on Constitutional and Political Theory, 249
Yale University, 6–7
Yangon University (YU), 215–18